Computers and Data Processing
CONCEPTS AND APPLICATIONS

WITH BASIC

Computers and Data Processing
CONCEPTS AND APPLICATIONS

Third Edition

WITH BASIC

Steven L. Mandell
Bowling Green State University

West Publishing Company
St. Paul   New York   Los Angeles   San Francisco

COPY EDITOR: Flora Foss
ILLUSTRATIONS: John Foster and Dave Pauly
COMPOSITION: The Clarinda Company

A study guide has been developed to assist you in mastering concepts presented in this text. The study guide reinforces concepts by presenting them in condensed, concise form. Additional illustrations and examples are also included. The study guide is available from your local bookstore under the title, *Study Guide to Accompany Computers and Data Processing: Concepts and Applications Third Edition,* prepared by Steven L. Mandell.

Library of Congress Cataloging in Publication Data

Mandell, Steven L.
  Computers and data processing.

Includes index.
  1. Electronic data processing. 2. Electronic digital computers. 3. BASIC (Computer program language)
I. Title.
QA76.M27472 1985   001.64   83–19522
ISBN 0–314–87560–3

PHOTO CREDITS

2 Courtesy of Apple Computer, Inc. **8** courtesy of International Business Machines Corporation. **9** courtesy, The Firestone Tire & Rubber Company. **10** courtesy of IBM. **14** courtesy of Flight Simulation. **18** courtesy of IBM. **21** courtesy of IBM. **22** (top) courtesy of the Science Museum, London. **22** (bottom) courtesy of IBM. **23** (top right) courtesy of IBM. **23** (bottom right) courtesy of Science Museum, London. **23** (bottom left) courtesy of IBM. **24** courtesy of IBM. **25** courtesy of IBM. **26** courtesy of IBM. **27** (top) courtesy of Iowa State of Science and Technology. **27** (bottom) courtesy of Sperry Univac, A Division of the Sperry Rand Corporation. Courtesy of Sperry Corporation. **28** courtesy of the Institute for Advanced Study. **29** courtesy of Sperry Univac. **30** (bottom) courtesy of the Department of the Navy. **31** courtesy of IBM. **32** (top) courtesy of International Business Machines Corporation. **32** (bottom) courtesy of IBM. **33** courtesy NCR Corp. **34** courtesy of Digital Equipment Corporation. **35** (bottom) courtesy of Intel Corporation. **38** courtesy of Radio Shack, a Division of Tandy Corporation. **39** courtesy of Apple Computers, Inc. **42** courtesy of The Department of the Navy. **46** courtesy of RCA. **53** (top) courtesy of IBM. **54** courtesy of AT&T, Bell Laboratories. **55** courtesy of AT&T, Bell Laboratories. **56** courtesy of Intel Corporation. **66** (top left) courtesy of Cray Corporation. **66** (bottom) courtesy of Cray Corporation. **67** courtesy of Sperry Univac. **68** courtesy of IBM. **72** courtesy of IBM. **74** courtesy of LKB Instruments, Inc. **79** Norma Morris. **81** courtesy of Wang Laboratories, Inc. **87** (bottom) courtesy of MSI. **89** courtesy of NCR Corp. **90** courtesy of Hewlett-Packard. **93** (top) courtesy of

(continued following Index)

CONTENTS

Chapter 4   Input and Output   74

Chapter 5   Storage Devices   106

SECTION III PROGRAMMING 183

Chapter 9   Programming and Software Development   206

Chapter 10   Programming Languages   237

Chapter 11   Structured Design Concepts   272

Chapter 12   Application Software   294

Chapter 15   Management Information and Decision Support Systems   394

SECTION V   COMPUTERS IN SOCIETY   419

Chapter 16   The Impact of Computers on People and Organizations   420

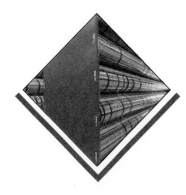

Chapter 17 Computer Security, Crime, Ethics, and the Law 452

Chapter 18 Computers in Our Lives: Today and Tomorrow 474

Appendix A Careers 501

BASIC SUPPLEMENT B-1

Glossary G–1

Index I–1

PREFACE

The revision work associated with this edition of the text has been even more productive and enjoyable than the efforts involved with both the original book and the second edition. Feedback from instructors using the text has provided an excellent road map for implementing necessary changes, and nothing can replace the actual classroom testing of material when attempting to improve the content. When prior editions have proven highly successful, critical time can be spent updating and refining the book rather than creating an entirely new version. The final result is a new, third edition of a textbook vastly improved in structure and substance.

It is appropriate at this point to thank the following people who reviewed the book and provided invaluable comments based on their experience using the second edition of *Computers and Data Processing*.

Michael J. Belluzzi
William Rainey Harper
Illinois

William R. Cornette
Southwest Missouri State University

J. Patrick Fenton
West Valley College
California

F. Paul Fuhs
Virginia Commonwealth University

Richard A. Grimes
DeKalb Community College
Georgia

David L. Herzog
*St. Louis Community College
at Florissant Valley*

Robert T. Keim
Arizona State University

James G. Kriz
Cuyahoga Community College
Ohio

James E. LaBarre
University of Wisconsin, Eau Claire

Don B. Medley
California State Polytechnic University, Pomona

Robert D. Smith
Kent State University
Ohio

J. Martin Stacy
Tarrant County Junior College
Texas

Louis A. Wolff
Moorpark Community College
California

NEW FEATURES

Readers familiar with the second edition of the text will notice several changes incorporated into the third edition:

- New articles and highlights
- New and updated applications
- Concept Summaries, a new feature, provide a clear and concise review of key topics

- Two new Consumer Guide sections help the would-be buyer of microcomputers and application software through the maze of products available on the market
- Increased coverage of semiconductor memory technology
- Reduced coverage of magnetic core memory
- Further reduction in punched card coverage
- New chapter on microcomputers
- Rewritten chapter on telecommunications including discussions on distributed data processing, local area networks, and electronic transmission of data
- Rewritten chapter on programming languages
- New chapter on application software
- Improved presentation of system analysis and design
- Rewritten file organization and data design chapter including data base concepts
- New section on decision support systems
- Increased coverage of computers in our society

The most inspiring lectures on computers that I have had the fortune to attend were presented by Commodore Grace Hopper, a legend in her own time. In analyzing her material, which always seemed so interesting, it became apparent to me that no new concept was permitted to remain abstract. Rather, actual examples were described, encouraging the listener to visualize their applications. In a like manner, each chapter in this book is followed by an application that shows how a corporation or government agency implements the concepts presented.

Several other important features are included within each chapter. The introductory section serves a dual purpose: as a transition between chapters and as a preview of material. An article that evokes attention and acts as a motivator follows. Highlights containing interesting computer applications or controversial topics are included to maintain reader interest. Concept summaries permit the student to quickly review the important key topics covered in the chapter. Chapter summary points and review questions are also provided. At the end of the text is a comprehensive glossary and a separate index.

I have had one paramount objective throughout the development of each edition of this book. The material is designed to be student oriented, and all incorporated approaches are designed to assist students in the learning process. Important concepts are never avoided, regardless of their complexity. Many books on data processing emphasize one of two aspects of data processing—either informational relationships or computer capabilities. This text attempts to balance and blend both subjects.

The material is structured according to an approach used successfully by several thousand business and computer science students in a course entitled "Introduction to Information Systems" at Bowling Green State University. The book is divided into five sections: Information Processing, Technology, Programming, Systems, and Computers in Society. The Information Processing section presents an introduction to the basic concepts of data processing and an historical perspective. The Technology section concentrates on computer hardware (both mainframe and micro), including internal and secondary storage and input/output devices. System and application software, program development, languages, and structural approaches constitute the Programming section. The Systems section provides a discussion of the methods and approaches to designing information systems. Finally, the Computers in Society section includes material concerning security, privacy and law, and computer impact on organizations and individuals, while presenting a view of the future.

In order to provide for a variety of teaching situations, there are two versions of this text available. First, a version with a very complete, expanded BASIC Supplement that includes more flowcharts, new programming problems, and debugging exercises. Second, a language free-version is also available.

SUPPLEMENTARY EDUCATIONAL MATERIALS

The study guide for this text includes numerous materials for student reinforcement. The instructor material is designed to reduce administrative efforts. Transparency masters are provided to adopters of the text as well as color slides (with a written script) of a tour of a modern computer facility. For qualified adopters there is also available a set of full color transparencies. WESTEST II and MICRO Test II, computerized testing services with over one thousand questions, are available from West Publishing Company.

Included with this version for qualified adopters of the text are two supplementary diskettes. The first diskette is a BASIC tutorial developed from the BASIC Supplement of the text. The diskette is designed to complement the BASIC material as a computer-assisted instructional device. The tutorial also includes an on-demand dictionary of terms from the BASIC Supplement. The second diskette contains educational versions of a word processor, electronic spreadsheet, data manager, and graphics package. The packages are available for a number of microcomputers and are designed to be used in conjunction with Chapter 12 of the text.

ACKNOWLEDGMENTS

Many individuals and companies have been involved in the development of the material for this book. The corporations and government agencies whose applications appear in this book have provided invaluable assistance. Many professionals provided the assistance required for completion of a text of this magnitude: Russ Thompson on student material; Karen McKee on BASIC; Bob Szymanski on applications; Sarah Basinger, Susan Moran, and Rhonda Raifsnider on highlights; Ed Fiscus and Kim Girnus on instructor material; and Norma Morris and Candy Streeter on manuscript development.

The design of the book is a tribute to the many talents of William Stryker. One final acknowledgment goes to my publisher and valued friend, Clyde Perlee, Jr., for his unfaltering support.

Steven L. Mandell

SECTION 1
INFORMATION PROCESSING

1

Introduction to Data Processing

INTRODUCTION

The computer has become a dominant force in society. Business corporations, government agencies, and other organizations depend on it to process data and make information available for use in decision making. Computers are responsible, to a large extent, for the standard of living typical in the United States today. As the costs for computer equipment continue to decrease, computers will become an even more integral part of daily life. It is therefore essential that people gain a basic understanding of computers—their capabilities, limitations, and applications.

This chapter gives a basic description of the computer and its uses and distinguishes between data and information. An example of computerized payroll processing is used to demonstrate how computers can be programmed to provide meaningful information. Finally, some of the major advances and problems that have resulted from using computers are presented as evidence of the computer's growing impact on all parts of society.

ARTICLE

When The Computer Is Down

Art Buchwald

The most frightening words in the English language are, "Our computer is down." You hear it more and more as you go about trying to conduct your business.

The other day I was at the airport attempting to buy a ticket to Washington and the attendant said, "I'm sorry, I can't sell you a ticket. Our computer is down."

"What do you mean your computer is down? Is it depressed."

"No it can't be depressed. That's why it's down."

"So if your computer is down, just write me out a ticket."

"I can't write you out a ticket. The computer is the only one allowed to issue tickets on the plane." I looked down the counter and every passenger agent was just standing there drinking coffee and staring into a blank screen.

"What do all you people do?"

"We give the computer the information about your trip, and then it tells us whether you can fly with us or not."

"So when it goes down, you go down with it."

"That's very good, sir. I haven't heard it put that way before."

"How long will the computer be down?" I wanted to know.

"I have no idea. Sometimes it's down for 10 minutes, sometimes for two hours. There is no way we can find out without asking the computer, and since it's down it won't answer us."

"Don't you have a backup computer, when the main computer goes down?"

"I doubt it. Do you know what one of these things costs?"

"Let's forget the computer. What about your planes? They're still flying, aren't they?"

"I couldn't tell without asking the computer, and as I told you . . . ."

"I know, it's down. Maybe I could just go to the gate and ask the pilot if he's flying to Washington," I suggested.

"I wouldn't know what gate to send you to."

"I'll try them all," I said.

"Even if the pilot was going to Washington, he couldn't take you if you didn't have a ticket."

"Why don't I give you the money and you could give me a receipt and I could show that to the pilot as proof that I paid?"

"We wouldn't know what to charge you. The computer is the only one who keeps track of air fares because they change every hour."

"How about my credit card?"

"That's even worse. When our computer is down it can't notify the credit-card computer to charge the fare to your account."

"Is there any other airline flying to Washington within the next few hours?"

"I wouldn't know," he said, pointing at the dark screen. "Only 'IT' knows."

"And at the moment 'IT' don't know nothing."

" 'IT' knows it," he said defensively, " 'IT' just can't tell me."

By this time there were quite a few people standing in lines. The word soon spread to other travelers that "the computer was down." Nobody knew exactly what this meant, but some people went white, some people started to cry and still others kicked their luggage.

A man in a red blazer came out. "Please don't get excited. Wichita has been notified."

"What's Wichita got to do with it?" I asked.

"That's where our main computer went down. But as soon as it gets over its glitch, it's going to buy everyone who missed his plane a free drink."

Reprinted with permission of the author, Los Angeles Times Syndicate, 1984.

Like the Wright Brothers at Kitty Hawk, computers can sometimes have a little trouble getting off the ground. Once they're airborne, however, they fly extremely high in accomplishing the data-processing tasks assigned to them by people. Much as the first flight at Kitty Hawk led to a significant change in society, so has the invention of the computer changed our lives and the world in which we live.

BACKGROUND

Many people envision an electronic marvel with mystical powers when they think of the word *computer*. The **computer** in its most basic form—a piece of hardware—is quite limited in what it can do, however. Its success can be directly attributed to the imagination of people. A computer cannot perform any tasks that a person has not predetermined. The computer, therefore, has no intelligence of its own but must rely on human intelligence to perform tasks as simple as addition.

Three basic functions computers can perform are:

1. Arithmetic operations (addition, subtraction, multiplication, and division).
2. Comparison operations (test the relationship of two values to see if they are equal, if the first is greater than the second, or vice versa; these values can be either numeric or alphabetic).
3. Storage and retrieval operations.

The number of unique instructions required to direct a computer to perform these three functions is quite limited, often fewer than one hundred. These instructions control the basic logical and arithmetical procedures such as addition, subtraction, and comparison. Together, they constitute the **instruction set** of the computer. Engineers design the instruction set into the electronic circuitry of the machine. By manipulating this small instruction set, people can create computer programs that harness the computer's power to help them achieve desired results.

Most computers can be used for many purposes. They are referred to as **general-purpose machines. Special-purpose,** or **dedicated, machines** are similar to general-purpose computers but have been specifically adapted to perform specialized tasks. In all cases, a human determines the combination of instructions that a machine will perform.

Computers derive most of their amazing power from three features: speed, accuracy, and memory. Two factors control the speed of a computer: the switching speed of the electronic circuits that make up the computer and the distances that electric currents have to travel. Recent advances in technology have made it possible to increase the switching speed of electronic circuits; other advances have made it possible to reduce the lengths of interconnections by packing circuits closer together. And technological breakthroughs continue with each passing year. Modern computers are capable of performing millions of calculations in one second. Their speed is fast reaching the physical limitation of the speed of light, which is about 186,000 miles per second. Generally, computer speed is expressed as the time required to perform one operation. The following units of time apply:

UNIT	SYMBOL	FRACTIONS OF A SECOND	
Millisecond	ms	one-thousandth	(1/1,000)
Microsecond	μs	one-millionth	(1/1,000,000)
Nanosecond	ns	one-billionth	(1/1,000,000,000)
Picosecond	ps	one-trillionth	(1/1,000,000,000,000)

In the past, the time required to perform one addition ranged from 4 microseconds to 200 nanoseconds, and it is estimated that it will be 200 to 1,000 times faster in the future.

The accuracy of computers is due in part to the inherent reliability of the electronic circuits that make up a computer. In our daily lives, we take advantage of this aspect of circuitry every time we switch on an electric device and assume it will come on. Our assumption is based upon our past experience; we expect the same activity to yield the same result. Similarly, in a computer, passing the same type of current through the same electrical circuits yields the same result. This constancy of computer-generated results is referred to as **accuracy.**

However, the accuracy of a computer relates to its internal operations. To say that a computer is accurate does not imply that what comes out of the computer is correct—that depends on what was put into it. If the **input** collected for use by the computer is incorrect or is not relevant to the problem being solved, then it is impossible for the computer to manipulate that input and produce meaningful **output.** This concept, called **garbage in–garbage out (GIGO),** is fundamental to understanding computer "mistakes." Incorrect processing instructions will also produce incorrect output; so the correctness of programs used to manipulate the data is also important.

The part of the computer that stores data that is to be operated on is the computer's **memory.** The amount of data a computer can store in its memory varies from computer to computer. While some of the smaller computers store as few as 16,000 characters, many large computers can store up to 1,000,000 characters within memory. The figures given, however, refer only to what is known as **primary memory.** External storage devices, referred to as **secondary storage,** may also be attached to the computer and can increase the data storage capacities in some cases by up to 40 times. Secondary storage holds data that is not immediately needed by the computer. When the data is needed, it is brought from secondary storage to primary memory.

Computers, therefore, can store a virtually unlimited amount of data and retrieve it at incredible speeds. We could store similarly vast quantities of data in paper files, but the files would become extremely bulky and require a good deal of storage space. Further, the job of manually extracting data from such a file would become increasingly tedious and time consuming as the size of the file increased. The computer's memory can store the same data in considerably less space and retrieve it in a fraction of the time.

The amount of storage available in today's computers can be increased or decreased according to user requirements. Users can purchase the amount of

- The **instruction set** is designed into the computer's electronic circuitry by engineers. It contains logical and arithmetical instructions for performing arithmetic operations, comparison operations, and storage and retrieval operations.
- Most of a computer's power is derived from its **speed, accuracy,** and **memory.**
- The computer's memory is used to store data that is to be operated on. A computer's memory is divided into **primary memory** and **secondary storage.**
- On large computers, primary memory can hold up to 1,000,000 characters, while secondary storage can increase storage capacities by as much as 40 times.

memory they need, and continuing advances in technology have led to steady reductions in its cost. Once data has been placed in the computer's memory, efficient and accurate processing and retrieval operations can be performed.

DATA PROCESSING

In the past, manual techniques of collecting, manipulating, and distributing data to achieve certain objectives were known as **data processing.** As technology advanced, electromechanical machines were developed to perform these functions. The term **automatic data processing (ADP)** was introduced to describe the use of such machines. Today, the electronic computer is used to achieve results formerly accomplished by humans and machines. This is known as **electronic data processing (EDP).** (The term *data processing* is sometimes used as a shorthand reference to EDP.)

The objective of all data processing, whether manual, electromechanical, or electronic, is to convert raw data into information that can be used in decision making. **Data** refers to raw facts that have been collected from various sources but not organized. Data cannot be used to make meaningful decisions. For example, a daily list of all checks and deposit slips of all branch offices may mean very little to a bank manager. But through manipulation of the data in one fashion or another, useful information may be provided—perhaps in the form of a summary report giving the number and amount of deposits and withdrawals at each branch. **Information,** then, is data that has been organized and processed. Information increases understanding and helps people make intelligent decisions.

To be useful to decision makers, information must meet several requirements. It must be accurate, timely, complete, concise, and relevant. That is, information should be delivered to the right person, at the right time, in the right place. If information fails to meet these requirements, it fails to meet the needs of those who must use it and is thus of little value.

To derive information from data, all data processing follows the same basic flow pattern: input, processing, and output (see Figure 1–1).

Input involves three steps: data must be **collected, verified,** and **coded.**

■ Collect: Collection involves gathering data from various sources and assembling it at one location.
■ Verify: After data has been gathered, its accuracy and completeness must be checked. This is an important step that helps to eliminate the possibility of garbage in—garbage out.
■ Code: Data must be converted into machine-readable form so that it can be entered into the data-processing system. Entering data via a computer terminal and keyboard is one example of coding.

The terms **classify, sort, calculate, summarize,** and **store** are used to refer to the steps in processing data.

■ Classify: Classification involves categorizing data according to certain characteristics so that it is meaningful to the user. For example, sales data can be grouped according to salesperson, product type, customer, or any other classification useful to management.
■ Sort: After it is classified, data may be sorted. This involves arranging the grouped data elements into a predetermined sequence to facilitate processing. For example, an employee file may be sorted by social security number

Cabbage Patch Kids Designed by Computers

Remember the successful debut of the Cabbage Patch Kids manufactured by Coleco Industries? The original dolls were the idea of Xavier Roberts, an artist from Cleveland, Georgia. To make sure each of the mass-marketed Kids was unique, Coleco's computers were used to design the dolls' features. In that way, no two look alike. Each doll stands 16 inches, has yarn hair, outstretched arms, and detailed fingers and toes. Each doll is different because the face mold, hair color, eye color, skin tones ranging from black to white, and other variables are changed for each doll.

Figure 1–1 ■ The Data-Processing Flow

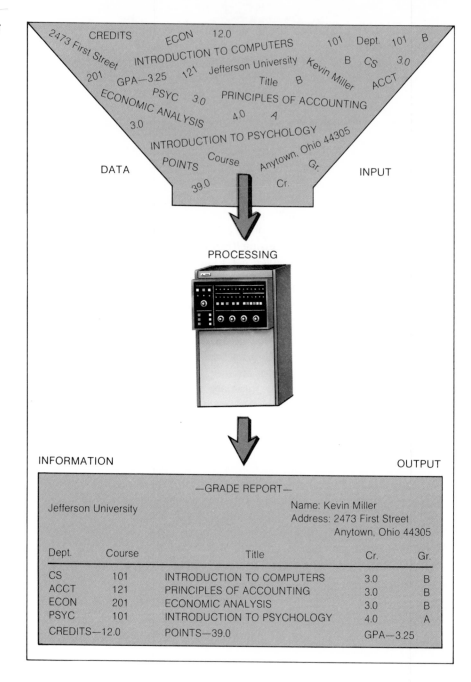

or by last name. Sorting can be done on numbers, letters, special characters (+, −, ¢, and the like), or a combination of these.

■ Calculate: The arithmetical or logical manipulation of data is referred to as calculation. Examples include computation of students' grade-point averages, customers' bank balances, and employees' wages.

■ Summarize: Reducing large amounts of data to a concise, usable form is called summarizing. This logical reduction of data is necessary to provide information that is useful. An example of reduced data is a top-management report that summarizes a company's accounting data to determine its profit performance.

■ Store: The data can be placed on a storage medium such as magnetic tape, magnetic disk, or microfilm for retrieval when needed. The cost of storage should not exceed the benefit of having the facts available for future use. Obviously, only facts that may be needed later should be stored.

Once data has been processed according to some or all of the steps above, information is available for distribution to the user. The three steps involved in the output phase of data flow are to **retrieve, convert,** and **communicate.**

■ Retrieve: The computer can retrieve stored information so that it can be referenced by the user.

■ Convert: Often people cannot use information in the form in which the computer stores it. Conversion involves translating such information into a form that humans can understand and use, such as a terminal display or a printed output. If several users require the information, it must be made available to all.

■ Communicate: Information must be in the right place at the right time. Communication occurs when information reaches the proper users at the proper time in an intelligible form.

To achieve effective data processing, data should be organized in an integrated way so that all anticipated needs of users for information can be met. For example, a business firm may want to maintain specific data about all employees—home address, social security number, wage per hour, withholding tax, gross income, and so on. Each of these categories is called a **field.** A collection of fields that relate to a single unit (in this case a single employee) is a **record.** A grouping of all related records (in this case all employee records) is a **file.** The structuring of data to satisfy a wider variety of information needs than can be supported by a single file is a **data base.** We shall consistently use the terms *field, record, file,* and *data base* in this manner (see Figure 1–2).

A DATA PROCESSING APPLICATION

One common application of data processing is payroll preparation. The inputs to this application are employee time cards and a personnel file. This data is processed to provide paychecks for all employees and a payroll report containing summary information for management (see Figure 1–3).

Figure 1–2 ■ **Organization of a Data Base**

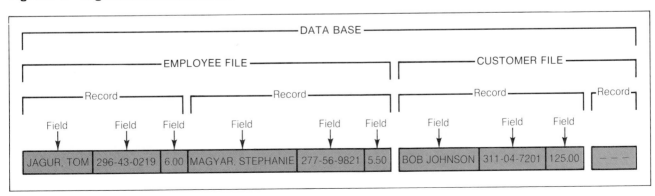

- **Data** is simply raw facts that have been collected and saved but not organized into a meaningful form. **Information,** on the other hand, is data that has been organized in a way that will help people in their decision making.
- The basic flow pattern of data processing is: **input, processing,** and **output.**
- Input involves collecting, verifying, and coding data.
- The processing portion of data flow can include the steps of classifying, sorting, calculating, summarizing, and storing.
- The output portion of data flow involves retrieving, converting, and communicating the data stored in the computer to human users.
- A **field** is a single data item, such as a social security number.
- A **record** is a collection of related fields, such as an employee record.
- A **file** is a grouping of related records, such as an employee file.
- A **data base** structures data so that a wider range of information needs can be supported than could be with a single file.

Payroll preparation is suitable for electronic data processing because it involves a well-defined, repetitive procedure and a large number of records. The computer must take the following steps in preparing a paycheck:

1. Read total hours worked from time card.
2. Compute gross pay by multiplying total hours worked by employee hourly wage rate.
3. Calculate withholding tax and social security tax.

Figure 1–3 ▪ Payroll Processing

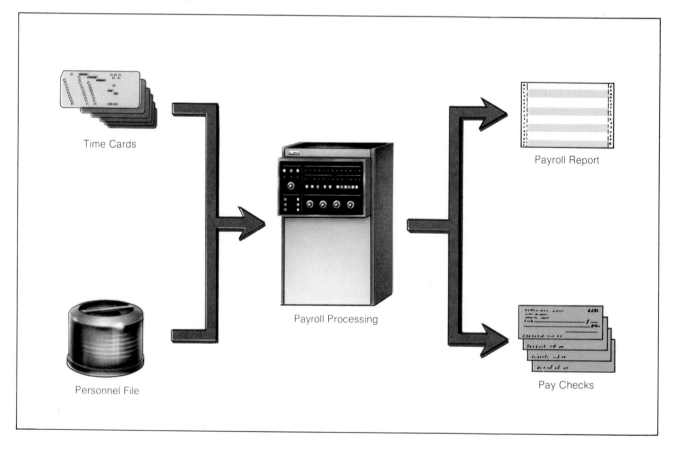

Time Cards

Personnel File

Payroll Processing

Payroll Report

Pay Checks

4. Deduct withholding tax and social security tax from gross pay to get net pay.

5. Write paycheck.

In most payroll applications, the computer must also check for other conditions, such as overtime, maximum or minimum allowable work hours, other deductions, and special wage rates for overtime work.

The payroll report includes summary information such as number of employees paid, total dollar value of payroll for the period, total withholding, and breakdowns of payments for all departments of the company. This report helps management to make decisions about labor costs, cash flow planning, and the like.

IMPACT OF COMPUTERS

We are in the midst of the computer revolution. The computer's ability to store, retrieve, and analyze data at tremendous speeds and at low cost has made possible such advances as space travel, electronic banking, and body scanners. The potential of computers seems unlimited—new applications appear every day. And as the costs of computers continue to decrease while human labor costs increase, more applications are inevitable.

Perhaps the greatest impact of computers has been on business. Today, nearly all businesses make use of, or come in contact with, electronic data processing. The power to process data rapidly and disseminate the results of processing to users is critical to technological progress. Further, business organizations are concerned with using scarce resources in an optimal manner to achieve their objectives of profit and growth. Often, in their attempts to achieve these goals, managers have had to make decisions in the face of uncertainty and with inadequate information. The computer, by providing information that is timely, concise, and relevant, has improved the decision-making process. The computer is also beginning to change the organization of the office itself. Information can be electronically transmitted from one office to another next door or across a continent. **Word processors** are facilitating many tedious jobs performed by secretaries, freeing them to perform other tasks.

The computer is much like any other tool used by humans. It has improved their efficiency, allowing them to perform new and different jobs that demand greater attention. The computer has enhanced their problem-solving capabilities and increased their capacity to handle complex relationships. Thus, computers are being used for straightforward clerical tasks (payroll processing, inventory control, and billing) and for complex applications (budgeting, facilities planning, market research, and corporate planning).

Government's use of computers parallels business's as far as conventional data processing is concerned. But the government also uses computers extensively in development of military weapons and defense systems. Examples of the latter include computerized radar systems and automatically guided missiles. The government also uses computers for land resource planning, health service planning, transportation planning, and police telecommunication systems.

Computers have had a significant impact on education—one of society's largest industries. Like business, it needs computers to store and process large

When you think of a cupid, a tiny figure with a bow and arrow usually comes to mind. And, cupids are generally thought of on Valentine's Day. However, a special cupid does point its arrow at one's heart.

Cupid is the name for a computer program used to train medical students. The program helps them learn to help a person whose heart has stopped beating. The message on the screen shows the current condition of the patient and a list of actions that the student can take. Depending on what the student "doctor" does, the computer "patient" will: (1) get better, (2) get worse, or (3) die instantly.

amounts of data. Recently, computers have begun to be used in teaching as well. **Computer-assisted instruction (CAI)** involves direct interaction between a computer and a student. This method of teaching holds promise, since the computer can deal with a large number of students on an individual basis.

In the health-care field, computers are being used for making medical diagnoses, maintaining medical histories, and monitoring patients. The advantage of computer monitoring of intensive-care patients is that critical factors like pulse rate, breathing, and body temperature can be checked several times a second. This type of monitoring could not be provided by individuals. Moreover, the computer does not suffer fatigue, and it makes no mistakes once it has been correctly set up.

The use of personal computers is also increasing. Decreasing costs have made computer use in the home possible and attractive. Home computers are being used to balance checkbooks, regulate fuel consumption, plan menus, and even turn lights and appliances on and off at prescribed times.

While many people are excited about all these uses of computers, many others are concerned about the problems they may create—problems like worker displacement, invasion of privacy, and depersonalization in business operations. The advantages of a new technology are often obvious, but the problems that may arise are much more difficult to assess. This was so with automobiles. It may very well be the case with computers. However, computers are here to stay. We could not maintain our present life styles without them. Indeed, it is essential that we be familiar with their capabilities, limitations, and real and potential social impact. This text introduces the basic workings of the computer, discusses recent computer innovations, and points to some of the issues that face the computer generations.

SUMMARY POINTS

- A computer possesses no intelligence. It can only perform tasks predetermined by humans.
- All computer processing involves the basic machine functions of performing simple arithmetic (addition, subtraction, and so on), comparing values (either numeric or alphabetic), and storing and retrieving information.
- The computer derives its power from three features: speed, accuracy, and memory.
- The speed of computer processing is limited by the switching speed of its electronic circuits and the distances that electric currents must travel through these circuits. Advances in technology have resulted in computers that can perform operations in nanoseconds (billionths of a second).
- Computers' accuracy is enhanced by the internal, self-checking features of electronic circuits. Although the internal operations of the computer are essentially error-free, its output will not be valid unless valid input was used. Understanding this "garbage in—garbage out" concept is fundamental to understanding computer "mistakes."
- The collection, manipulation, and dissemination of data is known as data processing. The use of machines to perform these functions is called automatic data processing. When an electronic computer is used, electronic data processing (EDP) is performed.
- Data refers to unorganized, raw facts. Information is data that has been organized and processed so that it can be used to make intelligent decisions.

In order for information to be useful, it must be accurate, timely, complete, concise, and relevant.

■ The conversion of data to information follows this pattern: Input through processing to output. Input involves collecting, verifying, and coding data. Processing involves classifying, sorting, calculating, summarizing, and storing it. Information retrieved and converted so that it can be communicated to the user in an intelligible form is output.

■ Data must be organized to be processed effectively. A data item is called a field; a collection of fields relating to a single unit, a record; and a grouping of related records, a file. The structuring of data to support the information needs of a wide variety of users creates a data base.

■ The capability of the computer to store, retrieve, and analyze data at tremendous speeds has made possible new advances such as space travel and electronic banking. Computers' impact on society is growing; we are becoming increasingly dependent on them in our daily lives.

REVIEW QUESTIONS

1. Although computer processing is essentially error-free, mistakes can and do occur. Explain how. What is meant by the phrase "garbage in–garbage out."

2. Distinguish between data and information. What are some of the functions performed in converting data into information? Give an example of how a computer can be used to perform these functions.

3. Describe the relationship that exists among data within a data base. (That is, what is a field, a record, a file, and a data base?)

4. List five ways in which the computer has had some impact on you.

5. What are some problems created by computers? Can these problems be solved? Discuss.

6. Describe a situation in which you feel the use of a computer would help to improve the current method used to perform a task. Describe the possible impact computerization might have on the individuals currently performing the task.

President and chief executive officer Albert L. Ueltschi founded FlightSafety International (FSI) in 1951. A native of Frankfort, Kentucky, Ueltschi was raised on a farm where his father, an electrical engineer, had retired. He learned to fly at a nearby airfield, soloing at 16. Borrowing $3,500.00 to buy an open-cockpit biplane, he gave flying lessons, put on air shows, and barnstormed around the country.

He joined Pan American Airways in 1941, eventually becoming personal pilot to its chairman, the late Juan Trippe. At airports where he ferried Trippe, he noted former military pilots were operating mostly reconfigured military aircraft as business aircraft without proper training. He established FlightSafety to meet this need, while still serving as Trippe's pilot. He retired from PanAm in 1968 to devote full time to the building of FSI.

FlightSafety International Inc. is the world's leading specialized supplier of high technology aircrew and maintenance technician training services. It has 24 learning centers in the United States, Canada, and France with more than 65 flight simulators. This is more than American Airlines, Pan American Airways, and TWA combined. Clients include corporations, U.S. and foreign commercial airlines, military and other government agencies including the FAA and NASA. A subsid-

iary, MarineSafety International, trains ship deck and engineering officers through the use of simulators. Recently the company joined with Babcock & Wilcox in setting up PowerSafety International for the high technology training of operator and maintenance personnel of electric power and industrial steam generating plants.

The company's learning centers are usually located near an aircraft factory or a service center. This makes it convenient for pilots to train while awaiting delivery of a new aircraft, or to take refresher training while aircraft are undergoing periodic maintenance.

The replication of the flight experience, including the practice of emergency procedures too dangerous to try in the air, has brought FlightSafety's simulator training into industry-wide acceptance. The FAA endorsement of simulator use, conservation of high fuel costs, and insurance company encouragement have also benefited the acceptance of FSI training.

THE FLIGHT SIMULATOR SYSTEM

The flight simulators built and used by FlightSafety International rely on computer simulation of actual flight for the training of pilots. The simulation software used by FlightSafety is written in Fortran and is designed to represent actual aircraft systems and respond to the pilot's actions in the cockpit just as the actual aircraft would respond in flight. The simulator program provides motion around and along six axes—pitch, roll, yaw, vertical, longitudinal, and lateral- a visual display, and actual manipulation of cockpit instruments and flight controls. A typical flight simulator system is diagrammed in Figure 1–4, and consists of the following components: (1) a hydraulically driven motion base, (2) an instructor's station, (3) a flight compartment, or cockpit, (4) an equipment cabinet which houses the circuitry necessary to interface the computer with the simulator itself, (5) an input/output controller, (6) a simulator computer, (7) an image-generator computer, and (8) the necessary peripheral devices.

The motion base is the device that actually simulates the velocity and acceleration cues. Motion is achieved through the use of six hydraulic cylinders. The cylinders are mounted in three pairs and are actuated by the simulator computer and the interface to produce the six types of motion.

The motion system is designed to also include kinesthetic sensations similar to those experienced in real flight. Rates of change of motion reflect actual aircraft

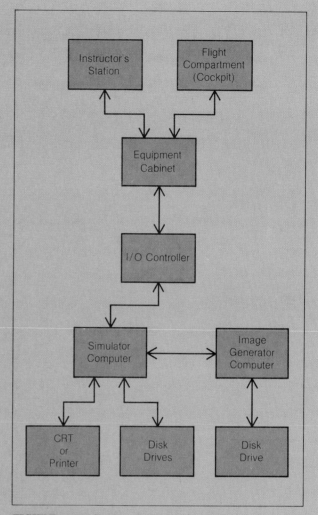

FIGURE 1–4 ▪ System Components

speed changes and cockpit instruments also accurately display the magnitude and direction of any changes the aircraft could experience under actual flight conditions.

The instructor's station is located within the simulator at a position where he or she can observe the students in the cockpit. A control panel, located at the instructor's station, can be used to control such things as meteorological conditions, aircraft systems, simulated emergencies, and visual images.

The flight compartment is an exact replica of the aircraft cockpit. The simulator cockpit is ordered from the aircraft manufacturer and is an actual production model.

The equipment cabinet, in conjunction with the input/output (I/O) controller, shown in Figure 1–4, serves as the interface between the simulator computer and simulator itself. Figure 1–5 illustrates this relationship in slightly greater detail. Many of the systems on the flight simulator require an analog input in order to perform their function. Therefore, the digital output produced by the simulator computer must be converted to an analog input for the particular system. The I/O system (the I/O controller and the equipment cabinet) thus converts the results of the computer's calculations into electrical signals used to perform such functions as positioning the cockpit instruments, developing sounds, and controlling the movement of the motion base.

These systems must also send information back to the simulator computer. In this case, the I/O system converts electrical input signals from controls and switches in the cockpit into digital quantities that can be understood and processed by the simulator computer.

The digital-to-analog conversion within the I/O system is performed by the D/A (digital/analog) converter, while the analog-to-digital conversion process is handled by the A/D (analog/digital) converter. Along with the D/A and A/D converters, digital input and output devices are also contained within the I/O system. These devices perform no conversions, but do allow data in a digital format to flow from the simulator computer to the simulator and vice versa.

The entire I/O process is repeated at extremely high speeds in order to present a dynamic situation to the students and the instructor at all times. A 300 nanosecond (a nanosecond equals one billionth of a second) cycle time of the CPU, which can perform up to 645,000 additions per second, helps to create this dynamic environment within the simulator.

The simulator computer, as well as interfacing with

FIGURE 1–5 ■ I/O System

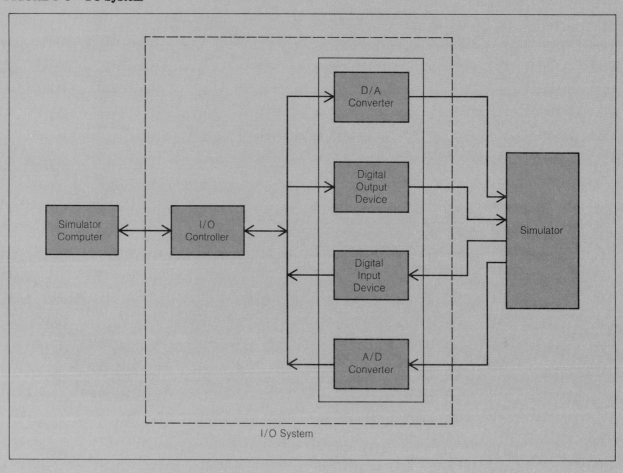

the I/O system, also interfaces with the image-generator computer. On the image-generator computer, the visual system creates realistic visual references for the students in the cockpit.

The visual system generates images that include navigation, runway and airport lighting as well as surface simulations representing the runways, buildings, and terrain. The visual system also has weather settings which range from very bad (cloud heights of 200 feet and visibility ¼ mile) to a very good (no clouds and unlimited visibility).

The visual system uses a TV-like display monitor to show the visual images within the cockpit. The visual images shown to the pilots represent to scale and location what would be seen at night. The images are created from maps, charts, and photographs. These images represent real locations such as Toledo, Denver, Wichita, Salt Lake, Seattle, Phoenix, Sacramento, Hong Kong, and Mexico City.

An interface assembly handles the communication between the two computers and also routes the visual-control selections made by the instructor from within the simulator to the simulator computer. The simulator computer sends the image-generator computer formatted data words that define the aircraft attitude and provide information relating to where the flight began within the program as a point of reference.

Once the data words are received through the interface assembly, the image-generator computer translates them into light points and surface images. After the entire image is created it is then sent to the display monitors in the front of the cockpit.

As stated earlier, this entire process is occurring at such a high rate of speed that the cockpit instrumentation, visual image, and motion reflect, in real time, what would be experienced in actual flight.

DISCUSSION POINTS

1. Discuss some of the benefits that computer simulation training offers over using actual equipment for training.
2. What other applications besides flight training could benefit from computer simulation training?

2
The Evolution of Computers

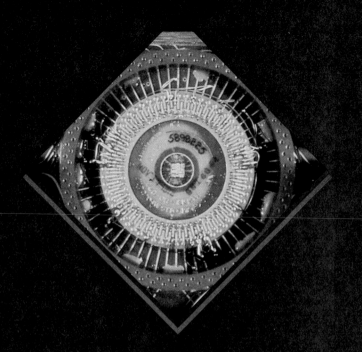

INTRODUCTION

Although the computer is a relatively recent innovation, its development rests on centuries of research, thought, and discovery. Advances in information-processing technology are responses to the growing need to find better, faster, cheaper, and more reliable methods of handling data. The search for better ways to store and process data is not recent—data-processing equipment has gone through generations of change and improvement. An understanding of the evolution of data processing is especially helpful in understanding the capabilities and limitations of modern computers.

This chapter presents significant events that lead to the development of the computer. A brief history of data processing is given, beginning with the earliest calculating machines and ending with the state of the art today. Since developments in computer programs **(software)** are as important as developments in computer equipment **(hardware),** major advances in both areas are presented.

Newport, R.I.—A bumper sticker for yachting traditionalists in these parts reads: "If God had wanted aluminum boats, He would have planted aluminum trees."

Richard McCurdy, an engineer who develops marine electronics, takes it a step further: "Actually," he says, "we all know that God also prefers wood to fiberglass and cotton over Dacron sails—certainly over Mylar."

If this is true, McCurdy concedes, then the deity must be horrified at what is happening on the America's Cup 12-meter racing yachts these days. In a word—computers. . . .

This year, what many call the most elaborate computer system ever will be hooked up to *Defender*, a boat designed by David Pedrick, a naval architect in Newport, and equipped by McCurdy. The onboard system is attached to instruments that monitor boat speed, wind speed, wind angle, heel angle (how far over the boat is leaning), compass heading, and elapsed time.

Today even very simple racing boats monitor these data, called "lay-line" information. However, *Defender's* computer is able to meld all the data together to find the "dead reckoning"—the path showing precisely where the boat has sailed relative to the mark she is headed for. "Then," says Pedrick, "the computer can tell you what you need to do to get there as fast as you can. It fig-

ures all that out and gives you updates twice a second." . . . .

Computers demonstrated some of what they have to offer in the last America's Cup competition. In 1980, when most competitors had limited computer aid to monitor weather and sea conditions, *Clipper* was able to make electronic pictures of the actual path it was sailing.

"You first have to understand how hard it is in a boat to know exactly where you are," says Pedrick. "That is, whether you're close to the approach line to one of the course marks or straying off it." A boat that moves off course even slightly loses valuable seconds, he says: a one-minute lead in a three-hour race is considered a comfortable margin.

"We had one particularly enlightening day on *Clipper*," says Pedrick. "*Clipper* and *Freedom* (her U.S. competitor) had a tacking duel [wherein one boat, turning from side to side through the wind, tries to force the other boat to lose position]. As the two boats were converging on the tacks that brought them together, the helmsman got nervous and turned toward the wind too soon, slowing down long before he made his tack."

Before the computer age, such an observation would have been impossible. But by analyzing the thousands of bits of performance data collected by the shore-side computer, McCurdy and Pedrick were

actually able to see the errors *Clipper's* crew was making.

Pedrick, an experienced ocean sailor, believes that as the computer systems designed for the 12-meter boats become standard equipment for all racing yachts, popular acceptance of computerized racing will follow. "What people will come to realize is that computers just don't know how to sail. They can't steer a boat, they can't take a look at a sail and decide if it looks good or not. People still have to sail. That's still the important factor of the sport.

"All the computer does," he says, "is give the human beings, who are trying to make the boat go as fast as it can, a lot more and faster information about whether they are succeeding."

Adapted from BOSTON GLOBE. Reprinted with permission from TECHNOLOGY REVIEW, copyright 1983.

Much as the invention of the Hollerith code brought about a new method of calculating the United States Census, computers are being used today in a variety of ways to improve human performance. As recent history has shown, many of the most recent startling accomplishments can be linked to our ability to adapt a computer to a specific use.

EARLY
DEVELOPMENT

Trying to piece together the separate inventions, discoveries, and events that culminated in the creation of the modern-day computer requires some guesswork, an open mind, and a little creative imagination. For one thing, at what point in history should such a search start? People always have had difficulty calculating answers to problems and keeping track of the answers. Ancient sheepherders tied knots in pieces of string in order to keep accurate counts of their herd. Could that have been a forerunner of today's computer?

Perhaps a more realistic start would be with the development of the abacus. It is one of the earliest known computational devices; its use dates back to antiquity. Although its creation is attributed to the Chinese, it emerged independently in several cultures. The abacus (see Figure 2–1) was a tool that aided the user in calculating answers to information problems and in storing the results. However, computing "instructions" were little more than carefully planned manipulations of the beads by someone well versed in its operation.

Mathematical discoveries also played their part in the history of the computer. John Napier, a Scotsman, discovered in the mid–1600s that he could multiply and divide numbers by simply adding and subtracting their representations in geometrical series called logarithms. Although the mathematical concepts behind logarithms are complex, it was the practical use to which he put this discovery that is noteworthy here. Napier placed the logarithms of numbers on a set of ivory rods (nicknamed "Napier's bones"). By sliding the "bones" up and down, in effect adding or subtracting the numbers' geometrical series, he performed multiplications and divisions (see Figure 2–2). His invention was translated into the slide rule around 1650 by Robert Bissaker, who placed those numbers on sliding pieces of wood instead of ivory rods. For the computer historian, these inventions represent the development of crude but effective manual calculators.

The development of the first real mechanical calculator is attributed to Blaise Pascal, around 1642. It added and subtracted numbers by using a se-

Figure 2–1 ■ The Abacus

Figure 2–2 ▪ Napier's "Bones"

ries of eight rotating gears, or wheels. As the first wheel counted out ten digits (one complete revolution), a pin on its edge would rotate the wheel next to it. This second wheel, in turn, would rotate the next, and so on (see Figure 2–3). (The same principle is used today in many odometers to keep track of a car's mileage.) Later in that century—around 1690—a German mathematician named Gottfried von Leibnitz developed a machine that could not only add and subtract but multiply, divide, and calculate square roots as well (see Figure 2–4). In both inventions, the "instructions" on how to do the calculations were programmed into the machines mechanically by the way the gears turned one another as they moved. Naturally, the instructions could not be changed without changing the operation of the machines.

One of the first developments in programmable instructions for machines came from the weaving industry in the early 1800s. In an attempt to automate the weaving process, a weaver named Joseph Jacquard developed a loom controlled by a series of punched cards. These cards, made of cardboard, were actual instructions "read" by the machine as they passed over a series of rods; the machine translated the holes in the cards into colors in the

Figure 2–3 ▪ Blaise Pascal and His Adding Machine

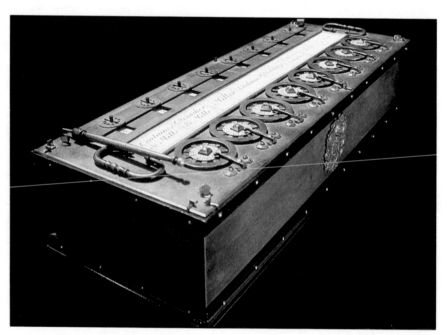

weave. Since each card represented one loop operation, a whole collection of cards were necessary to operate the loom (see Figure 2–5). This concept was a forerunner of what nearly everyone recognizes today as the **punched card.**

One of the tragedies in the history of the computer lies with Charles Babbage, a man truly ahead of his time. Babbage set out to develop a machine that could perform calculations without human intervention. The machine he envisioned would calculate logarithm tables and print the results, avoiding the printing errors so common in his day. In 1812 he managed to build a small model of what he called the **difference engine** (see Figure 2–6). The tragedy was that when he strove to make a larger version of the model, parts could not be manufactured to the tolerances required by his machine. The technology of his time was not sophisticated enough.

Undaunted, Babbage conceived of the idea of building a device which could perform any calculation—adding, subtracting, multiplying, or dividing—according to instructions coded on cards. Even intermediate results could be stored in a memory unit. This device, called the **analytical engine,** contained many features similar to those found in today's computers—in the early 1800s! An arithmetic unit called the "mill" performed the calculations;

Figure 2–4 ▪ Gottfried von Leibnitz and His Calculating Machine

Figure 2–5 ▪ Jacquard's Loom

Figure 2–6 ▪ Charles Babbage and His Difference Engine

and the memory unit, the "store," kept intermediate and final results as well as the instructions for each state of the calculations. Instructions and data were fed into the device by means of punched cards, and output was automatically printed. All of this, of course, was to be done mechanically, not electronically.

Although the analytical engine was originally conceived in 1833, Babbage died before it could be constructed. Nevertheless, a model based on his drawings and notes was put together in 1871 by his son. To his tribute, it worked. Although Babbage was never able to see his inventions become reality, they nevertheless earned him the reputation of being the "father of computers."

Babbage's vision of using punched cards for inputting data and instructions went relatively unnoticed until the late 1880s. At that time, Dr. Herman Hollerith, a statistician, put it to good use. It seems the United States Government was encountering problems in trying to process data gathered in the census. The last census, taken in 1880, had required some seven and a half years of manual calculations to tabulate. Significant population increases since then would make manual processing of the next census almost unthinkable. Hollerith was commissioned by the government to reduce the time required to process the census data.

To do this, he developed a series of machines that stored census data on cards. Each card had twelve rows and eighty columns, the same as the modern-day punched card. The coding scheme he developed for use in punching the cards is still used today. The **Hollerith code** permitted the machines to sort the census data according to the United States Government's information needs. His machines reduced the time required to process the census data to two and a half years, despite a population increase of three million (see Figure 2–7). Not only had Hollerith developed the first computer card, his project comprised the first large-scale data-processing environment.

His successful experience with the government led Hollerith to set up the Tabulating Machine Company to manufacture and market punched card

Figure 2–7 ▪ Herman Hollerith and His Census Machine

equipment for commercial use. His machines were first sold to railroads to be used to compute freight schedules. In 1911, his Tabulating Machine Company merged with several other corporations to form the International Business Machines Corporation (IBM). If Hollerith could only have known the future success of that merger!

In a different vein, William S. Burroughs was making advances with mechanical adding machines around the same time Hollerith's census machines were being put to use on the 1890 census. He developed a key-driven calculating-printing machine operated by a crank. The machine, which could record, summarize, and calculate, was patented and sold by the Burroughs Adding Machine Company, which also became a giant in the computer industry.

From the 1900s on, it becomes more difficult to sort out the different inventions, discoveries, and events that affected the development of the computer. In the late 1920s and early 1930s, significant advances in punched card equipment resulted in machines that could not only add and subtract, but multiply as well. As these machines were further enhanced with the ability to interpret alphabetic data, full-scale record-keeping and accounting functions could be supported. These enhanced machines were called **accounting machines,** or tabulators (see Figure 2–8).

The first real step toward the development of the computer as we know it, however, was made in 1944, by Howard Aiken of Harvard University. Harvard, IBM, and the U.S. War Department embarked on a joint project precipitated by the need to handle the high volume of number crunching (complex

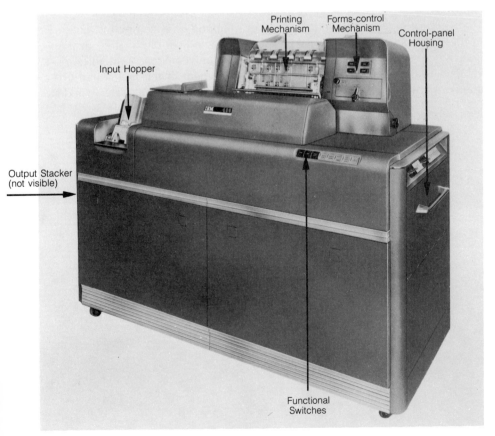

Figure 2–8 ▪ Accounting Machine

Printing Mechanism

Forms-control Mechanism

Control-panel Housing

Input Hopper

Output Stacker (not visible)

Functional Switches

equation solving) required in logistic calculation. The efforts of this team produced the first automatic calculator, which was called the **Mark I** (see Figure 2–9). It was not an electronic computer, but rather utilized electromagnetic relays and mechanical counters. When it ran, the clicking noise from the relays was deafening! Babbage's vision of automatic computation was realized in this machine. Instructions were fed into the Mark I by means of holes punched in paper tape, and results were obtained in the form of holes punched in cards.

Although there had been some question as to who invented the first electronic computer, a federal court in 1974 declared John Vincent Atanasoff to be the true inventor. Along with his assistant, Clifford Berry, Atanasoff completed a prototype electronic computer in 1939. Three years later at Iowa State, Atanasoff and Berry completed a working model of the **Atanasoff-Berry Computer (ABC),** a serial, binary electromechanical device (see Figure 2–10).

In competition with Atanasoff and Berry for the honor of developing the first electronic computer were J. Presper Eckert and John W. Mauchly of the University of Pennsylvania. Their project, completed in 1946, was sponsored by the War Department and considered classified. It resulted in a machine called the **ENIAC (Electronic Numerical Integrator and Calculator).** The ENIAC could perform a multiplication in three-thousandths of a second, compared with about three seconds required by the Mark I. The ENIAC was a huge machine; its 18,000 vacuum tubes took up a space ten feet high, ten feet wide, and some hundred feet long (see Figure 2–11). Since the ENIAC had no internal memory, instructions had to be fed into it by use of combinations of switches.

Not until Jon Von Neumann proposed a method of encoding instructions in the same language used for data did it become possible to store instructions within the computer–see Figure 2–12). Von Neumann's principles, developed in the late 1940s, spurred the development of the first **stored-program computer.** As it turned out, two groups of people were working

Figure 2–9 ▪ Howard Aiken and the Mark I

Figure 2–10 ▪ John Vincent Atanasoff, Clifford Berry, and the Atanasoff-Berry Computer

Figure 2–11 ▪ ENIAC

Figure 2–12 ▪ John Von Neumann and the EDVAC

simultaneously to create such a machine. In the United States, the University of Pennsylvania was developing the **EDVAC (Electronic Discrete Variable Automatic Computer),** while in England, Cambridge University was creating the **EDSAC (Electronic Delay Storage Automatic Computer).** History awarded the EDSAC the title of first stored-program computer, although it was completed only a few months before the EDVAC.

The EDSAC was the first computer to perform arithmetic and logical operations without human intervention, depending solely on stored instructions. It could perform a computation in three milliseconds. The EDSAC marked the end of the quest to develop a stored-program, self-sufficient calculating machine and marked the beginning of the computer age and the information-rich society it made possible. Refinements of the computer concept have focused on speed, size, and cost. The next section of the chapter is devoted to these developments, which can be usefully divided into four categories: first-generation, second-generation, third-generation, and fourth-generation computers.

FIRST GENERATION: 1951–1958

In 1951, the first commercial electronic computer was sold to the U.S. Census Bureau. It was the **UNIVAC I (Universal Automatic Computer),** built by John W. Mauchly and J. Presper Eckert, who had also been responsible for the development of the ENIAC. This event marked the beginning of **first-generation computers,** (see Figure 2–13).

Before the UNIVAC I, computers had been one-of-a-kind machines developed specifically for scientific and military purposes. However, the UNIVAC I was dedicated to business data processing applications. For the first time, business firms were exposed to the possibilities of computer data processing.

Figure 2–13 ▪ **The UNIVAC I Computer**

(Most first-generation computers, however, were still oriented toward scientific applications rather than business data processing.)

The characteristic that distinguished first-generation computers from subsequent machines was the use of vacuum tubes to control internal operations. The vacuum tubes were fairly large, and they generated considerable heat, much as light bulbs do. Thus, first-generation computers were huge, requiring a lot of space and special air-conditioning equipment to dissipate the tube-generated heat. Even with the considerable maintenance they required, their reliability was poor. Although first-generation computers were much faster than early mechanical or electromechanical devices, they were slow compared with today's computers, and their internal storage capacity was limited.

Many used **magnetic drums** as a storage medium. These cylinders, coated with magnetizable material, stored data as tiny magnetized spots on their outer surface. The drum was rotated at high speeds, and **read/write heads** above the drum surface could write or read data as required. Other types of storage media were also used. Operators performed input and output operations by using punched cards.

The computer, a binary machine, can distinguish between only two states—say, "on" or "off," or spots magnetized in one direction or the opposite. These early first-generation computers were programmed using "on" and "off" states called machine language. **Machine language** consists of strings of 0s and 1s that act as instructions to the computer, specifying the desired electrical states of its internal circuits and memory banks. Obviously, writing a machine-language program was extremely cumbersome, tedious, and time consuming.

To make programming easier, **symbolic languages** were developed. Such languages enabled instructions to be written with symbolic codes (called **mnemonics,** or memory aids) rather than strings of 0s and 1s. One word, or mnemonic, was used to represent a series of 0s and 1s that stood for a particular machine language instruction (see Figure 2–14). These symbolic instructions were then translated into corresponding binary codes (machine-language instructions). The first set of programs, or instructions, to tell the

Figure 2–14 ▪ Machine Language
versus Symbolic Language

MACHINE CODE TO ADD TWO FIELDS
11111010010000111000001000010100100000000010101100
SYMBOLIC CODE TO ADD TWO FIELDS
AP   TOTAL, AMOUNT

**Figure 2–15 ▪ Commodore Grace
Murray Hopper**

computer how to do this translation was developed by Commodore Grace Murray Hopper in 1952 at the University of Pennsylvania (see Figure 2–15). After this breakthrough, most first-generation computers were programmed in symbolic language. Of those first-generation computers used in business, most processed payroll and billing, since they were easy to program and to cost justify.

SECOND GENERATION: 1959–1964

In the late 1950s, tiny, solid-state **transistors** replaced vacuum tubes in computers. The elimination of vacuum tubes greatly reduced generated heat and made possible the development of computers significantly smaller and more reliable than their predecessors. These new computers were faster, had increased storage capacity, and required less power to operate. They were **second-generation computers.**

Magnetic cores replaced magnetic drums as the primary internal storage medium. Cores are very small, doughnut-shaped rings of ferromagnetic (magnet-like) material strung on thin wires. The passage of an electric current through wires on which a core is strung magnetizes the core to represent either an "on" or an "off" state and thus enables it to store data. Data stored in magnetic cores can be located and retrieved for processing in a few millionths of a second—faster than with magnetic-drum storage.

In many second-generation computer systems, the **primary memory** capacity of the computer was supplemented by the use of **magnetic tapes** for **secondary storage.** Substituting magnetic tapes for punched cards or punched paper tape increased input/output processing speeds by a factor of at least fifty (see Figure 2–16).

Other significant changes that occurred during this period were the development of magnetic disk storage, modular hardware, and improved input/output devices. **Magnetic disks** can be compared to phonograph records. Data is stored in circular tracks on the flat outer surfaces of the platter, or disk, which are coated with ferromagnetic material. The main advantage of disk storage is that it enables the user to locate a particular record on a set of disks rotating at high speeds in a fraction of a second. Unlike magnetic tape, records on disks do not have to be processed sequentially. The computer can go directly to the record it needs without having to read everything that comes before it. Thus, disks provide **direct,** or **random, access** to records in a file.

Figure 2-16 ▪ **A Second-Generation Computer System**

The modular-hardware concept involved using a building-block approach to the design of electronic circuits. With this approach, complete modules (sometimes called "breadboards") could be replaced in case of malfunctions, greatly reducing downtime, the processing time lost because of malfunctions. It also added flexibility, since new modules could be added to the system to increase its capabilities.

The improvement in input/output (I/O) devices could be seen in faster printing speeds and automatic detection and correction of input/output errors. These advances allowed the devices to be connected directly to the computer (to be **online**) without significantly lowering the overall efficiency of the computer system.

Second-generation computers were programmed in **high-level languages,** which resembled English a lot more than their predecessors had. These languages were **application-** and **problem-oriented** rather than **machine-oriented.** The first high-level language to achieve widespread acceptance was called **FORTRAN (FORmula TRANslator),** developed during the period from 1954 through 1957 by IBM. The version of the language known as FORTRAN IV was standardized in 1963 and is still used extensively for scientific applications.

Because FORTRAN lacked many features desirable for business data processing, another language, called *COBOL (COmmon Business-Oriented Language),* was developed in 1961. Among COBOL's significant features are its file-processing, editing, and input/output capabilities.

Second-generation computers, like their predecessors, were designed either for business data processing or for scientific applications. The most popular business-oriented computer was the IBM 1401. Typical applications included payroll processing, invoicing, and maintaining personnel records. All of these applications involved **batch processing**—the collection of data over a certain period of time and its subsequent processing in one computer run. Magnetic tape was the principal storage medium associated with batch processing.

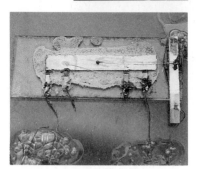

THIRD GENERATION: 1965–1970

Continued technological advances in electronics and solid-state physics brought further reductions in computer size, even greater reliability and speed, and lower costs. **Integrated circuits (ICs),** invented by Jack Kilby in 1958, replaced the transistors of second-generation equipment in machines referred to as **third-generation computers.** While employed by Texas Instruments, Kilby introduced the first silicon integrated circuit in September of 1958, and by February 1959, he had received a patent for the invention (see Figure 2–17). Through techniques like etching and printing, hundreds of electronic components could be included on silicon circuit chips less than one-eighth-inch square (see Figure 2-18).

The transition from the second to the third generation occurred when IBM introduced the System/360 computers. This "family," or series, consisted of six different computers, each offering a different main storage capacity. The series was designed to provide all types of processing; its computers were capable of supporting forty different input/output and auxiliary storage devices. Within a short time after the introduction of the System/360, other manufacturers announced their versions of third-generation computers. RCA, Honeywell, Univac, Burroughs, and others began competing with IBM, and before long over 25,000 third-generation computer systems were installed across the United States (see Figure 2–19).

Between 1965 and 1970, manufacturers invested millions of dollars in the research and development of **hardware** and **software** technologies. Competition was intense, and the cost to remain in the industry was high. As a result, some manufacturers did not survive. RCA left the computer business in 1972, followed by Xerox Corporation in 1975.

Although third-generation computers were smaller, faster, and less expensive than their predecessors, using them was not without problems. Many of the programs written for second-generation computers were based on an **ar-**

Figure 2–17 ▪ **Jack S. Kilby and the First Integrated Circuit**

Figure 2–18 ▪ **First-, Second-, and Third-Generation Components**

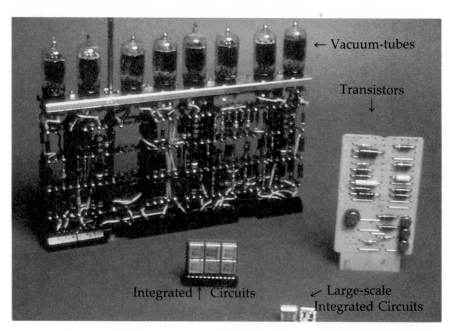

← Vacuum-tubes

Transistors ↓

Integrated ↑ Circuits

Large-scale Integrated Circuits

Figure 2–19 ■ **A Third-Generation Computer System**

chitecture, or internal design, significantly different from that of third-generation computers. Thus, these programs had to be rewritten. In addition, the skills of thousands of programmers became outdated with the introduction of this new architecture, resulting in a major need for re-education of programmers and operators.

Users also faced a problem—that of acquiring software and **operating systems.** When IBM announced the System/360 in 1965, an operating system was scheduled to accompany the installation of the hardware. However, the development of the operating system fell behind schedule, and it took several years to perfect the system.

Because of the overwhelming need for reliable software, a new industry—the software industry—emerged. Firms specializing in the development of software were able to cash in on the growing computer industry by selling **software packages.** Software packages gained widespread acceptance since many users found it more profitable to purchase the prewritten packages than to write the programs themselves.

The advances in solid-state technology that led to third-generation computers also led to the emergence of **minicomputers** (see Figure 2–20). A small computer manufacturer called Digital Equipment Corporation (DEC) introduced the first commercially accepted minicomputer in 1965 and has since grown into the largest manufacturer of minicomputers in the United States.

Other important improvements in third-generation equipment included:

■ Greater storage capacity.
■ Versatile programs (operating systems) that automated many tasks previously handled by human operators.
■ Greater compatibility of components, allowing easier expansion of computer systems.

Alan Turing: Unknown Genius

Alan Turing, a British mathematician, might be described as the unknown genius behind the development of the first electronic computer.

In the 1930s Alan Turing wrote a paper, "On Computable Numbers," that was considered a masterwork by the leading scientists of that time. The paper contained, among other things, the first academic proof supporting the concept of artificial intelligence.

Soon after Turing's paper was published, Britain went to war against Nazi Germany. The Germans had developed Enigma, a machine that could code military messages. Once messages were coded using Enigma, they were virtually impossible to decipher.

In 1939 M16, the British secret service, chose Turing to head a group including the best minds in England. Their assignment was to build a machine capable of deciphering Enigma coded messages. Shrouded in secrecy, the team constructed what some people regard as the world's first electronic computer, Colossus. Colossus was so successful that almost all secret messages intercepted from the Germans were instantly decoded. Historians believe the deciphering capabilities of Colossus had a major impact on the Allied victory in World War II.

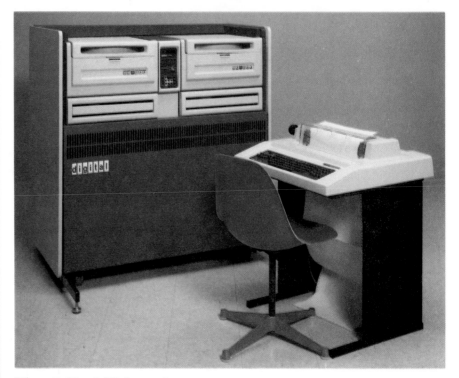

Figure 2–20 ▪ A Minicomputer That Uses Third-Generation Miniaturization Techniques

- Ability to perform several operations simultaneously.
- Ability to perform processing more sophisticated than simple batch processing.
- Capability to handle both business and scientific applications in the same machine.

Another third-generation innovation involved **remote terminals,** terminals placed at various geographic locations and used to communicate directly with a central computer. Using such terminals, many users could interact with the central computer at the same time and receive almost instantaneous results in what was called a **time-sharing** environment.

Third-generation computers, like those of the present, were used for such diverse applications as inventory control, scheduling labor and materials, and bank credit-card billing.

FOURTH GENERATION: 1971–?

State of the Art: The Present

In 1971, IBM began delivering its System/370 computers. This family of computers, and those developed by other large computer manufacturers in the

1970s, incorporated further refinements, among them monolithic semiconductor memories, self-diagnostic operating systems, wide-spread use of virtual storage techniques, and further miniaturization through **large-scale integration (LSI) circuits.** (LSI is a technological process that allows circuits containing thousands of transistors to be densely packed on a single silicon chip.)

Computers of this period are referred to as **fourth-generation computers,** because they offer significant performance and price improvements over third-generation computers. In addition, fourth-generation computers are gradually getting smaller, as evidenced by the emergence of microcomputers. In time, LSI was replaced by **VLSI (very-large-scale integration),** which has meant that computers are becoming smaller still.

Performance improvements in present-day computer systems include increased speeds, greater reliability, and storage capacities approaching billions of characters, all made possible by LSI and VLSI circuitry. The emphasis is on ease of use and application, often called being **user friendly.** Most systems have communication capabilities; they permit remote input and output via communication channels such as ordinary telephone lines. The use of TV-like display screens has become common.

Data-recording equipment to capture data at its point of origin in a form directly suitable for computer processing has been developed; common examples are magnetic-ink character recognition (MICR) devices and optical-character recognition (OCR) devices. The former are especially suited for applications like check processing for banks; the latter include point-of-sale (POS) terminals that record data about sales transactions as they occur. These devices do away with the need for a special data-entry step that uses other input devices. Thus, more accurate and faster entry of data for computer processing is achieved.

As computer technology progresses, computer hardware prices will continue to drop. A greater proportion of the cost of installing and maintaining a computer system is invested in personnel and software support costs (see Figure 2–21). Larger and larger portions of the costs go for personnel salaries. Even with the trend toward pre-written software packages, programmers are needed to tailor the package to fit the organization's needs and to provide ongoing maintenance to keep the programs up-to-date. This phenomenon has prompted greater research into software products to increase computer personnel productivity.

The fourth generation has also been marked by the growth of the home computer market. By using LSI technology, manufacturers are able to produce densely packed chips called **microprocessors.** The first microprocessor was invented in 1969; however, there is some debate whether Ted Hoff, developer of the 4004 microprocessor for Intel Corporation, or Victor Poor, developer of the 8008 microprocessor for Datapoint Corporation, should be given credit. Although the debate has not been resolved, Ted Hoff is usually recognized as the inventor of the microprocessor (see Figure 2–22).

Microprocessors are beginning to appear in many of the devices people use every day, such as microwave ovens, sewing machines, thermostats, and even automobiles. A microprocessor and other densely packed chips for storage and input/output operations form a **microcomputer.**

Table 2–1 provides a summary of the computer generations, their dates, computer system characteristics, and technological advancements.

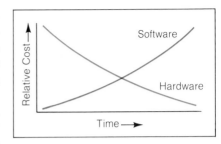

Figure 2–21 ▪ Historical Cost Pattern

Figure 2–22 ▪ Ted Hoff

Table 2–1 ▪ **Computer Advancements**

PERIOD	COMPUTER SYSTEM CHARACTERISTICS
First Generation 1951–1958	Use of vacuum tubes in electronic circuits Magnetic drum as primary internal-storage medium Limited main-storage capacity Slow input/output; punched-card-oriented Low-level symbolic-language programming Heat and maintenance problems Applications: payroll processing and record keeping Examples: IBM 650 UNIVAC I
Second Generation 1959–1964	Use of transistors for internal operations Magnetic core as primary internal-storage medium Increased main-storage capacity Faster input/output; tape orientation High-level programming languages (COBOL, FORTRAN) Great reduction in size and heat generation Increased speed and reliability Batch-oriented applications: billing, payroll processing, updating inventory files Examples: IBM 1401 Honeywell 200 CDC 1604
Third Generation 1965–1970	Use of integrated circuits Magnetic core and solid-state main storage More flexibility with input/output; disk-oriented Smaller size and better performance and reliability Extensive use of high-level programming languages Emergence of minicomputers Remote processing and time-sharing through communication Availability of operating-system programs (software) to control I/O and do many tasks previously handled by human operators Applications: airline reservation systems, market forecasting, credit-card billing Examples: IBM System/360 NCR 395 Burroughs B6500
Fourth Generation 1971–??	Use of large-scale integrated circuits Increased storage capacity and speed Modular design and compatibility between equipment (hardware) provided by different manufacturers (customer no longer tied to one vendor) Availability of sophisticated programs for special applications Greater versatility of input/output devices Increased use of minicomputers Introduction of microprocessors and microcomputers Applications: mathematical modeling and simulation, electronic funds transfer, computer-aided instruction, and home computers Examples: IBM 3081 Burroughs B7900 DEC 2010 (minicomputer) IBM PC-XT (microcomputer)

A HISTORICAL REVIEW OF THE COMPUTER INDUSTRY

Mainframe Computers

The **mainframe** sector is the oldest sector of the computer industry. Major competitors in this market include International Business Machines (IBM),

Burroughs, Digital Equipment Corporation (DEC), Honeywell, Sperry, Control Data Corporation (CDC), and Amdahl. These vendors appeal to potential users of large, sophisticated computers.

Entry into the market is restricted by the huge capital investment required. However, once in the market, companies can take advantage of economies of scale in research and development, hardware, and application and system software design. Large, well-established companies can spread these costs over a number of units; this gives them a pricing advantage.

Though the mainframe sector dominated the computer industry in the past, it has lost part of its market share during the past decade because of the changing nature of the computer business. At one time, the industry was almost purely a hardware business. The price of a computer system was dominated by the cost of the hardware; software costs were bundled in the total system price. With recent technological advances, the cost of hardware has been declining at a rate of 15 to 20 percent per year. In contrast, software and service costs have continued to increase significantly.

Most companies requiring the processing capabilities of large computers have already had them for some time. Purchases of newer mainframes are made only when the company needs expanded capability or when new price/performance ratios make them cost effective. The cost of maintaining large computer systems deters many firms from purchasing them. Some users are finding it more economical to purchase small computer systems. In short, the high end of the computer market is becoming saturated.

Minicomputers

Minicomputers have come a long way since their initial development for specific applications such as process control and engineering calculations. Current minicomputers are more flexible, provide greater capabilities, and support a full line of peripherals. The growth in minicomputer applications has led to the concept of distributed processing. Minicomputers are also used in time-sharing applications, numerical control of machine tools, industrial automation, and word processing.

One reason for the popularity of the minicomputer is its flexibility. Minicomputers can be plugged into standard electrical outlets; they do not require special facilities (such as air conditioning and water cooling); and they can be utilized in an unlimited number of configurations. Another important advantage of a minicomputer system is that it can be enlarged to meet the needs of a growing organization, since it can be implemented in a modular fashion. For example, a hospital may install one minicomputer in its outpatient section for record keeping and another in the pharmacy section or laboratory. As additional minis are installed, they can be connected to existing ones to share common data.

The minicomputer industry has been growing at a rate of 35 to 40 percent annually. However, recent analysis indicates that the growth rate of this sector of the market is declining and may stabilize in the near future. Leading manufacturers include Digital Equipment Corporation (DEC), Hewlett-Packard, Data General, Honeywell, General Automation, and Texas Instruments. Smaller manufacturers include Wang Laboratories, Systems Engineering Laboratories, Inc. (SEL), and Prime Computer, Inc. IBM and Burroughs have also entered this market.

HIGHLIGHT

World's Largest Computer

The world's largest computer weighed 300 tons and took up more space than a high school gymnasium. When it was delivered to McGuire Air Force Base, the equipment arrived in eighteen moving vans. Another thirty-five moving vans contained display screens and spare parts.

This computer, the IBM AN/FSQ-7, was the heart of the U.S. Air Force's system for air defense against attacking bombers. When the system was purchased in 1958, it cost $30 million; the Air Force bought fifty-six of these computers. The world's largest computer also set a record as being the longest-operating computer. It was in use until 1983.

Microcomputers

The rapid development of the microcomputer industry can be attributed to many ingenious and intriguing individual. One such individual is John Roach, the chairman of Tandy Corporation. Roach persuaded Charles Tandy to manufacture a microcomputer and market it through the Radio Shack stores that Tandy had bought in 1963. Roach had the foresight and marketing skill to create a situation where, for the first time, a person could walk into a retail store and purchase a low-priced personal computer. With the introduction of the TRS-80 microcomputer in September 1977, and later the TRS-80 Models II, III, and IV (see Figure 2–23), Radio Shack and Tandy Corporation have become a driving force in the microcomputer industry.

Another key figure, Jack Tramiel, the founder and vice chairman of Commodore Business Machines, had the ability to understand and predict possible outcomes in a given market. He once predicted that calculators would someday sell for as little as $10 at the neighborhood drugstore. Not knowing specifically what the computer could be used for, Commodore introduced its new computer at an electronics show in 1977. Demand for the computer was so great that people were told to send their money in so that they could be placed on a waiting list until enough computers could be manufactured to meet the demand. In one month Commodore received over $3 million for orders of the computers, signifying the potential demand for personal computers.

After acquiring control of MOS Technology, a semiconductor manufacturer, Commodore gained control of the 6502 microprocessor which was being developed at the time. Tramiel supplied additional financing to the development project, and the investment ultimately paid off. The 6502 microprocessor is used in the Commodore PET microcomputer and was also sold to Apple and Atari for use in various models of their microcomputers.

Two other individuals, Steven Jobs and Stephen Wozniak, have also had a great influence on the microcomputer industry. In 1976, Wozniak succeeded in building a small, easy-to-use computer, on which he had been working in his spare time. Wozniak was pleased with this clever machine, but Jobs had visions of its use in homes and small businesses and talked Wozniak into starting a business. By selling Job's Volkswagen and Wozniak's scientific cal-

Figure 2–23 ▪ John Roach and the TRS-80 Model II

culator, the two raised $1,300 to build the first Apple computers in Job's parents' garage.

From its humble beginnings in 1976, Apple Computer Company has become one of the leaders in the manufacture and sale of microcomputers (see Figure 2–24). With revenues of $983 million in 1983, Apple Computer Company has made Chairman of the Board Steven Jobs a modern-day folk hero and millionaire. Stephen Wozniak, on the other hand, left Apple to return to college while remaining a major stockholder.

Men are not the only success stories to be found in the area of microcomputers. Vector Graphics Inc. was founded in 1977 by Carole Ely and Lore Harp to market a microcomputer memory board designed by Lore Harp's husband. Six thousand dollars of inventory allowed the pair to begin assembly of the memory board in the Harp home, where packing materials were stored in a shower and the dining room was used for testing. The company has since grown to over 400 employees designing, assembling, and selling entire desk-top computers.

Although many of the innovators in the field of microcomputers have been, and continue to be, successful, the entrance into the market by such giants as IBM, DEC, NCR, Zerox, and Burroughs has created an extremely competitive environment. Adam Osborne, one of the early entrants into the market, for example, finally filed for Chapter XI under the federal bankruptcy laws.

Osborne, a scientist and technical writer born in Great Britain, established Osborne Computer Corporation using profits from the sale of twelve computer books he wrote and had translated into eight languages. The first Osborne personal computer was shipped in July 1981, and within sixty days of that shipment the company had reported a profit. By November 1981, Osborne Computer had reported profits of $10 million.

With the large number of firms that have entered the industry—nearly 200 manufacturers—and the success of microcomputers produced by companies such as IBM, competition is forcing firms like Osborne to claim bankruptcy. Many analysts feel that it will be IBM that will set the standards of the microcomputer industry in the future, much as they have in the mainframe

Figure 2–24 ▪ Steven Jobs, Stephen Wozniak, and the Apple II

computer market in the past. This is not to say that large manufacturers will dominate the market, but that all companies in the microcomputer industry must be prepared to do business in an extremely competitive environment. It is the analysts' opinion, therefore, that the companies with the lowest cost manufacturing or the greatest marketing strength will succeed in an industry with personal computer sales estimated at $28 million for 1987.

SUMMARY POINTS

■ Machines to perform arithmetic calculations were developed as early as the 1600s by Pascal and Leibnitz. The first machine employing concepts similar to those of a computer was the analytical engine designed by Charles Babbage in 1833. This machine was doomed to failure because its production was beyond the technology of its time.

■ The use of electromechanical calculating machines was first implemented by Herman Hollerith in the 1890 census. These machines used punched-card input and performed simple arithmetic calculations and card-sorting operations. Electromechanical punched-card machines such as accounting machines were used extensively in the early and mid-1900s. They were controlled by hand-wired control panels.

■ The Mark I was the first automatic calculator. Introduced in the late 1930s, the Mark I used electromagnetic relays and counters for performing calculations. It was an electromechanical rather than an electronic computer.

■ The first electronic computer—the Atanasoff-Berry Computer—was completed in 1942 by John Vincent Atanasoff and Clifford Berry.

■ In the mid-1940s, the ENIAC (Electronic Numerical Integrator and Calculator) was developed. The EDSAC (Electronic Delay Storage Automatic Computer) was completed in 1949. It was the first stored-program computer.

■ The first generation of computers (1951–1958) began with the introduction of the UNIVAC I (Universal Automatic Computer). First-generation computers used vacuum tubes to control internal operations. These machines were very large and generated a lot of heat. They were much faster than earlier machines, but very slow by today's standards.

■ Second-generation computers (1959–1964) relied on transistors for controlling internal operation. Transistors were much smaller, faster, and more reliable than vacuum tubes. In addition, significant increases in speed were obtained through the use of magnetic cores for internal storage, or memory. Other important innovations during the second generation were the introduction of high-level programming languages, modular hardware design, and improved input/output devices.

■ Third-generation computers (1965–1970) used solid-state integrated circuits rather than transistors to obtain reductions in size and cost, together with increased reliability and speed. These machines had a much larger storage capacity than second-generation computers. In addition, third-generation computers were supported by more sophisticated software. Many tasks previously handled by human operators were automated.

■ Fourth generation computers rely on large-scale and very-large-scale integration, and continue to offer improvements in size, speed, and cost.

■ Entry into the mainframe computer market is restricted by huge capital investment. The changing nature of the computer business has created a situation in which companies are turning to smaller computer systems, leaving the mainframe market saturated.

- Minicomputers have become popular because of their flexibility. Their modular design and ease of installation and maintenance have led to their current popularity.
- In 1977 Radio Shack and Tandy Corporation introduced the first TRS-80 model computer. It was the first time a microcomputer could be purchased in a retail store.
- Jack Tramiel, the founder of Commodore Business Machines, built a successful microcomputer manufacturing firm on the philosophy of selling "to the masses, not the classes."
- Apple Computer was begun by Steven Jobs and Stephen Wozniak, who sold a Volkswagen and a scientific calculator to raise $1,300 and begin making Apple computers in Job's parents' garage.
- Although dominated by small, innovative, engineering-oriented companies in its early history, the microcomputer industry is evolving into a highly competitive business environment.

REVIEW QUESTIONS

1. Calculating machines developed in the 1600s by Pascal and Leibnitz could perform many of the functions of modern computers. Besides the fact that these machines were mechanical rather than electronic, what was a major difference between these devices and computers?

2. In what way did the development of a loom by Jacquard affect the development of computing devices?

3. Charles Babbage attempted to build a machine employing the concepts now used in computers. What was this machine called and why was it never built?

4. What was the first automatic calculator? How did this machine differ from first-generation computers?

5. What are the chief characteristics that distinguish first-, second-, and third-generation computers?

6. Why has the development of large-scale integration had such an impact on the computer industry?

7. Many hardware innovations were accompanied by improvements in software. What were some of the software developments during the third generation of computers? Why were improvements in software necessary?

8. What was the marketing strategy employed by Jack Tramiel for selling Commodore computers? Why do you feel this strategy has proven successful?

9. How did John Roach and Radio Shack affect the microcomputer market (that is, what was unique about the way in which Radio Shack marketed its microcomputers)?

10. Describe the microcomputer market in general after the entrance of companies such as IBM, DEC, NCR, Xerox, and Burroughs. What impact will these companies ultimately have on the market?

APPLICATION

United States Navy

The United States Navy has provided a major impetus to the development of modern computers. Through the Office of Naval Research, much effort and money have been directed toward the development of concepts basic to today's computer. The most notable of these are stored programs and magnetic-core memory. Because of the increasing demands for national security, the Navy will no doubt remain at the forefront of technology.

WARTIME RESEARCH

The Navy's first major impact on computer development was its support of the Mark I, developed by Howard Aiken at Harvard and built by IBM. This project was first supported by the Bureau of Ships and then by the Bureau of Ordnance Computation Project. The Mark I was capable of performing the complex scientific calculations believed to be necessary for various applications relating to national security. In fact, some of the early calculations for the atomic bomb were performed on this machine.

Following the successful completion of the Mark I project, the Navy contracted Aiken to construct a machine for the computation of ballistic tables at the Bureau of Ordnance's Naval Proving Ground at Dahlgren,

Virginia. This machine, popularly known as the "Ballistic Computer," was a special-purpose, all-relay calculator and much faster than the Mark I.

In 1944, J. W. Forrester was contracted by the Navy Office of Research and Invention to build a computer system capable of simulating an airplane's performance. A pilot who provided input was to be part of the system, which was to respond to the pilot just as a plane would. Engineering changes to the plane could be simulated without the expense, time, and possible dangers inherent in building and operating a prototype plane.

POSTWAR ACTIVITIES

The Office of Naval Research (ONR) was established by Congress in 1946 as a postwar continuation of wartime projects initiated by the National Defense Research Committee (NDRC) and the Office of Scientific Research and Development (OSRD). The purpose of this organization was to encourage scientific research, which was believed to be vital to the maintenance of naval power and, in effect, the preservation of national security. For many years following World War II, the ONR was the primary and most reliable source of funds for scientific research in the United States.

After World War II, the Mathematical Sciences Division in the Natural Sciences group of the ONR provided heavy support for research in pure mathematics, applied mathematics, and mathematical statistics, including support for increasingly complex methods of numerical analysis. To implement these methods, researchers developed various computing devices and, eventually, large-scale electronic computers.

In 1946, the ONR began support of the Whirlwind I project at the Massachusetts Institute of Technology (MIT). This project was also under the direction of J. W. Forrester; while on the project, he developed and had operable by 1953 the magnetic-core memory that was to become the standard for all digital computers.

Also in 1946, a project under the cosponsorship of

the Army Ordnance Corps and the Office of Naval Research was set up. The project, under the direction of John Von Neumann, was known as the Electronic Computer Project of the Institute for Advanced Study. Four main components—an arithmetic unit, a memory, a control, and an input/output area—were developed for the project machine. These components exist in today's computers.

In 1952, the Naval Research Laboratory of the ONR developed a scientific calculator known as the Naval Research Laboratory Electronic Digital Computer (NAREC). Its primary function was the reduction of experimental data gathered from missile-control research. The internal storage of the machine consisted of electrostatic tubes. Auxiliary storage was provided by a magnetic drum.

The Naval Ordnance Research Calculator (NORC) was developed in a joint effort by the Naval Bureau of Ordnance and IBM in 1954. At the time of its development, the NORC represented the leading edge of technology. It was a one-of-a-kind device that used electrostatic storage tubes and was capable of performing multiplication in about thirty microseconds, a rate much faster than the six seconds needed by the Mark I to perform a similar calculation. The NORC was used to perform general scientific calculations in ordnance research, development, and testing at the Naval Proving Ground.

Beginning in about 1954, commercially available (mass-produced) computers began to replace one-of-a-kind computers. These machines, which could be adapted to a variety of purposes, began to appear everywhere in naval operations, from shipboard applications to weaponry and base control. As technology advanced, the Navy's use of computers became increasingly sophisticated.

Within this complex technological environment, ONR is searching for innovative concepts to reduce the costs of software development, improve understanding of the hardware-software interface, design automated systems to complement human decision making, improve industrial productivity, and substitute for human performance in hostile environments. Toward these ends, the ONR Information Sciences Program is currently supporting research activity in the following areas:

1. Computer Architecture: Computer architecture research relates to such factors as automated design and fabrication of digital computer components and provision of new concepts in memory technology.
2. Software Engineering: Research in software engineering is concerned with designing higher-level languages, providing program correctness, developing algorithms for computations, and developing support for large file systems.
3. Distributed Processing: ONR is studying the problems asociated with distributed processing, such as networking problems, allocation of the workload, and security.
4. Artificial Intelligence: The area of interest described as artificial intelligence spans the general fields of automated decision making and robotics, including efforts in knowledge representation, common-sense reasoning, natural language and speech understanding, and expert consulting systems. Within the robotics area, research is being performed on the development of machine vision, manipulation, sensing, and control.

In summary, the United States Navy has been operating at the forefront of computer technology for over a quarter of a century and will probably continue to do so. The advent of new technology makes possible increased national security, which is the prime concern of naval operations. The Navy will undoubtedly continue to push the development of computer technology into unexplored areas.

DISCUSSION POINTS

1. The Whirlwind I and NORC are members of which generation of computers? What characteristics place them in that generation?
2. What characteristics of third-generation computers allow them to be used in such advanced applications as aircraft and weaponry control?

SECTION II
TECHNOLOGY

3

Hardware

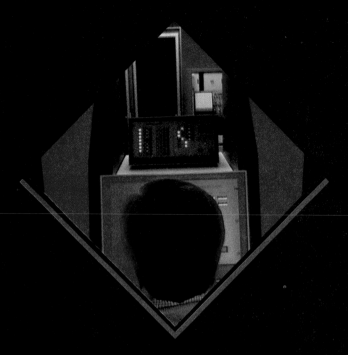

INTRODUCTION

One can acquire a general understanding of electronic
data processing without making a detailed study of the
computer technology involved. However, with a basic understanding of how the computer operates, the student of
data processing is better equipped to appreciate the
computer's capabilities and limitations and to relate this
knowledge to data-processing activities.

This chapter focuses on the parts of a computer system.
The heart of the computer is the central processing unit,
or CPU; its key components are identified and their functions explained. The chapter also examines various forms
of primary storage and briefly discusses read-only memory (ROM) and programmable read-only memory (PROM).
How data is represented in ways appropriate for computer
processing is also discussed. The chapter concludes with
a discussion of digital and analog computers, mainframe
computers, minicomputers, and microcomputers.

Computers of the Future: Will They Need Us?

Gordon Williams

It's become a cliche that today's computers are marvels. They're crammed with millions of electronic devices on silicon chips no bigger than lima beans, and are so swift, their computing speed is measured in billionths-of-a-second. But there are limits to how many electronic devices can fit on a silicon chip, and limits to how fast and powerful we can make computers, using existing technology. Besides, as efficient as today's computers are, they mostly do things you could do with paper and a pencil. They can add and subtract at super speeds, but they can't reason things out, and they can't learn.

In light of this, scientists are working to develop super computers that will be far faster and more complex; able to think and reason. They would be so powerful that no computing problem, no matter how difficult, would exceed their ability. Yet they would be made so minute, they could fit into our bodies—perhaps, for instance, to serve as "eyes" for a blind person.

The building block of our present computer is the silicon chip, with all the necessary electronic circuitry etched on its surface. The building block of the computer of the future would be a molecule, bred to perform some specific electronic function. A billion molecules would take no more space than a silicon chip, and the molecular computer would be a billion times faster and more powerful than existing computers.

No human could work with anything that tiny, so scientists will use genetic technology to make these molecular computers build themselves. In one theory, organic materials—marvelous new proteins—would be blended together in a biological stew to form "biochips." Whatever functions you wanted a biochip to perform, you'd program them in when you were growing the molecules.

One immediate advantage is that a biochip would be three-dimensional, with vastly greater capacity than a two-dimensional silicon chip. No one has built a molecular computer yet, but the model for one certainly exists. It's the human brain.

Biophysicist James McAlear and electrical engineer John Wehrung have spent a decade working on the biochip at their Gentronix Laboratories in Rockville, Md. McAlear has no doubt that a biochip computer can be built—not overnight, but in stages, with the power and speed of the computer gaining 1000-fold at each stage. He thinks we'll have the full-blown biochip computer around the dawn of the 21st century. Even before that, McAlear expects to see computers that far surpass the power of the human brain. "Anything is possible in a system you grow yourself," he says.

In the meantime, computer technologists are working to build bigger silicon chips. Trilogy Systems, of Cupertino, Calif., wants to make super chips with as many electronic devices as you'd find on 100 small chips. . . .

But even super chips would only be an improvement on what we have today—not a grand breakthrough to the future. . . . For the super chores that lie ahead—from tiny computers that could be implanted in our bodies to monitor our health or enhance our intellects, to super, *super* computers that will guide spaceships to the most distant stars—we need something faster, more powerful and much smarter.

That something may well be a molecular computer based on a biochip that grows itself—even if the first biochip hasn't been made, and the genetic technology needed to make one still doesn't exist.

But even if the first biochip computer is years off in the future, "you know it's the way it ought to happen," says Martin Cooper, former head of research and development at Motorola Inc., who now has his own company in the cellular telephone business. "You need a new technique," says Cooper, "and the new technique is to grow them."

Since the beginning of the first computer generation (1951), there has been a dramatic evolution in the area of computer hardware. As is indicated in this article, this technology is not static and will continue to change as we move further into the future. We can, therefore, only take a snapshot of hardware technology as it exists today, and speculate on its shape and form in the future.

CENTRAL PROCESSING UNIT

It is not necessary to acquire a working knowledge of the internal electronic circuitry of a computer in order to use it. However, a basic understanding of computer technology is essential. The simple diagram in Figure 3–1 shows the principal components of a computer system.

The input to a computer can take many forms: data can be entered from magnetic tape, through the pressing of keys on a terminal keyboard, and so on. Representing data on magnetic tape and entering it into the computer through a tape drive onto magnetic disk storage is one common method. (Input devices will be discussed in greater detail in Chapter 4.)

The **central processing unit (CPU),** also known as the **mainframe** on large systems, is the heart of the computer system. It is composed of three units: (1) the control unit, (2) the arithmetic/logic unit (ALU), and (3) the primary storage unit. Each unit performs its own unique functions.

The **control unit,** as its name implies, maintains order and controls activity in the CPU. It does not process or store data. Rather, it directs the sequence of operations. The control unit interprets the instructions of a program in storage and produces signals that act as commands to circuits to execute the instructions. Other functions of the control unit include communicating with an input device in order to begin the transfer of instructions and data into storage and, similarly, communicating with an output device to initiate the transfer of results from storage.

The **arithmetic/logic unit (ALU)** performs arithmetic computations and logical operations. Since the bulk of internal processing involves calculations or comparisons, the capabilities of a computer often depend upon the design and capabilities of its ALU.

The **primary storage unit (internal storage, primary memory,** or **main storage)** holds instructions, data, and intermediate and final results. At the start of processing, data is transferred from an input device to the primary storage unit, where it is stored until needed for processing. Data being processed and intermediate results of ALU calculations are also stored here. After all computations and manipulations are completed, the final results remain in memory until the control unit causes them to be transferred to an output device.

Among the most widely used of the many types of output devices are: printers, which provide results on paper; visual-display units, which project results on television-like screens; and tape and disk drives, which produce machine-readable magnetic information. (These devices will be discussed in Chapters 4 and 5.)

INSTRUCTIONS

Obtaining an overall perspective of the functions of each computer system component involves understanding the instruction and data flow through a computer system. A computer program is a series of instructions. Each computer instruction has two basic parts: the operation code and the operand. The **operation code (op code)** tells the control unit what function is to be performed (such as ADD, MOVE DATA, or COMPARE). The **operand** indicates the primary storage location of the data to be operated on. (Op codes and operands will be discussed in more detail in Chapter 10.)

Figure 3–1 ▪ **Computer System Components**

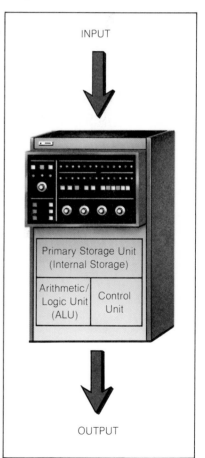

INPUT

Primary Storage Unit (Internal Storage)

Arithmetic/ Logic Unit (ALU)

Control Unit

OUTPUT

INPUT

Instructions

| 1 | 2 | 3 | 4 |

Input Area   Output Area

OUTPUT

Figure 3–2 ▪ Memory Segmentation

The computer performs instructions sequentially unless instructed to do otherwise. This **next-sequential-instruction feature** requires that the instructions that constitute a program be placed in consecutive locations in memory. Since input must be brought into the computer for processing, a separate area must be designated for the input. Output generated by the program also requires an area isolated from the instructions. Figure 3–2 shows this segmentation of memory.

It might be useful to illustrate how all three units interact. Initially, the control unit directs the input device to transfer instructions and data to primary storage. Then the control unit takes one instruction from storage, examines it, and sends appropriate electronic signals to the ALU and to storage, causing the instruction to be carried out. The signals sent to storage may tell it to transfer data to the ALU, where it is mathematically manipulated. The result may then be transferred back to storage.

After execution of an instruction has been initiated, the control unit takes the next instruction from the primary storage unit. Data may be transferred from storage to the ALU and back several times before all instructions are executed. When all manipulations have been completed, the control unit directs the storage unit to transfer the processed data (information) to the output device.

If more than one input record is to be processed, the steps which have been described will be repeated for each record.

These steps can be summarized as shown in Figure 3–3. Notice that computers, like humans, can only execute one instruction at a time. However, they work at incredibly high speeds.

STORED-PROGRAM CONCEPT

A **program** is a series of instructions to direct the computer to perform a given task. In early computers, instructions had to be either wired on control panels and plugged into the computer at the beginning of a job or read into the computer from punched cards in distinct steps as the job progressed. The latter approach slowed down processing because the computer had to wait for instructions to be fed in by a human operator. To speed up processing, the memory of the computer came to be used to store the instructions as well as the data, as explained earlier. This development—the **stored-program concept**—was significant; since the instructions were stored in the computer's memory in electronic form, no human intervention was required during processing. The computer could proceed at its own speed—close to the speed of light!

Most modern computers are stored-program computers. Once the instructions required for a particular application have been determined, they are placed into computer memory so that the appropriate operations will be performed. The storage unit operates much as a tape recorder does: Once a copy of the instructions has been stored, these instructions remain in storage until new ones are stored over them. Therefore, it is possible to execute the same instructions over and over again until the instructions are changed. This basic characteristic of memory is known as **nondestructive read/destructive write.** Each series of instructions placed into memory is called a **stored program,** and the person who writes these instructions is called a **programmer.**

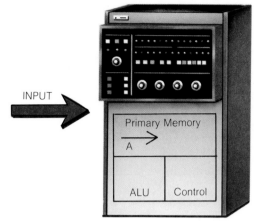

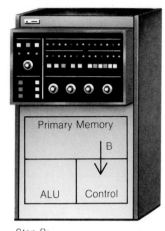

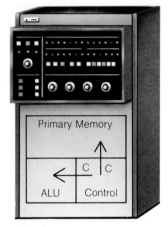

INPUT

Step A:
Instruction and data from the input device are stored in primary storage under direction of the control unit.

Step B:
The control unit examines one instruction and interprets it.

Step C:
The control unit sends appropriate electronic signals to the ALU and to primary storage.

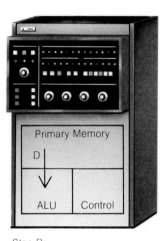

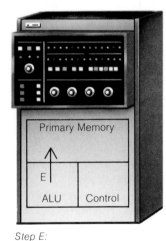

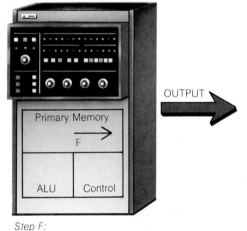

OUTPUT

Step D:
The required data items are transferred to the ALU, where calculations and/or comparisons are performed.

Step E:
The result is transferred back to the primary storage unit. B—E are continued until all instructions have been executed.

Step F:
The control unit signals the primary storage unit to transfer results to the output device.

Figure 3–3 ▪ CPU Operations

STORAGE

Storage Locations and Addresses

In order to direct processing operations, the control unit of the CPU must be able to locate each instruction and data item in storage. Therefore, each location in storage is assigned an **address.** A simple way to understand this concept is to picture computer storage as a large collection of mailboxes.

Figure 3–4 ▪ Each Mailbox
Represents a Location in Storage
with a Specific Address

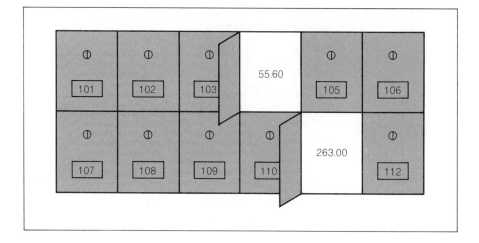

Each mailbox is a specific location with its own number or address (see Figure 3–4). Each can hold one item of information. Since each location in storage has a unique address, particular items can be located by use of stored-program instructions that give the addresses.

Suppose the computer is to be directed to subtract TAX from GROSS PAY to determine an employee's salary. Suppose further that TAX is stored at location 104 and has a value of 55.60 and that GROSS PAY is stored at location 111 and has a value of 263.00.

To accomplish this task, the programmer instructs the computer to subtract TAX from GROSS PAY. The computer interprets this to mean that it should subtract the contents of location 104 from the contents of location 111. It is easy to see why programmers must keep track of what is stored at each location. They are often aided in this task by the use of **variables**—meaningful names such as TAX and GROSS PAY. It is easier for the programmer to use such names, and the computer easily translates them into the addresses assigned to storage locations. The term *variable* arises from the fact that while the variable name (the storage address) itself does not change, the data stored at the location may. The values of TAX and GROSS PAY are likely to change with each employee. The addresses of TAX and GROSS PAY will not.

Primary Storage

Primary storage comprises all storage considered part of the CPU. It may, in some cases, be supplemented by **secondary** (also called **auxiliary,** or **external**) **storage,** which is separate from the CPU. Information is transferred between primary and secondary storage through electrical lines. The most common secondary storage devices are magnetic-tape and magnetic-disk units. (Secondary storage devices are discussed more fully in Chapter 5.)

As mentioned in Chapter 2, first-, second-, and third-generation computers contained primary storage units composed of magnetic cores. Each core could store one binary digit, or **bit** (short for *bi*nary digit). The cores' operation was based upon the principle that a magnetic field is created when electricity flows through a wire (Gauss's Law). The direction of the magnetic field, which depends upon the direction in which the electric current flows, determined which binary state a core represented. Magnetization of a core in a clockwise direction indicated an "on" (1) condition; a counterclockwise direction of magnetization represented an "off" (0) condition (see Figure 3–5).

Figure 3–5 ▪ Magnetizing a Core

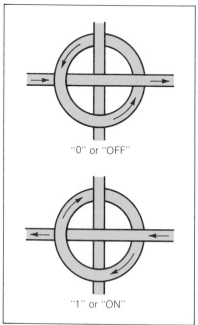

"0" or "OFF"

"1" or "ON"

Technological developments have led to the use of semiconductors in primary storage units. **Semiconductor memory** is composed of circuitry on **silicon chips.** One silicon chip, only slightly bigger than one core, may hold as much as thousands of cores can. The speed of processing with semiconductors is also significantly faster than that with cores. The main storage of recent computers consists mostly of semiconductors. Figure 3–6 illustrates the actual size of a silicon chip.

Semiconductors are designed to store data in locations called **bit cells,** which are capable of being in an "on" or "off" state. "On" is represented by a 1, and "off" by a 0. The bit cells of semiconductor memory are arranged in eight-row by eight-column matrices (see Figure 3–7). Unlike core memory, semiconductor memory does not store data magnetically. The bit cells indicate an "on" state when holding a charge and an "off" state when not containing a charge. The bit cell at which the current intersects, therefore, is holding a charge, while the remaining bit cells along the two lines are not holding a charge. As indicated by Figure 3–7, bit cells 2,3 and 6,4 are holding a charge and would be considered to be "on", while the remaining cells would be "off."

The bit cells of a semiconductor are arranged so that they can be written to or read from as needed. They have an inherent nondestructive read capability (since they either do or do not pass current). A diagram highlighting the actual makeup of a bit cell is also shown in Figure 3–7. The selection line is the row line, while the data line is the column line. Once current is passed through the selection line, all transistors along the row are turned on. The **transistor** is an on/off switch connecting the data line to the **capacitor** which holds the electrical charge. Once the data line and selection line both receive a charge, current passes through the transistor, causing the capacitor to take

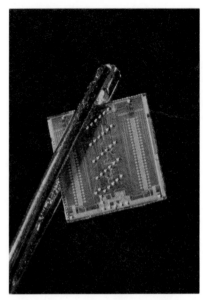

Figure 3–6 ▪ This Memory Chip Can Hold up to 64,000 Pieces of Information

Figure 3–7 ▪ A Portion of Semiconductor Memory

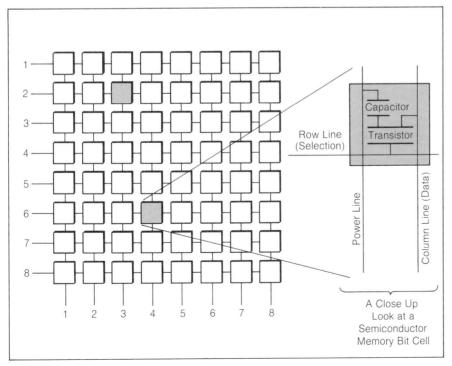

on a charge. If the selection line is not turned on, no current will pass through the transistor and the capacitor will have no charge.

One disadvantage of most semiconductor memory units is that they require a constant power source. Since they rely on currents to represent data, all their stored data is lost if the power source fails and no emergency (backup) system exists. This can be noted in Figure 3–7 by the fact that the capacitor is dependent on the power supply line for holding a charge. Core memory, on the other hand, retains its contents even if the power source fails because it relies on magnetic charges rather than on currents. Significant improvements in semiconductor technology have nevertheless increased the popularity of semiconductor memory over core.

A device called **bubble memory** has been introduced as a replacement medium not only for primary storage but also for secondary storage. This memory consists of magnetized spots, or **magnetic domains,** resting on a thin film of semiconductor material. The magnetic domains (called bubbles) have a polarity opposite that of the semiconductor material on which they rest. Data is stored by shifting the bubbles' positions on the surface of the material (see Figure 3–8). When data is read, the presence of a bubble indicates a 0 bit. The bubbles are similar to magnetic cores in that they retain their magnetism indefinitely. Bubbles are much smaller than magnetic cores; therefore, more data can be stored in a smaller area. A bubble memory module only slightly larger than a quarter can store 20,000 characters of data.

Some manufacturers have introduced bubble memories in computers; however, a more common use of bubble memories is to provide limited storage capabilities in input/output devices. High cost and difficulty of production have been major factors limiting wide industry and user acceptance of bubble memory.

An alternate method of producing primary storage, referred to as **biochip** technology, is currently in the research phase of development. Biochip technology uses groupings of molecules to create an electric circuit. The idea of being able to grow computer circuits rather than manufacture them is a very unique concept. Plans might also include the use of genetic engineering to aid in the design of molecular memory chips. Although the research in this area has just recently begun, its potential success is evidenced by the financial commitment major universities and corporations have made to the project.

Read-Only Memory (ROM)

Computers are capable of performing complex functions such as taking square roots and evaluating exponents. Such functions can be built into the hardware or software of a computer system. Building them into the hardware provides the advantages of speed and reliability, since the operations are part of the actual computer circuitry. Building them into software allows more flexibility, but carrying out functions built into software is slower and more prone to error.

When functions are built into the hardware of a computer, they are placed in **read-only memory (ROM).** Read-only memory instructions are **hard-wired;** that is, they cannot be changed or deleted by other stored-program instructions. Since ROM is permanent, it cannot be occupied by common stored-program instructions or data. The only method of changing its contents is by altering the physical construction of the circuits.

Figure 3–8 ■ Bubble Memory Section Magnified 1,500 Times

A direct result of this characteristic is microprogramming. **Microprograms** are sequences of instructions built into read-only memory to carry out functions (such as calculating square roots) that otherwise would have to be directed by stored-program instructions at a much slower speed. Microprograms are usually supplied by computer manufacturers and cannot be altered by users. However, microprogramming allows the basic operations of the computer to be tailored to meet the needs of users. If all instructions that a computer can execute are located in ROM, a complete new set of instructions can be obtained by changing the ROM. When selecting a computer, users can get the standard features of the machine plus their choice of the optional features available through microprogramming. Many minicomputers and microcomputers today are directed by instructions stored in ROM (see Figure 3–9).

A point worth emphasizing is that the concept of read-only memory is entirely different from that of nondestructive read. With nondestructive read, items in memory can be read repeatedly without loss of information; however, the contents of memory can be altered by reading in new values to replace old ones as directed by stored-program instructions. Read-only memory can be changed solely by reprogramming.

A version of ROM that can be programmed by the end user is **programmable read-only memory (PROM).** PROM can be programmed by the manufacturer, or it can be shipped "blank" to the end user for programming. Once programmed, its contents are unalterable. Thus, PROM can be programmed through conventional methods, but only one time. PROM enables the end user to have the advantages of ROM along with some flexibility to

Figure 3–9 ▪ **Microcomputer with CPU Chip, ROM Chip, and RAM Chip**

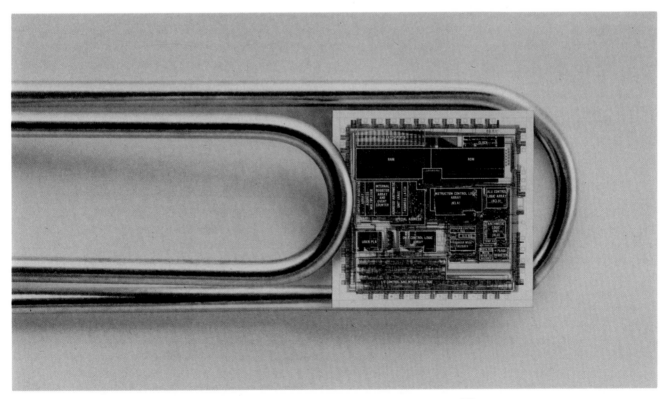

meet unique needs. A problem with it, though, is that mistakes programmed into the unit cannot be corrected. To overcome this drawback, **erasable programmable read-only memory (EPROM)** has been developed (see Figure 3–10). This memory unit can be erased, but only by being submitted to a special process, such as being bathed in ultraviolet light.

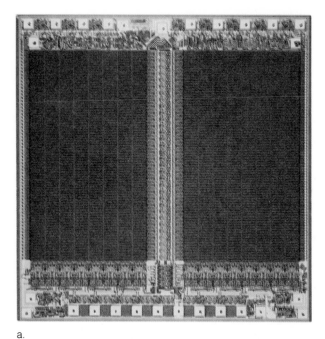

a.

b.

Figure 3–10 ▪ **EPROM**
a. EPROM chip.
b. EPROM chip mounted in a plastic carrier with pins that allow it to be plugged into a circuiting board.
c. Once the chip is mounted into its carrier, it can be plugged into this device where it can be programmed.

c.

Registers

Registers are devices that facilitate the execution of instructions by acting as temporary holding areas for instructions and data. They are located in the CPU but are not considered part of primary storage. Registers can receive information, hold it, and transfer it very quickly as directed by the control unit of the CPU.

A register functions much as a standard pocket calculator does. The person using the calculator acts as the control unit by transferring numbers from a sheet of paper to the calculator. This paper is analogous to the primary storage unit of the CPU. When the calculation is complete, the calculator displays the result. The person (control unit) then transfers the result displayed on the calculator (register) back to the sheet of paper (primary storage). This process is very similar to the way most modern computers work. Intermediate calculations are performed in registers, and the final results are transferred back to primary storage.

Cache Memory

Cache memory, also referred to as a high-speed buffer, is a portion of primary storage used to help speed the processing operations of the computer. Cache memory serves as a working buffer or temporary area to store both instructions and data that must be accessed a great deal by the program being executed. By storing the data in a temporary area of primary storage, the need to continually access secondary storage for the data or instructions is eliminated. Although more expensive than primary storage, cache memory increases processing speeds, which sometimes warrants its use.

DATA REPRESENTATION

Humans communicate information by using symbols that have specific meanings. Symbols such as letters or numbers are combined in meaningful ways to represent information. For example, the twenty-six letters of the English alphabet can be combined to form words, sentences, paragraphs, and so on. By combining the individual words in various ways, we construct various messages. This enables us to communicate with one another.

The human mind is much more complex than the computer. A computer is only a machine; it is not capable of understanding the inherent meanings of symbols used by humans to communicate. To use a computer, therefore, humans must convert their symbols to a form the computer is capable of "understanding." This is accomplished through binary representation and the "on" and "off" states discussed earlier.

Binary Representation

Data is represented in the computer by the electrical state of the machine's circuitry—magnetic states for core storage, current for semiconductor storage, and the position of magnetic bubbles for bubble memory. In all cases, only two states are possible, "on" and "off." This two-state system is known as a

- The **central processing unit (CPU),** or **mainframe** on large systems, is made up of three units: (1) the **control unit,** (2) the **arithmetic/logic unit (ALU),** and (3) the **primary storage unit.**
- The computer executes instructions in a **next-sequential** fashion which requires that program instructions be placed in consecutive locations in primary storage.
- A **program** is a set of instructions written to direct the computer to accomplish a given task.
- The **stored-program concept** allows instructions to be stored in primary storage during processing, thereby reducing human intervention.
- Each location in primary storage has an **address** which allows the CPU to identify it. **Variables** are used to identify storage locations within programs. The CPU then associates the variable with the address in memory.
- **Primary storage** is the memory portion of the CPU. **Secondary storage** is separate from the CPU and is most commonly found in the form of magnetic-tape or magnetic-disk units.
- Current primary storage is typically **semiconductor memory** composed of circuitry on silicon chips.

binary system, and its use to represent data is known as **binary representation.**

The **binary (base 2) number system** operates in a manner similar to the way the familiar **decimal number system** works. For example, the decimal number 4,672 can be analyzed as follows:

$$
\begin{array}{l}
4\ 6\ 7\ 2 \\
\quad 2 \times 10^0 = 2 \\
\quad 7 \times 10^1 = 70 \\
\quad 6 \times 10^2 = 600 \\
\quad 4 \times 10^3 = \underline{4000} \\
4672
\end{array}
\qquad
\begin{array}{cccc}
4 & 6 & 7 & 2 \\
| & | & | & | \\
10^3 & 10^2 & 10^1 & 10^0
\end{array}
$$

Each position represents a certain power of 10. The progression of powers is from right to left; that is, digits further to the left in a decimal number represent larger powers of 10 than digits to the right of them (see Figure 3–11).

The same principle holds for binary representation. The difference is that in binary representation each position in the number represents a power of 2 (see Figure 3–12). For example, consider the decimal number 14. In binary,

Figure 3–11 ▪ Decimal Place Values

10^5	10^4	10^3	10^2	10^1	10^0
100,000	10,000	1,000	100	10	1

Figure 3–12 ▪ Binary Place Values

2^6	2^5	2^4	2^3	2^2	2^1	2^0
64	32	16	8	4	2	1

the value equivalent to 14 is written as follows:

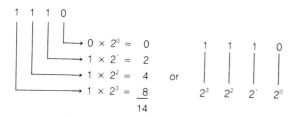

As a further example, the value represented by the decimal number 300 is represented in binary form below:

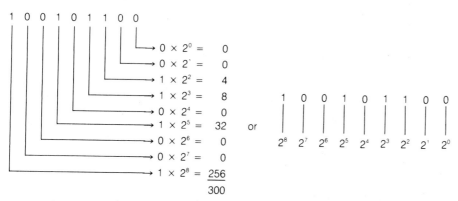

As indicated by the examples above, the binary number system uses 1s and 0s in various combinations to represent various values. Each digit position in a binary number is called a bit, as defined previously. A 1 in a bit position indicates the presence of a specific power of 2; a 0 indicates the absence of a specific power. As in the decimal number system, the progression of powers is from right to left.

Octal Number System

Although all digital computers must store data as 0s and 1s, the sizes of the storage locations do vary. These storage locations within primary memory are referred to as **words,** and one word is equal to one "mailbox" (see discussion on storage locations and addresses in this chapter). Word sizes are measured in bits and are typically 8, 16, 24, 32, 48, and 64 bits in length.

The **octal (base 8) number system,** which uses digits 0 to 7, can be employed as a shorthand method of representing the data contained within one word, or addressable memory location. In the case of 24 - and 48 -bit word size computers, the octal number system provides a shorthand method of representating what is contained in memory. This is true because three binary digits, or bits, can be represented by one octal digit and both 24 and 48 are divisible by three.

As was noted above, three binary digits can be represented by one octal digit. This is done by considering the first three binary place values from right to left which sum to seven—the highest single digit value in the octal number system.

1 1 1

$$1 \times 2^0 = 1$$
$$1 \times 2^1 = 2$$
$$1 \times 2^2 = \underline{4}$$
$$7$$

If we wanted to represent a binary value which was contained in a 24-bit word as an octal value, it could be converted as follows:

$$000 \quad 000 \quad 000 \quad 000 \quad 001 \quad 111 \quad 000 \quad 010$$
$$0 \quad\quad 0 \quad\quad 0 \quad\quad 0 \quad\quad 1 \quad\quad 7 \quad\quad 0 \quad\quad 2$$

If we then wanted to convert the octal value to its decimal equivalent, it could also be done. The octal number 1,702 is equivalent to the decimal number 962. Consider the conversion below, keeping in mind that each digit of the octal number represents a power of 8.

```
1  7  0  2
            → 2 × 8⁰  =     2     or    1    7    0    2
            → 0 × 8¹  =     0
            → 7 × 8²  =   448
            → 1 × 8³  =   512          8³   8²   8¹   8⁰
                          ———
                          962
```

$$2 \times 8^0 = 2$$
$$0 \times 8^1 = 0$$
$$7 \times 8^2 = 448$$
$$1 \times 8^3 = 512$$
$$962$$

For another example, the value represented by the decimal number 10,000 is displayed in octal form below:

```
2  3  4  2  0
               → 0 × 8⁰  =       0     or   2    3    4    2    0
               → 2 × 8¹  =      16
               → 4 × 8²  =     256
               → 3 × 8³  =   1,536
               → 2 × 8⁴  =   8,192         8⁴   8³   8²   8¹   8⁰
                             —————
                            10,000
```

$$0 \times 8^0 = 0$$
$$2 \times 8^1 = 16$$
$$4 \times 8^2 = 256$$
$$3 \times 8^3 = 1{,}536$$
$$2 \times 8^4 = 8{,}192$$
$$10{,}000$$

Hexadecimal Number System

When a program fails to execute correctly, it is sometimes necessary to examine the contents of certain memory locations to discover what went wrong. In such cases, the programmer often finds it useful to have a printout, or **dump,** of the contents of the memory locations (see Figure 3–13). If everything were printed in binary representation, the programmer would be staring at pages upon pages of 1s and 0s. Detection of the error would be difficult.

To alleviate this problem, the contents of storage locations in computers can be represented by symbols of the **hexadecimal (base 16) number system.** In the hexadecimal number system, sixteen symbols are used to represent the digits 0 through 15 (see Figure 3–14). Note that the letters A through F designate the numbers 10 through 15. The fact that each position in a hexadecimal number represents a power of 16 allows for easy conversion from binary to hexadecimal, since 16 is equal to 2^4. A single hexadecimal digit can be used to represent four binary digits.

As was noted above, four binary digits can be represented by one hexadecimal digit. This is done by considering the first four binary place values (from right to left) which sum to 15—the highest single digit value in the hexadecimal number system.

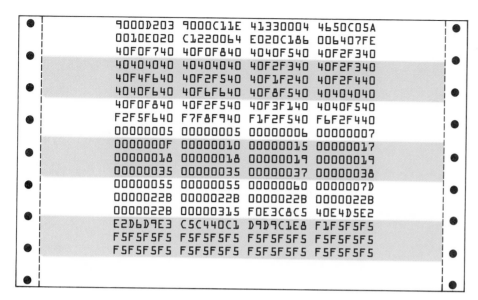

Figure 3–13 ■ Core Dump

```
9000D203  9000C11E  41330004  4650C05A
0010E020  C1220064  E020C186  006407FE
40F0F740  40F0F840  4040F540  40F2F340
40404040  40404040  40F2F340  40F2F340
40F4F640  40F2F540  40F1F240  40F2F440
4040F640  40F6F640  40F8F540  40404040
40F0F840  40F2F540  40F3F140  4040F540
F2F5F640  F7F8F940  F1F2F540  F6F2F440
00000005  00000005  00000006  00000007
0000000F  00000010  00000015  00000017
00000018  00000018  00000019  00000019
00000035  00000035  00000037  00000038
00000055  00000055  00000060  0000007D
0000022B  0000022B  0000022B  0000022B
0000022B  00000315  F0E3C8C5  40E4D5E2
E2D6D9E3  C5C440C1  D9D9C1E8  F1F5F5F5
F5F5F5F5  F5F5F5F5  F5F5F5F5  F5F5F5F5
F5F5F5F5  F5F5F5F5  F5F5F5F5  F5F5F5F5
```

```
1  1  1  1
|  |  |  └──→ 1 × 2⁰ = 1
|  |  └─────→ 1 × 2¹ = 2
|  └────────→ 1 × 2² = 4
└───────────→ 1 × 2³ = 8
                      ──
                      15
```

$$
\begin{array}{cccccccc}
1 & 1 & 1 & 1 \\
\end{array}
$$

$$1 \times 2^0 = 1$$
$$1 \times 2^1 = 2$$
$$1 \times 2^2 = 4$$
$$1 \times 2^3 = 8$$
$$\underline{}$$
$$15$$

If we wanted to represent a binary value which was contained in a 32-bit word as a hexadecimal value, it could be converted as follows:

```
0000  0000  0000  0000  0000  0010  0010  1011
  |     |     |     |     |     |     |     |
  ↓     ↓     ↓     ↓     ↓     ↓     ↓     ↓
  0     0     0     0     0     2     2     B
```

If we then wanted to convert the hexadecimal value to its decimal equivalent, it could also be done. Keep in mind that each digit of the hexadecimal number represents a power of 16.

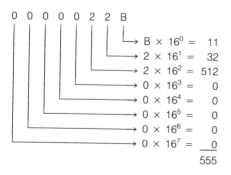

```
0  0  0  0  0  2  2  B
                     └──→ B × 16⁰ =   11
                  └─────→ 2 × 16¹ =   32
               └────────→ 2 × 16² =  512
            └───────────→ 0 × 16³ =    0
         └──────────────→ 0 × 16⁴ =    0
      └─────────────────→ 0 × 16⁵ =    0
   └────────────────────→ 0 × 16⁶ =    0
└───────────────────────→ 0 × 16⁷ =    0
                                    ────
                                     555
```

Computer Codes

Many computers use coding schemes other than simple binary notation to represent numbers. One of the most basic coding schemes is called **4-bit binary coded decimal (BCD).** Rather than represent a decimal number as a

Figure 3–14 ■ Binary, Hexadecimal, and Decimal Equivalent Values

BINARY SYSTEM (PLACE VALUES)				HEXADECIMAL EQUIVALENT	DECIMAL EQUIVALENT
8	4	2	1		
0	0	0	0	0	0
0	0	0	1	1	1
0	0	1	0	2	2
0	0	1	1	3	3
0	1	0	0	4	4
0	1	0	1	5	5
0	1	1	0	6	6
0	1	1	1	7	7
1	0	0	0	8	8
1	0	0	1	9	9
1	0	1	0	A	10
1	0	1	1	B	11
1	1	0	0	C	12
1	1	0	1	D	13
1	1	1	0	E	14
1	1	1	1	F	15

string of 0s and 1s (which gets increasingly complicated for large numbers), BCD represents each decimal digit in a number by using four bits. For instance, the decimal number 23 is represented by two groups of four bits, one group for the "2," the other for the "3." Representations of the number 23 in 4-bit BCD and in binary are compared below:

```
0 0 1 0    0 0 1 1          4-bit BCD
|_____|  |_____|
    2          3            Decimal
0000000000010111            Binary
```

The representation of a three-digit decimal number in 4-bit BCD consists of three sets of four bits, or twelve binary digits. For example, the decimal number 637 is coded as follows:

```
0 1 1 0    0 0 1 1    0 1 1 1     4-bit BCD
|_____|  |_____|  |_____|
    6          3          7        Decimal
0000001001111101                   Binary
```

Use of 4-bit BCD saves space when large decimal numbers must be represented. Furthermore, it is easier to convert a 4-bit BCD to its decimal equivalent than to convert a binary representation to decimal.

The 4-bit code allows sixteen (2^4) possible unique bit combinations. We have already seen that ten of them are used to represent the decimal digits 0 through 9. Since that leaves only six remaining combinations, this code in practice is used only to represent numbers.

To represent letters and special characters as well as numbers, more than four bit positions are needed. Another coding scheme, called **6-bit BCD,** allows for sixty-four (2^6) unique bit combinations. Thus, 6-bit BCD can be used to represent the decimal digits 0 through 9, the letters A through Z, and twenty-eight characters, such as the period and the comma.

The four rightmost bit positions in 6-bit BCD are called **numeric bits.** The two leftmost bit positions are called **zone bits** (see Figure 3–15). The zone

ZONE BITS		NUMERIC BITS			
B	A	8	4	2	1

Figure 3–15 ■ Bit Positions in 6-Bit BCD Representation

bits are used in various combinations with the numeric bits to represent numbers, letters, and special characters.

Another approach to data representation is an 8-bit code known as **Extended Binary Coded Decimal Interchange Code (EBCDIC).** An 8-bit code allows 256 (2^8) possible bit combinations. Whereas 6-bit BCD can be used to represent only uppercase letters, 8-bit EBCDIC can be used to represent uppercase and lowercase letters and additional special characters, such as the cent sign and the quotation mark. The EBCDIC bit combinations for uppercase letters and numbers are given in Figure 3–16.

In EBCDIC, the four leftmost bit positions are zone bits, and the four rightmost bit positions are numeric bits. As with 6-bit BCD, the zone bits are used in various combinations with the numeric bits to represent numbers, letters, and special characters.

The **American Standard Code for Information Interchange (ASCII)** is a 7-bit code developed through the cooperation of several computer manufacturers whose objective was to develop a standard code for all computers. Because certain machines are designed to accept 8-bit rather than 7-bit code patterns, an 8-bit version of ASCII, called **ASCII-8** was created. ASCII-8 and EBCDIC are similar, the key difference between them being in the bit patterns used to represent certain characters.

Bits, as described, are very small units of data; it is often useful to combine them into larger units. A fixed number of adjacent bits operated on as a unit is called a **byte.** Usually, one alphabetic character or two numeric characters are represented in one byte. Since eight bits are sufficient to represent any character, 8-bit groupings are the basic units of memory. In computers that accept 8-bit characters then, a byte is a group of eight adjacent bits. When

Figure 3–16 ■ EBCDIC Representation: 0–9, A-Z

Character	EBCDIC Bit Configuration		Character	EBCDIC Bit Configuration	
A	1100	0001	S	1110	0010
B	1100	0010	T	1110	0011
C	1100	0011	U	1110	0100
D	1100	0100	V	1110	0101
E	1100	0101	W	1110	0110
F	1100	0110	X	1110	0111
G	1100	0111	Y	1110	1000
H	1100	1000	Z	1110	1001
I	1100	1001	0	1111	0000
J	1101	0001	1	1111	0001
K	1101	0010	2	1111	0010
L	1101	0011	3	1111	0011
M	1101	0100	4	1111	0100
N	1101	0101	5	1111	0101
O	1101	0110	6	1111	0110
P	1101	0111	7	1111	0111
Q	1101	1000	8	1111	1000
R	1101	1001	9	1111	1001

large amounts of storage are described, the symbol **K** is often used. Generally, one K equals 1,024 (2^{10}) units. Thus, a computer that has 256K bytes of storage can store 256 $\times$ 1,024, or 262,144, characters.

Code Checking

Computers do not always function perfectly; errors can and do occur. For example, a bit may be lost while data is being transferred from the ALU to the primary storage unit or over telephone lines from one location to another. This loss can be caused by dust, moisture, magnetic fields, equipment failure, or other things. Thus, it is necessary to have a method to detect when an error has occurred and to isolate the location of the error.

To accomplish this task, most computers have at each storage location an additional bit, called a **parity bit,** or **check bit.** Computers that use parity bits are specifically designed always to have either an even or an odd number of 1-(or "on") bits in each storage location. Regardless of the type of code used, if an odd number of 1-bits is used to represent each character, the characters are said to be written in **odd parity.** Similarly, if an even number of 1-bits is used to represent each character, the characters are written in **even parity.** Internal circuitry in the computer constantly monitors its operation by checking to ensure that the required number of bits is present in each location.

For example, if the 6-bit BCD code is used, a seventh bit is added as a check bit (see Figure 3–17). Suppose the number 6 is to be represented in 6-bit BCD using odd parity (see Figure 3–18). In this case, the check bit must be set to 1, or "on," to make the number of 1-bits odd. If a parity error is detected, the system may retry the read or write operation occurring when the error was detected. If retries are unsuccessful, the system informs the computer operator that an error has occurred.

Notice that the checking circuitry of the computer can only detect the miscoding of characters. It cannot detect the use of incorrect data. In the previous example, for instance, the computer circuitry could determine whether a bit had been dropped, making the representation of the number 6 invalid. However, if the number 5 had been mistakenly entered into the computer instead of 6 (say, because of incorrect keying of a card), no error would have been detected.

Figure 3–17 ▪ Bit Positions of 6-Bit BCD with Check Bit

CHECK BIT	ZONE BITS		NUMERIC BITS			
C	B	A	8	4	2	1

Figure 3–18 ▪ Detection of Error with Parity Check (Odd Parity)

	C	B	A	8	4	2	1
Valid — →	1	0	0	0	1	1	0
Invalid— ←	1	0	0	0	0	1	0

- Data is represented in computer memory by the **binary number system** (0s and 1s), and its use to represent data is known as **binary representation.**
- The size of a storage location within memory is referred to as a **word.** Word sizes are normally measured in **bits** (binary digits), and are found in 8-, 16-, 24-, 32-, 48-, and 64-bit lengths.
- Computers use coding schemes to represent data within memory. A coding scheme called **6-bit BCD,** for example, uses 64-bit combinations to represent letters, special characters, and numbers.
- Coding schemes are a shorthand method of representing data in memory. Other coding schemes are: **4-bit BCD, EBCDIC, ASCII,** and **ASCII-8.**
- **Code checking** is a way of testing whether the computer is functioning correctly in relation to the way data is being stored. A **parity bit,** or **check bit,** is used to determine if the correct number of bits are in a particular memory location.

CLASSIFICATIONS OF COMPUTER SYSTEMS

Digital and Analog Computers

When the first section of this book used the term *computer,* it was talking about a specific type—the **digital computer.** However, there are also **analog computers.** It is important to distinguish between these two types.

A digital computer operates on the basis of discrete "on" and "off" states represented by binary digits. The digits can represent numbers, letters, or other distinct symbols in the form of groups of 1s ("on") and 0s ("off"). A digital computer receives input and produces output in the form of these 1 and 0 states. The states used for numbers, letters, and special characters can be represented by holes in punched cards or magnetized areas on tapes or disks. They can be translated to easily recognizable printing on paper.

Digital computers achieve varying degrees of accuracy, depending on their particular construction and machine characteristics. For example, some digital computers can provide results accurate to hundreds or even thousands of decimal places. Such computers are often used in scientific applications. For business applications, results accurate to only a few decimal places are sufficient. Therefore, computer manufacturers build various models of digital computers to meet the varied needs of the ultimate users of these machines.

In contrast to digital computers, analog computers do not operate directly on "on" and "off" states represented by binary digits. Instead, they measure continuous physical or electrical magnitudes such as pressure, temperature, current, voltage, length, or shaft rotations. For example, a gasoline pump contains an analog computer that measures (1) the quantity of gasoline pumped (to the nearest tenth of a gallon) and (2) the price of that gasoline (to the nearest penny). Another example of an analog computer is a car speedometer. Here, driveshaft rotations are measured and converted to a number that indicates the speed of the car.

It is important to note that while numerical results can be obtained from analog computers, they are arrived at indirectly. For this reason, analog com-

Figure 3–19

Inventor Seymour Cray and Cray Research president, John Rollwagen, left, pose with the Cray 2 computer as it sits in a tank of liquid coolant. So dense are the machine's circuits that the fluid must be used to dissipate heat generated during operation.

puters are less accurate than digital computers. It is not uncommon for a car speedometer to be "off" by one or two miles per hour. Because digital computers are commonly used in the applications discussed in this book, the remainder of the book focuses on digital computers.

Mainframe Computers

At the heart of a large-scale computer system is the mainframe, or CPU, (which consists, as you recall, of the control unit, ALU, and primary storage). A mainframe can process large amounts of data at very high speeds, hold millions of characters in its primary storage, and support many input, output, and auxiliary storage devices.

Although the current technology used in minicomputers and microcomputers has made it more difficult to clearly distinguish the three groupings of computers from each other, it is doubtful that either minicomputers or microcomputers will ever be considered equal to mainframe computers in overall power and capability.

Mainframe manufacturers sell their products to organizations requiring extensive data-processing capabilities. These organizations may process vast amounts of data or may need to perform millions of calculations per second. In some cases, demand exists for even higher processing speeds and efficiency. To respond to these needs, some vendors offer enormous, sophisticated computers called **supercomputers** or **maxicomputers.**

Supercomputer systems are very expensive, and their costs are justified in relatively few cases. The CRAY-2 computer, developed by Cray Research, Inc., is an example of a supercomputer system (see Figure 3–19). The CRAY-2 is offered at a base price of $4.5 million; it is used mainly in the scientific areas of weather forecasting, nuclear weapons development, and energy supply and conservation. Other supercomputers are used by large corporations and government agencies where the need for large data bases and complex calculation capabilities justify the costs of obtaining them. Such a configuration is shown in Figure 3–20.

Figure 3–20 ▪ Supercomputer Configuration

As hardware costs continue to decline, organizations that have not previously been able to afford a supercomputer may be able to pay the purchase price for one. Even then, however, the software costs associated with these systems would limit the number of users who could justify installing them.

Minicomputers

The distinction between minicomputers and mainframes has become blurred. When first introduced, minicomputers had the same types of capabilities as mainframe computers but contained smaller primary memories and were generally less powerful than mainframes. With advances in technology, minicomputers have tended to move up the ladder toward mainframe computers in terms of capability, memory size, and overall processing power. The minicomputers manufactured today are more powerful than the mainframes manufactured ten years ago, and their prices range from $15,000 to $250,000 (see Figure 3–21).

Microcomputers

Microcomputers have received a great deal of attention recently. When microcomputers first appeared, they were used by hobby-oriented engineers, programmers, electronics buffs, and other technically competent and inquisitive individuals. These computer hobbyists built their computers from scratch or purchased ready-to-assemble computer kits. Within a few hours, the hobbyist could put together a real computer, complete with a keyboard for data entry and a TV-like display tube.

Figure 3–21 ▪ Minicomputer System

Figure 3–22

Recent introductions to the microcomputer market include Apple's Macintosh and IBM's PCjr.

At the sight of a true consumer market, manufacturers began to offer user-oriented microcomputer systems. These small systems were preassembled and equipped with programs to do simple jobs, such as balancing a checkbook or playing a game of backgammon. The personal computing market started in 1975 when MIT introduced the Altair 8800, a computer kit for under $500. Today a wide range of personal computers is available, offering complete computing capabilities at low costs (see Figure 3–22). A computer for the home can be purchased for about the same price as a good stereo system; those available range in price from $100 to $5,000.

SUMMARY POINTS

■ The central processing unit, the heart of the computer, is composed of three units: the primary storage unit, the arithmetic/logic unit (ALU), and the control unit. The control unit maintains order and controls what is happening in the CPU; the ALU performs arithmetic and logical operations; and the primary storage unit holds all data and instructions necessary for processing.

■ Instructions are placed in consecutive locations in memory so that they can be accessed consecutively. This is called the next-sequential-instruction feature.

■ The stored-program concept involves storing both data and instructions in the computer's memory, thus eliminating the need for human intervention during processing.

■ The nondestructive read/destructive write characteristic of memory allows a program to be re-executed, since the program remains intact in memory until another is stored over it. The computer executes instructions sequentially (as accessed in consecutive locations in memory) unless instructed to do otherwise.

■ Each location in storage has a unique address, which allows stored-program instructions and data items to be located by the control unit of the CPU as it directs processing operations. Variables—names for storage addresses—are often used by programmers to facilitate data location.

■ One method of storing data in primary storage uses electrical currents to set magnetic cores to "on" and "off" states. Another form of storage is semiconductor memory, which uses circuitry on silicon chips. Semiconductor units are smaller and faster than cores, but they usually demand a constant power source. Bubble memory consists of magnetized spots that rest on a thin film of semiconductor material. These bubbles retain their magnetism indefinitely and have the ability to store much more data in a smaller space than core memory.

■ Biochip technology is an alternate method of creating primary storage, using groupings of molecules that are grown, not manufactured, to create a circuit.

■ Read-only memory (ROM), part of the hardware of a computer, stores items in a form that can be deleted or changed only by rewiring. Microprograms are sequences of instructions built into read-only memory to carry out functions that otherwise would be directed by stored-program instructions at a much slower speed.

■ Programmable read-only memory (PROM), can be programmed either by the manufacturer or by users to meet unique needs. Thus, it provides greater flexibility and versatility than ROM.

■ Registers are devices that facilitate the execution of instructions. They act as temporary holding areas and are capable of receiving information, holding it, and transferring it very quickly as directed by the control unit of the CPU.

■ Cache memory is a portion of primary storage designed to speed the CPU's processing of instructions or data.

■ Data representation in the computer is based on a two-state, or binary, system. A 1 in a given position indicates the presence of a power of a 2; a 0 indicates its absence. The 4-bit binary coded decimal (BCD) system uses groups of four binary digits to represent the decimal digits 0 through 9. The 6-bit BCD system allows for sixty-four unique bit combinations; alphabetic, numeric, and twenty-eight special characters can be represented. Both EBCDIC and ASCII-8 are 8-bit coding systems and are capable of representing up to 256 different characters.

■ Octal (base 8) and hexadecimal (base 16) notation can be used to represent binary data in a more concise form. For this reason, the contents of computer memory are sometimes viewed or printed in one of these notations. Programmers use these number systems to help in locating errors.

■ Parity bits, or check bits, are used to detect errors in the transmission of data.

■ Computers are usually classified as either digital or analog. Digital computers operate on distinct symbols (decimal numbers, letters, and the like) and are the computers commonly used in business applications. Analog computers measure continuous physical or electrical magnitudes such as pressure, temperature, current, or voltage and are less accurate than digital computers.

■ Classifications of computer systems can be made according to digital or analog and to mainframe computer, minicomputer, or microcomputer.

REVIEW QUESTIONS

1. Name the three major components of the CPU and discuss the function of each.

2. Explain what is meant by the stored-program concept and show why it is significant to electronic data processing.

3. What technological developments have occurred in primary storage media and what impact have these developments had on modern computers?

4. Explain the concept of read-only memory. How does it relate to microprogramming?

5. Why are computer codes necessary? What advantages does EBCDIC offer over 6-bit BCD?

6. Why are concepts of the binary number system important to an understanding of digital computers?

7. What is meant by the next-sequential-instruction feature?

8. What relationship do the first four binary place values (from right to left) have with the hexadecimal number system?

9. Convert the following binary value to a hexadecimal value. Then convert the hexadecimal value to a decimal value.

00110111

10. Convert the following binary value to an octal value. Then convert the octal value to a decimal value.

101100101

11. What is the purpose of code checking? By using a parity bit, or check bit, can incorrect data be detected?

12. Distinguish between analog and digital computers, giving examples of each.

In the 1880s, Herman Hollerith developed a mechanical method of processing census data for the United States Bureau of the Census. His method included two devices: one that coded population data as punched holes in cards, and another that sensed the data. The success of his method led Hollerith to form his own company in 1896 to manufacture and sell these devices. In 1911, the company became part of the Computing-Tabulating-Recording (CTR) Company, which manufactured commercial scales and tabulating and time-recording equipment. In 1924 CTR became the International Business Machines (IBM) Corporation.

Today IBM is a leader of the worldwide data-processing community and is the leading vendor of mainframe computers. IBM's Entry Systems Division is the second largest producer of small computers. IBM's products include data-processing machines and systems, information processors, electric typewriters, copiers, dictation equipment, educational and testing materials, and related supplies and services. Most products can be either leased or purchased through IBM's worldwide marketing organizations.

IBM's major business is information handling. IBM computers range from small, powerful minicomputers to ultra-high-performance computers for high-speed, large-scale scientific and commercial applications. The wide range of computer applications in scientific, industrial, and commercial areas today requires machines of different sizes and capabilities. For example, a computer used to forecast the weather has capabilities different from those of a computer used mainly for payroll processing. Consequently, computers with similar characteristics are usually grouped together into a family, series, or system. The family members differ from each other in terms of range of available memory, number of input-output channels, execution speed, and types of devices with which interface can be established.

For example, IBM's Series/1 is a family of low-cost, versatile, small computers. These computers are modular—that is, the user can acquire as much or as little processing power as needed. The Series/1 includes two processor versions. One, the 4952 processor, is available in three models. All offer 32K to 128K bytes of primary storage. Data can be transferred through input-output channels at a rate of 832,000 bytes per second, and the processor has a cycle time of 2,100 nanoseconds. The 4952 Model C processor offers the same functional capabilities and contains an integrated diskette drive.

The second version of processors for the Series/1 is the 4955 processor, which is available in four models. Primary storage capacities range from 32K to 512K bytes. The I/O channel rate is 1,650,000 bytes per second, and the cycle time is 660 nanoseconds. In addition, several optional devices and functions are available, such as an input-output expansion unit, a floating point processor, and a programmer console. Users can choose from many hardware attachments and support units. Disk storage units are offered in varying sizes, all nonremovable. Diskette storage units provide a removable direct-access medium. Five display station models and five printer models are available, most of them controlled by their own microprocessors. The 4955 version offers 3 to 3.5 times the internal performance of the 4952 version.

IBM also offers software to accompany the Series/1. Like the hardware, it is modular. The Series/1 was designed to facilitate extensive communication networks as well. Several processors and terminals may be tied together and share the same data. The Series/1 can also be used as a "front-end processor," or a link between a variety of peripherals and a central, or host, computer. The modular design and great flexibility of the Series/1 provide users of all types and sizes with a number of data-processing alternatives. Areas of application for the Series/1 include distributed processing (where there is a need for data entry, remote job entry, and inquiries to files); commercial applications (such as billing, inventory control, and sales analysis); sensor-

based applications (material and component testing, machine and process control, and shop floor control); and graphics.

In comparison, IBM's System/370 is a family of general-purpose large computers readily adaptable to a large number of applications. (Its predecessor, System/360, also a multipurpose system of computers, was named "360" to indicate ability to handle the "full circle" of applications.) The System/370's eleven processor models all have certain characteristics in common. Data can be transferred in blocks ranging in size from eight to sixty-four bits (one to eight bytes). The System/370 has the capability of addressing as many as 16,777,216 bytes of storage.

The System/370 models' main storage capacities vary from 65,536 bytes to 8,388,608 bytes (in comparison with the Series/1 scale, 32,768 to 524,288 byte capacities.) Model 168, designed for large-scale high-speed scientific and commercial applications, has the largest main storage capacity. Its scientific applications range from nuclear physics and theoretical astronomy to weather forecasting. The Model 168 can be used commercially as the control center of complex airline reservation systems, coast-to-coast time-sharing net-

works, and process-control systems. The power and speed of these advance systems are primarily the result of improved circuit technology. The machine cycle time of the System 370 devices is as fast as is eighty nanoseconds, eight times faster than that of the Series/1 computers.

The new IBM 3081 is IBM's most powerful processor. With faster internal cycle time and up to thirty-two million characters of high-speed main storage, it is meant for users with sizable data storage and data communication requirements. Three additional high-performance processors, the IBM 3031, 3032, and 3033, are appropriate for users who need increased speed and capacity but not to the extent provided by the IBM 3081. All four processors are compatible members of the System/370 family.

One of IBM's latest advances is the System/38 family, a general-purpose, data-processing system that supports both interactive (where the user can communicate with the computer and receive a response) and batch applications. Since the System/38 is designed as a growth system for some of IBM's previous computers, especially the System/3 and System 34, conversion techniques have been developed to allow the user to

Table 3–1 ■ Major IBM Computers

SERIES	MODELS	DATE INTRODUCED	COMMENTS
700	701	1953	Vacuum tubes
			Magnetic core
	702		
	704		
	705		
Type 650		1954	Magnetic-drum machine
1400	1401	1960	
	1410		Oriented to business
7000	7070	1960	Transistors, business-oriented
	7074		Scientific-oriented
1620		1960	Scientific-oriented, decimal minicomputer
1130		1962	Integrated circuits, small, special-purpose
1800		1963	Integrated circuits, small, special-purpose
360	20	1965	
	25		
	30		
	40		
	44		Systems designed for all purposes–business and scientific
	50		
	65		
	67		
	75		
	85		
	90		
	91		
System/7		1970	Replacement for 1800
System/3		1969	Midismall computer
370	115	1973	
	125		IBM's most popular system—extends capabilities of System/360
	135		
	138		
	145		
	148		
	158		
	168		
	3031	1977	IBM's most powerful processors
	3032		
	3033	1980	
System/32	3081	1975	Small system for business
System/34		1977	Small system for business
Series/1		1976	Versatile small computer for experienced users
System/38		1978	Powerful, general purpose supporting extensive data bases
5100		1975	Portable computer
5110		1978	Small business computer
5120		1980	Small business system
5520		1979	Administrative office system
Datamaster		1981	Small system with data, word processing
Personal Computer		1981	Microcomputer for home and office

convert to the new System/38 with as little reconstruction as possible.

The unique aspect of the System/38 is its use of a high-level "architecture" that involves a new use of hardware technology. The actual hardware is separated from the instruction set by two layers of microprogramming. Storage capacities range from 524,288 bytes to 2,097,152 bytes of primary storage. The System/38 is capable of translating secondary-storage addresses to main storage addresses.

The System/38 is composed of a processing unit, main storage, disk storage, console display, diskette drive, and optional I/O and communications facilities. One of the optional I/O devices is the IBM 5250 Information Display System, which consists of several models of display stations and printers.

Finally, the IBM 5520 Administrative System is an office system that integrates shared logic and resource characteristics. It is compatible with System/370 communications and data bases. It features text processing and document distribution. Through the text-processing functions, users can create, revise, share, print, and store documents. The file processing function can merge fields from one or two files with text to create reports or repetitive letters. Arithmetic expressions, if/else logic, record update, and multiple stored procedures provide a data-processing-like function for administrative users. The document distribution feature provides the capability to forward documents to other offices in the same building or across the country. There are four models, which differ in processing power and the amount of fixed and auxiliary storage supported. The 5520 is compatible with the System/370 model data bases, which allows for a very efficient method of controlling information and processing within an office system network.

Table 3–1 summarizes the major IBM series and their various models. As data-processing requirements have expanded, hardware capabilities such as those provided by IBM have been developed to provide the necessary support.

DISCUSSION POINTS

1. What characteristics do computers within a family have in common? How do family members within a series differ from each other?
2. Name some important hardware characteristics that must be considered when a computer is selected. How do these characteristics relate to processing requirements?

4

Input and Output

INTRODUCTION

A computer system is much more than a central processing unit. Auxiliary devices enter data into and receive output from the CPU. Data input and information output are important activities in any computer-based system because they are the communication links between people and the machine. If these people/machine interfaces are weak, the overall performance of the computer system suffers accordingly.

This chapter describes the primary media used for computer input—punched cards, magnetic tape, and magnetic disks. In addition, the chapter looks at the growing field of source-data automation. Specialized input devices are also discussed. Printers (the basic medium for computer output), terminals, and specialized output devices are discussed at the conclusion of the chapter.

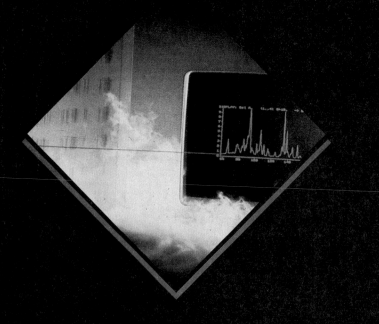

ARTICLE

The Computerized Creations of Raymond Kurzweil Can Talk, Listen and Sing

Within two years, you'll be able to buy a typewriter that takes dictation. Never mind that IBM and Bell Labs say it can't be done in less than five. Raymond Kurzweil promises it in two.

A Kurzweil promise is worth listening to. He's the man who, in 1976, introduced an optical scanner that can read—aloud—any printed text, no matter what the typeface. It's been called the greatest boon to the blind since Braille. It can also reprint what it reads. Kurzweil says IBM and Control Data have been trying to duplicate his technology, but so far they haven't caught up.

An accomplished pianist and the son of a Bell Symphony Orchestra conductor, Kurzweil also invented a unique music synthesizer that duplicates with disturbing accuracy the sound not only of a piano but of nearly every other acoustical instrument. With it, a single musician can "play" several instruments at once—and the synthesizer can simultaneously notate every sound played on it, of whatever speed or rhythm.

Now Kurzweil is working on a speech-recognition system that attaches to a word processor and "understands" 10,000 words at the rate of 150 per minute. . . .

There are already speech-recognition systems on the market that understand a few simple commands. Airport baggage handlers use them to route luggage; factory inspectors use them to keep track of product defects. But these systems can generally recognize only one word at a time. And their vocabulary is at most several hundred words.

Kurzweil's project is far more complex. It will incorporate two systems: One will analyze sound; the other will analyze grammar and syntax to distinguish between similar sounding words, such as "ware" and "wear."

Kurzweil's biggest challenge is that no person pronounces a word exactly the same way twice. . . . Kurzweil explains, "we're trying to identify the characteristics of pronunciation that don't change with the speaker or between utterances." . . . The system will be "speaker dependent"—trained to understand only one voice, at least at first—and the speaker will have to tell the machine how to punctuate. He will also have to pause very briefly between each word when dictating. But Kurzweil is confident he'll have his typewriter to market long before his competitors will. He predicts that his speech-recognition unit will be contained in an 18-inch cube and cost $5,000.

Raymond Kurzweil has been working with computers for 24 years. At 13, he designed software for statistical analysis that was distributed by IBM. At 16, he won seven national awards . . . for a computer program that could compose music in the style of Mozart. As a sophomore at MIT, he developed a program that matched students with appropriate colleges; he sold it a year later for $100,000 plus royalties.

In 1974, he founded Kurzweil Computer Products, which devel-oped the reading machine. In 1980, he sold the company to Xerox after an initial payment of $3.6 million. He continues with the company as its part-time chairman, reportedly at a six-figure salary. In 1982, he founded Kurzweil Music Systems (to make the synthesizer) and Kurzweil Speech Systems (to confront the challenges presented by the typewriter). He is president of both.

Though proud of his accomplishments, Kurzweil believes his future will eclipse his past. "I consider myself a) an inventor and b) an entrepreneur," he says. "Each of these tends to develop skills and get better with experience. It's a matter of combining your knowledge of the world with learning how to put people together and systems together. Inventions don't come to you, bang, in the shower. They come from analyzing needs, followed by years of painstaking research." The only difference is, Raymond Kurzweil seems to need fewer years per invention than everybody else.

Innovations such as those developed by Raymond Kurzweil, and others, will, in the future, revolutionize the ways in which computers can be used for data input and information output. A speech-recognition system such as the one being developed by Kurzweil will drastically change the way that we communicate with the CPU of a computer system.

DATA INPUT

Punched Cards

Punched cards were used in data processing long before the digital computer was developed, as we saw in Chapter 2. Today punched cards serve not only as a means of entering data into computers but also as user-oriented documents—time cards, bills, invoices, checks, and the like.

Punched-card processing involves two steps. Data must first be recorded on the cards; then the encoded cards are processed.

Data Representation The standard punched card has eighty vertical columns and twelve horizontal rows (see Figure 4 –1). It is appropriately called an **eighty-column punched card,** or a **Hollerith card,** after its developer Herman Hollerith. Each column can contain a single letter, number, or special character. Data is recorded as holes punched in a particular column to represent a given character. The pattern of holes used to represent characters is known as the **Hollerith code.**

The eighty-column punched card is divided horizontally into three sections. The lower ten rows, numbers 0 through 9, are called **digit rows;** they can be used to represent any digit from 0 through 9. The upper three rows, numbered 12, 11, and 0, are called **zone rows.** (The 0 row is both a digit row and a zone row.) Zone punches can be combined with digit punches in the same column to represent alphabetic and special characters. The third section (at the very top of the card), called the print zone, displays the actual character punched into a card column in a form easily read by humans.

For instance, in Figure 4 –1, the number 6 in column 21 is represented by a punch in the digit row 6; to represent a number, then, a hole is punched

Figure 4–1 ▪ Eighty-Column Punched Card and Hollerith Code

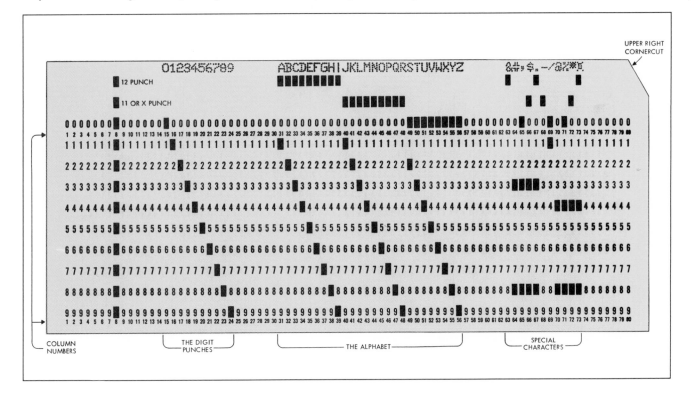

in the appropriate digit row. To represent letters or special characters, one zone punch is used in combination with one or two numeric punches.

When punched cards are used, data is generally grouped together and punched in specific columns on the cards. A group of related characters treated as a single unit of information is called a **field** and is composed of a group of consecutive columns (see Figure 4–2). A field may be from one to eighty characters in length. Related fields are stored on the same card if possible.

When one punched card contains all the necessary data about a transaction, it is said to be a **unit record**—a complete record. Figure 4–2 illustrates a unit record—a card containing all data pertaining to the sale of a particular item.

The eighty-column limitation of the Hollerith card presents major disadvantages to the establishing of unit records. First of all, when records require more than eighty columns, two or more cards must be used. This hinders processing of the cards, since punched-card machines are designed to operate on only one card at a time. Second, when less than an entire card is needed for a record, the remaining space is left unused and thus wasted. Another disadvantage of using the punched card is the possibility of mutilation during handling, which hinders the processing.

Card Punch   Data is most commonly recorded on punched cards through the use of a **card punch,** or **keypunch** (see Figure 4–3). An operator reads a source document and transcribes the data from the document onto cards by pressing keys on a keyboard, much as if he or she were using a typewriter. The machine automatically feeds, positions, and stacks the cards, thus allowing the operator to concentrate on the keying operation.

Keyboards on card-punch machines vary, depending on the uses for which

Figure 4–2 ▪ Unit Record

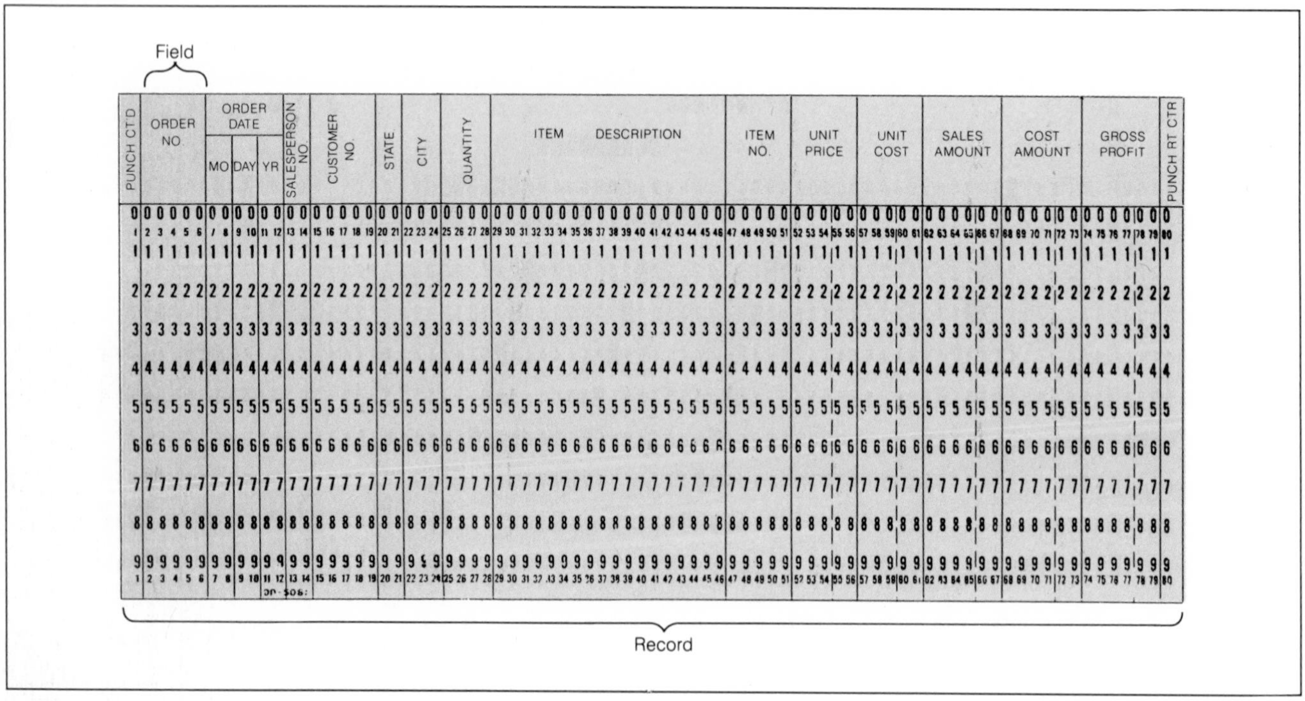

the machines are designed. For example, some keypunches have only alphabetic keyboards; some have only numeric keyboards; and others combine the two. Various sets of special characters and automatic skipping and duplicating are options usually available as well.

Regardless of the number of functions performed automatically (such as automatic skipping and duplicating), keypunching is probably the slowest and most costly operation in any computer system. One person is needed to operate each machine, and much time is spent keying data.

For many of the reasons discussed, keypunching and the eighty-column punched card have become obsolete methods of data entry. Many computer systems currently in use do not allow punched cards as a medium for data input.

Figure 4–3 ■ Eighty-Column Card Punch

Key-to-Tape, Key-to-Disk, and Key-to-Diskette

Key-to-tape and **key-to-disk** machines were developed to help solve an ever-worsening data entry problem: punched-card systems require much mechanized movement and have many limitations. With key-to-tape and key-to-disk machines, data is entered in much the same fashion as with the card punch, but it is stored not as punches on cards but as magnetized spots on the surface of a tape or disk. The data can be stored indefinitely because the spots retain their magnetism. It can be replaced with new data when desired. This reusability overcomes a major disadvantage of punched cards, which cannot be reused in this manner. Tapes and disks can also store much more data in a smaller space; for example, as many as 1,600 characters are commonly stored on one inch of magnetic tape. Finally, data stored on tape or disk can be read into the CPU more than twenty-five times faster than data on cards. Thus, use of magnetic tape or disk can significantly increase the efficiency of data-processing operations.

Key-to-Tape In a key-to-tape system, data is recorded on magnetic tape in reels, cartridges, or cassettes. The data recorder consists of a keyboard for entering the data; a small memory to hold data while it is being checked for accuracy; hardware to write the data on tape; and usually, a television-like screen to allow easy verification and correction by the operator.

Two general types of key-to-tape configurations are available to users. A **stand-alone key-to-tape device** is a self-contained unit that takes the place of a keypunch device. An operator keys the data onto a standard half-inch magnetic tape on reels, cartridges, or cassettes, which are then collected from all the stand-alone devices. The data from the various reels, cartridges, or cassettes are then combined onto a single magnetic tape, which is then used for computer processing.

A second configuration is known as a **clustered key-to-tape device.** Here, several keyboards are linked to one or two magnetic-tape units, which accept data from the operators and combine it as keying takes place. This type of configuration eliminates the extra step needed for the stand-alone devices. Clustered key-to-tape devices (also known as key-to-central-tape devices) tend to be less expensive than stand-alone devices because the hardware for recording the data onto the tape is centralized. The clustered devices are used in applications where large quantities of similar data are keyed.

An advantage of both types of key-to-tape configurations is that the data on the tape can be checked for accuracy and corrected if necessary prior to being forwarded to the computer for processing.

Key-to-Disk A typical key-to-disk configuration consists of several keying devices, all of which are connected to a minicomputer. Data is keyed onto magnetic disks (see Figure 4 – 4). Before that, however, the data is usually stored and checked for accuracy by the minicomputer. This editing is directed by the minicomputer's stored-program instructions. If an error is detected, the system interrupts the operator and ''stands by'' until a correction has been entered. The correct data is then stored on magnetic tape for input to the computer.

Key-to-Diskette An increasingly popular data-entry system is the key-to-diskette system. A **flexible** (or **floppy**) **diskette** is used instead of the conventional (hard) disk. The data is entered on a keyboard, displayed on a screen for verification, and recorded on the diskette. A key-to-diskette system can operate as a stand-alone device or in a cluster configuration (as described above). The data recorded on the diskettes is collected and pooled onto a magnetic tape for computer processing.

In summary, key-to-tape, key-to-disk, and key-to-diskette data-entry systems offer several advantages over traditional punched-card input:

1. Magnetic tapes, disks, and diskettes are reusable.
2. Errors can be corrected by backspacing and re-keying correct data over the incorrect data.
3. Since the key-entry devices work electronically rather than mechanically, they are much quieter.
4. Operators can transcribe data faster.
5. Record lengths are not limited to eighty characters. However, most key-to-disk systems can accommodate data in an eighty-column format, allowing use of old programs written to accept punched-card records.
6. Storage on tape, disk, or diskette is much more compact, which reduces data handling and saves storage space.

While key-to-disk, -tape, and -diskette systems offer many advantages over punched-card input, they also cost more. Generally, these systems are cost effective where large amounts of data are prepared for processing on medium-sized or large computers.

Figure 4—4 ▪ Key-to-Disk System

Source-Data Automation

Data entry has traditionally been the weakest link in the chain of data-processing operations. Although data can be processed electronically at extremely high speeds, significantly more time is required to prepare it and enter it into the computer system.

Consider a computer system that uses punched cards for data input. The data is first written on some type of coding form or source document. Then it is keypunched onto cards by an operator. Next, the data may be verified by duplication of the entire keypunching operation. Incorrect cards must be keypunched and verified a second time. After all data has been recorded cor-

Figure 4–5 ▪ Traditional Keypunch Data Entry Process

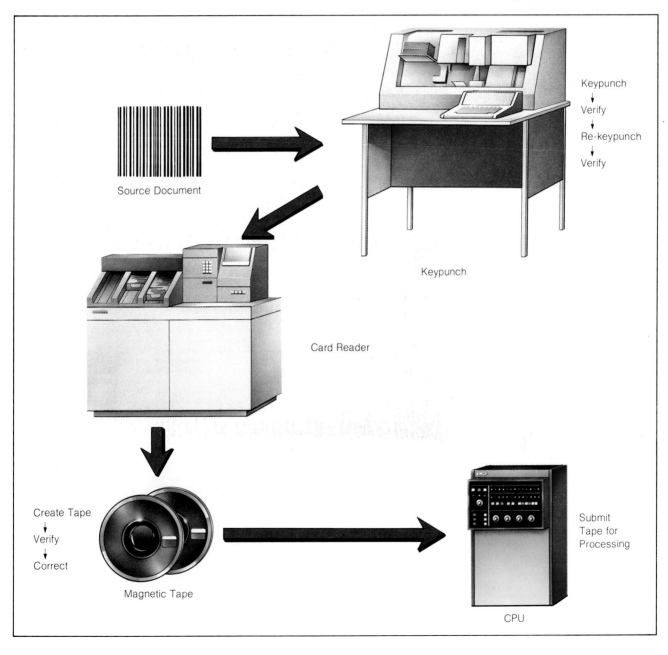

Source Document

Keypunch
↓
Verify
↓
Re-keypunch
↓
Verify

Keypunch

Card Reader

Create Tape
↓
Verify
↓
Correct

Magnetic Tape

Submit
Tape for
Processing

CPU

rectly on cards, operations such as sorting and merging may be required before the cards can be read into the computer. Generally, card files are copied onto magnetic tape for later input to the computer, because magnetic-tape files can be read into the computer much faster than card files. Figure 4–5 diagrams such a system.

This method of entering data into the computer is time-consuming and expensive. Some organizations have turned to the key-to-tape, -disk, or -diskette systems described above to simplify keypunching operations. Another approach to data collection and preparation is also gaining in popularity; it is called **source-data automation.** The purpose of source-data automation is to collect data about an event, in computer-readable form, when and where the event takes place. By eliminating the intermediate steps used in preparing card input, source-data automation improves the speed, accuracy, and efficiency of data-processing operations (see Figure 4–6).

Source-data automation is implemented by use of a variety of methods. Each requires special machines for reading data and converting it into machine language. The most common approaches to source-data automation are discussed below.

Magnetic-Ink Character Recognition   Magnetic ink was introduced in the late 1950s to facilitate check processing by the banking industry. Because magnetic-ink characters can be read by both humans and machines, no special data conversion step is needed. Magnetic-ink characters are formed with magnetized particles of iron oxide. Each character is composed of certain

Figure 4–6 ▪ Typical Methods of Source-Data Automation

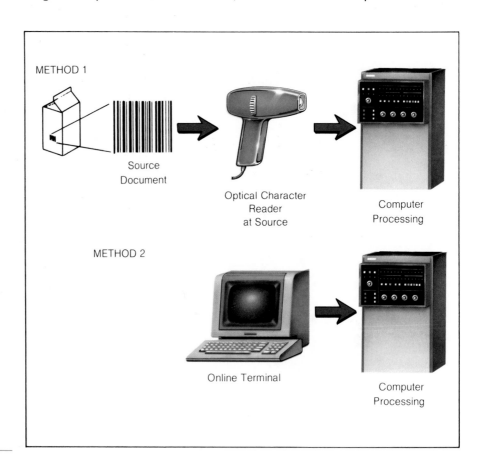

METHOD 1

Source Document

Optical Character Reader at Source

Computer Processing

METHOD 2

Online Terminal

Computer Processing

sections of a seventy-section matrix (see Figure 4–7a). The characters can be read and converted into machine code by a **magnetic-ink character recognition (MICR) device.**

With MICR each character area is examined to determine the shape of the character represented. The presence of a magnetic field in a section of the area represents a 1-bit; the absence of a magnetic field represents a 0-bit. Each magnetic-ink character is composed of a unique combination of 0-bits and 1-bits. When all sections in a character area are combined and translated into binary notation in this manner, the character represented can be determined. MICR devices automatically check each character read to ensure accuracy.

The processing of bank checks is a major application of magnetic-ink character recognition. The magnetic-ink characters are printed along the bottom of the check (see Figure 4–8). The **transit field** is preprinted on the check. It includes the bank number, which is an aid in routing the check through the Federal Reserve System. The customer's account number appears in an **"on-us" field.** A clerk manually inserts the amount of the check in the **amount field** after the check has been used and received at a bank.

All magnetic-ink characters on checks are formed with the standard fourteen-character set shown in Figure 4–7b. (Other character sets may be used in other applications.) As the checks are fed into the MICR device, it reads them and sorts them by bank number at a Federal Reserve Bank and by account number at the issuing bank. In this manner, checks are routed back to each issuing bank and then back to its customers. A MICR device can read and sort between 750 and 1,500 checks per minute.

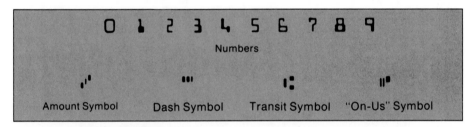

(a) Magnetic-Ink Character Set

Figure 4–7 ▪ Matrix Patterns for Magnetic-Ink Characters

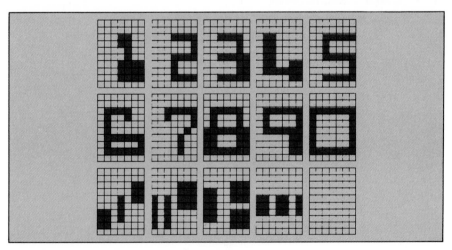

(b) Matrix Patterns for Magnetic-Ink Characters

Figure 4–8 ▪ **Magnetic-Ink
Character Recognition**

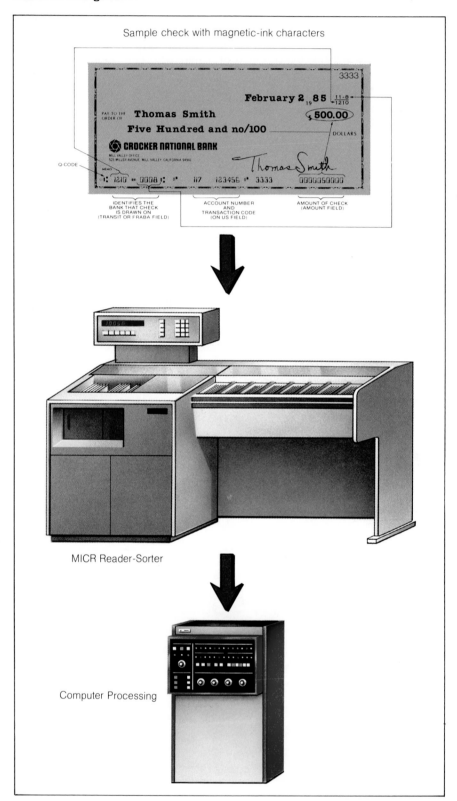

Sample check with magnetic-ink characters

MICR Reader-Sorter

Computer Processing

Optical Recognition Optical recognition devices can read marks or symbols coded on paper documents and convert them into electrical pulses. The pulses can then be transmitted directly to the CPU or stored on magnetic tape for input at a later time.

The simplest approach to optical recognition is known as **optical-mark recognition (OMR),** or **mark-sensing.** This approach is often used for machine scoring of multiple-choice examinations (see Figure 4–9), where a person taking the examination makes a mark with a heavy lead pencil in the location

Figure 4–9 ▪ Optical-Mark Recognition for Multiple-Choice Test

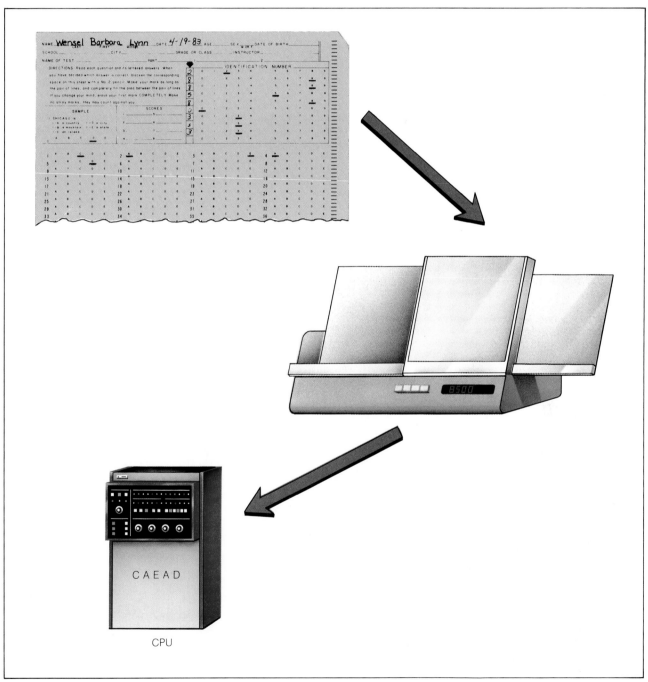

CPU

corresponding to each desired answer. The marks on an OMR document are sensed by an **optical-mark page reader** as the document passes under a light source. The presence of marks in specific locations is indicated by light reflected at those locations. As the document is read, the optical-mark data is automatically translated into **machine language.** When the optical-mark page reader is directly connected to the computer, up to 2,000 forms of the same type can be read and processed in an hour.

Optical-mark recognition is also used in order writing, inventory control, surveys and questionnaires, and payroll applications. Since optical-mark data is initially recorded by people, forms that are easy for them to understand and complete must be devised. Instructions, with examples, are generally provided to aid those who must use the forms. Good design helps to prevent errors and lessens the amount of time required to complete forms.

Another type of optical reader, known as a **bar-code reader,** can read special line, or bar, codes—patterns of optical marks. Some bar codes in use today are shown in Figure 4–10. They are suitable for many applications, including **point-of-sale (POS) systems,** credit card verification, and freight identification to facilitate warehouse operations.

Data is represented in a bar code by the widths of the bars and the distances between them. Probably the most familiar bar code is the **Universal**

Figure 4–10 ▪ Types of Bar Codes

Figure 4–11 ▪ **UPC Wand Reader**

Product Code (UPC) found on most grocery items. This code consists of ten pairs of vertical bars, which represent both the manufacturer's identity and the identity of the item but not the item's price. The code for each product is a unique combination of these vertical bars. The UPC symbol is read by a hand-held **wand reader** (see Figure 4–11) or by a fixed scanner linked to a cash-register-like device (see Figure 4–13). The computer system identifies the product, its brand name, and other pertinent information and uses this data to find the item's price. It then prints out both name and price. The computer keeps track of each item sold and thus helps the store manager to maintain current inventory status.

Optical-character readers can read special types of characters known as **optical characters.** Some **optical-character recognition (OCR)** devices can read characters of several type fonts, including both uppercase and lowercase letters. The most common font is shown in Figure 4–12.

A major difference between optical-character recognition and optical-mark recognition is that optical-character data is represented by the shapes of characters rather than by the positions of marks. However, both OCR and OMR devices rely on reflected light to translate written data into machine-readable form.

Acceptable OCR input can be produced by computer printers, adding machines, cash registers, accounting machines, and typewriters. Data can be

Figure 4–12 ▪ **OCR Characters**

ABCDEFGHIJKLMN
OPQRSTUVWXYZ ,.
$/*-1234567890

fed into the reader via a **continuous form** such as a cash-register tape or on **cut forms** such as phone or utility bills. When individual cut forms are used, the reader can usually sort the forms as well.

The most advanced optical-character readers can also read handwritten characters. However, the handwritten characters must be neat and clear; otherwise, they may not be read correctly. This is a major source of frustration because handwriting varies widely from individual to individual; and devices that must read handwriting are often very slow. Any characters that cannot be interpreted are rejected by the optical-character readers.

Machine-produced optical-character recognition has been used in credit-card billing, utility billing, and inventory-control applications. Handwritten optical-character recognition has been used widely in mail sorting. The reliability of optical-character recognition systems is generally very good.

Remote Input   Remote terminals collect data at its source and transmit it to a central computer for processing. Generally, data is transmitted over tele-communication equipment. The many types of remote terminals available can increase the versatility and expand the applications of the computer. Types of remote terminals to be discussed here are point-of-sale terminals, touch-tone devices, voice-recognition devices, and intelligent terminals.

Remote terminals that perform the functions of a cash register and also capture sales data are referred to as point-of-sale (POS) terminals. Such terminals have a keyboard for data entry, a panel to display the price, a cash drawer, and a printer that provides a cash receipt. A POS terminal typical of those found in many supermarkets is shown in Figure 4–13.

Figure 4–13 ▪ Point-of-Sale Terminal

As mentioned earlier, some POS terminals have wand readers that can read either the Universal Product Code (UPC) or the OCR characters stamped on or attached to an item. The sale is registered automatically as the checkout person passes the wand reader over the code; there is no need to enter the price via a keyboard unless the wand malfunctions. Thus, POS terminals enable sales data to be collected at its source. If the terminals are directly connected to a large central computer, useful inventory and sales information can be provided almost instantaneously to the retailer.

Touch-tone devices are remote terminals used together with ordinary telephone lines to transfer data from remote locations to a central computer. The data is entered via a special keyboard on the terminal. Generally, slight modifications must have been made to the telephone connection to allow data to be transferred over the line (see Figure 4–14).

There are several types of touch-tone devices. One type can read a magnetic strip on the back of plastic cards; this type is often used to verify credit-card transactions. Another type can store large amounts of data on a magnetic belt similar to a magnetic tape before transmitting it. This type of terminal is best suited for large-volume processing.

- A **field** is a group of related characters, or columns, that is treated as a single unit of information. A field designated to hold a social security number, for example, would be a single unit of information containing eleven characters (such as | 2 | 7 | 4 | - | 6 | 0 | - | 9 | 7 | 8 | 9 |).
- A **record** is a collection of related fields. These related fields (a record) may contain data on such things as an employee, a sales transaction, and an item in inventory.
- By reducing input to one step, **source-data automation** greatly speeds the data processing flow of input → process → output.
- The primary methods of source-data automation include: **magnetic-ink character recognition, optical recognition,** and **remote input.**

Figure 4–14 ▪ Touch-Tone Device

Specialized Input Devices

Voice-Recognition Devices   Terminals that use **audio input** or **voice-recognition systems** (see Figure 4–15) are suitable for low-volume, highly formal input and output. Users may enter data into the computer by punching keys on a terminal, perhaps a regular push-button phone terminal. Each key transmits a different tone over a telephone line. Or the user may "train" the computer to understand his or her voice and vocabulary. Here, the user must follow only the patterns the computer is programmed to recognize.

Currently, **voice-recognition modules (VRMs)** are available which can recognize a predetermined set of words and phrases. With word recognition accuracy of up to 99 percent, the system comes close to allowing the user to communicate with the computer using the natural speaking voice.

Available VRMs are compatible with high-level languages and can be interfaced to existing computer hardware. Then data can be entered by use of commands in natural spoken language, allowing greater accuracy in data entry.

The VRM has proven very effective for data entry, quality control, process control, computer-aided design, and word processing. In the future, many more uses will be found for this device.

Figure 4–15 ▪ Voice-Recognition System

Intelligent Terminals   **Intelligent terminals,** another type of remote input device, can be programmed by use of stored instructions. This capability distinguishes them from other terminals discussed earlier in this chapter (sometimes called dumb terminals), which cannot be programmed. Intelligent terminals have the same kinds of components as full-sized computers but are limited in their storage capability and in the set of instructions they can perform. They are useful for editing data prior to transmitting it to a central computer; editing and other manipulating functions are directed by programs stored in the terminal's primary storage unit.

Most intelligent terminals have a **cathode-ray tube (CRT)** and a printer built into them. The CRT is useful to show the data being edited and to display responses to inquiries. The terminal's programmable nature extends its applications into other areas as well. For example, an intelligent terminal can be connected to other input/output (I/O) devices and used as a stand-alone computer system for low-volume or special-purpose processing. Alternatively, such a terminal can be used to coordinate data entry from nonprogrammable terminals at other locations. In this case, the data is transmitted to the intelligent terminal for editing and validation and later transmitted as a part of batched input from the intelligent terminal to a large central computer.

The use of intelligent terminals will continue to grow as their cost continues to decrease and new applications for them are discovered. They can help in many ways to make data entry and retrieval easier for the user.

Touch-Sensitive Screens   **Touch-sensitive screens** (see Figure 4–16) permit the terminal screen itself to serve as an input device. Division of the terminal screen into a grid and placement of sensors in the screen allow the terminal to be used as an input device activated by touching the screen. The touch-sensitive screen should prove to be a significant time-saving input device in that it can eliminate a considerable amount of typing that is otherwise necessary.

As more and more computer applications are designed with touch-sensitive screens as an input device, considerable time will be saved. Applications using touch-sensitive screens are particularly appealing to business managers

Figure 4–16 ▪ Touch-Sensitive
Screen

and physicians for whom time is of the essence. Also, touch-sensitive screens
offer endless possibilities for the use of computers in the education of children.

Electronic Drawing Pens and Light Pens **Electronic drawing pens** and **light
pens** contain a photoelectric cell in the tip of a pen-shaped instrument. The
pens are used to draw lines on a terminal to create a drawing of an object.
The computer can identify the x and y coordinates of the pen when the photoelectric cell is placed on the terminal screen. Once the object is drawn on
the terminal screen, changes can be made to it until it meets the user's satisfaction. Light pens have seen the greatest amount of use in the areas of engineering and drafting (see Figure 4 –17).

Figure 4–17 ▪ Light Pen

Can a Pen Really Stop a Train?

Does this sound impossible? Thanks to the light pen and the computer, freight trains can be controlled easily at the Austrian Federal Railways freight yard, Austria. A rolling seventy-ton railroad car can be stopped when a yard controller draws a red bar at the appropriate spot on the video screen of a computer terminal. Another car can be sent along a clear track when the controller makes a green line on the screen. The system is connected to a fail-safe keyboard that can also direct the yard's switches. Moving a car around depots by computer is not uncommon in our country, but the use of the light pen is. In the future, light pen technology will be used in freight depots around the world.

Digitizers   **Digitizers** are also a graphics-oriented input device that can be added to a computer system. The digitizer is used to transform two- or three-dimensional drawings or representations into images on the display screen (see Figure 4–18). A three-dimensional digitizer is called a spacial digitizer. It requires special equipment for the user to input x, y, and z coordinates.

INFORMATION OUTPUT

Printers

Computer **printers** serve a straightforward basic function—printing processed data in a form humans can read (see Figure 4–19). This permanent, readable copy of computer output is often referred to as **hard copy.** To produce it, the printer first receives electronic signals from the central processing unit. In an **impact printer,** these signals activate print elements, which are pressed against paper. **Nonimpact printers,** a newer development, use heat, laser technology, or photographic techniques to print output.

Impact Printers   Impact printers can be further subdivided into character-at-a-time and line-at-a-time printers. **Character-at-a-time printers** print one character of data at a time, typically at speeds from 600 to 900 characters per minute. **Line-at-a-time printers** print an entire line of information at a time; generally, speeds up to 2,000 lines per minute can be obtained from such an impact printer.

Figure 4–18 ▪ Digitizer

Figure 4–19 ■ Printer

Printer-keyboards, dot-matrix printers, and daisy-wheel printers are the three principal character-at-a-time devices. The **printer-keyboard** is similar to an office typewriter except that a stored program, rather than a person, controls it (see Figure 4–20). All instructions, including spacing, carriage returns, and printing of characters, are sent from the CPU to the printer. A printing element with characters on its surface is generally used for printing. The keyboard allows an operator to communicate with the system—for example, to enter data or instructions. The usual speed of a printer-keyboard is about 900 characters per minute. Because these printers are slow, they are typically used for small amounts of output.

Dot-matrix (sometimes called **wire-matrix**) **printers** are based on a design principle similar to that of a football or basketball scoreboard. The matrix is a rectangle composed of pins; usually, it is seven pins high and five pins

Figure 4–20 ■ Printer-Keyboard

wide. Certain combinations of pins are activated to represent characters. For example, the number A and the letter 3 are formed by a combination of pins being pressed against paper, as shown in Figure 4–21. The dot combinations used to represent various numbers, letters, and special characters are also shown in Figure 4–21. Dot-matrix printers can typically print up to 900 characters per minute.

Daisy-wheel printers are similar to printer-keyboards in that they resemble office typewriters. The daisy wheel itself is a flat disk with petal-like projections (see Figure 4–22). Daisy wheels come in several type fonts that can be interchanged quickly to suit application needs. The daisy-wheel printer offers high quality type and is often used in conjunction with word processors to give output a professional appearance.

Types of line-at-a-time printers include print-wheel printers, chain printers, and drum printers. A **print-wheel printer** typically contains 120 print wheels, one for each of 120 print positions on a line (see Figure 4–23). Each print wheel contains 48 characters, including alphabetic, numeric, and special characters. Each print wheel rotates until the desired character moves into the corresponding print position on the current print line. When all wheels are in their correct positions, a hammer drives the paper against the wheels and an entire line of output is printed. Print-wheel printers can produce about 150 lines per minute.

A **chain,** or **train, printer's** character set is assembled in a chain or train that revolves horizontally past all print positions (see Figure 4–24). There is one print hammer for each column on the paper. Characters are printed when hammers press the paper against an inked ribbon, which in turn presses against appropriate characters on the print chain. Type fonts can be changed easily on chain printers, allowing a variety of fonts, such as italic or boldface, to be used. Some chain printers can produce up to 2,000 lines per minute.

Figure 4–21 ▪ Dot-Matrix Printer Character Set

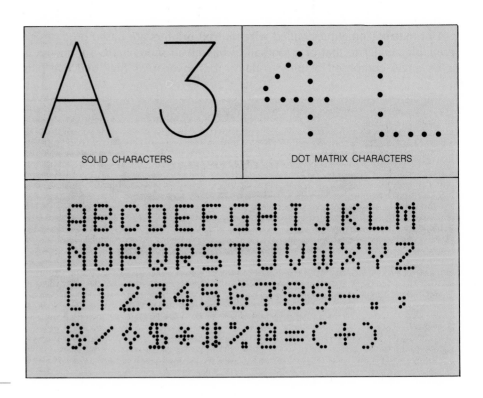

Figure 4–22 ■ **Daisy Print Wheel**

Figure 4–23 ■ **Print Wheel**

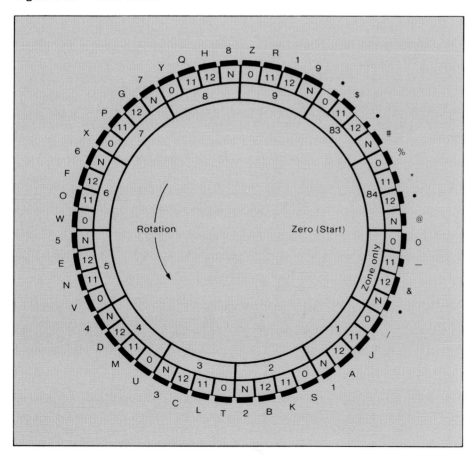

Figure 4–24 ▪ Print Element of Chain Printer

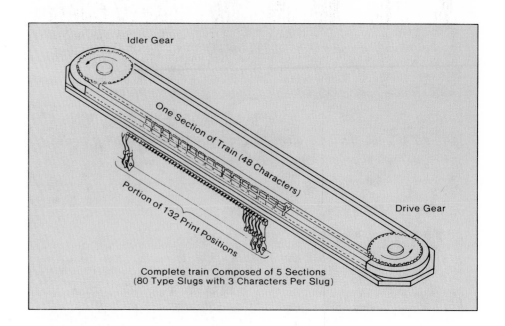

A **drum printer** uses a metal cylinder with rows of characters engraved across its surface (see Figure 4–25). Each column on the drum contains the complete character set and corresponds to one print position on the line. As the drum rotates, all characters are rotated past the print position. A hammer presses the paper against an ink ribbon and the drum when the appropriate character is in place. One line is printed for each revolution of the drum, since all characters eventually reach the print position during one revolution. Some drum printers can produce 3,000 lines per minute.

Nonimpact Printers   As mentioned earlier, nonimpact printers do not print characters by means of a mechanical printing element that strikes paper. Instead, a variety of other methods are used. Electrostatic, electrothermal, ink-jet, laser, and xerographic printers will be discussed here.

Figure 4–25 ▪ Print Drum

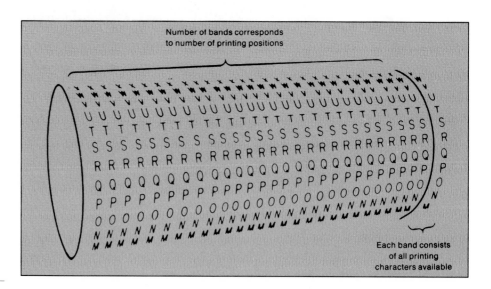

An **electrostatic printer** forms an image of a character on special paper using a dot matrix of charged wires, or pins. The paper is moved through a solution containing ink particles that have a charge opposite that of the pattern. The ink particles adhere to each charged pattern on the paper, forming a visible image of each character.

Electrothermal printers generate characters by using heat and heat-sensitive paper. Rods are heated in a matrix; as the ends of the selected rods touch the heat-sensitive paper, an image is created.

Both electrothermal and electrostatic printers operate silently. They are often used in applications where noise may be a problem. Some of these printers are capable of producing 5,000 lines per minute.

In an **ink-jet printer,** a nozzle is used to shoot a stream of charged ink towards the paper. Before reaching it, the ink passes through an electronic field that arranges the charged particles into characters.

Laser printers combine laser beams and electrophotographic technology to create output images (see Figure 4–26). A beam of light is focused through a rotating disk containing a full font of characters. The character image is projected onto a piece of film or photographic paper, and the print or negative is developed and fixed in a manner similar to that used for ordinary photographs. The output consists of high quality, letter-perfect images—the process is often used to print books. Laser printers operate at high speeds, up to 21,000 lines per minute.

Xerographic printers use printing methods much like those used in common xerographic copying machines. For example, Xerox, the pioneer of this type of printing, has one model that prints on single 8½-by-11-inch sheets of plain paper, rather than on a continuous sheet as the majority of printers do. Xerographic printers operate at 4,000 lines per minute.

Table 4–1 shows representative differences in print speeds of impact and nonimpact printers. Since nonimpact printers involve much less physical movement than impact printers, they are generally much faster. They also offer a wider choice of type faces and better speed-to-price ratios than impact

Figure 4–26 ▪ Laser Printer

Table 4–1 ▪ **Printer Types and Speeds**

PRINTER TYPE	APPROXIMATE PRINTING CAPABILITY
IMPACT PRINTERS	
Character-at-a-Time:	
Printer-keyboard	15 characters per second
Daisy wheel	50 characters per second
Dot-matrix (Wire-matrix)	120 characters per second
Line-at-a-Time:	
Print wheel	150 lines per minute
Print chain	2,000 lines per minute
Print drum	2,000 lines per minute
NONIMPACT PRINTERS	
Ink jet	200 characters per second
Xerographic	4,000 lines per minute
Electrothermal	5,000 lines per minute
Electrostatic	5,000 lines per minute
Laser	21,000 lines per minute

printers; and their technology implies a higher reliability because they use fewer movable parts in printing. The primary disadvantage of nonimpact printers is their inability to make carbon copies. However, they can make multiple printings of a page in less time than it takes an impact printer to make one multicarbon page.

Printing systems also combine many features of the printing process into one machine. For example, collating, routing, hole-punching, blanking out of proprietary information, and perforating may be performed. Some printers produce both text and form designs on plain paper; this reduces or eliminates the need for preprinted forms.

As the refinement of nonimpact printing technology continues, nonimpact printers will become the predominant means of producing hard-copy output.

Visual Display Terminals

Visual display terminals are output devices that display data on cathode-ray tubes (CRTs) similar to television screens (see Figure 4 – 27). A typical screen can hold twenty-four lines, each containing eighty characters. These termi-

Concept Summary 4–2

Printers

▪ The permanent, readable form of computer output produced by printers is referred to as **hard copy.** (This is in contrast to the output of visual display devices called **soft copy.**)

▪ Printers that have elements that strike the paper are **impact printers,** while **nonimpact printers** use heat, laser technology, or photographic techniques to print images on paper.

▪ Impact printers that can be subcategorized as **character-at-a-time printers** include: **printer-keyboards, dot-matrix printers,** and **daisy-wheel printers.**

▪ Impact printers that can be subcategorized as **line-at-a-time printers** include: **print-wheel printers, chain printers,** and **drum printers.**

▪ **Electrostatic, electrothermal, ink-jet, laser,** and **xerographic** printers are all types of nonimpact printers.

Figure 4–27 ▪ Visual Display Terminal

nals supply what is known as **soft copy** output; that is, the screen image is not a permanent record of what is shown. They are well suited for applications involving inquiry and response, where no permanent (printed) records are required, and can be used for capturing data to be transmitted from remote offices to a central computer. Data can be entered on a keyboard on the terminal and displayed on the screen for verification as it is keyed.

Visual display terminals have some advantages over printers. First, they can display output much faster than printers—some CRT terminals can display up to 10,000 characters in a second. Also, they are much quieter in operation than impact printers. It is usually possible to connect a printer or a copier to a CRT terminal; thus, hard-copy output of the screen contents can be provided.

Another type of CRT, known as a **graphic display device** is used to display drawings as well as characters on a screen (see Figure 4–28). Graphic display devices are generally used to display graphs and charts, but they can also display complex curves and shapes. Graphic display devices are being used in highly technical fields such as the aerospace industry to aid in the design of new wing structures. They are also being used heavily in computer-assisted design/computer-assisted manufacturing (CAD/CAM) areas where objects can be designed and tested and the manufacturing process specified on the computer system in an interactive fashion.

Specialized Output Devices

In some instances, printers and terminals cannot provide certain forms of output. At these times, special output devices are required.

Figure 4–28 ▪ Graphic Display
Device

Plotters A **plotter** is an output device that converts data from the CPU into graphic form. It can produce lines, curves, and complex shapes. The major difference between a plotter and a graphic display device is that the plotter produces hard-copy output (paper) whereas the graphic display device produces soft-copy output (screen image).

A typical plotter has a pen, movable carriage, drum, and chart-paper holder (see Figure 4–29). Shapes are produced as the pen moves back and forth across the paper along the y-axis while the drum moves the paper up and down along the x-axis. Both the paper movement and the pen movement are bi-directional. The pen is raised and lowered from the paper surface automatically.

The plotter can be used to produce line and bar charts, graphs, organizational charts, engineering drawings, maps, trend lines, supply and demand curves, and so on. The figures are drawn precisely because the pen can be positioned at up to 45,000 points in each square inch of paper. Some plotters can produce drawings in up to eight colors. The usefulness of the plotter lies in its ability to communicate information in easy-to-understand picture form.

Figure 4–29 ▪ Plotter

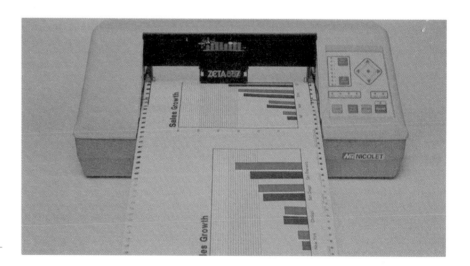

Computer Output Microfilm In situations where large volumes of information must be printed and stored for future reference, conventional paper output is not appropriate. It uses much storage space, and particular portions of it are often difficult to get to. A possible alternative is **computer output microfilm (COM),** which consists of photographed images produced in miniature by the computer. In some cases, the output is first recorded on magnetic tape. Special photocopying equipment is then used to reproduce the information on microfilm. In an interactive environment, the COM equipment is used to display output on a CRT screen. The screen is exposed to microfilm. The microfilm copy can be produced as a roll of film or a four-by-six-inch microfiche card. In such a system, the speed of recording can be twenty-five to fifty times faster than traditional printing methods.

The main advantage of COM is that much data can be stored compactly, reducing both space requirements and storage costs. Further, both character and graphic output can be recorded. Use of a transparent forms-overlay permits headings to be printed and lines superimposed so that output is highly readable. The cost of producing additional microfilm copies is very low. In the past, high initial investment costs and the inability of the computer to directly retrieve microfilmed data have been disadvantages. However, costs are declining, and the feasibility of attaining a COM system is increasing.

Voice Synthesizers **Voice synthesizers** constitute the output portion of a computerized voice communication system. Voice synthesizers can be used to provide verbal responses, or output, to the computer user. Although they have seem limited use to date, a voice synthesizer could be an invaluable component of a computer system used for the education of the blind, for example.

SUMMARY POINTS

- Data is recorded on punched cards by means of a card punch/keypunch machine. Data is typed from source documents by an operator. Options like automatic skipping and duplicating are available on most keypunches.
- The unit record concept implies that all necessary data pertaining to a transaction is contained on one punched card.
- The major disadvantages of punched cards are length limitations, possible mutilation during handling, and slow processing speed. Also, large card files take up space and increase handling costs.
- Key-to-tape, key-to-disk, and key-to-diskette devices are increasingly used because they overcome the disadvantages of punched cards. Tapes, disks, and diskettes allow easy correction of errors, are reusable, can store more data in less space than cards, and can transfer data at least twenty-five times faster than cards. These devices also allow data to be verified, formatted, and edited as it is recorded.
- Source-data automation refers to collection of data at the point where a transaction occurs. Common approaches to source-data automation employ optical-recognition devices and other types of remote terminals.
- Magnetic-ink characters can be read by humans and also by machines, since they are magnetically inscribed. Magnetic-ink character recognition (MICR) devices can convert the magnetic characters into machine code for computer processing. MICR devices are used extensively by the banking industry for processing checks.

- Optical-mark recognition devices can sense marks made with a heavy lead pencil and convert them into machine code. Other optical-character recognition devices are capable of reading bar codes, documents printed in various type fonts, and even handwritten characters. The main advantage of optical-character recognition is that it eliminates the intermediate process of transcribing data from source documents to an input medium.

- Remote terminals can collect data at its source and transmit it over communication lines for processing by a central computer. Each device satisfies distinct needs for input and output. Which device is most appropriate for a certain application depends on the particular I/O requirements.

- Specialized input devices including voice-recognition devices, intelligent terminals, touch-sensitive screens, electronic drawing pens and light pens, and spatial digitizers are used for data input in computer applications.

- Printers provide output in a permanent (hard-copy) form that people can read. Impact printers are most commonly used with computers. They can be classified as either character-at-a-time—such as printer-keyboards, dot-matrix printers, and daisy-wheel printers—or line-at-a-time—such as print-wheel printers, drum printers, and chain printers.

- Nonimpact printers are more recent developments that use photographic, thermal, or laser techniques to print output. They are faster than impact printers, offer a wider choice of type faces and better speed-to-price ratios, and are very reliable.

- Specialized output devices include plotters, computer output microfilm (COM) equipment, and voice synthesizers. Plotters provide computer output in hard-copy graphic form. COM, miniature photographed images of computer output, is suitable for applications that involve large volumes of information because it uses less space, thereby reducing storage costs. Voice synthesizers provide the computer user with a verbal form of output.

REVIEW QUESTIONS

1. What is a field? List three fields other than the one identified in Figure 4–2, which illustrates a record pertaining to the sale of a particular item.

2. Without considering any one particular input medium, does an input record have to be limited to eighty characters or less? Explain your answer.

3. Explain what is meant by a unit record.

4. What advantages are offered by key-to-tape, key-to-disk, and key-to-diskette devices? What are some disadvantages of key-to-tape data entry?

5. Explain source-data automation.

6. Discuss three types of optical-recognition devices. Identify applications in which each type can be used to advantage.

7. What advantages do visual display terminals offer over conventional printers?

8. What is an intelligent terminal? Give some examples.

9. Discuss the two types of printing devices. Which type is more common and why?

10. Distinguish between character-at-a-time printers and line-at-a-time printers, giving examples of each.

11. Describe what is meant by a point-of-sale (POS) system. Can you identify any retailers you think might be using POS systems?

12. What type of information is contained within the Universal Product Code? Why is price not included in the UPC?

APPLICATION
Gulf Oil Corporation

Spindletop, the most famous oil well in the world, roared in on January 10, 1901; it established Texas as a major oil source. The well was financed with $300,000 borrowed from a Mellon-controlled Pittsburgh bank. In May, Andrew W. and Richard B. Mellon organized the J. M. Guffey Petroleum Company and acquired the assets of the partnership that had drilled Spindletop (Mr. Guffey being one of them). The Gulf Refining Company was chartered by the Mellons on November 10, and construction began on a Texas-based refinery to manufacture and market Spindletop oil. Crude oil production was 670,000 barrels in that first year.

Today, Gulf Oil Corporation produces approximately 185 million barrels of oil per year. It employs some 42,000 people all over the world and has assets of $21 billion. In addition, Gulf has become a "total energy" company: it finds and produces crude oil, processes gas and gas liquids, mines coal and uranium, produces synthetic fuels made from coal, and manufactures chemicals and petrochemicals.

The Information Services Division (ISD) of Gulf Oil is responsible for computer- and communications-related services within the corporation. In the United States, programming and analysis personnel are in three major locations. Two major data centers—one in Houston, Texas, and one near Pittsburgh, Pennsylvania—handle the large "corporate systems" and those systems that apply to specific strategy centers, such as Corporate Finance, Product Inventory/Billing, Accounts Payable, and Payroll. Each of these large data centers consists of multiple large processors, mostly IBM or IBM-compatible equipment. A third data center in Atlanta, Georgia handles the Credit Card Accounts Receivable System. Approximately 900 employees make up the domestic ISD staff, including programmers, analysts, and operations personnel.

CREDIT CARD ACCOUNTS RECEIVABLE SYSTEM

The Atlanta Credit Card Center supports the complex process of credit card billing and is highly dependent on sophisticated data-capture techniques such as optical-character recognition (OCR). In a typical month, the Atlanta Center receives 13 million or more invoices for processing and creates almost 3 million customer billing statements. The Center computer equipment includes an IBM 3083 computer, an IBM 4341 computer, sixteen tape drives, and over forty disk drives to support the credit card processing system.

The credit card process begins at service or fuel stations when a customer presents a credit card as payment for products or services. The attendant uses an imprinter to record the customer's account number from the credit card and the dollar amount on an invoice. The invoices are sent to the Atlanta Center, where they are balanced and applied to customers' accounts. Finally, bills are prepared and mailed to the customers.

To handle the processing of credit card invoices and customer billing statements, the Atlanta Center utilizes TRACE (Transaction Capture and Encoding), OCR equipment manufactured by Recognition Equipment, Inc. The TRACE capture system reads data imprinted on the front of the invoice (account number, dealer code, expiration date, and amount) at the rate of approximately 2,400 documents per minute and sprays the data on the back of the invoice in bar-code representation. At the same time, a machine-generated sequence number that can be read by humans is assigned to each invoice and is ink-jet printed on the face of each document. This unique number is used for invoice corrections, if needed.

About 9 to 10 percent of the invoices are not readable by the TRACE capture system. Invoices can be rejected due to misregistered printing, smudged ink, and hand-written documents. The data from the rejected invoices are manually keyed into a file which is merged with the file from the invoices that were successfully scanned.

The information from the invoice is stored on a disk file. This disk file is transferred to a magnetic tape for the daily batch update of the customer master file, thus ensuring an up-to-date file for online viewing.

At cycle billing time (there are eighteen cycles per month), the customer statements are printed (listing all transactions applied since the last billing statement) and sorted into postage groupings for mailing. These statements are printed on an IBM 3800 laser printer at a speed of approximately 13,000 lines per minute. The statements, on continuous forms, are moved to special machines which burst the forms apart, fold, and stuff them into envelopes along with a return envelope, promotional material, and other inserts. The sealed envelopes are automatically weighed, postage is affixed, and bundles are taken to the post office sorted by ZIP Code.

The batch update is run nightly and is the focal point of credit card processing. This job updates customer account records, generates the alpha file (for online alphabetic inquiry to the customer master file), performs the billing routine on those accounts in the selected billing cycle, and generates records from which various control and management reports are prepared. The

customer master file contains records for more than 7.5 million accounts.

Gulf Oil also receives applications for new accounts at a rate of tens of thousands per month. The New Accounts Processing System is an online interactive terminal/computer system. When an application is received, a unique serial number is stamped on it. This number becomes the key for processing the application through the system.

The data from the application are entered onto a disk file via a CRT. At this time, an automatic search is performed against the online customer master file to detect if an account already exists for the applicant. Also, a search is performed against the new account file to detect if there is currently an outstanding application from the same applicant.

After the decision to accept the application is made, the data to set up the account are entered via a CRT. An account number is randomly assigned, and a new account is set up on the customer master file during that night's batch update. If the application is rejected, a declination letter stating the reason for rejection is sent to the applicant.

The Gulf Atlanta Center also utilizes a point-of-sale (POS) system for twenty-four-hour, seven-day-per-week telephone credit authorization services. The purpose of the POS system is to minimize bad-debt and fraud loss by allowing a Gulf dealer to check a customer's credit status at the time of the sale. The dealer places a toll-free call to the POS unit in Atlanta, where the up-to-date customer master file is accessible via CRTs. Credit authorization is required on all card sales above some dollar "floor limit," and the credit decision is usually available in twenty-five to thirty seconds. Failure to comply with this procedure may result in the invoices being charged back to the dealer if the credit would otherwise have been denied by the POS system. The POS system is made up of sixteen CRTs to handle the authorization calls from dealers, which can exceed 10,000 per day.

An improved POS system is replacing a substantial portion of the process used to input the transaction data. Some service stations are equipped with special terminals which can scan a magnetic strip on the credit card. Automatic credit authorization is performed by referencing an online file of "bad" credit card numbers. After the sale, the service station attendant keys into the terminal the dollar amount and a code for each product. The terminal then prints an invoice for the customer and transmits the entire transaction (card number, dealer code, product codes, and dollar amount) to Atlanta. This process eliminates voice telephone calls for credit authorization, approves all transactions and not just those above the floor limit, and eliminates most of the "float time" between the time of the transaction and the time at which the statement is sent to the customer.

As can be seen from Gulf's complex credit card processing system, sophisticated data-capture techniques are necessary for handling the massive volume of transactions occurring in a large credit card system. By automating data entry, the transactions are recorded at a rate of thousands per minute, and files are kept up-to-date for online inquiry to customer files.

DISCUSSION POINTS

1. Briefly discuss the process that is used for an invoice that cannot be read by the TRACE capture system. Why is this portion of the system important?
2. Discuss several reasons why data capture techniques like those used by Gulf Oil are critical to the overall success and timeliness of the credit card accounts receivable system.

5

Storage Devices

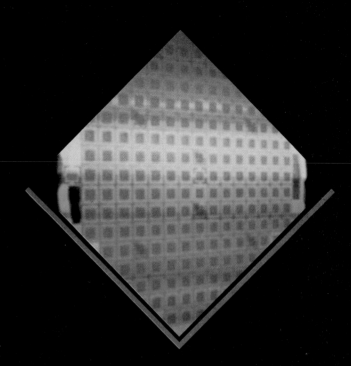

INTRODUCTION

Organizations store large volumes of data for a variety of purposes. Organizations that use electronic methods of processing this data must store it in computer-accessible form. Some storage media used in such situations have dual functions. For example, magnetic tapes and disks, which were mentioned in the previous chapter, are used for input and output and also for storage.

In discussing storage media, this chapter distinguishes between primary storage and secondary storage. Secondary storage devices are further classified according to whether they provide sequential access or direct access to stored data. The most common sequential-access storage medium is magnetic tapes. For direct access, magnetic disks are commonly used. Both are explained in detail here. The chapter also discusses the major advantages and disadvantages of mass storage systems.

ARTICLE

IRS Uses Robots as Collectors

William Giese—USA TODAY

The Internal Revenue Service continues to plunge ahead with its $107 million robot-dialing program to dun delinquent taxpayers—the folks who together owe about $24 billion in uncollected taxes.

IRS officials say it's still too early to pinpoint actual savings from the new program.

One preliminary analysis estimates that it costs the government $34 to close an average case using the new system, compared with $47 for the traditional paper-work approach.

"The purpose of the system is not so much to collect more (money) as to handle existing work more efficiently," an IRS spokesman says.

The IRS "automatic collection system" is operating 64 hours a week at six sites covering 10 states, mainly in the Midwest and Southeast.

When the computerized system is complete next summer, 31 sites will be wired to put the touch on tardy taxpayers across the USA.

The next big areas to go online, in March, are California, Hawaii and parts of New York and New Jersey.

As part of the program, computers retain records of delinquent taxpayers. Accounts are stacked in order of priority, which is determined by the amount owed and the length of time a taxpayer is delinquent. The taxpayers' phone numbers are on the list.

The computer simply begins dialing down its list; if it gets no answer or a busy signal, it automatically redials the number later.

An "office collection representative" handles the call if someone answers.

The operation runs continuously from 9 a.m. to 8 p.m. Monday through Friday and 9 a.m. to noon Saturday.

It is nearly impossible to imagine the tremendously large amounts of data that must be stored and accessed on the computer systems used by the IRS. The storage and retrieval of data on computer systems for data processing is, therefore, very critical to the success of an ADP or EDP system.

CLASSIFICATION OF STORAGE MEDIA

A computer system generally includes two types of storage: primary storage and secondary storage. **Primary storage,** discussed in Chapter 3, is actually part of the CPU and is used to store both instructions and data. Currently, semiconductor memory is the most widely used form of primary memory. Bubble memories are also seeing some limited use.

In many instances, the amount of data required by a program or set of programs exceeds the capacity of primary storage. In such cases, the data is stored in **secondary storage,** which is not part of the CPU. The most common types of secondary storage are magnetic tapes and magnetic disks. Media such as mass storage and magnetic drums are also used. These secondary storage media cost much less than primary storage and thus make storage of large volumes of data economically feasible.

The secondary storage devices are connected to the CPU, and once data has been placed in them it can be retrieved as needed for processing. However, the retrieval of items from secondary storage is slower than from primary storage. After processing has been completed, the data or results can be written back onto the secondary storage medium (see Figure 5–1).

Access to data in secondary storage can be either direct or sequential; the method depends on the storage medium used. Media such as magnetic tape and cassette tape provide **sequential-access storage.** With sequential storage devices, the computer must start at the beginning of a tape and read what is stored there until it comes to the desired data. In contrast, a medium such as a magnetic disk or magnetic drum does not have to be read sequentially; the computer can get access to the desired data directly—hence the name **direct-access storage.** Direct-access media, then, provide faster retrieval than do sequential-access media.

SEQUENTIAL-ACCESS STORAGE

Magnetic Tape

A **magnetic tape** is a continuous plastic strip wound on a reel, quite similar to the tape used in reel-to-reel stereo recorders. The magnetic tape's plastic base is treated with a magnetizable coating. Typically, the tape is ½ inch wide and is wound in lengths of from 400 to 3,200 feet. Magnetic tapes are also packaged in cartridges and cassettes for use with small computers.

Data is stored on magnetic tape by the magnetizing of small spots of the iron oxide coating on the tape. Although these spots can be read by the computer, they are invisible to the human eye. Large volumes of information can be stored on a single tape; densities of 1,600 characters per inch are common, and some tapes are capable of storing up to 6,250 characters per inch. A typical tape reel of 2,400 feet can store as much as 400,000 punched cards.

The most common method of representing data on tape uses a nine-track coding scheme, although other coding schemes, such as six-track and seven-track, are also available. When the nine-track method is used, the tape is divided into nine horizontal rows called **tracks** (see Figure 5–2). Data is rep-

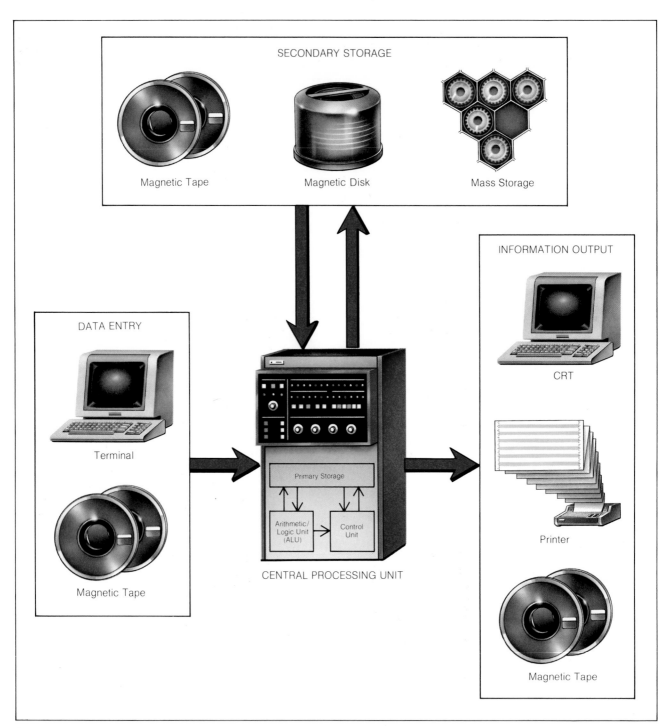

Figure 5–1 ▪ Schematic Drawing of a Computer System

resented vertically in columns, one character per column. The method of coding data is identical to the Extended Binary Coded Decimal Interchange Code (EBCDIC) used to represent data in primary storage (see Chapter 3). Thus, eight bits (and eight of the nine tracks) are used to represent each character. The ninth bit is used as a parity bit.

A magnetic tape is mounted on a **tape drive** (see Figure 5–3) when the

Figure 5–2 ■ Nine-Track Tape with
Even Parity

A B C D E F G H I J K L M N O P

Parity Bit

Zone Bits

EBCDIC

Numeric
Bits

NOTE: The parity bit is shown in the top tract to simplify visualization.

Figure 5–3 ■ Magnetic-Tape Drive

information it contains is needed by a program. The tape drive has a **read/write head** (actually an electromagnet) that creates or reads the bits as the tape moves past it (see Figure 5–4). When it is reading, the read/write head detects the magnetized areas and converts them into electrical pulses to send to the CPU. When writing, the head magnetizes the appropriate spots on the tape, erasing any previously stored data. Thus, writing is destructive, and reading is nondestructive.

Typical tape drives move tapes at speeds ranging from 25 to 200 inches per second. The **density** of the data on the tape determines how fast it can be transferred from the tape to the CPU. For example, if a tape has a density of 1,600 characters per inch and moves at a speed of 112.5 inches per second, then the data is transferred at a rate of 18,000 characters per second (1,600 characters per inch × 112.5 inches per second).

Individual records on magnetic tape are separated by **interrecord gaps (IRGs),** as shown in Figure 5–5. These gaps do not contain data but perform another function. A tape is rarely read in its entirety—without stopping.

Figure 5–4 ▪ Recording on Magnetic Tape

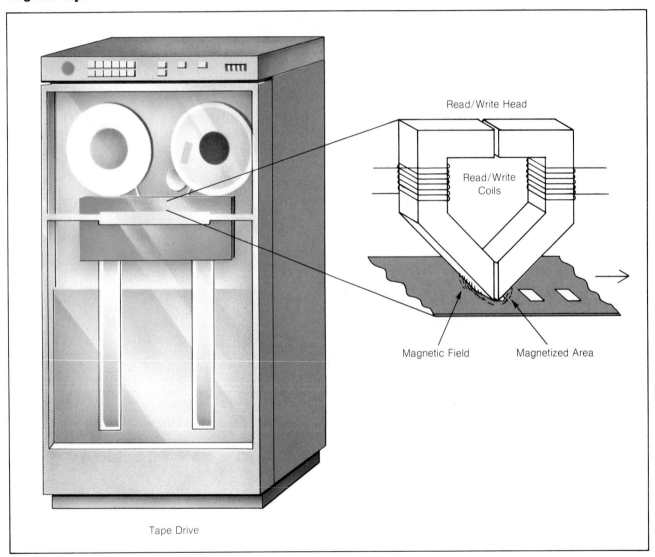

Tape Drive

Rather, it is stopped when the end of a record is reached. The tape reel must be rotating at the correct speed to allow the next record to be read correctly; otherwise, the result would be similar to what happens when a phonograph record is played at the wrong speed. The IRG allows the tape to regain the proper speed before the next record is read. The length of the interrecord gap depends on the speed of the tape drive; if the tape drive is very fast, longer gaps are needed, while slower speeds require shorter gaps.

The storing method shown in Figure 5–5, however, is not the only means of storing data on magnetic tape. Records may be grouped together, or blocked; this means condensing individual records separated by an IRG into a single block of records (see Figure 5–6). These **blocked records,** or **blocks,** are separated by **interblock gaps (IBGs).** The blocking of records on magnetic tape serves two purposes: (1) the amount of storage available on the tape is used more efficiently, and (2) the number of read/write (input/output) operations required in using the tape is significantly reduced, thus making computer resource use much more efficient.

Cassette Tape

Small computer systems may not need a large amount of secondary storage. For these systems, **tape cassettes** and **tape cartridges** have been developed. Tape cassettes look like those used in audio recording, and some can even be used with a typical cassette player/recorder. The major difference between the two types of tape cassettes is the tape; tape cassettes used for storing data use high quality, high-density digital recording tape (see Figure 5–7). The recording densities range from 125 to 200 characters per inch, and the common length is between 150 and 200 feet. Tape cartridges, on the other hand,

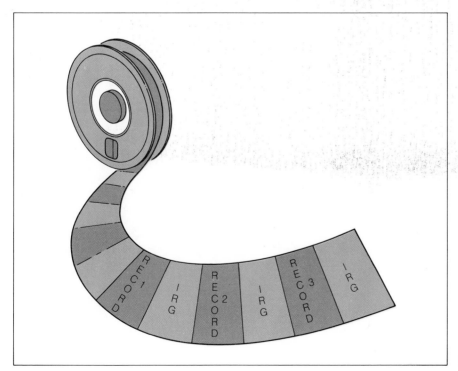

Figure 5–5 ▪ Magnetic Tape Records

Figure 5–6 ▪ **Blocked Records**

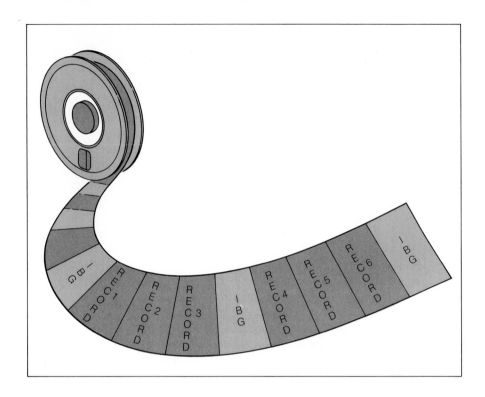

can store from 200 to 800 characters per inch, and come in 300, 450, and 555 foot lengths.

The advantages of using magnetic tape are as follows:

▪ Data can be transferred between magnetic tape and the CPU at high speeds.

Figure 5–7 ▪ **Tape Cassette**

■ Magnetic-tape records can be any length, while card records are usually limited to eighty characters.

■ Because of their high recording densities, magnetic tapes can store a large amount of data in a small amount of space.

■ Magnetic tape can be erased and reused.

■ Magnetic tape can provide high-capacity storage and backup storage at a relatively low cost. A 2,400-foot magnetic tape costs from $20 to $30.

■ Magnetic tape is perfectly suited for sequential processing. It is the most common storage medium in these types of systems.

Magnetic tape has the following disadvantages:

■ Since tape is a sequential medium, the entire tape must be read from start to finish when being altered. The amount of time required precludes its use where instantaneous retrieval of data is required.

■ All tapes and reel containers must be properly labeled and identified.

■ Humans cannot read the data on magnetic tape. When the validity of such data is questioned, the contents of the tape must be printed.

■ Environmental factors can distort data stored on magnetic tape. Dust, moisture, high or low temperatures, and static electricity can cause improper processing. Therefore, the environment must be carefully controlled.

DIRECT-ACCESS STORAGE

Magnetic Disks

The conventional **magnetic disk** is a metal platter fourteen inches in diameter coated on both sides with a magnetizable material like iron oxide. In many respects, a magnetic disk resembles a phonograph record. However, it does not have a phonograph record's characteristic grooves; its surfaces are smooth. Nevertheless, a disk unit does store and retrieve data in much the same fashion as a phonograph. The disk is rotated while a read/write head moves above its magnetic surface. Instead of spiraling into the center of the disk like the needle of a phonograph, however, the read/write head stores and retrieves data in concentric circles. Each of these circles is called a **track.** One track never touches another, as shown in Figure 5–8. A typical disk has from 200 to 500 tracks per surface.

In most disk storage devices, several disks are assembled to form a **disk pack** (see Figure 5–9) and mounted on a center shaft. The individual disks are spaced on the shaft to allow enough room for a read/write mechanism to move between them (see Figure 5–10). The disk pack in Figure 5–10 has 11 disks and provides 20 usable recording surfaces; the top and bottom surfaces are not used for storing data because they are likely to become scratched or nicked. A disk pack may contain anywhere from 5 to 100 disks.

A disk pack must be positioned in a disk storage unit when the data on the pack is to be processed. The **disk drive** rotates all disks in unison at a speed ranging from 40 to 3,600 revolutions per second. In some models, the disk packs are removable; in others, the disks are permanently mounted on the disk drive. Removable disk packs allow disk files to be removed when the data they contain is not needed. Users of removable disk packs typically have many more disk packs than disk drives (see Figure 5–11).

The data on a disk is read or written by the read/write heads located between the disks. Most disk units have one read/write head for each disk recording surface. All the heads are permanently connected to an **access mechanism.** When reading or writing occurs, the heads are positioned over the appropriate track by the in-and-out movement of the access mechanism (see Figure 5–10).

Figure 5–8 ▪ Top View of Disk Surface Showing 200 Concentric Tracks

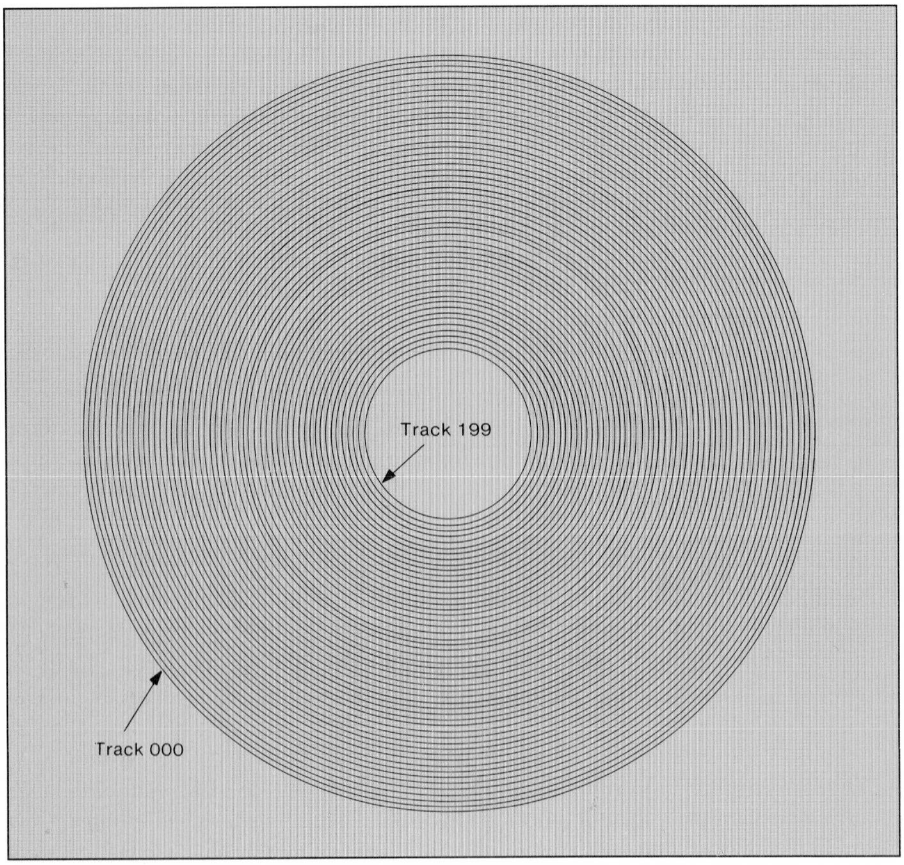

Figure 5–9 ▪ Disk Pack

Track 199

Track 000

Figure 5–10 ▪ **A Disk Pack**
a. Side View
b. Top View

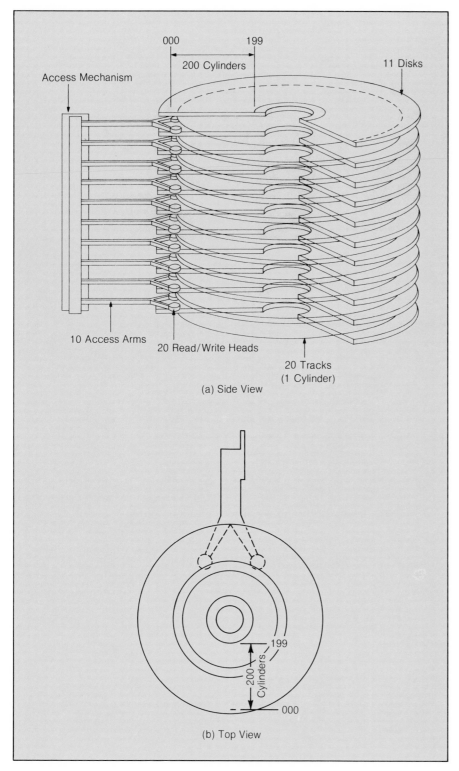

Figure 5–11 ▪ Disk Storage Units
with Removable Disk Packs

When data on the surface of one disk in the disk pack is required, all the heads move to the appropriate track, because they are connected to the same access mechanism. Because all the read/write heads move together, they are positioned over the same tracks on all disk surfaces at the same time. All the number-1 tracks on the disk surfaces form a **cylinder;** the number-2 tracks on all surfaces form another cylinder enclosed within the first; and so on (see Figure 5–10). The number of cylinders per disk pack equals the number of tracks per surface.

Some disk units have one read/write head for each track. The access time is much faster with this type of disk unit since the access mechanism does not need to move from track to track, but such units are rarely used because of their high costs. The placing of data on the disk pack, therefore, can be an important factor if the amount of access time is critical. If access time is a factor, it is best to store the data being accessed in the same cylinder or adjacent cylinders, because this will reduce the motion of the read/write heads and hence the access time.

Each track on a disk can store the same amount of data (even though the tracks get smaller toward the center of the disk). Consider a disk pack on which a maximum of 7,294 characters can be stored per track and 4,000 usable tracks (20 surfaces × 200 tracks per surface) are available. Such a disk pack could conceivably store 29 million characters of data.

Data stored on a magnetic disk is located by disk surface number, track number, and record number; this information constitutes a **disk address.** The disk address of a record immediately precedes the record (see Figure 5–12). Note that disk records are separated by gaps similar to the interrecord gaps on magnetic tape. Thus, although more data can be stored on a track by blocking several records together and reducing the number of gaps, the presence of gaps does reduce the amount of information that can be stored on a disk. In the disk pack described above, the usable storage capacity would be somewhat less than the potential capacity of 29 million characters of data.

Because disks provide direct access, they are typically used to store data

Figure 5–12 ■ Disk Address

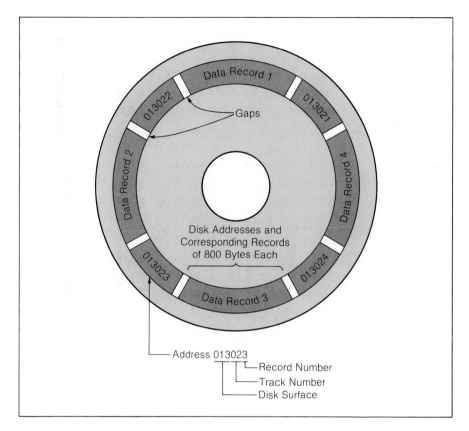

against which frequent inquiries are required. Depending upon the disk drive, read speeds of up to 850,000 characters per second are possible.

Floppy Disks

The **flexible disk, diskette,** or **floppy disk** was introduced in 1973 (see Figure 5–13) to replace punched cards as a medium for data entry, but it can also store programs and data files. These floppy disks are made of plastic and coated with an oxide substance. They are, in most respects, miniature magnetic disks. The diskettes often sell for as little as $2 and are very popular for use with minicomputer and microcomputer systems and point-of-sale terminals. They are reusable, easy to store, and weigh less than two ounces. They are readily interchangeable and can even be mailed. Because flexible disks are removable, they provide added security for a computer system. A typical disk can store as much as 12,000 punched cards.

The floppy disk comes in two standard sizes—8 inches and 5¼ inches; a 3½-inch size for use with microcomputers has recently been introduced. The disks are permanently sealed in a paper jacket (see Figure 5–14a). Data is stored as magnetized spots in tracks, as on conventional (hard) magnetic disks, and is addressed by track number and sector number (see Figure 5–14 b). There are seventy-seven tracks and twenty-six sectors on a standard 8-inch disk, forty tracks and eighteen sectors on a mini-floppy. The read/write head moves back and forth in the rectangular opening (the read/write notch) and can be placed on any track. Unlike the one in hard disk systems, this read/write head actually rides on the surface of the disk rather than being

Figure 5–13 ▪ Floppy Disks of 8 Inches, 5¼ Inches, and 3½ Inches

positioned slightly above it. The disk rotates at 360 revolutions per minute (as compared to 40 to 1,000 revolutions per second for hard disk drives).

Magnetic disks have several advantages over magnetic tape:

▪ Disk files can be organized sequentially and processed in the same way as magnetic tape, or they can be organized for direct-access processing.
▪ The fast access time offered by magnetic-disk storage allows data files to be changed immediately.
▪ Quick response can be made to inquiries (normally, response is made in seconds).
▪ Files stored on disks can be linked by software (stored-program instructions) to allow a single transaction to alter all files simultaneously.

The major disadvantages of magnetic-disk storage are:

▪ Magnetic disk is a relatively expensive storage medium; it may cost ten times as much as magnetic tape in terms of cost per character stored. However, reductions in disk costs and the introduction of flexible disks are making these storage devices more attractive from a cost standpoint.
▪ When data that exists on disk is altered, the original data is erased and the new data put in its place. Therefore, there is no backup file. If there are no other provisions for error checking and backup files, data can be lost.
▪ Disk storage requires more complicated programming for gaining access to records and updating files. The hardware itself is also highly complicated, and skilled technicians are required to maintain it.
▪ Security may be a problem because of the ease of gaining access to data on disk files.

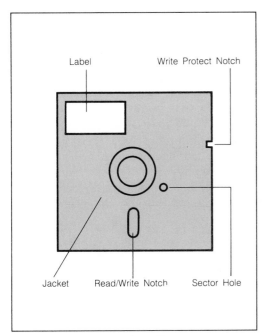

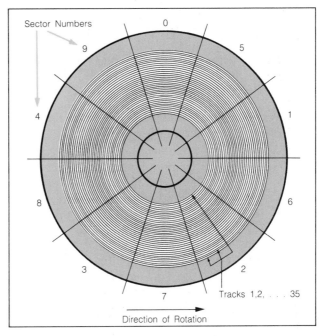

Figure 5–14 ▪ **Packaging of a Floppy Disk (a), and Sectors on a Floppy Disk (b)**

Concept Summary 5–2

Magnetic Disks

▪ A **disk pack** is an assembly of **magnetic disks** mounted on a center shaft and contained in a sealed enclosure.
▪ The disk pack is placed on a **disk drive** and the data stored on the disks is accessed by a read/write head connected to an **access mechanism.**
▪ **Cylinders** are formed by the vertical combination of the same track on each of the disks within the pack. (All number-1 tracks within the disk pack form a cylinder.)
▪ Cylinders are an important concept because of their ability to reduce the motion of the access mechanism and hence access time.
▪ **Floppy disks** are currently available in three sizes: 8-inch, 5¼-inch, and 3½-inch. Floppy disks are removable and used most heavily with microcomputers.

MASS STORAGE

Using primary storage is very fast because access to data is direct and requires no physical movement. The speed of electricity is, in effect, the limiting factor. However, primary storage is also very expensive. Disk storage is less expensive, and it provides direct-access capabilities. But even disk storage tends to be too expensive when very large amounts of data must be stored for direct-access processing.

To meet this need, **mass storage** devices have been developed. They allow rapid access to data, although their access times are much slower than those of primary storage or magnetic disk. Large files, backup files, and infrequently used files can be placed in mass storage at a relatively low cost.

Figure 5–15 ■ A Mass Storage Device Using Cartridge Tape

One approach to mass storage uses a cartridge tape as the storage medium (see Figure 5–15). The cartridges are similar to cassette tapes; however, the high-density tape used requires 90 percent less storage space than common magnetic tape. A mass storage system such as this can hold the equivalent of up to 8,000 tape reels. The mounting of the tapes is under the control of the system, rather than of an operator, and tends to be faster than the traditional operator-controlled mounting of magnetic tapes.

Mass storage is not limited to high-density magnetic tape. Recently, a mass storage system for minicomputers using small floppy disks as the storage medium was introduced. However, unlike the cartridge system described above, most mass storage devices require extensive physical movement, because the needed files must first be found and then mounted mechanically before data can be read or written. Although direct access is possible, the retrieval time is relatively slow (normally measured in seconds).

FUTURE TRENDS IN DATA STORAGE

Charge-Coupled Devices

As technology continues to advance, smaller, faster, and less expensive storage devices will become commonplace. Advances are rapidly being made in semiconductor and laser technology. A recent innovation in semiconductor technology is the development of **charge-coupled devices (CCDs)** for use in data storage. CCDs are made of silicon, similar to semiconductor memory. They are nearly a hundred times faster than magnetic bubbles but somewhat slower than semiconductor, random-access memories. As in semiconductor memories, data in CCDs can be lost if a power failure occurs.

Laser Technology

Laser technology provides an opportunity to store massive quantities of data at greatly reduced costs. A **laser storage system** can store nearly 128 billion characters of data at about one-tenth the cost of standard magnetic media. In a laser system, data is recorded by a laser beam's forming patterns on the surface of a polyester sheet coated with a thin layer of rhodium metal. To read data from this sheet, the laser reflects light off the surface, reconstructing the data into a digital bit stream. Laser data resists alteration, and any attempt to alter it can be detected readily; so it provides a secure storage system. Further, unlike magnetic media, laser storage does not deteriorate over time and is immune to electromagnetic radiation. Another advantage is that there is no danger of losing data because of power failures.

A very recent development is a laser system to be used as a mass storage device for minicomputers. This system uses a helium-neon laser, delivering about ten milliwatts of optical power to a disk coated with a film of nonmetallic substance (tellurium). Data is recorded when the laser creates a hole approximately one micrometer in diameter in the film. The disk used in this system is thirty centimeters in diameter and can store ten billion bits on its 40,000 tracks. The data cannot be erased once it is written, so this system is best suited for archival storage or for a great volume of data that must be maintained online.

Another recent development in laser technology is optical, or laser, disks. The **optical disks** are much faster than hard disks but are still fairly slow when compared to random-access memory. One big advantage, though, is their capacity. A single optical disk the size of a 12-inch record can hold the text equivalent to 1,735 books per side. Bits of data are stored on an optical disk as the presence or absence of a tiny pit burned into the disk by a pinpoint laser beam (see Figure 5–16). A line one inch long contains about 5,000 pits, or bits, of data.

RAM Chips

Accessing data on disks is relatively slow when compared with the speed at which a microprocessor can manipulate data. **Random-access memory (RAM) chips,** are, at present, the only type of storage device that can approximate the speed of a microprocessor. A new peripheral storage device using RAM chips is now available (see Figure 5–17). It plugs into the same slot a disk drive does and is indistinguishable from a disk drive to the computer. Since RAM chips require a continuous power supply, some manufacturers are providing battery back-up units for use in case of a power failure. A typical RAM chip for use with a microcomputer has up to 256K bytes of storage and has a retrieval rate fifty times faster than disk.

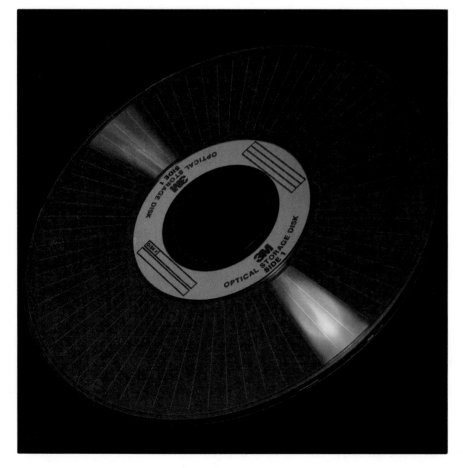

Figure 5–16 ▪ Optical Disk

Figure 5–17 ▪ **RAM Chip**

Josephson Junction

The **Josephson Junction** is a form of primary storage named for Brian Josephson, a British Nobel Prize winner. Josephson Junctions are in their early stage of development. However, when the technology is perfected, it is estimated that the speed at which primary storage operates will be increased ten-fold. Current semiconductor memory is slower than that proposed with Josephson Junctions because of the environment in which it is housed. By housing the circuits in liquid helium, the typical resistance to the flow of electricity that exists in semiconductor memory will, to a large extent, be eliminated. The use of the Josephson Junction, in conjunction with other technological advances, is expected to lead to further reduction in the size of computer hardware.

Technology advances so rapidly that accurate prediction of what future storage media will be like is nearly impossible. The objectives of making storage less expensive, faster, and smaller will continue to be pursued. The current state of the art will remain current for only a short time.

SUMMARY POINTS

▪ Secondary storage, which is not part of the CPU, can store large amounts of data and instructions at a lower cost than main storage. The most common secondary storage media are magnetic tapes and magnetic disks.

▪ Access to data in secondary storage can be either sequential or direct. Magnetic tapes on reels and in cassettes provide sequential-access storage, whereas conventional, or hard, magnetic disks and floppy disks provide direct-access storage.

■ Magnetic tape consists of a plastic base coated with iron oxide. Data is stored as small areas on the surface of the tape being magnetized.

■ Usually, data is represented on tape by a nine-track coding scheme, such as 8-bit EBCDIC with a ninth bit for parity.

■ Tape density refers to the number of characters that can be stored on one inch of tape. The transfer rate of data from tape to CPU depends on the density of the tape and the speed at which it travels past the read/write head.

■ Data is often recorded on magnetic tape in groups of records called blocks. Blocks are separated from each other by interblock gaps (IBGs). Blocking reduces overall input/output time and also makes more efficient use of available storage.

■ Tape cassettes are similar to audio cassettes. They can store up to 200 characters per inch and are used when small amounts of storage are required.

■ The major advantages of magnetic tape are high speed of data transfer, unlimited record length, reusability, and low cost. Disadvantages include requirement for sequential organization, data representation that humans cannot read, and susceptibility to environmental factors, which can distort data on tape.

■ A disk pack consists of 5 to 100 metal platters, or disks. In some packs, platters can have up to 500 tracks on which data is recorded in magnetic form. Data is read or written by read/write heads connected to an access mechanism.

■ A disk pack is positioned on a disk drive, which rotates all disks in the pack in unison. Some disk packs are removable; others are permanently mounted on disk drives.

■ Magnetic disks provide direct access. Any record can be located by reference to its disk surface number, track number, and record number. The read/write head can be positioned directly over the desired track.

■ Flexible, or floppy, disks provide low-cost, direct-access storage. Some can provide as much storage as 12,000 punched cards. Floppy disks are reusable, easy to store, and mailable. They are frequently used with minicomputers and microcomputers.

■ Advantages of disk storage include fast access times and provision for both sequential and direct-access file organizations. Major disadvantages are high cost, lack of backup, greater programming complexity, and need for greater security measures.

■ Mass storage devices are appropriate when large amounts of data must be stored at a low cost. They provide direct access, although access time is much slower than with disk. Commonly used mass storage media are cassette-type cartridge tapes and floppy disks.

■ Technological advances will continue to make storage devices faster, smaller, and less expensive. Charge-coupled devices and laser storage systems are two recent innovations.

■ Optical disks are another new branch of laser technology and are much faster than the conventional magnetic disk systems.

■ RAM chips, also a form of secondary storage, can increase data retrieval rates by as much as fifty times.

■ Josephson Junction technology allows primary memory to be housed in helium to eliminate the resistance to the flow of electricity currently found in semiconductor memory.

REVIEW QUESTIONS

1. Distinguish between primary and secondary storage. Name some common secondary storage devices.

2. Which storage media provide direct access and which provide sequential access? Explain how direct-access capabilities are achieved.

3. Compare magnetic tape and magnetic disk as secondary storage media. Identify applications for which each is suitable.

4. What is meant by density and when is it used in reference to magnetic tape? Does the density of the tape affect its use? Explain your answer.

5. Explain why interrecord gaps (IRGs) and interblock gaps (IBGs) are necessary on magnetic tape.

6. Explain blocking of records. What is its purpose?

7. What is the distinct advantage that direct-access storage devices have over sequential-access storage devices in a situation where there are a large number of records stored?

8. Give three reasons why you feel removable disk packs may be preferred over permanently mounted disk packs. Give three reasons why the opposite may be true.

9. Is there any reason why placing records on disk in certain locations may be preferred to allowing the records to be stored randomly on the disk pack? Explain your answer.

10. How does the manner in which the read/write heads function in a flexible disk system differ from their functioning in a hard disk system?

11. Describe two types of mass storage devices. What are the advantages and disadvantages of such devices?

12. What are the advantages of floppy disks? With what type of hardware are they typically used?

The Republic Iron and Steel Company was the outgrowth of a merger of thirty-five smaller midwestern iron companies. In its early days, Republic attracted some interesting people, among them John "Bet-a-Million" Gates. Along with some associates, Gates bought into Republic with the idea of using it as the basis for a great steel empire. Although the strategy failed in the Panic of 1906, Republic Iron and Steel grew quickly.

By 1927, Republic was in the hands of Cyrus Eaton, one of this country's most active, eccentric, and brilliant empire builders. It was Eaton's desire to use Republic Iron and Steel as the nucleus for a vast midwestern steel company. His progress was impressive. In 1928, Republic combined forces with Steel and Tubes, Inc., which had plants in Ohio, New York, and Michigan, and merged with Trumbull Steel. Republic's own plants in Youngstown, Ohio, gave Republic Iron and Steel much diversity. Union Drawn Steel, with plants in Ohio, Pennsylvania, Connecticut, Indiana, and Ontario, was added in 1929. The Republic Steel Corporation was officially born in 1930 as a result of mergers with three other steel and steel products companies.

Since then, Republic Steel has done better than most expected. Even before Republic's official birthdate, financial experts were predicting its death. Yet Republic has not died. Financially handicapped through most of the Depression, Republic nevertheless survived to grow in size and production capacity and continued to acquire smaller companies. During the 1960s, Republic's production of raw steel reached an all-time high of 10.7 million net tons (which was topped in 1973 with a total shipment of 11.3 million tons).

Today, Republic Steel is this country's fifth largest steel manufacturer. Recently, its sales reached an all-time high of $3.8 billion. Its corporate umbrella includes steel plants; steel and tubing divisions; and manufacturing, mining, and transportation interests.

Four large data centers, located in Cleveland, Warren, and Massillon, Ohio, and in Chicago, maintain the data-processing activities of the geographically dispersed steel plants. Each data center maintains several large CPUs. Specifically, the Cleveland data center utilizes two IBM 3000 Series computers and one Amdahl computer; the Massillon center operates three IBM System/370 model 158 computers; the Warren center operates two Amdahl computers; and the Chicago center uses two IBM System/370 model 158 computers.

In addition, Republic utilizes three other processing operations called satellite centers in other locations. The satellite centers are tied into the four large data centers described above and transfer data to them via remote job entry (RJE). Also hooked up to the large data centers are approximately 1,500 input/output terminals providing access to stored data.

Each data center handles a variety of data-processing applications. For example, the Cleveland data center computers handle the processing of corporate accounting procedures, such as accounts payable and accounts receivable, order entry and order processing, personnel, production control, and inventory control. Because of the necessity of gaining ready access to the large amounts of data needed for these applications, large and efficient data storage techniques are necessary. The Cleveland data center alone uses twelve IBM series 3350 disk drives and twenty-eight Control Data Corporation (CDC) double density model 33502 disk drives. Fourteen STC 3650 tape drives are used for processing.

The Cleveland data center performs processing in two ways: batch and online. The batch processing applications include payroll and accounting. Payroll data such as personnel records, tax records, and the like are stored on magnetic tape. When the payroll checks are to be processed, the data are transferred to magnetic disk and are accessed via direct-access storage devices (DASDs). Once the necessary files are updated and the payroll checks are processed, the updated files are transferred from disk to tape for storage. The magnetic tape provides a storage medium for files that are used periodically and also allows for file backup and archival storage.

The online processing is important for gaining imme-

diate access to data. Republic Steel has an extensive teleprocessing system. Data communication techniques are used to connect the 1,500 terminals to the data centers. An example of this online teleprocessing system is the order entry–customer billing system. Orders for Republic's products are entered on a CRT. The data are edited and verified, and a sales order is prepared. The information (customer name, items ordered, and so on) is stored on magnetic disk. A copy of the order is transmitted to the production department, where it is compared with other order and production data stored on disks. These data are also used by the accounting function to keep up-to-date records of accounts receivable, sales, and the like.

By storing data on magnetic disks, Republic has ready access to the files and can make inquiries to the customer files or change the dates or the instructions of a particular order.

The trend of Republic Steel's data-processing operation has been toward increased utilization of teleprocessing and data communication techniques. As the need for ready access to information grows, more and more information will be stored on disk devices, providing online availability of data.

DISCUSSION POINTS

1. Explain why a backup system of computer files is necessary. What methods of backup does Republic Steel use for its tape storage? For its disk storage?
2. What are the advantages of using disk storage for the order entry/billing system? How would tape storage be used in processing the order entry application?

6
Microcomputers

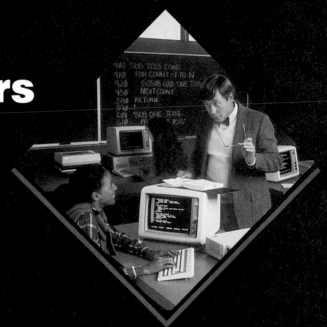

INTRODUCTION

As was seen in Chapter 2, microcomputers have had a short but eventful and colorful history. In addition, there have been a number of individuals who have figured prominently in helping to create and build the microcomputer industry into a multi-billion-dollar per year industry. Some relied on their technical expertise, while others used innovative marketing techniques to help build one of the fastest growing industries in modern history.

This chapter will begin by comparing the development of the microcomputer to that of the mainframe computer. After these development stages are reviewed, a discussion of hardware as it relates to microcomputers will be presented. The microprocessor, data storage, and microcomputer input/output devices will be discussed. The chapter will conclude with an exploration of uses for microcomputers that are expected to be popular in the future.

ARTICLE

The Computer Jungle

William D. Marbach

Though you can make the decision on purely economic grounds, buying a computer is often more like joining a religious cult. Buy an Apple, for example, and almost by default you join Apple chairman Steve Jobs in his crusade against IBM. Every machine has its "users' groups" and a band of loyal enthusiasts who tout its merits. That makes it all the more difficult for the uninitiated to decide what machine to buy. Students have a huge advantage, however. The computer companies are so eager for students' business (it builds "brand loyalty") that many offer huge discounts.

In the past six months, IBM, Apple and others have brought out new computers—and the fierce competition has forced prices down. But time is on your side: next year at this time you'd have even more choice and more computing power and features for the same price. On the other hand, this will probably be true for many years. So for those who need or want a computer now, here are some suggestions.

The most significant recent event was the introduction of Apple's Macintosh. A general-purpose computer for word processing, business spread sheets and programming, it is a radical departure from other machines because it is primarily designed to be easy to learn. And one of Apple's prime markets for the ma-

chine is the campus. (Apple priced it at $2,495 to retail customers, but students at colleges participating in Apple's program can buy it for about $1,000.) The Macintosh is a 17-pound transportable machine; the whole package fits into a canvas carrying case. It is built around a powerful Motorola 68000 microprocessor, a chip that processes information 32 bits at a time. (In contrast, the Apple IIe has an eight-bit microprocessor, and the IBM PC uses a 16-bit chip.) The computer has a built-in 3½-inch microfloppy disc drive and a high-resolution nine-inch black-and-white screen.

The inherent power of the Motorola 68000 chip and high-resolution graphics make the Macintosh easy to learn. Instead of needing to master dozens of arcane commands, users must only look to graphic symbols—icons of file folders, trash cans and the like. The Macintosh relies on a mouse—a tethered, plastic rodent about the size of a cigarette pack—to move the cursor around the screen. So instead of punching commands in at the keyboard, one uses the mouse: to erase a file, for example, the mouse will drag an icon of a tiny file folder across the screen to the image of a trash can.

Like any new machine, the Macintosh doesn't have much software available for it yet. Apple did not make the Macintosh software compatible with either its own Apple II family of computers or with the IBM world. For Macintosh to succeed,

Apple must encourage independent software companies to write programs for the machine. At the moment, Apple itself is offering two software packages with Macintosh, a word-processing program called MacWrite and a graphics program called MacPaint.

While it is an intriguing machine, the Macintosh does have handicaps: currently, the machine has 128K RAM (random access memory), too little to allow it to run many new business programs like Lotus 1-2-3, the spread-sheet program that has taken the business world by storm. Unlike the Apple IIe or the IBM PC, the Macintosh has no expansion slots on the computer board, so users cannot add memory. And the single disc drive can be a limitation.

This week Apple is expected to unveil another new computer: the Apple IIc. Unlike Macintosh, this machine is a direct descendant of the Apple II, the computer that launched Apple to stardom. Industry sources expect the Apple IIc to be a lightweight, eight-pound portable with a full keyboard and 128K of RAM; the machine uses a version of the same eight-bit processor at the heart of the Apple IIe. The new machine won't face a software gap: there is an enormous range of software available for the Apple II family. It is expected to be priced in the $1,000 to $1,300 range.

The Apple IIc will compete with IBM's new PCjr. IBM designed the

PCjr as a scaled-down version of the best-selling IBM PC. It uses the same microprocessor but has better sound and graphics than the larger machine. IBM is selling the machine in two versions. One, an entry model ($669), has 64K memory and no disc drive; programs can be loaded from ROM (read-only memory) cartridges, like a video-game machine. The enhanced version ($1,269) comes with 128K of RAM and a built-in disc drive. IBM designed the machine as an open system, with expansion slots so that more hardware can be added, and independent companies are building equipment for the PCjr.

IBM is encouraging software developers to write for the machine; some software—not all—that runs on the IBM PC will also run on the PCjr. The range of software includes word-processing programs, such as EasyWriter and HomeWord, entertainment, and business tools like the VisiCalc and Multiplan spread sheets. To use programs like Lotus 1-2-3 will require buying additional memory from another manufacturer.

The market is more than just a two-ring circus. One of the best values around is the Kaypro II, an eight-bit transportable computer for $1,295. The machine has a built-in nine-inch monochrome screen, two 5¼-inch disc drives and 64K of RAM. Unlike most computer prices, what you see in Kaypro II is what you get: the price includes all of the hardware and 10 software programs, including the WordStar word-processing program and a spread sheet accounting program. And its two disc drives make it easier to use than most smaller machines.

Transportable computers are not really meant to be carried too far. The Kaypro weighs 26 pounds, for example, and IBM's new portable IBM PC is a 30-pounder. The lap-size portables like Radio Shack's TRS-80 Model 100 are a better choice if you plan to carry a computer to class. The TRS-80 has a full-size keyboard with function and cursor keys and an eight-line LCD (liquid crystal display) screen; it can run with battery power; so that you don't need to be plugged in. Compared with desktop or transportable machines, lap models have only lim-

ited memory, thus making them less useful for longer papers. The limited eight-line screen also can make it more difficult to visualize and organize a longer work. Not a machine for business problems, the TRS-80 is a good lightweight computer for taking notes and simple word processing.

Better technology for lap-size computers is becoming available. One indication of what's to come is Hewlett-Packard's new machine, a nine-pound portable. The only trouble is that the new generation of machines, at least initially, will probably be priced higher than most student budgets allow. The consolation: they'll get cheaper.

As was pointed out in previous chapters, a great deal of research and development of new products is taking place in the computer industry. In no other area is this more prominent than that of microcomputers and microcomputer-related products. The introduction of the microcomputer in 1975 had a drastic affect on the computer industry and it will continue to do so in the future.

MICROCOMPUTERS TODAY

The Development of Microcomputers

The evolution of the microcomputer has differed greatly from that of the mainframe computer. As you will recall from Chapter 2, the first computers—such as the Mark I and ENIAC—were developed through large-scale research efforts funded by the U.S. government and private industry. The Mark I was developed at Harvard with funding from IBM and the War Department, while the ENIAC was developed at the University of Pennsylvania in a project sponsored by the War Department.

The first microcomputers, on the other hand, were developed by individuals or small companies using their own financial resources. The fact that Steven Jobs and Stephen Wozniak developed the first Apple computer in a garage after raising capital by selling a Volkswagen and a calculator helps demonstrate the difference in the environments in which the two types of computers were developed.

The type of people involved in developing the computers is also worth noting. In the case of mainframe computers, scientists and mathematicians were the key development figures. Microcomputers, however, were developed by entrepreneurs who were willing to risk their personal finances on the ideas they believed in.

The success of these entrepreneurs and their ideas is evidenced by the rapid acceptance of microcomputers. Since the introduction of the microcomputer in 1975, total sales have reached over 5 million units. Although differences make comparison difficult, mainframe computers did not enjoy an acceptance as rapid as that of microcomputers. It took mainframe computers nearly fifteen years to gain the level of acceptance microcomputers currently have. Because of this wide acceptance and their versatility, microcomputers have a great many potential uses.

Current uses ranging from home budgets to space flights demonstrate the great potential of microcomputers. Current and potential users of microcomputers include corporations, small businesses, home users, and educators. Corporations are finding microcomputers a valuable asset to managers in their decision making, either as stand-alone (self-contained) computer systems or as links to a minicomputer or mainframe computer within a distributed processing system. Owners of small businesses have found that microcomputers, in combination with packaged software, can help them manage their businesses more effectively and efficiently. Inventory control and financial accounting packages used on a microcomputer by small businesses can help reduce operating costs.

A large potential for the use of microcomputers in the home also exists. By connecting microcomputers to communication networks, services such as banking and consumer goods ordering can be done in the home. There are also endless possible uses of microcomputers in the field of education. The use of microcomputers in educating children and the handicapped has already shown great promise. The microcomputer, therefore, is an innovation that will have many positive effects on our lives and on society.

Microcomputer Applications

Profitable applications of microcomputers are found in small businesses and in the professions. An estimated one-third of all personal computers are located in private offices, where business people can use them to do word processing, accounting, inventory control, order processing, customer lists, client records, tax records, mailing labels, and evaluation of bids and contracts. School teachers can use them to devise exams and compute grades; doctors to keep patients' records; and college football coaches to figure out potent combinations of players and strategies.

The use of personal computers in small businesses has led to a new phenomenon known as telecommuting. **Telecommuting** is based on computer hookups between offices and homes that allow employees to work at home. This concept enables firms to employ labor resources that might not otherwise be available. For example, handicapped people, women who leave companies to raise families but still want the kind of work they did, and commuters who find the rising costs of gasoline prohibitive to taking jobs can be gainfully employed.

Many experiments with this new work environment are in progress. Control Data Corporation has employees involved in a voluntary work-at-home project. McDonald's is installing terminals in the homes of the handicapped so that they can write computer programs. Almost all employees at a British company, F International Ltd., work at home; about half of them use computer terminals. By offering the telecommuting option to employees who want to stay home, many companies have reduced their employee turnover.

Another area influenced by the low cost of microcomputers is word processing, the manipulation of text data to achieve a desired output. Wang Laboratories is the leading manufacturer of word-processing equipment, but many other manufacturers are also developing word processors.

Computer Stores

Personal computing was, until recently, primarily a mail-order business. Products were shipped directly from manufacturers to users. With the emergence of the home computer concept, however, a new retailing phenomenon has evolved—the **computer store.** These stores are structured to appeal to owners of small businesses and to personal users. Today, thousands of home computer stores exist in the United States. The best ones offer a variety of products and services manufactured by several firms. Demonstration systems are on display so that potential buyers can experiment with the systems, much as they would take test drives before purchasing a car. Microcomputer experts are available to answer questions and to provide technical guidance to the computer novice.

HARDWARE

The Microprocessor

At the heart of a microcomputer is the **microprocessor,** a single, integrated circuit that contains an arithmetic/logic unit as well as control capability for memory and input/output access. The microprocessor controls the sequence of operations and the arithmetic and logical operations, as well as storing data, instructions, and intermediate and final results, much the same as the CPU does on a mainframe computer. The CPU of a mainframe computer, however, is composed of a series of integrated circuits and is much more sophisticated than the microprocessor.

Although miniature in size, the microprocessor is, in some microcomputers, capable of performing up to 700,000 additions per second (see Figure 6–1). There are a number of differences between mainframe computers and microcomputers; however, the prefix *micro* should be interpreted in terms of size and cost rather than capability. The key differences between a microprocessor and a CPU and between microcomputers and mainframe computers are explored further in the following section.

Microcomputers versus Mainframes

As indicated, the microprocessor and mainframe CPU perform nearly identical functions, yet the manner in which each carries out these functions differs greatly. The CPU of a mainframe computer has a much larger and more powerful instruction set to choose from when performing its functions. A micro-

Figure 6–1 ▪ **A Microprocessor—the Heart of a Microcomputer**

computer, for example, may take several processing steps to perform a function performed in one processing step by a mainframe computer. As was discussed in Chapter 1, engineers design the instruction set into the electronic circuitry of the computer. The factors that affect the size of the instruction set are the register size and word size. Registers are the locations within the CPU that are used as temporary storage areas to facilitate the transfer of data and instructions. Word size is based on the size of the registers, and it is the word size that ultimately affects the instruction set designed into the computer. Therefore, the larger the word size, the greater the number of instructions in the instruction set.

The IBM 370/3033 mainframe computer, for example, has a word size of 64 bits, while the APPLE IIe microcomputer has an 8-bit word size, and the IBM Personal Computer has a 16-bit word size. The architectural design of the mainframe, therefore, permits a larger instruction set, access to more memory in a single step, and greater speed in processing large-number arithmetic computations. Also, since microcomputers have smaller register sizes for holding data, they perform arithmetic computations with less precision.

The number of registers is another significant factor to consider when comparing microcomputers to mainframe computers. Microcomputers also have fewer registers and because of this are considerably slower than mainframe computers when performing arithmetic computations.

Another difference between microcomputers and mainframe computers is that mainframes allow for multiple users, while most microcomputers allow for only one user at a time. Microcomputers are limited to one user because only one **communication channel** (see Chapter 7) is used to communicate with the computer's **peripheral devices.** Because only one channel is used, the software required to run the computer (the operating system) is significantly less complex.

Mainframes, on the other hand, use a concept called **parallelism** to allow for what appears to be simultaneous data movement through a number of communication channels. Mainframes are designed to accept a maximum number of communication channels with the ability to attach a maximum number of peripheral devices to each channel.

Microcomputers are very powerful in proportion to their size; in some cases their power is equal to that of early mainframe computers. To more fully understand the power of current microcomputers, we can compare micros to a mainframe computer introduced in the early 1960s. The IBM 360 Model 30 and the IBM Personal Computer will serve as examples for the comparison.

The 360 Model 30 (see Figure 6−2) required an air-conditioned room about eighteen feet square to house the central processing unit, the control console, a printer, and a desk for the keypunch operator. In addition, the CPU, which was five feet high and six feet wide, had to be water cooled to prevent overheating. The computer cost $280,000 in 1960 dollars and could perform 33,000 additions per second at full speed.

In contrast, IBM's Personal Computer (see Figure 6−3) can sit on a small desk or table top and contains a microprocessor which is smaller than a paper clip. Fully equipped, the IBM Personal Computer costs between $4,000 and $5,000 and can perform up to 700,000 additions per second. Although air conditioning is not required, many microcomputers now come equipped with a small fan to prevent overheating.

Data Storage on Microcomputers

For a microcomputer, or any computer, to be useful, the programs to be used and data to be manipulated must be readily available. Since the amount of

Figure 6−2 ▪ The IBM 360 Model 30

Figure 6–3 ■ **The IBM Personal Computer (PC)**

primary storage in a microcomputer is not capable of storing all the applications someone might have, peripheral methods of storing programs and data are necessary.

One such method is use of magnetic tape in the form of tape cassettes and cartridges (see Figure 6 – 4). Magnetic-tape cassettes and cartridges are well suited for the storage of short programs and data that can be retrieved and stored in a sequential format. For those who have no greater need, or whose budget won't allow more, the relatively low cost of this method of storage offers an affordable alternative to more expensive methods. It does, however, become time-consuming to load cassettes and cartridges into memory for long programs or large amounts of data. This is because they are slow compared with other peripheral storage formats and programs and data must be stored and accessed in them sequentially.

An alternative method of storage is flexible (floppy) disks (see Figure 6 – 5), which have, since the overall decrease in the price of microcomputer hardware, become the most widely used form of peripheral storage for microcom-

Figure 6–4 ■ **Magnetic-Tape Cassettes and Cartridges**

138

Figure 6–5 ▪ Flexible (Floppy) Disk

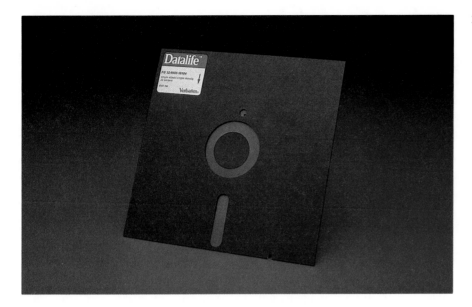

puters. The design of the floppy disks, as discussed in Chapter 5, allows programs and data to be accessed directly at many times the speed of tape cassettes or cartridges.

Data storage on floppy disks varies according to the density of storage on the surface of the disk and according to the side of the disk on which data is stored. The format for data storage on a floppy disk can take any of the following combinations: single-sided/single-density, single-sided/double-density, double-sided/single-density, and double-sided/double-density. A double-density format allows twice as much data to be stored on the disk's surface. Double-sided storage allows data to be stored on both surfaces of the floppy disk. It should be noted, however, that the format in which the data is stored on a floppy disk may not be compatible with the way in which another disk drive unit reads the disk.

As long as disks are used on the drives for which they are designed, there is usually no problem. However, if a system is capable of using a variety of disk drives, there is a danger that a disk designed for one drive may not operate properly on another disk drive unit. Unless stated otherwise by the manufacturer, some good rules of thumb are that double-sided disks cannot be used by single-sided disk drives and that double-density disks cannot be used by single-density disk drives; however, single-sided/single-density disks can be used by double-sided/double-density disk drives. There are also reversible disks that can be used on single-sided/single- or double-density disk drives. The disks can be flipped over, allowing data to be recorded on both sides of the disk; however, only one side of the disk can be accessed at a time.

Some users may require storage capacities greater than those provided by even the largest capacity floppy disks. Some microcomputer systems permit the use of hard magnetic disks, which provide larger storage capacities as well as greater speed in accessing data (see Figure 6 – 6). Hard disks come in two varieties: fixed and removable. The **fixed disk** is a totally sealed unit with no user access, while the **removable disk** allows for one disk to be removed and another inserted.

The fixed disk has a number of positive features: relatively low price, reli-

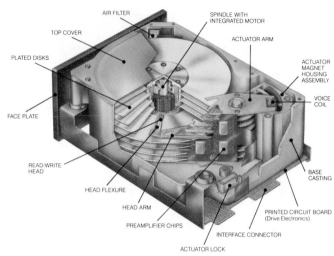

AIR FILTER
TOP COVER
PLATED DISKS
FACE PLATE
READ/WRITE HEAD
HEAD FLEXURE
HEAD ARM
PREAMPLIFIER CHIPS
ACTUATOR LOCK
SPINDLE WITH INTEGRATED MOTOR
ACTUATOR ARM
ACTUATOR MAGNET HOUSING ASSEMBLY
VOICE COIL
BASE CASTING
PRINTED CIRCUIT BOARD (Drive Electronics)
INTERFACE CONNECTOR

Figure 6–6 ▪ Hard Disk Unit without Enclosure and a Cutaway View

ability, security from damage by untrained persons, small size, and large storage capacity. The removable system, however, provides easier and quicker backup. For example, a typical basic fixed-disk system consists of a floppy disk for backup and the enclosed fixed-disk unit. If the floppy disk has, say, a storage capacity of 500,000 characters and the fixed-disk unit is capable of holding 5 million characters, there will be a significant imbalance when it comes to copying the data from the hard disk to the floppy disks. A box of ten floppy disks and at least twenty minutes would be necessary to complete the backup process.

This alone may not seem to be a great problem; however, it should be noted that standard software for file copying deals only with complete files, and any file that would spill over from one floppy disk to another could not be backed up without a special backup spill-over capability within the software. Therefore, it is advisable to make sure that a spill-over feature is available before purchasing a fixed-disk system. The disks in the removable system are physically detachable, allowing for a new disk to be inserted for the purpose of backup. At present, however, use of fixed hard disks predominates because of the high cost of removable disks.

Recent advances in technology will soon make available new types of storage devices. Some of these devices were discussed in Chapter 5.

Microcomputer Input/Output Devices

Monitors   The most common type of input/output device is the monitor. Monitors allow users to view information before sending it to the microprocessor for processing as well as to view information sent from the microprocessor. The information displayed on the monitor can be in the form either of characters or of some type of graphic display, such as a bar graph or pie chart.

Monitors are generally divided into four categories: (1) monochrome, (2) color, (3) RGB (red-green-blue), and (4) combination TV/monitors. Monochrome monitors display a single color, such as white, green, or amber, against a black background. Color monitors, on the other hand, display a composite of colors received in one signal. RGB monitors receive three separate color signals and can therefore offer a higher quality display than do the standard color monitors. Because RGB monitors receive three separate signals, they can display sharper images and are most commonly used for high quality graphic displays. Combination monitors are designed to double as TV receivers and color monitors.

Joysticks and Game Paddles **Joysticks** and **game paddles** are generally found on microcomputers that can run game applications. Both devices function as a means of positioning some object on the monitor screen. For example, joysticks (see Figure 6–7) are used to position the cursor displayed on the monitor. If the face of the monitor is viewed as an x/y plane, the joystick is used to control the movement of the cursor within that plane. Game paddles (see Figure 6–8) are used to position a figure that is required to move across or up and down the monitor screen for a particular video game.

The Mouse A **mouse** is a device that is used to position the cursor on a computer monitor. The object itself looks something like a mouse (see Figure 6–9) and fits in the palm of the hand. The significant advantage of the mouse is the fact that it eliminates a considerable amount of keyboard typing. By using the mouse to position the cursor, one can make choices and initiate programs without having to touch the keyboard.

MICROCOMPUTERS IN THE FUTURE

When introduced, microcomputers were generally envisioned for the home and small-business environments as stand-alone (self-contained) systems. Recently, however, they have begun to make their way into the management information systems of large corporations.

Figure 6–7 ▪ Joysticks

Figure 6–8 ▪ Game Paddle

141

Figure 6–9 ■ Mouse

It has been suggested that the entry of major mainframe and minicomputer vendors, such as IBM, Hewlett-Packard Company, Digital Equipment Corporation (DEC), and Xerox Corporation, into the microcomputer field has caught senior managers' attention and made them curious about the potential of microcomputer technology. Whatever the reason, the number of microcomputers being introduced into large corporations has increased dramatically.

A Manager's Tool for Decision Making

Different companies are taking different approaches to introducing microcomputers. Some, such as Ford Motor Company, are taking a cautious approach to this new technology. They are using their personal computers in

Concept Summary 6–1

Microcomputer Hardware

■ A **microprocessor** is a single integrated circuit in a microcomputer that functions much as the CPU of a mainframe computer. The microprocessor is the heart of the microcomputer.

■ Microcomputers generally have word sizes of 8 or 16 bits, while mainframe computers can have up to 64-bit word sizes.

■ Two types of secondary storage most commonly found on microcomputers are magnetic tape, in the form of **cassettes** and **cartridges,** and **flexible diskettes.** Tape cassettes and cartridges are typically less expensive, but are slow compared to diskettes and store data only in a sequential format.

■ **Hard disk** secondary storage systems are also available for microcomputers and can be found in either a **fixed disk** or **removable disk** configuration.

■ The most common type of input/output device used on microcomputers is the **monitor.** Monitors normally fall into one of four categories: (1) monochrome, (2) color, (3) RGB (red-green-blue), and (4) combination TV/monitors.

■ Other microcomputer input/output devices include **joysticks, game paddles,** and a **mouse.** Joysticks and game paddles are generally used in playing video games while the mouse is being used increasingly to help simplify the use of application software packages (see Chapter 12).

stand-alone mode only. Their strategy is to keep applications in a local mode, allowing no access to remote computer facilities and thus avoiding the potential problems of online use. Even in this restricted mode, Ford has reported an enthusiastic user response and annual average savings greater than the original cost of the microcomputers.

Companies are providing managers with microcomputers to help speed and increase the accuracy of their everyday decision making. Managers are performing such tasks as financial planning, budgeting, and resource planning using microcomputers in their day-to-day activities in a stand-alone mode.

Distributed Processing

General Electric has taken personal computers one step further. In addition to using microcomputers on a stand-alone basis for applications such as financial analysis and spreadsheets, presentations, and plotting, they are also allowing their microcomputers to have limited access to a remote computer. At present, though, they are employing no formal distributed processing strategy; instead they are waiting to see what the future brings.

North American Philips, one of the Pentagon's largest suppliers, with a company philosophy of **distributed data processing,** has approached microcomputers with an integrated, decentralized approach. The company plans to tie a hierarchy of supercomputers, minicomputers, and microcomputers together so that they can use the same data base. By linking together the mainframe computers and Apple, Radio Shack, and IBM personal computers, managers at various levels will be able to communicate among themselves or pass information up and down the organizational structure. The mainframes will continue to manipulate large data files, while the microcomputers will allow such applications as inventory analysis to be executed at the manager's desk.

Communication Networks

A. C. Markkula, Jr., President of Apple Computers, predicts that by the year 2000 a personal computer will be as necessary as an automobile is now. His projection is based on the anticipated use of microcomputers as telecommunicators between individuals and huge data banks. Nearly everyone will have as much information available as could be provided by the best of libraries—and it will be easier to access. Location will no longer keep the individual from access to good information; nor will the cost associated with transmission be prohibitive.

Electronic mail systems are being developed to replace conventional communication networks. For example, Easy Link, developed by Western Union, allows owners of microcomputers to send letters electronically over Western Union's existing communication lines.

Computer networks are not restricted to the ingenuity of the individual. There are several commercial network services available to subscribers. Two of the largest are *The Source* and *Dow Jones*. A third, *CompuServe, Inc.,* owned by H & R Block, provides an example of the development and growth of this industry. This firm offers a huge data bank full of interesting information. As can be seen from the partial listing that follows, the variety of topics offered is indeed wide.

Fiction on Disks

The book industry is taking a new direction. Recently, it has not been uncommon to access encyclopedias using computers. But now "interactive fiction" is becoming available for home computer users. The new fiction is available on cassette tape and floppy disks. Interactive fiction requires the reader to take an active role in the story. A basic story line is presented, and the reader is asked to search for the treasure or solve murders or dilemmas. One place of interactive fiction is *The Witness*, in which the reader solves two murders. Because the plot varies depending on the reader's interaction, it is unlikely that any two family members will read exactly the same story.

- Home record keeping.
- SAT test information.
- Silver prices.
- Stocks and bonds.
- Stamp collecting.
- *New York Times.*
- Trivia quizzes.
- Travel.
- Horse racing.
- Science and medical news.
- Theater listings.
- *Grolier's Encyclopedia.*
- College financial aid.
- *Los Angeles Times.*
- *Washington Post.*
- Tax advice.

With CompuServe, news, weather, and sports arrive via wire services; home information with supplementing articles from the current *Better Homes & Gardens* can also be accessed. Stocks and financial information, personal finance services, games, and even electronic editions of some major newspapers, such as the *New York Times* and *Washington Post,* are all popular listings.

Another form of communication network which is gaining in popularity is the electronic bulletin board. An **electronic bulletin board** uses an existing communications network to send messages to members of various user groups. Users of the bulletin board can choose topics that they believe relate to the manner in which they use their microcomputers. Members of the network with useful information relating to a particular, predefined user group can transmit the information to those network users. General information relating to numerous groups, or all users, can also be transmitted over the network. The use of a communication network in this selective manner provides users valuable information.

SUMMARY POINTS

- Since its beginning in the mid-1970s, the microcomputer industry has grown into a multi-billion-dollar annual revenue industry.
- Development of microcomputers and mainframe computers differed greatly, by comparison. Mainframe computers were developed using funding from the U.S. government and private industry, while microcomputers were developed by individuals and small businesses using personal funding.
- Individuals developing mainframe computers were typically scientists and mathematicians, whereas individuals developing microcomputers tended to be entrepreneurs.
- Potential users of microcomputers include large corporations, small businesses, individuals, and educators.
- The microprocessor, a single, integrated circuit, is the heart of the microcomputer.
- Although they perform nearly identical functions, the mainframe CPU and the microprocessor differ greatly in the manner in which they carry out these functions.

- Because of their architectural design, microcomputers offer less precision and are considerably slower than mainframe computers when performing arithmetic calculations.
- The majority of microcomputers are designed to allow for only one user, while mainframe computers can accommodate multiple users.
- Microcomputers are, in some cases, nearly equal in power and performance to some of the early mainframe computers.
- One method of program and data storage on microcomputers is on magnetic tape in the form of tape cassettes and cartridges.
- The design of floppy disks allows data to be accessed randomly at much greater speeds than with tape cassettes or cartridges.
- Data can be stored on floppy disks in one of the following formats: single-sided/single-density, single-sided/double-density, double-sided/single-density, or double-sided/double density.
- Hard disks can also be used on microcomputers and come in either fixed disk or removable disk models.
- Microcomputer input/output devices include monitors, joysticks, game paddles, and the mouse.
- Microcomputers are becoming an increasingly important tool for managers in large corporations.
- Microcomputers are being used for distributed processing and in communication networks.
- Microcomputer users can subscribe to services available from commmunication networks such as The Source, Dow Jones, and CompuServe, Inc.
- Some believe that in the future microcomputers will be an important, and in some cases essential, part of nearly everyone's day-to-day life.

REVIEW QUESTIONS

1. Contrast the development of the microcomputer with the development of the mainframe computer.
2. What functions does the microprocessor perform?
3. How does the microprocessor differ from the CPU of a mainframe computer?
4. Give a basic explanation of why microcomputers are typically less precise and slower than mainframe computers in performing arithmetic computations.
5. Explain why most microcomputers are capable of handling only a single user, while mainframe computers can handle mutliple users.
6. What is currently the most widely used form of external data storage on microcomputers? Explain why it is the most popular.
7. List the four formats of data storage for floppy disks. Why is it important to realize that the four formats exist?
8. Identify some of the popular input/output devices being used with microcomputers. List some applications in which each might be used.
9. It is believed that microcomputers will have a significant use in large corporations in the future. In what ways?
10. How do you think communication networks will affect our lives in the future? Do you think that the services provided by communication networks are essential or simply luxuries?

APPLICATION

Commodore

Commodore International Limited is a fully integrated manufacturer of advanced microcomputer systems, semiconductor components, consumer electronic products, and office equipment. Manufacturing facilities are located in North America, Europe, and the Far East. Marketing is worldwide. Research expenditures comprise over 5% of sales and are devoted primarily to the development of new products using solid state integrated circuitry, computer technology and consumer electronics.

Commodore International, as we know it today, began as a typewriter repair store and marketing organization for electro-mechanical office equipment in 1958. Since that time the company has grown out of its roots in Toronto to one of international dominance in the personal computer market.

Shipping more units world-wide than any other computer company, Commodore has grown from sales of $46 million in 1977 to over $680 million in 1983. And much of that success is due to the entrepreneurial instincts of Commodore's founder and president vice-chairman, Jack Tramiel. Over the past quarter-century Tramiel has led Commodore through adding machines, electronic calculators, digital watches, and the introduction of the personal computer age.

In 1976 Commodore purchased MOS Technology, Inc., one of its semiconductor chip suppliers, and worked its way toward becoming vertically integrated. Vertical integration allows Commodore to supply its own microprocessor needs and gives them significant lead time in new product development.

The next year was the watershed for the computer systems division when in 1977 the company introduced its first personal computer, the PET. The PET uses the MOS-designed 6502 microprocessor, which is also used by some of Commodore's competition. It was this machine that helped give birth to the personal computer market of today.

The PET sparked another period of rapid growth for Commodore, which is still underway today. It was marketed world-wide and really took hold in the European market because of the widespread, loyal dealer network Commodore had developed in its distribution of calculators. Commodore dominates the personal computer market in Europe today with more than 50 percent of the market in many countries.

After the PET 4000 and later the CBM 8000 series micros, the next major product was the popular VIC-20. Commodore sold 800,000 VIC-20s world-wide in 1982, reached the one million mark early in 1983, and is now shipping VICs at the rate of 100,000 units per month.

Commodore didn't stop with that success either, but continued research and development and in August, 1982, shipped the first Commodore 64. By March, 1983, the 64 was being shipped at the rate of 25,000 machines a month.

In addition to the obvious success the company has achieved in the home market, the Commodore name is familiar in both the business and education markets for personal computers. It is one of the leaders in small business computers with its SuperPET and CBM lines, and the 64 is also being used for a number of functions in small business.

MARKETING STRATEGY

As Commodore's president and founder Jack Tramiel has stated, "Our marketing strategy is clear. We produce for the masses—not the classes. Quality and service is our commitment. Our customers are mature and intelligent. We must give them the best because they will know if we don't."

The company's strategy continues to unfold—which is to continue their leadership role in the microcomputer industry not only in the home computing market, but in business and education as well, and in new microcomputer markets as they evolve.

PRODUCTS

By January 1983, more than one million VIC-20s had been sold, and the Commodore 64 is rapidly moving toward that level. The aftermarket for peripherals and software among these computer owners is becoming a major market for Commodore.

Home Computer Systems

During 1983, the majority of people who purchased home computers thought of the computer as a stand-alone console coupled with an inexpensive cassette tape recorder for storing and retrieving programs. VIC-20 and Commodore 64 owners listed their primary computing interests as entertainment and learning how to program. It is no surprise, therefore, that Commodore's best selling software included games like Bally Midway's "GORF" and "OMEGA RACE" and self-teaching courses in BASIC programming like INTRODUCTION TO BASIC and GORTEK.

Also in 1983, the price of a VIC-20 or a Commodore 64 computer system—computer, disk drive or cassette recorder, printer, modem, and software—fell below $1000. For the first time in history, the average consumer could afford to purchase a complete computer system . . . and benefit from wordprocessing, electronic spreadsheets, budgeting, home finance, and other applications.

Educational Systems

Commodore computers are also used worldwide for educational purposes. In Canada, the United Kingdom, and the United States, Commodore has been a leader in educational computing since the beginning of the microcomputer industry.

The PET 64—a monochrome version of the Commo-

dore 64 in a self-contained housing with a built-in monitor—was introduced in 1983 for use in education. Commodore has also successfully tested a low-priced networking system which can tie together all types of Commodore computers including the PET, VIC-20, and Commodore 64. This innovation will help in the networking of multiple systems within educational institutions.

Business Systems

Business computing represents one of Commodore's most promising expansion opportunities. The company believes that competitively-priced business microcomputers can be marketed in volume and made as attractive and "friendly" as home computers—but with the professional in mind.

Their new entry in the business marketplace—the Commodore "B" Series computer system—has been introduced and is being sold in Europe and North America. This low-cost 128K RAM version features an 80-column screen, an optional 16-bit microprocessor, and a 96-key professional-level keyboard. This powerful business microcomputer is being offered at prices comparable to or below many personal computers with far less internal RAM and less comparable features.

To provide the high capacity storage required by business users, Commodore's 9000-series Winchester hard disk units and CBM 8250 two megabyte, floppy-disk drives were introduced for sale in 1983, along with the Model 6400 letter-quality printer.

Portable Systems

Portable computing is becoming very popular among executives, students, and others who like to transport and use their computers in different locations. Commodore has entered the portable marketplace with the introduction of the Executive 64, the first affordable color portable computer. It is software compatible with the Commodore 64 and has a 170K built-in disk drive and built-in 5-inch color monitor.

RESEARCH AND DEVELOPMENT

Research and development expenditures have provided the basis for Commodore's growth as a leader in the microcomputer industry, and allows the company to take maximum advantage of the various technologies—at both the component and system level—which exist within the company.

Commodore's decentralized research organization promotes the development of individual projects in many centers around the world, where the employees are encouraged to work quickly—often simultaneously—on parallel projects. The ability to work on large-scale integrated circuit semiconductor devices, or "chips," at the same time the computer systems are being designed reduces not only development costs, but also the time it takes to complete and introduce a product—critical factors in the microcomputer industry.

Semiconductor Chip Design

In 1983, a major research effort was undertaken to develop a new family of "HMOS" chips. The HMOS process is an improved manufacturing technique which provides higher circuit density on a silicon chip; hence, for a given computer function, more chips per silicon wafer and consequent lower cost. New chips were also designed to reduce the overall component count of computer systems by up to half their previous number. Specifically, large-scale integrated circuits that have been designed by Commodore recently include:

- a new 6500-family microprocessor with optimized access to external memory,
- a color video controller which provides necessary timing functions for interface to a CRT and display data to control graphic and character format,
- a sound chip, called SID (Sound Interface Device), which provides the sounds used to generate sound effects and is the basis for music synthesis.
- a pair of related parts which generate the master clock for all logic components within a machine,
- a programmable logic array which contains "housekeeping logic,"
- a multi-purpose device used to reduce the component count in a number of Commodore products, encompassing a system controller, video controller, display processor, and voice generator.

These new chip designs, coupled with recent increases in memory density, will allow Commodore to field new generations of computers which will provide more computing power at less cost.

Operating Systems Software

Recently, much attention has also been devoted to adapting the MS/DOS, CP/M, Concurrent CP/M, and CP/M 86 operating systems to the company's line of computers—primarily the "B" Series business computer. These operating systems accompany the 8088 microprocessor board which was also developed for the "B" Series, and which allows the use of "industry-standard" applications software packages. The company has also designed and is now selling a CP/M cartridge for use with the Commodore 64.

THE FUTURE

As Jack Tramiel has said, "We're always looking at the future because we're helping to create that future . . . but the work is always done in the present."

DISCUSSION QUESTIONS

1. How has Commodore's marketing strategy contributed to its success? How do you think Commodore's strategy differs from other microcomputer manufacturers?
2. What is Commodore's strategy for producing and marketing microcomputers used in business? How do you think this type of strategy will affect the business microcomputer market?

A MICROCOMPUTER CONSUMER'S GUIDE

For a number of reasons, buying a microcomputer can be a difficult and time-consuming process. Recent and continuing technological advances in the field of microcomputers make it difficult to decide whether to buy a computer now or wait for future innovations. Technology within this field is currently moving at such a great pace that such a decision is complicated. As with stereo components and appliances, there are many models of microcomputers to choose from—each unique. Choosing one from over 150 models can seem like an impossible task. Currently, microcomputers can be purchased in retail stores ranging from K-Mart to Macy's to specialized microcomputer stores such as ComputerLand. Mail-order houses and microcomputer vendors themselves also market microcomputers. Deciding where to buy a microcomputer can also be confusing to the buyer.

This buyer's guide will attempt to make the buying process easier by discussing a number of the issues that must be considered when purchasing a microcomputer. The guide, however, is not designed to provide you with details concerning each and every model of microcomputer available; rather, it is intended to provide you with general information that will help you in your evaluation of microcomputers currently on the market. Issues such as whether to buy now or wait until later, as well as hardware considerations and choice of microcomputer sales location are discussed in an effort to help you become an informed consumer in what can be a complex and confusing market.

USES

Determining what you want to use a microcomputer for should be the first step in the buying process. By identifying what the microcomputer is going to be used for, you are beginning the buying process by narrowing the possible choices to only those that are capable of performing the task, or tasks, which you have specified. If, however, you can't specifically identify what you would like to use a microcomputer for, there may be no need to purchase one.

If you wish to use a microcomputer for playing video games only, buying one of the more expensive microcomputers designed for business use is not necessary.

Although these microcomputers are capable of playing games, they are priced significantly higher than those microcomputers designed for playing video games. If, however, you wish to use your microcomputer for such business or personal uses as word processing, data management, or electronic spreadsheet analysis, the microcomputers that are only capable of playing video games would not meet your needs.

If you have determined that you will require a microcomputer that is capable of both playing games and performing tasks such as word processing and data management, then you must shop for those microcomputers that perform both tasks to your satisfaction. By matching your microcomputer to your uses, you are likely to buy a system that meets your needs and is cost effective.

BUY NOW OR WAIT?

In any situation where technology moves as fast as it is currently moving in the field of microcomputers, the question arises: Should I buy now, or wait to see what will be available in the future? This is a difficult question to answer. The buyer asking this question when microcomputers were first introduced was much better off waiting. Prices on microcomputer hardware have fallen, while the level of technology has increased significantly since the microcomputer's introduction. Microcomputer buyers of today can get a great deal more for their money than when they were first introduced. However, there is no way to tell if this trend will continue.

On the other hand, there is a disadvantage to delaying the purchase of a microcomputer strictly in order to wait for possible technological advances and better prices. The time spent waiting is time that could be used for gaining experience in the use of microcomputers. Waiting also eliminates any benefits that might be gained through the use of microcomputers in business and in the home. Although patience can be a virtue, it could prevent you from realizing many of the benefits that technology has already provided. If some advantage can be realized through the purchase of a microcomputer, it might be best to go ahead and buy what current technology has to offer.

WHAT TO LOOK FOR

When shopping for a microcomputer, there are a number of things to look for or consider. Price is a very important consideration; however, it is not the only one. Other considerations include the software that you will be using on your microcomputer and the hardware that will be required based on your specified uses. This portion of the buyer's guide will review some things to consider in relation to price, software, and hardware.

Price

If you are a typical buyer, one of the first considerations to cross your mind is price. Don't be too price conscious, however. By identifying your intended uses, you have already begun to identify a price range. Microcomputers can cost as little as $50 or be as expensive as you wish, depending on desired peripherals. Portable microcomputers that can be placed in briefcases can be purchased for as little as $50, while microcomputer systems used for business, scientific, or engineering purposes can cost from $1,000 on up.

Generally, microcomputers that are purchased for home use, educational purposes, and for entertainment fall in the $50 to $2,000 price range. Some microcomputer manufacturers that offer products in this particular price range include: Apple, Atari, Coleco, Commodore, Epson, IBM, Mattel (Intellevision), Kaypro, Radio Shack, Texas Instruments, and Timex. Manufacturers that offer microcomputers for $2,000 and up include: Apple, Burroughs, Compaq, DEC, Epson, Hewlett-Packard, IBM, NCR, Radio Shack, TeleVideo, and Wang. As you can see, some manufacturers compete in both the low-end and high-end segments of the market.

Be cautious of low prices. A low price could mean lack of support or service, which could cost you more in the long run in both time and money. Again, identify your intended uses and then price shop within a category of microcomputers that can meet your needs.

Software

Once you have determined for what purpose you are going to use your microcomputer, the next step in the buying process is to determine your software requirements based on the uses you have specified. A microcomputer is a very powerful device, but it is the software that makes it a useful tool. It is very important, therefore, to shop for the software that will perform the necessary tasks and produce the desired results before the hardware is purchased.

Choosing your software first can be important because many software packages have specific hardware requirements. Your choice of software can affect the amount of internal memory your microcomputer will require and possibly the amount of secondary storage. Choosing the proper software package is discussed in a buyer's guide following Chapter 12.

The type of operating system (see Chapter 8) you choose is also an important software consideration. It is the operating system which directs the control of your microcomputer and also dictates the amount and type of software that it can use. Two of the more popular operating systems currently being used are CP/M, by Digital Research, and MS-DOS, by Microsoft Corporation. UNIX, an operating system developed by Bell Laboratories, is also becoming popular and may challenge the popularity of CP/M and MS-DOS in the future.

Hardware

The Microprocessor. The first microcomputers had 8-bit microprocessors, but advances in technology have led to 16-bit microprocessors. Depending again on your intended use, the 8-bit microprocessor may be adequate. The advantage of having a 16-bit microprocessor is that your microcomputer will be able to process instructions at a much faster rate and will also contain a larger instruction set. If you intend to use your microcomputer for such applications as electronic spreadsheet analysis, which can require a great deal of mathematical calculating, the 16-bit microprocessor would probably be the best choice.

Beginning to make their way into the market are 32-bit microprocessors. As was the case with the 16-bit microcomputers, 32-bit systems will offer significantly more processing power and the capability to run more sophisticated software. What the initial 32-bit microcomputers are offering is power and capabilities equal to those of minicomputers, but in a desktop version. The 32-bit microcomputers are also offering multi-user capabilities which, until now, have been somewhat limited on the

The IBM Portable Personal Computer

The Hewlett-Packard Portable Computer

16-bit microcomputers. Again, assessing your needs will be critical to matching your intended uses with one of the three sizes of microprocessors currently available.

Monitors. Some microcomputers, mostly portables, have a built-in video display. Most, however, will require the purchase of a separate video display or monitor. When purchasing a monitor, there are several things you should consider: the screen display dimensions; the color of the display; the monitor's resolution; and the focus, contrast, and brightness control of the display. Currently, microcomputer monitors come in either 40- or 80-column widths and 24- or 25-line displays. If you are going to be using your system for word processing, for example, you will find an 80-column screen more desirable. A standard 8½-inch piece of paper can fit on an 80-column display. An 80-column width monitor, therefore, would allow you to view the entire width of a document while typing. A 40-column display, on the other hand, would require you to use a wrap-around, or horizontal scrolling feature, to view the full width of the document.

There are two types of monitors when it comes to the color of display. Monochrome monitors display a single color—white, amber, or green—on a black or gray background. Choosing a color of display is usually a matter of personal preference; however, some users believe that amber monitors create less eyestrain than either green or white.

The second type, color monitors, are capable of displaying full color. This is particularly desirable for playing video games and also for the display of graphics.

There are two types of color monitors: the standard color monitor, which is very similar to a color TV in design, and an RGB (Red, Green, and Blue) monitor. Because of their design, RGB monitors produce higher quality color displays than do standard color monitors.

Possibly the most important factor to consider when buying a monitor is the resolution. Resolution refers to the clarity at which the characters are displayed on the monitor screen. The characters are created on a monitor by using small dots in patterns, or matrices, to create certain characters, much the same way a sports scoreboard does. The matrices used for creating a character vary from monitor to monitor in a range of a 5 × 7 dot matrix to a 17 × 19 matrix. The smaller the dots, the more densely packed they will be, and the clearer the display or resolution of the character.

The resolution is a particularly important consideration if you would like to use a television set as a monitor. Because of their design, television sets are not capable of matching the resolution of a monitor designed for use with a microcomputer. The standard television typically displays characters using a 5 × 7 matrix, which produces relatively poor resolution and also leaves off the tails, or descenders, of characters which extend below a line, such as y, j, p, q, and g.

Being able to control the contrast, brightness, and focus of the monitor's display is also important. By being able to control these factors, you can adjust the display to suit the lighting of the environment in which you are working. Also, be sure the monitor does not flicker or jump. This can also lead to eyestrain and can be very annoying.

Keyboards.   Keyboards for microcomputers can come in one of two forms. They can be attached to the microprocessor enclosure or detached from it. Keyboards that are detached are either connected to the enclosure with a cord or are operated using batteries instead of an electrical outlet.

One of the most important considerations when looking at a particular keyboard is its angle. Keyboards that are attached to the microprocessor enclosure can not be adjusted for angle, and can sometimes be difficult to type on for long periods of time. Some detachable keyboards can be adjusted to various angles.

The touch of the keys on a keyboard should also be considered. Most microcomputer manufacturers offer the standard touch-sensitive keys, but a few others offer a pressure-sensitive, mylar-covered keyboard which may be more suitable for use with young children. This type of keyboard is very difficult to type on and would not be suitable for applications such as word processing. Repeating keys are also a very convenient feature included on many microcomputers.

Microcomputer keyboards in some cases also contain numeric pads and function keys. Numeric pads are useful if large quantities of numbers are to be entered into the computer. Users of accounting software applications, for example, find numeric pads a definite asset. Function keys are designed to limit the amount of typing done on the keyboard; they can be programmed to enter text or issue commands with a single keystroke.

A final consideration when evaluating keyboards is the availability of upper- and lower-case letters. On some earlier microcomputer keyboards, only upper-case letters were available. This made entering text for applications requiring lower-case letters, such as word processing, difficult. Most manufacturers now offer upper- and lower-case capabilities, however.

Secondary Storage.   Three types of secondary storage devices are available for microcomputer systems: tape cassettes, floppy diskettes, and hard disks. Tape cassettes were one of the first methods of secondary storage used with microcomputers. They are currently the lowest priced form of storage in that they require only a standard tape cassette recorder to read and store data. This form of storage is somewhat limited in capability, however, and is used most on the low-end, less expensive microcomputer systems.

Tape cassettes are a sequential form of storage and for this reason can not be used for applications that require direct-access capabilities, such as data management. Tape cassette storage retrieval is also very slow compared to floppy diskette and hard disk forms of storage.

Floppy diskette storage is currently the most popular

The Apple Macintosh Keyboard

form of secondary storage used on microcomputer systems. Floppy diskettes are used with disk drives that can be purchased as peripherals or, in some cases, come as part of the standard microcomputer package. They can be used as a direct-access form of storage and are, therefore, faster and more versatile than tape cassettes.

Floppy diskettes come in three sizes according to their diameter. These sizes are: 3½ inch, 5¼ inch, and 8 inch. The 5¼-inch size is the most widely used and is capable of storing up to 320,000 characters. The 3½-inch diskettes have recently been introduced and are being used by some microcomputer manufacturers on their new microcomputer systems.

Hard-disk, secondary-storage devices are very similar to the magnetic disk devices used on mainframe and minicomputer systems. These storage devices can be purchased in either fixed-disk or removable-disk configurations. The fixed-disk systems are sealed to prevent dust and other outside elements from affecting the contents of the disks. Removable disks, on the other hand, can be removed from the disk drive in the same way floppy diskettes are. A removable hard-disk system, therefore, allows for greater storage capacities. Hard-disk drive systems for microcomputers can be purchased with storage capacities ranging from 5 million characters and up.

Printers. Printers can be one of the most expensive peripherals you can purchase for your microcomputer system. When evaluating printers, there are a number of features that should be considered. The speed of the printer is measured in characters per second, or cps. Depending on how you intend to use your system, printers can print as slow as approximately 10 cps, or as fast as 120 cps. We will look closer at printer speeds when we review the types of printers. The pitch of a printer refers to the number of characters printed within an inch horizontally and is measured in characters per inch, or cpi.

Printers can also print bidirectionally and have logic-seeking, or short-line, capabilities which can also affect the speed of the printer. Printers that are capable of printing bidirectionally can print from the left side of the paper to the right, and vice versa. This results in a more efficient use of the printer's motion because a carriage return is not required to return the print head back to the left-hand margin of the paper. Logic-seeking, or short-line, capabilities allow a printer to position its print head using the shortest path in moving from one print position to the next.

Printers can use either friction feed or tractor feed to pull the paper through the printer, and in some cases both can be used. Friction feed is the type of feed used by typewriters to pull paper through. Tractor feed, on the other hand, requires the use of special paper that has small holes on each side and is fed in as one continuous sheet. Tractor feeding prevents the paper from shifting while it is being pulled through the printer. Some printers allow both the continuous feed type paper and separate sheets of paper to be fed through. The separate sheet method of feeding paper is particularly useful if you hope to print letters on company stationary, for example.

A Hard Disk Unit

The Apple Image Writer 1 Dot-Matrix Printer

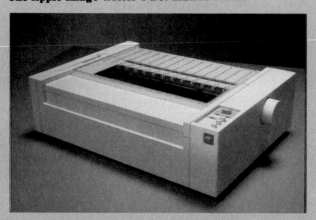

Some printers are also designed to read blocks of data and hold them in an internal buffer until they can be printed. This is known as buffering, or spooling, and can be helpful in freeing up the computer for use while the printer is operating. Printers also come in two standard carriage sizes. Carriage width can be either 80 columns or 132 columns wide. Applications such as an electronic spreadsheet may require a 132-column printer.

The quality of print available on printers varies depending on the method used to print images. A dot-matrix printer uses a predetermined character matrix similar to that discussed in the section on monitors. The most popular dot-matrix printers use either a 5 × 7, 7 × 9, or 9 × 9 dot-matrix for printing characters. As was true with monitors, the more dense the number of dots within the matrix, the better the quality. An overstrike, overprint, or double-strike capability can also be used by dot-matrix printers to improve print quality.

Letter-quality printers use what is referred to as a daisy-wheel to produce printed output. A letter quality, or daisy-wheel, printer is designed very much like a typewriter. Solid characters located on the petals of the daily-wheel are struck from behind by a hammer through a ribbon onto the paper's surface. Since solid characters are used, the print quality is much better than that of the dot-matrix printers. Dot-matrix and daisy-wheel printers possess further differences worth evaluating.

Dot-matrix printers use a matrix of pins that form a character which is struck by a hammer from behind the paper. These printers have very little motion and therefore can print at very high speeds—from 50 to 120 cps. Daisy-wheel printers, on the other hand, must wait for the daisy-wheel to spin around the hammer to print characters. Because of the amount of motion required to position the daisy-wheel, this type of printer is considerably slower. Daisy-wheel printers can print at a rate of from 10 to 75 cps.

A third type of printer that is also used with microcomputers is the ink-jet printer. An ink-jet printer forms a character much like a dot-matrix printer does; however, ink is sprayed onto the paper by an ink-jet. Ink-jet printers can print at speeds up to 110 cps but do lack some quality because of fuzzy characters created by spraying ink onto the paper. The primary advantage to an ink-jet printer is its quiet operation.

Other Hardware Devices. Again, depending on your intended uses and specific needs, your microcomputer system may require other specialized hardware devices. Hardware devices, or peripherals, that perform specific tasks include:

- joystick
- koala pad
- paddle
- modem
- light pen
- a mouse
- graphic tablet or spatial digitizer
- touch screen
- voice recognition and voice synthesizer systems

If you think that you may require any of these hardware devices, descriptions of how some of them work and their uses can be found in this text and in popular microcomputer literature such as magazines and paperback books.

Other Considerations

Training. If you will require some training or education after purchasing your microcomputer, there are a number of options available to you. Seminars offered by microcomputer software vendors and independent training firms are available for some of the more popular software packages. These seminars will teach you to use the software package and microcomputer for your desired applications. Classes or seminars to instruct you in the use of particular software packages are also offered by some local computer stores.

Community and local colleges also offer classes that are helpful to buyers of microcomputers. Microcomputer programming classes and classes covering microcomputer topics in general are often offered through the college's normal programs or through adult education programs. Local high schools may also offer adult education programs on microcomputer topics. Private lessons or tutoring are also possible means of acquiring knowledge concerning microcomputers, their use, and programming.

A final form of training or education is individual home study. Many hardware and software vendors are providing tutorials on the use of their products. These tutorials provide you the ability to get hands-on experience with the microcomputer while you are learning. The experience you gain can then be applied to whatever application for which you want to use your microcomputer. Independent firms are also beginning to provide self-teaching educational materials that can be used on your microcomputer. A wide range of topics are available and can be found in major bookstore chains such as B. Dalton.

Documentation. When you are considering various microcomputers for purchase, one of the most important considerations should be the system's documentation. The importance of documentation can be overlooked by hardware and software vendors; however, as a microcomputer user you will undoubtedly have to refer to documentation to resolve questions you will have. Good documentation, therefore, should be complete, accurate, and easy-to-use. A microcomputer with inadequate or difficult-to-read documentation may fail to provide needed answers in your daily use of the computer, and should not be purchased.

WHERE TO BUY

Once you have analyzed your needs and determined the appropriate software, where do you go to buy your computer? Actually, there are a number of sources from which you can buy a microcomputer. Microcomputer vendors, various types of retailers, and mail-order houses offer microcomputers and their peripherals.

Vendors

Computer vendors such as IBM, DEC, Burroughs, and NCR offer their line of microcomputers through a direct salesforce. Buying through a computer manufacturer can be beneficial for a number of reasons. Often, the salespeople are highly trained in the use of microcomputers in business and can assist you in determining the type of microcomputer system that will meet your needs. Microcomputer vendors can also provide you with maintenance contracts for on-site repair and can also offer replacement equipment if some part of your system should be unavailable for a period of time. This kind of service and support can be invaluable if your microcomputer is going to be used in a business environment.

Retailers

Microcomputer manufacturers are also marketing their products through department stores and computer specialty stores. Department stores such as Sears, J. C. Penney, Montgomery Ward, and Macy's currently offer microcomputers to their customers. Retail outlets like K-Mart and Toys "R" Us are also offering some of the lower-priced microcomputers on the market. Computer specialty stores such as ComputerLand, which has nearly 600 stores, also offer a full line of microcomputers and peripherals.

There are, however, some disadvantages to purchasing microcomputers in retail outlets such as department stores. Often the salespeople are not knowledgeable about microcomputers and are therefore unable to help you in putting together a microcomputer system to meet your needs. Also, department stores do not have a service department and often send the microcomputer back to the manufacturer for repair. If you are certain of what you want and can service your system yourself, or can do without it for an indefinite period of time, department stores can be a good place to buy. Because they purchase the microcomputers from the manufacturer in large quantities, they can sell them for less.

If you would like assistance in selecting the microcomputer and peripherals, and would prefer local service and support, computer specialty stores can be a good place to buy. Computer specialty stores are often staffed with knowledgeable salespeople and, in most cases, have an in-house service department. Microcomputers purchased from a computer specialty store will tend to cost more, however. Because of the service and support they provide, computer specialty stores tend to sell microcomputers for higher prices than do department stores and mail-order houses.

Mail-Order Houses

Buying from a mail-order house can be to your advantage if you are certain of exactly what you want to purchase. In many cases, mail-order houses also offer products for less than computer specialty stores. Before you buy from a mail-order house, however, determine exactly what you can expect in the way of services. For example, will the mail-order house provide service for your computer, or will you have to ship it to the manufacturer for an indefinite period of time?

A BUYER'S CHECKLIST

In the process of determining what you will be using your microcomputer for and in selecting a microcomputer, a checklist is often helpful. The following checklist is designed to help you identify the items you will need and to consolidate this information.

1. List the expected uses of your microcomputer.

2. Will you require a software package to accomplish what you would like to do with your microcomputer, or will you be programming the applications yourself?

a. If you will require packaged software, list those packages that are capable of meeting your designated needs.
b. If you will be writing the application programs yourself, list the programming languages that you will require.

3. Given the software requirements listed above, what are the specific hardware requirements of your microcomputer system?

THE MICROPROCESSOR
—8-bit microprocessor
—16-bit microprocessor
—32-bit microprocessor
—K Internal memory required

THE MONITOR
—40-column width
—80-column width

Monochrome display
—White
—Green
—Amber

Color display
—Standard color
—RGB

THE KEYBOARD
—Detachable keyboard
—Upper- and lower-case
—Repeating keys
—Numeric pad
—Function keys

THE PRINTER
—Dot-matrix
—Letter quality
—Bidirectional printing
—Logic seeking
—Friction feed
—Tractor feed
—Individual sheet feed
—Carriage width
  —80-Column
  —132-Column

OTHER HARDWARE DEVICES
—Joystick
—KoalaPad
—Track ball
—Paddle
—Modem
—Light pen
—A mouse
—Graphic tablet
—Touch screen
—Voice recognition
—Voice synthesizer

REQUIRED DOCUMENTATION QUALITY
—Excellent
—Good
—Average
—Poor

SOURCE
—Vendor
—Retail outlet
  —Department store
  —Discount store
  —Computer specialty store
—Mail-order house

7

Telecom-
munications

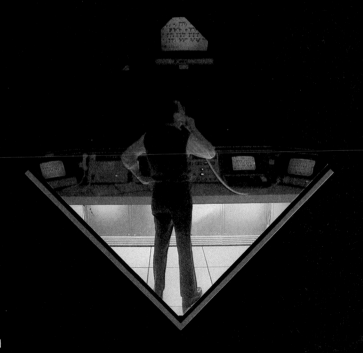

INTRODUCTION

Managing today's diverse businesses is a complex task. Management information needs extend beyond routine summary reports. A manager must have current knowledge of company operations in order to control business activities and to ensure that effective customer service is provided. Decisions must be made on short notice and on the basis of data gathered and analyzed from geographically remote locations. An efficient, fast way to capture, process, and distribute large amounts of data is needed. Data communication systems developed to meet this need help reduce delays in the collection and dissemination of data.

This chapter explains how communication systems allow users at remote locations to gain fast, easy access to computer resources. It discusses the concepts and techniques involved in message transmission and introduces the types of equipment that make data communication possible. It also presents alternative methods of using communications technology to implement management information systems.

ARTICLE

My First Videoconference

Carol Tomme Thiel

As I hurried into the conference room, an attendant whispered, "You're late. The broadcast started a minute ago." I'd missed the opening to this Headquarters Companies demonstration of AT&T's two-way video, two-way audio Picturephone Meeting service. I took my seat anyway and tried to get my bearings while the participants in Chicago were introduced to those in San Francisco.

The six of us in Chicago sat on one side of a curved table facing three large TV monitors. The middle monitor displayed slow-motion satellite-broadcast images of the meeting participants in San Francisco. The other two monitors displayed images of whoever in our room was speaking. . . .

When the participants in San Francisco spoke, their voices sounded normal, but their faces seemed frozen into unanimated smiles. Also, their eyes seemed to stare at the space behind our heads.

The frozen images distracted me throughout the broadcast. . . . Apparently, teleconferencing customers are willing to put up with the freeze-frame transmission because it costs half the price of sending the full-motion image—in this instance about $1,000 for 30 minutes. . . .

In the specially equipped, $500,000 conference room, several of the cameras are voice activated. When the man beside me spoke, I noticed that my image was also displayed on the monitor. It was so fas-

cinating to see myself on TV, I was tempted to stare at my image instead of paying attention to the meeting. . . .

Every now and then a pattern of tiny purple, pink, and green rectangles covered part or most of the faces being broadcast from San Francisco. According to the moderator, those were moments when we temporarily lost satellite transmission.

Suddenly the middle monitor screen was covered with the colored rectangles. The broadcast was over.

My first teleconference experience emphasized the prime rule for success with the medium: Be prepared. Activities that rob a minute here and there in face-to-face meetings are costly intrusions into a tightly produced teleconference. . . .

Many executives invest in training that teaches them how to behave in a video teleconference. Decker Communications, San Francisco, offers a special one-day training program for executives who participate in teleconferencing.

"We use intense video feedback—videotapes—to get executives to see themselves as others will see them on the video monitor," says Bert Decker, the company's president. . . .

Decker recommends the following:

Smile—"This is the thing to do in any kind of tension-making situation. You'll notice with amateurs that they tend to inhibit their energy—espe-

cially in their faces. If you look like you're at a funeral, people watching will tune out or disregard what you say. . . .

Eye communication—. . . You've got to look at the monitor that shows the people who are speaking. Because it's an artificial setting, you have to try harder to be natural, and this requires even more eye contact than you'd need in person."

Know your POV (point of view)—"There's a limited amount of time in a videoconference, so you've got to learn to say things concisely. . . .

And if at all possible, experts recommend that two-way video teleconferencing be used by people who've already met each other in person. This cuts down on the lag time spent wondering "whose voice was that?" Familiarity also makes the freeze-frame effect less distracting.

Reprinted from INFOSYSTEMS April 1984 Copyright Hitchcock Publishing Company.

Teleconferencing is one method used in managing businesses in today's complex business world. This type of communication system relies on satellite transmission of a conference between two distant locations. Teleconferencing, therefore, is one method of obtaining timely information needed for the day-to-day operations of many businesses. For this reason, teleconferencing is an alternative that is being considered for incorporation into many businesss' management information systems.

DATA COMMUNICATION

Data communication is the electronic transmission of data from one location to another, usually over communication channels such as telephone or telegraph lines or microwaves. In a data communication system, data are transmitted between terminals and a central computer or between two or more computers. As people and equipment become geographically dispersed, the computer and input and output devices, or **terminals,** are hooked into a communication network. The communication network provides the means for the input and output devices to communicate with both themselves and the computer(s) tied into the network. The combined use of communication facilities, such as telephone systems, and data-processing equipment is called **telecommunication.**

Data communication, using channels, can take place as near as within one room or as far as to peripheral devices located overseas, using an orbiting satellite as a communication channel.

Message Transmission

Data can be transmitted over communication lines in one of two forms: analog or digital. Transmission of data in continuous wave form is referred to as **analog transmission.** An analog transmission can be likened to the waves created in a pan of still water by a stick. By sending "waves" down a wire electronically, one causes messages to be sent and received. In the past, analog transmission was the major means of relaying data over long distances. This was due largely to the type of communication lines (see Figure 7–1a) provided by American Telephone and Telegraph (AT&T). **Digital transmission,** on the other hand, involves the transmission of data as distinct "on" and "off" pulses (see Figure 7–1b). Digital communications tend to be faster and more accurate than analog communications.

Analog transmission requires that the sender convert the data from the pulse form in which it is stored to wave form before transmitting it. This conversion process is called **modulation.** The opposite conversion—from wave form to pulse form—is required at the receiving end before the data is entered into the computer. This conversion is called **demodulation.** Both modulation and demodulation are accomplished by devices called **modems** or **data sets** (see Figure 7–2). The term *modem* is derived from the terms **mod**ulation and **dem**odulation.

As stated earlier, when digital transmission is used, data are transmitted in **pulse form,** as shown in Figure 7–1b. Since the computer stores data in pulse form, there is no need to convert the data to wave form. This reduces the time required to send messages. Digital transmission has also demonstrated a much lower error rate (about 100 times lower) than analog transmission. These two facts mean that users can transmit large amounts of data faster and more reliably.

Input/Output Operations

Control Units   One of the key functions of the input/output (I/O) subsystem of a computer system is the conversion of data into machine-readable code.

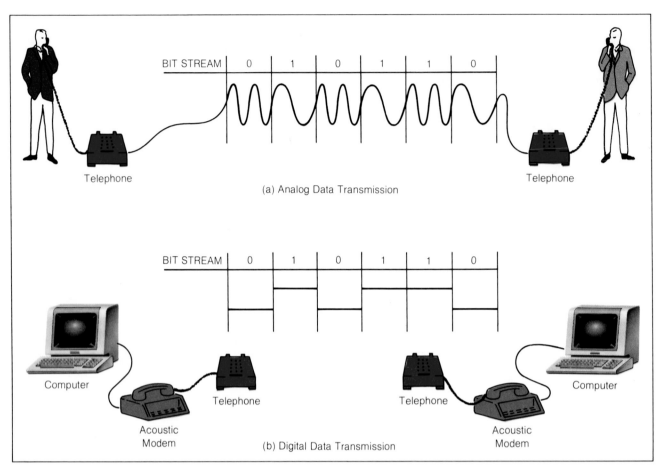

BIT STREAM | 0 | 1 | 0 | 1 | 1 | 0

Telephone   Telephone

(a) Analog Data Transmission

BIT STREAM | 0 | 1 | 0 | 1 | 1 | 0

Computer   Computer

Acoustic   Telephone   Telephone   Acoustic
Modem   Modem

(b) Digital Data Transmission

Figure 7–1 ▪ Analog and Digital Transmission

Figure 7–2 ▪ Modem

For instance, data on punched cards must be converted from Hollerith code into a machine code such as ASCII or BCD. Code conversion must be performed when data is entered from devices such as remote terminals and magnetic-ink character recognition devices. Code conversion is performed by a device known as an **I/O control unit.** This unit is different from the control unit of the CPU. It is located between one or more I/O devices and the CPU and is used only to facilitate I/O operations.

Besides code conversion, I/O control units perform another important function known as **data buffering.** A **buffer** is a separate storage unit (normally contained in the I/O control unit) for a particular input or output device. It is used as a temporary holding area for data being transferred to or from the CPU.

When data is read by an input device, it is converted to machine code and stored in a buffer. Once a certain amount of data has been collected in the buffer, it is transferred to the CPU. The buffer allows a large quantity of data to be transferred much faster than if the data items were transferred individually. For example, a buffer is used to temporarily hold data being entered from a remote terminal; this allows an entire record to be keyed on the terminal, held, and transferred all at once to the CPU. While the record is being keyed, the CPU processes other data (see Figure 7–3). The buffer serves a similar purpose when information is transferred from the computer to a printer or terminal as output.

Channels Although the CPU is very fast and accurate, it can execute only one instruction at a time. If it is executing an instruction that requires an input or output operation, it must wait while data is retrieved from or sent to an

Figure 7–3 ▪ Data Buffering

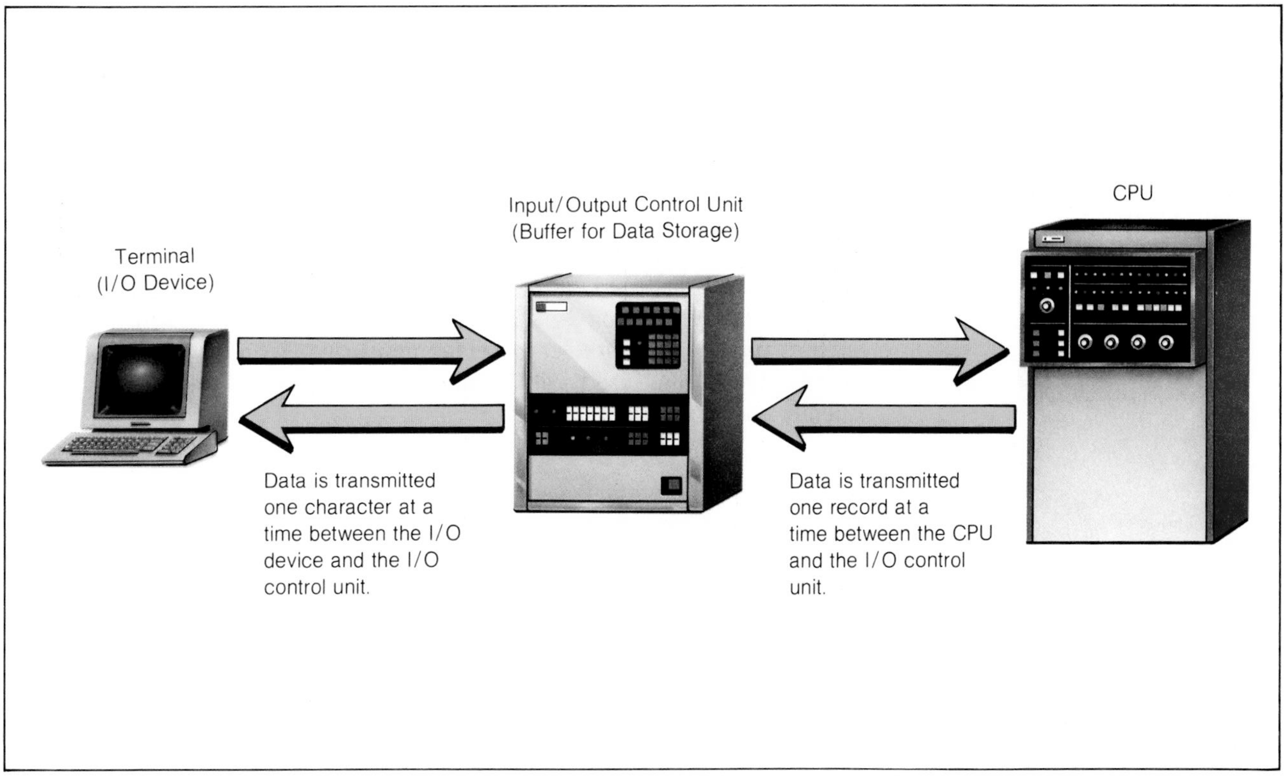

Terminal
(I/O Device)

Input/Output Control Unit
(Buffer for Data Storage)

CPU

Data is transmitted one character at a time between the I/O device and the I/O control unit.

Data is transmitted one record at a time between the CPU and the I/O control unit.

input/output device. Compared with the CPU's internal processing speeds, I/O speeds are extremely slow. Even high-speed I/O devices often work only one-tenth as fast as the CPU. When the CPU is slowed down because of I/O operations, it is said to be **input/output–bound.**

	TIME 1	TIME 2	TIME 3
Input	Item 1		
Process		Item 1	
Output			Item 1

The CPU is input/output–bound—it can operate on only one item at a time.

The flow of data shown in the table above indicates that in this system the CPU does the process step when it has the necessary data but sits idle while input and output occur. To increase use of the CPU, **channels** have been developed to take over the task of transferring data to and from it. Each channel is a small, limited-capacity computer that serves as a data roadway. It may be within the CPU or a separate piece of equipment connected to it. During processing, when the CPU encounters an instruction requiring input or output, it merely tells the channel what it needs. The channel then goes to the required input device for data or sends information to the appropriate output device. The CPU, meanwhile, is free to execute other instructions; it is relieved of its responsibility to transfer data and can process data more efficiently.

	TIME 1	TIME 2	TIME 3
Input	Item 1	Item 2	Item 3
Process		Item 1	Item 2
Output			Item 1

With the aid of channels, the CPU can be active a greater percentage of the time.

There are two types of channels: selector and multiplexor. A **selector channel** can accept input from only one device at a time and is used with a high-speed I/O device such as a magnetic-tape or magnetic-disk unit. A **multiplexor channel** can handle more than one I/O device at a time. A byte multiplexor channel is normally associated with multiple slow-speed devices such as printers, card readers, and terminals (see Figure 7– 4). A block multiplexor channel is used with multiple high-speed devices but is less frequently encountered.

Communication Channels

A **communication channel** is the link that permits transmission of electrical signals between **distributed data processing** locations; its purpose is to carry data from one location to another. The types of communication channels used for data transfer are telegraph lines, telephone lines, coaxial cables, microwave links, communication satellites, high-speed helical waveguides, and laser beams.

Figure 7–4 ■ **Channels, Control Units, and I/O Devices**

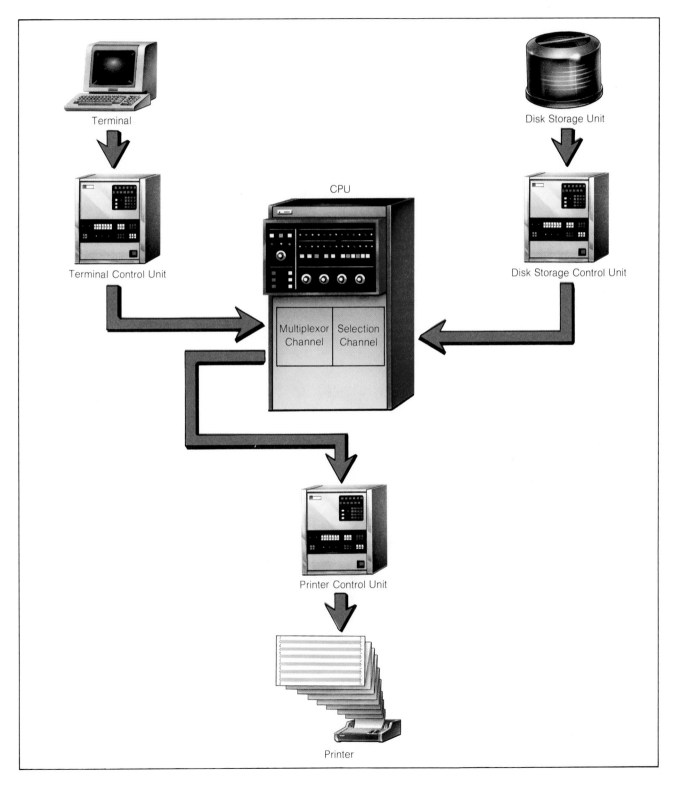

Terminal

Disk Storage Unit

Terminal Control Unit

CPU

Multiplexor Channel

Selection Channel

Disk Storage Control Unit

Printer Control Unit

Printer

Grades of Transmission   The **grade,** or **bandwidth,** of a channel determines the range of frequencies it can transmit. The rate at which data can be transmitted across the channel is directly proportional to the width of the frequency band. **Narrow bandwidth channels** can transmit data at a rate of 45 to 90 bits per second. Telegraph channels are typical narrow bandwidth channels.

Voice-grade channels have a wider frequency range; they can transmit at rates of from 300 to 9,600 bits per second. Voice-grade channels, such as telephone lines, are used by the Dataphone and Dataspeed equipment of AT&T's Bell Telephone System by similar equipment of the Wide Area Telephone Service (WATS), and by many others.

For applications that require high-speed transmission of large volumes of data, **broad-band channels** are most suitable. Coaxial cables, microwaves, helical waveguides, and laser beams belong in this grade. Leased broad-band services are offered by both Western Union and the Bell System. An example of a leased broad-band service is the Telpak system, which is capable of transmitting data at rates of up to 120,000 bits per second.

Modes of Transmission   Another method of classifying communication channels is by the mode of transmission they use. Depending on the application and the terminal equipment used, channels operate in one of three basic transmission modes (see Figure 7–5):

Figure 7–5 ▪ Channel Transmission Modes

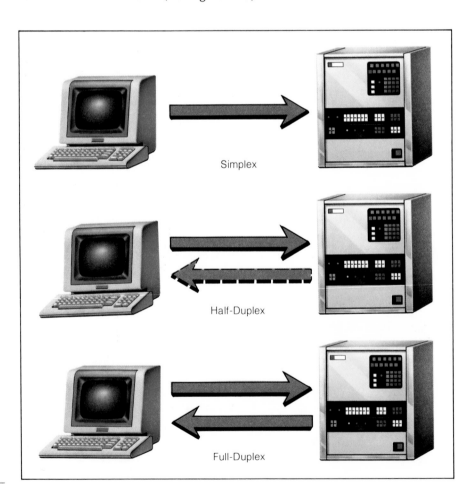

Simplex

Half-Duplex

Full-Duplex

- *Simplex.* A **simplex** channel provides for unidirectional, or one-way, transmission of data. A terminal that transmits via a simplex channel can either send or receive; it cannot do both.
- *Half-duplex.* In the **half-duplex** mode, communication can occur in both directions, but in only one direction at a time. The half-duplex mode is commonly used in telephone services and telephone networks for the transmission of data.
- *Full-duplex.* A **full-duplex** channel can transmit data in both directions simultaneously; thus it is the most versatile mode of transmission.

Multiplexers and Concentrators

Multiplexers and **concentrators,** also known as **datacom handlers,** increase the number of devices that can use a communication channel. This is necessary because I/O devices operate at a much slower speed (100 to 150 bits per second) than do communication channels (300 to 9,600 bits per second for voice-grade). Thus, a channel is not used to full capacity by a single I/O device.

Multiplexing can create more economical usage of the communication channel; it acts as a communication interface, combining the input streams from several devices into a single input stream which can be sent over a single channel to the computer system. This allows for a single communication channel (typically voice-grade) to substitute for many slower subvoice channels that might otherwise have been operating at less than full capacity. Once the computer system has completed processing, the output message is sent to the multiplexer, which then routes the message to the appropriate device.

A concentrator differs from a multiplexer in that it allows data to be transmitted from only one terminal at a time over a communication channel. The concentrator **polls** the terminals one at a time to see if they have any messages to send. When a communication channel is free, the first terminal ready to send or receive data will get control of the channel and will continue to control it for the length of the transaction. The use of a concentrator relies on the assumption that not all terminals will be ready to send or receive data at a single given time. Figure 7–6 shows communication systems with and without multiplexers and concentrators.

Programmable Communications Processors

A **programmable communications processor** is a device that relieves the CPU of many of the tasks typically required in a communication system. When the volume of data transmission surpasses a certain level, a programmable communications processor can handle these tasks more economically than the CPU. Examples of such tasks include handling messages and priorities, disconnecting after messages have been received, requesting retransmission of incomplete messages, and verifying successfully transmitted messages.

The two most frequent uses of communications processors are message-switching and front-end processing. The principal task of the processor used for **message-switching** is to receive messages and route them to appropriate destinations. A **front-end processor** also performs message-switching as well as more sophisticated operations such as validating transmitted data and preprocessing data before it is transmitted to the central computer.

Figure 7–6 ▪ **Communication Systems with and without Multiplexers and Concentrators**

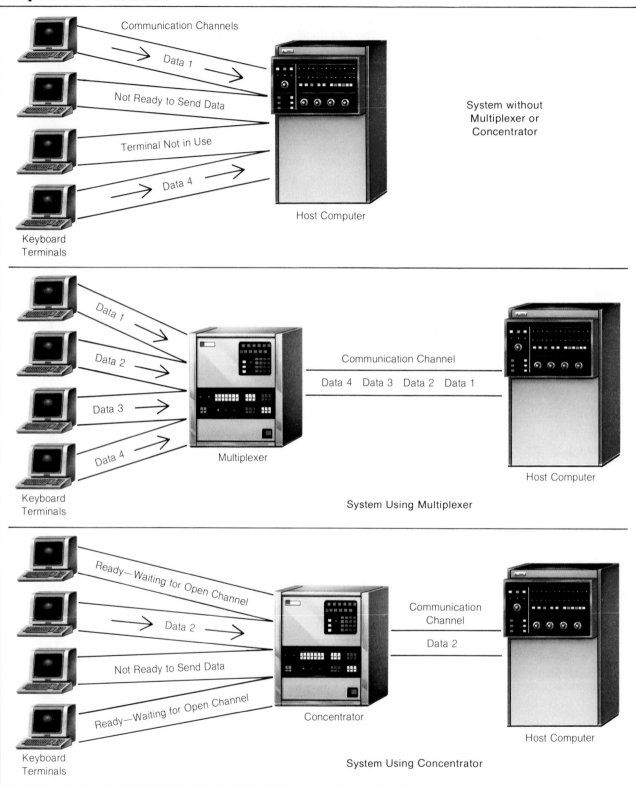

Communication Channels

Data 1

Not Ready to Send Data

Terminal Not in Use

Data 4

Keyboard Terminals

System without Multiplexer or Concentrator

Host Computer

Data 1

Data 2

Data 3

Data 4

Keyboard Terminals

Multiplexer

Communication Channel

Data 4   Data 3   Data 2   Data 1

Host Computer

System Using Multiplexer

Ready—Waiting for Open Channel

Data 2

Not Ready to Send Data

Ready—Waiting for Open Channel

Keyboard Terminals

Concentrator

Communication Channel

Data 2

Host Computer

System Using Concentrator

- **Telecommunication** is the combined use of communication facilities, such as telephone systems, and data processing equipment, such as terminals and computer systems.
- Data is transmitted over communication lines in one of two forms: **analog** or **digital.** An analog transmission is a continuous wave transmission, while a digital transmission is a series of "on" and "off" pulses sent over the communication channel.
- Since data in the computer is stored in an "on" and "off" state, it must be converted before it is sent out as an analog transmission. The process of converting digital pulses to a continuous wave is referred to as **modulation.** The conversion of the continuous wave back to digital pulses is called **demodulation.** The device which accomplishes these tasks is referred to as a **modem** (for *modulation/demodulation*).
- An **input/output control unit** is used to convert data from an input form to machine readable form, and from machine readable form to an output form.
- **Channels** are used in computer systems to relieve the CPU of the duty of communicating with the various I/O devices. When performing I/O operations, the CPU simply communicates with the channel.
- A **selector channel** can communicate with only one I/O device at a time, while a **multiplexor channel** can talk with more than one I/O device at a time.
- Channels can operate in one of three transmission modes: (1) **simplex,** (2) **half-duplex,** and (3) **full-duplex.**
- **Multiplexers** and **concentrators** are used to increase the number of I/O devices that can use one channel to communicate with the CPU.

COMMUNICATION SYSTEMS

Single CPU Systems

A typical computer system consists of a single mainframe linked to a variety of peripherals. If the peripherals are connected directly to the CPU, the system is said to be a **local system.** However, in recent years, advancements in computer technology have made it possible to place terminals (or other devices) in the hands of users in locations removed from the mainframe. These terminals are connected to the central computer by a communication channel. The resulting system is called a **remote system.**

Time-Sharing Systems Many businesses could benefit from the installation of a computer facility but are prohibited from doing so by its cost. Some organizations only infrequently need the power of a large computer system. To meet such needs in an economically feasible way, **time-sharing systems** have been developed. Under time sharing, two or more users with diverse tasks can access the same central computer and its resources and receive what seem to be simultaneous responses. Each user believes that he or she has total control of the computer, but in reality the computer is dividing its time among them. Each user is charged only for the computer resources he or she actually uses. This time-sharing system may be accessed by remote users via I/O devices and telephone lines, or by local users whose I/O devices are connected directly to the system.

A system that supports time sharing must have some method of allocating computing time to users. The purpose of the time-sharing system would be defeated if one user had to wait a long time while another monopolized the CPU's processing facilities. To solve this problem, a technique called **time slicing** is often used. Each user is allocated a small portion of processing time. If the user's program is completely executed during this time, or if the program reaches a point at which input or output activity must occur before the allotted time is used up, the CPU begins (or resumes) execution of another user's program. If execution of the program is not completed during the allocated time, control of the CPU is transferred to another user's program, and the first program is placed at the end of a waiting list. Once the program returns to the top of the list, execution is resumed at the point where execution was stopped when control of the CPU was transferred to another program. This switching of programs occurs at such a rapid rate that users are generally unaware of it.

There are two methods of establishing time-sharing capability. One is to set up a time-sharing system **in-house** to obtain quick answers to such problems as production and cost analysis, forecasting, and accounts receivable. The other is to purchase time-sharing capability from a service company which owns and maintains one or more computer systems. The latter approach is often taken by small organizations that cannot afford to purchase their own computers. Because of the intense competition in this area, many service companies have expanded to provide not only time-sharing capability but also specialized programs and technical assistance. Comshare, Tymshare and ADP (Automatic Data Processing) are three companies which have been very successful in providing time-sharing services.

The major advantages of time-sharing systems include the following:

- They provide an economical means for small users to utilize the resources of a large computer system.
- They allow each user to seem to possess a private computer.
- They provide quick response capabilities.
- Through resource pooling, they can provide access to greater numbers of application programs at a lower unit cost than privately owned and maintained computers.
- The user who purchases computer time from a service bureau does not need to worry about equipment obsolescence.

Time sharing also has inherent problems, some of which are identified below:

- Users connected to the system by telephone lines must worry about breakdowns in the lines or increases in communication costs. Furthermore, telephone lines are designed primarily for voice communication; they are not the best medium for transmission of data. Thus, applications involving extensive I/O operations may not be suited to time sharing.
- Because data can be accessed quickly and easily in a time-sharing system, concern for security must be increased. All programs and data must be safeguarded from unauthorized persons or use.
- When quick response is not a necessity, time-sharing capability may be a needless expense.
- System reliability may be lower than in non-time-sharing systems. The additional equipment and communication channels are possible areas for both mechanical and system-related problems.

Multiple CPU Configurations

As the complexity of business and scientific problems increases, the resources of a single CPU may not be sufficient to provide adequate response time to inquiries or to perform the complex calculations required. To provide adequate computing power for solving such problems, several CPUs may be linked together to form a **network.**

As with a single CPU and its terminals, the network's mainframes may be hooked together to form either local or remote systems. Several computers can be connected at a central location to enhance computing capabilities. The computers can also be dispersed geographically to the locations of data collection or information dispersal. These dispersed computers are connected by a communication network. The advantages of a distributed system include reduced organization impact, greater flexibility and responsiveness, and increased ability to withstand failure.

Different types of structures can be used to implement the multiple CPU concept (see Figure 7–7). In a **star configuration,** all transactions must go through a central computer before being routed to the appropriate network computer. The effect is to create a central decision point. This facilitates workload distribution and resource sharing, but it exposes the system to single-point vulnerability. An alternative approach uses a number of computers connected to a single transmission line in a **ring configuration.** This type of system can bypass a malfunctioning unit without disrupting operations throughout the network.

Figure 7–7 ▪ Multiple CPU Configurations

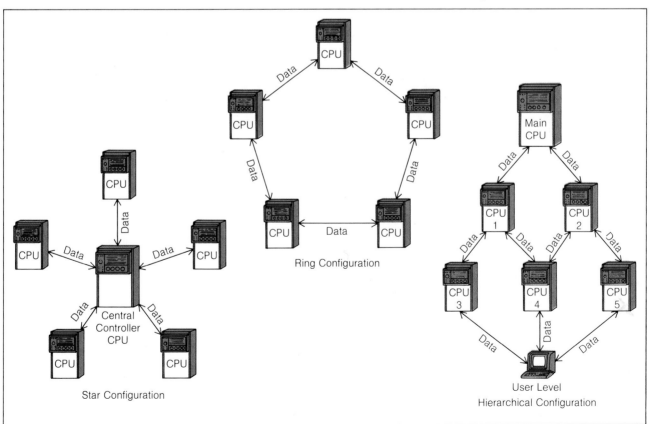

Star Configuration

Ring Configuration

User Level
Hierarchical Configuration

An interesting and more sophisticated approach is the **hierarchical configuration.** Under this approach, an organization's needs are divided into multiple levels, which are controlled by a single computer at the top of the hierarchy. The lowest is the user level, where only routine transaction processing power is supplied. This level is connected to the next higher level and its associated information system. At each higher level, the machine size increases, while the need for distribution decreases. Thus, such a system consists of a network of small computers tied in to a large central computing complex.

The networks discussed so far have relied on data communication channels that are earthbound. Today, however, many networks rely on the use of satellite communication channels to extend their ranges to other continents. Satellite-based networks are very expensive though, primarily because they need small dish-like antennas to send and receive messages from the satellites. Currently, such systems are cost effective only for users who process large volumes of information.

Distributed Data Processing

The concept of distributed data processing (DDP) involves processing, which to some degree is done at a site independent of the central computer system. The amount and type of processing that take place at a distributed site vary from company to company, depending on the structure and management philosophy of the company. Figure 7–8 illustrates a distributed system in which three dispersed minicomputers are connected by communication links to a large central computer. The three minicomputers, for example, may be located in three functional areas of the organization—finance, marketing, and production.

This type of approach to distributed processing gives the various functional areas the ability to process data independently of the central computer as well as to communicate data required by the entire organization to the central computer. Thus, some of the information generated in the functional areas can be communicated to the central computer to be used in corporate-wide planning and control.

Figure 7–8 ▪ Distributed System

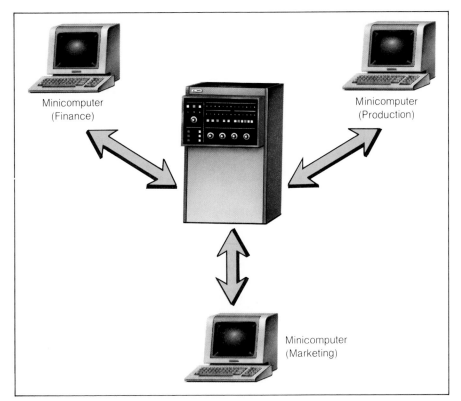

Minicomputer
(Finance)

Minicomputer
(Production)

Minicomputer
(Marketing)

The increase in popularity of microcomputers has led to their inclusion in distributed data processing systems. The use of microcomputers by managers for planning and control in a distributed system has seen a dramatic increase.

As we mentioned, a company's managerial philosophy normally determines the type of system and the amount of processing done at a distributed site. A company with a strong centralized managerial philosophy will normally do the majority of its processing at one centralized location. A company with a decentralized managerial philosophy will do a large amount of processing at distributed sites, with the central computer serving primarily as a communication link among various sites. As the technology in data communication improves and computers become more widely used at dispersed locations, the importance and use of distributed data processing will undoubtedly grow.

Local Area Networks

Local area networking, an alternate form of distributed processing, involves interconnecting computers in a single building or a complex of buildings. Microcomputers, for example, can be linked together, allowing them to share peripheral devices and information, and also to provide the ability to communicate between members of the network. Sharing peripheral devices such as printers and mass storage devices can reduce costs on a per-computer basis. For example, four or five microcomputers may share a high-speed, letter quality printer and a hard disk unit. The ability to share information is very important; information contained at a central location provides greater

A Micro in Every Home

Home computers are becoming so much a part of our lives that experts predict by the end of the century nearly eight out of ten households will include a personal computer. Hardware and software sales for personal computers are expected to exceed $12 billion before the end of the decade.

With the average complete system costing over $1,000, the home computer definitely falls into the category of a major purchase for most families. So how do people finance this investment?

The Aids Association for Lutherans (AAL), the nation's largest fraternal insurance society, has developed a plan for its employees that will allow them to buy personal computers. The company offers interest-free loans of up to $2,000 for any employee interested in purchasing a home computer system. Computers are vital to the insurance industry, and AAL is hoping their plan will encourage increased interest in computers among its employees.

Lunch-hour seminars conducted by the company help prospective buyers learn how to use personal computers and provide tips on selecting hardware and software.

With the help of companies like AAL, predictions like eight out of ten households owning personal computers will undoubtably prove to be correct.

data integrity and is accessed or updated in a timely fashion from any number of locations within the network.

The ability to communicate among members of the network is also an important consideration. **Electronic mail** is one means of network communication. Electronic mail allows one member of the network to send a message to another member. If the member receiving the message is not currently connected to the network, the message will be saved until the next time he or she connects to the network. Electronic mail, therefore, can eliminate many of the unnecessary calls and return calls of a telephone message process. The advantages of a local area network are numerous and should not be overlooked in an environment that uses multiple microcomputers.

Electronic Transmission of Data

Another type of communication system that has seen a dramatic increase in use recently is **electronic funds transfer (EFT).** More and more financial transactions are being handled electronically. In an EFT system, the accounts of the party or parties involved in a transaction are adjusted by electronic communication between remote I/O devices and a computer or between computers; there is no exchange of money in the form of cash or checks. Many people think that banking as we know it today will not exist in the future; rather we will live in a cashless and checkless society where all banking and credit transactions will be performed electronically.

Some of the more popular forms of EFT include direct deposit of pay checks, automatic withdrawal of payments from a borrower's account, and the use of **automatic teller machines (ATMs).** ATMs are remote I/O devices that communicate with the bank's computer (see Figure 7–9). They are normally available for use twenty-four hours a day and permit the customer to

Figure 7–9 ■ Automatic Teller Machine

perform transactions such as account balance inquiries, transfers of funds, deposits, withdrawals, and loan payments. Security for ATM systems includes identification numbers entered by the customers and used by the system to link the customers to the accounts.

SUMMARY POINTS

■ Data communication is the electronic transmission of data from one location to another, usually over communication channels such as telephone telegraph lines or microwaves. The combined use of data-processing equipment and communication facilities, such as telephone systems, is called telecommunication.

■ Modulation is the process of converting data from the pulse form used by the computer to a wave form used for message transmission over communication lines. Demodulation is the process of converting the received message from wave form back to pulse form. These functions are performed by devices called modems, or data sets.

■ Digital transmission involves transmitting data as distinct on and off pulses rather than as waves. This mode of transmission eliminates the specialized steps of conversion from pulse to wave form and subsequent reconversion from wave to pulse form at the destination.

■ I/O control units and channels are used in an I/O subsystem to increase the efficiency of the CPU. A control unit converts input data into machine code, and vice versa. It is also used in data buffering.

■ Channels control I/O operations and free the CPU to do other processing; this allows input, output, and processing to overlap. Selector channels can accommodate only one I/O device at a time and are used with high-speed devices; multiplexor channels can accommodate multiple I/O devices and are often used with low-speed devices.

■ A communication channel is the link permitting transmission of electrical signals from one location to another. Types of communication channels include telegraph lines, telephone lines, coaxial cables, microwave links, and communication satellites. Communication channels can be classified by (1) their grade, or bandwidth, or (2) the mode of transmission (simplex, half-duplex, or full-duplex).

■ Multiplexers, concentrators, and programmable communications processors are devices that reduce the costs associated with data transmission in a communication system.

■ A time-sharing system allows several users to access the same computer at the same time. An in-house time-sharing system can be installed, or time-sharing capability can be purchased from a service company.

■ Multiple CPU communication systems are characterized by several computers linked together in an earth-bound or a satellite-based communications network. Possible configurations for such systems include star, ring, and hierarchical designs.

■ Local area networks and electronic mail services are forms of distributed processing systems that can be utilized by managers for decision making and communication.

■ Electronic funds transfer (EFT) is a communication system that could revolutionize the banking industry. Automatic teller machines (ATMs) have become a very popular form of EFT.

REVIEW QUESTIONS

1. What are modems? What purpose do they serve in data communication systems?

2. What functions does an I/O control unit perform?

3. What are channels used for? Distinguish between selector channels and multiplexor channels.

4. Distinguish among simplex, half-duplex, and full-duplex transmission modes. Why are the transmission mode and bandwidth of communication channels of concern to an analyst designing a data communication system?

5. Explain the concept of polling.

6. How does the manner in which a concentrator communicates with an I/O device differ from the way in which a multiplexer performs the same function?

7. Distinguish between the terms *local system* and *remote system*. How does each apply to single and multiple computer systems?

8. What alternative is available to a firm that does not process a sufficient volume of data to justify the installation of a computer? What problems may arise?

9. Which configuration for multiple CPU systems has the disadvantage of single-point vulnerability? Why?

10. What is meant by distributed data processing?

11. What factors are instrumental in determining the degree to which processing will be done at a distributed site?

12. Based on what you've read about distributed data processing, describe how data-processing requirements for a large, international corporation with 98centralized managerial philosophy may vary from those for a similar firm with a decentralized managerial philosophy. (Note: There is no single correct answer; simply explain what you think some differences would be.)

APPLICATION
Bank of America

In October 1904, a small neighborhood bank opened for business in a remodeled tavern in the North Beach area of San Francisco. Its assets at the end of 1904 were $285,000. The founder of this bank, Amadeo Peter Giannini, had decided that small wage earners and small businesses should be offered the same banking services heretofore reserved for wealthy individuals and large companies.

Giannini's Bank of Italy (so named until 1930) was completely destroyed by the San Francisco earthquake of 1906, but Giannini was able to load $80,000 in cash on wagons and move the money to his home for safekeeping. Before the larger banks could reopen, he was lending money from a plank-and-barrel counter at the waterfront. Surviving the bank-closing panic of 1907, by 1918 the Bank of Italy had twenty-four branches in California—the leader in branch banking despite opposition from competitors and state officials. During the Great Depression, Giannini's newly named Bank of America survived while 8,000 other banks were liquidated, went bankrupt, or were forced to merge in order to stay afloat.

Today, Bank of America is one of the foremost banks in the world, with over $120 billion in assets; approximately 950 branches throughout California; and 104 branches, subsidiaries, and representative offices in 76 countries abroad. Its data-processing activities center around financial transactions and services such as check processing, savings services, Visa transactions, travellers' check services, and funds transfers. Two major data-processing centers handle the very large volumes of activity; one is located in San Francisco, and the other in Los Angeles.

The most significant data-processing work revolves around balancing the bank's books and determining its assets each night. Each day, paper records (in the form of checks and transaction records) and electronic records (in the form of magnetic tape and storage disks) are sent to the data centers from the approximately 950 branches, from internal bank departments, and from other banks with whom the Bank of America

does business. Bank of America has its own air and auto fleet to pick up and deliver the input and computer work from its branches and departments. Just to service the San Francisco data center, the fleets cover about 42,000 miles a day!

Once the balancing is completed, a multitude of reports are prepared to be used by the bank's branches and internal departments and by other banks with which it has direct correspondence. In addition, from the posted account information, numerous data bases (savings, checking, Visa, Versateller, student loans, travellers' checks, and many more) are updated to contain current customer information for the next processing day.

VERSATELLER

Bank of America uses many online applications of data communication technology. One is the Automated Teller Machine (ATM), known as the Versateller service. (See Figure 7–10.) More than 1,000 Versateller machines throughout California are connected with the mainframe computers in Los Angeles and San Francisco. (In addition, the system is linked with a nationwide PLUS System, accessing about 4,000 ATMs belonging to other member institutions in the consortium.)

FIGURE 7–10 ■ Bank of America's Versateller Service

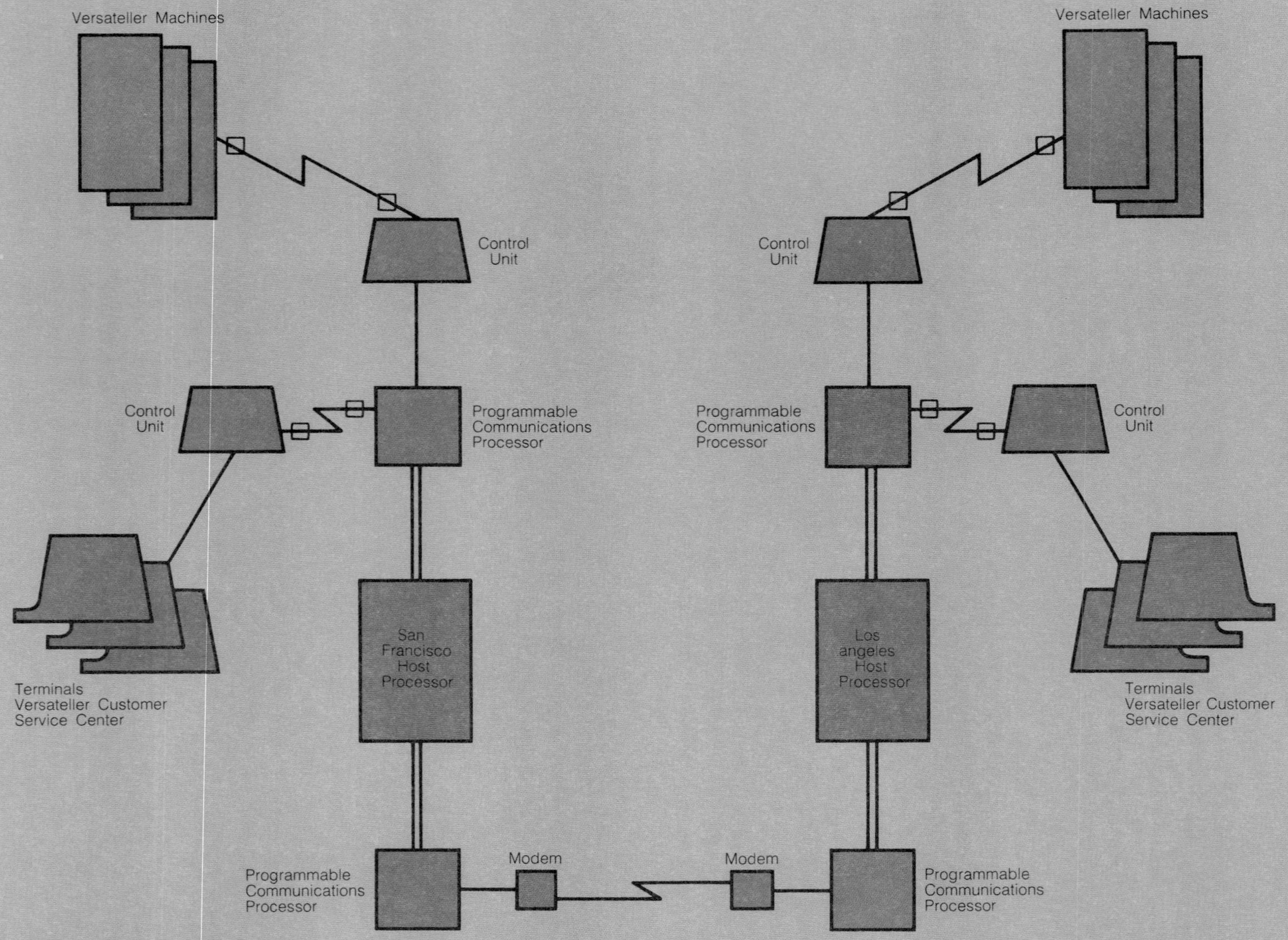

Versateller Machines

Control Unit

Versateller Machines

Control Unit

Programmable Communications Processor

Control Unit

Terminals Versateller Customer Service Center

Programmable Communications Processor

Los angeles Host Processor

Programmable Communications Processor

Modem

Modem

San Francisco Host Processor

Programmable Communications Processor

Control Unit

Terminals Versateller Customer Service Center

The two host computers are tied together by a communication link that uses telephone facilities. Programmable communications processors and modems at each end of the link convert the data in the form of signals from digital to analog and back again. Along the link, signals are sometimes carried on telephone lines, other times via microwave receivers or a combination of telephone and microwave, depending upon the distance involved.

Each host computer also supports a sub-network of terminals used by its Versateller Customer Service Center for updating and inquiring into the customer data base; communication takes place over telephone circuitry. Within the customer service center, coaxial cables link the control units with the terminals themselves.

Each host supports a subnetwork of Versateller machines as well. In this sub-network, the programmable control units are located in the data center; from there, telephone circuitry provides the communication link between the Versateller machines and the control units. A single control unit can support up to eighteen Versateller machines. As with all transmission over telephone circuitry, modems at each end of the line must make the digital/analog conversions.

DISTRIBUTED COMPUTING FACILITY

A second major network using communication facilities is the Distributed Computing Facility (DCF). (See Figure 7–11). This network is actually attached to the ATM network. It centers around a group of minicomputers connected to an IBM host computer that runs the Versateller network; this system is set up in both San Francisco and Los Angeles. Six high-speed digital lines pass customer account transaction information between the host computer and the distributed minicomputer system used by DCF. This process allows account balances to be kept up to the minute for all the Bank's customers.

The branch teller network is the facility by which tellers in the branches can inquire against and update information on customer account balances. Several specialized terminals are located in each branch and connected by coaxial cable to a control unit, which is also located in the branch bank. From the control unit, telephone circuitry is again used to transmit data to the DCF minicomputers at the data centers. During the early 1980s, Bank of America introduced new online services from its DCF branch network. But without a major addition of computer hardware, the minicompu-

ter-based system could not be modified to handle the additional high-volume, high-function transaction workload. The bank decided to add this application processing to the host by means of IBM's Information Management System (IMS). The strategy hinged upon integration of the bank's massive retail customer data bases into one segmented file. This file, controlled and accessed by IMS, would be used by both the branch teller network and the Versateller ATM network. By now, all application and database functionality has migrated from DCF to the IMS host, controlled at the branch terminals. A replacement for the DCF facility, to control the entire retail network, is planned for 1985. At that time, Versatellers and branch terminals will be able to share the same physical network facilities and control units, greatly reducing network expense.

MONEY TRANSFER SERVICE

A third major network handling Bank of America's activities is the Money Transfer Service. This network, composed of multiple minicomputers, utilizes telegraph lines, fiber optics, multiplexers, and satellites. It is responsible for sending and receiving messages between minicomputers in the San Francisco data center and those throughout the world. For example, the bank's private network links its San Francisco processing center with its subsidiary in New York, and with BofA offices in other U.S. and overseas locations. In addition, the system interfaces with several external funds-transfer or financial communications networks. These include FedWire, BankWire, and the Society for Worldwide Interbank Financial Transactions (S.W.I.F.T.). BofA's system also interfaces with Telex. The technologies needed to perform this message-switching depend upon the countries to which the messages are being sent or from which the messages are being received. For example, messages to and from South America primarily use telegraph interfaces provided by Western Union; messages to Hong Kong are transmitted via satellite. Communication to London is provided by a wide variety of communication links. (See Figure 7–12.)

The London-bound line leaving a money transfer minicomputer is first fed into a multiplexer. Here it is combined onto a higher-speed line with other Bank of America lines headed for London. This line in turn is fed into a concentrating modem, where it is combined with two other high-speed lines. This single line travels via telephone circuitry to a satellite earth station servic-

FIGURE 7–11 ■ Bank of America's Distributed Computing Facility

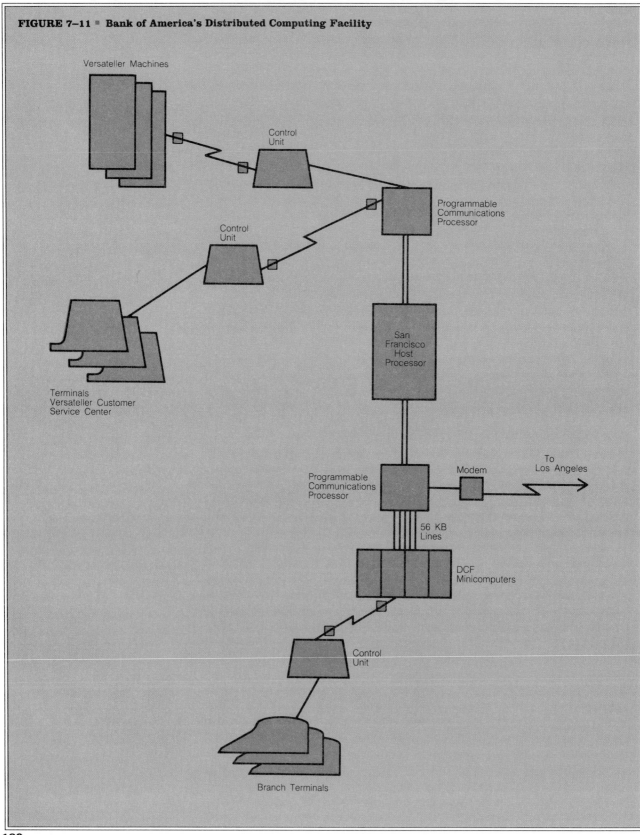

Versateller Machines

Control Unit

Control Unit

Terminals
Versateller Customer
Service Center

Programmable
Communications
Processor

San
Francisco
Host
Processor

Programmable
Communications
Processor

Modem

To
Los Angeles

56 KB
Lines

DCF
Minicomputers

Control
Unit

Branch Terminals

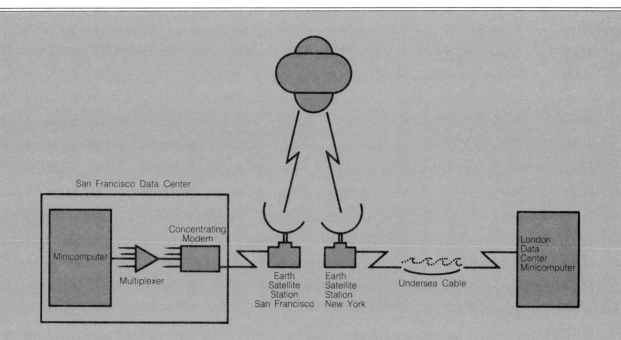

FIGURE 7–12 ▪ **Communication Channels for Bank of America's Money Transfer Service**

ing the San Francisco Bay area. The signal is passed via satellite to New York where it is carried by telephone circuitry to Western Union International's undersea cable. Through this cable, it crosses the Atlantic to London, where it is dispersed through additional multiplexing equipment onto telephone circuits for its final journey to the bank's London data center's message-switching minicomputers. A reverse procedure is used in sending messages to San Francisco from London. Fiber optics are now being widely used as the primary local area network tool for the Money Transfer System.

These three networks, only a few of the many communication networks at Bank of America, show how greatly data communication technologies have increased the capabilities and efficiency of data process-

ing in the banking industry. Bank of America's next stage of systems architecture development, called International Banking System and scheduled for completion in 1988, will change its technological environment from a series of stand-alone systems to a common database system.

DISCUSSION POINTS

1. Explain how Bank of America's data-processing system provides up-to-the-minute account balances for its customers. Why is such an operation important?
2. The Money Transfer Service allows the bank to communicate with associates all over the world. What other industries might need this type of communication?

SECTION III
PROGRAMMING

8
System Software

INTRODUCTION

The computer is a powerful machine that can solve a variety of problems. Previous chapters have covered the major hardware components of a computer system and have shown how these components are used to store and process data and generate information. However, the computer cannot solve problems without using computer programs. Programming is a critical step in data processing; if the system is not correctly programmed, it delivers information that cannot be used.

This chapter examines several aspects of computer programming, or software. It explains differences between system programming and application programming and discusses the various functions performed by operating system software. The chapter also describes some of the more advanced software developments that have occurred in recent years. The concepts of multiprogramming and multiprocessing are introduced, and the use of virtual storage to avoid limitations of primary storage is discussed in detail.

ARTICLE

The Research: One Step at a Time

Every 30 minutes, someone in America is paralyzed by spinal cord injury. There are more than half a million paralyzed people in this country. Most have been told they will never walk again. But history was made and hope ignited a year ago when a 22-year-old student named Nan Davis walked with the aid of a small computer.

That computer was developed in Dayton, Ohio, the culmination of 13 years of research into the link between computer wiring and the human spinal cord. Doctors contributing to the effort were Jerrold Petrofsky, Roger Glaser, and John Gruner.

Dr. Petrofsky, the director of Wright State University's biomedical engineering laboratory, is an electronics wizard and avid tinkerer who knows Nan's first step was just that—the first step in getting dormant limbs to function again. Even more heartening than Nan's walk last year was her graduation from Wright State last June. At that event, just five years after an automobile accident on her high school graduation night left her paralyzed from the waist down, she walked to the commencement platform to receive her college diploma.

This was the first time since the accident that Nan had walked outside a laboratory setting, and she did it with the aid of a portable computer that electrically stimulated her paralyzed muscles. This portable system differed markedly from the stationary computer system she had used last year. She originally wore a safety harness and walked holding on to parallel bars. These precautions were no longer needed because of advances in Petrofsky's computerized system, and because of the strengthening of Nan's bones and muscles from an exercise regimen devised by Dr. Glaser.

The computer itself has been miniaturized from a full-size desk-top model to one small enough to be carried in a purse. Balance is achieved with "level detectors" that tell the computer the position and movement of the legs so the computer knows which muscles to stimulate electrically to achieve coordinated movement. With this sytem, Nan can not only stand and walk, but walk backwards and sit down as well. Petrofsky says that if an electrode wire breaks or the person using the system trips, the computer is able to compensate and stimulate other muscles to keep the person from falling.

Petrofsky is convinced that the next few years will bring many more advances. He says, "We will be working on further miniaturization of the computerized portable walking system and at implanting the electrodes in the body over the next year or two."

Petrofsky says the size of the computer could shrink to the size of a small calculator or even a postage stamp, but only if a big electronics company gets involved. The entire system could be a small microprocessor, implanted pacemaker-style. Petrofsky hopes his walking system will be ready for commercialization within a decade. . . .

And the cost? It's hard to know for sure, but Petrofsky expects the microchip implant (to send and receive messages) to cost about $500 for the hardware. . . .

All in all, the new computerized systems will go a long way toward helping paralyzed people. But Petrofsky cautions against hope for instant results with walking. "There are still a lot of questions we're trying to answer," he says. "This is a research project, and that's often misunderstood. We're just getting into the clinical use now . . . but we have a long way to go."

Although some of the success of this project relies on computer hardware, software also plays a very critical role. The computers used in biomedical engineering must be programmed to respond accordingly to information sent to the system by its sensors. Once the information is received, the program must decide what muscles need to be stimulated. Software and programming, therefore, are also key factors to the successful use of computers by humans.

PROGRAMS

Despite the apparent complexity and power of the computer, it is merely a tool manipulated by an individual. It requires step-by-step instructions to reach the solution to a problem. As stated earlier, this series of instructions is known as a *program,* and the individual who creates the program is the *programmer.* There are two basic types of programs: (1) **system programs,** which coordinate the operation of computer circuitry; and (2) **application programs,** which solve particular user problems.

System Programming

System programs directly affect the operation of the computer. They are designed to facilitate the use of the hardware and to help the computer system run quickly and efficiently. For example, a system program allocates storage for data being entered into the system. We have already seen that computers differ in primary storage capacity, in the methods used to store and code data, and in the number of instructions they can perform. Consequently, system programs are written specifically for a particular type of computer and cannot be used (without modification) on different machines.

System programming is normally provided by the computer manufacturer or a specialized programming firm. Thus, system programs are initially written in a general fashion to meet as many user requirements as possible. However, they can be modified, or tailored, to meet a particular organization's specific needs.

A system programmer maintains the system programs in good running order and tailors them, when necessary, to meet organizational requirements. Since system programmers serve as a bridge between the computer and application programmers, they must have the technical background needed to understand the complex internal operations of the computer. Because each organization uses a different set of application programs, system programs must be modified (tuned) to ensure computer efficiency at each organization's installation.

Application Programming

Application programs perform specific data-processing or computational tasks to solve the organization's information needs. They can be developed within the organization or purchased from software firms. Typical examples of application programs are those used in inventory control and accounting; in banks, application programs update checking and savings account balances.

The job of the application programmer is to use the capabilities of the computer to solve specific problems. Application programs can be written by a programmer without an in-depth knowledge of the computer. The application programmer instead concentrates on the particular problem to be solved. If the problem is clearly defined and understood, the task of writing a program to solve it is greatly simplified. Application software will be discussed in greater detail in Chapter 12.

Patents on Software?

What is the best way to protect software from illegal copying? Is it by patent, copyright, or a combination of the two?

The software industry is estimated to generate $3.7 billion in sales each year. With increased software piracy, there is much concern about software protection.

According to the Copyright Office's policy planning adviser, Michael Keplinger, more than 1,000 computer software programs are being registered for copyright each month. But copyright does not protect the software idea; it protects only the mathematical algorithm used, that is, the order of the logic used to solve the problem.

The U.S. Patent and Trademark Office is considering the possibility of making computer programs patentable inventions. In the past, patents were granted only to ideas that were new, useful, and innovative. Many people believe that computer program ideas are not innovative, and so not patentable, because they are based on mathematical algorithms. The software patent idea is still in the early stages of consideration by the office.

OPERATING SYSTEMS

In early computer systems, human operators monitored computer operations, determined the order in which submitted programs were run (the priority), and readied input and output devices. While early electronic development increased the processing speeds of CPUs, the speed of human operators remained constant. Time delays and errors caused by human operator intervention became a serious problem.

Development of Operating Systems

In the 1960s, **operating systems,** which are a collection of system programs, were developed to help overcome this problem. An operating system is used by the computer to manage its own operations. This approach provides a control system that can operate at computer speeds. Instead of a human operator preparing the I/O devices to be used for each program and loading the programs into storage, the operating system assumes responsibility for all jobs to be run.

Functions of Operating Systems

The functions of an operating system are geared toward attaining maximum efficiency in processing operations. Eliminating human intervention is one method. Allowing several programs to share computer resources is another; the operating system allocates these resources to the programs requesting them and resolves conflicts that occur when, for example, two or three programs request the use of the same tape drive of primary storage locations. In addition, the operating system performs an accounting function—it keeps track of all resource usage so that user fees can be determined and the efficiency of CPU utilization evaluated.

Another important function performed by the operating system is scheduling jobs on a priority basis. Although it may seem logical to run programs in the order in which they are submitted, this is not always the most practical approach. For instance, assume five programs are submitted for processing within a short period of time. Suppose one program requires one minute of CPU time and the other four require one hour each. It may be reasonable to process the short program first. Or suppose one program will produce a vital report and the others' output is less important. The more important program should probably be processed first. A system of priorities can be established based on considerations such as the required processing time and the need for the expected output.

Types of Processing Handled by Operating Systems

There are two basic types of operating systems: **batch** and **online.** In a batch processing environment, several user programs (jobs or job steps) are grouped into a batch and processed one after the other in a continuous stream. For example, in the morning an operator may load all jobs to be processed during the day onto a tape drive and enter them into the system. The batch operating system will direct processing without interruption until all jobs are complete, thus freeing the operator to perform other tasks.

An online operating system can respond to spontaneous requests for system resources, such as management inquiries entered from online terminals.

Operating systems currently in use on mainframe and minicomputer systems can handle both batch and online applications simultaneously. These operating systems direct the processing of a job but also respond to **interrupts** from I/O devices such as online terminals, printers, and secondary storage devices which must communicate with the CPU through the operating system. When an I/O device sends a message to the CPU, normal processing is suspended (the CPU is interrupted) so that the CPU may direct the operation of the I/O device. It is the function of the operating system, therefore, to manage the resources of the CPU in its handling of batch and online processing and its control of peripheral devices.

COMPONENTS OF OPERATING SYSTEMS

An operating system is an integrated collection of subsystems. Each subsystem consists of programs that perform specific duties (see Figure 8–1). Since all operating system programs work as a "team," CPU idle time is avoided and utilization of computer facilities is increased. Operating system programs are usually stored on a secondary storage device known as the **system residence device.** The secondary devices most commonly used are magnetic tape (TOS—tape operating system) and magnetic disk (DOS—disk operating system). Magnetic-drum technology allows for the fastest processing times, but many existing operating systems use magnetic-disk technology.

Two types of programs make up the operating system: **control programs** and **processing programs.** Control programs oversee system operations and perform tasks such as input/output, scheduling, handling interrupts, and communicating with the computer operator or programmers. Processing programs

Figure 8–1 ▪ Operating System in Primary Storage and System Residence Device

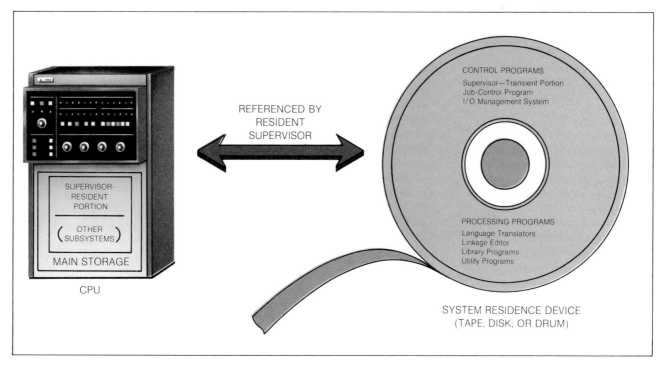

REFERENCED BY RESIDENT SUPERVISOR

SUPERVISOR-RESIDENT PORTION

(OTHER SUBSYSTEMS)

MAIN STORAGE

CPU

CONTROL PROGRAMS

Supervisor—Transient Portion
Job-Control Program
I/O Management System

PROCESSING PROGRAMS

Language Translators
Linkage Editor
Library Programs
Utility Programs

SYSTEM RESIDENCE DEVICE
(TAPE, DISK, OR DRUM)

are executed under the supervision of control programs and are used by the programmer to simplify program preparation for the computer system.

Control Programs

The **supervisor program** (also called the monitor or executive), the major component of the operating system, coordinates the activities of all other parts of the operating system. When the computer is first put into use, the supervisor is the first program to be transferred into primary storage from the system residence device. Only the most frequently used components of the supervisor are initially loaded into primary storage. These components are referred to as **resident routines.** Certain other supervisor routines, known as **transient routines,** remain in secondary storage with the remainder of the operating system. Supervisor routines call for these nonresident system programs as needed and load them into primary storage. The supervisor schedules I/O operations and allocates channels to various I/O devices. It also sends messages to the computer operator indicating the status of particular jobs, error conditions, and so on.

The operating system requires job-control information in order to perform its mission. (A *job* is a task to be processed by the CPU.) A **job-control language (JCL)** serves as the communication link between the programmer and the operating system. Job-control statements are used to identify the beginning of a job, to identify the specific program to be executed, to describe the work to be done, and to indicate the I/O devices required. The **job-control program** translates the job-control statements written by a programmer into machine-language instructions that can be executed by the computer.

In most computer systems, the data to be processed is stored on high-speed input devices such as magnetic-tape units or disk units. In these systems, job-control statements are entered from an input device other than the device in which the data is stored. For example, the JCL may be entered as a series of statements from magnetic tape as shown in Figure 8–2a. Among other things, these statements specify which data files and I/O devices are required.

In other systems, programs and data are read into storage from the same device used to submit the JCL (see Figure 8–2b). No additional I/O devices are required in this instance, but it is not an efficient method for processing large programs or data files. This method is most often used when programs are being tested, before they are stored on secondary storage devices. Figure 8–3 is a sample JCL used to translate a COBOL program (to machine readable form—1s and 0s) which reads transactions (program data), processes them against a test master file, and prints the results on a line printer.

The first statement uniquely identifies the job and indicates what system messages will be displayed concerning the translation. The second statement identifies the particular step of the overall job and invokes the COBOL language translator. Although this JCL contains only one step, multiple steps can be contained in a single job, as demonstrated in Figure 8–2. The third statement identifies the beginning of the COBOL source program, and the fourth statement identifies the beginning of the program data. The source program would be placed between statements three and four and the data between statements four and five. Statement five defines the master file to be used which, in this case, is a disk file. The final statement simply identifies the line printer as the output device.

A job is often thought of as a single program entered by a user into the computer. In fact, most data-processing jobs require the execution of many

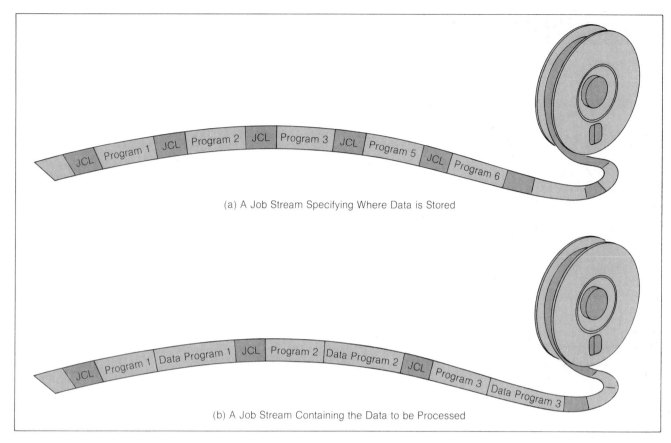

(a) A Job Stream Specifying Where Data is Stored

(b) A Job Stream Containing the Data to be Processed

Figure 8–2 ■ **Continuous Job Streams for a Batch Processing System**

related programs. For example, processing a weekly payroll job may require that programs execute the following tasks:

1. Entering the payroll cards through a card reader, editing the data, and transferring the information to tape.
2. Sorting the records into some order, such as by employee number.
3. Matching the resultant transaction file with the master payroll file.
4. Processing the matched data to produce payroll checks, a payroll check register, and various payroll reports.

Thus, several job-control statements are needed to indicate which operations are to be performed and the devices needed to perform them.

The control programs of the operating system must be able to control and coordinate the CPU while receiving input from channels, executing instructions of programs in storage, and regulating output. I/O devices must be assigned to specific programs, and data must be moved between them and

Figure 8–3 ■ **Sample JCL**

```
//PAY JOB ACCT, '***PAYROLL***', MSGLEVEL=(1,1)
//STEP1 EXEC COBVCG
//COB. SYSIN DD *

//GO. SYSIN DD *

//GO.FILE1 DD DSN=MASTER.FILE , DISP = SHR
//GO.OUTPUT DD SYSOUT=A
```

Game Story

Arcade games have increased in complexity since the days when Defender and Pac Man first appeared. Defender was created by two men, Eugene Jarvis and Sam Dicker, in a very short time. Today, dozens of individuals may be involved in the successful development of a single video game.

Williams Electronics followed an involved series of steps before they released the game Sinister on the market. The plot for the game was created at a brainstorming session with a dozen of the company's top people. After the plot was developed, a team of graphic artists created a storyboard (a detailed game outline) and then began making sketches of the game characters, while hardware specialists determined memory requirements and chip arrangements. Next, each section of the game was assigned to a different programmer for programming. A software designer created a program that linked the game sections together.

The above steps took months to complete. Following the design process, the game was tested in an arcade. Problem areas were identified and corrected before full-scale production began. A year after the initial brainstorming session, Sinister appeared in the arcades.

specific memory locations. The **input/output management system** oversees and coordinates these processes.

Processing Programs

The operating system contains several processing programs that facilitate efficient processing operations by simplifying program preparation and execution for users. The major processing programs contained in the operating system are the language translators, linkage editor, library programs, and utility programs.

Application programs are seldom (if ever) written in machine language, because of the complexity and time that would be required to write them. Instead, most programs are written in a language closely resembling English. A **language-translator program,** as its name implies, translates English-like programs written by programmers into machine-language instructions (1s and 0s).

A number of application programming languages are available; common examples include FORTRAN, COBOL, BASIC, AND PL/I (all discussed more fully in Chapter 10). The programmer must specify (in a job-control statement) the language in which a program is written. When the program is to be executed, the job-control program interprets that job-control statement and informs the supervisor which language translator is needed. The supervisor then calls the appropriate language translator from the system residence device. The language translator converts the program (called the **source program**) into machine language so it can be executed.

The translated application program (called the **object program**) is often placed on the system residence device until the supervisor calls for it to be loaded into primary storage for execution. It is the task of the **linkage editor** to "link" the object program from the system residence device to primary storage. It does this by assigning appropriate primary storage addresses to each byte of the object program.

Library programs are user-written or manufacturer-supplied programs and subroutines that are frequently used in other programs. So that these routines will not have to be rewritten every time they are needed, they are stored in a **system library** (usually on magnetic disk or tape) and called into primary storage when needed. They are then linked together with other programs to perform specific tasks. A **librarian program** manages the storage and use of library programs by maintaining a directory of programs in the system library; it also contains appropriate procedures for adding and deleting programs.

Operating systems also include a set of **utility programs** that perform specialized functions. One such program transfers data from file to file, or from one I/O device to another. For example, a utility program can be used to transfer data from tape to tape, tape to disk, card to tape, or tape to printer. Other utility programs, known as **sort/merge programs,** are used to sort records into a particular sequence to facilitate updating of files. Once sorted, several files can be merged to form a single, updated file. Job-control statements are used to specify the sort/merge programs; these programs or routines are then called into primary storage when needed.

Additional Software

As mentioned at the beginning of the chapter, system programs are available from a variety of sources. Each data-processing department must decide which subsystems to include in its operating system. The original operating system is usually obtained from the manufacturer of the CPU. However, in some cases alternative operating systems may be purchased from software vendors.

Once the essential operating system has been purchased, optional subsystems may be obtained. These subsystems either improve an existing subsystem or provide additional capabilities to the operating system. For example, the operating system for a bank's computer might be supplemented with a subsystem to interface with MICR equipment (discussed in Chapter 4). Applications requiring the use of light pens with display terminals also demand special subsystems.

■ **Operating systems** were developed in the 1960s to take advantage of a computer's speed. An operating system allows the computer to manage its own operations rather than requiring human intervention.
■ Operating systems handle two types of processing: **batch processing** and **on-line processing.**
■ Operating system programs are normally stored on a secondary storage device (usually a magnetic disk) called a **system residence device.**
■ The **supervisor program** coordinates the activities of all other parts of the operating system, which include the **language-translator programs, library programs,** and **utility programs.**

MULTIPROGRAMMING

When the CPU is very active, the system as a whole is more efficient. However, the CPU frequently must remain idle because I/O devices are not fast enough. The CPU can operate on only one instruction at a time; furthermore, it cannot operate on data that is not in primary storage. If an input device is slow in providing data or instructions, the CPU must wait until I/O operations have been completed before executing a program.

In the earliest computer systems with simple operating systems, most programs were executed using **serial processing**—they were executed one at a time. Serial processing was terribly inefficient because the high-speed CPU was idle for long periods of time as slow input devices loaded data or output devices printed or stored the results.

Multiprogramming increases CPU active time by effectively allocating computer resources and offsetting low I/O speeds. Under multiprogramming, several programs reside in the primary storage unit at the same time. Although the CPU still can execute only one instruction at a time, it can execute instructions from one program, then another, then another, and back to the first again. Instructions from one program are executed until an interrupt for either input or output is generated. The I/O operation is handled by a channel, and the CPU can shift its attention to another program in memory until that program requires input or output. This rotation occurs so quickly that the execution of the programs in storage appears to be simultaneous. More precisely, the CPU executes the different programs **concurrently,** which means "over the same period of time." This process is often referred to as **overlapped processing,** and is illustrated in Figure 8–4.

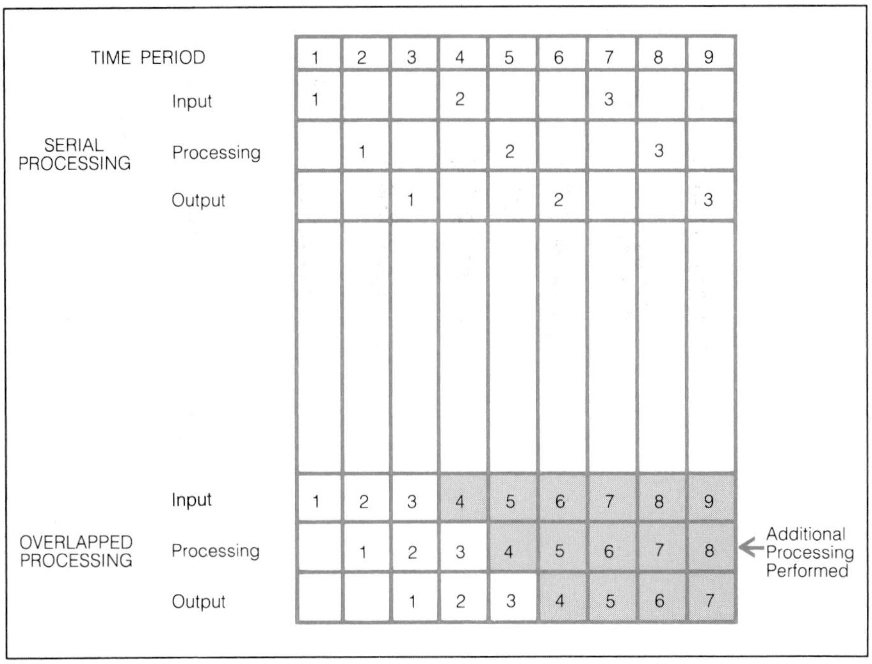

Figure 8–4 ▪ **Comparison of Serial and Overlapped Processing**

Although multiprogramming increases the system's flexibility and efficiency, it also creates some problems. First, the programs in primary storage must be kept separate. This is accomplished through the use of **regions** or **partitions.** Keeping programs in the correct region or partition is known as **memory management,** or **memory protection.** A similar situation exists with I/O devices—two programs cannot access the same tape or disk drive at the same time. These problems are handled by operating system control programs.

A second problem that arises with multiprogramming is the need to schedule programs to determine which will receive service first. This requires that each program be assigned a priority. In a time-sharing system, the programs being used for online processing must be capable of responding immediately to users at remote locations. Thus, these programs are assigned the highest priority. The highest-priority programs are loaded into **foreground partitions** and are called **foreground programs.** Programs of lowest priority are loaded into **background partitions** and are called **background programs** (see Figure 8–5). Background programs are typically executed in batch mode. When a foreground program is interrupted for input or output, control is transferred to another foreground program of equal or lower priority or to a background program.

For large systems with several foreground and background programs, scheduling is not a simple task. Two programs of the same priority may request CPU resources at the same time. The method of deciding which program gets control first may be arbitrary; for example, the program that has been in primary storage longer may receive control first. Fortunately, the operating system is capable of handling such problems as they occur, and in most instances makes the process of multiprogramming invisible to the user.

Figure 8–5 ▪ Foreground and Background Programs in a Multiprogramming Environment

MAIN STORAGE

Supervisor Program

Foreground Program

Foreground Program

Background Program

Background Program

Other Programs

VIRTUAL STORAGE

Multiprogramming increases system efficiency because the CPU can concurrently execute programs instead of waiting for I/O operations to occur. A limitation of multiprogramming, however, is that each partition must be large enough to hold an entire program; the program remains in memory until its execution is completed.

Another limitation of this approach is that all the instructions of a program are kept in primary storage throughout its execution, whether they are needed or not. Yet, a large program may contain many sequences of instructions that are executed infrequently. For example, the program may consist of several logical sections, but most of the processing may be done by only one or two of them. While this processing occurs, those not being used are occupying primary storage that could otherwise be used more efficiently. As processing requirements increase, the physical limitations of memory become a critical constraint, and the productive use of memory becomes increasingly important.

For many years, the space limitations of primary storage have been a barrier to applications. Programmers have spent much time trying to find ways to trim the size of programs so that they could fit into available primary storage space. In some cases, attempts have been made to segment programs (break them into separate modules) so that they could be executed in separate job steps; but doing this manually is both tedious and time consuming. While hardware costs have decreased and storage capacities have increased, this storage problem still exists in high-volume processing systems that require large programs.

To alleviate the problem, an extension of multiprogramming called **virtual storage** (sometimes called **virtual memory**) has been developed. Virtual storage is based on the principle that only the immediately needed portion of a program be in primary storage at any given time; the rest of the program and data can be kept in secondary storage. Since only part of a program is in primary storage at one time, more programs can reside in primary storage simultaneously, allowing more programs to be executed within a given time period. This gives the illusion that primary storage is unlimited.

To implement virtual storage, a direct-access secondary storage device such as a magnetic-disk unit is used to augment primary storage. The term **real storage** is usually given to primary storage within the CPU, while virtual storage refers to the direct-access storage (see Figure 8–6). Both real and virtual storage locations are given addresses by the operating system. If data or instructions needed are not in the real storage area, the portion of the program containing them is transferred from virtual storage into real storage, while another portion currently in real storage may be written back to virtual storage. This process is known as **swapping.** If the portion of the program in real storage has not been modified during execution, the portion from virtual

Figure 8–6 ▪ Schematic Drawing of Virtual Storage and Swapping

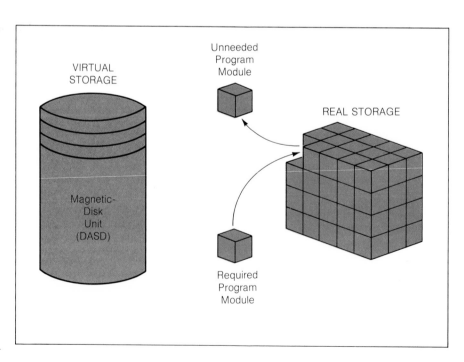

storage may be simply laid over it, because copies of all parts of the program are kept in virtual storage.

There are two main methods of implementing virtual-storage systems, both of which use a combination of hardware and software to accomplish the task. The first method is called **segmentation.** Each program is broken into variable-size blocks called **segments** which are logical parts of the program. For example, one segment may contain data used by the program; another segment may contain a **subroutine** of the program; and so on. The operating system software allocates storage space according to the size of these logical segments.

A second method of implementing virtual storage is called **paging.** Here, primary storage is divided into physical areas of fixed size called **page frames.** All page frames for all programs are the same size, and this size depends on the characteristics of the particular computer. In contrast to segmentation, paging does not consider the logical portions of the programs. Instead, the programs are broken into equal-size blocks called **pages.** One page can fit in one page frame of primary storage (see Figure 8–7).

In both paging and segmentation, the operating system handles the swapping of pages or segments whenever a portion of the program that is not in real storage is needed during processing.

Virtual storage offers tremendous flexibility to programmers and systems analysts designing new applications; they can devote their time to solving the problem at hand rather than to fitting programs into storage. Moreover, as already explained, the use of primary storage is optimized, since only needed portions of programs are in primary storage at any time.

One of the major limitations of virtual storage is the requirement for extensive online secondary storage. Also, the virtual-storage operating system is highly sophisticated and requires significant amounts of internal storage. If virtual storage is not used wisely, much time can be spent locating and ex-

Figure 8–7 ▪ Paging

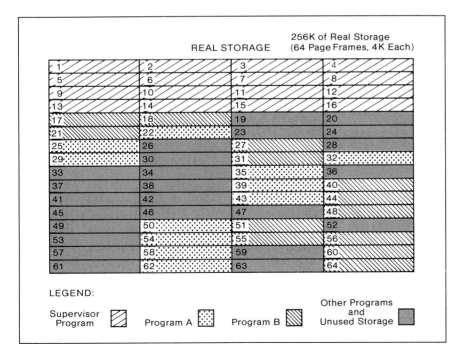

REAL STORAGE — 256K of Real Storage (64 Page Frames, 4K Each)

LEGEND:

Supervisor Program   Program A   Program B   Other Programs and Unused Storage

- **Multiprogramming** increases CPU efficiency by executing instructions of a program while another program's I/O operations are being handled by a channel. This reduces CPU idle time significantly.
- Multiprogramming is accomplished by using **partitions** or **regions** in primary storage to keep programs separate. This partitioning of memory is known as **memory management** or **memory protection.**
- The highest-priority programs are held in primary storage in **foreground partitions.** Lower-priority programs are held in **background partitions.**
- **Virtual storage** is an extension of multiprogramming that gives the impression that primary storage is unlimited in size. Portions of programs are stored on secondary storage devices and brought into primary storage when required using this concept.
- Two methods of implementing virtual storage are **segmentation** and **paging.**

changing program pages or segments; in some programs, little actual processing occurs compared with the amount of swapping. (This is known as **thrashing**.)

MULTIPROCESSING

Multiprocessing involves the use of two or more CPUs linked together for coordinated operation. Stored-program instructions are executed simultaneously, but by different CPUs. The CPUs may execute different instructions from the same program, or they may execute totally different programs. (In contrast, under multiprogramming, the computer appears to be processing different jobs simultaneously but is actually processing them concurrently.)

Multiprocessing systems are designed to achieve a particular objective. One common objective is to relieve a large CPU of tasks such as scheduling, editing data, and maintaining files so that it can continue high-priority or complex processing without interruption. To do this, a small CPU (often a minicomputer) is linked to the large CPU. All work coming into the system from remote terminals or other peripheral devices is first channeled through the small CPU, which coordinates the activities of the large one. Generally, the small CPU handles all I/O interrupts and so on, while the large CPU handles the "number crunching" (large mathematical calculations). A schematic diagram of this type of multiprocessing system is shown in Figure 8–8. The small CPU in Figure 8–8 is commonly referred to as a **front-end processor.** It is an interface between the large CPU and peripheral devices such as online terminals.

A small CPU may also be used as an interface between a large CPU and a large data base stored on direct-access storage devices. In this case, the small CPU, often termed a **back-end processor,** is solely responsible for maintaining the data base. Accessing data and updating specific data fields are typical functions a small CPU performs in this type of multiprocessing system.

Many large multiprocessing systems have two or more large CPUs. These large CPUs are no different than those used in single-CPU (stand-alone) configurations. Each may have its own separate memory, or a single memory may be shared by all of them. The activities of each CPU can be controlled

Figure 8–8 ▪ Multiprocessing System with Small Front-End Processor and Large Mainframe

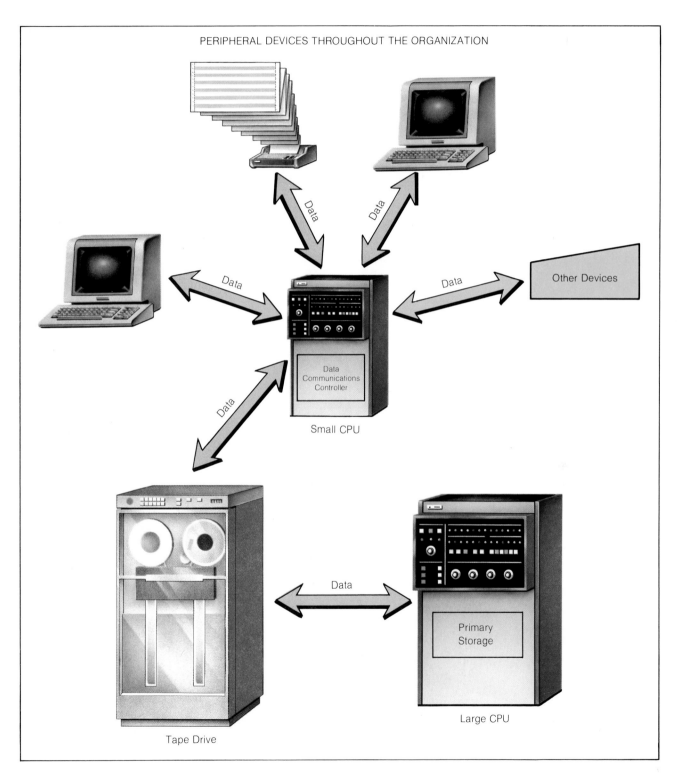

PERIPHERAL DEVICES THROUGHOUT THE ORGANIZATION

Data

Data

Data

Data

Other Devices

Data Communications Controller

Small CPU

Data

Tape Drive

Data

Primary Storage

Large CPU

Figure 8–9 ▪ **Multiprocessing**
System Using Multiple Large CPUs

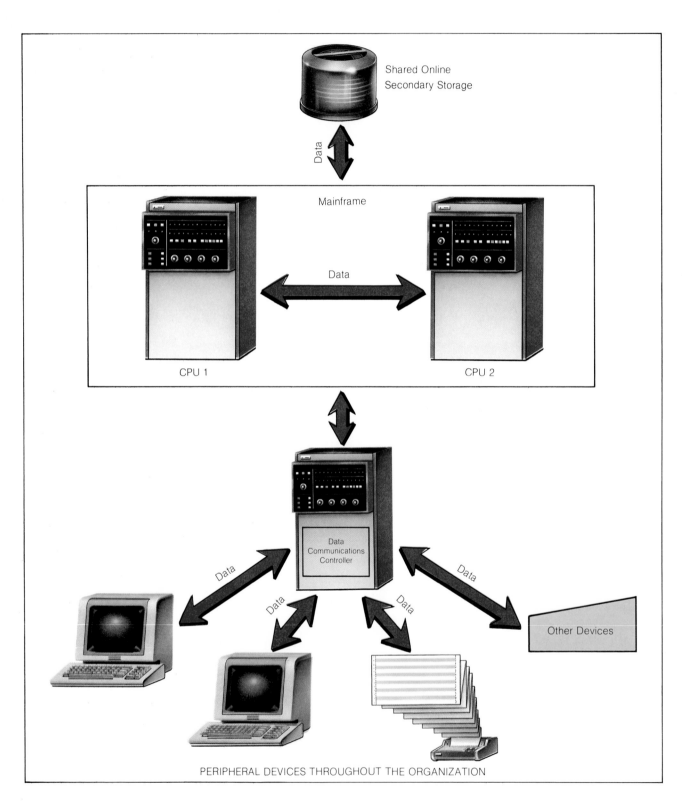

Shared Online Secondary Storage

Data

Mainframe

CPU 1

Data

CPU 2

Data Communications Controller

Data

Data

Data

Data

Other Devices

PERIPHERAL DEVICES THROUGHOUT THE ORGANIZATION

in whole or in part by a common supervisor program. This type of system is used by organizations with extremely large and complex data-processing needs. Each large CPU may be dedicated to a specific task such as I/O processing or arithmetic processing. One CPU can be set up to handle online processing while another handles only batch processing. Alternately, two CPUs may be used together on the same task to provide rapid responses in the most demanding applications. Many multiprocessing systems are designed so that one or more of the CPUs can provide backup if another malfunctions. A configuration that uses multiple large CPUs is depicted in Figure 8–9. This system also uses a small CPU to control communications with peripheral devices and perform ''housekeeping chores'' (input editing, validation, and the like).

Coordinating the efforts of several CPUs requires highly sophisticated software and careful planning. The scheduling of workloads for the CPUs involves making the most efficient use of computer resources. Implementing such a system is a time-consuming endeavor that may require the services of outside consultants as well as those provided by the equipment manufacturers. The payoff from this effort is a system with capabilities extending far beyond those of a single-CPU system.

SUMMARY POINTS

■ A program is a series of step-by-step instructions required to solve a problem. Application programs solve user problems, whereas system programs coordinate the operation of all computer circuitry.

■ System programs are generally provided by the computer manufacturer or a specialized programming firm. Application programs can be developed within the organization or purchased from a software firm.

■ An operating system is a collection of programs designed to permit a computer system to manage its own operations. It allocates computer resources among multiple users, keeps track of all information required for accounting purposes, and establishes job priorities.

■ Batch operating systems allow uninterrupted processing of a batch of jobs without operator intervention. Online operating systems can respond to spontaneous requests for system resources, such as management inquiries entered from online terminals. Operating systems that handle both batch and online applications are standard.

■ An operating system consists of control programs and processing programs stored on the system residence device. The supervisor program, the major component of the operating system, controls the other subsystems.

■ A job-control language (JCL) is the communication link between the programmer and the operating system. Job-control statements identify the beginning of a job, identify the specific program to be executed, and describe the work to be done.

■ The input/output management system is part of the operating system control programs. It receives input from channels, regulates output, assigns I/O devices to specific programs, and coordinates all I/O activities.

■ Language translators convert English-like programs into machine-language instructions.

■ Library programs consist of programs and subroutines frequently used in other programs; they are stored in a system library (usually on magnetic tape or disk) and called into primary storage when needed.

■ The linkage editor links the object program on the system residence device to primary storage by assigning appropriate primary storage addresses to each byte of the object program.

■ Utility programs perform specialized functions like sorting and merging and transferring data from one I/O device to another.

■ Operating systems can be developed in a modular fashion by addition of components to the original operating system.

■ The CPU may be idle for a significant amount of time because of the speed disparity between the CPU and I/O devices. Multiprogramming is used to increase the efficiency of CPU utilization.

■ With multiprogramming, several programs reside in the primary storage unit at the same time. Instructions from one program are executed until an interrupt for either input or output is generated. Then the CPU shifts attention to another program in memory until the program requires input and output.

■ When multiprogramming is used, the programs in primary storage are kept separate by use of partitions or regions. Memory protection and a method of assigning priorities to programs are required. High-priority programs are loaded into foreground partitions, and low-priority programs are loaded into background partitions.

■ Multiprogramming is limited by primary storage space limitations. A complete program may not fit into a partition; also segments of some programs may take up space but be executed infrequently. These problems are alleviated by use of virtual storage.

■ Virtual storage involves loading only the part of a program needed in primary storage, while keeping the remainder of the program in secondary storage. This gives the illusion that primary storage is unlimited.

■ Segmentation is a method of implementing virtual storage whereby each program is broken into segments of variable size. Each segment is a logical subunit of the complete program. Paging, another method of implementing virtual storage, uses equal-size blocks called pages without considering logical parts of the program.

■ Multiprocessing involves the use of two or more CPUs linked together for coordinated operation. Separate programs or separate parts of the same program can be processed simultaneously by different CPUs.

■ Small computers can be linked to mainframes as either front-end processors or back-end processors. The former act as interfaces between the CPU and I/O devices; the latter act as interfaces between large CPUs and data bases stored on direct-access storage devices.

■ Large CPUs can be linked together to handle extremely large and complex data-processing needs. Each CPU may be assigned to a specific task, or it may be used with other CPUs on the same task to provide rapid response.

REVIEW QUESTIONS

1. Distinguish between application programs and system programs. Give examples of each and explain why they belong in that particular category.

2. What are the major functions performed by an operating system? Is an operating system that can handle batch processing more complex and sophisticated than one that allows online processing? Explain.

3. What are the major components of an operating system? Briefly explain the functions of each component.

4. What is the function of the supervisor program?

5. What is the primary purpose of a job-control language?

6. Distinguish between a source program and an object program.

7. Why is a language translator important to an application programmer?

8. Who is most likely to use utility programs and why?

9. Distinguish between multiprogramming and multiprocessing. What are some of the problems that must be solved in a multiprogramming environment?

10. What is the purpose of placing programs in either foreground or background partitions of memory?

11. Why were virtual-storage systems developed? Compare and contrast the two techniques—segmentation and paging—used to implement virtual-storage capabilities.

12. A corporation is implementing a large data-base management system that can respond to inquiries from online terminals. What multiprocessing configuration would be most suitable for this application?

The cash register was invented in 1879 by a Dayton cafe owner, James Ritty, and his brother John. By 1883, the National Manufacturing Company had been formed to manufacture the new device. John H. Patterson, who was using two cash registers in his small store in Coalton, Ohio, found that they proved to be the difference between operating at a loss and making a profit. Patterson bought twenty-five shares of stock in the National Manufacturing Company. He became its secretary and a member of the board of directors; and in 1884, he purchased a controlling interest and changed the company's name to the National Cash Register Company.

Patterson's first factory employed thirteen people and produced as many as five cash registers a week. By 1900, the company's registers were widely used throughout the United States and overseas. Today, almost a hundred years later, the corporation employs 65,000 people and has sales and service facilities in more than a hundred countries.

To more accurately reflect the corporation's expanded activities, the board of directors changed the company's name in 1974 from the National Cash Register Company to the NCR Corporation. While NCR is still involved in the design and manufacture of retail systems, its market has expanded to encompass many other types of products.

NCR Corporation today is a multinational organization engaged in developing, producing, marketing, and servicing business equipment and computer systems. Its product line includes electronic data-processing systems; electronic point-of-sale terminals for retail stores and financial institutions; a variety of data-entry and retrieval terminals; communication equipment such as modems, adapters, concentrators, etc.; individual free-standing business equipment; business forms; supplies; and related accessories. In addition, NCR has recently acquired a communications firm in St. Paul, Minnesota, called COMTEN, and a firm named ADDS (Applied Digital Data Systems) that specializes in general-purpose CRTs, and a firm called DPI (Data Pathing

Inc.) that specializes in manufacturing control terminals and systems.

MISSION

NRC develops application software as well as system software to support its equipment. A major new application is NCR MISSION (Manufacturing Information System Support Integrated On-Line). One of the largest applications ever undertaken by the company, MISSION can be used as a single- or multiple-plant system for the complete control of an industrial company's manufacturing operations. This application requires the use of a data-base management system and a transaction processor. The DBMS used is CINCOM's TOTAL. The transaction processor (communications monitor) was developed by the MCS organization and is called TRAN-PRO.

Numerous NCR plants across the nation and abroad are involved in the design and manufacture of hardware and software for NCR products. The plants are decentralized; each has a separate management information system (MIS) department to support it and produce the systems it needs. In an attempt to incorporate all common manufacturing systems used by the plants, a group called the manufacturing control system (MCS) was formed to oversee all the MIS departments. This overall MIS function was staffed with application programmers from outside the company to bring ideas to NCR. The group interviewed the plant managers to determine their individual needs and found these needs to be not only common among NCR management but also similar to those found in any type of manufacturing plant. The MCS group broke the system into subunits and assigned these subunits to separate plants for development. The design of system files, transaction processing, and I/O interfaces was required.

A design review committee of user personnel from three plants was established to evaluate the design and documentation produced by the various developing plants and to ensure that the systems satisfied user

specifications. After the final design was agreed on, the MIS department within each plant proceeded with application programming.

The total system design includes many application modules that work together and draw upon common resources. Eight of these modules, or subsystems, have been completed: the Bill of Material, Material Management, Inventory Management, Cost, Routing, Order Processing, Capacity Requirements Planning, and Material Requirements Planning.

The only difference between MISSION and an application designed specifically for customer use is that MISSION was originally designed for use in NCR's own manufacturing plants. Therefore, the system had to go through the tests given to systems designed for sale to customers before it was approved for use. The first of these tests is known as BETA test. For MISSION, it was a complete in-house system test of the completed application subsystems. This was followed by GAMMA test, which ensures the quality of the application. The final procedure was the Customer Verification Test (CVT). Normally, the system is installed in a user site for this test; in the case of MISSION, the system was installed in one of NCR's plants.

Because MISSION's debut was successful, the completed subsystems have been made available to NCR customers. Each application subsystem is made up of 25 to 200 separate programs; for example, the Bill of Materials application contains 100 separate programs, half of which accept input from online terminals.

VRX

Since its debut, MISSION has been converted to run under VRX (Virtual Resource Executive). VRX is a group of software modules comprising an operating system that allows multiprogramming, virtual storage, and multiple virtual machine capabilities.

In a multiprogramming environment, VRX schedules and runs up to thirty-five jobs concurrently. Real memory, processor time, and peripheral use are automatically allocated, and the user can exercise as much or as little control over job processing as needed.

The VRX handles a virtual storage environment by assigning currently active portions of virtual storage to real memory. The virtual memory, which is stored on a high-speed, random-access peripheral device, is divided into pages. The entire virtual storage operation is transparent to the application running in the system; that is, the programs are totally unaware of the environments created for them.

The virtual machine capabilities make it possible to tailor a system to operate on a specific programming language. The language compiler translates the source code into an intermediate, object-level code that is interpreted by firmware (small hardware chips that contain complete programs). In most cases, one source-code instruction (which usually requires many object-level commands) translates to one object-level command. Therefore, programs are compiled and executed much faster and far more efficiently than on machines that are not language oriented.

DISCUSSION POINTS

1. Describe how the VRX software allows the virtual machine capabilities. What are the advantages of a language-oriented computer system? What are the disadvantages?
2. What are the advantages of purchasing an applications package such as MISSION instead of developing it in-house? What are the disadvantages?

9

Programming and Software Development

INTRODUCTION

People often solve problems intuitively, without having to identify each step they use. Computers lack this human capability. Therefore, using a computer to help solve a problem requires a lot of planning. All the steps required to solve the problem must be identified and coded into a logical instruction sequence—a program—before the computer can be used to perform the computations and get the correct result.

This chapter identifies and discusses the five stages involved in developing a program: defining the problem; designing a solution; writing the program; compiling, debuggin, and testing the program; and documenting the program. The chapter explains the four traditional, basic patterns of program logic that can be used to solve any problem and also discusses pseudocode and flowcharts. Special considerations in solution design and a programming case study are also included in the chapter.

A visually impaired computer programmer for the Federal Aviation Administration is succeeding in the sighted world by using a closed-circuit television system that enlarges print to 60 times its normal size.

A legally blind computer support analyst for the Electric Power Research Institute flourishes in his position through the aid of a Versa-Braille device (a Braille word processor) and an Optocon instrument, a book-sized mechanism that scans a printed page and translates it into vibrations the user can decipher.

A 29-year-old foreign affairs analyst who has been blind since the age of three is thriving in a competitive electronics firm by means of the Braille word processor and a "talking" computer that turns the written word on the display into speech.

These are but three of nearly 400 blind, deaf or otherwise handicapped individuals prospering in the competitive work world as a result of special technological devices and training coordinated by the Sensory Aids Foundation (SAF), a Palo Alto, CA-based nonprofit organization. This year alone at least 50 handicapped people have found jobs or have been able to retain their jobs as a result of the SAF's work, according to Susan Phillips, SAF director of employment programs.

Handicapped Now Competitive

"Technology is opening up a new world for disabled workers, who at long last can be genuinely competitive with the non-handicapped working population," says Phillips.

Phillips acts as a coordinator between those seeking employment and participating companies. In many instances, this requires her to first analyze the work site and the specific nature of the potential employee's disability, and then recommend appropriate aids for the job. These sometimes expensive devices are made available to the employee through the employing company's funds or from the California Dept. of Rehabilitation.

The foundation was started in 1973 by Marjorie Linville, the wife of a Stanford electrical engineering professor, as a result of the Linvilles' own struggle to help their blind daughter achieve independence and career fulfillment. The daughter, Candy Linville, lost her sight when eight months old.

Her father embarked on seven years of research to develop the Optocon, an electronic device that "reads" ordinary printed material and translates it into vibrating images the user can feel with the index finger. An invaluable aid now used by more than 9,000 people worldwide, the Optocon enabled Candy to graduate from Stanford University with a PhD in clinical psychology and to pursue a successful career in her field.

SAF Expands

"The SAF organization was originally started to provide low-interest loans to handicapped users wanting to purchase the Optocon device, but the group has since expanded its efforts to job placement for people with a whole range of disabilities," notes Phillips.

For example, research is now underway on a speech recognition device that would enable the deaf to interact normally in the world of sound. Dubbed the "Vidvox" system (Latin for "I see a voice"), the electronic gadget would display a stream of phonetic symbols to the viewer while a speaker talked into the machine. Thus the deaf person could "read" what someone was saying. By all accounts it is an enormously ambitious project.

"We're only in the early stages of development on the Vidvox and probably will not see the fruition of it for several more years," says Phillips. "But we think it may pave the way to employment for many people who would otherwise be hopelessly dependent on government support—and that's what we're all about."

Reprinted from INFOSYSTEMS January 1984. Copyright Hitchcock Publishing Company.

Because of the enormous number of ways computer technology can be used to assist us in our pursuits, programming and software development have become critical factors in developing useful computer systems. Presented with the problem of designing a program to help a handicapped person requires a problem-solving methodology that leads to the development of software that guides the computer in its efforts to aid the handicapped individual.

Most people think computers are cold, calculating machines. In all fairness to computers, they are. They process tax returns and paychecks with equal impartiality. Computers have no emotion, independent thought, or voluntary action. How is it, then, that computers have come to dominate our present-day business society?

From the beginning, this book has described the computer as a machine that is incredibly fast and accurate but has an IQ of zero. It performs step by step only what it has been told to do. On the one hand, this appears to limit the tasks that computers can perform; on the other hand, it suggests that computers are limited only by people's ability to break down a problem into steps that computers can use to solve it. As economist Leo Cherne suggested, "The computer is incredibly fast, accurate, and stupid. Man is unbelievably slow, inaccurate, and brilliant. The marriage of the two is a force beyond calculation."

The evolution of the computer from the first mechanical machine to the vastly complex electronic marvel of today is a tale of human ingenuity. When it appeared that computer applications would be limited because all instructions had to be coded in machine language, someone devised a method of having the computer itself translate English-like commands into its own language. When this middle-level language in turn became cumbersome, several higher-level languages were developed. All these innovations did nothing more than make it easier for humans to give instructions to the computer.

The previous chapter introduced system programs that help the computer to manage its own operations. These programs are designed, written, and maintained by programmers. If a computer is able to oversee its vastly complex operations, it is only because someone has been able to understand what operations were required and how they were to be performed and has then programmed the computer to execute them. This chapter discusses the sometimes complicated task of breaking down a problem and its solution into the logical series of steps required for computer problem solving.

COMPUTER
PROBLEM SOLVING

As any seasoned programmer will tell you, the computer does not "solve" problems the way we do. Humans solve problems by using reason, intelligence, and intuition. Computers solve problems according to instructions provided by programmers. Any "intelligence" the computer seems to possess is given to it by these programmers. At present, the computer cannot even take general instructions like "calculate each employee's net pay" and turn them into programmatically correct statements it can use to perform the task. Instead, the computer has to be told how to calculate an employee's net pay, step by step. It is nothing more than an overgrown calculator!

Each program, then, has to be well thought out. Instructions must be ordered in a logical sequence. The problem must be analyzed to such a level of detail that all logical conditions that may be encountered during processing are anticipated in advance. If an unanticipated condition arises during processing, the program will be executed incorrectly or, in some cases, not at all.

Problem-Solving Process

When programs were first written, there were few rules for programmers to follow because there were few things computers could do. Today, however, with the vast array of programming languages, processing techniques, storage devices, and printing media, a programmer is well advised to use a structured approach to problem solving and program development. Five steps have been found helpful in this process:

- Defining the problem.
- Designing a solution.
- Writing the program.
- Compiling, debugging, and testing the program.
- Documenting the program.

Defining the problem and designing a solution are two steps that can be followed regardless of the programming language used. They are also usually the most difficult, because the analyst/programmer not only must be adept at analyzing a problem but also must establish a method of solving it with current computer capabilities.

The other three steps—writing the program; compiling, debugging, and testing the program; and documenting the program—involve translating the solution into one of several computer programming languages. This requires a good understanding of the advantages and limitations of the language used, as well as a logical and structured approach to program writing.

DEFINING THE PROBLEM

The first step in defining a problem begins with recognizing a need for information. This need may be expressed as a request from management, users, or a systems analyst performing a system study. The analyst/programmer receiving the request must analyze the problem thoroughly in order to understand what is required of its solution. Since such problem-solving skills often differ from the skills required of a programmer, some companies use the **systems analyst** to define and design a solution to the problem (see Chapter 13). The tasks of writing, compiling, debugging, and testing, and documenting the program would then be performed by members of the company's programming staff.

Output

Whether the systems analyst, the programmer, or both together define the problem, its solution must be stated in terms of clear, concise objectives. One of the ways to do this is to first define what output is required of the program; this output represents the information requirements of users and management. The analyst/programmer often prepares report mock-ups based on user requests to verify the output requirements of the program to be written. In this way, the analyst/programmer can quickly determine whether any omissions or incorrect assumptions about the program were made.

Input

Next, the input required to provide this output must be determined. The analyst/programmer reviews current systems to see what data may be available and to determine what new data items must be captured in order to provide the required information.

Processing

Finally, given (1) the output specifications developed by the analyst/programmer in close cooperation with the users and management and (2) the required input established by careful evaluation of the current systems, the processing requirements can be determined. Once they are known, the analyst/programmer proceeds to the next step—designing a solution.

Defining the Problem—Payroll Example

The accounting department's payroll section is not functioning properly. Checks are issued late, and many are incorrect. Most of the reports to management, local and state governments, and union officials are woefully inadequate. The payroll section's personnel often work overtime to process the previous week's payroll checks.

The problem is fairly obvious—company expansion and new reporting requirements have strained the accounting department beyond its capacity. A new computerized payroll system has been suggested. Management has agreed with this assessment and has contacted the computer services department for help in solving the problem.

Output   Defining this problem in terms of determining what functions are actually performed in the company's payroll system is difficult. Most functions can be determined by observing the output of the payroll section. Naturally, it issues paychecks. It also sends a statement of weekly and monthly payroll expenses to management and an updated list of changes in employee salaries and positions to the personnel department. The local, state, and federal governments require a monthly report of income taxes withheld, and the union receives payment of employee dues deducted by the payroll section. Not only the checks but all of these reports must be included in a computerized system.

Input   The next step in defining the problem is to determine the inputs to the payroll system. One input is the employee time card, which contains the employee number and the hours worked each day of the week. Another input, dealing with new employees and changes in pay scales, is sent by the personnel department. Supervisors provide a special form regarding employee promotions. The tax section sends updates of tax tables used to calculate local, state, and federal withholdings. The union provides information about the withholding of dues.

Processing   Given the output reports generated by the accounting department and the inputs provided to it by various sources, the processing required of the new computerized payroll system can be determined (see Figure 9–1).

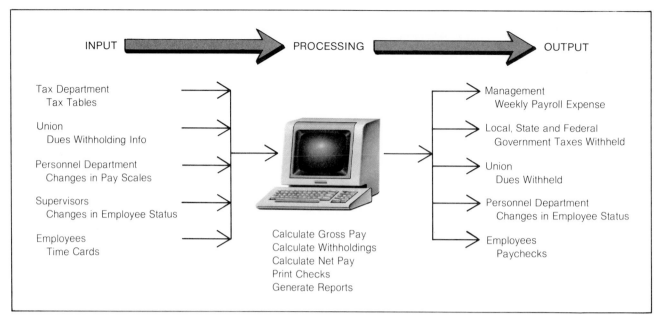

INPUT → PROCESSING → OUTPUT

Tax Department
  Tax Tables

Union
  Dues Withholding Info

Personnel Department
  Changes in Pay Scales

Supervisors
  Changes in Employee Status

Employees
  Time Cards

Calculate Gross Pay
Calculate Withholdings
Calculate Net Pay
Print Checks
Generate Reports

Management
  Weekly Payroll Expense

Local, State and Federal
  Government Taxes Withheld

Union
  Dues Withheld

Personnel Department
  Changes in Employee Status

Employees
  Paychecks

Figure 9–1 ▪ Problem Definition Step for Payroll Example

First, each employee's gross pay must be calculated from the employee's time card and pay scale. Second, each deduction regarding taxes and union dues must be determined from the tax rates provided by the tax department and the information regarding union dues provided by the union, and these deductions must be subtracted from the gross pay to arrive at the net, or take-home, pay. Third, the employee's paycheck must be printed. Totals must be kept of all employees' gross pay and net pay values as well as of taxes and union dues withheld. These totals are used to generate reports to management, government, and union officials. In addition, changes in any employee's work status must be reported to the personnel department. Once the problem has been defined to the level of detail required, the analyst/programmer must design a structured solution to the problem.

DESIGNING A SOLUTION

When the definition of the problem has been completed, the design of the solution begins. This design may take the form of one or more programs. The programmer takes each of the segments uncovered in the definition step and works out a tentative program flow. By approaching each segment separately, the programmer can concentrate on developing an efficient and logical flow for that segment.

The programmer does not need to know which programming language is to be used in order to develop a tentative flow. (In fact, knowing the processing requirements first helps the programmer to select the language best suited to those requirements.) To develop a tentative flow, the only thing a programmer needs to know are the four basic logic patterns used by the computer.

Basic Logic Patterns

There is nothing magical about writing a computer program. In fact, the computer can understand and execute only four basic logic patterns: simple sequence, selection, loop, and branch. High-level languages may have more complicated statements, but they all are based on these four patterns.

Simple Sequence   **Simple sequence** logic involves the computer's executing one statement after another in the order given by the programmer. It is the most simple and often-used pattern; in fact, the computer assumes that all statements entered by the programmer are to be executed in this fashion unless it is told otherwise. Figure 9–2 demonstrates the simple sequence pattern as it would relate to the payroll example.

Selection   The **selection** pattern requires that the computer make a choice. The choice it makes, however, is not based on personal preference or taste, but on pure logic. Each selection is made on the basis of a comparison that determines whether one memory location is equal to, less than, or greater than another. In fact, these are the only comparisons the computer can make. Complex selections, which involve choices such as determining whether one memory location is less than or equal to another or greater than or equal to

Figure 9–2 ▪ Simple Sequence Logic Pattern

Calculate Gross Pay
Calculate Withholdings
Calculate Net Pay
Print Checks
Generate Reports

Primary Memory

CENTRAL PROCESSING UNIT

another are made by combining two comparisons. Figure 9–3 illustrates the selection pattern by demonstrating how the logic of the payroll example would consider overtime pay.

Loop   The **loop** pattern enables the programmer to instruct the computer to alter the normal next-sequential-instruction process and loop back to a previous statement in the program. The computer then re-executes statements according to the simple sequence flow. This is especially useful if the same sequence of statements is to be executed, say, for each employee in a payroll program; the programmer need not duplicate the sequence of statements for each set of employee data processed.

When using the loop, the programmer must establish a way for the computer to get out of the loop once it has been executed the required number of times. For instance, once all employee data has been processed, control of execution should shift to the statement immediately following the loop. Two basic methods of controlling loops are through the use of trailer values

Figure 9–3 ▪ **Selection Logic Pattern**

and counters. A **trailer value** is a unique item that signals the computer to stop performing the loop. It is also referred to as an "end of-file" item, since it can be used to signal the end of the input data. The programmer tests for this trailer value within the program. Since it will cause the computer to exit from the loop, it should be a value that will not be encountered in the input data.

The second method of loop control uses a **counter,** which regulates the number of times the loop is executed. A counter can be entered at the time of program execution as a value in an instruction in the program, or computed within the program. To use a counter to control a loop, the programmer must set up a method of increasing the counter and testing its value each time the loop is executed. When the proper value is reached, the execution of the loop can be terminated. The looping pattern is illustrated in Figure 9– 4.

Branch The last and most controversial pattern is the **branch,** which is often used in combination with selection or looping (see Figure 9–5). This pattern

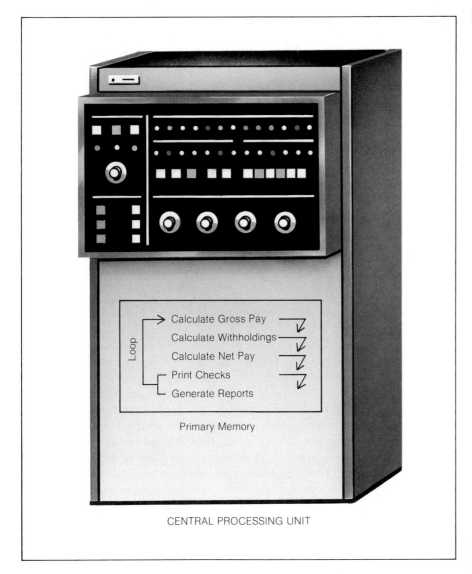

CENTRAL PROCESSING UNIT

Figure 9—4 ▪ **Loop Logic Pattern**

Figure 9–5 ■ Branch Logic Pattern

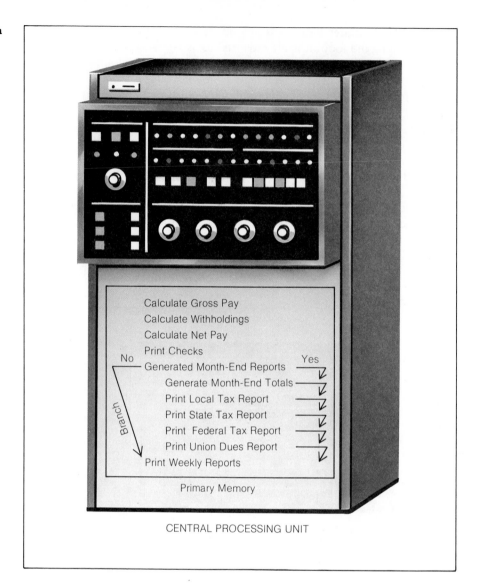

CENTRAL PROCESSING UNIT

allows the programmer to skip past statements in a program, leaving them unexecuted.

Branching is controversial for several reasons. If a program uses it too often, the computer must jump frequently from one part of the program to another. This is inefficient and makes it difficult for other programmers to follow the logical flow of the program. Such programs are difficult and time consuming to maintain. For these reasons, Chapter 11 is devoted to structured programming, which seeks to reduce the use of branching techniques.

It is easy to see why the solution of a problem must be well thought out before programming is started. The programmer has to work creatively around the computer's limitations. The problem must be stated in such a way that it can be solved by use of a series of simple sequence instructions, selections, loops, and, in some cases, branches. Even the selections have to be simplified so that they involve only equal-to, less-than, and greater-than comparisons.

When faced with the task of writing programs designed to solve complicated problems, the programmer can easily make omissions and errors in processing logic. Pseudocode and flowcharting are techniques that can help the analyst/programmer avoid such omissions and errors.

Pseudocode

Pseudocode can be thought of as narrative descriptions of processing steps to be performed in a program. The programmer arranges these descriptions in the order in which corresponding program statements will appear in the program. Using pseudocode allows the programmer to focus on the steps required to perform a particular process by eliminating the need to determine how they should be phrased in a computer language. (As will be explained in Chapter 11, coding statements in a computer language often requires strict adherence to syntactical rules.)

Figure 9–6 shows an example of pseudocode used to lay out the processing steps required to calculate a company's payroll. Correctly written, each pseudocode statement can be translated into one or more program statements. It is easy to see from the example how useful pseudocode can be.

Flowcharts

A **flowchart,** sometimes called a **block diagram** or a **logic diagram,** provides a visual frame of reference to the processing steps in a program. Instead of using the English-like statements of pseudocode, flowcharting uses easily recognizable symbols to represent the type of processing performed in a program. These symbols are arranged in the same logical sequence in which corresponding program statements will appear in the program.

Flowcharts provide excellent documentation of a program. For maintenance, the flowchart can be used to guide the programmer in determining what statements are required to make any necessary changes and where to locate them. Once the flowchart is updated to reflect these changes, it provides good documentation of the revised program. Because of their potential value, flowcharts should be completed, up-to-date, and easy to read. To help achieve the latter objective, the **American National Standards Institute (ANSI)** has adopted a set of flowchart symbols, which are commonly accepted and used by programmers.

Figure 9–7 shows some of the ANSI flowchart symbols. The symbol ⬭ represents the start or termination of a program and so appears at the start and end of a program flowchart. The symbol ▯ shows a process step such as addition, subtraction, multiplication, or division. Most of the data manip-

Figure 9–6 ▪ Pseudocode Example

```
Start
Read employee's hours worked and hourly wage
Do until end of items
    Calculate gross pay
    Calculate withholdings
    Calculate net pay
    Print check
End loop (no more data)
Generate reports
Stop
```

ulation performed in a program is represented by process symbols. A comparison, or decision, uses the symbol $\diamond$ to represent a program statement that directs the computer to compare values. The computer may take either of two paths for a decision step. If the result of the comparison is true, one

Figure 9–7 ▪ Flowchart Symbols

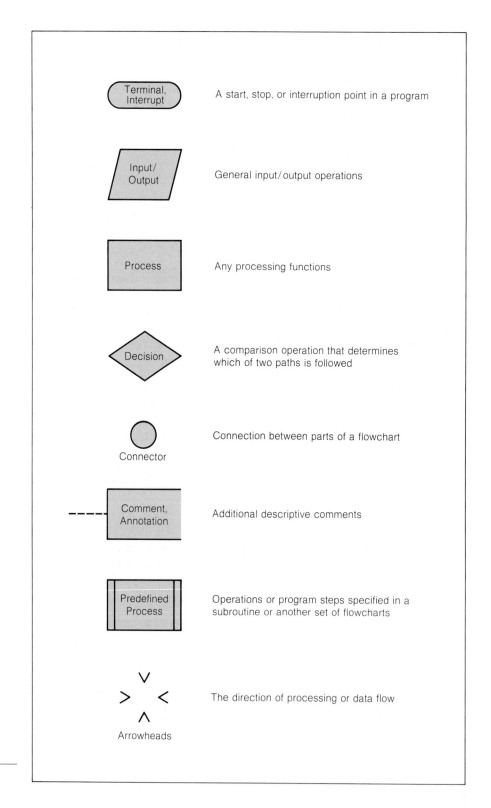

path is executed; if the result is false, the other is taken. Finally, the symbol ⬜ indicates that the program requires either input or output of data.

Figure 9–8 shows a grocery bill calculation expressed in flowchart form. It is important to notice several things in the figure. First, the symbols are arranged from top to bottom, left to right. **Flowlines** connect the symbols and visually represent the implied flow of logic from statement to statement. Arrowheads indicate the direction of flow. Notice also the very brief instructions written within the symbols to provide a more detailed description of the activities represented by the blocks.

It is useful to connect the earlier discussion of basic logic patterns to the flowchart symbols (see Figure 9–9). The first basic logic pattern, simple sequence, is implied by the top-to-bottom arrangement of symbols in the flowchart. The flowlines connecting the symbols arranged in this order merely help to make this flow more apparent. The second pattern, the selection, is represented by the decision symbol, ◇. The loop pattern is represented by a flowline from the last symbol included in the loop up to the first block to be re-executed. Notice that the arrow on the loop flowline indicates that the direction is opposite the normal flow. Finally, the branch is represented by a flowline pointing away from the normal flow to a circle with a number in it. Another circle with the same number appears later in the flowchart, pointing back into the flowchart's logical flow. The numbers within the circles connect the branch exit and re-entry points. The three other flowchart symbols—start or stop, ⬭ ; processing, ⬜ ; and input/output, ⬜ —are used to differentiate the types of programming statements used by the programmer and help him or her to visualize the logical processes followed within the program.

Flowcharts can be used to provide an overview of the major components of a program or to detail each of the processing steps within a program. A flowchart that outlines the general flow and major segments of a program is called a **modular program flowchart,** or **macro flowchart.** The major segments of the program are called **modules.** Macro flowcharts are useful to highlight possibilities for independent program development and are especially useful in implementation of structured programming techniques (discussed in Chapter 11). **Detail,** or **micro, flowcharts** depict the processing steps required within a particular program and often involve a one-to-one correspondence between flowchart blocks and program statements. Figure 9–10 shows both modular and detail flowcharts.

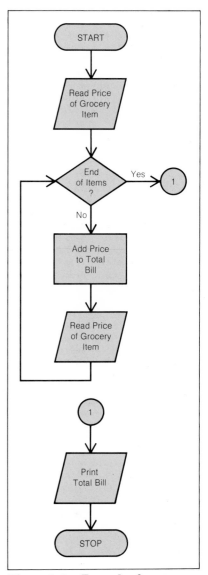

Figure 9–8 ▪ Example of a Flowchart

Designing a Solution—Payroll Example

It was determined in the definition stage of the payroll problem that several processing steps are required. First, an employee's gross pay must be calculated. Next, the employee's check can be printed. Finally, a series of reports is required for management and for government and union officials (see Figure 9–11 for a modular flowchart of these functions).

The first step to planning a solution is to take each of these processing segments and work out a tentative program flow. First, to determine an employee's gross pay, the hours worked during the week are multiplied by the hourly wage. Next, to calculate the employee's withholdings, the appropriate rate and union dues must be determined. For the purposes of this example, assume that a weekly salary over $150 is taxed at a 10 percent rate, while all salaries less than that are taxed 6 percent. Union dues are $15 per week. To calculate net pay, the taxes and union dues are subtracted from the gross

Figure 9–9 ■ Four Traditional Program Logic Patterns

1. Simple sequence pattern
   One statement after another, executed in order as stored (A then B).

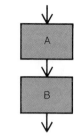

2. Selection Pattern
   Requires a test; depending on the result of the test, one of two paths is taken. For instance, IF A is true THEN do B; ELSE do C.

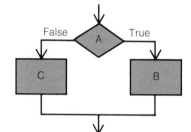

3. Loop pattern
   Execution of E and F continues in a loop fashion as long as D is true. If D is false, the loop is exited; E and F are not executed. The logic is DO E and F WHILE D is true.

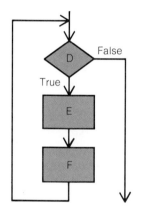

4. Branch pattern
   Control is transferred from the simple sequence flow to another portion of the program. For instance, if G is false, GO TO J. The flow of the program continues with execution of J (rather than H) whenever G is false.

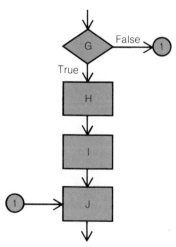

Figure 9–10 ▪ Modular Flowchart and Detail Flowchart

Figure 9–11 ▪ Modular Flowchart for Payroll Problem

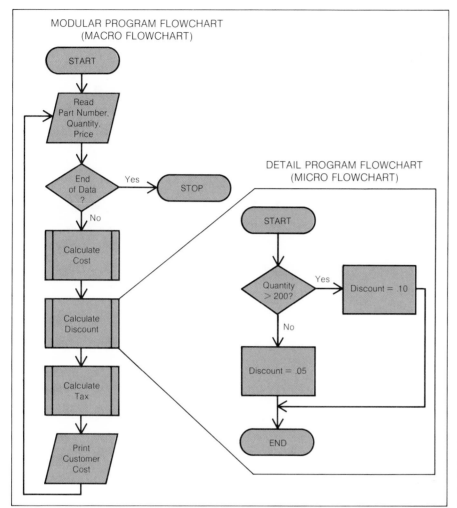

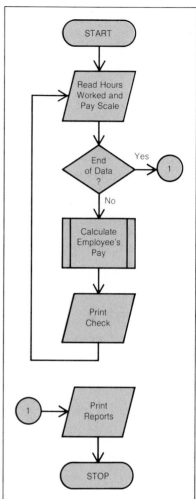

pay. The paycheck is printed next, and then the calculations are repeated until there are no more time cards for processing.

The steps required to calculate an employee's net pay can be illustrated in a detail flowchart, as shown in Figure 9–12. The steps required to solve the payroll processing problem can also be represented in pseudocode, as shown in Figure 9–13. As can be seen, each of the pseudocode statements corresponds to either a modular or detail flowchart symbol in Figures 9–11 and 9–12.

If all payroll programs were this easy, programmers would soon be out of jobs. There are many more processing steps in an actual payroll system. For instance, employees who work more than forty hours in the week are entitled to overtime pay. A payroll program would be required to test the number of hours worked and calculate the overtime "premium" for hours over forty. Similarly, it is likely that not all employees belong to the union. For example, office workers may be excluded from union membership. A payroll program handling this processing problem would be required to bypass union dues

Problem Definition and Solution Design

Figure 9–12 ▪ Detail Flowchart for Payroll Problem

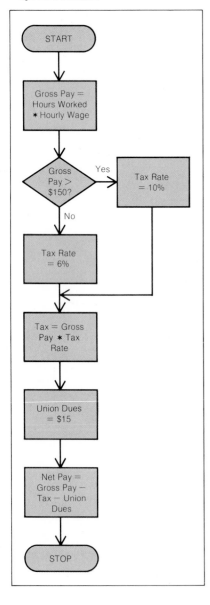

calculations for these employees. These two problems, as well as any others that may occur, would have to be designed into the solution before the program could be written.

Accumulators

The loop is a powerful tool not only for reducing the number of program statements required to perform a particular task but also for accumulating totals. For instance, as each employee's gross pay is calculated, it can be added to the total gross salary paid to all employees. This is also true of the employee's net pay, tax, and union dues. When all employee data has been processed, these totals can be printed on summary reports required by management, government, and the union. An important point to remember, however, is that these totals can be used only after all employee data has been read and processed. Although the **accumulators** are positioned within the

Figure 9–13 ▪ Pseudocode for Payroll Problem

```
Start
Read employee's hours worked and hourly wage
Do until end of items
    Multiply hours worked times hourly wage to get gross pay
    If gross pay is greater than $150
        Then tax rate is 10 percent
        Else tax rate is 6 percent
    Multiply tax rate times gross pay giving tax
    Union dues are $15
    Subtract tax and union dues from gross pay giving net pay
    Print check
    Read next employee's hours worked and hourly wage
End loop (no more data)
Print reports
```

loop, the reporting of their values must occur outside the loop after it has been executed the required number of times.

In order to accumulate totals in a program that uses a loop, the programmer must do two things. First, he or she must include statements within the loop to accumulate the desired totals. These statements must appear at the correct logical points of the loop. For instance, a statement accumulating gross pay should be inserted directly after the statement that calculates the gross pay for an employee, not before it. Second, the programmer must provide for printing or storing the total outside the loop once the loop has been executed the desired number of times (see Figure 9–14).

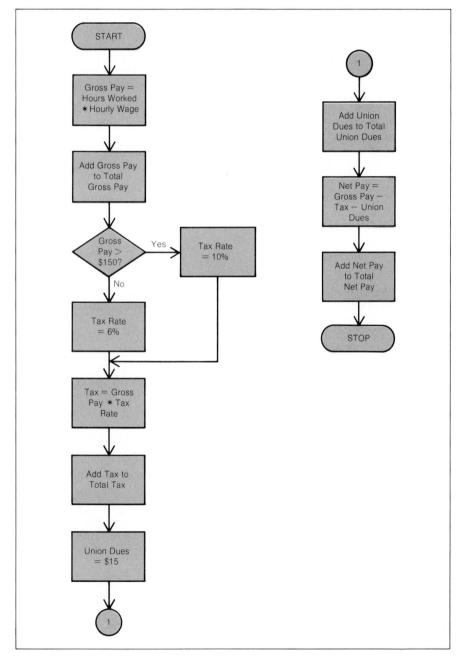

Figure 9–14 ▪ Detail Flowchart with Accumulators

WRITING THE PROGRAM

After the programmer has defined the problem and designed a solution, the program is written in a specific programming language. High-level languages are usually designed for specific types of applications. Although definition and solution of a problem do not depend on a particular programming language, the proposed solution may limit the choices of languages that can be used. Other constraints outside the scope of the problem and its solution may also affect the choice of a programming language. For example, FORTRAN is a language designed primarily for scientific applications; COBOL is normally used for business applications. A programmer may have no part in the selection of a language for a particular application—there may be a business requirement to use COBOL, for instance, because of its readability. Programming languages are discussed further in Chapter 10.

Types of Statements

Certain types of programming statements are common to most high-level programming languages; they are comments, declarations, input/output statements, computations, transfers of control, and comparisons.

Comments   The type of statement known as the remark or comment has no effect on program execution. Comments are inserted at key points in the program as documentation—notes to anyone reading the program to explain the purposes of program segments. For example, if a series of statements sorts a list of names into alphabetical order, the programmer may want to include a remark to the effect: "This segment sorts names in ascending alphabetical order."

Declarations   The programmer uses declarations to define items used in the program. Examples include definitions of files, records, initial values of counters and accumulators, reusable functions, and the like.

Input/Output Statements   Input statements bring data into primary storage for use by the program. Output statements transfer data from primary storage to output media such as hard-copy printouts or displays on video terminals. These statements differ considerably in form (though not so much in function) from one programming language to another.

Computations   Computational instructions perform arithmetic operations—addition, subtraction, multiplication, division, and exponentiation. Languages vary in their facilities for invoking the computer's arithmetic capabilities.

Transfers of Control   Another type of instruction allows the sequence of execution to be altered by transferring control. A conditional transfer of control alters the sequence only when a certain condition is met. An unconditional transfer always changes the sequence of execution.

Comparisons   The final type of statement is the comparison, which allows two items to be compared. Based on the result of the comparison, either input/output, computation, or transfer of control could occur.

Desirable Program Qualities

As the program is being coded, the programmer should be aware that generating the correct output is not the only requirement of a good program. There is always more than one way to code a program to provide a correct solution; however, one program can be better than another. The programmer should try to incorporate the following qualities into any program:

- Programs should be easy to read and to understand. Data names should be descriptive. Short data names that do not reflect the data represented should be avoided. Statements should be placed in a format that is easy to read and to follow. In other words, the programmer should write the program in such a way that someone else can easily read and understand it.
- Programs should be efficient. In general, this means that programs should execute in as little time as possible. Computers are very expensive, and CPU time is a valuable resource. Some companies charge users hundreds of dollars for *one minute of CPU time*. An efficient program could save a user thousands of dollars per year.
- Programs should be reliable; that is, they should consistently produce the correct output. All formulas and computations, as well as all logic tests and transfers of control, must be accurate.
- Programs should be robust; they should work under all conditions. Reliability alone is no guarantee of a successful program. Internal logic may be correct, but an incorrect data item (garbage in) could produce incorrect output (garbage out). For example, a program that uses the age of a person may want to test for incorrect ages in the data stream. How would the program react if someone's age were 4,692 or −35?
- Programs should be maintainable. They should be easy to update and modify. Programs should be written in independent modules so that a change in one module does not necessitate a change in others.

COMPILING, DEBUGGING, AND TESTING THE PROGRAM

After the program has been written, it is submitted to the computer for translation. Levels of language and language translation are discussed here to illustrate how a high-level language program is altered to a form the computer can use.

Levels of Language

The programmer uses a sequence of instructions to communicate with the computer and to control program execution. As computers have developed in complexity, so have programming languages. Today there are three language levels—machine language, assembly language, and high-level language (see Figure 9–15).

Machine language is as old as the computer itself. It is the code that designates the proper electrical states in the computer and is expressed as combinations of 0s and 1s. It is the only language the computer can execute directly; therefore, it can be called the language of the computer. **Assembly**

Figure 9–15 ▪ Language Levels

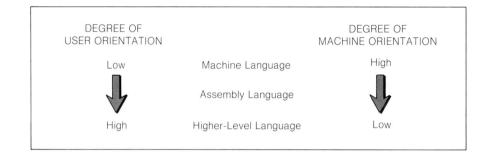

language is one step removed from machine language. Programmers using assembly language must be very conscious of the computer and must designate not only the operations to be performed but also storage locations, as when using machine language. However, assembly language is more easily understood by humans. Instead of the 0 and 1 groupings of machine language, convenient symbols and abbreviations, known as **mnemonics,** are used.

High-level languages are so called because they are furthest removed from the hardware; they least resemble the 0 and 1 combinations of machine language. Whereas one assembly-language instruction is generally equivalent to one machine-language instruction, one high-level-language statement can accomplish the same result as a half-dozen or more machine-language instructions, principally because the addresses for many of the required storage locations do not have to be specified; they are handled automatically.

Language Translation

Assembly and high-level languages are much more widely used by programmers than machine language. Since these languages cannot be executed directly by computers, they are converted into machine-executable form by a **language-translator program.** The sequence of instructions written by the programmer—the **source program**—is transformed by the language-translator program into a machine-executable form known as the **object program,** which accomplishes the same operations as a program originally written in machine language.

The translator program for an assembly language is called an **assembler program.** A high-level-language translator can be either a **compiler program** or an **interpreter program.** Assemblers, compilers, and interpreters are designed for specific machines and languages. For example, a compiler that translates a source program written in FORTRAN into a machine-language program can only translate FORTRAN.

During the compilation, or assembly (the translation process), the object program is generated. The programmer receives an assembly listing or a source-program listing that contains indications of any errors the assembler or compiler detected during translation. The errors are usually violations of the rules associated with the particular programming language. For example, if a statement that should begin in column 8 on a line begins in column 6, an error message will be generated. Similarly, an error message will be generated if language keywords such as WRITE or COMPUTE are misspelled.

To help the programmer, the compiler can provide a listing of all compiler-detected errors. The error-message listing may give the number of each statement in error and may also describe the nature of the error (see Figure 9–16). Only after all errors preventing compilation have been corrected can the object program be created and submitted to the computer for execution. Several attempts at successful compilation or assembly may be needed. The complete process of compilation and execution of a high-level language is shown in Figure 9–17. In this case, the source program has been entered using a visual display terminal, and the data provided as input to the object program has been stored on magnetic tape.

An **interpreter,** a language translator that has been used extensively on microcomputer systems, unlike assemblers and compilers, evaluates and translates a program one statement at a time. The interpreter reads a program statement by statement—first checking **syntax,** then translating the statement, and finally executing the statement—before proceeding to the next statement. This is in contrast to an assembler or compiler, which first checks the entire program for syntax and then translates the entire program into an object program that can be executed. An interpreter program is typically smaller than an assembler or compiler program. For this reason, and because there is no need to store an object program in the computer, interpreters are popular on microcomputer systems. An interpreter, however, can be inefficient. Program statements that are used more than once in a program's execution must be evaluated, translated, and executed each time the statement is used.

Like assemblers and compilers, interpreters also provide the programmer with error messages that can be used for correcting syntax errors. Since the interpreter is designed to process a program statement by statement, a statement must be entered correctly by the programmer before the next statement can be entered. This immediate error reporting can be helpful in resolving syntax errors (see Figure 9–18).

Debugging the Program

The language translator can detect grammatical or syntax errors such as misspellings and incorrect punctuation. However, logical errors must be detected by the programmer and are often found through testing. Such errors may result when the programmer does not fully understand the problem or does not account for problems that may arise during processing.

Figure 9–16 ▪ Compiler-Detected Errors

Statement Number	Error Code	Error Messages
1972	IKF1080I-W	PERIOD PRECEDED BY SPACE. ASSUME END OF SENTENCE.
1999	IKF1080I-W	PERIOD PRECEDED BY SPACE. ASSUME END OF SENTENCE.
2074	IKF1043I-W	END OF SENTENCE SHOULD PRECEDE 02. ASSUMED PRESENT.
2399	IKF2126I-C	VALUE CLAUSE LITERAL TOO LONG. TRUNCATED TO PICTURE SIZE.
2432	IKF1043I-W	END OF SENTENCE SHOULD PRECEDE 02. ASSUMED PRESENT.
2481	IKF1080I-W	PERIOD PRECEDED BY SPACE. ASSUME END OF SENTENCE.
2484	IKF1080I-W	PERIOD PRECEDED BY SPACE. ASSUME END OF SENTENCE.
2623	IKF1004I-E	INVALID WORD NOTE. SKIPPING TO NEXT RECOGNIZABLE WORD.
2623	IKF1007I-W	MINUS SIGN NOT PRECEDED BY A SPACE. ASSUME SPACE.
2623	IKF1007I-W	**NOT PRECEDED BY A SPACE. ASSUME SPACE.

Figure 9–17 ▪ High-Level Programming Language Translation and Execution

The process of translating and executing a high-level language
program begins by compiling the source program. Once
the program is compiled and the object program created,
the link/loader links the object program with any system
programs that may be needed for execution. The object
program and system library programs combine to form the
load program. The load program, which is in object form, is
then executed using input data and the desired output is created.

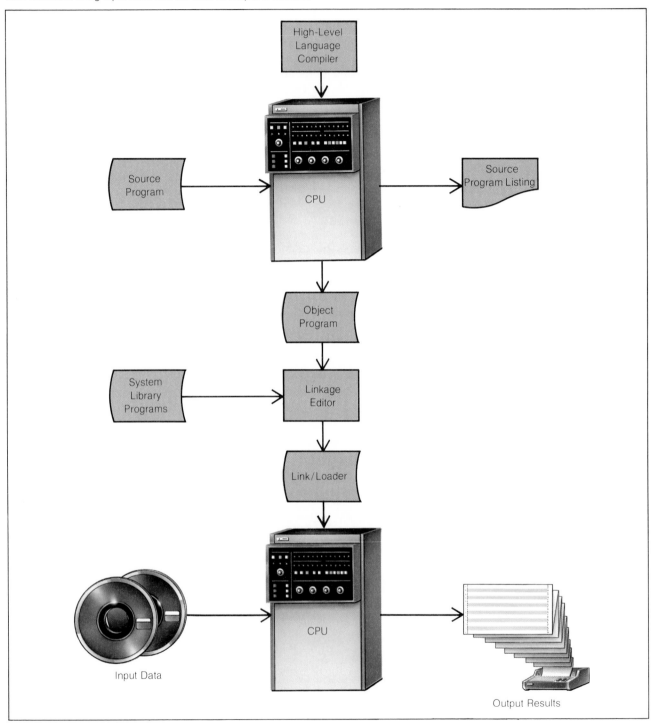

Figure 9–18 ■ Interpreter-Detected
Errors

```
100 REM THIS PROGRAM WILL ADD 5 INDIVIDUAL GRADES
110 REM FOR A STUDENT, CALCULATE THE AVERAGE, AND THEN
120 REM DETERMINE THE STUDENT'S FINAL GRADE
130 PRNT "NAME","AVERAGE","FINAL GRADE"
*** SYNTAX ERR
130 PRINT "NAME","AVERAGE","FINAL GRADE"
140 PRINT
150 REAS N$,G1,G2,G3,G4,G5
*** SYNTAX ERR
150 READ N$,G1,G2,G3,G4,G5
155 IF N$ = 'END OF DATA' THEN 999
160 LET T = G1 + G2 + G3 + G4 + G5
170 LET A = T / 5
180 IF A >= 90 THEN 240
190 IF A >= 80 THEN 260
200 IF A >= 70 THEN 280
210 IF A >= 60 THEN 300
220 LET F$ = 'F'
230 GOTO 310
240 LET F$ = 'A'
250 GOTO 310
260 LET F$ = 'B'
270 GOTO 310
280 LET F$ = 'C'
290 GOTO 310
300 LET F$ = 'D'
310 PRINT N$,A,F$
320 GOTO 150
330 DATA 'FRED J. SMITH', 70, 65, 24, 100, 98
340 DATA 'JASON R. JACKSON', 97, 96, 59, 78, 60
350 DATA 'JOHN S. LAWSON', 90, 94, 88, 98, 96
360 DATA 'SUSAN EAKINS', 83, 76, 87, 89, 95
370 DATA 'MARY Q. JOHSON', 66, 79, 83, 75, 70
380 DATA 'END OF DATA', 0, 0, 0, 0, 0
999 END
```

Errors in programs are called bugs, and the process of locating, isolating, and eliminating bugs is called **debugging.** The amount of time that must be spent in debugging depends on the quality of the program. However, a newly completed program rarely executes successfully the first time it is run. In fact, one-third to one-half of a programmer's time is spent in debugging.

Testing the Program

When a compilation without errors is achieved, it is time for a test run. This run involves executing the program with input data that is either a representative sample of actual data or a facsimile of it. Often, sample data that can be manipulated easily by the programmer is used so that the computer-determined output can be compared with the programmer-determined correct results. The output should be easy to recognize so that the programmer can see if it is correct.

A complex program is frequently tested in separate units so that errors can be isolated to specific sections, helping to narrow the search for the cause of an error. The programmer must correct all mistakes; running and rerunning a specific unit may be necessary before the cause of an error can be found. The programmer then rewrites the part in error and resubmits it for another test. Care must be taken so that correction of one logical error does not give rise to several others.

PROGRAMMING AND SOFTWARE
DEVELOPMENT

The First Computer "Bug"

The first "bug" in a computer program occurred in a very strange way. In the summer of 1945, something went wrong with the Mark II, the large electromechanical device used by the Department of Defense for making calculations. Though the machine was not working properly, no obvious problems could be found. The personnel operating the machine continued their search and finally discovered the cause of their problems. A large moth had become stuck in one of Mark II's relays, preventing the circuit from being completed and thereby causing an error. The solution to the problem was to remove the bug from the relay, and thus the term *debugging* came into existence.

Each section of the program must be tested (even sections that will be used infrequently). If instructions for handling exceptions are part of the program, the sample input data should include items that test the program's ability to spot and reject improper data items. The programmer often finds **desk-checking (desk-debugging)** helpful. With this method, the programmer pretends to be the computer and, reading each instruction and simulating how the computer would process a data item, attempts to catch any flaws in the program logic.

After a programmer has worked for a long time to correct the logic of a program, he or she may tend to overlook errors or assume a clarity that in reality does not exist. For this reason, programmers sometimes trade their partially debugged programs among themselves. The programmer stepping through a "fresh" program may uncover mistakes in logic that were hidden to the original programmer.

In many cases, program errors prove especially difficult to locate. Two commonly used diagnostic procedures usually available to the programmer in such cases are dump programs and trace programs.

A **dump program** lists the contents of registers and primary storage locations. The dump is often useful in locating an error because the values that were in the registers and primary storage at the time the error occurred can be checked for correctness. If an incorrect value is found, it can be used to help locate the error.

A **trace,** produced by a **trace program,** is apt to be easier to use than a dump. The trace lists the steps followed during program execution in the order in which they occurred. The programmer can specify that all or portions of a program be traced. The trace is often used in combination with the desk-checking procedure described above to see if the correct flow of execution has occurred. The values of selected variables (memory locations) can also be displayed in the trace; this can be helpful in determining whether the necessary calculations have been performed correctly.

DOCUMENTING THE PROGRAM

Documentation consists of written descriptions and explanations of programs and other materials associated with an organization's data-processing systems. Documentation of system and program designs is one of the most important (and, unfortunately, one of the most neglected) requirements for success in a data-processing application. The importance of complete documentation has long been known, but many firms are only now beginning to insist that complete documentation be a prerequisite to implementing a new program or changing an existing one.

Everyone who uses the computer needs such documentation at some time. The groups that need documentation the most include computer operators, programmers, and management personnel. Proper program documentation serves as a reference guide for programmers and analysts who must modify or update existing programs and system procedures. Without it, a programmer may have to spend days or weeks trying to ascertain what a program does and how it does it. Further, in many cases, programs are designed to operate under a fixed set of conditions and constraints. When organizations change and grow, program modifications must keep pace with their changing

- The types of programming statements that are common to most high-level programming languages include:
  (1) Comments
  (2) Declarations
  (3) Input/output statements
  (4) Computations
  (5) Transfers of control
  (6) Comparisons
- Programs should be easy to read and understand, efficient, reliable, robust, and maintainable.
- The three levels of programming languages are (from most machine dependent to least machine dependent):
  (1) Machine-language
  (2) Assembly language
  (3) High-level language
- The program statements, or instructions, written by the programmers are called the **source program.** The source program is transformed into machine-executable form—the **object program**—by the **language-translator program.**
- A language translator used for assembly language is called an **assembler,** while either a **compiler** or **interpreter** is used to translate high-level languages.
- **Bugs** are errors within programs. **Debugging** is the process of locating, isolating, and eliminating program bugs.
- **Desk-checking,** a **dump program,** and a **trace program** can be used in the testing of a program.

needs. Documentation helps management to evaluate the effectiveness of data-processing applications and to determine where changes are desirable.

Documentation is also essential to those who must perform manual functions required by the system. When staff changes occur, new employees need complete documentation of all clerical procedures within the system. This information helps them to understand their jobs and how to carry them out. Finally, documentation provides instructions to the computer operator about the requirements (tape drives, card readers, and the like) for running particular programs.

The process of documentation is an ongoing one. It begins with the initial request for information. The individual making the request should be identified. So should those who will be charged with the responsibility of designing the system and the required programs. The names of the persons who must approve the request should be provided.

During the problem-definition phase, the problem should be described clearly in a short narrative statement. The objectives of the program that will be created to solve the problem should be included with the problem statement. Several other descriptions are necessary:

- A complete description of the contents and formats of all data inputs, outputs, and files to be used.
- A statement of the hardware requirements for running the program, such as magnetic-tape drives, disk drives, and card readers, as well as estimated processing time and storage requirements.
- A statement of software requirements, such as utility programs and library programs; this statement may also identify the programming language to be used and list the reasons for choosing it.

In the planning phase, the most important documentation produced is the flowchart. If the application is complex, both modular and detail program flowcharts should be prepared. Descriptive comments may be included for each processing step. Completeness and accuracy are essential. If changes are made to the program, they must be reflected in the flowchart so that all program documentation stays up-to-date.

An operator's manual, sometimes known as a **run book,** should also be prepared. It contains the instructions needed to run the program and will be used primarily by the computer operator. All the documentation for a program or system can be combined to form a user's manual, which contains documentation designed to aid persons not familiar with a program in using the program.

PROGRAMMING CASE STUDY

The objective of this problem is to calculate the average numerical grade for each student in a course and to determine the final letter grade for each. Our input will be the students' names and the five numerical grades each received during the course. Our output requirements are to print the names of the students, their average numerical grades, and their final letter grades under the headings "Name," "Average," and "Final Grade."

The final grade for each student is to be based on the following grade scale:

AVERAGE	FINAL GRADE
90–100	A
80–89	B
70–79	C
60–69	D
0–59	F

Thus, the job requirements have been defined: the input will be the students' names and grades; the required computation will be the determination of average and final grades; and the required output will be the students' names, averages, and final grades listed under appropriate headings. It is important to remember that the problem solution must be defined logically and that the computer must be given all relevant data and instructions.

The first step in designing a problem solution is to determine a basic instruction flow. Output headings can be printed before the student data is read as input. Since each student has five grades, the student's name and five grades must be input and the grades added together. When the addition has been completed, the average can be calculated. Once the average has been determined, the appropriate final letter grade can be assigned according to the grade scale. After the final letter grade has been established, the name, average, and final grade can be printed. When the data for one student has been processed, the data for the next student can be read and processed, and so on, until no more statistics are available.

The pseudocode representing the logical flow of the solution is found in Figure 9–19.

A flowchart for the solution of this problem is given in Figure 9–20. The

Figure 9–19 ■ Pseudocode for Case Study

```
Start
Print Headings (Step 1)
Do until End of Items (Step 7)
    Read Student's Name and Grades (Step 2)
    Calculate Student's Grade Total (Step 3)
    Calculate Student's Grade Average (Step 4)
    Determine Final Letter Grade (Step 5)
    Print Name, Average, Final Grade (Step 6)
End Loop (No More Data)
Stop (Step 8)
```

Figure 9–20 ▪ Flowchart for Case Study

Note: The characters enclosed in ( ) are the variable names used in the BASIC program.

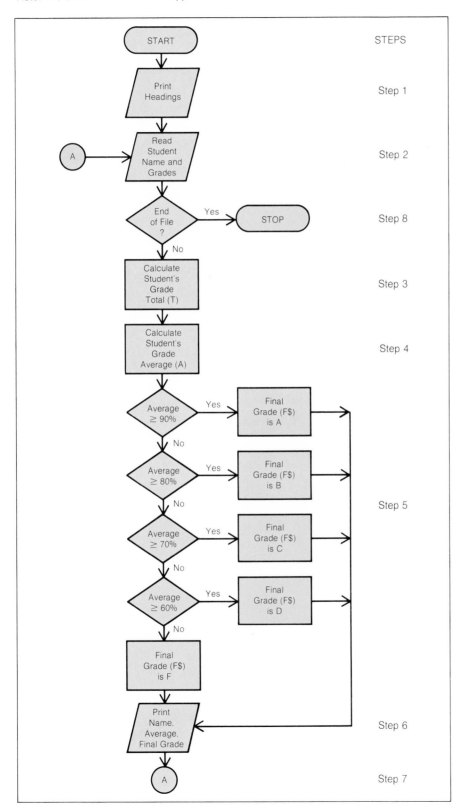

relationship between the pseudocode above and the blocks on the flowchart is also pointed out.

After the flowchart has been constructed and the logic reviewed, the next task is to express the solution in a programming language—in this case, BASIC. The completed source program can then be entered into the computer via the keyboard of a terminal. Then it can be translated into an object program. A listing of the source program and notification of errors (if any) detected by the language translator can be generated. Then the program can be executed. Figure 9–21 shows the source-program listing and the output produced during the execution of the program.

Figure 9–21 ▪ BASIC Program with Sample Data for Case Study

```
100 REM THIS PROGRAM WILL ADD 5 INDIVIDUAL GRADES
110 REM FOR A STUDENT, CALCULATE THE AVERAGE, AND THEN
120 REM DETERMINE THE STUDENT'S FINAL GRADE
130 PRINT "NAME",,"AVERAGE","FINAL GRADE"
140 PRINT
150 READ N$,G1,G2,G3,G4,G5
155 IF N$ = "END OF DATA" THEN 999
160 LET T = G1 + G2 + G3 + G4 + G5
170 LET A = T / 5
180 IF A >= 90 THEN 240
190 IF A >= 80 THEN 260
200 IF A >= 70 THEN 280
210 IF A >= 60 THEN 300
220 LET F$ = "F"
230 GOTO 310
240 LET F$ = "A"
250 GOTO 310
260 LET F$ = "B"
270 GOTO 310
280 LET F$ = "C"
290 GOTO 310
300 LET F$ = "D"
310 PRINT N$,A,F$
320 GOTO 150
330 DATA "FRED J. SMITH    ",70,65,24,100,98
340 DATA "JASON R. JACKSON",97,96,59,78,60
350 DATA "JOHN S. LAWSON  ",90,94,88,98,96
360 DATA "SUSAN EAKINS    ",83,76,87,89,95
370 DATA "MARY Q. JOHNSON ",66,79,83,75,70
380 DATA "END OF DATA",0,0,0,0,0
999 END
```

Output

```
RUN
NAME                          AVERAGE      FINAL GRADE

FRED J. SMITH                 71.4         C
JASON R. JACKSON              78           C
JOHN S. LAWSON                93.2         A
SUSAN EAKINS                  86           B
MARY Q. JOHNSON               74.6         C
Ok
```

SUMMARY POINTS

■ The computer is incredibly fast and accurate, but it has an IQ of zero. Any intelligence the computer appears to have is given to it by the programmer. The programmer must tell the computer how to solve a problem, step by step.

■ There are five steps in the problem-solving process—defining the problem; designing a problem solution; writing the program; compiling, debugging, and testing the program; and documenting the program.

■ Defining the program begins with recognizing the need for information. This need can be in the form of a request from users, management, or a systems analyst conducting a system study.

■ The second step in defining the problem requires determining what output the system should provide. This is determined either by the systems analyst or by the programmer and verified by users and management.

■ The next step is to determine what input is available from current systems and what new data items need to be provided.

■ The final step is to determine what processing steps the program should include based on the output required and the input provided to the system.

■ Planning a problem solution requires only that a programmer know the four basic logic patterns used by the computer to solve problems: simple sequence, selection, loop, and branch.

■ When it uses the simple sequence pattern, the computer executes program statements one after another in the order given by the programmer.

■ Selection requires that the computer make a comparison between two items to determine whether one is equal to, less than, or greater than the other.

■ The loop sends the computer back to a previous program statement. That statement is re-executed, and processing continues with the next statement in accordance with simple sequence logic.

■ The branch logic pattern makes the computer skip over certain program statements. If used too often, it can be inefficient and confusing.

■ Pseudocode refers to narrative descriptions of the processing steps required in a program. These descriptions help the programmer determine the program's logical flow.

■ Flowcharts are pictorial representations of the processing logic in a program. Modular flowcharts depict the major processing segments, while detail flowcharts show each processing step.

■ Accumulators are used to keep totals of certain items in a program. The statement accumulating the total is placed within the loop. The reporting of the final value of the accumulator takes place outside the loop after the loop has been executed the required number of times.

■ Once the problem solution has been planned and the appropriate language chosen, the program can be written. Several types of programming statements are common to most languages.

■ Programmers should strive to write high-quality programs that are easy to read and understand, efficient, reliable, robust, and maintainable.

■ There are three levels of language groups: (1) machine language is expressed as combinations of 0s and 1s and is the only language the computer can execute directly; (2) assembly language provides convenient symbols and abbreviations for writing programs; and (3) high-level languages are English-like languages.

■ A sequence of instructions written in assembly language or high-level language is called a source program. The language translator converts the source program into a machine-language equivalent known as an object program.

■ The translator program for an assembly language is called an assembler program. A high-level language translator is called a compiler program or an interpreter program.

■ After programs have been written, they are debugged and tested. Dump programs and trace programs provide diagnostics to help debug programs. Testing is done on sample data so that the computer-determined output can be compared with predetermined correct results.

■ Program documentation is essential throughout the programming cycle. It simplifies modification and updating of existing programs and system procedures and is a must for the success of any program.

REVIEW QUESTIONS

1. What are the five steps of the problem-solving process? Identify the steps that could be performed by a systems analyst. By a programmer.

2. What is important about the desired output of a computerized system? In what stage of the problem-solving process is an evaluation of desired output most important?

3. What are two techniques of illustrating a logic flow used in designing a solution to a computer problem?

4. Is it important for a systems analyst/programmer to have a specific programming language in mind when performing the first two steps of the problem-solving process? Why or why not?

5. Consider the problem of finding an apartment. Can you define the problem well enough that a computer could be used to solve it? (Assume that data on all vacant apartments is available.) Design a solution to your problem once you have defined it.

6. What are some of the advantages of using flowcharts? Pseudocode? As a systems analyst/programmer, which would you prefer to use—pseudocode or flowcharts—and why?

7. Draw a flowchart that depicts the steps necessary to convert Fahrenheit temperatures to Celsius and print both temperatures.

8. Write the pseudocode that illustrates the steps necessary to test for and sum the prime numbers between 1 and 1,000. (Note: Prime numbers are those numbers that are divisible evenly by *only* 1 and themselves.)

9. List and describe the types of statements used in most high-level programming languages.

10. Discuss the qualities that can make one program better than another. How can these qualities make a program better?

11. After a program has been written and submitted to the computer, how does the computer translate it into usable form?

12. List the three types of language translator programs. How do the three differ?

13. What is documentation, and at what steps of program development should it be included? Why is documentation important?

14. What groups in particular should receive documentation of a computer program? Identify the types of documentation required by each group.

On May 10, 1876, Colonel Eli Lilly, a Civil War veteran, began operating a small laboratory in downtown Indianapolis, Indiana, to manufacture medications. With total assets of $1,400 in fluid extracts and cash, Lilly began producing pills and other medicines. In 1881, the firm, which had since incorporated as Eli Lilly and Company, moved to the location just south of downtown Indianapolis that today continues to house its principal offices and research headquarters.

Two of the best-known medical discoveries toward which Lilly provided substantial contributions are insulin and the Salk polio vaccine. More recently, the company has developed a number of important antibiotics and cancer treatment agents. Besides manufacturing pharmaceutical products, Lilly has diversified into agricultural products, cosmetics, and medical instrument systems through its subsidiaries.

Products are manufactured and distributed through the company's own facilities in the United States, Puerto Rico, and 33 other countries. In 17 countries, the company owns or has an interest in manufacturing facilities. Its products are sold in more than 130 countries.

With interests in business and research scattered across the globe, Eli Lilly and Company has developed an extensive data-processing operation to support every department of the corporation. The Scientific Information Systems Division handles activities related to research and development. Corporate Information Systems and Services supports the firm's business data-processing needs. The Corporate Computer Center consists of five large IBM computers and three Digital Equipment Corporation computers that receive and process data transmitted to the center via online teleprocessing, remote job-entry (RJE), and time-sharing terminals located in user departments of the corporation in U.S. and overseas locations. The Corporate Computer Center supports more than 300 time-sharing terminals, more than 2,000 teleprocessing devices, and at least 100 RJE stations. In a typical business day, more than 12,000 programs are executed and about 600,000 teleprocessing transactions are processed. More than 300 personal computer workstations for professionals have been acquired, and about 500 secretarial workers now use office terminals.

The Information Systems Development Division, which employs approximately 400 people, is responsible for the design, development, and maintenance of business information systems. The division is composed of functional development groups; each group works with line management and staff groups to develop application programs designed to reduce operating expenses and provide information for more effective management. Marketing activities, manufacturing departments, financial systems, all phases of engineering, patent and general legal affairs, corporate affairs, and industrial relations are supported by this organization.

When a user department requests a major new application, a project is initiated to begin a multiphase process called PLAD (Process for Lilly Application Development). Figure 9–22 illustrates the flow of the PLAD phases and their related activities.

1. The first phase of the process requires documentation of the objectives and requirements of the requested system. Some projects warrant the review and approval of a separate objectives document before the detailed requirements are studied. These documents are carefully prepared to serve several purposes:

- User and management sign-off helps assure that the system will meet the business need.
- Technical reviews provide the opportunity for computer operations, system programming, data management, and other support groups to verify feasibility and resource availability.
- Cost/benefit analysis provides the basis for management approval.

After systems and user management have approved the objectives/requirements documents, the design phase begins.

Figure 9–22 ■ PLAD

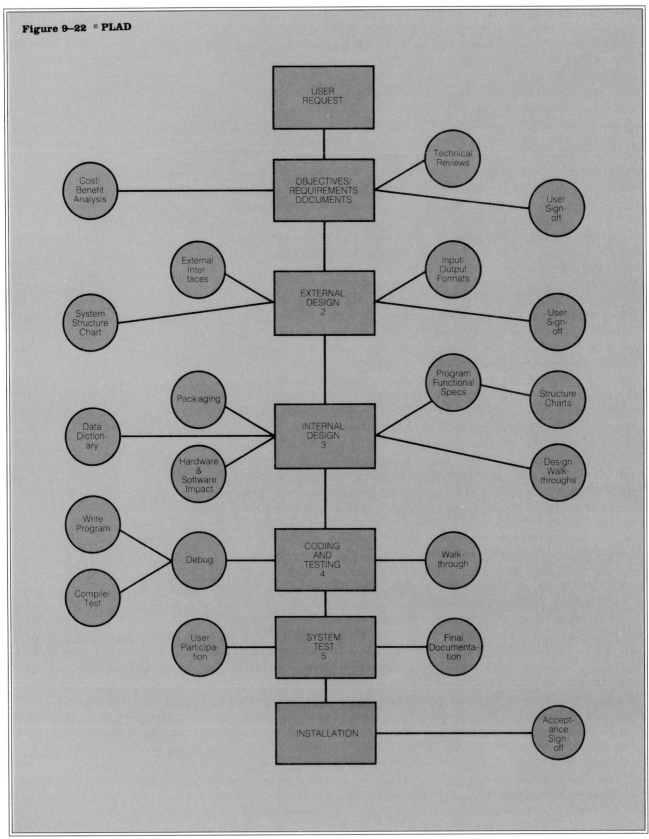

2. In the external design phase, the users are provided a detailed understanding of how the system will work so that they can verify that the system as planned by the designer will meet their specific needs. Logical system structure charts explain the flow and the transactions for each part of the system. Users participate in the design of reports, screen formats, and inquiries. The external design report documents the architecture of the system and provides plans for the following phases.

3. The next phase, internal design, produces the blueprints for the construction of the system. The user language of the external design phase is translated into technical terms. The system structure is divided into subsystems and programs. Specifications describe the functions performed by each program. All data elements are defined to the data element dictionary. Data files used for communications between programs are specified. Experienced designers, not a part of the project team, conduct the design walk-through. The internal design report includes plans for the coding, testing, and installation phases to follow.

4. During the coding and unit-test phase, additional members often join the project team. With the information from internal design and firm staffing plans, the project leader is able to project a fairly reliable finish date. Each team member begins detailed design and coding of assigned programs. When coding is completed, the program is submitted for compilation. Any clerical errors should be detected during the compilation process. This step is repeated until an error-free compilation is achieved.

The programmer then conducts a walk-through, explaining the purpose of the program to a previously uninvolved third party. This person, usually a fellow programmer, can provide fresh insights into areas where the purpose of the program is unclear (and thus requires additional comments). The person can also desk-check the program to identify logic errors that the programmer has overlooked.

At this point, before the actual testing, the program is usually recompiled according to a compiler program that optimizes the machine-language code (builds instruction sequences that will be most efficient for repetitive processing purposes). It may also provide diagnostic messages indicating possible logic problems.

The program is now ready to be executed using real, or "live," test data that represents what may be processed in real-life situations. If the data is processed correctly, the program is ready for use. However, correct processing seldom occurs on the first run. To identify the causes of errors, the programmer may submit trial runs with abnormal terminations that produce core dumps at the end of execution. Occasionally, an error is so subtle that the programmer cannot determine its cause by analyzing a dump. In this case, a trace program can be used to indicate the execution flow through the entire sequence of instructions. The programmer can then determine if the flow has mistakenly entered a wrong section of the program.

5. The system-test phase involves heavy user participation and is actually the beginning of user training. Each subsystem is thoroughly tested using user-supplied input data. Finally, the entire system is tested, usually running in parallel with the old system.

After the system has been thoroughly tested, a final review of the application is made by members of the staff who will be involved in its operation. This review includes a check to see that (1) the system conforms to established standards; (2) user and system development documentation requirements have been satisfied; and (3) the system is ready to be assigned to "production" status. If the total application is found to be acceptable, it is released for implementation.

The application is allowed to operate for two to three months following implementation. After this period, the user area and operations staff review the application and either document their acceptance or suggest revisions.

The complexity of activities involved in the development of a new application, from the objectives document through completion of the system test, is justified by the financial and business factors associated with such an undertaking. Failure to properly perform any of the steps in the process can result in, at best, considerable difficulty and, at worst, a complete failure of the application. For this reason, the stringent standards described above have been adopted by Eli Lilly and Company.

DISCUSSION POINTS

1. Why does Eli Lilly involve users so heavily in the designing of a new application? In what ways are users incorporated into the application development process?
2. What procedures are used to test the applications prior to their implementation?

10
Programming Languages

INTRODUCTION

The hardware capabilities of computers have grown tremendously during the past decade. However, benefits from the hardware technology cannot be realized unless there are complementary developments in software; thus, various programming languages have been developed to increase the usefulness of computers. The future of information processing appears to depend less on the development of better machine technologies than on the effectiveness with which we use existing capabilities. Thus, developments in software and programming technologies can be expected to play a key role in the future success of computer-based systems.

This chapter highlights the major programming languages used today. It discusses the unique features and characteristics and the advantages and disadvantages of each and identifies typical applications. The payroll program developed in Chapter 9 is used here as a sample program to illustrate use of the various languages. The chapter ends with a critical comparison of the languages that points out the factors to be considered in selecting the most appropriate one for a particular application.

ARTICLE

Are Computers Hazardous to Creativity?

Carol Tomme Thiel

How many of you bought personal computers for your children this Christmas?

Perhaps you justified the purchase on the basis that "it will help my child in school." But did you ever consider that it might hurt your child's creativity?

"We're a society that quantifies and analyzes structured data to make decisions," says Steve Kassay, founder of Kassay Consulting Services, Playa Del Rey, CA. "This is taught in our schools whether you're trained to be an engineer, an MBA or a social worker. The machine that enables us to quantify easier and faster is the computer."

But what are we doing as a society to increase our creative and intuitive capabilities? Kassay asks.

"Computers are machines of programmed logic, of rules and man-designed boundaries or limits," says Kassay, "while creativity means to originate, to bring into being. Computers use "reason." Therefore they are not expanding our intuitive abilities. But creativity and intuition are needed for problem solving."

Kassay notes that young children often produce wonderfully creative art, but "outgrow" this talent as they begin to learn the rules of color, composition and reality. "Our creativity and imagination are overpowered at an early age by our pragmatic rule system," he points out. "And today's child is experiencing the computer at a young age for

Reprinted from INFOSYSTEMS October 1984 copyright Hitchcock Publishing Co.

recreation and learning, but what kind of learning?"

On a recent NOVA program called "Talking Turtle," Seymour Papert, the designer of the Logo language, said use of computers in school for things like drills in arithmetic or language is a "misuse of the computer" and not really education.

"Education has little to do with explanation and more to do with falling in love with the material," says Papert. At least with Logo, he says, children can develop analytical skills, make and create procedures. There is no right way and no wrong way to program things, but children quickly learn to debug when they don't like the way the result looks.

Some educators don't agree that the computer is a danger to creativity, however. In a *Wall Street Journal* article (6/28/83) about computer use at Carnegie-Mellon University in Pittsburgh, some professors said students in the music, design, drama and other liberal arts departments "love" using the computer for taking tests, self-tutoring, and word processing. . .

Today's college students didn't grow up using computers, however. They grew up playing with old-fashioned toys like electric trains, erector sets, tinker toys and toy soldiers. They had a chance to develop their imaginations and now they are applying that creativity in their use of computers.

But what about children who are growing up with the computer? If they aren't limited to rote learning—

and if they are provided tools that let them explore and experiment—their creativity might expand beyond anything we've encountered so far. . .

Think about how you use the computer. If you're not very technical or haven't read all your system documentation, you're probably limited by the packaged programs you use: programs that someone else has written for you; programs limited by that person's intelligence and imagination. . .

If computers are used in schools merely to automate uncreative methods of learning, we might be risking computerization of our children. But if we can harness what Papert calls the "intensity and holding power" that computers are capable of, we can make learning more personal and more effective. And we've got to teach children computer skills that go beyond what someone else has programmed for them.

In reality, computer programming languages allow the computer to be used in a creative manner. Programming languages can be used to write programs that draw upon the user's own creativity. Some programs are used to produce creative works of art such as computer drawings and written documents. In many ways, computer programs can be used to help bring out an untapped creativeness in individuals. Programming languages, therefore, serve as the link between a person's creativity and the computer's processing power.

BATCH PROGRAMMING VERSUS INTERACTIVE PROGRAMMING

Batch Programming

Batch programming is used to solve problems for which immediate responses are not required. A batch program is submitted to the computer and is placed in a batch program **queue** by the operating system. The program can be submitted with a set of data or can access a file on secondary storage which contains the required set of data. Once the program has been moved to the CPU, processing takes place without intervention from programmers or users.

Batch programs are not executed as they are submitted to the computer. Instead, several batch programs are stored temporarily in the batch queue on a secondary storage device until the CPU is ready to execute them. Several batch program jobs may be submitted to the queue at the same time but processed at different times during the day or night, depending on their priorities. Batch programs on the whole normally have a low priority during hours when online programs require the resources of the CPU. Quick responses are critical to online applications and would be slowed if both online and batch programs were permitted to run at the same priority, thereby sharing the resources of the CPU.

Most batch programs are used to solve specific problems that occur according to some predetermined schedule. For example, payroll processing is usually done in batch mode, since the same payroll processing functions must be performed each week or month. The batch program can be executed at slack times, instead of monopolizing the CPU during prime-time hours. A batch program that contains the steps necessary to process the payroll can be written once and then used repeatedly to process different sets of data. Other common uses of batch programs include the generation of weekly or monthly reports and the generation of unscheduled reports which are not needed immediately.

Interactive Programming

Interactive programming allows the programmer or program user to communicate directly with the computer in a conversational fashion. Programs and data can be submitted directly to the computer from remote terminals. The programs are translated and executed, and the results are returned to the remote terminal in a matter of seconds. (In contrast, programs submitted in a batch environment may spend several hours in a queue before they are executed and the results returned to the user.)

The number of programs written for interactive computing has increased significantly in recent history. Nearly all programming languages are now capable of being used interactively. With the increase in demand for online systems, interactive programming has become quite common. Applications such as accounts receivable, inventory control, and billing, which were traditionally written as batch programs, have now been converted to online applications using interactive programming. Interactive programming, therefore, is the key to online applications.

MACHINE-ORIENTED LANGUAGES

Machine Language

The earliest computers were programmed by the arranging of various wires within the components. Up to six thousand switches could be set on the ENIAC to perform a program. However, when a new program was to be run, all of the switches had to be reset. Clearly, this was highly undesirable. The EDSAC, the first stored-program computer, allowed instructions to be entered into primary storage without the need for rewiring or setting switches, but some form of code was needed to enter these instructions. These codes came to be known as **machine language.**

Machine language is the language of the computer, the only language that the computer directly understands. It also functions as the object language of higher-level language programs, since all high-level languages must be translated into machine language in order for the computer to execute them.

Remember from Chapter 3 that data in digital computers is stored as either a 1 or a 0, an "on or "off" electrical state. Therefore, machine language must take the form of 1s and 0s to be understood by the machine. But coding a program in this binary form is very tedious, so machine language is often coded in either octal or hexadecimal codes.

The programmer using machine language must specify *everything* to the computer. Every step the computer must take to execute a program must be coded. This means that the programmer must know exactly how the computer works. Actual numerical addresses of storage locations for instructions and data must be specified. Every switch and register must be known. It should be noted, however, that due to the ease of use of higher-level languages, machine language is seldom used for application or system programming.

In order to accomplish the necessary specificity, each machine language instruction must have two parts. The **op code** (short for operation code) tells the computer what function to perform. The **operand** tells the computer what data to use when performing that function. The operand takes the form of the specific storage addresses where the data is located. Figure 10–1 shows examples of machine-language instructions.

Figure 10–1 ▪ Machine-Language Instructions Expressed in the Hexadecimal Number System

48	00	23C0	
4C	00	23C2	
40	00	2310	
D2	01	2310	2310
48	00	2310	
4E	00	2028	
F3	17	3002	2028
9G	F0	3003	

ADVANTAGES AND DISADVANTAGES The greatest advantage of machine language is that it is the most efficient in terms of storage area use and execution speed. It also allows the programmer to fully utilize the computer's potential for processing data.

On the other hand, programming in machine language is extremely tedious and time consuming. The instructions are difficult to remember and to use. Programs written in machine language will execute only on the specific machine for which they were written, so they must be rewritten if a new computer is purchased. Machine language is therefore totally unstandardized, unlike some high-level languages.

Assembly Language

Assembly languages were developed to alleviate many of the disadvantages of machine-language programming. When programming in an assembly language, the programmer uses symbolic names, or mnemonics, to specify machine operations; thus, coding in 0s and 1s is no longer required. Mnemonics are English-like abbreviations for the machine-language op codes. For example, Table 10–1 shows some common arithmetic operations coded in an assembly language and in binary.

Many of the operations listed in Table 10–1 involve the use of registers. Further, the mnemonic codes for assembly-language instructions differ depending on the type and model of computer. Thus, assembly-language programs, like machine-language programs, can be written only for the computers that will execute them.

There are three basic parts in an assembly-language instruction: an op code and an operand, as in machine language, and a label (see Table 10–2). The **label** is a programmer-supplied name that represents the first storage location to be used for an instruction. When the programmer wishes to refer to the instruction, he or she can simply specify the label, without regard to its storage location.

The op code, as in machine language, tells the computer what operation is to be performed, but it is in mnemonic form (refer again to Table 10–1). The operand, also in mnemonic form, represents the address of the item to be operated on. Each instruction may contain one or two operands. The remainder of the coding-form line can be used for remarks that explain the operation being performed (the remarks are optional).

Table 10–1 ▪ Examples of Assembly-Language Mnemonic Codes

OPERATION	TYPICAL ASSEMBLY-LANGUAGE MNEMONIC CODE	TYPICAL BINARY OP CODE
Add memory to register	A	01011010
Add (decimal) memory to register	AP	11111010
Multiply register by memory	M	01011100
Multiply (decimal) register by memory	MP	11111100
Subtract memory from register	S	01011011
Subtract (decimal) memory from register	SP	11111011
Move (numeric) from register to memory	MVN	11010001
Compare memory to register	C	01011001
Compare (decimal) memory to register	CP	11111001
Zero register and add (decimal) memory to register	ZAP	11111000

Table 10–2 ▪ The Parts of an Assembly-Language Instruction

LABEL	OP CODE	OPERANDS A AND B	REMARKS
OVERTIME	AP	OVERTIME, FORTY	BEGIN OVERTIME COMPUTATION
	MP	OVERTIME, WKRATE	
	AP	GROSS, WKRATE	
	SP	WKHRS, FORTY	COMPUTE OVERTIME PAY
	MP	WKHRS, ONEHLF	
	MP	GROSS, WKHRS	
	MVN	GROSS + 5(1), GROSS + 6	
	ZAP	GROSS(7), GROSS(6)	
	AP	GROSS, OVRTME	
TAXRATE	CP	GROSS, = P'25000'	BEGIN TAX COMPUTATION

For Adults Only

No longer are computer camps just for kids. Now, there are camps for adults from all backgrounds—not just executives.

Activities at a computer camp do not revolve solely around computers. There are opportunities to relax on the beach, go horseback riding, hiking, and much more.

Although adults can take a night class in computers, some people feel a computer camp has more advantages. Rather than just devoting a fraction of a day a few times a week to studying computers, many feel the idea of devoting an entire week to studying computers is more effective. A computer camp offers this.

Not all camps are recreational. Adult computer camps held at universities tend to be more academic than recreational. Also, the camp costs vary.

ADVANTAGES AND DISADVANTAGES   There are several advantages to using assembly language: First, it can be used to develop programs highly efficient in terms of storage space use and processing time. The programmer has tight control of the machine. Second, the assembler program performs certain checking functions and generates error messages (as needed) that are useful in debugging. Third, assembly language encourages modular programming techniques, which break a program into a number of separate modules, or programming units. The advantage of this technique is that it makes the logic of the total program more manageable; instead of one extensive program, it creates a group of small, easily handled segments.

The main disadvantage of assembly language is that it is cumbersome to use. Generally, one assembly-language instruction is translated into one machine-language instruction; this one-for-one relationship leads to long program preparation times.

Another disadvantage of assembly language is the high level of skill required to use it effectively. As with machine language, the programmer must know the computer to be used and must be able to work with binary or hexadecimal numbers and with codes such as EBCDIC. The task of writing the solution to a problem in assembly language is often the most difficult phase in the solution process.

Finally, assembly language is machine-dependent; a program written for one computer generally cannot be executed on another. Thus, equipment changes may require substantial reprogramming.

Assembly language is often used for operating systems. Because operating systems are designed for particular computers, they are machine-dependent. The potential efficiency of assembly language also makes it well suited for operating-system programming.

HIGH-LEVEL LANGUAGES

Procedure-Oriented versus Problem-Oriented Languages

In contrast to the machine orientation of machine language or assembly language, high-level languages are either procedure-oriented or problem-oriented. A procedure-oriented language places programming emphasis on describing the computational and logical procedures required to solve a problem. Commonly used procedure-oriented languages include COBOL, FORTRAN, and PL/I. A problem-oriented language is one in which the problem and solution are described without the necessary computational procedures being detailed. The most popular problem-oriented language is RPG.

Beyond being categorized as either procedure-oriented or problem-oriented, high-level languages can also be classified according to their functional orientation. Some languages have been designed for and function best in scientific applications. Others see their greatest use in business applications, while some have been designed primarily for use in education. There are those languages, however, that have been designed with no particular orientation in mind and can be used for problem solving in a number of different applications.

- A **batch program** is submitted to the computer and placed in a **queue,** where it will stay until sufficient CPU time is available to run the program.
- **Interactive programs** allow the user to communicate with the computer in a conversational manner.
- **Machine language** is the only language that can be directly understood by the computer. Machine language programs, therefore, are written using the binary number system—Os and 1s.
- **Assembly languages** are a step above machine language and use mnemonics to specify machine operations.
- **High-level languages** can be classified as either **procedure-oriented** or **problem-oriented. Procedure-oriented languages** emphasize computational and logical procedures, while **problem-oriented languages** emphasize the problem to be solved and not the computational procedures.

Scientific-Oriented Languages

FORTRAN FORTRAN (FORmula TRANslator) is the oldest high-level programming language. It originated in the mid-1950s, when most programs were written in either assembly language or machine language. Efforts were made to develop a programming language that resembled English but could be translated into machine language by the computer. This effort, backed by IBM, produced FORTRAN—the first commercially available high-level language.

Early FORTRAN compilers contained many errors and were not always efficient. Moreover, several manufacturers offered variations of FORTRAN that could be used only on their computers. Although many improvements were made, early FORTRAN continued to suffer from this lack of standardization. In response to this problem, the American National Standards Institute (ANSI) laid the groundwork for a standardized FORTRAN. In 1966, two standard versions of FORTRAN were recognized—ANSI FORTRAN and Basic FORTRAN. They were very similar to two earlier versions, FORTRAN IV and FORTRAN II. A group from the University of Waterloo in Ontario developed a subset of FORTRAN—WATFOR (Waterloo FORTRAN)—specifically for the beginning or student programmer. Improvements were added to WATFOR, and the enhanced version was called WATFIV. In spite of the attempts to standardize FORTRAN, however, most computer manufacturers have continued to offer their own extensions of the language. Therefore, compatibility of FORTRAN remains a problem today.

In 1957, when FORTRAN was first released, the computer was primarily used by engineers, scientists, and mathematicians. Consequently, FORTRAN was developed to meet their needs, and its purpose has remained unchanged. FORTRAN is a procedure-oriented language with extraordinary mathematical capabilities. It is especially applicable where numerous complex arithmetic calculations are necessary. However, it is not well suited for programs involving file maintenance, editing of data, or production of documents. Figure 10–2 shows the sample payroll program in FORTRAN.

The basic unit of a FORTRAN program is a statement. There is only one statement that must appear in every program: END. A FORTRAN program is one unit that incorporates all storage declarations, computations, and in-

Figure 10–2 ▪ Payroll Program in FORTRAN

```
FORTRAN IV G LEVEL 21        MAIN                DATE = 81214

        WRITE (6,1)
    1   FORMAT('1','EMPLOYEENAME',5X,'NETPAY'/'')
    2   READ (5,3) NA,NB,NC,ND,NHOURS,WAGE,IEND
    3   FORMAT (4A4, 12, 2X, F4.2, 54X, 12)
        IF (IEND.EQ.99) STOP
        IF (NHOURS.GT.40) GO TO 10
        GROSS = FLOAT(NHOURS)*WAGE
        GO TO 15
   10   REG = 40.*WAGE
        OVERTM=FLOAT(NHOURS-40)*(1.5*WAGE)
        GROSS=REG+OVERTM
   15   IF (GROSS.GT.250.) GO TO 20
        RATE = .14
        GO TO 25
   20   RATE = .20
   25   TAX=RATE*GROSS
        PAY = GROSS - TAX
        WRITE (6,50) NA,NB,NC,ND,PAY
   50   FORMAT (' ', ,4A4, 3X, F6.2)
        GO TO 2
        END
```

Output

EMPLOYEE NAME	NET PAY
LYNN MANGINO	224.00
THOMAS RITTER	212.42
MARIE OLSON	209.00
LORI DUNLEVY	172.00
WILLIAM WILSON	308.00

put/output definitions. Also, FORTRAN does not require that most variables be declared before use. Record descriptions are contained in FORMAT statements within the program.

Four types of statements are used in FORTRAN programs: control statements, arithmetic statements, input/output statements, and specification statements. Control statements determine the sequence in which operations will be performed and govern operations such as choosing between alternatives and branching to another part of the program. Arithmetic statements direct the computer to perform computations. Input/output statements instruct the computer to read data from, or write data to, an I/O device. Specification statements tell FORTRAN *how* to interpret data read from an input device and how to write data to an output device.

Numbers are represented by two kinds of variables: real number variables and integer variables. Variable names beginning with the letters I through N are reserved for integers. A variable name is usually limited to a length of six characters.

In FORTRAN, a string of **alphanumeric** characters (numeric, alphabetic, or special) must be divided into groups of four characters each. Thus, to store alphanumeric data consisting of more than four characters, more than one variable is needed. For example, assume a data card contains an employee's name in the first sixteen columns. The programmer can use four **single,** or **simple, variables,** each of which stands for a single data item. (Refer to line 3 of Figure 10–2.)

Notice that only two characters are stored in the locations set aside for the variable name ND. The remaining space is filled with blanks.

FORTRAN also allows **array variables** which can be used to represent groups of similar data items. The elements of the array are referred to by **subscripts.** The same employee name shown above could be represented by an array name N with four elements.

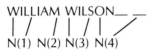

ADVANTAGES AND DISADVANTAGES FORTRAN was designed for use by engineers, scientists, and mathematicians and is used with great success in scientific applications. Use of FORTRAN for certain types of business applications is increasing; for example, FORTRAN is often used for quantitative analysis involving techniques such as linear programming and regression analysis.

In general, however, FORTRAN is not a good business language, primarily because it was designed for scientific purposes. It has limited ability to process alphabetic data and files and to format printed reports, which are all necessities for a good business language. Also, as Figure 10–2 shows, FORTRAN does not closely resemble English and so requires good documentation.

APL **APL** (A Programming Language) was conceived in 1962 by Kenneth Iverson, who described it in his book *A Programming Language,* and worked with IBM to develop it. APL became available to the public through IBM in 1968 and, over the years, has been expanded and has gained many enthusiastic supporters.

The full power of APL is best realized when it is used for interactive processing via a terminal. A programmer can use APL in two modes. In the **execution mode,** the terminal can be used much like a desk calculator. An instruction is keyed in on one line, and the response is returned immediately on the following line. In the **definition mode,** a series of instructions is entered into memory and the entire program is executed on command from the programmer. The APL user enters statements to develop a source program, system commands to communicate with the operating system, and editing commands to modify the source program. However, APL bears little resemblance to any high-level programming language we will discuss.

Both character-string data and numeric data can be manipulated when APL is used. It is especially well suited for handling tables of related numbers known as **arrays.** To simplify the programmer's task, a number of operations (up to fifty or more) are provided for array manipulation, logical comparisons, mathematical functions, branching operations, and so forth. The operators are represented by symbols on a special APL keyboard (see Figure 10–3). Some examples of APL coding are shown in Table 10–3. Figure 10–4 illustrates an interactive APL session.

Figure 10–3 ▪ APL Keyboard

ADVANTAGES AND DISADVANTAGES APL operators can be combined to perform some very complex operations with a minimum of coding. APL's lack of formal restrictions on input and output and its free-form style make it a very powerful language. It can be learned quickly by programmers. APL is also available through time-sharing networks for organizations that need only a limited amount of data processing.

APL involves a few disadvantages as well. It is very difficult to read. Further, as mentioned above, a special keyboard is required to enter APL statements; fortunately, however, the large offering of new, low-cost terminals capable of handling several type fonts has greatly reduced this problem. Many people do not believe that APL is suitable for handling large data files. Another limitation of APL is the large amount of primary storage required by its compiler. Usually, only large and medium-sized systems are capable of supporting APL. However, if a network of remote terminals is connected to a large central computer, APL can be made available to users at the remote sites. (Indeed, time-sharing networks such as this have led to increased use of APL.) Finally, APL is not as widely offered by vendors as other high-level languages.

Business-Oriented Languages

COBOL COBOL (COmmon Business-Oriented Language) is the most frequently used business programming language. Before 1960, no language well suited to solving business problems existed. Recognizing this inadequacy, the Department of Defense called together representatives of computer users, manufacturers, and government installations to examine the feasibility of establishing a common business programming language. That was the beginning of the **CODASYL** (Conference of Data Systems Languages) Committee. By 1960, the committee had established the specifications for COBOL, and the first commercial versions of the language were offered later that year. The

Table 10–3 ▪ APL Coding

APL CODING	ENGLISH TRANSLATION
A + B	A plus B
A ← 25	A = 25
ALB	Finds the smaller of A and B
V1 ← 2 5 11 17	Creates a vector of 4 components and assigns this vector to V1
r/ V1	Finds the maximum value in the vector V1

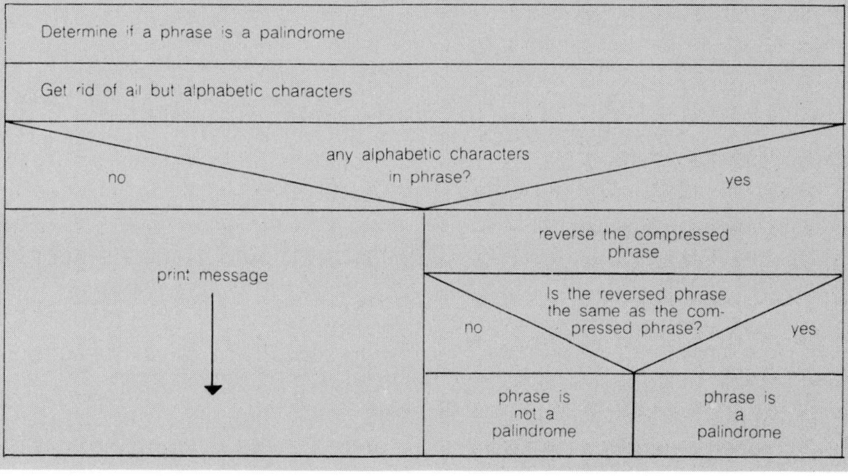

Figure 10—4 ■ Interactive APL Session

```
      ∇PALINDROME[□]∇

    ∇ PALINDROME PHRASE;ALPHA;COMPRESSED;REVERSE
[1]   A  PROGRAM TO DETERMINE IF A PHRASE IS A PALINDROME
[2]   A  THE PHRASE MUST BE CHARACTER DATA AND HAVE AT LEAST ONE
[3]    ALPHA←'ABCDEFGHIJKLMNOPQRSTUVWXYZ'
[4]    COMPRESSED←(PHRASE∈ALPHA)/PHRASE
[5]    →(0 =ρCOMPRESSED)/NONE
[6]    REVERSE←COMPRESSED[∇ιρCOMPRESSED]
[7]    →( ∧/REVERSE=COMPRESSED)/YES
[8]    PHRASE,'  IS NOT A PALINDROME'
[9]    →0
[10]  YES:PHRASE,'  IS A PALINDROME'
[11]   →0
[12]  NONE:'THERE ARE NO ALPHABETIC CHARACTER IN PHRASE'
    ∇


      PALINDROME 'MOM'
MOM  IS A PALINDROME


      PALINDROME 'THIS'
THIS  IS NOT A PALINDROME


      PALINDROME 'MADAM IN EDEN I''M ADAM'
MADAM IN EDEN I'M ADAM  IS A PALINDROME


      PALINDROME '1 21'
THERE ARE NO ALPHABETIC CHARACTER IN PHRASE
```

government furthered its cause in the mid-1960s by refusing to buy or lease any computer that could not process a program written in COBOL.

One of the objectives of the CODASYL group was to establish a language that was machine-independent—that could be used on any computer. Thus, when several manufacturers began offering their own modifications and extensions of COBOL, a need for standardization became apparent. Consequently, in 1968 ANSI established and published guidelines for a standardized COBOL that became known as ANSI COBOL. In 1974, ANSI published a revised version of the standard in which the language definition was ex-

Figure 10–5 ▪ Payroll Program in COBOL

```
    IDENTIFICATION DIVISION.
    PROGRAM-ID. PAYROLL.
    INPUT-OUTPUT SECTION.
    FILE-CONTROL.
        SELECT CARD-FILE ASIGN TO UR-S-SYSIN.
        SELECT PRINT-FILE ASSIGN TO UR-S-OUTPUT.

    DATA DIVISION.
    FILE SECTION.
    FD  CARD-FILE
        LABEL RECORDS ARE OMITTED
        RECORD CONTAINS 80 CHARACTERS
        DATA RECORD IS PAY-RECORD.
    01  PAY-RECORD.
        03  EMPLOYEE-NAME        PIC A(16).
        03  HOURS-WORKED         PIC 99.
        03  WAGE-PER-HOUR        PIC 99V99.
        03  FILLER               PIC X(58).

    FD  PRINT-FILE
        LABEL RECORDS ARE OMITTED
        RECORD CONTAINS 132 CHARACTERS
        DATA RECORD IS PRINT-RECORD.
    01  PRINT-RECORD             PIC X(132).

    WORKING-STORAGE SECTION.
    77  GROSS-PAY                PIC 9(3)V99.
    77  REGULAR-PAY              PIC 9(3)V99.
    77  OVERTIME-PAY             PIC 9(3)V99.
    77  NET-PAY                  PIC 9(3)V99.
    77  TAX                      PIC 9(3)V99.
    77  OVERTIME-HOURS           PIC 99.
    77  OVERTIME-RATE            PIC 9(3)V999.
    77  EOF-FLAG                 PIC X(3)        VALUE 'NO'.

    01  HEADING-LINE.
        03 FILLER               PIC X           VALUE SPACES.
        03 FILLER               PIC X(21)       VALUE
            'EMPLOYEE NAME'.
        03 FILLER               PIC X(7)        VALUE
            'NET PAY'.

    01  OUTPUT-RECORD.
        03 FILLER               PIC X           VALUE SPACES.
        03 NAME                 PIC A(16).
        03 FILLER               PIC X(5)        VALUE SPACES.
        03 AMOUNT               PIC $$$$.99.
        03 FILLER               PIC X(103)      VALUE SPACES.

    PROCEDURE DIVISION.
    MAIN-LOGIC.
        OPEN INPUT CARD-FILE
             OUTPUT PRINT-FILE.
        PERFORM HEADING-ROUTINE.
        READ CARD-FILE AT END MOVE 'YES' TO EOF-FLAG.
        PERFORM WORK-LOOP UNTIL EOF-FLAG = 'YES'.
        CLOSE CARD-FILE
              PRINT-FILE.
        STOP RUN.

    HEADING-ROUTINE.
        WRITE PRINT-RECORD FROM HEADING-LINE
              BEFORE ADVANCING 2 LINES.
```

Figure 10–5 ▪ Continued

```
WORK-LOOP.
    IF HOURS-WORKED IS GREATER THEN 40
        THEN
            PERFORM OVERTIME-ROUTINE
        ELSE
            MULTIPLY HOURS-WORKED BY WAGE-PER-HOUR
                    GIVING GROSS-PAY.
    PERFORM TAX-COMPUTATION.
    PERFORM OUTPUT-ROUTINE.
    READ CARD-FILE AT END MOVE 'YES' TO EOF-FLAG.

OVERTIME-ROUTINE.
    MULTIPLY WAGE-PER-HOUR BY 40 GIVING REGULAR-PAY.
    SUBTRACT 40 FROM HOURS-WORKED GIVING OVERTIME-HOURS.
    MULTIPLY OVERTIME-HOURS BY 1.5 GIVING OVERTIME-RATE.
    MULTIPLY OVERTIME-HOURS BY OVERTIME-RATE
            GIVING OVERTIME-PAY.
    ADD REGULAR-PAY, OVERTIME-PAY GIVING GROSS-PAY.

TAX-COMPUTATION.
    IF GROSS-PAY IS GREATER THEN 250
        THEN
            MULTIPLY GROSS-PAY BY 0.20 GIVING TAX
        ELSE
            MULTIPLY GROSS-PAY BY 0.14 GIVING TAX.
    SUBTRACT TAX FROM GROSS-PAY GIVING NET-PAY.

OUTPUT-ROUTINE.
    MOVE EMPLOYEE-NAME TO NAME.
    MOVE NET-PAY TO AMOUNT.
    WRITE PRINT-RECORD FROM OUTPUT-RECORD
            BEFORE ADVANCING 1 LINES.
```

Output

```
    EMPLOYEE NAME           NET PAY

    LYNN MANGINO            224.00
    THOMAS RITTER          212.42
    MARIE OLSON            209.00
    LORI DUNLEVY           172.00
    WILLIAM WILSON         308.00
```

panded. The CODASYL Committee has continued to examine the feasibility of modifying or incorporating new features into COBOL and has proposed a new version (COBOL '80) that has not yet been accepted.

Another key objective of the designers of COBOL was to make the language look like English. Their intent was that programs written in COBOL should be understandable even to casual readers, and hence self-documenting. You can judge how successful they were by looking at Figure 10–5, which shows the payroll application coded in COBOL.

COBOL programs have a formal, uniform structure. Many types of statements must appear in the same form and position in every COBOL program. The basic unit of a COBOL program is the sentence. Sentences are combined to form paragraphs; paragraphs are joined into sections; and sections are con-

SOURCE: *Datamation* April, 1981. Reprinted by permission

"By Jove. . . this is written in COBOL!"

tained within divisions. COBOL programs must have four divisions: IDENTI-FICATION, ENVIRONMENT, DATA, and PROCEDURE. The divisions appear in the program in this order and are identified by headings, as in Figure 10–5.

The IDENTIFICATION DIVISION provides documentation of the program. At a minimum, a unique name is assigned to the program. The program's author, the date it was written, the compilation date, and relevant security requirements may also be provided.

In theory, the ENVIRONMENT DIVISION is the only machine-dependent division of a COBOL program. Its purpose is to specify the computer to be used when the program is compiled and executed. File information is related to input/output devices. Therefore, if the program is run on different computer systems, adjustments to the ENVIRONMENT DIVISION may be required.

The DATA DIVISION describes the variable names, records, and files to be used by the program. Variables—words chosen and defined by the programmer to represent data items referred to in the program—are mnemonics for the storage locations of data. Each data name may be up to thirty characters long; since letters, numbers, and embedded hyphens can be used, this allows for very descriptive data names. In COBOL, the programmer need only know the variable name; the COBOL language keeps track of actual data locations in storage. Figure 10–5 shows some examples of data names. The input and output formats of data are also specified in the DATA DIVISION. These formats tell the program how data is to be brought in and how it is to be written to an output or storage device.

The PROCEDURE DIVISION contains the actual processing instructions. In keeping with its English-like nature, COBOL uses verbs in its statements to perform various functions—for example, READ, MULTIPLY, ADD, SUB-TRACT, MOVE, and WRITE. Since these verbs have special meanings in COBOL, they are called reserved words. In all, more than 250 words are contained in COBOL's reserved word list.

ADVANTAGES AND DISADVANTAGES COBOL offers many advantages as a business programming language. Because of its English-like nature, programs that use it require little additional documentation; well-written COBOL programs tend to be self-documenting. COBOL is much easier to learn than either machine language or assembly language, since learning it does not involve learning detailed machine functions. Testing and debugging are simplified, because the logic of the program is easy to follow.

COBOL also has strong file-handling capabilities, unlike FORTRAN and other languages used primarily in scientific applications. It supports sequential, indexed, and relative files (to be discussed in Chapter 14). Although many COBOL application programs are written for batch processing, COBOL is being used increasingly in an interactive mode.

One final advantage of COBOL is its standardization, which allows a firm to switch computer equipment with little or no rewriting of existing programs. Because COBOL is widely supported, many programmers know it through previous experience or college training. Thus, organizations are able to acquire experienced programmers to maintain and enhance their applications.

The effort to make COBOL as English-like as possible has resulted in some disadvantages. A large and sophisticated compiler program is needed to translate a COBOL source program into machine language. Such a compiler occupies a large portion of primary storage. As a result, COBOL cannot be used on some small computers. (However, there are some COBOL compilers supporting subsets of the language that can be used with microcomputers.)

Another disadvantage is COBOL's tendency to be wordy. Using COBOL may require that many more statements be made to solve a problem than would be needed with a more compact language such as FORTRAN. Certain features of COBOL make it less than ideal for structured programming (discussed in Chapter 11). Finally, COBOL's computational abilities are limited; for this reason, it is seldom used for scientific and mathematical applications.

Regardless of COBOL's disadvantages, it is likely to remain a popular language for many years. Polls indicate that over 80 percent of business application programs are written in COBOL. Converting these hundreds of thousands of COBOL programs to other languages and retraining thousands of programmers would not be easy tasks for the business community.

RPG RPG (Report Program Generator) is a problem-oriented language originally designed to produce business reports. Basically, the programmer using RPG describes the type of report desired without having to specify much of the logic involved. A generator program is then used to build (generate) a program to produce the report. Therefore, little programming skill is required to use RPG.

Since RPG was initially intended to support the logic of punched-card equipment, it is used primarily with small computer systems. Many firms that formerly used electromechanical punched-card processing equipment have upgraded their data-processing operations to small computer systems. These firms usually have relatively simple, straightforward data-processing needs. In such cases, a small computer system supporting RPG can provide signifi-

A Countess Is Honored

Aren't the names of most common programming languages dull? Really. There's BASIC, RPG, FORTRAN, PL/I, APL, all acronyms and all very—well—basic.

But the new state-of-the-art language developed by the U.S. Department of Defense is named after a real, flesh-and-blood person with an interesting name: Ada Augusta Byron, Countess of Lovelace and daughter of the poet Lord Byron. The language is called Ada in honor of Lady Lovelace's achievements, which became the foundation for modern computer programming.

Lady Lovelace was a prodigy in mathematics. She worked with Charles Babbage, the English mathematician who designed the difference engine and the analytical engine, both prototypes of the modern computer. Lady Lovelace's ideas earned her the title ''the first programmer.'' She introduced the looping technique for repeating like instructions and suggested the binary system instead of the decimal system for Babbage's engine.

Ada is no beginner's language. It may take a skilled programmer six months to become proficient in Ada. The language, a derivative of Pascal, will be used to standardize American military computers. Now what if it had been named LOVE for Lovelace?

cantly improved data-processing operations. Management reports can be produced in a fraction of the time required by electromechanical methods.

RPG is now used for processing files as well as for preparing printed output. The programmer does not code the statements required; instead, he or she completes specification forms such as those shown in Figure 10–6. All files, records, and fields to be manipulated must be defined by entries in specific columns on the specification forms. The operations to be performed and the content and format of output files are described similarly. The entries on the RPG forms are keypunched, combined with job-control cards, and submitted to the computer. The RPG program builds an object program from the source program, and the object program is executed by the computer (see Figure 10–7).

Like other programming languages, RPG is constantly being improved. IBM introduced a new version named RPGII in the early 1970s for use on its IBM System/3 computers. This new version has been widely accepted and is now supported by many computer manufacturers; in fact, it has essentially replaced the original RPG. A third version introduced in 1979, RPGIII, features the ability to process data stored on a data base.

ADVANTAGES AND DISADVANTAGES RPG is easy to learn and to use because the basic pattern of execution is fixed. Since it does not require large amounts of primary storage, it is one of the primary languages of small computers and minicomputers. RPG provides an efficient means for generating reports requiring simple logic and calculations; it is commonly used to process files for accounts receivable, accounts payable, general ledgers, and inventory.

However, the computational capabilities of RPG are limited. Some RPG compilers can generate machine-language instructions for up to thirty different operations. However, compared with COBOL, FORTRAN, and PL/1, RPG's looping, branching, and decision capabilities are restricted. It is not a standardized language; therefore, RPG programs may require a significant degree of modification if they are to be executed on a computer other than the one for which they were initially written. This is especially true if a firm changes computer manufacturers. However, if a firm stays with a particular manufacturer's equipment, its RPG programs can generally be run on a similar but more powerful computer with only slight modifications.

Ada Ada is a relatively new, high-level programming language developed for use by the Department of Defense. Ada is named after Agusta Ada Byron, Countess of Lovelace and daughter of Lord Byron the poet. Agusta Ada Byron worked with Charles Babbage, programming his difference engine (see Chapter 2), and for this reason is often referred to as the first programmer. Ada is derived from Pascal, another high-level language which will be discussed later in the chapter.

The need for a language such as Ada was determined by a Department of Defense study conducted in 1974, which found that over $7 billion was spent on software in 1973. Through further study it was found that no current high-level language could meet the needs of the Department of Defense and a new language would have to be developed. In 1980 the Department of Defense approved the initial Ada standard, and in 1983 ANSI approved the Ada standard. Because of the considerable influence the Department of Defense has had and continues to have in this area, it is believed that Ada will some-

**Figure 10–6 ▪ RPG Program
Specification Forms**

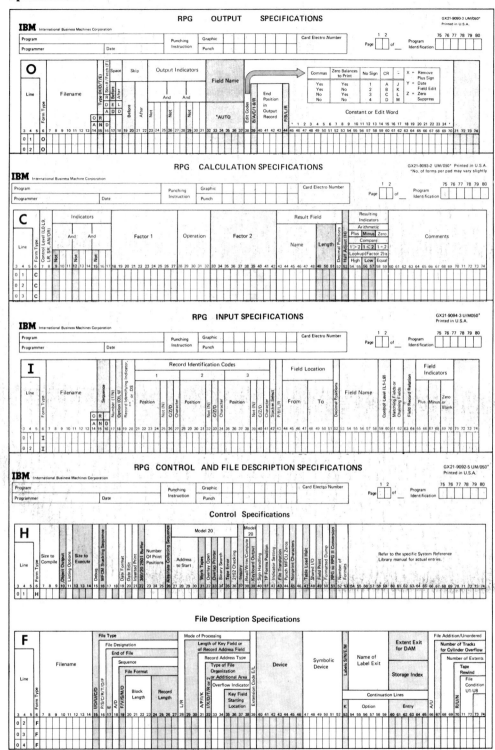

Figure 10–7 ▪ **Payroll Program in RPG**

```
00010H         0003          132
00020F*                          PAYROLL EXAMPLE
00030FCDIN    IP  F  80  80              READ01
00040FPRINTR  O   F 132 132     OF    PRINTER
000501* DEFINES INPUT
000601ICDIN    ZZ  01  80  CD
000701                                1   6 DATE
000801         ZZ  02
000901                                1  10DEPT   L1
001008                                2   5 EMPNO
001101                                6  92HRS
001201                               10 133RATE
001301                               14 140EXEMP
00510C*TO FIND GROSS PAY, NET PAY
00511C    40              SETOF                        30
00512C    N40 02          SETON                      3040
00520C    02      HRS     COMP  40.00            100909
00530C    02 09   RATE    MULT  HRS     GROSS 52H
00540C    02 10   HRS     SUB   40.00   OTHRS 42
00550C    02 10   RATE    MULT  40.00   REG   52
00560C    02 10   RATE    MULT  1.5     OTRT  43
00570C    02 10   OTHRS   MULT  OTRT    OVER  52
00580C    02 10   REG     ADD   OVER    GROSS 52
00590C    02      EXEMP   MULT  14.40   EXAMT 52H        EXEMPT AMT
00600C    02      GROSS   SUB   EXAMT   BASE  52
00610C    02      BASE    MULT  .12     INCTX 52HN       INCOME TAX DED
00620C    02      GROSS   SUB   INCTX   NET   52
00630C    02      GROSS   ADD   DGROSS  DGROSS 62
00640C    02      HRS     ADD   DHRS    DHRS  52
00650C    02      GROSS   ADD   GGROSS  GGROSS 72
00660C    02      HRS     ADD   GHRS    GHRS  62
001400* DEFINES HEADINGS AND OUTPUT
001500OPRINTR   H 0201    01
001600        OR          OF
001700                              10'DATE'
001800                      DATE    19'  /  /  '
002100                              67'PAYROLL'
002200                             120'PAGE'
002300                      PAGE   125'  0'
002400          H 02      L1
002500        OR          OF
002600                              10'DEPT'
002700                              24'EMP NO'
002800                              37'HOURS'
002900                              49'RATE'
003000                              63'GROSS'
003100                              81'EXEMPTIONS'
003200                             100'INCOME TAX'
003300                             115'NET PAY'
003400          D 02      02
003500                      DEPT
003510            L1
003510            30        DEPT     8
003600                      EMPNO   23
003700                      HRS     37'  .  '
003800                      RATE    49'  .  '
003900                      GROSS   63'  0.  '
004000                      EXEMP   76
004100                      INCTX   97'  0.  '
004200                      NET    114'  0.  '
004300          T 33      L1
004400                              27'DEPARTMENT
004500                      DGROSS B 63'  , $0.  '
004600                      DHRS   B 37'  0.  '
004700          T 30      LR
004800                              29'GRAND TOTALS
004900                      GGROSS B 63'  , $0.  '
005000                      GHRS   B 39'  0.  '
```

Figure 10–7 ▪ Continued

```
//GO.PRINTR DD SYSOUT=A
//GO.CDIN   DD =
052775
10029400031753
10087410029002
10141420044401
10160400026754
10387445049954
10401510037502
10403400029003
20037300024502
20098400029701
20201400044501
20221440041503
20485478541705
/*EOF
```

Output

```
                                        PAYROLL

   DEPT   EMP NO    HOURS    RATE     GROSS    EXEMPTIONS    INCOME TAX    NET PAY


   1       0029     40.00   3.175    127.00        3           10.06       116.94
           0087     41.00   2.900    120.35        2           10.99       109.36
           0141     42.00   4.440    190.92        1           21.18       169.74
           0160     40.00   2.675    107.00        4            5.93       101.07
           0387     44.50   4.995    233.51        4           21.11       212.40
           0401     51.00   3.750    211.87        2           21.97       189.90
           0403     40.00   2.900    116.00        3            8.74       107.26

   DEPARTMENT
   TOTALS           298.50          $1,106.65

   DEPT   EMP NO    HOURS    RATE     GROSS    EXEMPTIONS    INCOME TAX    NET PAY


   2       0037     40.00   2.450     98.00        2            8.30        89.70
           0098     40.00   2.970    118.80        1           12.53       106.27
           0201     40.00   4.450    178.00        1           19.63       158.37
           0221     44.00   4.150    190.90        3           17.72       173.18
           0485     47.85   4.170    215.90        5           17.27       198.63

   DEPARTMENT
   TOTALS           211.85           $801.60

   GRAND TOTALS     510.35          $1,908.25
```

day replace COBOL as the most widely used programming language in business.

Education-Oriented Languages

BASIC   **BASIC** (Beginners' All-Purpose Symbolic Instruction Code) was developed at Dartmouth College in 1965 for use by students on time-sharing systems. Because BASIC is easy to learn, it can be used by those who have little or no programming experience—novice programmers can write fairly complex programs in BASIC in only a matter of hours.

The growth in the use of time-sharing systems has been accompanied by an increase in the use of BASIC. Most computer manufacturers offer BASIC support on their computers. Although BASIC was originally intended to be used by colleges and universities for instructional purposes, many companies have adopted it for their data-processing needs. In addition, the increasing popularity of microcomputers in homes is furthering the use of BASIC, since it is the language most often supported by these microcomputers.

A BASIC program consists of a series of sequentially numbered statements. Each statement occupies a separate line. Following the line number is a keyword, such as PRINT or READ, which identifies the type of statement. Figure 10–8 shows the payroll program coded in BASIC.

Writing a BASIC program involves typing three types of entries from the terminal:

- Programming-language statements are used to write the BASIC program. BASIC statements such as IF, GO TO, PRINT, and INPUT correspond to similar statements used in other high-level languages.
- System commands are used to communicate with the operating system. For example, the terminal user must type a system command such as RUN to

Figure 10–8 ▪ Payroll Program in BASIC

```
10  REM THIS PROGRAM CALCULATES A WEEKLY
20  REM PAYROLL FOR FIVE EMPLOYEES
30  PRINT "EMPLOYEE NAME",,"NET PAY"
40  PRINT
50  READ N$,H,W
60  IF N$ = "END OF DATA" THEN 270
70  IF H > 40 THEN 100
80  LET G = H * W
90  GOTO 130
100 LET R = 40 * W
110 LET O = (H - 40) * (1.5 * W)
120 LET G = R + O
130 IF G > 250 THEN 160
140 LET T = .14
150 GOTO 170
160 LET T = .2
170 LET T2 = T * G
180 LET P = G - T2
190 PRINT N$,P
200 GOTO 50
210 DATA "LYNN MANGINO  ",35,8.00
220 DATA "THOMAS RITTER ",48,4.75
230 DATA "MARIE OLSON   ",45,5.50
240 DATA "LORI DUNLEVY  ",40,5.00
250 DATA "WILLIAM WILSON",50,7.00
260 DATA "END OF DATA",0,0
270 END
```

Output

```
RUN
EMPLOYEE NAME              NET PAY

LYNN MANGINO               224.00
THOMAS RITTER              212.42
MARIE OLSON                209.00
LORI DUNLEVY               172.00
WILLIAM WILSON             308.00
```

direct the computer to begin program execution. To terminate program execution, the user types the system command STOP.

■ Editing commands are used for inserting changes in, or deleting parts of, the source program. For instance, the programmer can delete an incorrectly keyed letter or number simply by pressing the backward arrow (←) key and then typing the correct character.

ADVANTAGES AND DISADVANTAGES   Among BASIC's most attractive features are its simplicity and flexibility. It is very easy to learn. It can be used for both scientific and business applications. And although BASIC was intended for use as an interactive programming language, it is finding increased use as a batch language.

The simplicity of BASIC has led many manufacturers to offer different versions of the language. A BASIC standard was established in 1978, but it covers only a small subset of the BASIC language.

BASIC programs written for one system may need substantial modification before being used on another. Many extensions to BASIC have been developed, but only at the expense of increasing the difficulty of learning and using the language. As firms continue to expand online programming applications, however, the use of BASIC will no doubt continue to increase.

Logo   **Logo** is a procedure-oriented, interactive programming language developed initially by Seymor Papert at MIT in 1966. Logo's main attraction is that it allows children of all ages to begin to program and communicate with the computer in a very short period of time. Logo allows the user to draw images, animate them, and color them using very simple instructions.

Logo accomplishes this interactive programming of graphics through a triangular object called a **turtle**, which leaves a graphic trail in its path. The user can easily command the turtle to draw straight lines, squares, or other objects as his or her skill level increases. Figure 10−9 contains a Logo program that illustrates statements that can be used to draw a square. When graphics mode is first entered, the turtle is located near the center of the monitor screen and is pointing to the 0 degree position. To draw a square with sides of 30 screen units in length, the program in Figure 10−9 could be used.

Figure 10−9 ▪ A Logo Program to Draw a Square

```
 10   GR:   CLEAR
 20   GR:   GOTO -15,5
 30   GR:   DRAW 30
 40   GR:   TURN 90
 50   GR:   DRAW 30
 60   GR:   TURN 90
 70   GR:   DRAW 30
 80   GR:   TURN 90
 90   GR:   DRAW 30
100   GR:   TURN 90
110   E:
```

The GR is used to indicate a graphics command. Line 10 clears the screen of any previous drawings and line 20 positions the turtle at location −15, 5 to begin the drawing. Line 30 directs the turtle to draw a straight line 30 units long and line 40 turns the turtle 90 degrees. The program continues in this fashion until the square is completed in line 100. The E of line 110 signals the end of the program.

ADVANTAGES AND DISADVANTAGES   Logo has been developed as an education-oriented language; its strengths lie in its ability to help the inexperienced user to learn. Primarily, Logo helps the user to realize and develop the procedures required to solve a given problem using the computer. It also helps the user learn to communicate with the computer and to develop an understanding of what programming is all about, including the debugging of programs. Logo's main advantage, therefore, is its simplicity, which helps the inexperienced computer user adjust to the programming environment.

The primary disadvantage of Logo is its limited overall capability. Currently, very few, if any, applications exist for Logo outside the area of education, while BASIC is now being used extensively for many business applications. Taken, however, as the introductory educational tool for which it was designed, Logo is very adept at accomplishing its goals.

Multi-Purpose Languages

PL/I PL/I (Programming Language I) was designed to be an all-purpose, procedure-oriented language for both scientific and business applications. With the increased use of management-science techniques such as linear programming and regression analysis, the business programmer needed a language with greater computational capabilities than COBOL. By the same token, a language with greater file-manipulation ability than FORTRAN was desired by the scientific programmer. PL/I combined the best features of both COBOL and FORTRAN; it is a flexible high-level language. PL/I was introduced in 1964 for use with IBM System/360 computers and is still primarily an IBM-sponsored language, although it is used on other computers.

Most languages impose some rather strict coding rules on the programmer. Column restrictions are prevalent. In contrast, PL/I is a free-form language with very few such restrictions.

The basic element in a PL/I program is the statement, which must be terminated by a semicolon. Statements are not confined to individual lines or paragraphs and need not begin in certain columns, as long as they are between columns 2 and 72 (see Figure 10–10).

In additon to its free-form characteristic, PL/I has many other desirable features. PL/I programs can be constructed in a modular fashion; separate logical procedures, called blocks, can be combined to form a complete program. This simplifies writing of the program and facilitates the use of structured programming techniques (to be discussed in Chapter 11).

The PL/I compiler has certain default features. A **default** is a course of action chosen by the compiler when several alternatives exist but none has been explicitly stated by the programmer. The default has been determined by the designers to be the alternative most often required. For example, if the programmer does not specify the types of data to be represented by particular variable names, the compiler assumes that data items beginning with the letters I through N represent integer values. Thus, the number of statements needed in a program is reduced.

The PL/I compiler also contains several **built-in functions,** SQRT (for taking square roots) and LOG (for finding logarithms). The availability of these built-in functions greatly simplifies the programmer's task; he or she need only refer to a required function by name to cause the corresponding pretested, correct routine to be executed and the results returned to the program. Many of these functions are also offered in FORTRAN but have no equivalents in COBOL.

PL/I was designed to be used by both novice and expert programmers. The beginning programmer can learn to write programs using basic features of the language. As knowledge of the language increases, the programmer can use more powerful features to write programs to solve complex problems.

Various subsets of PL/I containing only portions of the full language have been developed. These subsets are especially geared toward educational use (just as WATFIV is geared to educational use for FORTRAN). The PL/I program in Figure 10–10 is actually written in PL/C, a subset of PL/I developed at Cornell University.

Figure 10–10 ▪ Payroll Program in PL/I

```
PAYROLL: PROCEDURE OPTIONS (MAIN);

PAYROLL: PROCEDURE OPTIONS (MAIN);
DECLARE NAME        CHARACTER (16);
DECLARE HOURS       FIXED DECIMAL (2);
DECLARE WAGE        FIXED DECIMAL (3,2);
DECLARE GROSS_PAY FIXED DECIMAL (5,2);
DECLARE TAXRATE     FIXED DECIMAL (2,2);
DECLARE TAX         FIXED DECIMAL (4,2);
DECLARE NET_PAY     FIXED DECIMAL (5,2);
PUT PAGE LIST ('EMPLOYEE NAME','NET PAY');
PUT SKIP;
START: GET LIST (NAME,HOURS,WAGE);
ON ENDFILE GO TO FINISH;
IF HOUR>40 THEN
    GROSS_PAY=40*WAGE + 1.5*WAGE*(HOURS-40);
  ELSE GROSS_PAY = HOURS*WAGE;
IF GROSS_PAY>250 THEN TAXRATE=.20;
  ELSE  TAXRATE=.14;
TAX=TAXRATE*GROSS_PAY;
NET_PAY=GROSS_PAY - TAX;
PUT SKIP (1) LIST (NAME, NET_PAY);
GO TO START;
FINISH: END PAYROLL

PAYROLL      14:50      AUGUST 3RD, 1984
```

Output

```
    EMPLOYEE NAME          NET PAY

    LYNN MANGINO           224.00
    THOMAS RITTER          212.42
    MARIE OLSON            209.00
    LORI DUNLEVY           172.00
    WILLIAM WILSON         308.00
```

ADVANTAGES AND DISADVANTAGES The greatest strength of PL/I is its power, which lends the language many attractive features. PL/I's powerful features make it good for system programming. It is less wordy than COBOL and is well suited for short programming projects. Its default and modularity features make it easier to learn. Facilities that allow use of structured programming techniques are another distinct advantage of PL/I.

PL/I is not free of disadvantages, however. Because it is such a broad, powerful language, a large amount of storage is required for its compiler. This prohibits its use on small computers. As data processing becomes increasingly distributed, this restriction may make using PL/I impossible for some businesses. Further, the breadth of PL/I makes learning all the features of the language difficult.

PL/I was developed after COBOL and FORTRAN, and programmers experienced in those languages often resist having to learn a new one. Also, the need for a computer large enough to support the compiler has restricted the teaching of PL/I in colleges and universities. Finally, PL/I is used primarily with IBM computers; there has been no government support to increase its use as there was with COBOL and Ada.

Pascal **Pascal** is named after the French philosopher and mathematician Blaise Pascal. (Remember from Chapter 2 that Pascal invented the first mechanical adding machine.) Niklaus Wirth, a computer scientist from Switzerland, developed Pascal between 1968 and 1970. The first Pascal compiler became available in 1971.

Like BASIC, Pascal was first developed to teach programming concepts to students but is rapidly expanding beyond its initial purpose and finding increased acceptance in business and scientific applications. Pascal is well suited for both batch and interactive modes, although most Pascal business applications are batch oriented.

Pascal is a relatively new language, developed and offered after the concept of structured programming began to receive support. Thus, it is designed to be compatible with structured programming concepts (which will be explained in Chapter 11). Each Pascal program has two basic parts: a heading (in which definitions and declarations are made) and a body (in which input, processing, and output are accomplished—see Figure 10–11). Pascal also discourages the use of GO TO (branching) statements (although it makes them available), by offering alternative logic patterns such as:

REPEAT-UNTIL, WHILE-DO, FOR-TO/DO,
IF-THEN-(ELSE), and CASE -OF.

ADVANTAGES AND DISADVANTAGES   Pascal receives avid support from its users because, while it is relatively easy to learn (like BASIC), it is also powerful (like PL/I). As mentioned, it can be used in both batch and interactive modes. Unlike PL/I, Pascal is available on microcomputers and seems to be a good alternative to BASIC for use on personal computers. Pascal's suitability for structured programming and its graphics capabilities (described below) make it a very good language for educational purposes.

Unlike FORTRAN, Pascal allows variable names of any length, although only the first six characters have meaning to the computer. Thus Pascal is more English-like than FORTRAN.

Pascal does not have many default features. Thus, there are fewer compiler-generated errors to be debugged. The compiler provides fast translation of the source program. Also, Pascal is good for system programming.

Unlike COBOL and FORTRAN, Pascal has very good graphics capabilities. Programmers can create intricate, detailed objects using Pascal on properly equipped display terminals. This feature is attractive to scientists and increasingly so to business personnel as well.

At first, Pascal's availability was limited. But as time passes, more computer manufacturers are offering Pascal compilers with their machines. Perhaps the major disadvantage of Pascal is that it is not yet standardized. Many versions and enhancements are available from manufacturers, which may cause programs written in Pascal to differ depending upon the specific compiler used. In addition, some people believe that PASCAL has poor input-output capabilities.

Natural Languages

Natural languages, or **query languages** as they are sometimes called, are programming languages that use English-like sentences for the purpose of accessing information usually contained in the data base. A sentence such as "HOW MANY WOMEN HOLD A POSITION AT LEVEL 10 OR ABOVE?"

Figure 10–11 ■ Payroll Program in Pascal

```
PROGRAM PAYROLL (INPUT,OUTPUT);
VAR HOURS,REGULAR,WAGE,OVERTIME,GROSS,TAX,NETPAY : REAL;
NAME : ARRAY (.1..17.) OF CHAR;
I : INTEGER;
BEGIN
WRITELN('1','EMPLOYEE NAME','             NET PAY');
WRITELN(' ');
WHILE NOT EOF DO
    BEGIN
    FOR I:=1 TO 17 DO
        READ (NAME(.I.));
        READLN (HOURS,WAGE);
        IF HOURS>40
            THEN BEGIN
                REGULAR:=40*WAGE;
                OVERTIME:=(HOURS-40)*(1.5*WAGE);
                GROSS:=REGULAR + OVERTIME
            END
            ELSE BEGIN
                GROSS:=HOURS*WAGE
            END;
        IF GROSS>250
            THEN BEGIN
                TAX:=0.20*GROSS;
                NETPAY:=GROSS-TAX

            ELSE BEGIN
                TAX:=0.14*GROSS;
                NETPAY:=GROSS-TAX
            END;
    WRITE (' ');
FOR I :=1 TO 17 DO
    WRITE(NAME(.I.);
    WRITELN(NETPAY:12:12);
    END
END.
```

Output

EMPLOYEE NAME	NET PAY
LYNN MANGINO	224.00
THOMAS RITTER	212.42
MARIE OLSON	209.00
LORI DUNLEVY	172.00
WILLIAM WILSON	308.00

may be entered by a member of the personnel department to gain information for reporting purposes. In some cases, if the natural language processor does not fully understand the inquiry, it may request further information from the user in order to process the given inquiry.

The natural languages have been designed primarily for the novice computer user for use as an online, data-base, query language. The natural language processor normally is designed to be used with a vocabulary of words and definitions that allow the processor to translate the English-like sentences

PROGRAMMING LANGUAGES

to machine executable form. Currently, natural language sentences are typed on a keyboard; however, in the future the combination of voice recognition technology and natural languages could result in a very powerful tool for computer users. The ability to interface natural language systems with graphics software also provides a valuable tool for managers in decision making. Although limited to mainframe computers in the past, natural language systems are being developed for minicomputer and microcomputer systems as well.

PROGRAMMING LANGUAGES—A COMPARISON

Implementing an information system involves making an important decision concerning the type of programming language to use. The decision is based almost entirely on the application involved. Some questions must be asked:

- What languages does the selected (or available) computer system support?
- Will the application require mostly complex computations, file processing, or report generation?
- Is a fast response time crucial, or will batch processing be satisfactory?
- Are equipment changes planned for the future?
- How frequently will programs need modification?
- What languages do the programmers who will program and maintain the system know?

The size of the computer system is an obvious constraint on language choice. The limited primary storage capacity of small computers usually prohibits the use of languages such as COBOL, FORTRAN, PL/I, and APL, which require significant amounts of primary storage and sophisticated hardware. The computational capabilities of RPG are limited, but in many cases they can supply sufficient information for the management of small firms. If interactive processing is desired, BASIC and Pascal, which can be used on many microcomputers and minicomputers, should be considered. Subsets of PL/I, COBOL, and FORTRAN that can be used on small systems have also been developed.

For large systems, the type of processing is the key consideration in choosing a language. Business applications typically involve large amounts of data on which relatively few calculations are performed. Substantial file processing (requiring many I/O operations) is required; thus, many business applications are **input/output–bound.** In such cases, COBOL and PL/I provide the necessary power for efficient operations. When choosing between COBOL and PL/I, management must weigh the importance of standardization versus ease of programming. Although PL/I has been standardized, it is still primarily an IBM language. In contrast, COBOL is available on all large computers but may require greater programming effort because of its wordiness. If a new system is to be developed from scratch, or if a system is to be converted from one language to another, new languages (such as Ada) and their characteristics must also be considered.

Scientific programming applications usually require many complex calculations on relatively small amounts of data. Therefore, they tend to be **process-bound.** The computational capabilities of FORTRAN make it ideal for such applications. Another alternative is PL/I, which becomes more attractive as more manufacturers offer PL/I compilers. Pascal is a third possibility for scientific programming. It has good mathematical and graphics capabilities, and it is available on all sizes of computers, unlike PL/I.

Because of the diversity of programming languages, many firms choose to use several. For example, a firm can write scientific programs in FORTRAN, and file-updating programs in COBOL. It is also possible to write part of a program in one language and another part in a different language; this involves compiling the various portions of the program in separate steps and linking together the resultant object programs. These steps can be specified in job-control statements. For example, a program written in COBOL may call up an assembler program to perform extensive sorting of alphanumeric data, since assembler language can sort more efficiently than COBOL and can save processing time.

Nevertheless, there has been a definite trend away from programming in assembly language. Because of the one-to-one relation between assembly-language instructions and machine-language instructions, programming assembly language is very time consuming. Assembly-language programs may be efficient, but writing them is laborious. In contrast, high-level languages shift the programming emphasis away from detailed computer functions toward procedures for solving problems. High-level language compilers require significant amounts of primary storage capacity, but the languages are much easier to use than machine-oriented languages.

As hardware costs have decreased, more firms have determined that they could afford computers capable of supporting high-level languages. At the same time, labor costs have increased, and program development and maintenance have become significant expense items. Thus, high-level languages have increased in popularity. However, in systems where primary storage capacity is a critical constraint and virtual storage capabilities are not available, assembly languages are the best, if not the only, alternative available. This situation is frequently encountered in microcomputer systems.

Like choosing hardware, choosing software involves many considerations. A comparison chart reflecting some of the most important ones is shown in Table 10–4.

Table 10–4 ▪ Comparison of Programming Languages

	ASSEMBLY LANGUAGE	FORTRAN	COBOL	PL/I	RPG	BASIC	APL	PASCAL	LOGO
Strong math capabilities	X	X		X		X	X	X	X
Good character-manipulation capabilities	X		X	X		X	X	X	X
English-like			X	X				X	X
Available on many computers	X	X	X		X	X		X	X
Highly efficient	X								X
Standardized		X	X	X					
Requires large amounts of storage			X	X			X		X
Good interactive capability						X	X	X	X
Procedure-oriented		X	X	X		X	X	X	X
Problem-oriented					X				
Machine-dependent	X								

SUMMARY POINTS

- Programming can be placed into two categories—batch and interactive.
- Batch programming provides for better utilization of computer resources because batch programs are run at times when other, higher priority, programs are not being run.
- Interactive programming allows the user direct communication with the computer in a conversational mode. Response time is almost immediate.
- Machine language is the language of the computer, the only language that the computer directly understands. Machine language must take the form of 0s and 1s to be understood by the computer.
- Machine-oriented languages include machine and assembly languages, which require extensive knowledge of the computer. Procedure-oriented languages like COBOL, FORTRAN, and PL/I emphasize the computational and logical procedures for solving a problem. Problem-oriented languages such as RPG describe a problem without detailing the computational steps necessary to solve it.
- Programs in problem- and procedure-oriented languages are simpler to code but require more execution time than comparable programs written in lower-level, machine-oriented languages.
- An assembly-language program uses symbolic names for machine operations, making programming less tedious and time consuming than when machine language is used. Assembly-language programs can be very efficient in terms of storage and processing time required. However, assembly-language programming requires a high level of skill, and the language itself is machine-dependent.
- FORTRAN was the first high-level language developed. It is well suited for scientific and mathematical applications.
- APL is a powerful interactive language that can be used in an execution mode or a definition mode. Both character-string data and numeric data can be manipulated easily. Because APL includes a large number of unique symbols as operators, it requires a special keyboard. The APL compiler needs a large amount of primary storage; this restricts its use to medium-sized and large computers.
- COBOL is the most popular business programming language. It was designed to be English-like and self-documenting. Standardization of COBOL has helped to make it machine-independent. The main disadvantage of COBOL is that a large and sophisticated compiler is required to convert a COBOL source program into machine language.
- RPG is designed to produce business reports. The output format must be specified, but the RPG generator program can build a program to provide the output. Thus, little programming skill is required to use RPG. It is popular with users of small computers and minicomputers. However, it has limited computational capabilities and is not totally machine-independent.
- Ada is a new, high-level language which is a derivative of Pascal, and is thought to be the language that will replace COBOL in the future.
- BASIC is an easy-to-learn language, well suited for instructional purposes and ideal for time-sharing systems. Because many features of the language are not standardized, it is machine-dependent.
- Logo is an interactive, education-oriented language that uses an object called a turtle to help students become familiar with the computer and computer graphics.

- PL/I is a multi-purpose language combining the best features of COBOL and FORTRAN. Its modularity facilitates structured programming. PL/I compilers require a large amount of storage and are not available on small computers.
- Pascal is also easy to learn and well suited for instructional purposes. It is useful in both business and scientific applications. Structured programming techniques work well with Pascal because of the language's modular features.
- Natural languages (or query languages) are designed to allow the novice computer user to use the computer's capabilities more easily. Easy to write and understand English-like sentences allow the user to access information in a data base, for example.
- Factors to consider when selecting an appropriate programming language include: What languages can the computer support? Are computations simple? What response time is required? Are equipment changes planned in the future? How often will programs be modified?
- Decreasing hardware costs and increasing labor costs have helped create a trend toward the use of high-level, procedure-oriented languages.

REVIEW QUESTIONS

1. How does batch programming differ from interactive programming? If you were developing an airline reservation system, would you choose batch programming or interactive programming? Explain your choice.
2. Explain why batch programs normally have a lower priority than interactive programs during prime-time hours.
3. Distinguish between machine languages and assembly languages. What are the advantages and disadvantages of each?
4. If you were developing an application system for a microcomputer in which processing time was a critical factor, would you choose to program in a high-level language or an assembly language? Why?
5. How does a procedure-oriented language differ from a problem-oriented language? List some common procedure-oriented languages and problem-oriented languages.
6. What are some common characteristics of scientific-oriented programming languages? How do these characteristics differ from business-oriented programming languages?
7. What does CODASYL stand for? What were the objectives of the CODASYL Committee in relation to COBOL?
8. Describe some of the key advantages associated with the COBOL language.
9. Although they are both education-oriented languages, how do BASIC and Logo differ? Do you see any use for Logo outside the area of education? If so, where?
10. In comparison to BASIC, what advantages would Pascal have if it were used for developing application systems on microcomputers?
11. Tell what each of the following programming language names, or acronyms, stands for: COBOL, FORTRAN, APL, RPG, BASIC, PL/I.
12. List and discuss some of the factors that should be considered when a programming language is to be chosen for use with a particular computer system or application.

APPLICATION

Ohio Citizens Bank

Ohio Citizens Bank opened for business in Toledo on March 28, 1932, with twenty-five employees and capital funds totaling $350,000. After a 1959 merger with the Spitzer-Rorick Trust and Savings Bank, the bank's total deposits exceeded $100 million. At December 1983, its total assets exceeded $670 million.

Through the years, the bank has pioneered and popularized many services in the greater Toledo area, including personal loans, drive-up windows, money orders, charge cards, freight payment, payroll systems, and statement savings. In 1975, the bank introduced an automatic loan plan called CheckLOAN, which provides extra funds whenever needed for approved checking customers. The twenty-four-hour teller machines, OC24 Banks, were also introduced during that year.

"OC Transfer," the first bank telephone transfer system offered in the marketplace, was developed in 1977. This system allows a customer to transfer funds among checking, savings, and CheckLOAN.

In September of 1982, Ohio Citizens Bank, with over $600 million in assets, became a part of National City Corporation. Including Ohio Citizens, National City Corporation became the largest bank-holding company in Ohio.

Ohio Citizens Bank purchased the Owens-Illinois, Inc. building in May 1981 and moved the bank headquarters to this facility in March 1982. The bank occupies approximately 50 percent of this structure and also maintains the Corporate Data Processing Operations, formerly located at 133 N. St. Clair Street. The Port Lawrence parking facility and atrium adjoining the Ohio Citizens Bank Building was completed in mid-1983 and further recognized in dedication ceremonies in September 1983.

The pace of the bank's progress quickened with the transition from the OC24 ATM system to The Money Center™. This improved automatic teller system generated substantial increases in the number of cardholders and active card users. This step forward in electronic banking positions Ohio Citizens to join National City

Bank and other major banking organizations throughout Ohio in a state-wide ATM network "Money Station," planned for 1984.

Offering financial services to both retail and commercial communities, the bank processes an average of 700,000 transactions per week. Millions of dollars worth of computers and other facilities are used to record and process nearly 133,000 transactions daily.

The corporate data-processing facilities utilize two mainframe computers. The IBM 4341 processors provide information support for all departments. Each CPU has a four-megabyte memory. One is used primarily to support online applications, while the other is used for batch processing. Both systems are completely switchable, however, to insure minimal interruption of online service in case of equipment failure.

Charge-card processing, installment loans, and stock transfers are supported by remote data-entry stations in the appropriate departments. Entrex, the primary key-entry system, is a key-to-disk data-entry system in which the data are collected, stored, retrieved, and forwarded to the application computer systems for processing. The data are entered on a keyboard with a visual display screen and stored directly on a disk; the data on the disk are transferred to tape or transmitted through telecommunication facilities for daily processing. Entrex is also a dual system to insure uninterrupted service.

Ohio Citizens' data-processing applications use three programming languages: COBOL, BASIC, and assembly language. The controller's division of the bank uses BASIC on an IBM PC and on an IBM 5100 microcomputer with a CRT to process special accounting-oriented financial reports. These applications use online, real-time programming; data are submitted directly to the computer from remote terminals, and results are returned in seconds. Accounting applications on the microcomputers are conducive to BASIC programming because the same procedure is used every day; it involves only entering data in an interactive style. The controller's division also uses BASIC for two programs

that are not run daily. One is a Return-on-Investment Analysis program, which determines instantaneously the bank's return on investment. The other is a Budget Modeling program; because the BASIC program can be changed quickly and simply, it provides an excellent environment for manipulating alternative budget models.

In the data-processing department, programs are written in assembly language and COBOL. Originally, all programming was done in assembly language. Because the department's first IBM System/360 computer was a Model 30—a small computer with only 32K bytes of main storage—it was necessary to use a compact language, such as assembly language. The transition to large equipment has made the use of COBOL possible; new development is in COBOL, and many programs have already been converted to the COBOL language.

All batch applications in the department will eventually be written in COBOL and all new or replacement applications are written in COBOL. The Installment Loan and Payroll applications are two original assembly language. COBOL has been selected as the application language of the future because of its standardization and readability and because it is easy for programmers to use.

written for System/360 machines can be run on current equipment. Because of its speed and efficiency, assembly language will continue to be used for teleprocessing monitors and MICR support. Also, some applications require I/O devices that can only be supported with assembly language provided by the equipment manufacturer. These programs and the operating systems will also continue to be programmed in assembly languages.

The three languages just discussed were selected by Ohio Citizens in order to match the requirements of the applications with the strengths of the languages. The online, real-time microcomputer programs are written in BASIC so that results can be obtained quickly. Operating systems and programs that require assembly-language I/O support will continue to be written in assembly languages. COBOL has been selected as the application language of the future because of its standardization and readability and because it is easy for programmers to use.

In addition to the three standard programming languages used at Ohio Citizens, the programming facilities use another product called EASYTRIEVE, marketed by Pansophic Systems, Inc. EASYTRIEVE is an information-retrieval and data-management system that can be used to produce reports from any number of input files on a variety of output media. Programs to do relatively simple jobs such as file-to-file or file-to-printed-output can be set up and run with very little effort. It is used for special-request reports, file analysis, and file repair. EASYTRIEVE is ideal for producing one-time reports that are needed quickly.

DISCUSSION POINTS

1. Ohio Citizens has chosen COBOL as the primary application language. Which programs has it decided are better suited for assembly language?
2. Why is BASIC ideal for applications such as budget modeling?

11

Structured Design Concepts

INTRODUCTION

With recent advances in computer technology, hardware costs have continued to decrease while capabilities have expanded. Unfortunately, the same cannot be said of program and system development costs. Modern business environments have become more complex and dynamic. Systems designed to supply information to management must be continually redesigned or modified to respond to changing needs. As more time is spent in system design and maintenance, the costs of such services continue to rise dramatically in relation to hardware costs.

These problems have caused greater emphasis to be placed on simplicity and well-thought-out logic in system and program design. A sound methodology for program and system development is a necessity. This chapter first discusses the concept of top-down design and the tools for its implementation. These techniques apply to both system and program development. A later section deals specifically with structured programming. Finally, the chapter describes the management of system projects.

ARTICLE

Chip of the Decade

Chips come and chips go. Rarely, however, has a chip garnered as much early attention as the 65816. Silicon Valley programmers argue about it on days off and computer firms from Sunnyvale to Cambridge, England, are scrutinizing the very first samples fresh from the lab.

The reason for the excitement is simple. For the first time in the short history of personal computers, a chip gives manufacturers the ability to build powerful new computers without abandoning the software that's written for customers who own their older models. It may even be possible to upgrade existing computers—such as the Apple II—by pulling out the old chip and dropping in the 65816. "It will be," predicts one industry observer, "as if you could turn your Volkswagen into a Porsche, with an engine switch that takes 30 seconds."

The 65816 is a descendant of the venerable 6502, which (in various forms) powers Apple II, Atari and many Commodore computers. The new chip, however, will not only run the software already written for those older machines, it will also function as a much more powerful 16-bit microprocessor, capable of using vast amounts of memory, at very high speeds. Early tests suggest that in its 16-bit mode, the 65816 will be more than twice as powerful as the chip used in the IBM PC.

The 65816 was developed by 39-year-old William D. Mensch Jr., founder of the Western Design Center in Mesa, Arizona six years ago. WDC is a modest enterprise: Mensch's sister is the layout-design manager; his wife, a former school-teacher, trains other layout designers, and the company headquarters is a former residence (with pool) on the main street of town.

Mensch now has 15 microcomputer-chip designs hanging on his wall in Mesa. All have been hits: the royalties from those designs alone should earn him $50 million to $100 million over the next 10 years. But Mensch has larger plans, and foresees a vast family of related chips, ranging from the tiny microcomputers that control dishwashers to the chips in mainframe computers, all running related software. And all designed by Mensch.

Mensch's unalloyed enthusiasm for his own products would border on the megalomanic, were it not for the universal enthusiasm his first efforts have generated. A steady stream of investment bankers and venture capitalists have been visiting the little shop in Mesa, and sooner or later Mensch—who now owns every share of stock himself—may go public. "But I want to do it perfectly," he says. "It will be as well-planned as my chips."

Access, Fall 1984. Copyright 1984 by Newsweek, Inc.

New advances in microcomputer technology such as that discussed in relation to the 65816 may, in the future, decrease the need for software technology to keep pace with hardware developments. This type of hardware development, therefore, could indirectly help to increase programmer productivity.

THE NEED FOR STRUCTURED TECHNIQUES

Data processing has come a long way since the days of the UNIVAC I, when the leading scientists of the period projected that the world would need only ten such machines for the rest of time. Today the world has millions of computers with processing capabilities billions of times greater than ten UNIVAC Is, and the demand for computing power continues to increase. In the first generation of computers, hardware was expensive, accounting for 80 percent of costs, while software accounted for 20 percent. Today, those figures are reversed, and it appears this trend will continue for a long time.

As the pace of technological innovation accelerates, data processing departments are hard pressed to keep up. In fact, most are unable to. Software development is far behind existing technology because software development is extremely labor intensive. Thus, data processing departments today face a productivity problem: They must obtain greater software development for each dollar invested. The basic ways of increasing productivity are: (1) to automate the software development process, (2) to require employees to work harder or longer or both, and (3) to change software development methodologies. This chapter focuses on the third option, improving methodology.

In the early days of data processing, programming was very much an art. It was a new skill, with no standards and no concrete ways of doing things. Programmers considered programs their own creations. Very often, like artists, they would not allow anyone to see their creations until they were finished. Much has been learned since those early days. Thousands of programs have been written; studies have been done; and the body of knowledge regarding program development has grown accordingly. Attempts are now being made to use this knowledge to develop standardized techniques of program development.

One growing body of knowledge is concerned with structured techniques. Most of these techniques have existed only since the early 1970s and are being continually expanded and refined. While structured techniques are not universally accepted in the data-processing community, their use is increasing as managers recognize their ability to improve productivity. Three of these techniques—structured design, structured programming, and structured review—will be discussed in the remainder of this chapter.

STRUCTURED DESIGN METHODOLOGY

Top-Down Design

Chapter 9 mentioned that it is possible to simplify a problem by breaking it into segments, or subunits. This is known as a **modular approach** to problem solving. A problem solution is defined in terms of the functions it must perform. Each step, or **module,** in the solution process consists of one or more logically related functions. Thus, a problem solution may consist of several independent modules that together perform the required tasks.

The use of modules greatly facilitates the solution-planning process. But the modules must be meaningfully organized. **Top-down design** is a method of organizing a solution by defining it in terms of major functions to be performed and further breaking down these major functions into subfunctions.

The most general level of organization is the main control logic; this overall view of the problem is the most critical to the success of the solution. Modules at this level contain only broad descriptions of steps in the solution process. These steps are further broken down into several lower-level modules that contain more detail as to the specific steps to be performed. Depending on the complexity of the problem, several levels of modules may be required, with the lowest-level modules containing the greatest amount of detail.

The modules of the problem solution are related to each other in a hierarchical manner. These relationships can be depicted graphically on a **structure chart.** Figure 11–1 shows a portion of such a chart for an inventory processing application.

The highest level in the hierarchy is the **main control module,** which is represented in Figure 11–1 by the block labeled "Inventory Processing." This module is further broken down into lower-level modules that correspond with the inventory-processing application's three basic functions: reading a master inventory record and a sales transaction record, computing the reorder quantity, and writing an updated master file and purchase orders. The "Compute Reorder Quantity" module can be further divided into "Compute Current Inventory" and "Compute Order Requirements" modules. Finally, computing the current inventory involves two modules: "Determine Beginning Inventory" and "Determine Units Sold." Notice how the level of detail increases at the lower level.

Figure 11–1 ▪ Portion of Structure Chart for Inventory Processing Example

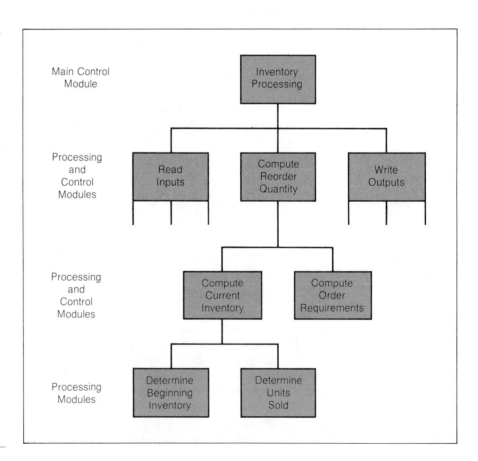

The flow of control in the structure chart is from top to bottom, demonstrating the top-down design of the solution. In other words, each module has control of the modules directly below it and is controlled by the module directly above it. The higher-level modules are both processing modules and control modules; they describe processes and also control modules below them in the hierarchy. At the lowest level, modules involve only processing.

The complete structure chart for the inventory processing application is shown in Figure 11–2.

When top-down design is used, certain rules must be followed. First, each module should be independent of other modules; in other words, each module should be executed only when control is passed to it from the module directly above it. Similarly, once a module has been executed, control should be passed back to the module directly above. The return process continues until the main control module is reached.

Another rule of the modular approach is that each module should be relatively small to facilitate the translation of modules into program statements. Many advocates of the modular approach suggest that each module should consist of no more than fifty or sixty lines of code. When module size is limited in this manner, the coding for each module can fit on a single page of computer printout, which simplifies testing and debugging procedures.

Yet another rule is that each module should have only one entrance point and one exit point. This makes the basic flow easy to follow and also allows easy modification of program logic to accommodate system changes.

When top-down design is used, the complete solution is not established

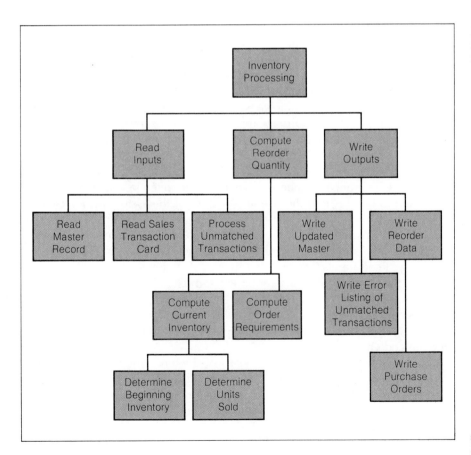

Figure 11–2 ▪ Structure Chart for Inventory Processing Example with Four Levels of Processing Modules

Is Your Program Full of—Er—Spaghetti?

The term *spaghetti thinking* was first introduced by a well-known programmer, Edsger Dijkstra. He scorned programmers who just fiddled with their programs until they came out right. He wanted to curb the use of one of the common programming structures, the transfer, also known as the GOTO statement. In March 1968, Dijkstra wrote a letter in the *Communications of the ACM* (Association for Computer Machinery) saying the GOTO statement was an invitation to messy programming and many kinds of errors. If a person took a program and drew a line from each GOTO statement to where it transferred, the resulting picture would look like a plateful of spaghetti. Since Dijkstra's famous letter, people have referred to excessive GOTOs in a program as the "spaghetti code."

One common language that seems to encourage excessive use of GOTO is BASIC. Recently, proponents of BASIC such as Arthur Luehrmann have favored structuring BASIC rather than scrapping the language. BASIC programmers should start with a top-down approach, Luehrmann says. They should define the problem in general steps first, then program the individual steps in chunks called modules, using GOSUB statements. This discourages the impulsive programming techniques of spaghetti thinking.

until the lowest-level modules have been designed. However, this does not prevent higher-level modules from being coded and tested at earlier stages in the development cycle. To do this, programmers create **dummy modules** and use them in place of the lower-level modules for testing purposes. Significant errors in higher-level modules can be isolated by the testers' observing whether control is correctly transferred between the higher-level modules and the dummy modules. As the lower-level modules are designed and coded, they can replace the dummy modules and be similarly tested. Thus, by the time the lowest-level modules have been coded, all other modules have already been tested and debugged.

Documentation and Design Tools

The structure charts described above provide an excellent means of documentation. However, structure charts show only functions, their relationships, and the flow of control; they do not show the processing flow, the order of execution, or how control will be transferred to and from each module. Therefore, structure charts must be supplemented with system charts, program flowcharts, record layouts, and so on. Chapter 9 discussed program flowcharts and layout forms. System charts will be discussed in Chapter 13. Two design and documentation aids—HIPO and pseudocode—are discussed in this section.

HIPO   The term **HIPO** (Hierarchy plus Input-Process-Output) is applied to a kind of visual aid commonly used to supplement structure charts. Whereas structure charts emphasize only structure and function, HIPO diagrams show the inputs and outputs of program modules.

A typical HIPO package consists of three types of diagrams that describe a program, or system of programs, from the general level to the detail level. At the most general level is the **visual table of contents,** which is almost identical to a structure chart but includes some additional information. Each block in the visual table of contents is given an identification number that is used as a reference in other HIPO diagrams. Figure 11−3 shows a visual table of contents for the inventory-processing application introduced in Figure 11−1.

Each module in the visual table of contents is described in greater detail in an **overview diagram** which includes the module's inputs, processing, and outputs. The reference number assigned to the overview diagram shows where the module fits into the overall structure of the system as depicted in the visual table of contents. If the module passes control to a lower-level module in the hierarchy for some specific processing operation, that operation is also given a reference number. An overview diagram for the inventory processing "Read Inputs" module (1.0) is shown in Figure 11−4.

Finally, the specific functions performed and data items used in each module are described in a **detail diagram.** The amount of detail used in these diagrams depends on the complexity of the problem involved. Enough detail should be included to enable a programmer to understand the functions and write the code to perform them.

HIPO diagrams are an excellent means of documenting systems and programs. The varying levels of detail incorporated in the diagrams allow them to be used by managers, analysts, and programmers to meet needs ranging from program maintenance to the overhaul of entire systems.

Pseudocode   Flowcharts are the most commonly used method of expressing program logic, but pseudocode is becoming increasingly popular for that pur-

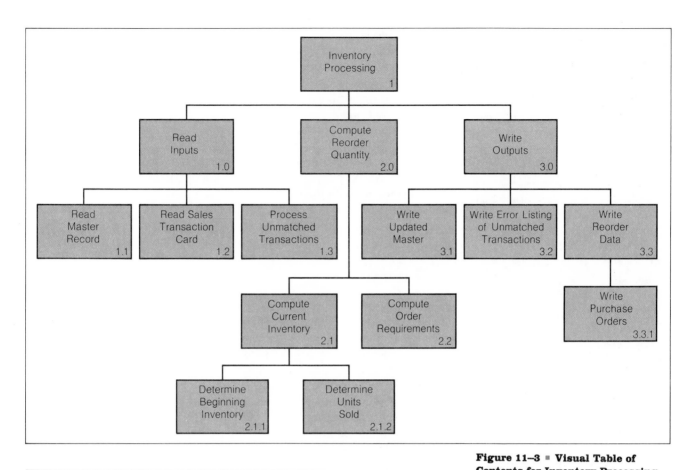

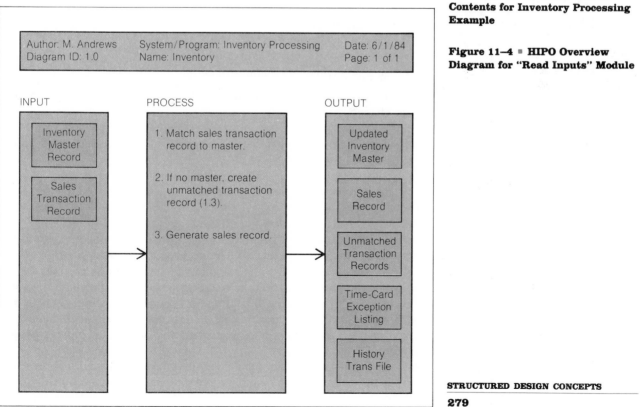

Figure 11–3 ▪ Visual Table of Contents for Inventory Processing Example

Figure 11–4 ▪ HIPO Overview Diagram for "Read Inputs" Module

Computers Go Sailing

Computers are being used to design the hulls of twelve-meter racing yachts and to design the best pattern for the sails.

Computers have been used both on board and on shore to assist in sailing. These computers inform crew members of the boat's time in the race and its position. They even suggest a correction to position the boat if it is off course.

Not only does the computer on the racing yacht keep track of the boat's speed, the wind speed, and where the boat is directed, but it also considers this information to show the exact path that the boat has taken. Data is collected and analyzed by the computers both on board and on shore; then the computer provides updates on the path of the boat every two seconds using this information. Before computers were used, the crew based many decisions on educated guesses.

pose. Pseudocode, as you may recall from Chapter 9, is an English-like description of the processing steps in a program. At times, flowcharts become lengthy and difficult to read, especially those for complex programs. In some cases, it is difficult to express the logic of processing steps with the commonly used flowcharting symbols. When pseudocode is used, the program solution follows an easy-to-read, top-down sequence.

Although certain keywords such as IF, THEN, and ELSE are used in pseudocode, no rigid set of rules must be followed. Thus, pseudocode is a simple technique to learn and use. Figure 11–5 contrasts pseudocode with program flowcharting. As the example indicates, pseudocode is understandable even to those unfamiliar with the program logic. The actual program can be easily coded directly from the pseudocode.

STRUCTURED PROGRAMMING

Emphasis on the art of programming and on the flexibility that high-level languages provide has sometimes encouraged poor programming techniques. For example, many programs contain numerous branches that continually alter the sequential flow of processing. These programs may work successfully, but their often confusing logic can be understood only by the original programmer. This increases the costs and difficulties associated with program maintenance. Furthermore, without a standardized method of attacking a problem, a programmer may spend far more time than necessary in determining an appropriate solution and developing the program. To counter these tendencies, **structured programming** has been widely publicized.

Structured programming has four objectives:

1. To reduce testing time.
2. To increase programmer productivity.
3. To increase clarity by reducing complexity.
4. To decrease maintenance time and effort.

More simply stated, programs should be easy to read, easy to maintain, and easy to change.

Structured programming encourages well-thought-out program logic. The top-down, modular approach discussed earlier in this chapter is used during development of the program design. The structured program itself uses only three basic control patterns: simple sequence, selection, and loop (see Figures 11–6 and 11–7). When these three patterns and the modular approach are used, programs can be read from top to bottom and are easier to understand. An attempt is made to keep programs as simple and straightforward as possible; structured programming discourages the use of "tricky" logic that is likely to confuse program users (sometimes even the original programmer).

A basic guideline of structured programming is that each module should have only one entry point and one exit point. This allows the flow of control to be followed easily by the programmer. When the modular approach is used, the one-entry/one-exit guideline is easy to incorporate into the program. A program that has only one entrance and one exit is called a **proper program.**

Several features should be included in structured programs to make them easy to read. Comment statements, or remarks, should be used liberally. Var-

FLOWCHART

START

Read
Record

A

Data
Record
?

No → B

Yes

Balance
<100?

No

Yes

Penalty =
.02 × Balance

Penalty =
.03 × Balance

B

Balance =
Balance +
Penalty

Write
Statement

Read
Record

A

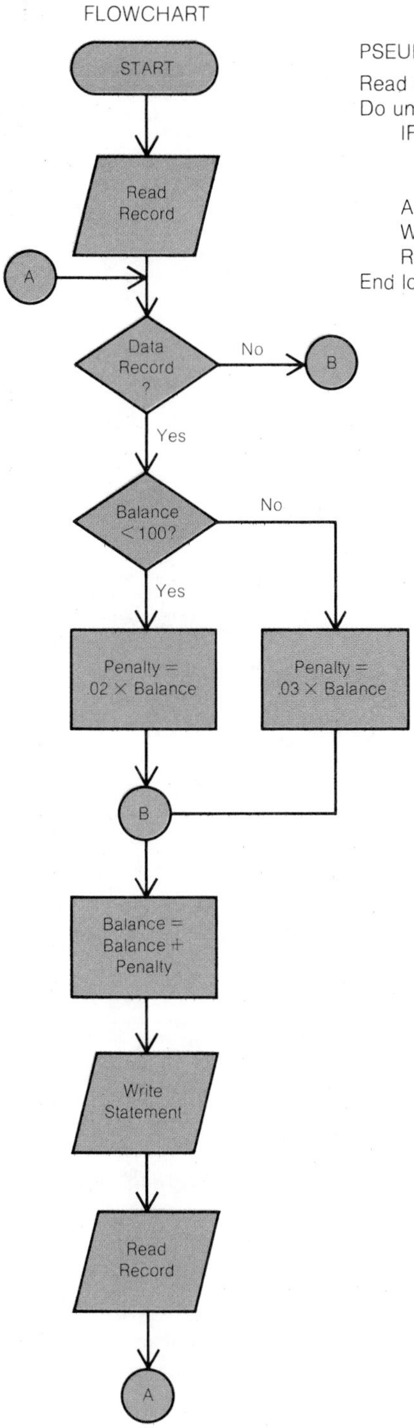

PSEUDOCODE
Read record
Do until there are no more data records
　IF balance is less than $100
　　　THEN calculate penalty at 2% of balance
　　　ELSE calculate penalty at 3% of balance
　Add penalty to balance
　Write customer statement
　Read record
End loop (no more data records)

Figure 11–5 ▪ Comparison of Pseudocode and Flowcharting

Figure 11–6 ▪ Basic Structured Programming Control Patterns

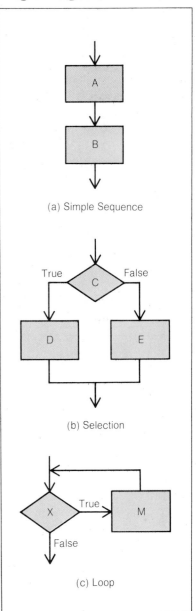

A

B

(a) Simple Sequence

True   False

C

D   E

(b) Selection

X   True   M

False

(c) Loop

Figure 11–7 ▪ Sample Flowchart of
Structured Programming

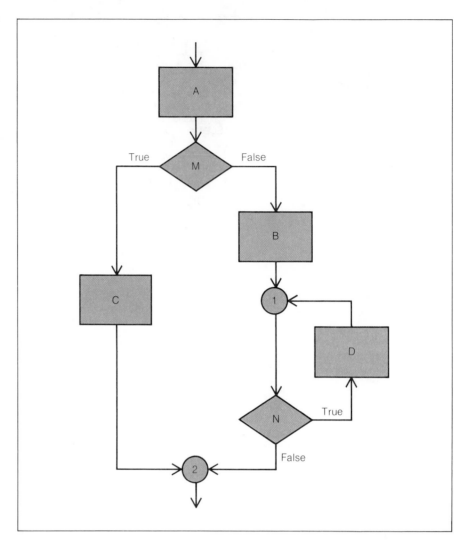

iable names should be definitive. Finally, indentation and spacing of program statements should be used.

It must be emphasized that the branch pattern, characterized by the GO TO statement, is not advocated in structured programming. (In fact, structured programming is sometimes called "GO-TO-less" programming or "IF-THEN-ELSE" programming.) A GO TO statement causes an unconditional branch from one part of the program to another. Excessive use of GO TO statements results in the continual changes in execution flow mentioned earlier. Often the flow is transferred to totally different logical sections of the program. Programs containing many GO TO (branching) statements are difficult to modify because they are obscure and complicated. A programmer may not know how a change in one part of the program will affect processing in other parts. In contrast, structured programming logic flows from the beginning to the end of a program, without backtracking to earlier sections (see Figure 11–7). This is not to say that a structured program may not have any GO TO statements, but that they should be used only to implement structured logic.

Some programming languages are better suited to structured programming than others. Especially well suited are Pascal, PL/I, and ALGOL (a language developed by a coordinated effort of user groups and computer manufacturers that is in widespread use in Europe). Languages such as FORTRAN and BASIC lack some features that many people consider essential for structured programming. For example, it is sometimes difficult to avoid the use of GO TO statements in these languages. However, careful planning and well-placed GO TO statements can result in well-structured programs, regardless of the language used.

Figure 11–8 compares structured and unstructured versions of a portion of a payroll program written in COBOL. The structured version is preferred to the unstructured version because it is written with a top-down design using processing and control modules such as MAIN-LOGIC and WORK-LOOP to call on processing modules. The structured version, therefore, uses a flow of control which is from top to bottom. The MAIN-LOGIC module passes control to modules below it, and once processing is complete, control is passed back up to it for termination of the program. The unstructured version, on the other hand, passes control from module to module with no particular consistency and terminates the program in a processing module rather than a control module.

Management's difficulties in implementing structured programming may originate in a resistance to change. However, the use of structured programming not only significantly improves programming practices but also represents potential cost savings.

MANAGEMENT OF SYSTEM PROJECTS

This chapter has presented various tools—top-down design, modular design, HIPO diagrams, pseudocode, and structured programming—intended to aid in designing an efficient, easy-to-maintain system in a minimal amount of time. However, even the most organized and well-structured system may contain errors and omissions that can render it useless. Thus, continuous review of the system during the development cycle is essential. While errors

```
00001     MAIN-LOGIC.
               .
               .
               .
00011          GO TO WORK-LOOP.
               .
               .
               .
00032     WORK-LOOP.
00033          READ CARD-FILE AT END GO TO FINISH.
00034          IF HOURS-WORKED IS GREATER THAN 40 THEN GO TO
00035               OVERTIME-ROUTINE.
00036          MULTIPLY HOURS-WORKED BY WAGE-PER-HOUR
00037               GIVING GROSS-PAY.
00038          GO TO TAX-COMPUTATION.

00039     OVERTIME-ROUITNE.
00040          MULTIPLY WAGE-PER-HOUR BY 40 GIVING REGULAR-PAY.
00041          SUBTRACT 40 FROM HOURS-WORKED GIVING OVERTIME-HOURS.
00042          MULTIPLY WAGE-PER-HOUR BY 1.5 GIVING OVERTIME-RATE.
00043          MULTIPLY OVERTIME-HOURS BY OVERTIME-RATE GIVING
00044               OVERTIME-PAY.
00045          ADD REGULAR-PAY, OVERTIME PAY GIVING GROSS-PAY.

00046     TAX-COMPUTATION.
00047          IF GROSS-PAY IS GREATER THAN 250 THEN MULTIPLY
00048               GROSS-PAY BY 0.20 GIVING TAX ELSE MULTIPLY
00049               GROSS-PAY BY 0.14 GIVING TAX.
00050          SUBTRACT TAX FROM GROSS-PAY GIVING NET-PAY.
00051          MOVE EMPLOYEE-NAME TO NAME.
00052          MOVE NET-PAY TO AMOUNT.
00053          WRITE PRINT-LINE.
00054          GO TO WORK-LOOP.

00055     FINISH.
00056          CLOSE CARD-FILE, PRINT-FILE.
00057          STOP RUN.
```

and oversights will almost certainly surface after a system becomes operative (sometimes even months or years later), such problems can be minimized through careful planning, coordinating, and review.

Chief Programmer Team

An important first step sometimes taken to coordinate a system design effort is the formation of a **chief programmer team (CPT),** which is a small number of programmers under the supervision of a chief programmer. The goals of the CPT approach are: to produce a software product that is easy to maintain and modify, to improve programmer productivity, and to increase system reliability. Organizations have applied the CPT concept to implement systems well ahead of schedule and with minimal errors.

The chief programmer is responsible for the overall coordination, development, and success of the programming project. The chief programmer, therefore, has managerial responsibilities as well as the responsibility for high-level design and the coding of some modules. A lead analyst works with the chief programmer in large system projects. In such cases, the lead analyst may supervise the general system design effort while the chief programmer concentrates on the technical development of the project.

Figure 11–8 ▪ Continued

```
00001    MAIN-LOGIC.
              .
              .
              .
00011        READ CARD-FILE AT END MOVE 'TRUE' TO EOF-FLAG.
00012        PERFORM WORK-LOOP UNTIL EOF-FLAG = 'TRUE'.
00013        CLOSE CARD-FILE, PRINT-FILE.
00014        STOP RUN.
              .
              .
              .
00034    WORK-LOOP.
00035        IF HOURS-WORKED IS GREATER THAN 40
00036            THEN PERFORM OVERTIME-ROUTINE
00037            ELSE PERFORM STANDARD-ROUTINE.
00038        PERFORM TAX-PAY-COMPUTATION.
00039        PERFORM PRINTING.
00040        READ CARD-FILE AT END MOVE 'TRUE' TO EOF-FLAG.

00041    STANDARD-ROUTINE.
00042        MULTIPLY HOURS-WORKED BY WAGE-PER-HOUR.

00043    OVERTIME-ROUTINE.
00044        MULTIPLY WAGE-PER-HOUR BY 40 GIVING REGULAR-PAY.
00045        SUBTRACT 40 FROM HOURS-WORKED GIVING OVERTIME-HOURS.
00046        MULTIPLY WAGE-PER-HOUR BY 1.5 GIVING OVERTIME-RATE.
00047        MULTIPLY OVERTIME-HOURS BY OVERTIME-RATE GIVING
00048            OVERTIME-PAY.
00049        ADD REGULAR-PAY, OVERTIME-PAY GIVING GROSS-PAY.

00050    TAX-PAY-COMPUTATION.
00051        IF GROSS-PAY IS GREATER THAN 250
00052            THEN MULTIPLY GROSS-PAY BY 0.20 GIVING TAX
00053            ELSE MULTIPLY GROSS-PAY BY 0.14 GIVING TAX.
00054        SUBTRACT TAX FROM GROSS-PAY GIVING NET-PAY.

00055    PRINTING.
00056        MOVE EMPLOYEE-NAME TO NAME.
00057        MOVE NET-PAY TO AMOUNT.
00058        WRITE PRINT-LINE.
```

Usually, a backup programmer is assigned as an assistant to the chief programmer. The backup programmer is a highly qualified specialist who may help in system design, testing, and evaluation of alternative designs. The chief programmer and backup programmer normally code the most critical parts of the overall system. Separate modules of the system are programmed and tested by different programmers. The chief and backup programmers then work with one or more other programmers to integrate all parts into a complete system. This approach uses both structured programming and top-down design.

The CPT also includes a **librarian** to help maintain complete, up-to-date documentation of the project and to relieve the team programmers of many clerical tasks they would otherwise have to perform. The librarian's duties include:

▪ Preparing computer input from coding forms completed by programmers.
▪ Submitting inputs and picking up computer output.
▪ Maintaining up-to-date source-program listings in archives available to all programmers.
▪ Updating test data and implementing changes in programs and job-control statements as required.
▪ Maintaining up-to-date documentation.

A librarian enhances communication among team members because he or she makes all program descriptions, coding, and test results current and visible to everyone involved in the effort. In addition, this approach enables the chief programmer to maintain control of costs and of human and computer resources and to ensure adherence to standards.

The organizational structure of a chief programmer team is shown in Figure 11–9. As mentioned previously, the structure varies depending on the complexity of the project.

Structured Review and Evaluation

Obviously, an important goal of a system design effort is to produce an error-free system in the shortest possible time. This requires that the system be carefully reviewed before it is implemented. Early detection of errors and oversights can prevent costly modifications later.

One approach used in the early phases of system development is an **informal design review.** The system design documentation is studied by selected management, analysts, and programmers, usually before the actual coding of program modules. After a brief review period, each person responds with suggestions for additions, deletions, and modifications to the system design.

A **formal design review** is sometimes used after the detailed parts of the system have been sufficiently documented. The documentation at this point may consist of program flowcharts, pseudocode, narrative descriptions, or combinations of these methods. Sometimes called a **structured walkthrough,** the formal design review involves distributing the documentation to a review team of two to four members, which studies the documentation and then meets with the program designers to discuss the overall completeness, accu-

Figure 11–9 ▪ Organization of Chief Programmer Team

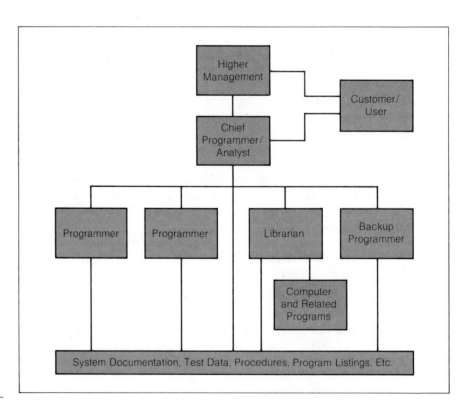

racy, and quality of the design. The reviewers and program designers often trace through the programs using desk-checking as discussed in Chapter 9. Both valid and invalid data are used to ascertain the program's exception-handling and standard procedures.

After programs have been coded and executed on the computer, their outputs can be compared with hand-calculated results for verification. Any discrepancies can be noticed and problems corrected. When this approach is used, few, if any, errors remain undetected when the system finally becomes operative.

Egoless Programming   Another method of improving program quality is the concept of egoless programming. As was stated earlier in the chapter, programming was at one time considered an art, and like many artists, programmers would not permit others to see their programs and would take personally any criticisms made of their programs.

Egoless programming, in contrast, is a concept that involves establishing a program review process to determine if programs are being coded consistently and in adherence to predetermined coding standards. This type of programming encourages attitudes more likely to facilitate smooth development and maintenance of computer programs and is particularly applicable in environments utilizing programming teams. The concept of egoless programming is not intended to minimize the creativity of the programmers but to help increase productivity and maintainability of programs.

SUMMARY POINTS

■ Software now accounts for a greater share of data-processing budgets than does hardware, a reversal of the situation in the 1950s.

■ Data-processing departments are lagging behind in program development. Thus, programmers' productivity must increase.

■ Top-down program design and structured programming are techniques that have been developed to reduce program development and maintenance costs.

■ In the top-down approach, a program is broken into functional modules. At the highest level is the main control module, which is further divided into lower-level modules. Structure charts are used to graphically depict the program modules and their relationships. The flow of control in the structure chart is from top to bottom.

■ When using top-down design, the programmer codes the higher-level modules first and tests them. Lower-level modules are then coded and tested. This facilitates debugging because errors can be isolated to particular modules.

■ Two methods of documentation used with top-down design are HIPO diagrams and pseudocode. HIPO diagrams show the input, processing steps, and output of each module. HIPO documentation consists of three types of diagrams: a visual table of contents, overview diagrams, and detail diagrams. Program logic can be expressed in pseudocode, an English-like description of the processing steps in a program. In pseudocode, the program solution follows a top-down sequence. The technique is easy to learn and use.

■ Structured programming is a "GO/TO-less" programming concept. It uses only three basic control patterns: simple sequence, selection, and loop. Some languages, like Pascal, PL/I, and ALGOL, are especially well suited to structured programming.

■ The chief programmer team (CPT) concept involves organizing a small number of programmers under the supervision of a chief programmer. Usually, the chief programmer is assisted by a highly qualified backup programmer. These two people code the most critical parts of the overall system. A librarian maintains complete, up-to-date documentation. The organization of the CPT varies according to the complexity of the project.

■ Systems must be reviewed before they are implemented. In an informal design review, the system design documentation is reviewed before coding takes place to determine any changes that may be desirable. After a detailed system design is complete, a formal design review is held to check for completeness, accuracy, and quality. Desk-checking and test data are used to check all programs.

■ Egoless programming is a programming methodology designed to determine whether programs are being coded consistently and in adherence to predetermined coding standards.

REVIEW QUESTIONS

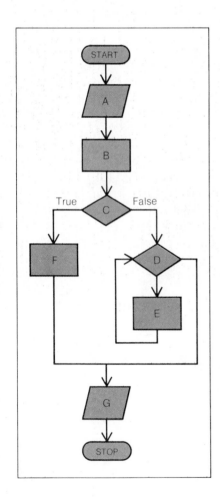

1. Briefly explain why there is a need for structured techniques in a data-processing environment.

2. Explain what top-down design is and why it is being used for system and program design.

3. Describe a module. Using the programming case study from Chapter 9, use your judgment to break the solution presented there up into modules (use Figure 9–20 as a guide).

4. Using top-down design, prepare a structure chart for the payroll example presented in Chapter 9.

5. What is the role of HIPO and pseudocode in structured design methodology? Do these tools offer any significant advantages over traditional methods of documentation? Explain.

6. Using top-down design and HIPO, develop a visual table of contents, overview diagram, and detail diagram for the payroll example presented in Chapter 9.

7. What are the objectives of structured programming? In general, how are these objectives consistent with increasing programmer productivity?

8. Structured programming avoids the use of GO TO statements. Does this reduce the flexibility of the programmer and make coding more difficult?

9. What benefits can be realized by using structured programming? Give reasons to support your answer.

10. Given the following flowchart, identify the basic structured programming control patterns that are present.

11. Explain the chief programmer team concept. What is the role of the librarian in this approach to system design?

12. Identify and give a brief explanation of the approaches used for structured review and evaluation.

APPLICATION
Armco Inc Butler Plant

In the late 1880s, a young man named George M. Verity, mananger of a small roofing company, was looking for a reliable source of quality steel sheets. These sheets were not easy to find, and Verity decided to become his own supplier. He organized the American Rolling Mill Company—the first company to bring together all the steps necessary to make steel; roll it flat into sheets; and galvanize, corrugate, and fabricate the sheets into a finished product. Today, Armco, Inc, is a highly diversified company headquartered in Ohio. Employing 50,000 people, Armco is one of the nation's largest producers of steel, in the past ranking third in the industry in assets, sales, and profits. In terms of shipments, Armco traditionally ranks fifth or sixth.

At the Armco plant in Butler, Pennsylvania, about 2,800 employees make the steel used in electrical equipment such as transformers, motors, and other devices that generate, distribute, and use electric power. This plant is now the world's largest producer of electrical steels; it also makes large quantities of stainless steel sheets and strips.

Throughout the data-processing structure at Armco, large computers, minicomputers, and microcomputers are used. More specifically, these systems include IBM, Four-Phase, and Modcomp hardware. The regional CPUs are located at Armco corporate headquarters in Middletown, Ohio. They consist of two IBM mainframe computers (a 3081 and a 370/168) with disk and tape units. All general office and Butler regional applications are processed on this equipment. Butler jobs are handled by an IBM remote job-entry (RJE) terminal, and keypunch data is transmitted by a Four-Phase key-to-disk system with six display-entry stations.

The data-processing center at Butler houses two IBM System/7 (S/7) minicomputers and one IBM Series 1 (S/1) minicomputer, which are tied to the regional equipment at Middletown. With this communication capability, the Butler plant can transfer any data it processes to the equipment at headquarters. Butler also has a Modcomp 7870 machine that communicates with the regional facility. It has a communications attach-

ment that handles line traffic from approximately 100 data collection devices. The S/7 computers are strictly application machines that depend on the S/1 for handling communications. Figure 11–10 illustrates the hardware configuration for the Regional Computer Center and the Butler Plant. The minicomputers and attached disks handle the Butler Information Management System test and production systems, time-sharing option, and load applications development. Many other interactions exist within the cluster, and many more will be possible in the future.

The data-processing department at Butler presently has thirty-five employees. Computerized data processing is used in the areas of payroll, cost accounting,

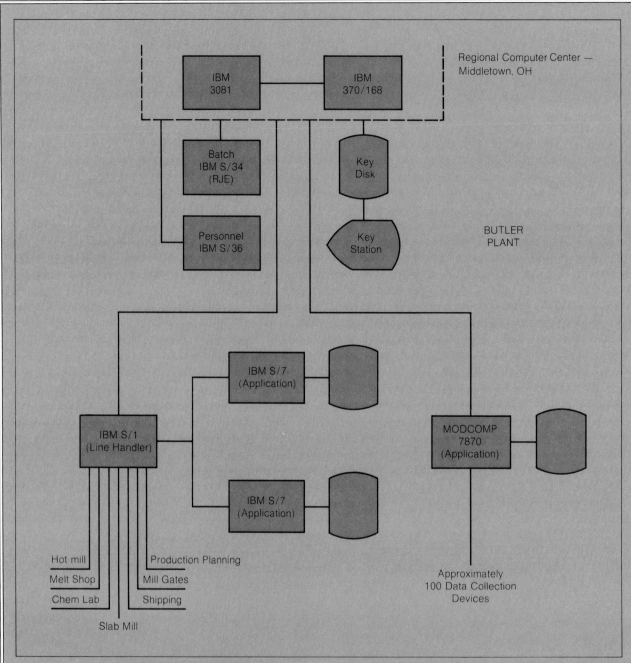

Figure 11–10 ▪ Armco Inc Computer Operations

production inventory control, metallurgical testing of customer shipments, forecasting of production requirements, and preparation of management information reports. Other applications include an automated shipping system that tracks shipping inventory and prints out necessary shipping documents, a personnel data system that keeps complete employment records of all employees, a badge reader and time-keeping system, and a maintenance job-order control system.

The data-processing department uses a structured approach to analyze business problems and to design, program, and test solutions to these problems. All computer systems are developed through a defined project life cycle that consists of several steps, starting with a system study and ending with the system's operating on a scheduled basis. The programming step lies about in the middle of the project, and structured programming techniques are used. The typical flow constructs are established. Coding rules for statements, comments, segmentation, indentation, and so on, are applied. In setting out the procedures they would follow, the EDP personnel chose the structured features they considered most applicable to their philosophy and discarded others. For instance, they do not use a librarian or detailed HIPO diagrams. However, they have implemented the use of structure charts. PL/I and Pascal are used in coding because of their structured qualities.

During the design steps of the project life cycle, every program in the system is identified. Then, before programming begins, these programs are grouped into units, each containing from one to five programs. The programs are developed through a process known as a unit development procedure. The project leader assigns a unit to a team member. Documentation developed during the design steps and a brief description by the project leader identify the programs in the unit and the functions they are to perform. The team member creates a unit development plan (UDP) to estimate the effort needed to develop that particular unit. The UDP clarifies early, and in writing, the specific functions that a program is to perform. It is valuable as a feedback mechanism to ensure that the team member understands the function to be performed. Errors are frequently detected during review of the UDP, before any code has been written. The UDP also provides a means of scheduling checkpoints with the program user, thus promoting user involvement with project development.

As stated, the UDP is initiated by a brief and general written assignment statement from the project leader to a team member. The assignment statement includes a definition of the task, recommendations for establishing its interface with other tasks, and a target completion date. It also includes recommendations regarding procedures such as edits, timing, and important tests (see Figure 11–11).

When the team member receives the assignment statement, he or she sets up a schedule of subtargets and prepares the unit development plan. Three standard items must be included in the UDP:

▪ Data definition list and flow plan: The definition list is an itemization of all input and output. The flow plan

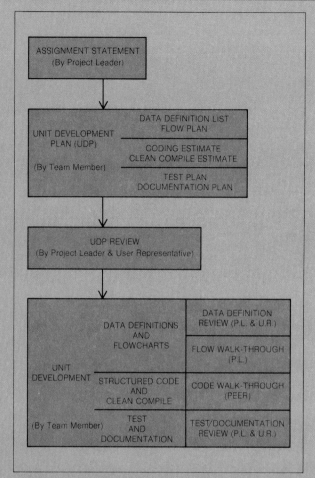

Figure 11–11 ▪ **Relationship among Plan, Review, and Development Processes of Project**

specifies the flows needed, the approach to be used on them (structured, top-down, or the like), and an estimate of the time needed to complete the flows.
▪ Coding and clean-compile estimates: These are estimates of the time needed to code the program, key in the code, and clean-compile the program (eliminate all compiler-detected errors).
▪ Test and documentation plans: The test plan defines the editing needs and the test conditions that will be used to validate the program. It may also include an estimate of the number of compilations and test runs anticipated. The documentation plan includes a list of documentation and training considerations.

Throughout the development of the UDP, the team members meet once a week to discuss their progress. After each UDP is completed, it is reviewed by the project leader and a user representative. At this time, the team member and project leader review the target dates that each has estimated. A final target date is assigned. The project leader and user representative can then either approve the UDP or meet with the team member to resolve any differences. The approved UDPs are then assembled, and the whole project plan is reviewed for approval. Upon approval, the team members begin the unit development effort.

Figure 11–11 illustrates the relationship of the UDP to the actual unit development. The development begins with establishment of data definitions and flow charts. Typical flow constructs have been established as standard:

* Every structure has one entrance and one exit.
* Every connector has two arrows going in and one arrow coming out.
* Every structure should have the potential of being compressed into one box.
* Each modular structure must be independent of other modular structures.

These initial steps end with a data definition review by the project leader and user representative and a flow walk-through by the project leader.

The next step for the programmer is the actual program coding. Some structured-programming conventions have been established for use with PL/I:

* Every procedure must be a proper program, with one entry and one exit.

* No GO TO or RETURN statements are allowed.
* There must be only one statement per line and only one data characteristic (attribute) per line.

The code is key entered via a time-sharing option by the programmer, compiled, and then reviewed by the programmer and another team member. Next, the program is validated with data that tests its conditions and editing needs; finally, it is documented. Both the test and the documentation are reviewed by the project leader and user representative.

Armco's Butler plant is committed to the structured approach because of the many benefits derived from it. The major benefit relates to planning and organizing projects. The modular approach and the weekly team reviews have led to a tremendous reduction in errors. For example, one of the projects included fifty programs and, after implementation, was found to have only two errors. Furthermore, the discussions of logic flow among team members aid greatly in any follow-up and documentation.

DISCUSSION POINTS

1. What specific benefits have Armco's Butler plant personnel found in the structured approach? What are some of its other advantages?
2. In what states of the programming process does this group use the structured approach? Do you think that might be typical of many businesses or unique to this one?

12
Application Software

INTRODUCTION

Recently, the use of prewritten application software packages has increased dramatically. This increase can be attributed largely to two factors: (1) the increased cost of developing application software, and (2) the rise in popularity of microcomputers. For medium to large companies, the costs associated with developing and maintaining application software have become a very significant cost of doing business—one that can be reduced by purchasing prewritten software packages. In the case of microcomputer users, many would be forced to write application software themselves or to hire programmers to do it for them if application software packages were not already available. The availability of these packages, therefore, provides businesses and computer users with an alternative means of acquiring application software.

This chapter will discuss four of the more popular types of application software packages: word-processing packages, data-management packages, modeling packages, and graphics packages. Each section on a particular type of application software will define the particular type, explain its uses, and discuss some features found in that type of package. The chapter will conclude with a brief explanation of integrated software.

ARTICLE

Electronic Parenting

Seated one day recently at his personal computer, a *Forbes* reader known to us was restless, ill at ease and feeling guilty about how tough it is to stay in touch with his kids, all three of them semigrown and away at school. The kids were keeping up their end. It was our reader-parent who was laggard. One thing led to another as his fingers wandered idly over the not very noisy keys, and the result appears below. Here, he told us in a covering note, is an answer for loving, busy parents hoping to cement relations.

‹MONTH, DAY›, 1983
Dear ‹NAME OF CHILD›:

It was truly wonderful and special to receive your letter and ‹NUMBER OF CALLS› phone calls. It sounded as if you were right next door, instead of ‹NUMBER OF MILES› miles away.

Your concerns about individuality are not well founded. ‹NAME OF CURRENT WIFE› and I regard each of our children as special and apart, ‹NAME OF CHILD›. Your lovely ‹HAIR COLOR› hair, ‹EYE COLOR› eyes and personality traits of ‹FIRST TRAIT› and ‹SECOND TRAIT› make you very dear to us.

What have we been up to? We've been relaxing and enjoying the ‹SEASON›. On ‹MOVIE DAY› evening, we saw ‹NAME OF MOVIE›. It was ‹POSITIVE MOVIE ADJECTIVE›, although somewhat ‹NEGATIVE MOVIE ADJECTIVE›. We also went to the theater with ‹THEATER PERSON› and saw a ‹THEATER ADJECTIVE› production of ‹NAME OF PLAY›. It's about ‹PLAY ABOUT›.

Have you been following the terrible events in ‹COUNTRY OR REGION›? The actions of the U.S. seem questionable, at best. On the other hand, the atrocities committed by the ‹GOVERNMENT OR GUERRILLA?› forces are a serious provocation threatening peace in the area. Moving on to more important things, we've just paid a fortune to have the ‹CAR OR APPLIANCE› fixed. It was ‹CAR OR APPLIANCE SYMPTOM›.

Mom has been keeping quite busy working on a report for the ‹NAME OF ORGANIZATION›. As usual, there's quite a bit of back-stabbing between the pro-‹ISSUE› and anti-‹ISSUE› factions. I am working quite hard on ‹NAME OF SICK COMPANY›. I think things there seem to be ‹DETERIORATING OR IMPROVING›.

‹NAME OF COUPLE› are waiting and we must rush off to ‹NEXT FUN EVENT›, so I'll cut this letter short. It took forever to write, as I thought about the things I wanted to tell you and only you, ‹NAME OF CHILD›. We've also heard from ‹NAME OF FIRST OTHER CHILD› and ‹NAME OF SECOND OTHER CHILD›, but I'll let ‹NAME OF CURRENT WIFE› fill you in on that when she writes.

I love you a lot and would write you more frequently, but I fear a certain sameness to my letters. Perhaps it's just my imagination, ‹NAME OF CHILD›.

Love,

If the idea appeals, you will want to know that our reader composed his loving letter on an Apple 2 Plus microcomputer, using the "form fill-in" feature of the Word Handler word processing program. He is proud of it but, understandably, does not wish his name attached to it.

As you can see, application software can help to improve productivity and can even help a busy father to keep in touch with his children. Word processors, data managers, electronic spreadsheets, and graphics packages all offer a way of automating manual, time-consuming tasks. Application software, therefore, turns the computer into a useful tool for a wide variety of users.

WORD-PROCESSING SOFTWARE

A Definition

When word processing is discussed, three terms appear often: word processor, word processing and word-processing system. A **word processor** is an application software package designed to allow the user to enter, manipulate, format, print, store, and retrieve text. **Word processing** is the term used to describe the process of manipulating text using the word processor. The term **word-processing system** is used to describe the computer system, or a portion of the computer system, used for the task of word processing.

A word-processing system can be found in one of two configurations. One is a **dedicated word-processing system,** which is designed solely for word processing and is normally found in businesses where large quantities of word processing must be done. The second is found in the form of software packages used on multipurpose digital computers. Because businesses or computer users may want to use their computer systems for more than a single application, a word processor may be only one of a number of application software packages that can be used on the computer system. Word processing involves two steps: text editing and print formatting.

Text Editing   In the **text-editing** process, a user enters text into the computer via a word processor. After the text is entered, it is stored in the computer system, where it can be edited and a new version saved. Word processors are designed to edit text in one of two ways. A **line editor** allows you to operate on only one line of text at a time. A **screen editor,** on the other hand, can be used to edit the text shown at a given time on the entire screen—as much as twenty-four or twenty-five lines.

Because of their design, line editors do not give the user a true picture on the screen of how the text will be printed. Often, line editors require the commands for such things as centering text and indenting for paragraphs to be contained in the text file prior to the line that would be centered or indented. The command then takes effect when the document is printed; thus, only after the document is printed does the user see how it will look. A word processor that is set up as a screen editor, however, is designed to give the user a true picture on the screen of what the document will look like when it is printed. If a center command is given, the text is centered on the display screen. If an 80-column display is used with a screen editor, the entire width of an 8½-inch-wide document can be seen on the display screen. A 40-column display, however, would require the use of horizontal scrolling (see section on word-processor features) to view a line of text that is to be printed on an 8½-inch-wide piece of paper.

Word processors can also vary in the way the text is entered and edited. Some word processors have what is referred to as write mode and edit mode. The write mode permits the user to enter text, while the edit mode permits editing of a document that has already been saved. Other word processors simply have a single mode that allows the user to both enter and edit a document without switching modes. Many word-processor users find the single mode more convenient and easier to use.

Word processors may also treat text files differently. A **page-oriented word processor** treats a document as a series of pages. When using a page-oriented word processor you can display and edit only one page at a time. The manner in which a word processor treats a text file also determines how it uses the computer's internal memory and secondary storage. If the word processor is page oriented, it will permit one page of text to be in internal memory at a time. If another page is required, the word processor will copy it into the computer's internal memory in place of the page that was there.

A **document-oriented word processor** treats a text file as one long document. This way of handling a text file eliminates the need to work on pages separately. It also allows a greater portion of a file to be held in internal memory, thereby reducing the number of times secondary storage must be accessed for retrieving and storing text.

Print Formatting   The second step of word processing—**print formatting**—occurs when the word processor communicates with the printer, through the computer system, to tell it how to print the text. Print formatting allows the user to do such things as the following:

- Set margins and tab stops.
- Request single, double, or triple spacing.
- Set the position of headers and footers.
- Select page numbering.
- Indicate what is to be underlined and typed in boldface.
- Determine subscripts and superscripts.

Different word processors, however, do have different print formatting capabilities.

Uses

Word processors are used in business as well as in the home. The word processors most widely used in the home fall into the $50 to $100 price range, while word processors used for business purposes tend to fall in the $150 to $500 price range.

In the home, word processors can be used for such things as writing letters, memos, and formal papers. In business they are used for generating reports, producing formal correspondence, writing memos, and creating form letters, just to mention a few functions. There are also some specialized uses of word processors—for example, the creation of documents in foreign languages.

Other word-processing features, which in some cases are added-cost items, allow the word processor to be used for additional tasks. Most word processors contain a mail-merge option that allows the user to insert names, addresses, and other variables into a form letter entered and saved using the word processor. Some word processors also offer a speller, dictionary, and a thesaurus (usually at an additional cost) that can be used in conjunction with the word processor.

Features

A number of common features are offered in nearly all word processors. These features are normally selected by a simple keystroke and fall into one of three categories: (1) writing and editing, (2) screen formatting, and (3) print formatting.

Writing and Editing The **cursor,** which is normally a blinking line or box on the display screen, is used to identify the current position on the display and indicates where the next character will be typed. Cursor positioning is a very important part of word processing because you must be able to position the cursor at various locations on the screen to be able to edit a text file. The following list identifies some of the more common cursor positions:

- Home: Upper left-hand corner of display screen.
- Top of page: First character at top of current display screen.
- End of page: Last character at bottom of current display screen.
- Tab: Predefined positions from left margin of display screen.
- Page up: Displays top portion of current page and positions cursor to first character.
- Page down: Displays bottom portion of current page and positions cursor to last character.
- Next word: First character of the following word.
- Previous word: First character of the last word.
- Next page: Displays top portion of next page and positions cursor to first character.
- Previous page: Displays top portion of previous page and positions cursor to first character.
- Go to: Positions cursor to designated location in text (such as: GO TO PAGE 5).

Other common writing and editing features of word processors include: word wrap, scrolling, insertion, deletion, move, search, and undo. **Word wrap,** or word wraparound, automatically positions the text you type to fit within predefined margins. For example, as the user is typing and comes to the right margin, word wrap automatically positions a word that extends beyond the margin on the beginning of the next line. To end a line prior to reaching the right margin—at the end of a paragraph, for example—one simply presses a carriage return.

Scrolling allows the user to position a particular portion of text file onto the display screen. Since, in most cases, only a part of the document can be viewed at one time, this feature is valuable for viewing it in its entirety. Vertical scrolling, the most common form of scrolling, allows the user to scroll through a document from top to bottom or vice versa. When the system being used cannot display the entire width of the document, horizontal scrolling can be used.

The **insertion** and **deletion** features available on word processors are very similar in the way they can be used. The insertion feature allows characters, words, sentences, or blocks of text to be inserted into a document, while the delete feature allows deletion of characters, words, sentences, or blocks of text.

Many word processors also provide block movement features, which allow the user to move an entire block of text from one location to another, copy a block of text into a designated position within the document, save a block of text on secondary storage, and delete an entire block of text.

The valuable **search** feature is found on many word processors. A search and find feature allows the user to specify a word or set of characters to be searched for throughout the document. The word processor will search for the string of characters, positioning the cursor at the first character of the string when it finds it. A search and replace feature allows the user to search for a particular string of text and then replace it. Once the word processor finds the designated string, it will replace that string with the one provided. This feature can be particularly helpful in correcting misspellings throughout a document.

The **undo** feature of a word processor allows the user to recover text that has been accidentally deleted. Some word processors can save text that has been deleted in a special text buffer. If you wish to recover what you have deleted, the word processor can retrieve it from the text buffer. The size of these buffers varies from word processor to word processor, however, and in some cases only the last block of text deleted can be saved.

Screen Formatting   **Screen formatting** features control the way that text is displayed on the screen as well as provide the user with status information concerning the document being entered or edited. The display of upper- and lower-case letters is considered to be a screen formatting feature and is controlled by either the shift key or capital lock key. Status information concerning the location of the cursor on the display screen (row, column, and line number), along with information such as the current page number, the available memory, the number of words the document contains, tab settings, and page breaks are also screen formatting features.

Print Formatting   Some of the more common **print formatting** features found in word processors include: margin settings, line spacing, centering, automatic pagination, headers and footers, and character enhancements.

Some word processors allow the user to set all four margins, while others allow the setting of only one or two margins. Left and right justification is also available on some word processors.

Single spacing is available on all word processors, and many can switch to either double or triple spacing. Note, however, that on many word processors the spacing will only occur when the document is printed; document display is single spaced.

Nearly all word processors provide centering and automatic pagination. In most cases, centering is done automatically once the command has been given. Some word processors allow the user to choose where the page number will be printed; some do not.

Headers and footers are a very important feature if the word processor is used for creating manuscripts or formal reports. In most cases one can define the header or footer once, and the word processor will insert it at the top or bottom of each page. The numbering of pages, for example, can be placed in the text as a header if the page numbers should appear at the top of the page, or as a footer if they are placed on the bottom of the page. The placing of footnotes in a formal paper prepared using a word processor would be done using a footer.

Character enhancement features allow one to underline, boldface, subscript, or superscript text within a document. Both the word processor and printer must be capable of providing these enhancements, however.

Additional features that are found in some word processors include: disk formatting, disk copying, cataloging, file renaming, document copying, and document deleting.

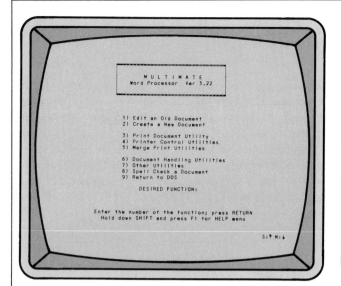

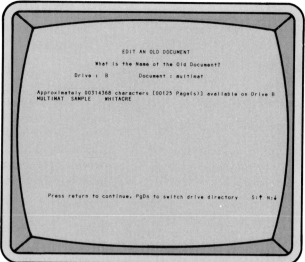

MultiMate's Main Menu is the starting point from which you proceed through a series of menus and screens for the option you select. For instance, selecting number 6, Document Handling Utilities, gives you choices including "Copy a Document," "Move a Document," "Delete a Document" and "Rename a Document." These functions can all be performed without leaving MultiMate.

Selecting Main Menu number 1, "Edit an Old Document" will give you a screen listing all the documents on your document disk, giving you some information about disk space, and asking you for the name of the document you want to edit. In this case we have typed in "MULTIMAT." (Only the first eight characters are recognized by the word processor.)

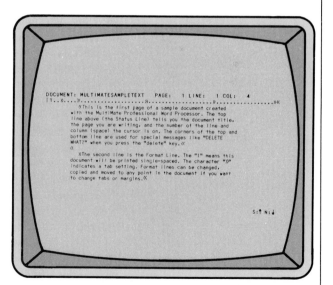

Pressing the RETURN key after you have entered the file name takes you to MultiMate's Document Summary Screen, with the name of your document at the top. You can use its blank "fields" to briefly describe the document. The date is entered automatically. Later, MultiMate can search the Document Summary Screens of all the documents on your disk.

Pressing F10 takes you from the Document Summary Screen to the document itself. This screen is from a sample document explaining what you see on the screen itself. The top line (the Status Line) tells you the document title, the page you are writing, and the number of the line and column (space) the cursor is on.

DATA-MANAGEMENT SOFTWARE

A Definition

Data managers (or data-management packages) are application software packages that computerize the everyday tasks of recording and filing information. The traditional manual filing system, using pencil, paper, file folders, and file cabinets, is replaced by a computer system where data managers are used. Data is recorded using a computer terminal and keyboard and is stored on the computer's secondary storage devices where it can be accessed.

Most data-management packages contain a number of standard features, including the following:

- The ability to add or delete information within a file.
- The ability to search a file for information based on some criterion.
- The ability to update information within a file.
- Sorting of information into some order.
- The ability to print reports or even mailing labels.

There are, however, two types of data managers, and although many of the standard functions discussed above are contained in both types, the two types differ greatly in their capabilities. The two types of data managers are file handlers and data base packages.

File Handlers   File handlers and data base packages differ mostly in the way in which the data is stored and hence how it can be accessed. One way to view the difference between the two types of data managers is by reviewing their development through time.

File handlers were developed first and were designed to duplicate the traditional manual methods of filing. Before the use of computers for filing, sections or departments in a business generally kept records that pertained only to their particular area of interest. The payroll department, for example, might keep an employee's name, number, address, salary, and number of deductions to facilitate the writing of paychecks. The personnel department, on the other hand, might keep each employee's name, number, salary, job title, address, employment history, and spouse's name. Each department would keep its own information independently for its own use.

Computers and computerized recordkeeping made it possible for the procedures and methods of recording and filing data to be converted from paper, file folders, and file cabinets to computer software and storage devices. Computer access allowed each department to maintain its own independent files. The personnel department would have access to the employee file, while the payroll department would have access to the payroll file.

File handlers, therefore, can access only one data file at a time. They also cause duplication of data between files when used in a situation where many files containing similar information must be maintained—as often happens in a large corporation. This is not to say, however, that file handlers are not useful in certain situations. A small business, for example, can benefit greatly from the use of a file handler package that helps to organize and properly maintain the business's inventory.

Data Base Packages   File handling software did have some drawbacks for companies that had enormous amounts of data and limited computer resources. Because of the duplication of data and difficulty in accurately keeping one piece of information, such as an employee address, across several files, large companies began to develop data bases.

Data bases consolidate various independent files into one integrated whole from which all users can have access to the information they need. Such consolidation means that a piece of data needs to be located in only one place, making it easier to maintain. Users can still search for, update, add, or delete data as with a file handler; it is the way in which the data is organized and stored that differs.

A data base, therefore, could be likened to a large, centrally located room with file cabinet after file cabinet of information. Because it is kept in a central location and all personnel can have access to the information they require, information is easy to access, can be updated in one location, and is not duplicated.

A file handler, on the other hand, can be likened to a single file cabinet kept in a particular department where only the department's employees have access to the data. Another department's employees would find it difficult to get access to the data, and it would therefore be duplicated across departments within the organization.

Uses

Data managers have a number of uses in the home, in business, and in specialized situations. Data managers—file handlers in particular—have proven to be very popular software packages for use in the home. They can be used for such things as creating a computerized Christmas card list, compiling a computerized recipe index card file, and balancing the checkbook. The data manager software package can be used for just about any type of record keeping and filing done in the home.

Other possible uses of data managers in the home include: keeping a personal-property inventory, creating a listing of important documents and their locations, keeping a computerized address book and phone listing, creating a mailing list, keeping an appointment calendar, and keeping track of works within a personal library. File handlers simply offer a means of computerizing a manual record-keeping task—that of keeping organized, readily accessible records.

File handlers are also popular with small businesses that can benefit from the conversion of manual record-keeping processes to computerized record keeping. This process of converting manual filing systems to computerized filing systems has been possibly the greatest single use of data managers. Any aspect of a business that uses some form of file system, such as a rolodex file or file cabinet, could potentially be computerized using a data manager. Business applications that are easily adapted to use with a data manager include the keeping of employee records, inventory control, and listings of suppliers and customers.

There are, however, some data managers that are designed for use in special, or unique, situations. One such specialized use of data management software is in the area of mass mailing. A popular application is creating mailing lists. Mailing list data managers provide the user with the ability to store, update, sort, and print data that can be used for creating mailing lists or mailing labels. Not only can these data managers be used to create mailing lists, they can also be used along with word processors to generate form letters.

Features

Many of the popular data managers offer a standard group of features. In most packages, these features can be selected through choices displayed in menus (a list of options available to the user). These standard features include: adding records, deleting records, searching for and/or updating records, sorting the data file, printing, and making some mathematical calculations. Additional features contained in some data managers include creating screen displays, and displaying "help" screens containing available menu choices and explanations to guide the inexperienced user.

Add/Delete   Once a file has been created, data is entered into the file using the add feature. The add feature simply allows one to place a record of information in the data file. The delete, or remove, feature serves just the opposite function; it erases a record of information from the data file.

Search/Update   The search feature of a data manager allows the user to search an existing data file for a record or records based on certain criteria. If, for example, one wants to find all softball bats in a sports equipment inventory with a price of over $15, he or she would use the search feature. The update feature, on the other hand, allows one to change the value of a data field once one has located it. If the price of the softball bats has changed from $15 to $17.50, one would use the update feature to make the change within the inventory file. In many of the data managers the search and update features are used in conjunction with each other to locate a record and then to change it.

Sort   The data in a file is generally stored in the order it is entered; the sort feature provides the user with a way to alter that order of storage. For example, a data file containing the names and addresses for a mailing list can be sorted according to last names prior to printing the list. This would allow the list to be printed in alphabetical order.

Print   The print feature can be valuable, but some packages have limited printing capabilities. Some software publishers offer an independent report-generating package or package add-ons to use with the data files created using the data manager. For the purpose of printing mailing lists and mailing labels, most data managers have adequate print capabilities.

Mathematical Calculations   Some data managers are capable of making mathematical calculations on the data contained within a file. These calculations can be as simple as subtotalling or totalling a particular field within the data records, or can be as complex as calculating statistics such as means or averages. File handlers, for the most part, offer limited mathematical capabilities while data base management packages typically permit more complex computations.

Additional Features   A special feature in many data managers allows one to design the screen on which the data will be displayed. By designing the

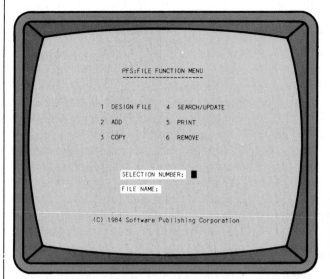

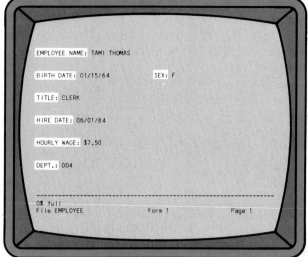

This screen represents the main menu of the PFS: File data management package for the Apple IIe by Software Publishing Corporation. The first time this screen is encountered, a selection number and file name must be entered. For our purposes, we will choose to ADD a record to the file titled EMPLOYEE.

The second screen shows the information that would be entered for the employee Tami Thomas. The Tab key would be used to position the cursor to the input locations and a CONTROL-C key combination would store the information in the EMPLOYEE file.

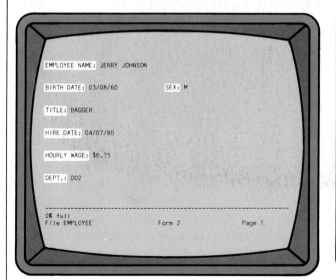

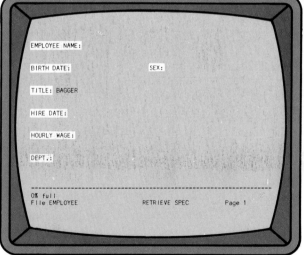

Jerry Johnson's information would be entered as shown above. Note the status information that is provided at the bottom of the screen. With one record added the EMPLOYEE file is 0% full and Page 1 of the second Form is being displayed. The ESC key would be pressed to stop entering records.

This screen represents what the user would see if he or she had chosen selection number 4 from the main menu after the employee records were added. In this case, we are searching for employers with the TITLE of BAGGER. The Jerry Johnson screen as shown above would be displayed.

screen display format, one indicates to the data manager the fields that will be contained within a record of the data file. Data managers that do not allow the creation of a display format generally require users to declare data fields that will be contained in a record.

Some data managers also can display help screens upon request. If the user is confused about available choices at a certain point within the program, he or she can request a display of the available options and possibly even a brief explanation of what each option will do. This feature is valuable for the inexperienced user of the package, although once he or she has gained experience, the need for the help screens will decrease. Since the screens are displayed only on request, the experienced user is not slowed by the additional display of menu screens and explanations of available choices.

Concept Summary 12–1

Word Processing and Data Management

■ An application software package designed to enter, manipulate, format, print, store, and retrieve text is called a **word processor. Word processing** is the term used to describe this process, and a **word processing system** is the computer system used for word processing.

■ Word processing involves two steps: **text editing** and **print formatting.**

■ A word processor referred to as a **line editor** can operate on only one line of text at a time. A **screen editor,** on the other hand, can operate on an entire screen of text (24 or 25 lines).

■ Word processing features are usually chosen using a simple keystroke and fall into one of three categories: (1) writing and editing, (2) screen formatting, and (3) print formatting.

■ **Data managers** (or data management packages) are application packages designed to computerize the everyday tasks of recording and filing information.

■ There are two types of data managers, **file handlers** and **data base packages.** File handlers are designed to duplicate traditional methods of manual filing, while data base packages are designed to consolidate independent files into an integrated whole.

■ Standard features found in data managers include: adding records, deleting records, searching for and/or updating records, sorting the data file, printing, and making some mathematical calculations.

MODELING SOFTWARE

A Definition

Modeling software, as the name implies, is based on a mathematical model. A **model** is a mathematical representation of a real world situation. For example, the relationship of a monthly payment to an amount borrowed and an annual interest rate can be shown with a mathematical equation, or model. A model used to calculate monthly payments, therefore, might look like the following:

$$\frac{\text{Monthly}}{\text{Payment}} = \frac{\text{Interest rate}}{12} \times \frac{\text{Amount}}{\text{Borrowed}} \times \left(\frac{\left(1 + \frac{\text{Interest rate}}{12} \right) \text{Number of Months}}{\left(1 + \frac{\text{Interest Rate}}{12} \right) \text{Number of Months} - 1} \right)$$

Once the model has been developed, it can be entered into the computer using a modeling application software package. A **modeling package** uses the power and speed of a computer to perform mathematical calculations. Depending on the particular package, modeling software can also create printed reports and graphic displays.

Modeling software has a wide variety of potential uses; however, one of its most popular uses is to assist business managers in decision making. By developing a model, entering it into the computer via the modeling software, and then altering values of the variables within the model, a manager can see how changes in the variables will affect the outcome of the model. This type of process is known as **simulation** and will be discussed in greater detail in Chapter 15.

Modeling software used on microcomputers is called an electronic spreadsheet, while modeling, or planning, packages are used on minicomputers and mainframe computer systems. This chapter will focus on electronic spreadsheets, their uses, and features, and Chapter 15 will take a closer look at a planning package—IFPS (Interactive Financial Planning System).

Electronic Spreadsheets   A **spreadsheet,** or ledger sheet, is primarily used in business by accountants for performing financial calculations and recording transactions. An electronic spreadsheet is simply a computerized version of a traditional spreadsheet. Electronic spreadsheets, however, are being used for more than just doing financial calculations and recording transactions. An **electronic spreadsheet** is a table of rows and columns used to store and manipulate any kind of numerical data.

Some spreadsheets are as large as 254 rows by 64 columns, which means that a user can only view a portion of the spreadsheet at one time. The display screen acts as a window to view a selected portion of the spreadsheet. As in viewing documents using a word processor, vertical and horizontal scrolling are used to position a portion of the spreadsheet onto the display screen.

The point in a spreadsheet where a particular row and column meet is called a **cell.** Each cell is a unique location within the spreadsheet, and in the case of a 254 by 64 spreadsheet, there would be 16,256 cells. Cells can contain labels, values, and formulas. The formulas that can be entered into a cell can contain operators that perform addition, subtraction, multiplication, division, and exponentiation. Some spreadsheets also have predefined math functions that can be placed in a cell, including sum, minimum, maximum, and average.

Most spreadsheets also have a **status area** at the top of the display that indicates the location of the cursor and what was entered into a particular cell. A **command area** at the bottom of some spreadsheets displays the commands available to the user.

Uses

Like word processors and data managers, electronic spreadsheets can be used at home as well as in business. In business, electronic spreadsheets are being used increasingly by managers as an aid to decision making. By constructing a model where inputs and outputs are identified, the manager can use the spreadsheet to experiment with the outcome of the model. This is much faster than doing this type of analysis by hand using pencil, paper, and a calculator.

Along with the modeling and simulation performed by managers, electronic spreadsheets are being used in the areas of finance and accounting for traditional purposes. The tasks of preparing financial reports and recording transactions are greatly simplified through the use of an electronic spreadsheet.

At home, electronic spreadsheets can be used for a variety of purposes. Home budgeting, interest calculations, and just about any task that requires the manipulation of numeric data can be done using an electronic spreadsheet.

Features

Variable Column Width Spreadsheets that have variable column widths allow the user to adjust the columns to a desired width. This can be very helpful when either large values, long variable names, or large formulas are required.

Automatic Spillover Automatic spillover is a feature of some spreadsheets that have fixed column widths. It allows extra-long labels to "spill over" into the next cell.

Insert and Delete Insert and delete features allow a user to insert or delete rows or columns as desired. If a particular cell is inserted or deleted that would be contained in a formula, the spreadsheet will automatically compensate for the row or column's addition or deletion.

Graphics Some spreadsheets offer the user the capability to create graphs using data contained in the spreadsheet. Horizontal graphs using asterisks, simple pie charts, or line charts are often available.

Templates A **template** is a predefined set of formulas that are used on a continuing basis. By saving the formulas as a template, they can be retrieved and new values can be substituted for calculation. This eliminates the need to enter the formulas each time the calculations are required.

Locking Cells The locking, or protecting, of cells prevents them from being altered or destroyed. A cell that is critical to the outcome of a formula cannot be accidentally deleted or changed if the cell is locked.

Hiding Cells Hiding cells within the spreadsheet prevent the contents of a cell from being displayed. This would prevent the user from seeing the results when data is entered for manipulation, for example. This could be used as a security measure to prevent sensitive information, such as an employee's salary, from being seen by unauthorized personnel.

Naming Cells Cells can be referenced according to either their location within the spreadsheet (a cell at column B, row 6, for example, would be named B6), or by a name provided by the user. Naming cells is more convenient if you wish to include a cell in a formula. Rather than having to search through the spreadsheet for the cell's location, one simply refers to the cell by name in the formula.

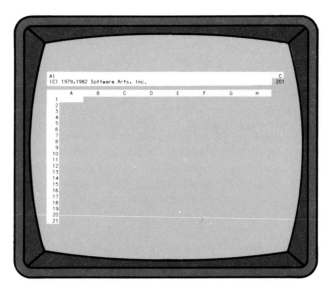

The screen represents the initial screen of the VisiCalc electronic spreadsheet for the IBM PC by Software Arts, Inc. The letters horizontally across the screen identify the columns (A-H) while the numbers running vertically down the screen identify the rows (1-21). The upper left-hand corner of the screen identifies the current cell location.

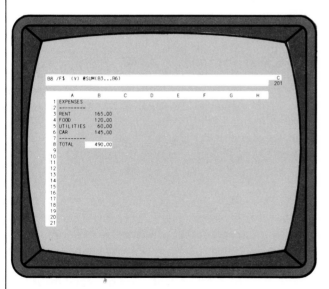

This screen demonstrates how a spreadsheet can be used to calculate a monthly budget, for example. Labels are entered in column A and B. Cell B8 sums the value contained in cells B3 through B6.

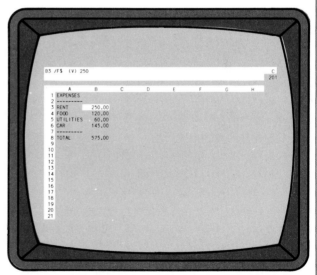

In order to alter the budget, the cursor can be positioned to cell B3 and the value of RENT changed to 250.00. Once the new RENT value is entered the TOTAL is recalculated to reflect the change.

Windows Windows permit the user to divide the display screen into several independent displays that bring separate portions of the spreadsheet into view.

Titles If one is using the first column of a spreadsheet for the purpose of titling the rows, the title feature allows the first column of the spreadsheet to stay locked in place while the remainder of the columns will scroll as desired.

Copy The copy, or replication, feature allows the user to copy a cell, or group of cells, to another location within the spreadsheet. This eliminates the need to retype cells that must be duplicated throughout the spreadsheet.

Manual Recalculation A manual recalculation feature lets the user choose when the outcome of the spreadsheet should be recalculated. Normally, when a value of a cell is changed, the spreadsheet automatically begins a recalculation. With the manual recalculation feature, more than one cell can be altered before the recalculation is started.

Sort The sort feature in a spreadsheet provides for the ordering of information contained within the spreadsheet.

GRAPHICS SOFTWARE

A Definition

Graphics software packages are designed to allow the user to display images on a computer monitor or terminal or to print images on a printer. The images that can be created range from a bar chart to detailed designs of objects created by an engineer, for example.

The operation of graphics packages can be as simple as selecting choices from a menu of available options, or as complex as being given control of the individual dots on the display screen, called **pixels,** to create images. Each display screen has a certain number of pixels that are used to make any image that is displayed on the screen. By controlling these pixels, the user can create graphic images with virtually any degree of detail desired.

Uses

Applications for graphics software packages range from business uses to artistic uses. Within business itself, they are used for a number of differing applications. Graphic packages that produce graphs such as pie charts and bar graphs are used by managers to summarize data for presentation purposes. The graphs that are created can be used for presentations on monitors or can be printed for distribution to those attending a presentation. The printed output from these packages can also be used to create slides or transparencies.

Graphics packages are also being used in business to design entire objects or parts. Computer-aided design, for example, employs a graphics software package to allow an engineer to design products as complex as automobiles.

Art is another area that is seeing increasing use of graphics packages. Computer artists can now use this kind of software to "paint" images or pictures on the display screen. This technique is particularly appealing because the images on the display screen can be changed easily if the artist is dissatisfied with the image.

Graphics packages are also being used heavily in the creation of computer video games. Developers of these games can use the packages to create display screens that they can then save and call up for display while the game is running.

Features

Some features that are common to nearly all types of graphics software packages are discussed below.

Two- and Three-Dimensional Display   Some graphics packages are capable of only two-dimensional display, while some are capable of displaying three dimensions. Depending on the application, a two-dimensional display may be sufficient.

Save   The save feature can be particularly useful. By being able to save screen displays, a program written for a particular application can call display screens from secondary storage while the program is running. The save feature is also helpful in a case where display screens used in other applications are similar to some already saved. The saved display screens can be modified to meet new programs' needs and saved under another name. This eliminates the need to create a new display screen from scratch each time one is needed.

Cursor Positioning   Many packages use the positioning of the cursor to create graphic images. In some cases, arrows (found on many keyboards) or control characters are used to position the cursor. In other cases, input devices such as joysticks, game paddles, koala pads, graphic tablets, or a mouse can be used to position the cursor.

High-Resolution Graphics   The ability of a graphics package to take advantage of the computer's high-resolution graphics capability means that the images the user can create will be sharper than they would be if they were displayed in the normal display mode. High-resolution graphics provides for a greater total number of pixels on the display screen in order to sharpen the images.

Color   Many computers also have the ability to display images in color. If a computer system has a color monitor and the capability to display color, the graphics package can then make images much more appealing.

Animation   Animation involves the moving of an image about the display screen. The image can be moved either horizontally, vertically, or diagonally; it can also be rotated about a point. Such mobility is critical in the preparation of video games and the design of certain types of objects.

- A **model,** a mathematical representation of an actual situation, is the basis of a modeling software package.
- Modeling software packages used on microcomputers are called **electronic spreadsheets.** An electronic spreadsheet is a table of rows and columns used to store and manipulate numerical data.
- A **cell** is a unique location within a spreadsheet where a particular row and column meet.
- Cells of a spreadsheet can contain labels, values, and formulas. Addition, subtraction, multiplication, division, and predefined math functions such as sum, minimum, maximum, and average can be used in the formulas contained within cells.
- Graphics software packages allow the user to create images that can be displayed on the computer's monitor or printed on paper using a graphics printer.
- **Pixels** are individual dots on the display screen used to create images. The control of these pixels allows a graphics package user to create images with a very high degree of detail.

INTEGRATED SOFTWARE

Vertical Integration versus Horizontal Integration

Currently, there are two ways of viewing software integration. From a business-oriented perspective, software integration is based on what the software is designed for. With this type of orientation, **horizontal software integration** refers to those application software packages that are general in nature and are capable of being used for a number of different types of applications. For example, a word-processing package that can be used by anyone who desires to manipulate text is said to be horizontally integrated. On the other hand, **vertical software integration** indicates specificity of purpose. A word processor designed for use in creating legal documents, for example, would be considered a vertically integrated package because it is used for one specific purpose.

Viewing software integration from a different perspective—that of software design—horizontal integration can be used to describe the combination of application packages—such as a word processor, data manager, spreadsheet, and graphics package—into one package that can share data. Although application software packages are very powerful as stand-alone packages, the ability to combine packages and pass data between them can offer even greater potential. By combining an electronic spreadsheet with a graphics package, for example, one obtains a very powerful, integrated application package to support decision making.

Vertical integration in a software design context is used to refer to the enhancement of a single package. For example, adding a spelling program, dictionary, or thesaurus to a word processor would be considered vertical integration.

Windows

A relatively new type of software package referred to as a window, or window environment, allows for a software design using horizontal integration.

This screen represents the main menu of the PFS: GRAPH
graphics package for the Apple IIe and IIc by Software Publishing Corporation. Once a graph has been created it can be
saved and displayed as many times as desired. SELECTION
NUMBER five allows the user to GET a graph that has been
saved on disk.

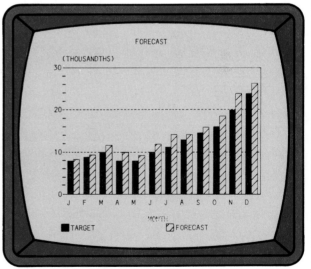

The second screen lists all the graphs available and prompts
the user for a CHART NAME. Software Publishing provides a
diskette of sample graphs and we will choose FORECAST.
The chart name is followed by a CONTROL-C key combination.

Once the name is chosen the graph is then displayed.

Windows, or **window environments,** are an enhancement to the normal operating system of a computer and allow more than one application software package to run concurrently. Windows are currently found primarily on microcomputers and are considered to be on the leading edge of microcomputer software technology.

A windowing software package gives the user the ability to look through a number of "windows" at application packages that are currently in use or capable of being used. As an enhancement to or extension of the normal operating environment, windows have a number of advantages over conventional application software packages, including the following:

- A more user-oriented, or user-friendly, environment.
- The potential for a consistent command structure across application packages.
- The ability to transfer data between applications.
- The use of a mouse or other pointing device.

Most of the window packages that are available use a desktop design that treats the computer display screen as a desktop. By doing so, the window package allows the user to shuffle the packages within the window environment much as he or she would the papers on a desktop. An individual application package such as word processing or data management is available to the user at all times. The user simply selects the desired application and can move from one application to another as required.

Windows can also provide the user with a consistent command structure. Depending on the design of the window package, the manner in which menu choices and commands are displayed and the manner in which commands are issued are consistent across the various applications available for use. Windowing packages also provide for some means of passing data among the various applications.

In many cases, window packages are designed to be used with a mouse or some other pointing device that makes for easier use. Windows will undoubtedly be used to a greater extent in the future because of their ability to both simplify and enhance the environment in which the computer user has to work.

SUMMARY POINTS

- A word processor is an application software package designed to permit the user to enter, manipulate, format, print, store and retrieve text. Word processing is the process of manipulating text using a word processor.
- A word-processing system is the computer system, or portion of a computer system, used for the task of word processing. A dedicated word-processing system is used exclusively for word processing, while a multipurpose digital computer can be used for word processing and many other applications.
- The process of word processing involves two steps: text editing and print formatting.
- A line editor operates on only one line of text at a time, and a screen editor can operate on an entire screen of text at a time.
- A word processor that holds only one page of text in internal memory at a

time is referred to as a page-oriented word processor. A document-oriented word processor treats a file as one continuous document.

■ A few uses of word processors include creating formal reports, letters, memos, and manuscripts.

■ Features included in word processors normally fall into one of three categories: (1) writing and editing features, (2) screen formatting features, and (3) print formatting features.

■ Data managers are used for the same purpose as manual filing systems—the recording and filing of information.

■ There are two types of data managers: file handlers and data base packages. File handlers were developed first to replace manual filing systems, while data base packages were developed later to organize independent files into an integrated whole.

■ Data managers can be used for such tasks as creating a Christmas card list, keeping a personal calendar, maintaining inventory control, and cataloging lists of customers and suppliers.

■ Features considered to be standard in nearly all data managers include: adding or deleting records, searching for records and updating them, sorting records, and printing information from records. Additional features include: screen display formatting and mathematical calculation capabilities.

■ A model is a mathematical representation of an actual situation. One of the most popular uses of modeling software packages is to assist business managers in decision making.

■ Modeling software used on microcomputers is called an electronic spreadsheet, while modeling or planning packages are used on minicomputer and mainframe computer systems.

■ An electronic spreadsheet is a computerized version of a traditional spreadsheet, that is, a table of columns and rows used to store and manipulate numerical data. A cell is the point at which a specific row and column meet within the spreadsheet. Cells can contain labels, values and formulas.

■ Electronic spreadsheets are used for such purposes as assisting managers in their daily decision-making tasks, and also for financial and accounting purposes.

■ Graphics packages allow the computer user to display images, such as a pie chart, on a monitor or terminal, or to print images on a printer. A pixel—the smallest element displayed on a monitor or terminal—is a small dot that, when combined with other dots, creates characters or images for display.

■ Graphics application software packages are used by such people as business managers, engineers, artists, and video game programmers.

■ Horizontally integrated software, in a business sense, refers to those application software packages that are general in nature and can be used for a variety of purposes. In a software design sense, horizontally integrated software refers to the combination of two or more application packages into a single package that is capable of sharing data.

■ Vertically integrated software, in a business sense, refers to packages designed and used for a specific purpose, such as creating legal documents. In a software design context, however, vertical integration refers to the enhancement of a single package.

■ Windows, or window environments, are software packages designed to accomplish horizontal integration in a software design context; they are capable of creating a more user-oriented environment for the application software user.

REVIEW QUESTIONS

1. Define the terms *word processor, word processing,* and *word-processing system.*

2. What are the two primary functions of a word processor? Briefly explain each.

3. How does a line editor differ from a screen editor? What is the difference between a page-oriented word processor and a document-oriented word processor?

4. What is a cursor, and how might controlling its movements help a user of a word processor to edit a document? List and briefly describe five of the cursor positioning features.

5. What is a data manager, and how is it used?

6. Give a brief explanation of the difference between a file handler and a data base package.

7. List and briefly describe four of the more common features contained in data management software packages.

8. What is modeling, and how can it be beneficial to business managers?

9. What is the process used by managers to explore possible outcomes by changing variables within the model?

10. What is a cell? What type of information can it contain?

11. What is a pixel? Show how it is used to create characters or images on a display screen using a blown-up drawing of the letter x.

12. What are some of the advantages horizontally integrated software can offer to the application software user if the package has been developed using a software design perspective?

APPLICATION

Microsoft Corporation

The microcomputer industry began to form in the mid-1970s, and since then has experienced rapid growth. Most visible have been the successes of various hardware suppliers—Apple Computer, Tandy Corporation, Osborne Computer, and more recently, IBM. It was the marked achievements of the hardware suppliers that initiated development of a number of related business concerns—most notably, companies whose efforts were directed toward the design and manufacture of software to run on the new machines.

Founded in 1974, Microsoft Corporation has quickly become the largest developer of software for microcomputers in the United States, establishing itself as a pioneer in an industry teeming with pioneers. Since 1977, sales have doubled every year, staffing has jumped from 5 to over 500, and the company's new quarters were outgrown in less than one year. Microsoft has given new meaning to the concept of rapid expansion.

Beginning with Microsoft's initial product, the first BASIC language for microcomputers (still an industry standard), the company established a reputation for developing innovative, state of the art products. One of the most notable features of Microsoft's design standards is that each new generation of software is compatible with the software of the previous generation.

Microsoft was begun as a partnership between William H. Gates and Paul G. Allen. It was recognized as a privately held corporation in 1981 with Gates as Executive Vice President and Chairman of the Board and Allen as Executive Vice President. Jon Shirley joined the company as President in August of 1983.

Today Microsoft is the leading, innovative, independent software supplier of easy-to-learn and well supported productivity tools, languages, and operating systems. With dealers nationwide, three offices in Europe, and branches in Japan, Australia and Korea, Microsoft is growing and changing to meet the needs of the worldwide software industry.

MICROSOFT'S COMPLETE LINE OF PRODUCTS

Microsoft has the most comprehensive range of microcomputer software products of any company in the world, maintaining a full line of language compilers, interpreters, operating systems, business tools, and even entertainment packages.

In 1980, Microsoft licensed the UNIX operating system from Bell Labs and began to develop its own enhanced version for microcomputers which is called XENIX. UNIX is a powerful, multi-user operating system designed for microcomputers, and Microsoft successfully adapted it, with a number of improvements, to run on the 16-bit-microprocessor. With the release of the XENIX operating system, Microsoft began providing maintenance, support, and even application assistance to original equipment manufacturers (OEMs) and end-users. As a result, Microsoft rapidly became the main supplier of a popular, standardized, high-level 16-bit operating system that was powerful, yet also accessible to almost every microprocessor on the market. The XENIX operating system was developed to run on multi-user computers with 16-bit microprocessors and on DEC's PDP-11 series. To date, forty companies in eight different countries have licensed XENIX.

Also in 1980, Microsoft developed and introduced the Microsoft SoftCard, a plug-in board that allows Apple II owners accessibility to both Microsoft BASIC and the CP/M operating system for the Zilog Z-80 microprocessor, and thereby tens of thousands of software packages. The first year on the market, Microsoft sold 25,000 units, and since then SoftCard has been installed in more than 100,000 Apple systems.

Approached by IBM, and then working closely with them, Microsoft developed a new 16-bit operating system. When IBM introduced its personal computer in August, 1981, Microsoft MS-DOS was the only operating system for which IBM provided additional software. Within a year, IBM had announced full support of twelve Microsoft products, and by June 1982, thirty other companies had released software designed to run on Microsoft MS-DOS. Microsoft also adapted a number of 8-bit languages to the 16-bit microprocessor. Those languages include Microsoft BASIC Interpreter and Compiler, as well as Business BASIC, Pascal, COBOL, C, and FORTRAN Compilers.

Microsoft has developed a number of second-generation software packages and tools, such as Multiplan electronic worksheet, a sophisticated electronic planning and modeling tool designed to be the friendliest and most powerful on the market. By the end of 1982, Multiplan was offered by thirty-six different microcomputer manufacturers and was available in seven languages. According to recent surveys, Multiplan has become the leading program for business, displacing the original electronic spreadsheet, VisiCalc ®.

Microsoft also offers productivity tools that help consumers to design and quickly build customized Multiplan electronic worksheets. The Budget expert system for budget planning and control and the Financial Statement expert system for performing financial statement ratio analysis were both released in the spring of 1983 and have received overwhelming acceptance from business managers and professionals.

In March of 1983, Microsoft introduced SystemCard, designed for the IBM Personal Computer to integrate serial and parallel interface with additional memory (up to 256K bytes of RAM) and a clock/calendar, all on one card. This card will save space in the expansion-limited IBM PC system unit.

Following the release of SystemCard, Microsoft introduced a low cost, handheld input device, called the Microsoft Mouse. Mouse is small and lightweight and is used to quickly insert, delete, and reposition the cursor or blocks of text within a document without having to use the keyboard. Microsoft Mouse has been developed for use with the IBM Personal Computer and other systems that run on the MS-DOS operating system.

With the release of the Microsoft Mouse, Microsoft is also introducing a highly sophisticated word processing software package, Microsoft Word. With features like style sheets, footnotes, glossaries, columnar formatting, and multiple windows, Word is expected to set the pace for the competition. Typical of Microsoft's careful planning, Word has been designed to take advantage of anticipated developments in computer printers by allowing users to specify not only paper and type sizes, but also special character sizes, ink colors, and up to 64 different type fonts.

In the area of entertainment software, the most significant software package released by Microsoft is Flight Simulator, which has become one of the biggest selling programs for the IBM Personal Computer. With Flight Simulator, the players "pilot" an aircraft (similar to a Cessna Skylane) through takeoffs and landings at over twenty different airports. They may alter the environment to simulate various weather conditions, as well as daytime or nighttime flight.

Microsoft will continue to develop other consumer applications and tools, and is committed to the philosophy of constantly improving software and developing upwardly compatible versions of all established products for the new generation of 16-bit computers.

MICROSOFT LOOKS TO THE FUTURE

Microsoft has anticipated several key issues facing it and other software developers today—none of which have easy answers. However, the stand that the major software developers take on these issues will determine the future direction of software design. Three of the major issues that Microsoft sees it must face are: integration, user interface, and expanding the definition of what an operating system is.

Integration has been a byword in the software industry for some time. But the issue here is not superficial integration. We are not talking about taking our products and calling them by similar names. We are not even talking about moving data back and forth between the products through some sort of low-level numeric description, where special commands must be given each time the user wants to move data from one application to another.

The two key features of real integration, then, are that it must capture all data descriptors, and that it must be automatic. That is, to get two applications to work together, there should be no need to continually move the data back and forth manually. If, for example, a user needs to combine data from his Balance Sheet and his Income Statement to do his monthly reports, he should be able to specify what data he wants the reports to include and what format he wants it printed in, and the rest should be automatic—graphs, charts, and all—without any need to go back in and reinput or redescribe the data.

This, then, is how fully integrated software will work. But the big question is, how do we get there? Basically, there are two possible approaches: either we build one single application that does everything, or we find better ways of moving data between separate applications.

The first approach has a definite appeal, in view of the fact that no one has yet developed a way of moving data between applications in a high-level form. But there are three significant drawbacks to the idea of building a single applications package that does it all.

First, there is the problem of specialized expertise. Even if one software developer had the expertise to build a complete set of generic applications—time scheduling, project scheduling, data base development, electronic spreadsheets, and the like—it would be impossible to find a single vendor who had the expertise to build all the necessary vertical applications. And vertical packages, specific to different professions or companies, are going to be a major segment of the software market. This need, then, points to the importance of developing an approach to integration that lets different parties with specialized types of expertise come in and provide specific vertical applications of the various packages.

A second problem with the approach of developing a single application that does it all is that it requires the selection of a single data structure. Since a data structure that is ideal for one application may be clumsy and inefficient for another, the net effect of this approach is that it compromises individual applications. For example, an in-memory data structure that is well-suited to a spreadsheet application may be poorly suited for a data-base package. In fact, it may be totally unusable. If a user wants to develop graphs from the data stored in all the separate cells of a spreadsheet, for example, and he has to move the cells around and give a special set of commands each time he needs a graph drawn, he's not going to be likely to use the application very frequently. Clearly, different applications require different data structures to make them easy to use.

The third difficulty with the single-application approach is that the command structure can easily become overstrained. The number of different commands and decision trees can become a significant problem.

For all of the above reasons, Apple and Microsoft are in agreement that the best solution is to have multiple products that can easily pass data back and forth. This doesn't mean that they can't all be on the screen at one time. But it does mean that they will be based on different data structures and will use different command structures.

A second key decision area facing software developers today involves the development of standards for user interface issues. We do today have general agreement on some of these issues. For example, it is generally accepted that packages should include on-line ''help'' files, so users can immediately call up a piece of help text that is designed for the specific context in which they find themselves. Similarly, menus written in standard English and the use of full-sentence prompts are generally accepted. Visicorp, for example, is moving away from the use of coded commands (/) and toward the use of English words.

The big issue today in the area of user interface is the introduction of a new element into the picture: graphics. ''Graphics,'' to many people, implies the drawing of bar charts, isometric charts, and the like. But the graphics issue is, in reality, far broader than that.

The issue is really one of how we present data on the screen. So far, we have been fairly confined in how we use the screen to present data. For a long time, we could only put characters—and monospaced ones, at that—in specific positions on the screen. This may not seem like a problem at first glance. But stop and think for a minute: if, everytime you went to use a piece of paper, or a chalkboard, you had to take little letters and place them where you wanted them, wouldn't you find this approach to be restricting? You might find yourself using the paper or chalkboard a great deal less than you do now, when you have the freedom to put arbitrary images there in any form you want them.

The new graphic technology—with its use of pixels, bit-mapping, and the like—is bringing this same richness to the computer screen. This ability to view the screen as a piece of paper, and to put arbitrary images on it, means that graphics are going to be used for a great deal more than just drawing graphs. The use of icons, for example, to tell the user what is happening is a much more compact and compelling approach than using words to say the same thing. Cursor displays to show the user his position are another form of visual feedback. For example, when the user is deleting something, the screen could show scissors moving around the material being deleted. Even graphs and diagrams will be revolutionized by the new graphics technology, because the time and effort required to produce them will be significantly reduced. In fact, what the new graphics technology represents is a revolution in user interface.

The bottom line is that graphics are going to be a standard part of all computers. No machine that costs more than $1,000 will be without a built-in bit-map graphics screen. And the software analog of that hardware statement is that, one year from today, no decent application software family, no decent language family, and no decent operating system will be without extremely high-level support for this type of graphics capability. It will be no small task for the software developers to achieve this graphics integration—but it is a necessary task. Furthermore, the graphics capability is not going to be in the form of an add-on package that the user goes out and buys after he has bought his computer; it will be part of the definition of the machine itself. As such, it will require very high-level primitives to allow the user to easily access the graphics capabilities.

As the above observations indicate, software developers are going to have to agree on some user-interface standards to allow the full power of this graphics revolution to be felt. First, they will need to develop some standards for incorporating the graphics capability into the machine. Apple is already moving in this direction with its development of a strong operating system as a foundation for such built-in features. Second, they will need to agree on some high-level operating-system commands to make the graphics capabilities readily accessible to the user.

A third important development that we will be seeing in the near future is a greatly expanded definition of what an operating system is. Microsoft, for example, as the vendor of one of today's most popular operating systems, MS-DOS, is planning to incorporate an increasingly higher number of functions into that system. Graphics capabilities, user interface capabilities, networking—all will be incorporated into the operating system. Instead of these functions being considered as add-on products, they will automatically be a part of every machine. This means that application software developers will be able to assume that they are there, and design their packages accordingly.

THE SOFT WORLD IS HERE

As the above observations indicate, a revolution is taking place in the world of computers today, and software is where the innovation is coming from. No longer do we need to go out and build better, more powerful hardware to achieve productivity improvements: we simply develop a new software package, and people can put it to use immediately in their existing machines. The revolution is here—and it is soft.

DISCUSSION POINTS

1. What key issues does Microsoft consider critical to software developers in the future? Briefly explain why these issues are so important.
2. Explain why the development of standards for user interface is an important consideration for a software developer. Why are graphics important to this issue?

A MICROCOMPUTER CONSUMER'S GUIDE

Once you've made the decision to purchase some software, whether it is a word processor, a data manager, or some other type, what do you do next? There are so many programs available that choosing the best one for you may seem as likely as finding the proverbial needle in the haystack.

This guide will provide you with some general guidelines for buying any type of application software as well as some specific considerations for buying word processors, data managers, spreadsheets, and graphics software packages.

ANALYZE YOUR NEEDS

The first step to a successful software purchase is to have a thorough understanding of your needs. Start by determining the type of output you will require. Look at it in terms of what type of information you will need the program to supply and what form or forms in which you want the information or output presented to you. Next determine the inputs that will be used. Based on the inputs used and the required output, determine the processing that is needed to convert the input into the desired output. You may not need to know all the specifics of the processing, such as exactly how some calculations are done, but you will have to know the general types of operations needed. For example, if you need a data manager, you need to determine if the program will need to sort the data items and how sophisticated the sorting feature needs to be. Most will sort on at least one field, but if you need to be able to sort on multiple fields, then make sure that the package you choose can accomplish this.

Make sure you allow room for future expansion when determining your needs. For example, you may presently only need a word processor capable of short, informal documents. However, in the near future you might be starting school, in which case you'll need a word processor capable of handling larger and more formal documents.

After you have a complete picture of your processing and output needs, group them by relative importance. Since the chances of one program providing you with the easiest and most efficient means of accomplishing every one of your needs is fairly slim, you'll want to make sure that the most important and most used features are easy and efficient to operate. For example, if your business needs to provide quick order information to a customer over the telephone, you would want a data manager program that is very fast in providing that information. In this case, because speed is very important, you may be forced to choose a program that is efficient in this area, but not so efficient in other areas that are not as important to the application as access speed.

DETERMINE YOUR CONSTRAINTS

The biggest constraint you are likely to have is money. Your budget may not allow you to purchase the program that will do everything you would like it to. You might have to settle for a moderately priced program that does the basics but foregoes any extras. A word of caution: be careful about letting price be your only guide. Many buyers fall into the trap of either over- or under-buying. Some people feel that if they buy expensive software it will undoubtedly have all the features they need. This may or may not be true; however, studies have shown that many people who purchase higher-priced software use only one-third to two-thirds of the program's capabilities. On the other extreme are those so thrift conscious that they buy low-priced software, only to discover upon using it that it doesn't meet their needs or that their needs soon expand beyond its capabilities.

The point here is that while you may be forced to choose from a certain price range, there are good and bad software packages at both the high and low price ranges. Make certain you know your needs and the capabilities of the programs in question so you may select the best possible choice for your needs.

If you already own the computer hardware that you intend to use, then this will impose another constraint. The software that you choose will have to be compatible with this hardware. For certain computers, this can pose a severe restriction on the number and types of software packages available. Ask yourself the following questions: Does your present hardware system have enough memory to support the program? Do you have the correct number of disk drives needed to run the program? Many programs require that you have at least two disk

Microcomputer software packages are often packaged in colorful binders that include the original diskette and user's manual.

drives to operate them. Does the package you want require special hardware? For example, a graphics package may require a specific video display. Does your computer have the required operating system? Most computers support more than one operating system, so you will need to know which operating system you will be using and the operating system under which the software runs.

EVALUATE THE SOFTWARE

When evaluating software packages, you will want to match the time and money spent on the evaluation to the importance of the software in question. If the software serves only a secondary need and is not vital to the efficiency or effectiveness of your application, then there is no need to spend hundreds of hours selecting it. Simply gathering the names of a few well-known packages and selecting one that will adequately do the job is the best approach. However, if the software is vital to the application in question and it will be used by many persons, then spending considerable time and money to find the best software available is justified.

In many cases the person evaluating the software and the person(s) using the software are not the same. If this is the case, carefully consider those who will be using the software. Spend time with them to get their opinions and desires. This will help assure that the software package you select can both accomplish your intended purpose and be satisfactory to the people using it.

After you have determined the appropriate amount of time and money to spend on the evaluation step and have determined the attitudes and desires of the personnel who will be using the software, then start researching what is available.

RESEARCH

A good place to start would be the technical magazines and journals for manufacturers' ads and for reviews of the software. Other sources of information include present users of the software package in question, computer stores, and information available directly from the manufacturer. Remember, however, that because many of the sources from which you get information may either own or be trying to sell the software in question, their viewpoint may be biased. In general, this should not be a big problem, and with the information gathered from the above sources you should be able to put together a list of the packages most likely to meet your needs.

HANDS-ON TESTING

At this point you'll want to arrange a hands-on demonstration to see for yourself what the software packages can do and how easy they are to implement and use. You should test more than one program in a specific application to help you get a perspective on what is available and the different approaches taken. Whether you will have to go to a computer store for a demonstration or can arrange for the manufacturer to come to you will depend on the type of software or the amount of the purchase. For example, if you are buying an operating system for a mainframe or minicomputer, the manufacturer will more than likely come to you for the demonstration. The same might be true if you are going to buy a large number of a particular piece of software and to enter into an ongoing business relationship with the software manufacturer. Buying a single piece of software for personal use, however, will necessitate making arrangements for a demonstration at one of the local software or computer stores.

A successful hands-on demonstration depends on several factors. One is to be prepared. If you have thoroughly analyzed your needs, you should have either a written or mental checklist of the type of functions you need in the program and have ordered them in a hierarchy based on their importance. If you already own your hardware, run the demonstration on the same type of system you have to make sure there are no compatibility problems. Make sure that the software in question can perform all the functions you need and that the most important and most used functions are accomplished effectively and efficiently. Remember, when constructing this list, it is also important to consider the future. Will your applications expand or change over the next few years? Asking yourself this question will help you select software that can grow with your needs.

To get the most out of a demonstration, do not let the salesperson guide you through. When you run the demonstration, keep in mind the types of reports and documents you need to produce. Tailoring the demonstration to your needs rather than to just what the salesperson wants you to see may help you discover important pluses or minuses that can help you in your decision. You should test demo copies with real, not test, data. For example, if you need a data management program that allows fast access to any record and the salesperson demonstrates the speed of that package using only the demonstration file of ten records, you may be quite surprised when you discover later that it does not zip along quite so fast when you have all 1,000 of your records implemented.

GENERAL PROGRAM CONSIDERATIONS

There are many things to consider when choosing a program. We'll take a look at a number of these in the following sections.

Difficulty Level of a Program

One of these considerations is the difficulty level of the program. You should try to find a program that matches your or the user's background and interest in learning. The best choice for a beginner might be a simple but less powerful package that is easy to use and does not require much time spent on learning to use the program. For the serious user, however, relatively comprehensive software that requires more effort to learn may be more appropriate. Users of more sophisticated software packages should be prepared to spend time on reading, training, and experimenting. A good program will let you "grow into" the package and not limit you as your experience increases. It should allow you to run the program using only the basic commands needed to accomplish the application and allow you to incorporate the more sophisticated commands as you learn them.

There is an important distinction to be made when considering the difficulty level of a program. You must distinguish between the technical background necessary to set up a program for use and the background needed to operate it once installed. For example, a complex communications program might be difficult to configure for the remote systems with which you want to communicate, but easy to operate once it is set up. You can usually obtain help from the manufacturer or place of purchase to initially install a program. While a program that is easy to use is the ideal for any application, take a careful look at those that use this point as a major selling factor. It may be that they are easy to use because they have very limited capabilities and might not be suited to your particular needs.

Program Organization and Appearance

The overall organization and appearance of a program provide many areas for differences. You should look for a clear and logical screen appearance. A screen that is cluttered and poorly organized will take more time to learn and will not be as efficient to use. Most programs have several different modes or sections. Look at how the program handles movement between the program modes. To make things simple and to help avoid disaster or annoyance from striking a wrong key, look for a program that moves from one mode to another simply and consistently. For example, a program may use special function keys or a single key such as the escape key to switch between modes.

 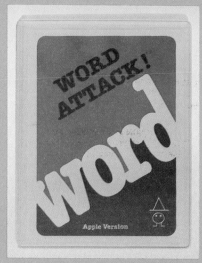 

Available software includes such packages as a speed reading and comprehension program, a vocabulary building program, and a mathematics skills program.

Command Style

The type of command style used also bears looking at. Command style refers to the approach used in implementing a program's commands. Several approaches to command style include: the display of a full menu of commands with explanation; the display of a single command only with explanation; and no displayed menus at all, in which case the available commands must be memorized. Beginners will probably find a program with menus easier to use. More experienced users might want to look at programs without menus because they are faster to operate once you are trained in the use of the program.

Help Screens

Make sure the help screens are truly helpful. Help screens that you can call from any point in the program and that return you to where you left off are probably the most efficient and helpful.

Default Values

Examine the program for the presence of defaults. A default is a value that the computer assumes when you don't tell it what value to use. For example, many word processors are set up to produce a standard business letter on 8½-by-11 inch paper without your having to specify this size. Default values are desirable because they make the program more flexible to your needs. They should be easy to change, allowing you to set them so that the most used format will automatically be used when the program is run. They should also be easy to temporarily override while you are using the program.

Macro Commands

Not essential but very helpful is the program's ability to use macro commands. A macro command allows you to string together several commands and define them as a single key. When that key is struck, the sequence of commands is executed automatically. Macros can increase the efficiency and ease of use of a program.

Error Handling

Determine how the program deals with errors. Error handling capability is an area that, if overlooked in the selection of a program, can spring up as one of the most annoying and disastrous aspects of the program. You should consciously try to make the program you are testing fail to see how it handles the error condition. A good program will let you recover from common error conditions. For example, if you are in the middle of a save operation and you get the error message that the disk is full, the program should allow you to replace the disk and then redo the save operation without losing any of your data. Check for commands that are designed to help you recover from inadvertent errors. Many programs now include an undo command providing a way to recover from errors. For example, when you make a change in the data, the old data is temporarily stored in a buffer instead of being deleted and can be recalled to the screen if desired.

Size Limitations

Make sure that the package you choose can support a large enough data area to meet your needs. For example, check the number of records a data manager can support, the number of pages of text a word processor can work with, or the number of columns and rows that a spreadsheet can support.

Copy Protection

The question of copy protection can be an important consideration to some users—especially microcomputer users. Being able to copy a program gives you a great deal of flexibility. If the software in question is copy protected, then it may be difficult, if not impossible, to use that software with a hard disk, local area network, or an electronic disk simulator because the program cannot be moved from its floppy diskette. Also, if you want to or think you might have to modify a program, make sure that the source code is available before you buy the program. Source code is the sequence of instructions written in either assembly or high-level language by the programmer.

Documentation

The quality of documentation can tell you a lot about the quality of the software package. Look for thorough, well-written manuals that are organized clearly and logically. When you are testing the program, pick up the manual and see if you can easily run some aspect of the program using only the instructions provided. Reference cards that you can place by your computer for quick reference to the program's commands are very helpful. For use with more sophisticated programs, look for tuto-

rials that will guide you step by step through the program's operation.

WHERE TO PURCHASE SOFTWARE

Before you purchase software from any source, familiarize yourself with the past record and policies of the vendor—especially if you are going to make a large purchase. If you are a novice, it is best to look for a vendor that is willing and able to answer your questions before and after you've purchased the software.

Two good ways for the novice or home user to discover the best sources for software in the area are to talk with friends who have a computer or visit a local computer club and talk with its members. The most common software sources for the average home user include software specialty stores, computer hardware stores, department stores, and mail-order houses. Software specialty stores deal exclusively in software, and you can find a wide variety of software for most popular computers. Many computer hardware stores also carry software compatible with the hardware they sell. Software from department stores or mail-order houses can be cheaper; however, these vendors also typically offer little technical advice or support for the software.

If you are purchasing a very expensive piece of software, such as an operating system for a mini- or mainframe computer, or a large number of programs, then it is probably best to go straight to the manufacturer rather than to a distributor or retailer. In most cases manufacturers are willing to make special arrangements with large customers, such as contracts for quantity purchases at substantial discounts and licensing agreements to make unlimited copies of a program and its documentation.

The old adage "let the buyer beware" certainly applies to software purchasing. While the legal considerations involved with software are often hazy at best, you can avoid most problems by simply asking questions before you buy. Don't be afraid to ask; there are no stupid questions. If the salesperson doesn't answer your questions satisfactorily, then it might be wise to try another source. Two of the most important general questions to ask are: How long? and how many? For example, how many records can the program hold? How long does it take to access a record when the maximum number of records are implemented? How many accounts will fit on a single disk? How long can each file name be? How long a document can this word-processing program handle? Well, you get the idea. Ask questions continually and as soon as you think of them so you won't forget them. It is also a good idea to have a pencil and pad to jot down notes about the software.

Some other questions that the more sophisticated user might ask include the following: What will happen when new versions of the operating system under which your program runs appear on the market or when errors are discovered and enhancements are made to the program? Find out if there is a contract to cover software maintenance and updates. Will the updates or corrections be supplied free or at a minimal cost? In addition, ask if training is available and if you will have access to a support person for consultation and assistance, preferably through a toll-free "hot line."

SPECIFIC PROGRAM CONSIDERATIONS

Here are some specific buying considerations for word processors, data managers, spreadsheets, and business graphic packages. When buying one of these packages, consider these points as well as the general guidelines presented above.

Word Processors

The amount of internal memory or internal storage capacity needed to run the word-processing program is an important concern. If you only have a 64K machine but the program requires 128K to run, then you obviously would not be able to run the program without first increasing the amount of memory in your computer. Another consideration is in the size of the document the word processor can work with. Some word processors severely limit the size of the document, forcing you to break up large documents into several smaller ones. Some, however, do allow these smaller segments to be merged during printing. If you will be using the word processor for writing large texts, you will find the ability to work with them as one document advantageous.

There is a wide range of features available for word processors. Finding the program with the right features for you requires that you have heeded the advice given earlier and have thoroughly considered your needs. The two general areas to consider are the typing and editing features and the formatting features available. The typing and editing features include such things as copy

and move commands, cursor positioning features, and search features. The formatting features include those features that determine how your text will appear when it is printed, such as character enhancements, margin settings, headers, and footers. Which features you will need will depend on the type and amount of writing you intend to do.

The flexibility of a word processor refers to its ability to meet your specific needs through the implementation of its available features as well as its ability to use enhancement programs such as spelling and grammar checkers. One example of a program's flexibility is its ability to act as a text editor for writing programs that can then be saved in a format that allows your computer to run them without any modifications. If you will be writing formal letters or papers for presentation, then the ability to use spelling and grammar checkers may also be an important consideration for you. In a business setting requiring a lot of correspondence, the ability to use a mail-merge program is valuable. Another example of a word processor's flexibility is its ability to merge data with another package, such as merging a portion of a spreadsheet into a document created on the word processor.

Data Managers

The storage capacity of the data-manager package is a very important consideration. Many software publishers specify either how many characters can be stored using the package, or how many average-sized records can be stored. If the record is used as a means of determining how much data can be stored in a file, the publisher will normally provide some means of calculating the number of average-sized records that can be stored. If the number of characters is used, you will have to determine the average number of characters a record will contain to determine how many records can be stored in a file. This storage capacity must be adequate for your needs. For example, if you have 1,000 records, but the program only allows for 800 records, the package will be of very little value to you. So determine your storage capacity requirements before you shop for a data manager.

You will also want to examine the features offered by each data manager you are considering. If you know that it will be necessary to do many mathematical calculations when using a data manager, consider only those packages capable of the necessary mathematical calculations. If you require the creation of detailed reports, evaluate only those packages that provide the necessary printing capabilities. If you require a great deal of sorting, then consider only those packages that offer sorting as an available feature.

The flexibility of a particular data manager should also be examined. If you intend to use your data manager to create data files for use with your word processor, then consider only those packages that can create compatible data files. Consult with the data manager manual or the software salesperson to determine if the data managers you are considering will create compatible data files.

Spreadsheets

One of the questions you should ask is how big a worksheet you will need. The worksheet or matrix size of spreadsheets varies considerably. For example, some programs provide 20 columns by 40 rows for a total of 800 cells, whereas others provide as many as 1,000 columns by 50,000 rows for a total of 50 million cells. Also consider how many entries you will need to make. This factor depends on the amount of memory available and not the number of cells, so it is important to know how much memory the program takes up and how much memory you have available in your computer.

Another important consideration is how many display options you want. Many programs have split screens or windows which let you do simultaneous manipulations of different sections of your spreadsheet. For example, if you want to see what impact a change in one portion of

your spreadsheet would have on another portion, you could set up vertical or horizontal windows with each window containing one of the desired areas. You can then make a change in one window and see immediately what result it has on the values in the other windows. With this type of feature, you won't have to scroll through possibly hundreds of rows and columns to see the results of the change.

Make sure that the spreadsheet you choose can support the type of calculations you need to do. Check to see if the common arithmetic functions you need are built into the spreadsheet. Can you build your own arithmetic functions to handle your special needs? Also decide what other special commands you would like. For example, does the program support copying rows and columns, global search and replace, sorting, and so on?

Ask yourself in what form you require your output. Does the spreadsheet allow you to vary column width enough to place the headings you want into it? Can your worksheet be printed in report form as well as in matrix form? Some spreadsheets will also allow you to change worksheets into graphs and charts if your computer and printer have these capabilities. If you need text-editing functions such as underlining and indenting, make sure the spreadsheet is capable of these. If your needs vary, you might also want a spreadsheet that allows you to design your own output form.

Graphics Packages

In graphics software, more than with any of the other software packages discussed, the limits of your hardware dictate the level of complexity you can achieve.

Business graphics packages can create bar graphs such as the one shown below.

Packages can also be purchased to do payroll.

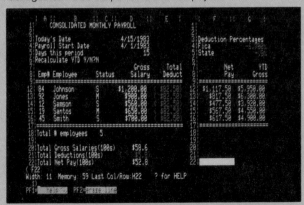

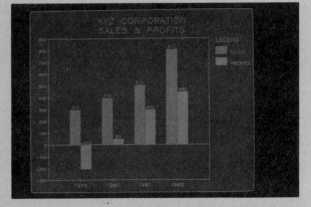

Graphics packages can be used to create artistic works such as the one here.

For example, the type of display screen you have is a limiting hardware factor. Even the most sophisticated graphics packages won't produce high quality graphics on a low quality display screen.

Storage requirements are another important consideration when working with graphics. Graphics can eat up a lot of memory. Each monochrome pixel is represented in memory by 1 bit, a four-color pixel requires 2 bits, eight-color pixels require 3 bits each, and so on. It's easy to see that a graphic image of any reasonable size will require a lot of memory to store it. A pixel is the smallest individual element on a display screen that can be lighted up. The number of these pixels determines the resolution. The higher the resolution, the better the detail you can achieve.

There are different types of graphics packages, so you will need to determine what kind of graphics work you need to do. Do you want a package that can be used to create business graphics (such as line, bar, and pie charts) or one that can be used to create more artistic graphics? If you are looking for business graphics, you will need to decide how good the quality of your graphics needs to be. There are two basic types, analytical or presentation quality graphics. Analytical graphics give you line, bar, and pie charts designed for everyday analysis needs rather than for presentations at stockholders' meetings. Presentation graphics, on the other hand, offer higher resolution, more typefaces, and greater formatting capabilities.

The ability to integrate your graphics with other programs, such as a word processor program, is an important feature for many business users. Of more concern to the graphics artist are the total number of colors from which to choose and the number of colors that can be used on the screen at one time. Some programs are limited in the colors they provide; others have a fairly large selection of colors but only allow you to work with a few at a time; still others have both a large selection of colors and the ability to work with a large number of these at a time. Check to make sure that any other features you want are included in the package, such as the ability to move, copy, rotate, or change the size and shape of graphic images.

There are a number of ways in which a graphics program might accept input. The same is true for the other types of software; however, the manner of input takes on a greater importance for graphics software because of the difficulty and tediousness of programming graphic images. Common methods of input include programming, using a light pen, using a mouse, or using a graphics tablet. Devices such as the light pen, mouse, and graphics tablet make it easier and faster to create complex graphic images. You will need to determine your preference and choose a program that can accommodate it.

SECTION IV
SYSTEMS

13

System Analysis and Design

INTRODUCTION

In computer-based information systems, the hardware and software technologies discussed in earlier chapters are applied as tools for the collection, storage, and retrieval of information that is either helpful to management or required for routine business practices. Information that is helpful to management might include sales analyses, while information that is required for normal business practices might include payroll processing or income tax reporting. It is necessary to understand the hardware and software technologies in order to use them in developing an effective management information system.

This chapter focuses on the application of hardware and software technologies to the development of computer-based information systems. The chapter begins by discussing what a system is. It also discusses the importance of using the system approach to problem solving. The chapter then provides a detailed description of the steps required to develop an information system—analysis, design, programming, implementation, and audit and review.

ARTICLE

Birth of the Killer Robots

Michael Rogers

In the 1951 science-fiction novel "I, Robot," Isaac Asimov promulgated his now famous "Three Laws of Robotics"—the most important of which forbids robots to injure humans. It is only recently that the evolution of real robots began, but Asimov's law will almost certainly be broken soon. Already there have been several accidental deaths caused by industrial robots. And work is now under way, in both military and commercial areas, to create robots capable of killing people on purpose. Last week a prototype of one such machine was completed: the Prowler, by Robot Defense Systems of Thornton, Colo.

The Prowler (which stands for Programmable Robot Observer With Logical Enemy Response) is a mobile robotic sentry, resembling a miniature tank. In final form, the robot will be equipped with microcomputers, artificial intelligence software and distance-ranging sensors, allowing it to patrol the perimeters of an area, such as a military base or airfield, and to identify intruders. Purchasers will specify the sensors and weaponry they desire—and also whether or not the robot will need human permission (from a remote monitoring station) before it opens fire.

Moral Issues: The prototype Prowler is equipped with two M60 machine guns and a grenade launcher. "In the United States, we

don't forsee the Prowler armed with lethal weapons," says Walt Lee, RDS marketing coordinator. "Or, if it is, there will always be a human required in the loop for activation. But there are countries where there aren't the same political or moral considerations." RDS president Christy Peake suggests that armed robots are "an ideal way to protect pipelines, air bases, palaces, when you're outnumbered." Bechtel National, the huge international construction firm, has already proposed the use of RDS robots for a security installation in an unnamed Middle Eastern country. Peake reports that a royal family in that region is currently considering a $4 million robot purchase; RDS has also received inquiries from both Iran and Iraq.

Due to the initial cost (perhaps $200,000 per robot), Bechtel National has yet to install its first RDS robot, but Don Davis, the company's physical-security specialist, considers robot sentries inevitable. "The driving factor is the cost of a 24-hour guard," says Davis, which can be as high as $300,000 a year for highly trained military postings. "In the long run, a robot is cheaper, and it doesn't get bored, lonesome or fall asleep. Plus, a robot will always do what you tell it."

Davis cautions that security robots are still crude devices, capable at best of following limited instructions, and not necessarily to be trusted with lethal weapons. But even as they are, robot sentries could prove

useful. This fall, Denning Mobile Robotics, in Woburn, Mass., will test a robot prison guard, capable of patrolling prison corridors at night, detecting stray inmates, telling them to stay put and then broadcasting a warning to human guards. Benjamin Wellington, Denning's vice president of marketing, also expects industrial applications, patrolling confined areas such as warehouses and factories. He doubts, however, that Denning's robots will ever be armed. "In the military, if someone is in the wrong place and gets shot, they're shot. But you can't get away with that if you're guarding Sears."

Meanwhile, military development of battlefield robots has taken a sharp upswing. The Department of the Army has requested nearly $8 million in its fiscal 1985 budget to start development of an "autonomous land vehicle"—a tanklike device capable of maneuvering around an open battlefield using its own computerized "intelligence." A prototype is expected by 1988. And last month the Defense Advanced Research Projects Agency (DARPA) requested proposals from Martin Marietta, FMC and General Dynamics for a similar machine as part of their massive Strategic Computing Program. "What they're all working toward," says one observer, "is the time when you can tell a machine to go kill enemy tanks, and it will go out by itself, hide, identify friend from foe, kill the enemy and scamper off."

SYSTEM THEORY

Information is data that has been processed and is useful in decision making. It helps decision makers by increasing knowledge and reducing uncertainty. Modern businesses cannot be run without information; it is the lifeblood of an organization. An information system, therefore, is designed to transform data into information and make it available to management in a timely fashion. System analysis and design is an approach used to develop and maintain information systems that supply managers with needed information. System theory will be the basis used to discuss system analysis and design throughout the remainder of the chapter.

Definition of a System

The system approach is based upon system theory. System theory defines a **system** as a group of related elements that work together toward a common goal. One example of a system is a single cell in a human body; each molecule in the cell performs important functions, and all these molecules work together in order for the cell to survive.

A system is made up of inputs, processes, and outputs. **Inputs** enter the system from the surrounding environment. For the cell, the inputs might be oxygen and nutrients. These inputs are transformed by some **process** into outputs. The cell processes its inputs into energy and wastes. Most of the **outputs** leave the system, going to the environment; but some may stay within the system. The energy output from cell processing is kept for survival. Wastes are returned to the environment (see Figure 13–1).

Feedback is another important concept in system theory; it can take the form of either internal or external communication. That is, information can flow within the system or between the system and the environment. Its purpose is to inform the system whether or not predetermined standards or goals

Figure 13–1 ▪ **A Cell as a System**

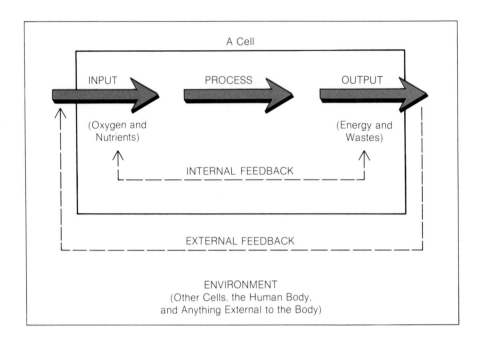

are being met. The feedback for a cell would be the information it needs to survive. If the cell does not have enough oxygen or nutrients to survive, it tries to get more. If an attack from the outside environment threatens its survival, the cell may alter its chemistry by taking in more oxygen or nutrients to try to deter the threat. In system theory a system's primary goal is survival, and feedback is one means used by the system to survive.

The System's Interaction with Other Systems

The body contains many different types of cells—blood cells, nerve cells, lung cells, and so on. Each of these groups can be thought of as a system— blood cells are part of the circulatory system, nerve cells are part of the nervous system, lung cells are part of the respiratory system. These systems, in turn, collectively form a still larger system called a human body. Each of the systems can be viewed in terms of its inputs, processes, outputs, and feedback mechanisms.

The boundaries between systems are not always easy to define. Neither are the elements of a system that might stand alone as systems in themselves. The determination depends on the level or scope at which one views the system. A doctor who is a general practitioner views the body as the system; an ophthalmologist views the eye as the system.

The fact that one system may belong to another, larger system is an important concept in system theory. It implies the existence of interaction among systems. All of these concepts are put to good use when system theory is used to view the organization.

The Organization as a System

The concepts of system theory can be applied to a business firm. It has a group of related elements (departments or employees) working together towards a common goal (survival and profit). Figure 13–2 shows a business

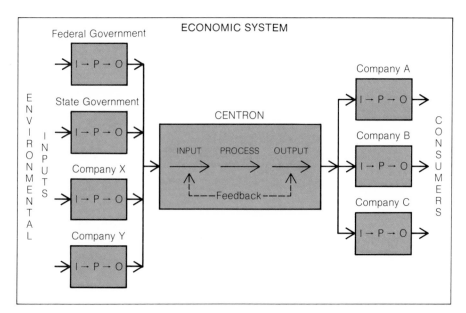

Figure 13–2 ▪ Interacting Systems

firm as a system within a system—the economic system of today's business world. The Centron system is shown using inputs from the surrounding environment to create outputs through a transformation process.

As Figure 13–2 shows, Centron is affected by external environmental factors outside its control. Government regulations, competition, and the economy are examples of such external factors. Internal factors affecting Centron include the quality of its managers, its management/labor relations, its departmental relationships, and its internal communication channels. An analysis of Centron's information needs must take into account both its internal and external environmental factors.

Each department within Centron can also be thought of as a system. A planner in the production department (a system) needs information about forecast sales from the sales department (another system). In making sales forecasts, the sales department probably uses past history and information from its own salespersons (internal environment) as well as stated customer intentions and projected economic conditions (external environment). Information about the availability of raw materials is provided by the purchasing department, which communicates with suppliers. The list of interactions goes on and on (see Figure 13–3).

Modeling Reality: The System Approach

A business is too complex to study directly. A systems analyst needs tools to help analyze the complex information flows that affect it. Just as the person who cannot see the forest for the trees needs to take a few steps backwards, the analyst needs to step back and consider the entire organization rather than focusing on its smaller elements.

The system approach to system analysis provides the analyst with a way to better understand and evaluate information systems by removing their complexities. It is a model that aids in the analysis of information systems by attempting to mirror actual events while reducing the complexity of the activities involved in those events. The systems model highlights important rela-

**Figure 13–3 ▪ The Company as a
System and Its Interactions**

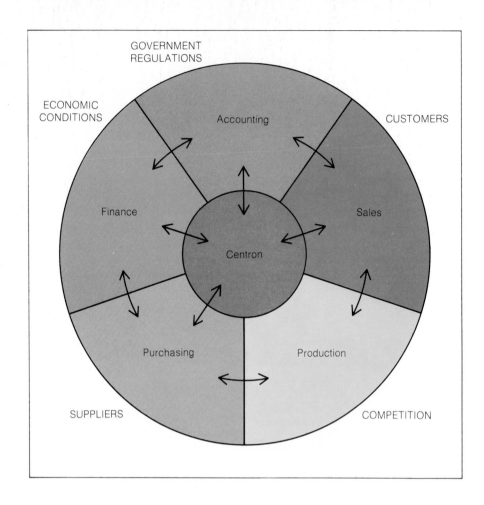

tionships, patterns, and flows of information. Instead of accurately representing each tree in the forest, the model shows the overall pattern of the trees,
their outline, and the countryside bordering their edges.

The system approach to problem solving, therefore, views an organization
as an integrated whole, and not as a grouping of independent functional
areas. This philosophy could be equated to viewing the overall pattern of
trees rather than looking at each individual tree to gain an understanding of
how the forest works. The system approach relies on the assumption that
individual cells of an organization (or system), although somewhat self-sufficient or independent, still contribute to and shape the overall character of the
whole organization. In fact, removal of one of the cells from the whole would
change the character of the overall organization.

Traditionally, problem solving involved breaking an organization into cells
so that each cell could be analyzed separately. This method of problem solving involved viewing the organization from the bottom up, whereas the system approach involves viewing an organization from the top down. This top-
down view emphasizes that an accurate evaluation of an organization and its
relationships, patterns, and information flows requires an understanding of
how that organization functions as a whole, not as individual cells. Important
relationships, patterns, and flows of information among the individual cells
of the whole organization can be determined using the system approach.

System Methodology

An information system is designed to satisfy the needs of decision makers. Some information systems are computerized; others are manual. Both must provide management with the information it needs or they will become unused and outdated. However, even when there are reasons to review an existing system, it does not necessarily follow that a new system should be developed. Developing a new information system to replace another may cost hundreds or even millions of dollars. It is a complex and time-consuming process. The decision to develop a new system should be based on need. Developing a system involves the following steps: analysis, design, programming, implementation, and audit and review (see Figure 13–4).

SYSTEM ANALYSIS

The first step of **system analysis** is to formulate a statement of overall business objectives—the goals of the system. Identifying these objectives is essential to the identification of information the system will require. The next step is for the analyst to acquire a general understanding of the scope of the analysis.

The analyst, by viewing the system from the top down, determines on what level the analysis should be conducted (see Figure 13–5). This level should be agreed upon with management and reviewed in the form of a proposal to

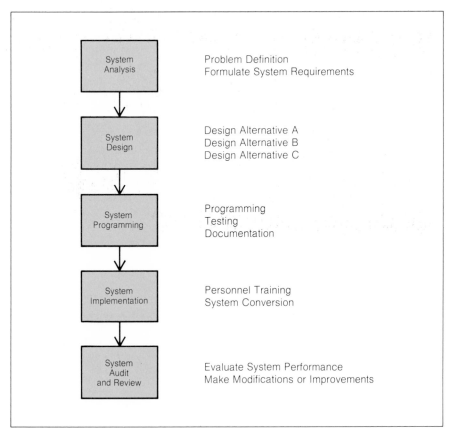

Figure 13–4 ▪ System Methodology

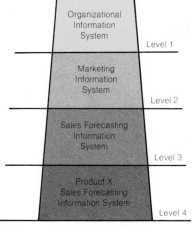

Figure 13–5 ▪ Top-Down View of an Organization's Information System

conduct system analysis. The proposal to conduct system analysis should provide management with the following:

- A clear and concise statement of the problem, or reason for the system analysis.
- A statement clearly defining the level of the system analysis and its objectives.
- An identification of the information that must be collected and the potential sources of this information.
- A preliminary schedule for conducting the analysis.

The proposal ensures that management knows what resources will be required during the system analysis and also helps the system user to be sure the analyst has identified the problem correctly and understands what the analysis should accomplish. Because system analysis is costly and time consuming, the scope should be clarified in this way before the analysis continues.

Once the proposal has been accepted, the analysis can proceed. Data relevant to decision makers' information needs is gathered and analyzed. When the analysis is completed, the analyst communicates the findings to management in the **system analysis report.** On the basis of this report, management decides whether or not to continue with the next step in system development—system design.

Reasons for Conducting System Analysis

System analysis is performed for various reasons, and the reason for the analysis determines its scope, or magnitude. The gathering and analyzing of data occurs at different levels of intensity, depending upon the scope of the analysis. System analysis may be required because of a need to solve a problem, respond to new information requirements, incorporate new technology into a system, or make broad system improvements. Each of these reasons is discussed below.

Solving a Problem   Sometimes information systems do not function properly and thus require adjustment. Perhaps a particular manager is not getting a report at the time when it is needed. Or an insufficient number of copies of a certain report may be printed. Or the information a report provides may be incorrect.

In attempting to solve such a problem, the analyst may find that the effort snowballs into a broad system improvement; one problem may lead to another, which leads to another, and so on. Analysts must use discretion and discipline in solving the problem at hand. This is another of the main reasons for determining the scope of the system analysis at the outset of the project, as described earlier.

Responding to New Requirements   Information systems should be designed to be flexible, so that changes can be made without much trouble. Unfortunately, it is often difficult to anticipate future information needs. New requirements more often than not cause change, which in turn requires a new system analysis. For example, oil companies have experienced a series of changes in government regulations in recent years. Passage of the windfall profits tax followed by the earlier-than-expected deregulation of domestic oil prices created instant headaches for the companies and instant projects for systems analysts. Information systems, especially for the accounting departments, had to be updated very rapidly in order to comply with new laws.

Another area in which government regulations have affected business information systems is personnel. Regulations governing hiring and firing practices are constantly changing. Privacy is another area; more and more information must be kept confidential with each passing year.

New requirements also originate from nongovernment sources. A company may add a new product line, requiring a whole new series of reports. A new labor agreement may require new benefits and new deductions or a different way of paying overtime or calculating base pay.

Implementing New Technology   The introduction of new data-processing technology can cause major changes in information systems. Many companies started with punched-card, batch-processing environments. When magnetic tape became available, larger files could be processed and more information could be stored. The introduction of magnetic-disk technology opened up direct-access processing, causing many information systems to change drastically in the late 1960s. New input devices such as visual display terminals began to replace paper forms and punched cards for data entry.

In banking alone, the introduction of MICR (magnetic-ink character recognition—see Chapter 4) technology eliminated thousands of bookkeeping jobs because it allowed electronic posting of entries to accounts instead of manual posting. In grocery stores and other retail stores, bar-code readers and optical-character readers are being combined with point-of-sale devices to dramatically change internal accounting and checkout procedures. The list goes on and on. Changes in data-processing technology often lead to changes in information systems.

Making Broad System Improvements   There may be times when an organization wants to update its entire information system, perhaps because of an increase in its size or sales volume or a competitive incentive to operate as efficiently and effectively as possible.

One example of a broad system improvement is the introduction and use of online ticketing by major airlines. As soon as the first company converted to this new method, other airlines had to follow suit to remain competitive. The new method forced changes in the airlines' entire accounting and reservation systems.

Numerous companies discovered their information systems were out of date during the boom years of the 1950s and 1960s. Some growth was natural, but much was due to mergers and acquisitions. Many companies found that it was advantageous to update their entire information systems rather than to just keep patching them.

A broad system improvement normally requires an extensive system analysis, because it has a very broad scope.

Data Gathering

After the proposal to conduct system analysis has been accepted, the analyst sets out to gather data. The type and amount of data gathered depend upon the scope and goal of the system analysis. Data can be supplied by internal and external sources.

Internal Sources Four common sources of internal information are interviews, system flowcharts, questionnaires, and formal reports.

INTERVIEWS. Personal interviews can be a very important source of data. Preliminary interviews provide data about current operations and procedures and the users' perception of what the system should do. The analyst must be diplomatic, yet probing. Often the analyst discovers informal information in the form of reports, personal notes, and phone numbers that indicate how the current information system really works. Unless interviews are conducted, these "extras" might never appear. Follow-up interviews and discussion sessions provide checkpoints to verify the accuracy and completeness of the procedures and documentation within the system.

SYSTEM FLOWCHARTS After gathering the documents that provide the system input, the processing steps needed are illustrated in system flowcharts. The devices and files used, the resulting output, and the departments that use the output are identified. (System flowcharts are discussed in detail later in this chapter.)

QUESTIONNAIRES. Questionnaires are used to collect more details about system operations. By keying questions to specific steps in a system chart, the analyst can obtain detailed data on the volume of input and output. The frequency of processing, the time required for various processing steps, and the personnel and equipment used can also be identified.

Questionnaires are useful only if they are properly constructed. Further, the analyst must be careful to make note of who filled out a particular questionnaire; a manager might respond differently than an employee. The analyst must also be sure to follow up if a questionnaire is not returned (see Figure 13–6).

FORMAL REPORTS. Formal reports, the major outputs of many systems, should be studied carefully by the analyst (see Figure 13–7). The processing steps taken to convert data to information are usually apparent from these reports. The number of copies made and who receives them helps to identify the flow of information within the organization. How and where a report is stored may indicate the degree of sensitivity and importance of the information it contains. With the advent of inexpensive paper copiers, the task of determining all users of a particular report may be extremely difficult; the ease with which copies can be made is not always an advantage in this case.

External Sources Systems analysts should (within budgetary constraints) leave no stones unturned during the data-gathering stage. External sources of information can be very helpful. Standard sources are books, periodicals, brochures, and product specifications from manufacturers. Customers and suppliers are sometimes good sources. For example, analyzing an accounts receivable system might involve asking customers what information they would like to see on an invoice. Analysts should also attempt to contact other companies that have developed or implemented similar information systems.

Data Analysis

After data has been collected, it must be organized and integrated to be seen in proper perspective. Whereas the focus during data collection is on *what* is

Figure 13–6 ▪ Sample
Questionnaire

TITLE   *Report Analysis—Batch Payroll Report*
NUMBER   *378-Batch-Pay*
PURPOSE *To determine demand for and timing of Batch Payroll Report*

1. Do you currently receive, or would you like to receive, the Payroll Report?
   ☐Yes   If yes, please answer the remaining questions.
   ☐No   If no, please go to the end of the questionnaire.

2. How often would you like to receive the Payroll Report?
   ☐Weekly   ☐Quarterly   ☐Annually
   ☐Monthly   ☐Semiannually

3. What would you be using the report for?
   ☐Department budgeting of payroll expenses
   ☐General information only
   ☐Other _____

4. How do you rank this report in relation to other reports you receive?
   ☐Above average   ☐Average   ☐Below average

5. Do you require more payroll information than is contained on the report?
   ☐Yes   ☐No
   If yes, please list the additional information you require:

6. Please indicate any other information that would be useful in revising or updating
   the Payroll Report.

   _____

   _____

                              Thank you for your cooperation.

Signed _____ Title _____

Department _____ Date _____

being done, the focus during data analysis is on *why* certain operations and procedures are being used. The analyst looks for ways to improve these operations.

Information Needs   An analysis should be conducted to determine management's information needs and what data will be required to meet those needs. This will have a great impact later when input/output requirements are being determined.

Determining information needs requires that the analyst use a system approach. In a magnetic-tape-oriented, file-processing environment, it is relatively easy to create and manipulate files. But many companies are rapidly moving into data-base environments. Creating and maintaining an effective data base requires that data items be independent. This means that the data must be analyzed and organized from a corporate-wide perspective. A file can no longer be created for use by a single department; data must be accessible to many other departments as well. The goal is to properly relate each data item to all other data items, ignoring departmental boundaries.

SYSTEMS ANALYSIS AND DESIGN

Figure 13–7 ▪ **Example Formal Report**

```
                              GB ELECTRIC AND GAS COMPANY
                                    PAYROLL REPORT
                                    NOVEMBER, 1982


   12/21/82                                                          PAGE      2

   DEPT. NO.      ID       EMPLOYEE        HOURS     GROSS PAY      TAX        NET PAY
     1          12345    BUXBAUM, ROBERT    75.0    $  750.00    $  60.00    $  690.00
                23488    COSTELLO, JOSEPH B  82.1    $  623.63    $  49.89    $  573.74


   12/21/82                                                          PAGE      3

   DEPT. NO.      ID       EMPLOYEE        HOURS     GROSS PAY      TAX        NET PAY
     2          24567    ANDERSON, DAVID    80.4    $  760.86    $  60.87    $  699.99
                31578    BREWER, BETTY      43.2    $  791.85    $  63.35    $  728.50


   12/21/82                                                          PAGE      4

   DEPT. NO.      ID       EMPLOYEE        HOURS     GROSS PAY      TAX        NET PAY
     3          15422    CALDWELL, SUSAN    75.9    $  348.38    $  13.94    $  334.44
                16882    CLANCY, BETTY      55.7    $  426.10    $  25.57    $  400.63


   12/21/82                                                          PAGE      5

   DEPT. NO.      ID       EMPLOYEE        HOURS     GROSS PAY      TAX        NET PAY
     4          23451    ALEXANDER, CHARLES 90.2    $  952.10    $  95.21    $  856.89
                32155    BROWN, WALLACE     77.5    $  792.05    $  63.36    $  728.69
                54202    DUNIGAN, HENRY     66.5    $  964.25    $  96.43    $  867.82
                70123    JACKSON, KENNETH   75.9    $  977.59    $  97.76    $  879.83

                                    TOTAL EMPLOYEES          4
                                    OVERTIME EMPLOYEES       1
                                    TOTAL TAX          $   352.76
                                    TOTAL NET PAY      $ 3,333.23


   12/21/82                                                          PAGE      6

   DEPT. NO.      ID       EMPLOYEE        HOURS     GROSS PAY      TAX        NET PAY
     5          20988    FOX, WILLIAM       90.0    $1,941.80    $ 233.02    $1,708.78
                31254    HALLECK, FRANCES  120.0    $4,277.20    $ 513.26    $3,763.94
                32611    HEFNER, ELMER     110.4    $  753.60    $  60.29    $  693.31
                52319    HORNE, ALBERT      92.0    $  980.00    $  98.00    $  882.00
                67822    SAWYER, DAVID      80.0    $  444.00    $  26.64    $  417.36
                78200    SIPE, CHARLES      75.0    $1,101.25    $ 141.75    $1,039.50
                89212    SMITH, JERRY       60.0    $  539.40    $  32.36    $  507.04

                                    TOTAL EMPLOYEES          7
                                    OVERTIME EMPLOYEES       4
                                    TOTAL TAX          $ 1,105.32
                                    TOTAL NET PAY      $ 9,011.93


   REPORT TOTALS

                                    TOTAL EMPLOYEES         39
                                    OVERTIME EMPLOYEES      14
                                    TOTAL TAX          $ 4,980.01
                                    TOTAL NET PAY      $50,730.91
```

Some of the techniques used to analyze data are grid charts, system flow-charts, and decision logic tables. These techniques are explained below. This list is not all-inclusive, however. Analysts should use whatever tools and techniques they can devise to analyze the gathered data.

Grid Charts   The **tabular,** or **grid, chart** is used to summarize the relation-ships among the components of a system. Figure 13–8 is a grid chart indicating which departments use which documents of an order-writing, billing, and inventory-control system.

System Flowcharts   As was discussed in Chapter 9, program flowcharts are concerned with operations on data. They do not indicate the form of input (for example, terminal keyboard, cards, or tape) or the form of output (for example, display, document, disk, or tape); they simply use a general input/output symbol (⬚) for all forms.

In contrast, **system flowcharts** emphasize the flow of data through the en-tire data-processing system, without describing details of internal computer operations. A system flowchart represents the interrelationships among var-ious system elements.

The general input/output symbol used in program flowcharting is not spe-cific enough for system flowcharting. A variety of specialized input/output symbols are needed to identify the wide variety of media used in input/output activities. The symbols are miniature outlines of the actual media (see Figure 13–9).

Similarly, specialized process symbols are used instead of the general pro-cess symbol (⬚) to represent specific processing operations. For example, a trapezoid is used to indicate a manual operation such as key-to-tape data entry (see Figure 13–10).

The difference in emphasis in the two forms of flowcharting is due to the difference in the purposes they serve. A program flowchart aids the program-mer by providing details necessary to the coding of the program. In contrast, system flowcharts are designed to represent the general information flow; of-ten one process symbol is used to represent many operations.

Figure 13–8 ▪ Grid Chart

Document \ Department	Order Writing	Shipping	Billing	Inventory	Marketing	Accounts Receivable
Sales Order	X				X	
Shipping Order	X	X	X	X		
Invoice			X		X	X
Credit Authorization					X	X
Monthly Report					X	X

Figure 13–9 ▪ **Specialized Input/Output Symbols for System Flowcharting**

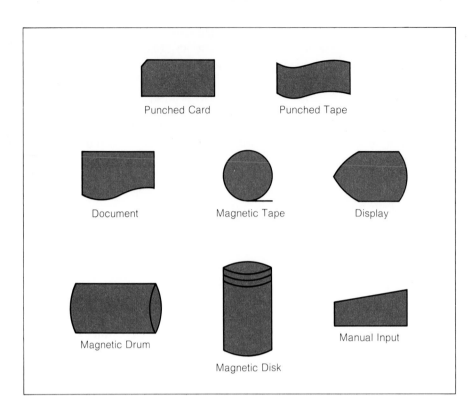

Figure 13–10 ▪ **Specialized Process Symbols for System Flowcharting**

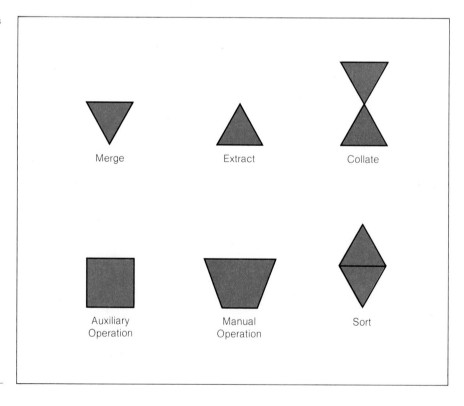

Figure 13–11 is a sample system flowchart that shows the updating of an inventory master file. The **online storage symbol** ($\boxed{}$) indicates that the file is kept on an online external storage medium such as disk or tape. The file is used to keep track of the raw materials and finished products of the organization. How current this information is depends on how often the master file is updated. If it is updated as soon as a product is shipped or a raw material supply depleted, then the information it provides is up-to-date. Usually, however, the updating is done on a periodic basis. All changes that occur during a specific time period are batched and then processed together to update the inventory master file. Reports from the shipping, receiving, and production departments are collected. The data from this set of documents are entered into the computer via a CRT. The data entered on the CRT and the inventory master file then serve as input for the updating process.

The flowchart in Figure 13–11 outlines the steps in this process. In addition to updating the inventory master file, the system generates three reports,

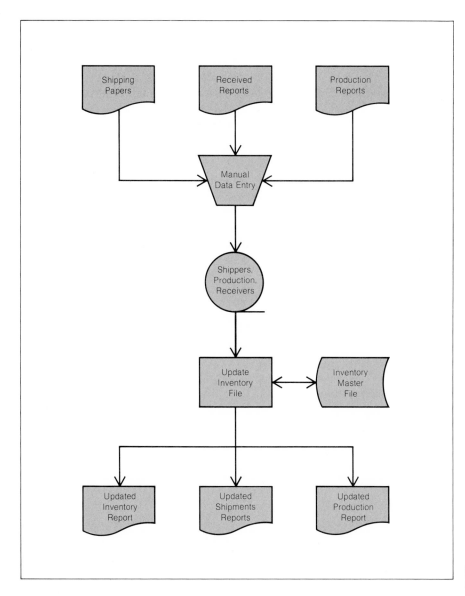

Figure 13–11 ▪ Sample System Flowchart

which give management information about inventory, order shipments, and production. Notice that in the system flowchart, one process symbol encompasses the entire updating process. A program flowchart must be created to detail the specific operations to be performed within this process.

Decision Logic Tables A **decision logic table (DLT)** is a tabular representation of the actions to be taken under various sets of conditions. Thus, the decision table expresses the logic for arriving at a particular decision under a given set of circumstances. The structure within the table is based on the proposition "if this condition is met, then do this."

The basic elements of a decision logic table are shown in Figure 13–12. The upper half lists conditions to be met, and the lower half shows actions to be taken. That is, the **condition stub** describes the various conditions; the **action stub** describes the possible actions. **Condition entries** are made in the top right section. **Action entries** are made in the bottom right section.

A decision table is not needed when conditions can be communicated and understood easily. However, where multiple conditions exist, a decision table serves as a valuable tool in analyzing the decision logic involved. Figure 13–13 shows a decision table for selecting applicants for an assembly-line job.

The rules for selecting applicants are based on the age, education, and experience of the candidates. The applicants must be at least eighteen years old to be considered for the position. They must have at least a high school education or a year's experience to be interviewed for further evaluation. They are hired directly if they meet both requirements. The Ys in the table mean yes, the Ns mean no, and the Xs indicate what actions are to be taken. The decision table is read as follows:

- *Rule 1:* If the applicant's age is less than eighteen years, then reject him or her.
- *Rule 2:* If the applicant is at least eighteen years old but has no high school education and less than one year's experience, then reject him or her.
- *Rule 3:* If the applicant is at least eighteen years old, has no high school education, but has experience of more than one year, then call him or her for an interview. Once a candidate has been selected for an interview, another decision table may be needed to evaluate the interview.
- *Rule 4:* If the applicant is at least eighteen years old, has a high school education, but has less than one year's experience, then call him or her for

Figure 13–12 ▪ Decision Logic Table

HEADING	Rule Numbers							
	1	2	3	4	5	6	7	8
CONDITION STUB	Condition Entries							
ACTION STUB	Action Entries							

Figure 13–13 ■ Decision Logic Table for Selecting Applicants

SELECTING APPLICANTS		Rules				
		1	2	3	4	5
CONDITIONS	Age < 18 Years?	Y	N	N	N	N
	High School Education?		N	N	Y	Y
	Experience > 1 Year?		N	Y	N	Y
ACTIONS	Reject	X	X			
	Interview			X	X	
	Hire					X

an interview. Again, another decision table might be used to evaluate the interview.

■ *Rule 5:* If the applicant is at least eighteen years old, has a high school education, and has more than one year's experience, then hire him or her.

A more detailed decision logic table is shown in Figure 13–14. The first step in constructing such a table is to determine what conditions must be considered. In this case, these conditions are: (1) Is the customer's credit rating AAA? (2) Is the quantity ordered above or equal to the minimum quantity for a discount? (3) Is there enough stock on hand to fill the order? The conditions are listed in the condition stub section of the decision table.

The next step is to determine what actions can take place. These are: Either (1) bill at a discount price or (2) bill at a regular price; and either (3) ship the total quantity ordered or (4) ship a partial order and back-order the rest. These possibilities go in the action stub.

Once the conditions and possible courses of action have been identified,

Figure 13–14 ■ Decision Logic Table for Order Processing

ORDER PROCESSING	Rules							
	1	2	3	4	5	6	7	8
Credit Rating of AAA	Y	Y	Y	Y	N	N	N	N
Quantity Order >= Minimum Discount Quantity	Y	N	N	Y	Y	N	Y	N
Quantity Ordered <= Stock on Hand	N	Y	N	Y	N	Y	Y	N
Bill at Discount Price	X			X				
Bill at Regular Price		X	X		X	X	X	X
Ship Total Quantity Ordered		X		X		X	X	
Ship Partial and Back-Order Remaining Amount	X		X		X			X

the conditions can be related to corresponding action entries to indicate the appropriate decision. Thus, Rule 4 could be interpreted as follows: "If the customer has a credit rating of AAA and the quantity ordered is equal to or above the minimum discount quantity and there is enough stock on hand, then the customer is to be billed at the discount price and the total order is to be shipped."

Decision tables summarize the logic required to make a decision in a form that is easy to understand. They are used to record facts collected during the investigation of the old system and can also be used to summarize aspects of the new system. In the latter case, they guide programmers in writing programs for the new system.

System Analysis Report

After collecting and analyzing the data, the systems analyst must communicate the findings to management. The system analysis report should include the following items:

- A restatement of the scope and objectives of the system analysis.
- An explanation of the present system, the procedures used, and any problems identified.
- A statement of all constraints on the present system and any assumptions made by the analyst during this phase.
- A preliminary report of alternatives that currently seem feasible.
- An estimate of the resources and capital required to either modify the present system or design a new one. This estimate should include costs of a feasibility study.

Only if management approves this report can the systems analyst proceed to the detailed system design.

Concept Summary 13–1

System Theory and Analysis

- A **system** is a group of related elements that work together toward a common goal. A system consists of **inputs, processes,** and **outputs.**
- Information that informs the systems whether predetermined standards or goals are being met is referred to as **feedback.**
- The system approach to system analysis acts as a model in analyzing information systems by attempting to mirror actual events while reducing their complexities.
- The system approach views an organization as an integrated whole, and not as a grouping of independent functional areas.
- Reasons for conducting a system analysis include: (1) solving a problem, (2) responding to new requirements, (3) implementing new technology, and (4) making broad system improvements.
- The type and amount of data gathered during system analysis depends upon the reason for conducting an analysis and the goal of the analysis. Data can be supplied by internal sources including: interviews, systems flowcharts, questionnaires, and formal reports. There are also external sources such as: books, periodicals, brochures, and product specifications from manufacturers.
- Tools such as **grid charts, system flowcharts,** and **decision logic tables** are used to analyze data collected during system analysis.
- Once the data has been collected and analyzed, the systems analyst must communicate the findings to management through the **system analysis report.**

SYSTEM DESIGN

If, after reviewing the system analysis report, management decides to continue the project, the system design stage begins. Designing an information system demands a great deal of creativity and planning. It is also very costly and time consuming. In system analysis, the analyst has focused on what the current system does and on what it should be doing according to the requirements discovered in the analysis. In the design phase, the analyst changes focus and concentrates on how a system can be developed to meet the information requirements.

Several steps are useful during the design phase of system development:

- Reviewing goals and objectives.
- Developing system model.
- Evaluating organizational constraints.
- Developing alternative designs.
- Performing feasibility analysis.
- Performing cost/benefit analysis.
- Preparing system design report and recommendation.

Reviewing Goals and Objectives

The objectives of the new or revised system were identified during system analysis and stated in the system analysis report. Before the analyst can proceed with system design, these objectives must be reviewed, since any system design offered must conform to them.

In order to maintain a broad approach and flexibility in the system design phase, the analyst may restate users' information requirements so that they reflect the needs of the majority of users. For example, the finance department may want a report of customers who have been delinquent in payments. Since this department may be only one subsystem in a larger accounts-receivable system, the analyst may restate this requirement more generally. It might more appropriately be stated as (1) maintain an accurate and timely record of the amounts owed by customers, (2) provide control procedures that ensure detection of abnormal accounts and report them on an exception basis, and (3) provide, on a timely basis, information regarding accounts receivable to different levels of management to help achieve overall company goals.

A well-designed system can meet the current goals and objectives of the organization and adapt to changes within the organization. In discussions with managers, the analyst may be able to determine organizational trends that help to pinpoint which subsystems require more flexibility. For instance, if the analyst is developing a system for an electric company, strong consideration should be given to providing flexibility in the reporting subsystem in order to respond to changing regulatory reporting requirements.

Developing System Model

The analyst next attempts to represent symbolically the system's major components to verify his or her understanding of the various components and their interactions. The analyst may use flowcharts to help in the development of a system model or may simply be creative in the use of diagrammatic representations.

In reviewing the model, the analyst refers to system theory to discover any possible omissions of important subsystems. Are the major interactions among subsystems shown? Are the inputs, processes, and outputs appropriately identified? Does the model provide for appropriate feedback to each of the subsystems? Are too many functions included within one subsystem?

Once a satisfactory system model has been developed, the analyst has an appropriate tool for evaluating alternative designs (discussed later in this section). Each alternative can be evaluated on the basis of how well it matches the requirements of the model. Figure 13–15 is an example of a conceptual model of an accounts-receivable system.

Evaluating Organizational Constraints

No organization has unlimited resources; most have limitations on financial budgets, personnel, and computer facilities and time constraints for system development. The systems analyst must recognize the constraints on system design imposed by this limited availability of resources.

Few organizations request the optimal design for their information requirements. Businesses are profit-seeking organizations. Only in an extremely rare case does an organization request an all-out system development with no cost constraints. (Competition or technological developments, for example, may make such an uncharacteristic decision mandatory.)

The structure of the organization also affects subsequent designs developed by the analyst. A highly centralized management may reject a proposal for distributed processing. Similarly, an organization with geographically dispersed, highly autonomous decision centers may find designs that require routing reports through the central office unsatisfactory.

Human factors are also an organizational constraint that must be evaluated during the system design phase. In particular, consideration must be given to the users of the system. A proposed system design must be **user friendly**. In

Figure 13–15 ▪ Model of an Accounts-Receivable System

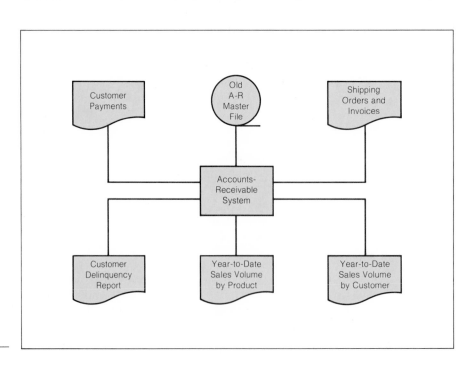

other words, the system must be designed not only to meet the needs of the user, but also to meet those needs through an easy-to-use, understandable design.

A **menu-driven** system design, for example, guides the user through the computerized system, helping him or her to attain the needed information. A menu-driven system displays to the user "menus" explaining available choices or actions (see Figure 13–16). With the menu-driven system, the user can be guided through the process of using the system.

Technological advances such as touch-sensitive screens, a mouse, and voice recognition/voice synthesizer systems may also help make a system design more compatible for its human users. The human factors of system design, in many cases, are the most important.

Before proceeding with system design, the analyst must be fully aware of the various organizational constraints and critically evaluate their impact on the system design.

Developing Alternative Designs

Systems can be either simple or complex. Simple systems require simple controls to keep processes working properly. Complex systems, on the other hand, require complex controls. A business is a complex system; it requires vast numbers of interactions among its many interrelated subsystems. It naturally follows that information systems developed for business use must be complex, since they model the actual business.

There is more than one way to design a complex information system, and systems analysts are generally required to develop more than one design alternative. This requirement is useful because it forces the analyst to be creative. By designing several possible systems, the analyst may discover valuable parts in each that can be integrated into an entirely new system. The alter-

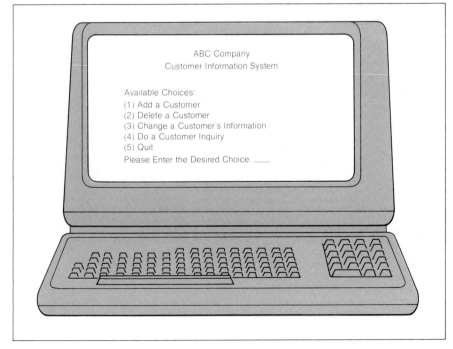

Figure 13–16 ▪ Sample Menu

native systems may also be designed in ascending order of complexity and cost; since management often desires alternatives from which to choose, designing alternative systems in this fashion is quite appropriate.

The analyst must work with a number of elements in designing alternative systems. Computerized information systems have many components. Inputs, outputs, hardware, software, files, data bases, clerical procedures, and users interact in hundreds of different ways. Processing requirements may also differ in each alternative. For example, one may require batch processing and sequential organization of files; another may provide random-access processing using direct-access storage and online terminals. The data collection, processing, storage, retrieval, and update procedures vary, depending on the alternative selected.

Each alternative developed by the analyst must be technically feasible. In some instances, analysts try to design at least one noncomputerized alternative. Although this may be difficult, it often reveals unique methods of information processing that the analyst has not considered when developing the computerized systems.

In designing each alternative, the analyst should include tentative input forms, the structures and formats of output reports, the program specifications needed to guide programmers in code preparation, the files or data base required, the clerical procedures to be used, and the process-control measures that should be instituted.

With the increasing use of online systems, the input forms are often input screens. These screens must be designed in as much detail as their hard-copy counterparts. The analyst, in consultation with those who will be inputting the data, must design each screen to maximize efficiency in data input. The screen format must be easy for users to view and understand (see Figure 13–17).

Figure 13–17 ▪ **Screen Format**

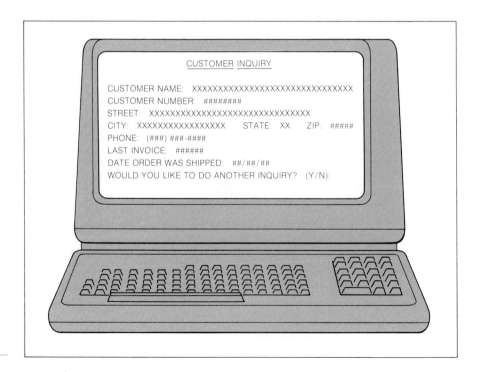

Output reports must be designed so that users can quickly and easily view the information they require. The analyst often prepares mock-up reports that approximate how the actual computer-generated report will look (see Figure 13–18). Most contain sample data. It is easier for users to relate their needs to such sample reports than to discuss them in abstract form with the analyst in an interview. Mock-up reports also allow the analyst to verify once again his or her understanding of what is required of the system.

Once the input forms or screens and output reports have been designed, a detailed set of programming specifications for each alternative must be prepared. The analyst must determine what processing is to occur in each of the system designs. He or she often works in conjunction with the programming staff to determine these requirements and to develop cost estimates for program coding.

File and data-base specification is particularly important. The analyst must be aware of the physical layout of data on a file. The storage media and keys used to access data on the files need to be determined (this topic is discussed further in Chapter 14). The analyst should also determine the potential size of each file, the number of accesses and updates that may take place during a particular time period, and the length of time for which users may wish to retain each file. Since each of these specifications requires the use of computer facilities, such estimates help the analyst determine the potential cost of each design alternative.

The analyst must carefully examine each clerical procedure required in a particular system alternative. In a sense, the analyst must imagine himself or herself actually performing the steps required. From the receipt of data through the processing steps to the final output, the analyst must determine the most efficient methods for users to perform their required tasks.

Process-control measures were easier in the days of batch processing. With online systems, however, changes made to files and data bases are instantaneous. If the changes are made on the basis of incorrect data, incorrect values will be stored, accessed, and reported. The analyst must institute controls from initial data capture and entry through processing and storage to final reporting. Methods to restore data bases when errors in data entry occur should be developed. Security procedures should be instituted to prevent unauthorized access to stored data. Since the advent of privacy legislation (discussed in Chapter 17), the development of control procedures has become increasingly important.

Performing Feasibility Analysis

While developing each alternative system, the analyst must keep asking the question, "Is this feasible?" A design may require certain procedures the organization is not staffed to handle; the design, therefore, must be discarded, or the appropriate staff acquired. The analyst may discover an alternative with great potential for reducing processing costs but may find that the company does not own the hardware required to implement it. The analyst may choose to present this alternative to management rather than disregard it. The analyst must use personal judgment and experience to eliminate infeasible alternatives.

The users' educational backgrounds and organizational positions must be taken into consideration. The lack of familiarity of some employees with computer-based information systems may prohibit the use of a complex sys-

Figure 13–18 ■ Output Report Format

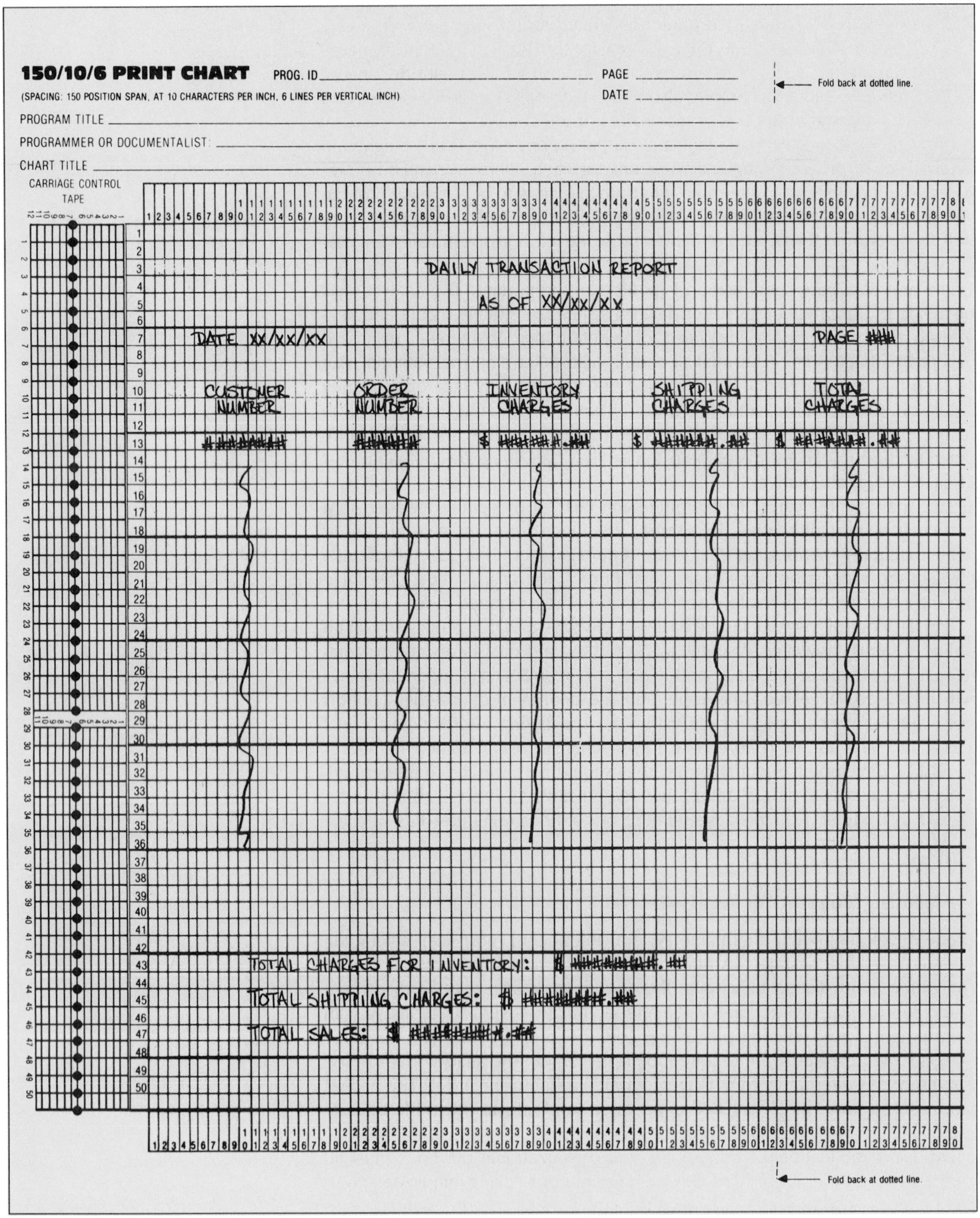

tem. Highly educated managers may resist a simple information system because they feel uneasy working with it. Companies in rural locations may be unable to properly staff data-processing departments.

Analysts must also determine whether there are legal constraints that affect the design of the system. For example, several U.S. presidents have proposed to Congress the creation of a massive, integrated data base about citizens receiving benefits from the government. Their objective was to reduce fraud, inefficiency, and multiple payments. However, the possibility that such a data base might violate privacy laws had to be considered (see Chapter 17). Although the system is feasible in other respects, the controls that would have to be incorporated into it to conform with the legal constraints have hindered its development.

Time is frequently a limiting factor. A time constraint may appear before system development begins, during the development process, or during implementation. The required completion date may preclude the selection of a complex alternative, necessitate changing the selected design to one less complex, or require that the system be developed in stages different from those suggested by the analyst.

The economic feasibility of a project is paramount. Many systems have fallen by the wayside because of budgetary constraints. The system's economic feasibility is determined by cost/benefit analysis, which is discussed below. In performing this analysis, the analyst must be extremely careful. Costs that at first appear to exceed the budget may in fact give rise to greater benefits. The expression "you have to spend money to make money" is often applicable here. It is up to the analyst to foresee such possibilities.

Performing Cost/Benefit Analysis

Cost/benefit analysis is a procedure commonly used in business decision making. A firm has limited financial resources. They must be allocated to projects that appear to offer the greatest return on the costs of initial development. In order for cost/benefit analysis to be performed, both costs and benefits must be quantified. Costs are easier to determine than benefits. Some benefits are tangible (or realizable as cash savings). Others are intangible (not necessarily giving rise to obvious reduction in costs). Naturally, intangible benefits are especially difficult to determine. How does one estimate the benefit from an improved information system that provides better customer service?

An analyst might approach the cost/benefit analysis of an accounts receivable system in the following fashion. A company is unable to respond to 20 percent of customer orders because of inefficiencies in its current information system. A proposed new system will reduce lost sales by increasing the customer service level so that only 5 percent of orders remain unprocessed. By observing the current sales level and predicting how much sales will increase if the new system is implemented, the analyst can approximate the cash benefits of the alternative.

The costs of an alternative include direct costs like the initial investment required for materials and equipment; setup costs required to create computer files from old manual systems, to install data-processing equipment, and to hire personnel; and educational costs to educate the users of the new system. Ongoing expenses resulting from employee salaries, computer operations, insurance, taxes, and rent must also be identified.

It is not always necessary for positive economic benefits to exist for an alternative to be considered feasible. For example, environmental impact statements are required of some companies by law. Design alternatives for a system that must produce such reports must allow for provision of accurate and timely information in spite of the cost/benefit relationship involved. However, the resources required to develop such a system should be kept to a minimum.

The analyst can also use statistics in determining costs and benefits of large system designs. Sampling and modeling enable the analyst to provide cost/benefit figures not readily apparent from available information. By modeling the complex interactions of accounts-receivable, inventory, and service levels, the analyst may be able to determine how savings in one area affect costs in another. Other techniques, ranging from judgment to common sense to experience, are useful to the analyst attempting to choose the best alternative.

Which design alternative management selects often depends on the results of cost/benefit analysis. The analyst must ensure that a comprehensive cost/benefit study has been performed on all alternatives.

Preparing Design Report

Once the analyst has completed all of the steps described above, he or she must prepare a report to communicate findings to management. The **system design report** should explain in general terms how the various designs will satisfy the information requirements determined in the analysis phase. The report should also review the information requirements uncovered in the system analysis, explain in both flowchart and narrative form the proposed designs, detail the corporate resources required to implement each alternative, and make a recommendation.

Since many organizational personnel may not have participated actively in the analysis stage of system development, the analyst restates information requirements in the design report to tell these decision makers the constraints considered in creating alternative designs. The restatement also shows that the analyst understands what information the new system should provide.

Each of the proposed alternatives should be explained in easy-to-understand narrative form. Technical jargon should be avoided. The purpose of the design report is to communicate; using words unfamiliar to the reader will hinder this communication process. Flowcharts of each alternative should be provided as well.

From the detailed design work performed on each alternative, the analyst should glean the important costs, benefits, and resources required for its implementation. This, more than any other portion of the report, will be analyzed carefully by those empowered to make a design selection. Their decisions will be based on the projected benefits of each design versus the corporate resources required to implement it.

Finally, the analyst should make a design recommendation. Because of the analyst's familiarity with the current system and with each alternative design, he or she is in the best position to suggest the one with the greatest potential for success. If the analyst has been thorough in analyzing resource costs and potential benefits, as well as objective in viewing corporate goals, this recommendation is apt to be adopted by management.

After evaluating the system design report, management can do one of three things: approve the recommendation, approve the recommendation with changes (this includes selecting another alternative), or select none of the alternatives. The "do nothing" alternative is always feasible. If the design of the system is approved, the analyst proceeds to implement it.

SYSTEM PROGRAMMING

Programming

A computerized information system depends on computer programs for converting data into information. If the analyst does not program, the system design specifications must be communicated to people who do. Programmers must completely understand what is expected of the system before programming begins. If the design of the system has been thorough, there will be few changes to make in programs during conversion. If, on the other hand, the analyst has not fully considered all processing requirements, considerable time may be spent in reprogramming.

The analyst, in conjunction with the programming department, may wish to evaluate software packages designed to perform tasks similar to those required of the selected design as an alternative to in-house programming. Evaluations should be made on the basis of compatibility and adaptability. Are the package controls and clerical procedures similar to those in the analyst's design? Can the package be readily adapted to this particular application?

To maintain flexibility, programs should be developed in independent modules, which make the system easier to maintain and change (review Chapter 11). If the programs are to be written in-house, a decision regarding the language to use must also be made.

Testing

Before a system becomes operational, it must be tested and debugged. Testing occurs at various levels. The lowest level is program testing. Programs are divided into distinct logical modules. Each module is tested to ensure that all input is accounted for, the proper files are updated, and the correct reports are printed. Only after each module has been debugged should the modules be linked together and the complete program tested.

Once all program testing is complete, system testing can proceed; this level of testing involves checking all the application programs that support the system. All clerical procedures used in data collection, data processing, and data storage and retrieval are included in system testing.

Two test methods discussed in Chapter 9—desk-checking and processing test data—are often used in system testing. Desk-checking involves mentally tracing the sequence of operations performed on a particular transaction to determine the correctness of the processing logic. This approach is least costly, but it is not always reliable. Processing test data involves taking a sample of "live" data that has already been processed by the old system and processing it in the new system. If the results from the two systems match, the new system is functioning properly.

Documentation

Until recently, one of the most neglected parts of system development was documentation. Many systems developed in the early 1970s were implemented with sparse documentation. This presented no problems when the systems were first implemented. Over time, however, changes in the businesses and their information requirements necessitated making systems and programming changes. It was at that point that organizations painfully realized the need to have extensive system documentation. It was often difficult to understand programs written five to ten years earlier. Changes made to them often caused errors in other programs. Thus, most organizations have adopted a system development methodology requiring adequate documentation.

Creating system documentation requires taking an overview of the purpose of the entire system, its subsystems, and the function of each subsystem. Documentation of subsystems usually includes system flowcharts depicting the major processing flows, the forms and computer files input to the subsystem, and the reports and computer files output from the subsystem. This provides a frame of reference for system maintenance as information needs change.

Program documentation includes explanations of major logical portions of the program. The programmer may construct program flowcharts to allow other programmers to locate areas to be changed and to observe how the changes will affect other programs. File declarations explaining the layouts of data elements on computer files are also included as part of this documentation.

Procedure documentation instructs users how to perform their particular functions in each subsystem. These documents are designed so that users can quickly and easily get the information they need. User documentation is particularly important, since the best-designed system can fail if users perform their functions incorrectly. Procedures must be established to keep user documentation up-to-date with the latest system changes.

Special Considerations

In designing solutions to business problems, analysts and programmers must be aware of other considerations besides developing the programs required to help solve a particular problem. Since system analysis and design concentrate on inputs, processing, and outputs, the following issues must be considered: (1) The form of input to the program determines how the program should ask for data. (2) Processing steps should verify the accuracy of data and identify potential errors. (3) The program may be required to produce output that is not in hard-copy form.

Input   Today's computer systems give users a variety of ways to communicate with programs. Given the vast array of input devices discussed in Chapter 4, it is not difficult to see why. The programmer must know in advance which input devices will be used to put data into the program. For instance, if input will be in the form of tape, the program must be prepared to accept the data in the same way it was stored on the tape. If a data base will provide input, the program may need to actively search and retrieve data from the data base.

Different input devices require different input considerations. The input devices and forms of data input must be precisely defined before solution design begins. Considerable time may otherwise be required to rework programs designed to accept input in an inappropriate format.

Processing   Businesses are naturally concerned with the accuracy of data used to provide the information managers use to make decisions. Programmers must do their part to help keep data error free; merely designing a program with logically correct processing statements providing the required output may not be enough. Most programmers are required to include extensive edit checks on the data before storing it in data files. **Edit checks** are processing statements designed to identify potential errors in the input data.

Several broad types of edit checks can be incorporated into the solution design; reasonableness, range, type, and correct code are a few possibilities. A reasonableness check looks at a data item to see if its stated value is possible, given the type of data it represents. For instance, if the program requires input of the effective date of a purchase, the program could check that date against today's date. Any date that is not equal to or greater than today's date could be reported to the users for further investigation. It may be difficult for some users to remember to use the new year's date during January processing. A reasonableness check of this type would quickly identify such incorrect dates.

A range check evaluates the data item to see if its value lies within an established range. For instance, if a company sells bulk gasoline to truck tankers, experience may have shown that a normal load varies between 8,000 and 12,000 gallons. A value lower or higher would be highlighted for the users to verify.

A type check verifies that the data value is in the right form. If the program is expecting someone's age, the data item entered should be numeric, not alphabetic. Similarly, if the user is requested to enter a number between 1 and 3, the letter x would be an incorrect type. Catching type errors can greatly reduce processing reruns.

Verifying the correct code requires matching a data value to specific numbers or values used in the company. A product number is one example of a code; employee type and status are others. When a code is received as input, the program looks it up in a computer table. If the code is there, it is valid. If it is not, it will be reported for user investigation.

In some situations, combinations of these edit checks are required. The determination of how many and what kinds of edit checks should be performed on input data is usually made by all personnel involved in the solution design. The users, management, systems analyst, and programmers should all be involved in ensuring the integrity of input data.

Output In modern systems, not all data is entered directly into a program by users nor output fed directly to hard-copy reports. Many systems require the use of interdependent programs in which the output from one program is used as input to another, and so on. The reason for this is that each program may perform a specialized function. If the program design requires this type of processing, programmers need to ensure that output from one program is in a form acceptable as input to another. Similarly, if the first program in the processing cycle has done extensive edit checks on the input data, later programs need not do verification. (Once data items are put into the computer for processing, they will not change.)

If the output will be hard-copy reports, the reports should be easy to read. If they seem imposing or confusing to users, the reports will likely be used incorrectly or not at all.

The trend in computer systems today is to design programs that process data immediately after it is entered by the user. The user usually provides the input at a CRT terminal and receives the output from the program at the same terminal. This type of processing is quite useful in business, but it imposes stringent processing constraints. The program must perform edit checks on each data item as it is entered by the user, even if the item was also entered and checked in an earlier step. To the program, the data item appears new each time it is entered.

Another problem is that, in order for immediate output to be provided, data items may be stored on computer files during processing. Once the processing is completed, there is no way of checking the data further. Input processed for modern data bases faces this type of problem; all types of edit checks must be made during the input of data by the user, before it is accepted, processed, and written to the data base.

Finally, the way in which the programmer designs the program to ask the user for data input can have an important effect on how the user feels about the system. Computer specialists like to refer to programs that ask for input effectively as being user friendly. Frustration, panic, or boredom can result from improperly designed input segments.

SYSTEM IMPLEMENTATION

In the implementation stage of the system methodology, the analyst is able to see the transformation of ideas, flowcharts, and narratives into actual processes, flows, and information. This transition is not performed easily, however. Personnel must be trained to use the new system procedures, and a conversion must be made from the old system to the new one.

Personnel Training

Two groups of people interface with a system. The first group includes the people who develop, operate, and maintain the system. The second group includes the people who use the information generated by the system to support their decision making. Both groups must be aware of their responsibilities regarding the system's operation and of what they can and cannot expect from it. One of the primary responsibilities of the systems analyst is to see that education and training are provided to both groups.

The user group includes general management, staff personnel, line managers, and other operating personnel. It may also include the organization's customers and suppliers. These users must be educated as to what functions they are to perform and what, in turn, the system will do for them.

The personnel who operate the system must be trained to prepare input data, load and unload files on secondary storage devices, handle problems that occur during processing, and so on.

Such education and training can be provided in large group seminars or in smaller tutorial sessions. The latter approach, though fairly costly, is more personal and more appropriate for complex tasks. Another approach, used almost universally, is on-the-job training. As the name implies, the employee learns while actually performing the tasks required.

Personnel training and education are expensive, but they are essential to successful system implementation.

Conversion

The switch from an old system to a new one is referred to as a conversion. Conversion involves not only the changes in the mode of processing data but also the changes in equipment and in clerical procedures.

Several approaches can be used to accomplish the conversion process. The most important ones are explained below:

- *Parallel conversion.* When **parallel conversion** is used, the new system is operated side-by-side with the old one for some period of time. An advantage of this approach is that no data is lost if the new system fails. Also, it gives the user an opportunity to compare and reconcile the outputs from both systems. However, this method can be costly.
- *Pilot conversion.* **Pilot conversion** involves converting only a small portion of the organization to the new system. For example, a new system may be implemented on one production line. This approach minimizes the risk to the organization as a whole, in case unforeseen problems occur, and enables the organization to identify problems and correct them before implementing the system throughout the organization. A disadvantage of this method is that the total conversion process usually takes a long time.
- *Phased conversion.* With **phased conversion,** the old system is gradually replaced by the new one over a period of time. The difference between this method and pilot conversion is that in phased conversion the new system is segmented, and only one segment is implemented at a time. Thus, the organization can adapt to the new system gradually over an extended period while the old system is gradually being phased out. One drawback is that an interface between the new system and the old system must be developed for use during the conversion process.
- *Crash conversion.* **Crash** (or **direct**) **conversion** takes place all at once. This approach can be used to advantage if the old system is not operational or if the new system is completely different in structure and design. Since the old system is discontinued immediately upon implementation of the new one, the organization has nothing to fall back on if problems arise. Because of the high risk involved, this approach requires extreme care in planning and extensive testing of all system components.

SYSTEM AUDIT AND REVIEW

Evaluating System Performance

After the conversion process is complete, the analyst must obtain feedback on the system's performance. This can be done by conducting an audit to evaluate the system's performance in terms of the initial objectives established for it. The evaluation should address the following questions:

1. Does the system perform as planned and deliver the anticipated benefits? How do the operating results compare with the initial objectives? If the benefits are below expectation, what can be done to improve the cost/benefit tradeoff?
2. Was the system completed on schedule and with the resources estimated?
3. Is all output from the system used?
4. Have old system procedures been eliminated and new ones implemented?
5. What controls have been established for input, processing, and output of data? Are these controls adequate?
6. Have users been educated about the new system? Is the system accepted by users? Do they have confidence in the reports generated?
7. Is the processing turnaround time satisfactory, or are delays frequent?

- The design phase of system development involves the following steps:

  (1) Reviewing goals and objectives
  (2) Developing a system model
  (3) Evaluating organizational constraints
  (4) Developing alternative designs
  (5) Performing feasibility analysis
  (6) Performing cost/benefit analysis
  (7) Preparing a system design report and recommendation

- Step two of design, developing a system model, involves identifying major subsystems and their interactions and identifying inputs, processes, and outputs so that an accurate model of the system can be developed. The model is then used for evaluating alternative designs.
- The **system design report** is prepared by the analyst to present design alternatives and their requirements to management. The analyst may also recommend a particular design alternative.
- The system programming phase of system development involves writing, testing, and documenting the programs required by the accepted system design.
- Documentation has become one of the most important parts of system development. The documentation provides a frame of reference for system maintenance by including system flowcharts, the forms and computer files used by the system, and the reports and computer files generated by the system.
- System implementation involves personnel training and system conversion. Methods of system conversion include: **parallel conversion, pilot conversion, phased conversion,** and **crash conversion.**

All persons involved in developing the system should be aware that a thorough audit will be performed. The anticipated audit acts as a strong incentive; it helps to ensure that a good system is designed and delivered on schedule.

As a result of the audit or of user requests, some modification or improvements of the new system may be required.

Making Modifications and Improvements

A common belief among system users is that after a system has been installed, nothing more has to be done. On the contrary, all systems must be continually maintained. System maintenance detects and corrects errors, meets new information needs of management, and responds to changes in the environment.

One of the important tasks of the analyst during the system audit is to ensure that all system controls are working correctly. All procedures and programs related to the old system should have been eliminated. Many of the problems that the system analyst deals with during system maintenance and follow-up are problems that were identified during the system audit.

A well-planned approach to system maintenance and follow-up is essential to the continued effectiveness of an information system.

Responding to Change

A well-designed information system is flexible and adaptable. Minor changes should be easily accommodated without large amounts of reprogramming.

This is one of the reasons why structured programming was emphasized in Chapter 11; if each program module is independent, a minor change in one module will not snowball into other changes.

No matter how flexible or adaptable a system is, however, major changes become necessary over time. When the system has to be redesigned, the entire system cycle—analysis, design, programming, implementation, and audit and review—must be performed again. Keeping information systems responsive to information needs is a never-ending process.

SUMMARY POINTS

- A system is a group of related elements that work together toward a common goal. Inputs are transformed by some process into outputs. Feedback provides information to the system about its internal and external environments.
- Most systems are collections of subsystems and are themselves subsystems of larger systems.
- A business is a system made up of subsystems (departments). It interacts with other systems (suppliers, customers, governments) and is also a subsystem of larger economic and political systems.
- The system model highlights important relationships, patterns, and flows of information within the organization. It is a tool often used to model reality.
- System development or revision consists of the following phases: analysis, design, programming, implementation, and audit and review.
- System analysis is conducted for any of four reasons: to solve a problem, to respond to a new requirement, to implement new technology, or to make broad system improvement.
- Problem solving is an attempt to correct or adjust a currently malfunctioning information system. The analyst must balance the desire to solve just the problem at hand with an attempt to get at the most fundamental causes of the problem. The latter could snowball into a major project.
- A new requirement is caused by either internal or external change. A typical example is a new law or a change in government regulations.
- New technology can force system analysis by making formerly infeasible alternatives feasible.
- The most comprehensive system analysis is conducted for a broad system improvement, which can be necessitated by rapid sales or rapid internal growth or by desire to redesign the present system.
- Data is gathered during system analysis from internal and external sources. Interviews are an excellent way of collecting data and often lead to unexpected discoveries. System flowcharts help the analyst to get a better understanding of how the components in a system interrelate. Questionnaires can be helpful, but they are sometimes difficult to design, administer, and interpret. Formal reports tell the analyst much about the present workings of the system.
- An analyst should also collect data from external sources, such as customers, suppliers, software vendors, hardware manufacturers, books, and periodicals.
- Data should be analyzed in any manner that helps the analyst understand

the system. Grid charts, system flowcharts, and decision logic tables are three of the tools analysts use to accomplish this task.

■ The final result of the system analysis stage is the system analysis report, a report to management reviewing the results of the analysis and the feasibility of proceeding with system design and implementation.

■ If the system analysis report is approved, the analyst begins the design stage. Goals and objectives of the new or revised system are reviewed. A system model is developed, and organizational constraints are evaluated.

■ Alternative designs should always be generated in the design phase. There is always more than one way to design a system; and management likes to have alternatives from which to select.

■ When developing the various alternatives, the analyst must include tentative input forms or screens, output report formats, program specifications, file or data-base designs, clerical procedures, and process-control measures for each alternative.

■ Each alternative should undergo a feasibility analysis. This involves looking at constraints, such as those imposed by hardware, software, human resources, legal matters, time, and economics.

■ A cost/benefit analysis should be conducted to determine which alternative is most viable economically. While tangible costs and benefits are easy to determine, intangible benefits are difficult to quantify.

■ The final step in system design is preparing a design report to present to management. This report should explain the various alternatives and the costs, benefits, and resources associated with each. The report includes the analyst's recommendation.

■ The next stage of the system methodology is system programming. Programming is one of the most time-consuming parts of the system methodology and begins almost immediately after management has approved a design.

■ Testing is performed when each program module is completed. When all program testing is done, system testing commences.

■ Documentation is a necessary part of system and program development. System documentation provides an overview of the entire system and its subsystems. It includes system flowcharts and narratives describing the input forms and computer files as well as the output reports and computer files. Program documentation provides an explanation of the logical portions of the programs and may also include program flowcharts. Procedure documentation provides users with instructions on how to perform the functions of each subsystem.

■ During implementation, converting to a new system can be done in several ways. In parallel conversion, the old and the new system operate together for a period of time. In pilot conversion, the new system is first implemented in only a part of the organization to determine its adequacies and inadequacies; the latter are corrected before full-scale implementation. In phased conversion, the old system is gradually replaced with the new system a portion at a time. In crash conversion, the new system is implemented all at once.

■ Once a new system is operational, it must be audited to ascertain that the initial objectives of the system are being met and to find any problems occurring in the new system. System maintenance is the continued surveillance of system operations to determine what modifications are needed to meet the changing needs of management and to respond to changes in the environment.

REVIEW QUESTIONS

1. How will the structure of an organization affect the design of its information system? Considering distributed processing and centralized processing, briefly describe the organizational structure that would be best suited to each type of processing.

2. Briefly explain what is meant by a system.

3. Describe what is meant by the environment, compared on page 336 to "the countryside bordering the edges of the forest." What relationship, if any, exists between the system and the environment?

4. What is the purpose of the proposal to conduct system analysis? How will the definition of the scope of the analysis affect the overall system analysis?

5. Identify and briefly describe the possible reasons for conducting a system analysis.

6. What four internal sources of data do analysts frequently use? Which one appears to be most effective?

7. Briefly describe what a decision logic table is and how it can be used by a systems analyst and a programmer.

8. What type of information should be contained in the system analysis report?

9. How does the focus of system design differ from that of system analysis?

10. Why is it difficult to design a perfect information system?

11. What information should be contained in the system design report? Who is the report to be presented to, and how should it be presented?

12. What are some of the methods used to train personnel in new system procedures? What groups of individuals must undergo training?

13. Explain why the documentation of both systems and programs is important to the long-term success of a system.

14. List and briefly explain the types of conversion available for a system implementation. Given a situation in which a new computer-based information system is replacing a manual system, what method of conversion might be best?

15. Why is a system audit important? What is the difference between system audit and system maintenance?

APPLICATION

Marathon Oil Company

Marathon Oil Company is a fully integrated oil company; exploration, production, transportation, and marketing of crude oil and natural gas, as well as refining, transporting, and marketing of petroleum products, are its primary activities. The pursuit of these activities has led to its establishing significant international operations extending to six continents and involving over 19,000 employees.

Four distinct computer centers are maintained by the Marathon Oil Company. One is the Computer Sciences Department at its research center in Littleton, Colorado. The primary function of this department is support of petroleum engineering, geophysical, and research work conducted at the research center. The computer system itself is a dual processor Burroughs B7900 mainframe and the necessary tape and disk drives. Several pieces of online equipment directly associated with research activities are also used.

A second computer facility is located at Marathon's international office in London, England. This computer facility consists of one IBM 3083 and a variety of peripherals that support the BRAE project, which is concerned primarily with the construction and operation of large offshore drilling and production platforms.

The remaining two computer facilities are primarily devoted to business-related computing. Two IBM 3081s located at Marathon's corporate headquarters in Findlay, Ohio, and an IBM 3081 located in its Houston, Texas, office are connected in a multiprocessor arrangement with a variety of peripheral devices. One processor in Findlay is used mainly for batch processing, while the second processor is used for data-base online applications. The processor located in Houston is used as a test and backup machine.

The Computer Services Organization at Findlay encompasses three functional areas: Systems Development, Technical and Remote Computing, and Computer Operations. The applications developed and operated at Marathon range from a simple payroll procedure to computer control of refining operations. It is not unusual to find one project development group updating an existing billing system while another group is developing a highly sophisticated engineering applica-

tion. Thousands of programs have been developed to handle user requests. An average of 4,500 jobs (17,000 programs) are processed each day.

The Systems Development Division of the Computer Services Organization employs approximately 260 analysts and programmers who are concerned with the maintenance of current systems and the development of new systems arising from user requests. Marathon uses PRIDE, a standard methodology for system development marketed by M. Bryce & Associates. In all, seven phases of system analysis and design are outlined in the PRIDE methodology.

Phase I is essentially a feasibility study comprising the following steps:

1. **Project Scope.** The overall nature of the project is defined; emphasis is placed on what the study intends to accomplish.
2. **Information Requirements.** Data is collected during extensive interviews with individuals who will interface with the new system and become its primary users.
3. **Recommendations and Concepts.** A general flowchart of the proposed system is developed; it depicts the flow of key documents through the system. A narrative is included to explain the flow.
4. **Economics.** The projected costs of developing the proposed system and the annual costs associated with its operation are determined. Savings generated by the system, as well as a payout schedule, are included.
5. **Project Plan.** A calendar schedule outlining the time required to complete the proposed system is set up.

Several alternatives are usually generated during Phase I. These alternatives are presented to management, which selects the one it considers most feasible. The chosen alternative is then carried forward into Phase II.

During Phase II, all major functions of the system are identified. The total system is divided into logical subsystems. Each subsystem is thoroughly documented through the use of flowcharts. Included in the flowcharts are subsystem identification, the inputs and outputs associated with the subsystem, and the files to be accessed, referenced, or updated by the subsystem.

Any output report generated by the subsystem is also formatted at this time. A narrative is included to clarify any points not represented by the flowcharts. The entire package is then presented to management for final approval. Once the design has been approved by management (at the end of Phase II), no other formal presentation of the entire system is made, although the final details of each subsystem are reviewed.

Phase II entails subsystem design and focuses directly on the project plan for each subsystem. Administrative procedures and computer procedures are thoroughly documented in a subsystem design manual. Flowcharts and narratives are again used as documentation tools. During this phase it is not unusual to discover overlooked outputs, such as control totals, that the system should provide. These changes are incorporated, and the final formats for all output reports are developed.

In Phase IV, the activities of analysts and programmers are separated. The analysts begin work on the administrative procedure design, which is denoted as Phase IV–1. The key activity here is the development of a users' manual. The system design manual generated during Phase II generally becomes the first chapter of this manual; the remaining chapters are devoted to the component subsystems. Necessary input documents are designed and added to each subsystem definition. The previously designed output documents are usually carried forward. The procedures or methods to be used in inputting data are defined.

While the analysts are developing the users' manual, programmers are busy with program design, Phase IV–2. Extensive use of HIPO techniques occurs during this phase, which eventually leads into Phase V. During Phase V, the actual programs are produced. This phase tends to be overlapped with Phase VI, during which each program module is tested.

The activities of the analysts and programmers are carefully coordinated so that the users' manual and the programs are completed at approximately the same time. The entire system is now ready to begin the final phase outlined in the PRIDE methodology—a complete systems test. Phase VII involves extensive volume tests and comprehensive training of the system users.

An example of a system developed internally by this method is the Medical Claims System, designed to speed the processing of medical claims submitted by Marathon employees. Before this system was developed, each claim was processed manually. First, a medical claims processor thoroughly checked the claim's validity. After all the medical bills associated

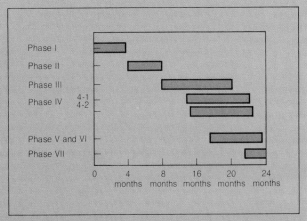

Figure 13–19 ▪ **Medical Claims System Time-Phased Development Chart**

with the claim had been received, the processor filled out a worksheet to complete the claim. The processor was then able to prepare a check to the employee.

The new system greatly simplifies and speeds this processing. Once the entire claim has been collected, it is entered into the system via a CRT. This is the last human interface with the claim; the system handles all subsequent processing, including generation of the check.

The bar chart in Figure 13–19 indicates the time involved in each phase of the development of this system. More than 4,600 person-hours were required for development. This means that if one person were to devote 40 hours a week to the development of such a system, over two years would be required to finish it.

During 1983, the Systems Development Division was actively involved in the development of many new systems as well as in maintaining systems already in operation. (Despite their continual efforts to satisfy users' demands, a sizable backlog of requests remains.) As users continue to become more comfortable with computer interaction, the demands on this division will undoubtedly continue to grow.

DISCUSSION POINTS

1. The structured approach outlined in the PRIDE methodology is an effective technique for conducting systems analysis, design, and implementation. Should such a detailed procedure always be followed? Why?
2. What types of documentation are included in the PRIDE methodology? During what phase or phases is documentation prepared?

14

File Organization and Data Design

INTRODUCTION

All business organizations maintain a wide variety of files that contain data about production, employees, customers, inventory levels, and so forth. An organization's method of processing this data is determined largely by specific job requirements. To facilitate the processing of data, an organization can tailor its files to meet certain objectives. For example, files can be structured to decrease overall processing time and to increase processing efficiency.

This chapter examines three types of file arrangement, or data design: sequential, direct access, and indexed sequential. It describes representative applications of these methods to clarify how they are used and discusses the advantages and disadvantages of each method. The chapter also explains the data-base concept and how it uses physical and logical design. Finally, it describes data-base management systems and software packages available for various data-base systems.

ARTICLE
Database Confusion Reigns
Doran Howitt

A computer is better than a human at keeping track of things, and software makers know it. File managers and database managers by the hundreds are flooding the market as vendors battle for a share of a lucrative—and growing—market.

Buyers, though, are in trouble. They are finding they must fend for themselves in a sea of claims, counterclaims, and confusion. With more complicated products being introduced every month, consumers may do their homework and still find, months later, that they haven't solved their information management problems.

"The market is very confusing," says C. J. Date, author of *Database: A Primer,* published by Addison-Wesley of Reading, Massachusetts. "I don't think anybody can keep up with it. For a decade, truly relational databases were just a theory. None existed, not even for mainframes. Now, in the past two or three years, suddenly there are perhaps a hundred or more on the market." The *One Point Electronic Catalog,* produced by ITM of Walnut Creek, California, listed 188 data-base-management systems in June. (This figure includes some educational packages about database programs, but does not include non-business-oriented products.)

Microcomputer database-management systems generally are divided into two groups: simpler programs, sometimes referred to as file managers, and more sophisticated

programs, usually relational database-management systems. Software Publishing's PFS:File and PFS:Report packages lead the market at the low end, and Ashton-Tate's dBase II leads at the high end. (Ashton-Tate has announced that dBase III, a more advanced version of its program, will soon be available.) There's a spectrum of programs with capabilities between these two. Integrated software packages such as Lotus' 1-2-3 incorporate data-management capabilities like those of file manager rather than a true relational database.

To add to the confusion, the "relational" moniker can be misleading. Simply put, a relational database makes it possible to merge information from different files. For example, one could take a list containing customers' names, addresses, and zip codes and combine it with data from another file containing customers' names and the products they ordered. In that way one might create a list of products ordered, sorted according to the purchaser's zip code. Most programs, Date explains, have various constraints on the capability to merge data. He says, to paraphrase writer George Orwell, "Some databases are more relational than others."

Choosing a package probably won't get any simpler very soon. The advanced programs generally require much more effort to master than do the leading spreadsheet or word processing packages. To

complicate matters, software publishers are gearing up their promotional efforts, trying to capture a market share before the industry settles on a winner.

Perhaps a sign of how complicated the issue can get is the growth of *Data Based Advisor,* a magazine published by Data Based Solutions, a software development company in San Diego. The magazine was originally intended for the company's dBase II applications, but the circulation and ad revenues started to take off when it began covering other database-management systems, too. Now, revenue from the magazine overshadows the company's other lines of business.

The real contest may have just begun. Relational database packages are commanding multimillion-dollar promotional campaigns, after Lotus demonstrated success with this same strategy in spreadsheets. For example, Hayes Microcomputer Products of Norcross, Georgia, best known for its modems, plans to spend nearly $3 million in the coming year—about a third of the company's annual advertising budget—to promote Please, its new entry in the database arena.

Microrim and Ashton-Tate plan similar campaigns. Microrim is trying to bolster its position by introducing a companion package called Conversational Language Option, or Clout. The add-on permits the user to build up a vocabulary of plain English commands that the R:Base products will understand; other publishers are also working on these so-called Natural Language command shells. Ashton-Tate's dBase III is said to feature extensive on-screen assistance and menus.

In the face of this competitive fervor, the industry lacks a consensus as to how many products the market really can support. Many assert that, ultimately, only a few of the new offerings will become successful products, though others are more sanguine about the survival of a wider variety of database products.

Adam Green, president of the SoftwareBanc, of Arlington, Massachusetts, a dBase II training firm, holds the former point of view. He predicts that there eventually will be only a handful of products left. "I already have a shelf full of database-management products that seem to have disappeared from the market," he says.

"Retailers want simplicity," Green says. "All these products confuse them. They ask a customer, 'Do you do programming?' If the answer is yes, they'll sell you dBase II. If it's no, they'll tell you about PFS."

David Irwin, technical editor of *Data Based Advisor,* agrees that the market will soon narrow significantly. "A lot of the programs on the market now are not well-supported," he says. "They won't be able to compete with the big-budget products."

David Kruglinski, president of Tenon Software Services of Seattle and author of *Data Base Management Systems* (Osborne/McGraw-Hill), sees integrated products that include some information management capabilities as stiff competition for file managers. "I don't see how all the low-end programs can survive competing against the integrated-software packages," he says. The inclination of many buyers, he feels, will be to try to buy one software package that fulfills all their basic needs—spreadsheet, word processing, and data management.

But at the other end of the market, Kruglinski believes that a variety of products can succeed. "At the high end, each product has its unique advantages, and these can correspond to variations in users' experience and needs," he says. "If you're looking to accomplish a particular task, you can probably find a package that will do it. It's tough to find one that does everything well."

Robert Leff, president of Softsel, a major software wholesaler based in Culver City, California, notes that many of the less popular products will still survive because they are sidelines for a company with other successful products. "A software package doesn't need to be a huge hit to make money," he says.

Most computer stores carry only a small selection of database products—and may actively hustle even fewer. For example, the Harvest Computer Store in Cambridge, Massachusetts, an independent retailer, carries about 15 database-management products, counting both low- and high-end products for Apple and IBM machines. But it is gradually expanding its product line, adding a new package every month or two. Charles Strange, assistant sales manager, says the store could handle quite a few more easily. "I can learn to demonstrate another 10 programs," he says.

Which database package should a buyer select? Experienced users advise outlining in detail the tasks the database-management system is expected to do. Buyers should try to anticipate all combinations and permutations of data needed—and then ask whether a particular software package can accommodate them. After that, the main concern is how easy the program is to learn and use, experts say.

InfoWorld, July 16, 1984. Copyright 1984 by Popular Computing, Inc. All rights reserved.

The data base approach to file organization has existed for a number of years on mainframe computers, however, it is just beginning to be used heavily on microcomputers. Although recent focus has been on data base concepts, the other types of file organization are still used heavily. In some applications, for example, an indexed sequential organization may be better suited than a data base would be.

Computers Aid Police Departments

Computers are and have been for some times assisting police in solving crimes. Angola, Indiana, police chief Russell Long uses a microcomputer in his patrol car to have easy access to crime statistics. Police stations in almost every city with a population of over one million use computers to keep track of mug shots and fingerprints.

New York City and New Orleans police departments are particularly successful in their application of computers. The New York City department now has an automated mug-shot file. Prior to the computerized file, witnesses and victims had to look for hours through files of mugshots. With the computerized system, the number of photos of suspects can be narrowed by giving the computer information about distinguishing features such as marks or scars. Then the witness has to select from only a few photos.

The New Orleans police department has computerized records of 150,000 known offenders in the area. These records contain addresses, fingerprints, and information about the hangouts of the offenders.

FILE PROCESSING

File processing is the operation of periodically updating permanent files to reflect the effects of changes in data. Files can be organized in several ways, with or without the use of a computerized system. Without computers, files must be recorded on paper and manually updated. For example, consider the case of ABC Company, a small sports equipment supplier. The company carries an inventory of fifty types of items, supplies equipment to thirty customers, and maintains a staff of twenty employees. All of ABC's records are kept on paper, and transactions are recorded manually.

Every time a customer places an order, a clerk must prepare a sales order. The customer's file is checked to obtain all necessary information about the customer, such as billing and shipping addresses and credit status. The clerk fills in the type and quantity of equipment ordered, and the sales order is sent to the warehouse where the inventory is stored. At the warehouse, an employee determines if the requested equipment is available. This operation requires a physical count of inventory. If the inventory is available, it can be packaged and prepared for shipping. If the order cannot be filled, the employee must prepare a back-order. The sales order is forwarded to the accounting department, where the customer's bill is prepared. In this department, a clerk consults a company catalog to determine the cost of each item. The total bill is calculated, including tax and shipping rates; this total is recorded on the customer's record; and the order is shipped.

Even this simplified transaction includes many time-consuming and inefficient activities. In addition, ABC Company must prepare a monthly payroll as well as purchase orders to replenish depleted inventory. Obviously, ABC Company could benefit from computerizing its activities.

Several computerized files could be arranged to facilitate ABC's operations. First, an employee file could be set up; each individual employee record might contain the employee's home address, social security number, wage per hour, withholding tax, and gross income. So that this data can be used in a variety of ways by various individuals, it is stored in a file that can be accessed by users who require the information. Figure 14–1 shows a portion of an employee file and reintroduces several terms useful in a discussion of data design. Recall from Chapter 1 that a **field** is a data item; a **record** is a collection of data items that relate to a single unit; and a **file,** or **data set,** is a grouping of related records.

The company could also use an inventory file with one record for each item carried in inventory. Each record could contain a description of the item, the quantity on hand, the cost of the item, and the like. Finally, a customer file containing such fields as billing and shipping addresses, current balances owed, and credit status would be useful.

Each of these files would be accessed, or read, in different ways. For example, the entire employee file would be read every time the payroll was prepared. The inventory file, however, would only need to be accessed one record at a time—that is, only one record would be read each time an order was placed for a particular item. The customer file would be accessed in two ways. First, when a customer placed an order, only the particular record containing data about that customer would be read. Second, the entire file would be read each time ABC Company prepared customer bills or needed a report on outstanding customer balances.

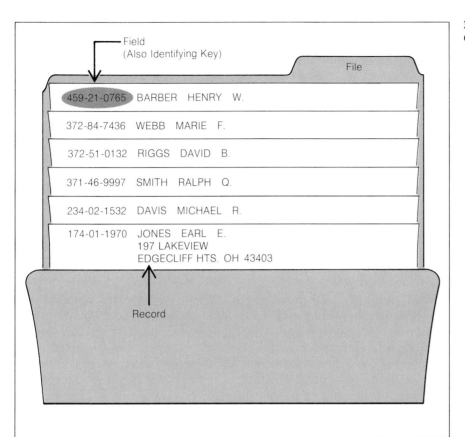

Figure 14–1 ■ Employee Data—ABC Company

Field
(Also Identifying Key)

File

459-21-0765 BARBER HENRY W.

372-84-7436 WEBB MARIE F.

372-51-0132 RIGGS DAVID B.

371-46-9997 SMITH RALPH Q.

234-02-1532 DAVIS MICHAEL R.

174-01-1970 JONES EARL E.
197 LAKEVIEW
EDGECLIFF HTS. OH 43403

Record

The following sections will discuss the three types of file arrangements that would be used in these three cases.

SEQUENTIAL DESIGN

If we need to find a particular record and the set of records in a file is very small, then it may not be difficult to search the file from beginning to end to find the record. For files containing large numbers of records, however, this method is impractical. A special ordering technique is needed so that records can be retrieved more easily. For this reason, employee records, for example, may be arranged according to social security number (look again at Figure 14–1), or records in an inventory file may be arranged according to item number. The identifier used to locate a particular record in the file is called a **key.** Since a key is used to locate a particular record, it must be unique— that is, no two records in a file can have the same key value. The records ordered according to their key values form a **sequential file.**

Updating involves two sets of files; the basic file containing all existing records is called the **master file,** and the file containing changes to be made to the master file is called a **transaction file.** The master file is organized according to the identifier chosen as a key. Since the changes, or transaction records, must be matched against the master records, processing is greatly enhanced if the transaction records are ordered according to the same key. That is, the transaction file should also be sequentially organized.

In updating, both the master file and the transaction file serve as input to the computer system. The computer compares the key of the first master record with the key of the first record on the transaction file. If the keys do not match, the next record on the master file is read. When a match between the transaction record and a master record occurs, the master record is updated. If a master record has no matching transaction record, it is left unchanged. If a transaction record has no matching master record, an error or warning message may be generated.

The updated master record can be longer or shorter than it was before the updating occurred. Since records are stored one after another on a sequential file, a new record may overwrite the next record following it or may leave a gap before it. In some applications, an unmatched transaction causes an entirely new master record to be inserted between two other master records. In others, some transactions may cause old master records to be deleted. To allow such processing, a new master file is created whenever changes have to be made to the old master file. Every master record not deleted explicitly must be written to the new master file, whether or not it is changed.

When such **sequential processing** is utilized, there is no way to directly locate the matching master record for a transaction. Every time a given master record is to be updated, the entire master file must be read and a new master file created. To eliminate a great deal of unnecessary processing, transactions are collected for a given time period and then processed against the master file in one run. This approach, you may remember from earlier chapters, is called **batch processing** (see Figure 14–2).

The amount of time required to update a record in the sequential processing mode includes the time needed to process the transaction, read the master file until the proper record is reached, update the master record, and rewrite the master file. To reduce the time needed, the transactions are sorted to reflect the order of the master file. For security, the old master file and the transaction records are retained for a period of time; then, if the new master is accidentally destroyed, it can be reconstructed from the old master and the transaction files.

Example of Sequential Processing

Billing operations are well suited to sequential processing. Customers' bills must be prepared, but only at scheduled intervals. Standard procedures apply, and large numbers of records must be processed.

Processing customer records results in the preparation of bills for customers and updates of the amounts they owe. Magnetic tape is an appropriate medium for this application because the customer records can be arranged in customer number order and processed in sequence accordingly.

The procedure for preparing the billing statements involves the following steps:

■ *Step 1:* The transaction records indicating which items have been shipped to customers are keyed-to-tape, verified, and edited. One record is used for each item shipped. The key-to-tape operation also provides a report of invalid transactions so that they can be corrected (see Figure 14–3a).
■ *Step 2:* The transaction records are sorted according to customer number because the customer master file is arranged in customer number order (see Figure 14–3b).
■ *Step 3:* The sorted transactions are used to update the customer master file.

Figure 14–2 ▪ Sequential Processing

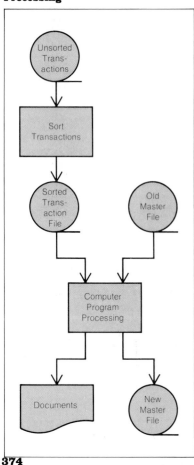

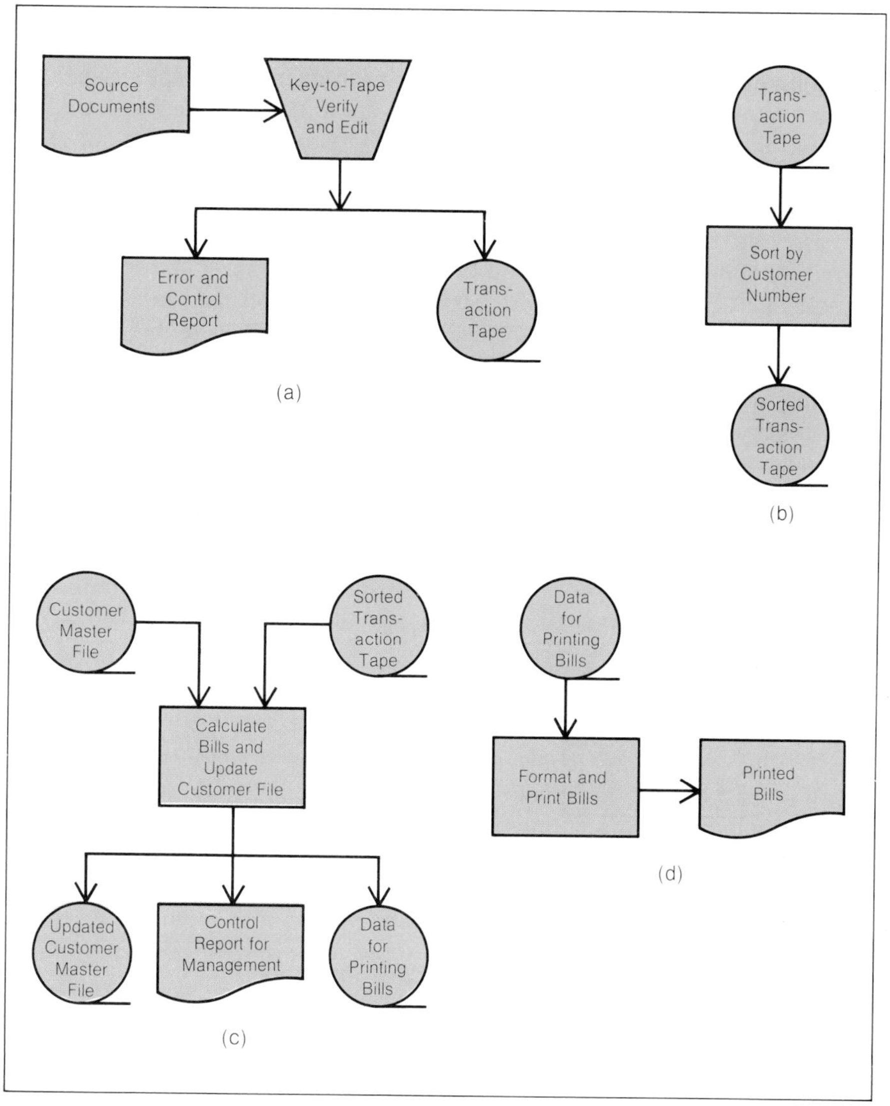

Figure 14–3 ▪ Billing Operations (Using Sequential Processing)

The process involves reading the transaction records and master records into main storage. There may be more than one transaction record for a master record. The master record is updated to reflect the final amount owed by the customer. Usually, during an update, a report is also printed for management. For example, during the billing update, a listing of customers who have exceeded their credit limits may be printed (see Figure 14–3c).

▪ *Step 4:* The customers' bills are prepared from the data generated in the previous step (see Figure 14–3d).

Interrogating Sequential Files

How inquiries into a sequential file on magnetic tape are handled depends on the type of inquiry. Let us consider the following inquiries into the employee file shown in Figure 14–1.

1. List the records of employees with social security numbers 234–02–1532 and 372–84–7436.
2. List all employees from the area with zip code 43403.

The employee file is sequenced according to social security number. In the first case the file will be searched for the correct social security numbers from the beginning of the file, but only the key of each record will be checked. As soon as the required social security numbers are located, the records will be listed and the search stopped. Of course, if the numbers are in the last two records on the file, then the entire file must be searched.

For the second inquiry, the entire file will again have to be searched. In this case, the zip code field of each record must be checked to see if it matches 43403. This illustrates one problem with referring to a nonkey field on sequential files. If an inquiry is based on a field other than the key, then a great deal of time is wasted in the search process. To alleviate this problem, a temporary employee file, ordered by zip code, could be created. A sort procedure would be used to order the file, which would only be needed until the necessary report was created and the program finished. Some programming languages, such as COBOL, offer a sort procedure which uses a temporary sort file such as the one just discussed.

Assessment of Sequential Design

Some advantages of sequential processing and file design are:

■ It is suitable for many types of applications—payroll, billing, preparation of customer statements, and so forth—that require periodic updating of large numbers of records.
■ Economies of scale are achieved when the number of records processed is high. If at least half the records in a master file are updated during a processing run, the large volume of transactions reduces the processing cost per record.
■ The design of sequential files is simple.
■ Magnetic tape, a low-cost medium, can be used to maximum advantage.
■ Input and output rates are higher than those achieved with direct input of transactions from terminal keyboards.

The disadvantages of this mode of processing include the following:

■ The entire master file must be processed and a new master file written even if only a few master records have to be updated.
■ Transactions must be sorted in a particular sequence; this takes time and can be expensive.
■ The master file is only as up-to-date as the last processing run. In many instances, the delay in processing the master file results in use of old and thus incorrect information.
■ The sequential nature of the file organization is a serious handicap when unanticipated inquiries must be made.

DIRECT-ACCESS DESIGN

Direct-access processing is suited to applications involving files with low activity and high volatility. **Activity** refers to the proportion of records processed during an updating run, and **volatility** refers to the frequency of changes to a file during a certain time period.

In contrast to a batch-processing system, a direct-access system does not require that transaction records be grouped or sorted before they are processed. Data is submitted to the computer in the order it occurs. Direct-access storage devices (DASDs) such as magnetic disks make this type of processing possible. A particular record on a master file can be accessed directly and updated without all preceding records on the file being read. Only the key to the record need be known. Thus, use of direct-access design in combination with online processing can provide up-to-the-minute information.

For example, assume Ralph Smith's address in the employee master file in Figure 14–1 had to be changed. With direct-access processing, the computer can locate the record to be updated without sequentially processing all records that precede it.

A major consideration in the use of direct-access processing is finding the record to be updated. For the record to be located, its address, or location, in secondary storage must be known. The address is usually a number from five to seven digits in length that is related to the physical characteristics of the direct-access storage device. The address can be obtained either through transforming the record key (also called **randomizing** or **hashing**) or from searching a **directory,** or table, which associates record keys with corresponding record addresses.

When randomizing, or hashing, is used to locate a record's address, an arithmetic manipulation of the record key is performed to create an address. For example, suppose we need a three-digit disk address. The nine-digit Social Security number could be converted as follows. First, we select a number such as 995. We then divide every social security number by 995 and the result is a quotient and a remainder. The employee's record is stored at the address equal to the remainder. Thus, Ralph Smith's record would be stored at address 677. (371469997 ÷ 995 = 373336 with a remainder of 677.)

A problem that sometimes arises with randomizing is that of duplicate addresses. This situation would occur when two or more keys divided by the chosen number result in the same remainder. The problem can be resolved by either developing another randomizing routine, or by storing the record in an alternate address which is somehow linked to the initial address. Some operating systems do provide a linking mechanism for direct-access files.

Directories, on the other hand, list record keys along with their corresponding address in storage. During processing the computer sequentially searches the directory to locate the address of a particular record. For example, assume that the ABC Company's employee master file (refer again to Figure 14–1) is on a direct-access storage device and that the addresses are contained in a directory. The directory, or table, would consist of two data items; the first would contain the key of the record (social security number) and the second the address of the record associated with that key (see Figure 14–4). To find Ralph Smith's record, the computer would search the directory until it found his social security number. It would then pick up the corresponding address from the second data item and access the record stored at that location.

Examples of Direct-Access Processing

Many applications are not suited for sequential processing. One example is an airline reservation system. Airline employees who assign seats on flights must have up-to-date information. Sales efforts must be coordinated so that a

Figure 14—4 ▪ **Sample Directory for the ABC Company**

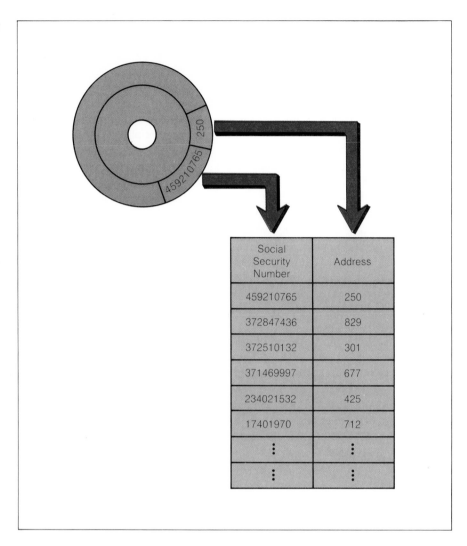

Social Security Number	Address
459210765	250
372847436	829
372510132	301
371469997	677
234021532	425
17401970	712
⋮	⋮
⋮	⋮

passenger in Cleveland and one in Detroit do not purchase the same seat on the same flight to New York. If data for an airline were processed once a week, plane flights would often be oversold. With a direct-access system, on the other hand, a ticket agent can submit a flight number and quickly determine the number of seats available. This is possible because not all flight records must be read—only the record of the flight in question. The computer system has up-to-date information on all flights at all times.

Another example of direct-access processing is a savings account system at a bank. The bank can maintain a current status of all savings accounts by updating each account as soon as a deposit or withdrawal is made. Customer records are stored on a DASD. Terminals are installed at all branch offices and connected to the computer by communication facilities (for example, telephone lines); the terminals are used for both input and output (see Figure 14–5).

When a bank customer makes a deposit or withdrawal, the amount of the transaction, the type of transaction (deposit or withdrawal), and the customer's account number are communicated to the central computer through the typewriter-like terminal at the branch office. The computer immediately lo-

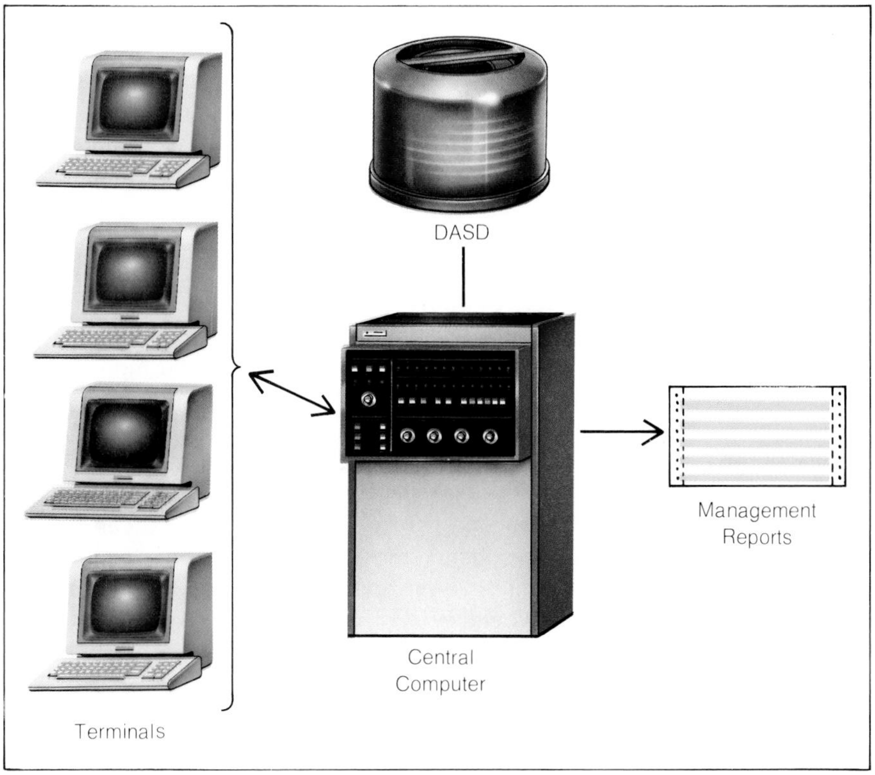

Figure 14–5 ■ Direct-Access Processing

DASD

Management
Reports

Central
Computer

Terminals

cates the record containing that account number on the DASD, updates the account, and sends a message giving the current balance back to the terminal. The message is printed on the customer's savings book.

It is important to note that the desired record can be directly located on the DASD and that only one record is updated. Using the direct-access method can be compared to finding a particular landmark on a city map by means of coordinates. Knowing these coordinates, we can immediately zero in on the exact location of the landmark. Sequential processing is unsuitable for this kind of application.

Interrogating Direct-Access Files

To see how direct-access files handle inquiries, let us look again at the two inquiries discussed in connection with sequential files:

1. List the records of employees with social security numbers 234–02–1532 and 372–84–7436.
2. List all employees from the area with zip code 43403.

With regard to the first inquiry, the records of the two employees can be located directly because the addresses can be found by use of either a directory or randomizing, as described earlier (assuming social security number is used as the key).

The approach used for the second inquiry will depend on the organization of the file. If much processing is done based on a geographic breakdown of employees, a directory relating zip codes and their record addresses can be created (see Figure 14 – 6). However, if ABC is a small company, a directory

Figure 14–6 ■ Directory for Zip Codes

ZIP CODE	ADDRESS
43403	12043
43403	12140
44151	12046
44153	12143
44200	12146
44201	12045

to locate employee records by zip code may have little value. In this case, we encounter the same situation we did with sequential files: The entire file must be read to obtain the desired information. This could take a great deal of time.

Assessment of Direct-Access Design

The following are advantages of direct-access processing and file design:

- Transaction data can be used directly to update master records via online terminals without first being sorted. Transactions are processed as they occur.
- The master file is not read completely each time updating occurs; only the master records to be updated are accessed. This saves time and money.
- It takes only a fraction of a second to gain access to any record on a direct-access file.
- Direct-access files provide flexibility in handling inquiries.
- Several files can be updated concurrently by use of direct-access processing. For example, when a credit sale is made, the inventory file can be updated; the customer file can be changed to reflect the current accounts-receivable figure; and the sales file can be updated to show which employee made the sale. Several runs would be required to accomplish all of these operations if sequential processing was used.

Disadvantages of direct-access design include the following:

- During processing, the original record is replaced by the updated record. In effect, it is destroyed. (In batch processing, a complete new master file is created, but the old master file remains intact.) Consequently, to provide backup, an organization may have to make a magnetic-tape copy of the master file weekly and also keep the current week's transactions so that master records can be reconstructed if necessary.
- Since many users may have access to records stored on direct-access devices in online systems, the chances of accidental destruction of data are greater. Special programs are required to edit input data and to perform other checks to ensure that data is not lost. Also, there exists the possibility of confidential information falling into unauthorized hands; additional security procedures are necessary to reduce this risk.
- Implementation of direct-access systems is often difficult because of their complexity and the high level of programming (software) support that such systems need.
- When the randomizing technique is used with direct-access file organization, some file locations can be unused. It is necessary to keep track of these unused locations for use as overflow areas for later additions.

INDEXED-SEQUENTIAL DESIGN

Sequential processing is suitable for applications where the proportion of records processed in an updating run is high. However, sequential files provide slow response times and cannot adequately handle file inquiries. On the other hand, direct-access processing is inappropriate for applications like payroll, where most records are processed during a run. When a single file must be used for both batch processing and online processing, neither direct-access nor sequential file organization is appropriate. The same customer file that is used in a weekly batch run for preparing bills by the accounting department may be used daily by order-entry personnel to record orders and check credit status. To some extent, the limitations of both types of file design can be minimized by using another approach to file organization—**indexed-sequential** design.

In this structure, the records are stored sequentially on a direct-access storage device. In addition, an **index,** or directory, containing record keys and their corresponding addresses is also established. A record within the file can be accessed directly by using the index, which can have multiple levels. By dividing the index into levels, the amount of searching required to locate the desired record can be reduced. In Figure 14–7, for example, a search for the forty-fifth record in the employee master file would require searching six elements of the index and five records to reach the desired record. This would be in comparison to searching forty-five records in a sequential search of the file. The indexed-sequential file, therefore, can be accessed directly by matching the record key to an element of the index table to get an approximate address for the required record. The computer then goes to the address in storage and checks records sequentially until the desired record is found.

Thus, an indexed-sequential file provides direct-access capability through the use of indexes. Also, since all the records are ordered according to a key, it also allows efficient sequential processing.

Thus, an indexed-sequential file provides direct-access capability. Since all the records are ordered according to a key, it also allows efficient sequential processing.

Examples of Indexed-Sequential Processing

The customer file referred to earlier in this chapter is an example of a file suitable for indexed-sequential processing. The file could be read sequentially for the billing operation. In addition, it could be accessed one record at a time for order-entry transactions. The following steps outline the procedures involved in preparing a customer order:

■ *Step 1:* A customer mails or phones an order to ABC Company for equipment. The clerk receives the order and enters the customer number on a visual display terminal. This number acts as a key to the file.
■ *Step 2:* The customer file is searched until a match is found between the number entered and the appropriate record. Once the appropriate record is found, the information appears on the terminal's screen. The clerk verifies shipping and billing addresses.
■ *Step 3:* The order is entered on the keyboard, and a sales order is generated by a printer connected to the system.
■ *Step 4:* The customer's record is updated to reflect the current order.

Assessment of Indexed-Sequential Design

Advantages of indexed-sequential design include the following:

■ Indexed-sequential files are well suited for both inquiries and large processing runs.
■ Access time to specific records is apt to be faster using an index than it would be if the file were sequentially searched.

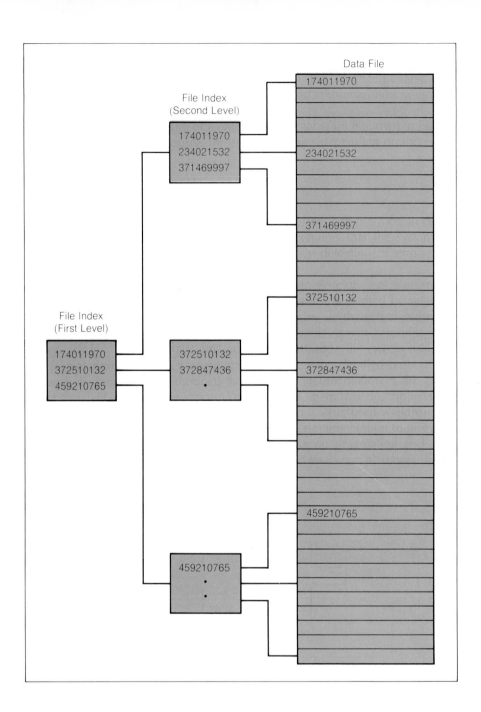

Figure 14–7 ▪ **Example of an Indexed-Sequential File Index**

Disadvantages of indexed-sequential design include the following:

▪ More direct-access storage space is required for an indexed-sequential file than for a sequential file holding the same data because of the storage space required for indexes.
▪ Processing time for specific record selection is longer than it would be in a direct-access system.

Each of the types of file organization discussed in this chapter describes the physical organization of computer files—that is, how the data is arranged on a particular storage medium. In a sequential file, for example, the records are physically placed one after another. Many organizations maintain a file for every application program; one for accounting, one for billing, one for inventory, and so on. This may result in the same data being recorded in several files.

There is another approach to data organization in which a file is not treated as a separate entity. This method uses a **data base**—a single collection of related data which can be used in many applications. The duplication of data is therefore eliminated.

Data-base organization allows the user or application programmer to concentrate on *logical,* rather than physical, structures. In logical structures, data is organized in a way that is meaningful to a particular user, who is not concerned with the physical arrangement of data on a storage medium. Data-base organization and logical data structures are discussed in the following section.

- A file that must be searched from beginning to end to locate a record, and that is organized according to **key** values, is a **sequential file.**
- The process of **updating** involves a file containing all existing records—the **master file**—and a file containing the changes to be made to the master file—the **transaction file.**
- Sequential file organization is best suited to applications that can use **batch processing.**
- Direct-access processing is best suited to applications that have a low **activity** and high **volatility** and require online processing.
- Direct-access processing is made possible through the use of direct-access storage devices such as magnetic disk.

DATA-BASE CONCEPTS

As was mentioned above, separate departments often have their own separate data files and collect their own input for processing. The accounting data files are set up to suit the preparation of financial accounts; the marketing data files, the preparation of sales reports; and the production data files, the preparation of production schedules and the monitoring of inventory levels. These files frequently contain duplicate data about customers, employees, and products.

In contrast, the data-base concept requires the use of some form of general data storage. The organization's data must be stored in such a way that the same data can be accessed by multiple users for varied applications. This can be accomplished by using a data base which groups, or structures, data elements to fit the information needs of an entire organization rather than specifically for one application or functional area. Thus, multiple departments can use the data, and duplication of files is avoided.

In addition to reducing redundancy and increasing data independence, the data base increases efficiency. When a particular item is to be updated, the change needs to be made only once. There is no need for multiple updates as required with separate files. The integration of data also permits the results of updating to be available to the entire organization at the same time. Furthermore, the data-base concept provides flexibility because the system can respond to information requests that previously may have had to bridge several departments' individual data files.

Data Organization

The design of data for a data base is approached from two perspectives. **Physical design** refers to how the data is kept on storage devices and how it is accessed. **Logical design** deals with how data is viewed by application programs or individual users. The logical data design is performed by the systems analyst and data analyst (see Chapter 13). Together, they attempt to model the actual relationships that exist among data items. Logical records should be designed independent of physical storage considerations. The physical design is often performed by the data-base administration (DBA) team. Taking into account such problems as data redundancy, access time, and storage constraints, this team tries to implement the logical data design within the physical records and files actually stored on the data base.

A logical unit can extend across more than one physical file. That is to say, what one user views as a logical unit of data may include data from the employee file and the payroll file. Conversely, one physical file may contain parts of several logical units of data. One user's logical unit may include only an employee's name and address; another may include only the employee's number and job code. In both of these cases, the data is only a part of one physical file: the employee file (see Figure 14–8).

Figure 14–8 ▪ Example of Company ABC's Data Base

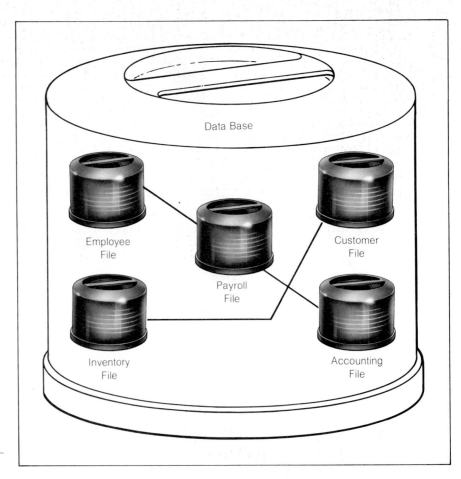

Data Base

Employee File

Payroll File

Customer File

Inventory File

Accounting File

- A type of file organization that combines the characteristics of sequential and direct-access file organization is called **indexed-sequential design.**
- Indexed-sequential files permit a record to be located either sequentially or directly through the use of an **index.**
- Indexed-sequential file organization is best suited to applications that require both batch and online processing.
- Data-base organization allows the user or application programmer to concentrate on logical data structures rather than physical structures.
- Data bases reduce redundancy, increase data independence, and increase efficiency.
- **Physical design** refers to how the data is stored on the computer's secondary storage devices and whether it is accessed sequentially or directly. **Logical design** refers to the way in which the data is viewed by the users or applications programmers.

Manipulation, Retrieval, and Inquiry

Data-base systems depend on direct-access storage devices (DASD) to permit easy retrieval of data items. The capabilities provided by a DASD are needed to handle the variety of logical relationships that exist among data elements. Routines can be established to retrieve various combinations of data elements from any number of DASDs.

In data-base systems, several methods are used to store and retrieve data from storage devices. A **simple structure** (or **list**) is a sequential arrangement of data records. All records are viewed as independent entities, as illustrated in Figure 14–9. If the records are ordered—that is, arranged in a specific sequence—then the list is referred to as a **linear structure.**

A list can be subdivided into groups to provide valuable information. Each such group has one "owner" record and any number of "member" records. This is called a **hierarchical,** or **tree, structure.** Such a list, a customer-order file, is illustrated in Figure 14–10. The owner record of each group contains the customer's number, name, and address. Each member record consists of the item number, item description, quantity ordered, and total price.

A typical file with a simple structure is shown in Figure 14–11. Each record in this file has five characteristic fields called **attributes**—name, title, education, department, and sex. Simple file structure is appropriate for generating large reports but cumbersome for handling inquiries. To overcome this limitation, an **inverted structure** can be used.

The inverted structure is better suited to responding to unanticipated inquiries. It contains indexes for selected attributes in a file, similar to those used in indexed-sequential files, and the addresses of records having those attributes (see Figure 14–12). Thus, the indexes rather than the actual files can be searched, and complex inquiries can be handled easily. Search criteria can be given for multiple files or for several attributes within one file. Once the search criteria have been satisfied and the addresses of the desired records obtained, the actual physical records can be retrieved from the file.

The major advantage of the inverted structure is that it enables a variety of inquiries to be handled quickly and efficiently. A major disadvantage is that the attributes to be used in searches must be indexed. In some cases, the indexes for a particular file may be larger than the file itself.

Some typical inquiries and responses relating to the inverted file in Figure 14–12 follow:

Figure 14–9 ▪ **Example of a Simple Structure**

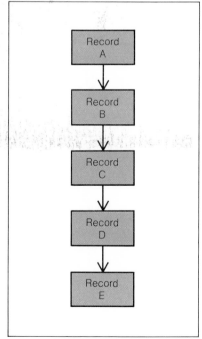

Figure 14–10 ■ Customer-Order File with Owner and Member Records (A Hierarchical Structure)

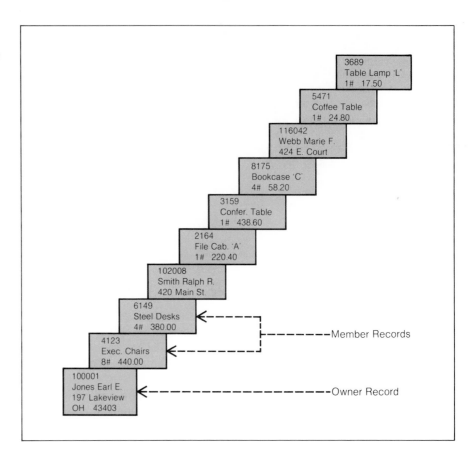

Member Records

Owner Record

Question: How many female assistant professors do we have and what are their names?

Response: Total of 2—Deluse, Cross.

The computer checks the attribute list for sex until it finds Female. It then goes to the attribute list for title and locates assistant professor. Record addresses for those two values are compared. After Female there are two addresses. Both of them match addresses listed for Assistant Professor in the title index. The computer goes to each of these addresses in the master file, finds the record, and returns the name.

Figure 14–11 ■ File with Simple Structure

ADDRESS	NAME	TITLE	EDUCATION	DEPARTMENT	SEX
018021	Borgelt	Asst. Prof.	Ph.D.	Marketing	Male
018024	Henkes	Professor	D.Sc.	Management	Male
018046	Pickens	Instructor	M.S.	Accounting	Male
018020	Deluse	Asst. Prof.	Ph.D.	Marketing	Female
018016	Kozak	Assoc. Prof.	Ph.D.	Accounting	Male
018412	Gadus	Assoc. Prof.	Ph.D.	Accounting	Male
018318	Cross	Asst. Prof.	M.B.A.	Management	Female

| NAME | | TITLE | | EDUCATION | | DEPARTMENT | | SEX | |
Value	Address	Value	Address	Value	Address	Value	Address	Value	Address
Borgelt	018021	Instructor	018046	M.S.	018046	Marketing	018021	Male	018021
Henkes	018024	Asst. Prof.	018021	M.B.A.	018318		018020		018024
Pickens	018046		018020	Ph.D.	018021	Management	018024		018046
Deluse	018020		018318		018020		018318		018016
Kozak	018016	Assoc. Prof.	018016		018016	Accounting	018046		018412
Gadus	018412		018412		018412		018016	Female	018020
Cross	018318	Professor	018024	D.Sc.	018024		018412		018318

Figure 14–12 ▪ File with Inverted Structure

Question: List the name of each employee who has a Ph.D.

Response: Borgelt, Deluse, Kozak, Gadus.

The computer checks the education list for Ph.D. Since there are no other search criteria, it goes to the addresses listed and prints the corresponding names.

In addition to the two file structures discussed, there are other, more complex structures, such as the network structure, which are suitable for applications that require multiple linkages among data items. A detailed explanation of these structures is beyond the scope of this text.

Data-Base Management Systems

To facilitate the use of a data base, an organization can use a **data-base management system (DBMS)**—a set of programs that serves as the major interface between the data base and its three principal users: the programmer, the operating system, and the user. By purchasing an available DBMS, an organization greatly reduces the need to develop its own detailed data-handling software.

One of the major purposes of a DBMS is to effect the physical data independence mentioned earlier. This physical data independence permits the physical layout of data files to be altered without necessitating changes in application programs. Such insulation between a program and the data with which it interacts is extremely desirable. The programmer does not have to pay attention to the physical nature of the file. He or she can simply refer to the specific data that the program needs.

Most existing DBMSs provide the following facilities:

▪ Integration of the data into logical structures that model the actual relationships among data items.
▪ Provision for storing the volume of data required to meet the needs of multiple users.
▪ Provision for concurrent retrieval and updating of data.
▪ Methods of arranging data to eliminate duplication and thereby avoid inconsistencies that arise from duplication.
▪ Provision for privacy controls to prevent unauthorized access to data.
▪ Controls to prevent unintended interaction or interference among programs that run concurrently.

■ Capability for data-base interface from within application programs coded in high-level programming languages.

Assessment of the Data-Base Approach

Using a data base has a number of advantages:

■ Data redundancy is minimized.
■ Data can be stored in a manner that is useful for a wide variety of applications.
■ Updating involves only one copy of the data.
■ The system can handle requests that previously may have spanned several departments.

Limitations of the data-base approach include the following:

■ An error in one input data record may be propagated throughout the data base.
■ Design and implementation of a data-base system requires highly skilled, well-trained people.
■ Major attention must be given to the security of the system, since all the data resources of the organization are collected in a repository that is readily accessible to data-base users.
■ Traditional processing jobs may run slower.

SUMMARY POINTS

■ File processing is the process of periodically updating permanent files to reflect current data. Files are accessed in different ways, depending upon the organization of the file.
■ Sequential processing involves storing records in a sequence based on a unique identifier called a key. These records form a master file. All changes to be made to the master file are collected and processed in a batch to create the new master file. The changes to be processed against the master file form a transaction file; they must be ordered in the same sequence as the records in the master file. After processing, there is a new master file, an old master file, and a transaction file.
■ Sequential processing is normally used when files are large and need to be updated only periodically, such as for payroll or billing. However, sequential file organization is not well suited to responding to inquiries, since the file must be read from beginning to end to locate a desired record.
■ In a direct-access system, transaction records are processed as they occur, without prior sorting or grouping. This method requires the use of high-speed, direct-access storage devices (DASDs) and online processing.
■ To find a record in a direct-access file, the user must know its address, or location, on a particular storage device. The addresses can be found through use of randomizing or a directory containing the key of the record and its address on DASDs.
■ Direct-access processing is most often used when changes are frequent but only a small proportion of master records must be updated at any single time.
■ Indexed-sequential file organization is suitable where the proportion of records to be processed in an updating run is high. Records are stored in se-

quence on a direct-access storage device. An index to selected record keys and their corresponding addresses is established. When a record in an indexed-sequential file must be located, the index gives the approximate address of the record. The records near that location are read sequentially until the correct one is found. Both indexed-sequential and direct-access file organizations are well suited to responding to inquiries into data files.

■ A data base is a grouping of data elements structured to fit the information needs of all functions of an organization. The data base reduces data redundancy and increases data independence and flexibility.

■ Storage of data in a data base reflects both logical and physical structures. Physical structure refers to the location of a data item on a storage device. Logical structure refers to how the data is viewed by the programs that use it.

■ The physical design of files describes the manner in which data is stored on a particular storage medium. Logical design describes the way data is organized to be meaningful to a user.

■ Logical structures can be placed on physical storage devices in several ways. The two basic methods use simple and inverted structures. A simple structure organizes records sequentially; each record is viewed as an individual entity. (If the records are organized in a specific sequence, the structure is linear.) An inverted structure creates indexes for selected attributes of the record for easy cross-referencing.

■ A data-base management system (DBMS) is a set of programs that provides, among other things, (1) a method of arranging data to limit duplication; (2) an ability to make changes to the data easily; and (3) a capability to handle direct inquiries.

REVIEW QUESTIONS

1. What is meant by file processing? What is meant by updating a record or file?
2. How are the records within a sequential file organized? Explain the process of updating a record of a sequential file.
3. Give a brief description of each of the following files: (a) master file, (b) transaction file.
4. Under what circumstances is sequential processing applicable? What are its limitations?
5. Explain how direct-access processing differs from sequential processing.
6. What are two commonly used ways of finding addresses in direct-access files? Explain briefly the differences between them.
7. Direct-access processing is best suited to what types of applications?
8. Contrast indexed-sequential file organization with sequential and direct-access file organization. What advantages does indexed-sequential organization have over the other two approaches?
9. What is a data base? How can it be structured to respond to a variety of inquiries?
10. Explain what is meant by the physical design and logical design of a data base. Who performs each of the two design tasks?
11. Draw a diagram that depicts the relationship the DBMS has with both the data base and the application programs.
12. Should a data base be designed to handle all possible inquiries? Explain.

APPLICATION
Dana Corporation

Dana's origins date to 1904, when Clarence Spicer, a mechanical engineering student at Cornell University, adopted the idea of replacing the sprockets and chains being used to transmit the power from the engine to the rear axle in automobiles with a universal joint and drive shaft. The Spicer Manufacturing Company was founded in Plainfield, New Jersey, to manufacture and market these universal joints. When an order for ninety-six sets of universal joints and drive shafts was received in 1905 from the Wayne Automobile Company, nearly sixteen weeks of around-the-clock production were required to fill it. Today, Dana produces and ships 2.5 million joint sets in a similar sixteen-week period.

Dana's major products today are axle parts, transmissions, universal joints, clutches, industrial products, engine parts, and frame and chassis parts. International sales have grown from about $1 million in 1950 to over $390 million in the late 1970s. Total sales have increased from $153 million to almost $1.8 billion during the same period.

The Spicer Transmission Division of Dana has an extensive data-processing center that supports the division itself and another plant in Jonesboro, Arkansas, and also maintains some financial information and centralized accounts receivable for the corporate headquarters. Fifteen management personnel and three data-entry operators are involved in programming, operations, and the preparation of data for subsequent processing at this facility.

Two IBM 4341 CPUs with a combined main storage capacity of 12 million characters are used to service more than 120 remote work stations. More than twenty remote terminals are used in the centralized accounts-receivable system. Twelve terminals are located at the World Headquarters for Financial Control and Marketing. Seventy-six additional remote terminals at the Spicer plant complex are used for online sales, new product development, and personnel record-keeping applications.

The variety of needs of users at the Spicer Transmission Division requires both online/direct-access and batch/sequential modes of processing. Most application programs are written in COBOL. (The entire COBOL program library contains some 2,000 programs.) Although recent emphasis has been placed on the development of online applications, batch processing remains a vital aspect of the overall data-processing activities.

One system that operates in a batch mode is the material requirements planning (MRP) system, which is extremely important to the production and purchasing departments of the division. Production planning schedules depend heavily on a sufficient supply of the parts required in the assembly of a given product. A shortage is extremely expensive, because the entire

Figure 14–13 ▪ Data-Processing Environment at Dana Corporation's Spicer Division

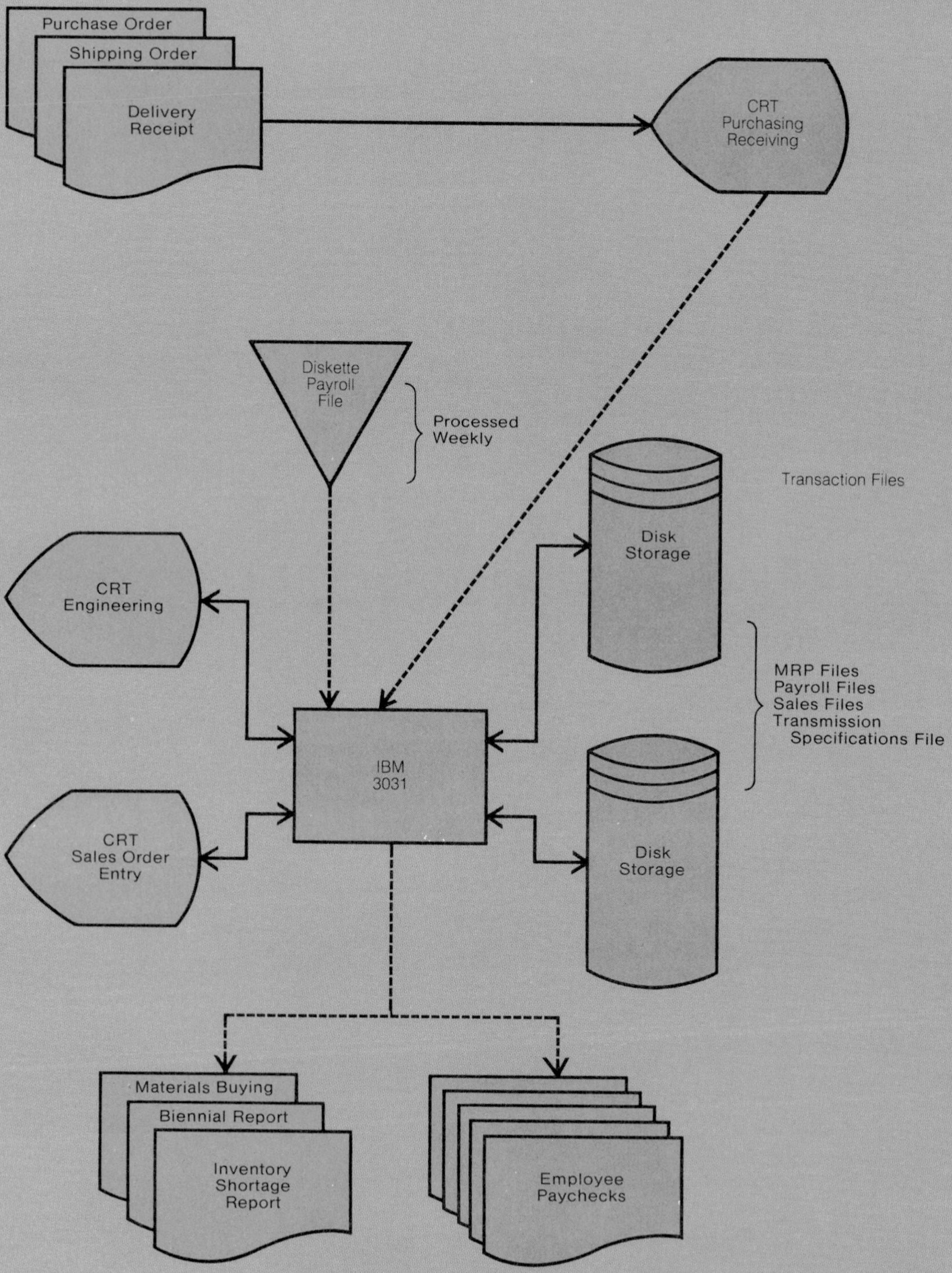

Purchase Order

Shipping Order

Delivery Receipt

CRT Purchasing Receiving

Diskette Payroll File

Processed Weekly

Transaction Files

Disk Storage

CRT Engineering

MRP Files
Payroll Files
Sales Files
Transmission
　Specifications File

IBM 3031

CRT Sales Order Entry

Disk Storage

Materials Buying

Biennial Report

Inventory Shortage Report

Employee Paychecks

assembly line must either be halted until the needed parts arrive or be converted to another assembly process. Carrying a large supply of parts in inventory is also expensive, so the purchasing department must strive to have no more inventory than is needed to meet demand.

Any transactions affecting inventory have an impact on the MRP system. During a typical day, many such transactions occur—deliveries of goods, shipments of goods, withdrawals of goods from inventory, and so on. As these transactions occur, they are entered directly into the computer via online cathode-ray tube terminals (CRTs). The transactions are stored on a transaction file that is processed nightly against the master files in the MRP system. These master files can be used to produce planning reports, inventory shortage and overage reports, and material-buying reports.

Approximately 150 reports are available through the MRP system. They can be generated at regular intervals or on user demand. Consider, as an example, an inventory shortage report. This report can include item number, description, quantity on hand, quantity on order, expected future requirements, requirements during past periods, shortage quantities, the division placing the orders, and even the specific buyer responsible for the item. Such comprehensive, up-to-date reports are invaluable to management.

Another batch-processing application is the payroll system. The office staff and production workers are paid on a weekly basis. The salaried management personnel are paid on a semimonthly basis. Employees are normally paid for forty hours per week; an additional complication arises when exceptions to that work period are reported by supervisors. The exceptions are encoded on magnetic diskettes. These data are sequentially processed against an employee master file, which uses the employee number as a key. Together, the diskette file and the master file contain all the data necessary for the calculation of employees' pay and the computer generation of paychecks. The entire payroll can be processed in five to six hours.

The two batch systems discussed above adequately serve certain user needs. However, many users also need immediate access to data to effectively perform their jobs. The engineering department is an example of such a user group.

The Spicer Transmission Division has produced approximately 5,000 different types of transmissions over the years. The specifications for these transmissions are maintained in a transmission file. When a customer submits specifications for a new product, such as a heavy truck transmission, the engineering department must determine how that product will be produced. When the order is received, an engineer keys into the keyboard of a CRT any number of major component specifications for the ordered transmission. The computer searches the transmission file and indicates which of those transmissions contain the largest number of parts identical to the new specifications. With this information, the engineer can determine the development or retooling necessary to produce the new product and provide the purchaser with accurate time and cost estimates.

A vitally important online/direct-access system used extensively by the Spicer Transmission Division is the one used to enter sales orders. This sytem makes use of a complex data base containing data about customers and pricing as well as a part-number interchange. When an order is received, a sales-entry clerk uses a CRT to obtain customer data such as the shipping address, terms, and party to be charged. The order information and part number are then entered. Since the part number the customer uses is often different from the number used by Dana to represent the same part, the data base converts the customer's part number to the appropriate Dana classification. The order is then submitted for processing. A computer-generated shop order is produced and entered into the manufacturing system, and a customer acknowledgment form is created for mailing to the buyer. The customer's order is also entered into an open-order file. Through this file, a sales representative can inquire into the status of a customer's order at any time. This capability is used hundreds of times a day in response to customer inquiries.

A schematic diagram of the data-processing environment at Dana's Spicer Division is presented in Figure 14–13.

DISCUSSION POINTS

1. What criteria determine if an application will be processed batch/sequential or online/direct access?
2. Describe the type of file organization used in the processing of sales orders. Why might this particular file organization have been chosen?

15

Management Information and Decision Support Systems

INTRODUCTION

For many years, computers have been used to perform routine and repetitive operations formerly done manually. Person hours are saved when functions such as payroll preparation and order writing are done by computer, but these types of applications are not especially helpful to management when it must plan for the future or control daily activities. Simply having a computer does not ensure that management has an effective information system. To achieve its full potential, the computer must be integrated with people and procedures to provide information useful in decision making.

This chapter emphasizes the decision-oriented reporting of a management information system. It discusses decision support systems and decision models and the role they currently play, and may play in the future, within an organization's management information system. The chapter also discusses the various levels of management and the information needs of each and presents several approaches to designing an information system to meet these needs.

ARTICLE

Old Inn Prospers with New System

The Hawthorne Inn, in historic Salem, Mass., goes to great lengths to recreate the comfortable atmosphere of an early American hostelry. With 89 guest rooms, a meeting space that accommodates 350, and eight smaller conference rooms, providing guests with the amenities modern travelers expect is no easy task. Without its 20th century computer, however, running the Inn would be a lot harder. It's not just a question of adding to the comfort of the guests. Even with the same occupancy rate, the controls the computer makes possible contribute to a healthier bottom line.

A new group of seasoned hoteliers has been running the Hawthorne Inn for the last two years. Unlike some of his associates, Ken Boyle, the general manager, a 20-year veteran in the industry, knew little about data processing when the group took over. The others had seen it in operation. Among them, they owned an Apple II computer and a high speed printer. Determined to keep abreast of their operation electronically, they bought a monitor to complete the installation and brought in Todd Reidel, a consultant whose First Micro Group is located in nearby Boston.

Using off-the-shelf software, Reidel set up a fully integrated budgeting system for them. Starting the job in July of 1983, he had the inn online by the beginning of September.

Reprinted by permission from the January/February 1984 issue of D & B Reports magazine, a Dunn Bradstreet publication.

What Reidel and the Apple have accomplished for the business has made a data processing fan out of Boyle. "In my previous experience, I always had trouble getting an updated list for payables and receivables," he says. "Now we can look at these things as frequently as we want to, as long as we keep updating our transactions each week, which isn't much of a job at all."

Forecasting Is Key

Running out of supplies such as towels or eggs, on the one hand, or acquiring too many of them, on the other, are the Scylla and Charybdis of the hospitality business. That's why fast forecasting is so essential to making a success of it. "Forecasting is the area where we use the computer most heavily," Boyle says. "Nothing beats having a continual look at the operation and comparing it to the forecast. From the daily results we are able to make decisions which will affect our operations. The computer updates the historical data with information about new bookings supplied by the front office. The department heads use the results to schedule purchasing and payroll."

The Apple II installation has not reduced the cadre of employees on the Inn's payroll, Boyle says, but it has permitted them to take a "systematic rather than a haphazard approach to their basic tasks. All of us have become more goal-oriented

because of it. We all have guidelines. If the housekeeper knows we are coming into a period of slow occupancy, what she should buy in sheets and pillowcases is determined for her in advance."

Like any other business manager, Boyle tries to spot trends in operations as soon as they develop. But in his previous experience, he found the details escaping him because he was so immersed in them, or they piled up too fast for him to assimilate them. "You were not able to see the expenses creeping higher than the budget or higher than the previous year, but the computer has all the information you need. All you have to do is interpret it."

Identifying Savings

How the Hawthorne Inn has monitored its energy costs is a good example of the data processor's endless ability to package information in whatever form will best serve a proprietor's needs. "We set out to reduce the heat and power factor in our overhead," Boyle says. "We had put in 242 storm window-screen combinations and contracted for some boiler improvements. In no time at all, all by myself, calling up the summary of operations from the computer, I can identify the savings in heating bills month by month. On a cumulative basis I have justified the investment."

By now, the computer has penetrated into every aspect of the Inn's busy life. It allocates costs and expenses by department, including rooms, food, beverages, phone and laundry. It provides a detailed, year-to-date consolidated income report, simultaneously boiling it down to a one-page summary. In another report on the fiscal budget, it compares actual performance with projections, permitting management to adjust to new conditions as they develop. And the banks are impressed by its crisp, professional documentation.

"Our hotel is decorated in authentic federal style with candelabras, antique ship models, oriental rugs, solid brass hardware and so forth," Boyle says. "It summons up a lot of nostalgia. But the key to making the operation work, even with all the nice ingredients, is a system that lets you carry out the job in a timely and effective manner. Thanks to the computer, we are running a traditional business in a modern way— and our results show it."

The primary goal of a management information system is to provide information to managers that is useful in making decisions. As has been proven at the Hawthorne Inn, a computerized management information system can be used to help run a business more efficiently and effectively. Management information systems, therefore, should concentrate on providing decision-oriented information in their reports.

ELEMENTS OF MANAGEMENT INFORMATION SYSTEMS

Data-processing systems are found in most organizations. Typical data-processing activities involve collecting and manipulating data to produce reports. Managers have found that, with computer help, such activities can be performed faster, more accurately, and at a lower cost than is possible otherwise. Recently, managers have recognized that the possibilities for computer use extend beyond normal reporting to generating information to support decision making. This application is known as a **management information system (MIS).** An MIS is a formal information network using computer capabilities to provide management with information necessary for making decisions. The goal of an MIS is to get the correct information to the appropriate manager at the right time.

No matter what types of operations an organization performs, its management information system must provide:

■ *Reports that are decision-oriented.* Decision-oriented reports provide information that is accurate, timely, complete, concise, and relevant. If the information does not have these characteristics, then the reports are not useful for decision making.
■ *Room for expansion and growth.* The survival and growth of an organization depends on how well it adapts to a changing environment. Therefore, the MIS must be flexible enough to handle the organization's changing needs. It should also be able to handle any increase in user requirements.
■ *Results that the user needs.* As noted above, the primary objective of an MIS is to provide management with information necessary for decision making. An MIS cannot be successful if it does not meet the users' requirements.

To better understand the concept involved in such a system, we will look separately at each element of the term *management information system.*

Management

Three levels of management generally exist within an organization, and managers at each level participate in certain characteristic decision-making activities. These levels are depicted in Figure 15–1.

Top-Level Management—Strategic Decision Making   At the top level, activities are future-oriented and involve a great deal of uncertainty. Examples include establishing goals and determining strategies to achieve the goals. Such strategies may involve introducing new product lines, determining new markets, acquiring physical facilities, setting financial policies, generating capital, and so forth.

Middle-Level Management—Tactical Decision Making   The emphasis in middle levels is on activities required to implement the strategies determined at the top level. Thus, most middle-management decision making is tactical. Activities include planning working capital, scheduling production, formulating budgets, making short-term forecasts, and administering personnel. Much of the decision making at this level pertains to control and short-run planning.

Lower-Level Management—Operational Decision Making   Members of the lowest level in the management hierarchy (first-line supervisors and foremen) make operating decisions to ensure that specific jobs are done. Activities at this level include maintaining inventory records, preparing sales invoices, determining raw material requirements, shipping orders, and assigning jobs to workers. Most of these operations are structured and the decisions are deterministic—they follow specific rules and patterns established at higher levels of management. The major function of lower-level management is controlling company results—keeping them in line with plans and taking corrective actions if necessary.

In addition to the breakdown of an organization into three management levels, there exists a breakdown of the organization by function. Each functional group generates a separate stream of information flow (see Figure 15–2). For example, one such group, the marketing department, might produce detailed sales reports for each product but might send only a summary of these reports showing divisional sales levels to middle-level marketing management. This summary report might again be summarized to show sales figures for the whole company in a report to top-level marketing management.

Figure 15–1 ▪ **Levels of Decision Making**

Information

Managers at all levels must be provided with decision-oriented information. The fact that the nature of decisions differs at the three levels creates a major difficulty for those attempting to develop an MIS: The information needs of each level differ, and the information system must be tailored to provide appropriate information to all levels.

Decisions made at the lower level are generally routine and well defined. The needs of first-level supervisors can be met by normal administrative data-processing activities such as preparation of financial statements and routine record keeping. Although this level of decision making is fairly basic, it provides the data-processing foundation for the entire organization. If the information system is faulty at this level, the organization faces an immediate crisis.

Tactical decision making is characterized by an intermediate time horizon, a high use of internal information, and significant dependence on rapid processing and retrieval of data. Many middle-level decisions are also ill structured and difficult to plan for. The major focus of tactical decisions is how to make efficient use of organizational resources.

The main problems in MIS design arise when planners attempt to define and meet the information requirements of top-level management. It is extremely difficult, if not impossible, to clearly define these information needs. Most problems are nonrepetitive, have great impact on the organization, and involve a great deal of uncertainty. Most information systems serve the needs of the two lower levels but are not adequately designed to cope with the variety of problems encountered by top management. However, well-designed management information systems can help.

Table 15–1 summarizes the differences among the three levels of decision-making. Since the information needs at the three levels differ, data has to be structured differently at each level. For routine operating decisions such as payroll preparation and replenishment of inventory, separate employee and inventory files are adequate. To serve the middle and top levels, the data should be organized to provide query capabilities across functional lines and to handle routine information reports.

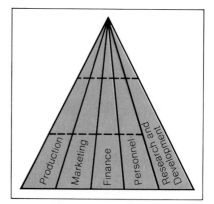

Figure 15–2 ▪ Functional Information Flow

Systems

As you may recall from Chapter 13, in a system, inputs are processed to achieve outputs; and feedback—information received by the system, either internally or externally—is used in adjusting future output. For example, in a manufacturing system, input takes the form of raw materials, which are processed by manufacturing facilities, resulting in output in the form of finished goods. Feedback occurs in the form of quality control standards and customer complaints. Processing can respond to feedback by adjusting output. These four elements are present in all systems and can thus be used to analyze them.

A business firm is composed of a multitude of such systems. By carefully integrating the data required to meet its systems' information needs, a business positions itself to cope with internal and external changes. It can compete more effectively in the marketplace because it faces fewer unknowns.

Table 15–1 ▪ Characteristic Differences in Levels of Decision Making

CHARACTERISTICS	LEVELS OF DECISION MAKING		
	Operational	Tactical	Strategic
Time Horizon	Daily	Weekly/Monthly	Yearly
Degree of Structure	High	Moderate	Low
Use of External Information	Low	Moderate	Very High
Use of Internal Information	Very High	High	Moderate/Low
Degree of Judgment	Low	Moderate	Very High
Information Online	Very High	High	Moderate
Level of Complexity	Low	Moderate	Very High
Information in Real Time	High	High	High

In almost 40 percent of the nation's restaurants, there are no waitresses taking orders to the kitchen. Instead, computerized ordering devices are now being used in many restaurants to take orders back to the kitchen. This allows waiters and waitresses to spend more time in the dining room with the customers. The American Cafe in Washington, D.C., is one restaurant using one of the new systems, The Expediter. Systems like this one allow restaurant managers to learn more about their operations. For example, the Expediter told the manager that ninety-four cups of coffee had been sold by mid-afternoon and that these sales accounted for 38.12 percent of the beverage sales. With this type of system, a restaurant manager can take stock of a certain item's popularity, adjust menus, restock inventory, and analyze sales accordingly. Because eight of ten new restaurants now fail, restaurant managers will probably look upon computers as a helpful way to improve cost control.

The designer of The Expediter, Richard W. Hayman, foresees robot arms scooping chicken into buckets in fast-food outlets within three years.

DECISION-ORIENTED REPORTING

Information Reports

Management information systems typically generate several types of reports, including scheduled listings, exception reports, predictive reports, and demand reports.

Scheduled Listings   Scheduled listings are produced at regular intervals and provide routine information to a wide variety of users. Since they are designed to provide information to many users, they tend to contain an overabundance of data. Much of it may not be relevant to a particular user. Such listings constitute most of the output of current computer-based information systems.

Exception Reports   Exception reports are action-oriented management reports. The performance of business systems is monitored, and any deviation from expected results triggers the generation of a report. Such reports can also be produced during routine batch processing. Exception reports are useful because they ignore all normal events and focus management's attention on abnormal situations that require special handling.

Predictive Reports   Predictive reports are used for planning. Future results are projected on the basis of decision models. Such models can be very simple or highly complex. Their usefulness depends on how well they can predict future events. Management can manipulate the variables included in a model to get responses to "what if" kinds of queries. Thus, such models are suited to tactical and strategic decision making.

Demand Reports   Demand reports are produced only on request. Since they are not required on a continuing basis, they are often requested and displayed through online terminals. The MIS must have an extensive and appropriately structured data base if it is to provide responses to unanticipated queries. No data base can provide everything, but the data base of a well-designed MIS should include data that may be needed to respond to such user inquiries. Providing demand reporting can be expensive, but it permits decision makers to obtain relevant and specific information at the moment they need it.

Management and MIS

Although an MIS can help management make decisions, it cannot guarantee the decisions will be successful. One problem that frequently arises is determining what information is needed by management. To many, decision making is an individual art. Experience, intuition, and chance affect the decision-making process. These inputs are all but impossible to quantify. In designing a system, the analyst should rely on the user to determine information requirements. Frequently, lacking precise ideas of what they need, managers request everything the computer can provide. The result is an overload of information. Instead of helping the manager, this information overload creates another problem—how to distinguish what is relevant from what is irrelevant.

After the MIS has been installed, management does not always consider the change beneficial. In some cases, however, the people who must use the system were not involved in the analysis and design; thus, their expectations are unrealistic. Managers frequently expect that decision making will be totally automatic after implementation of an MIS; they fail to recognize that unstructured tasks are difficult to program. Even though routine decisions (such as ordering materials when inventory stock goes below a certain point) can be programmed easily, decisions that depend on more than quantitative data require human evaluation, because the computer system has no intuitive capability.

Other problems may arise. As the computer takes over routine decisions, managers may resist further changes. They may fear that their responsibility for decision making will be reduced or that the computer will make their positions obsolete. They may fail to realize that the availability of good information can enhance their managerial performance.

The success of an MIS depends largely on the attitude and involvement of management. An MIS is most apt to be successful when it is implemented in an organization already operating on a sound basis, rather than in an organization seeking a miracle.

Concept Summary 15–1

MIS and Decision-Oriented Reporting

- In general, a **management information system (MIS)** must provide:
  (1) Reports that are decision-oriented.
  (2) Room for expansion and growth.
  (3) Results that the user needs.
- The three levels of management that generally exist within an organization and the type of decision making that they are concerned with are:
  (1) Top-level management—strategic decision making.
  (2) Middle-level management—tactical decision making.
  (3) Lower-level management—operational decision making.
- The types of reports typically generated by an MIS include: scheduled listings, exception reports, predictive reports, and demand reports.

DECISION SUPPORT SYSTEMS

Closely related to management information systems is the decision support system. A **decision support system (DSS)** provides information through computerized processes to assist managers in relatively unstructured decision-making tasks. Although DSS seems to overlap with the fundamental nature of MIS, there are some professionals in the information field who feel that a distinction must be made between the two. They claim that MIS has become associated with systems that emphasize structured or operational decisions, whereas DSS focuses on the unstructured managerial decision-making process. Others, however, feel that decision support systems are only subsystems of the larger MIS and have only recently become a reality because of technological advances in computer hardware and software.

The Purpose and Scope of a DSS

DSS separates structured (or operational) decision making from unstructured (or strategic) decision making. For example, a purchase order for a certain product may be generated automatically if an inventory stock level falls below a certain quantity. Such a structured decision can be handled by a computer.

A decision support system, on the other hand, places more emphasis on semistructured or unstructured decisions. While the computer is used as an analytical aid to decision making, the DSS does not attempt to automate the manager's decision making or impose solutions. For example, an investment manager must make recommendations to a client concerning the client's portfolio. The manager's decision is based on stock performance and requires a judgmental process. The computer can be used to aid the decision but cannot make the actual recommendation to the client.

The primary use of computer technology within decision support systems has been to speed the processing of large amounts of data which may be necessary if the manager is to consider the full effects of a possible decision. It also allows for the consideration of a greater number of alternatives by managers—alternatives which otherwise might not have been considered due to time constraints. But as previously stated, decision support systems, and within them the use of computers, must be a normal and comfortable extension of the manager's overall method of problem solving and decision making.

Advocates of DSS, therefore, claim that its emphasis is toward improving the effectiveness and quality of decision making. The purpose of the decision support concept is not to replace management information systems but to enhance them. Because advances are being made in applying computer technology to the areas of tactical and strategic decision making, the rewards that can be realized are even greater than those that have occurred in the area of operational decision making. Computer applications in the areas of tactical and strategic decision making are a logical step forward in the application of computer technology to management science and a logical addition to, and advancement in, the area of management information systems.

A Model: The Heart of a DSS

As was stated in the section on decision-oriented reporting, predictive reports are based on decision models which are used to project future results. As was also noted, such models are suited to tactical and strategic decision making, which is the focus of a DSS.

A **model** is a mathematical representation of an actual system. Although the representation may not be all inclusive, it contains independent variables (the inputs) which are the factors that determine the value of the dependent variable (the output). In the case of advertising, for example, advertising expenditures function as an independent variable while sales of the product serve as the dependent variable. This relationship implies that the ultimate value of sales is dependent on the level of advertising expenditures and could be represented by the following mathematical relationship, where sales is a function of advertising expenditures:

$$\text{SALES} = f(\text{ADVERTISING EXPENDITURES}).$$

This relationship could then be expressed as a mathematical equation which would represent the relationship between advertising expenditures and sales.

The manager who will be using the decision support system should be responsible for the development of the model. The model, therefore, will represent the manager's perception of the real-world system. Since the model is developed by the manager, it is based on his or her judgment of how the system works and also on the experience the manager has gained in his or her contact with the system.

It is the fact that each manager must have a decision model based on his or her perception of the system that has made the implementation of decision support systems so difficult. Managerial styles, as well as the environments in which people manage, are unique to nearly each and every manager; and in order for the DSS to be useful, it must be designed to aid a manager in his or her particular decision-making style.

Commercial Planning Packages

There are a number of commercial software packages available that allow a manager to interactively probe a computerized model for results concerning various decision alternatives. The fact that a computerized model can be used in an interactive fashion is consistent with the goal of a decision support system—aiding the manager in making decisions in a manner compatible with his or her decision-making processes. Some packages that are available in the area of marketing and include a predefined model include: ADBUDG, which models the advertising expenditure, product price, and market share to sales relationship; MARKETPLAN and BRANDAID, which help in preparing marketing plans; CALLPLAN and DETAILER, which aid in the allocation of a sales force; and MEDIAC, which helps to prepare advertising media schedules. The major disadvantage of these types of commercial packages is the fact that a model has already been incorporated within the system, thus precluding the manager's valuable input to the model's development.

An alternative to the packages mentioned above is the Interactive Financial Planning System (IFPS). IFPS is a planning, or modeling, package that is interactive and centers around a model based on a manager's perception of the real-world system. IFPS, marketed by EXECUCOM Systems Corporation, can be considered a generalized planning or modeling system. As a generalized system, IFPS can be used for such applications as balance sheet and income statement preparation, operating budgets, forecasting, strategic planning, risk analysis, and capital budgeting. Because IFPS does not incorporate a specific model, it offers management a great deal of flexibility.

Figure 15–3 illustrates a simple example using IFPS. A model titled AD-SALES, which represents one possible relationship between advertising expenditures and product sales, has been entered into the system and can be listed to verify its contents. Line 10 of the model indicates the columns of data within the model. Line 50 contains the model, which uses three independent variables: the advertising budget from two years ago (line 20), the budget from last year (line 30), and the potential budget for this year (line 40), about which a decision must be made. Based on the three independent variables, the dependent variable—budgeted sales—is estimated to be $35,222,582, the amount displayed in the report produced using IFPS.

Although currently available only for microcomputers, commercial pack-

Figure 15–3 ▪ Sample IFPS Session

```
@IFPS
INTERACTIVE FINANCIAL PLANNING SYSTEM - 9.0 DP
ENTER NAME OF FILE CONTAINING MODELS AND REPORTS
? ADSALES
FILE ADSALES PROCESSED
READY FOR EXECUTIVE COMMAND
? MODEL ADSALES
READY FOR EDIT, LAST LINE IS 50
? LIST
^L
MODEL ADSALES   VERSION OF  07/28/84  10:53
10 COLUMNS 1985
15 *
20 BUDGET TWO YEARS AGO = 43283400
25 *
30 BUDGET LAST YEAR = 64036300
35 *
40 BUDGETED EXPENDITURES = 75003000
45 *
50 BUDGETED SALES = .999764 + (.582415 * L40) - (.17528 * L30) + (.06385 * L20)
END OF MODEL
? SOLVE
MODEL ADSALES  VERSION OF  07/28/84  10:53 - 1 COLUMNS 4 VARIABLES
ENTER SOLVE OPTIONS
? GENREPORT RPSALES
```

```
                              Shrock Brewing Company
                           Advertising Budgeting Model
                                    (for 1985)

                                     08/19/84

                                                      1985


        BUDGET TWO YEARS AGO                  $ 43,283,400
        BUDGET LAST YEAR                      $ 64,036,300
        BUDGETED EXPENDITURES                 $ 75,003,000

        BUDGETED SALES                        $ 35,222,582
```

ages such as VISICALC and MULTIPLAN can be used in a similar fashion as IFPS. These types of packages, known as spreadsheets (see Chapter 12), also permit a model to be entered and the values of variables changed to determine the outcome of a potential decision. These packages are also capable of generating reports.

Simulation

Using a decision model to gain insight into the workings of an actual system is referred to as **simulation.** Used to identify key variables, analyze the effects of changing key variables, and identify optimal solutions for decision alternatives, simulation can eliminate the need to experiment with a real-world system. Assuming that the decision model closely resembles the real-world system, simulation using a decision support system can be a great aid to both the manager and the organization as a whole.

Sensitivity Analysis   One method of simulation is referred to as sensitivity analysis. **Sensitivity analysis** uses the decision support system, incorporating the decision model, to determine how the variables of the real-world system affect its ultimate outcome. Sensitivity analysis is an attempt to identify those sensitive, or key, variables that warrant management's attention. Once key variables are found, sensitivity analysis can be used to evaluate the effect the alteration of a key variable will have on the ultimate outcome of a real world system. Figure 15–4 demonstrates how altering advertising expenditures from a base of $70,000,000 within a range of −4 percent to 4 percent in 2 percent increments, can be used to determine the effect advertising expenditures have on budgeted sales.

"What If" Analysis   Another form of simulation is "what if" analysis. **"What if" analysis** allows the manager to interactively process various decision alternatives, quickly exploring the possible outcomes of these alternatives. In cases where models consist of more than one key variable, it may be useful to use "what if" analysis to isolate a variable that appears to greatly affect the output of a system and then use sensitivity analysis to probe the effects of a

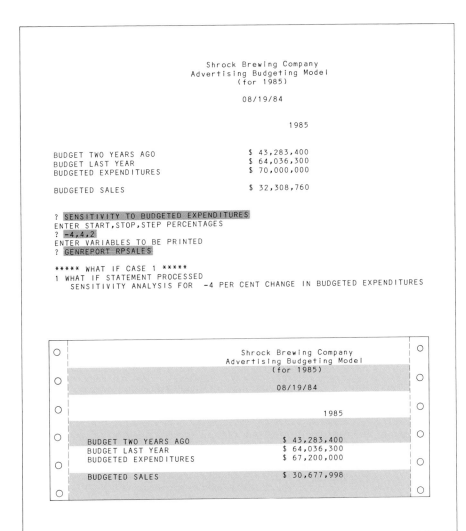

Figure 15–4 ▪ Sensitivity Analysis Example (continued on next page)

Figure 15—4 ■ **(Continued)**

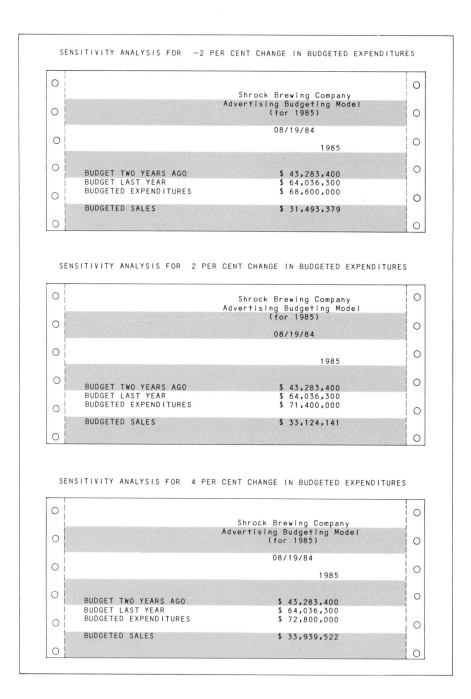

range of the variable's values. Figure 15—5 demonstrates the use of "what if" analysis using the sales-to-advertising-expenditure model.

Goal Seeking A third method of simulation is goal seeking. **Goal seeking** allows the manager to select an independent variable that can be altered to achieve a given output from the decision model. The manager specifies the desired output and the decision support system then determines the value of the independent variable necessary to achieve the desired goal. For example, this method allows the manager to specify the desired level of sales, and the decision support system, using the relationship expressed in the decision

Figure 15–5 ▪ "What If" Analysis
Example

```
? MODEL ADSALES
READY FOR EDIT, LAST LINE IS 50
? WHAT IF
MODEL ADSALES   VERSION OF  07/28/84  10:53 - 1 COLUMNS 4 VARIABLES
WHAT IF CASE 1
ENTER STATEMENTS
? BUDGETED EXPENDITURES = 70000000
? SOLVE
ENTER SOLVE OPTIONS
? GENREPORT RPSALES


***** WHAT IF CASE 1 *****
1 WHAT IF STATEMENT PROCESSED
```

```
                    Shrock Brewing Company
                    Advertising Budgeting Model
                          (for 1985)

                           08/19/84


                             1985


    BUDGET TWO YEARS AGO          $ 43,283,400
    BUDGET LAST YEAR              $ 64,036,300
    BUDGETED EXPENDITURES         $ 70,000,000

    BUDGETED SALES                $ 32,308,760
```

model, calculates the level of advertising expenditures needed to achieve the sales goal. This method is illustrated in Figure 15–6.

The methods of simulation discussed enable the manager to alter the values of the model in order to gain greater understanding of the modeled relationship and to evaluate the results associated with alternative decisions. Using these options, the manager can explore a number of alternatives in a short period of time. With this added insight to the effect changes in variables will have, the manager's decision-making ability should be enhanced considerably.

Figure 15–6 ▪ Goal Seeking
Example

```
? MODEL ADSALES
READY FOR EDIT, LAST LINE IS 50
? GOAL SEEKING
GOAL SEEKING CASE 1
ENTER NAME OF VARIABLE(S) TO BE ADJUSTED TO ACHIEVE PERFORMANCE
? BUDGETED EXPENDITURES
ENTER 1 COMPUTATIONAL STATEMENT(S) FOR PERFORMANCE
? BUDGETED SALES = 36000000


***** WHAT IF CASE 1 *****
1 WHAT IF STATEMENT PROCESSED


***** GOAL SEEKING CASE 1 *****

                         1985

BUDGETED EXPENDITURES = 76337818
```

- A **decision support system (DSS)** is a portion of the overall MIS and is designed to improve the effectiveness and quality of decision making.
- A **model** is the heart of a DSS and is a mathematical representation of an actual system.
- **Simulation** is the process of using a DSS to gain insight into the workings of an actual system.
- **Sensitivity analysis** is a form of simulation that attempts to identify sensitive, or key, variables within a model.
- **"What if"** analysis allows a manager to interactively process a number of decision alternatives, quickly exploring their outcomes.
- **Goal seeking** permits a manager to specify the desired outcome of a model. In doing so the DSS provides him or her with the required value of a variable needed to achieve the desired outcome.

The Future of DSS

Management   One of the key factors, if not the key factor, in the acceptance of decision support systems within business is management. How management of a company views modeling and decision support systems is the critical factor that determines whether they are successfully implemented and used or not. Although decision modeling is used in a large number of firms, it must still overcome obstacles such as management resistance, a lack of management sophistication, and interdepartmental communication problems if its full potential is to be realized.

It is felt that the acceptance and use of decision modeling and decision support systems in business is being slowed by the resistance of top management. A skeptical attitude toward scientific management techniques and unwillingness to accept and have confidence in these techniques often slows or even prevents the implementation of decision support systems. In addition, management is also sensitive to a situation in which the promise of what can be done with computers is far different from that which is finally accomplished. Before management will fully accept the use of computers and decision support systems, promises of what can be accomplished must be realistic. Until these promises can be realized, management's willingness to accept new decision-making aids will be hindered.

Simultaneous DSS   Until now decision support systems have been discussed in a functional context. Each functional area of an organization may have its own DSS. In the past ten years, however, there have been movements made toward what are referred to as **simultaneous decision support systems,** or **corporate planning models.** The primary goal of simultaneous decision support systems has been to combine into one system the various functional areas of an organization which affect the performance and output of other functional areas. The marketing areas of a firm, for instance, must coordinate their advertising and sales efforts with that of production to insure that the demand generated for a product can be met.

Organizations have come to realize that consistent, overall strategic planning is required if the organization is to survive in a dynamic environment. For this reason, firms are attempting to develop simultaneous decision support systems which can coordinate the functional areas of a corporation as well as aid the organization's strategic and tactical planners. Figure 15–7 illustrates a possible structure for a simultaneous decision support system.

Although the number of organizations using simultaneous decision support systems or corporate planning models is relatively few, there is little doubt that the future of decision support systems lies in this direction. Further advances must be made in the areas of decision model development and applying computer technology to managerial decision making, however, before simultaneous decision support systems will gain widespread acceptance and use. Once decision modeling and decision support technology have become common and widely accepted, it only seems logical to progress in the direction of simultaneous decision support systems.

DESIGN ALTERNATIVES

The development of a management information system is an integrated approach to organizing a company's activities. The company's MIS must be structured in a way that will allow it to fully realize the benefits of integration. When considering alternative MIS designs, the analyst faces virtually unlimited possibilities. When conducting the system analysis, the systems analyst should consider the organizational structure because it will be a critical factor in choosing an overall system design. The MIS should be designed to take full advantage of integration, but must also fit in to the organizational structure if it is to be successful. This section describes four basic design structures: centralized, hierarchical, distributed, and decentralized. These structures should be viewed as checkpoints along a continuous range of design alternatives rather than as separate, mutually exclusive options. For example, a system design may incorporate attributes from both the distributed system

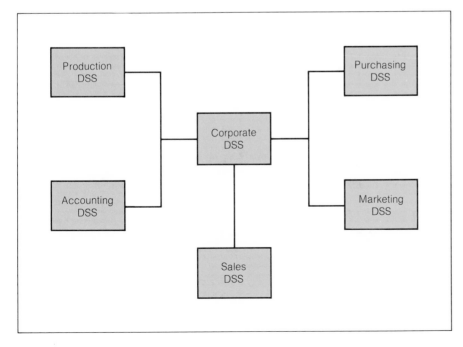

Figure 15–7 ■ **Possible Framework for Simultaneous Decision Support Systems**

and the decentralized system. Whatever design is used, the resulting MIS system must meet the needs of the organization it is to serve.

Centralized Design

The most traditional design approach involves the centralization of computer power. A separate electronic data-processing (EDP) department is set up to provide data-processing facilities for the organization; this department's personnel, like other staff personnel, support the operating units of the organization. All program development, as well as all equipment acquisition, is controlled by the EDP group. Standard regulations and procedures are employed. Distant units use the centralized equipment through remote access via a communication network. A common data base exists, permitting authorized users to access information (see Figure 15−8a).

Figure 15−8 ▪ Sample Design Structures

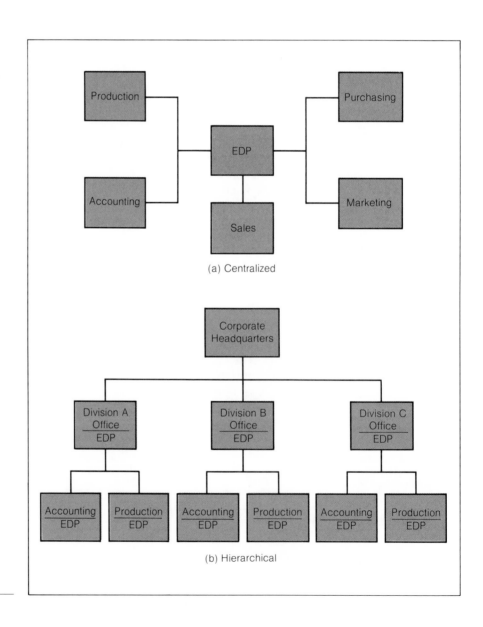

(a) Centralized

(b) Hierarchical

The advantages of the centralized approach are that it permits economies of scale, eliminates redundancy and duplication of data, and results in efficient utilization of data-processing capability. However, a centralized design is not always best suited to all divisions of an organization. Response to division needs is generally slow because priorities are assigned based on overall organizational needs. Also, many managers prefer to control their own data-processing needs; they are reluctant to relinquish authority to a central EDP staff group.

Hierarchical Design

When hierarchical design is used, the organization consists of multiple levels with varying degrees of responsibility and decision-making authority. In addition, the organization may have functional subdivisions based on geograph-

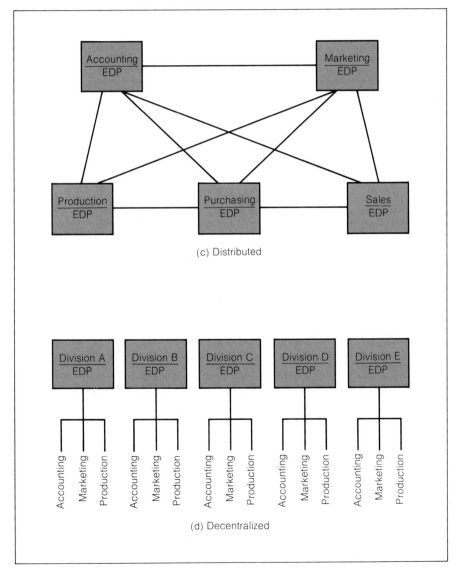

(c) Distributed

(d) Decentralized

Figure 15–8 ▪ (Continued)

A computerized dating service for horses? With data-base management software, Brad Baker of Moondrift Farms, a Colorado horsebreeding ranch, matches horses.

Detailed information is kept on all horses at the ranch. This information includes how many times a mare has been bred, what she's been fed, and even information on the mare's personality traits. Information such as this increases the success of the system because a mare's traits can be more easily matched to an appropriate stallion.

Brad has a similar program for stallions. This system makes it easy for mare owners to check any stallion's background.

Other programs that Brad has set up include a medical history program for his horses and even a program to keep track of repair work that needs to be done on the farm's equipment.

ical considerations. Information flows among the various levels of management. Requests for information come down the levels, and summarized information flows up. Communication among the subdivisions is limited.

In hierarchical design, each management level is given the computer power necessary to support its task objectives. At the lowest level, limited support is required, because the work is considered technical in nature. Middle-level support is more extensive, because managerial decisions at this level require more complicated analysis (hence, more information processing). Finally, top-level executives seek little detailed information. They deal with general issues, requiring information that can be obtained only with greater processing and storage capabilities.

Data bases are usually segregated along regional or functional lines. The data bases at each level may or may not be standardized. Communication among levels is essential, but the line of responsibility for computer systems is normally traced through several levels rather than handled within all levels of the organization. The tendency, then, is for the largest group of people and machines—those at the top level—to assume responsibility for coordination and control. An example of this design approach is shown in Figure 15–8b.

Distributed Design

The distributed design approach identifies the existence of independent operating units but recognizes the benefits of central coordination and control. The organization is broken into the smallest activity centers requiring computer support. These centers may be based on organizational structure, geographical location, functional operations, or a combination of these factors. Hardware (and often people) are placed within these activity centers to support their tasks. Total organization-wide control is often evidenced by the existence of standardized classes of hardware, common data bases, and coordinated system development. The distributed computer sites may or may not share data elements, workload, and resources, depending on whether or not they are in communication with each other. An example of the distributed design approach is given in Figure 15–8c.

Decentralized Design

In a decentralized design, authority and responsibility for computer support are placed in relatively autonomous organizational operating units. These units usually parallel the management decision-making structure. Normally, no central control point exists; the authority for computer operations goes directly to the managers in charge of the operating units. Since there is no central control, each unit is free to acquire hardware, develop software, and make personnel decisions independently. Responsiveness to user needs is normally high because close working relationships are reinforced by the proximity of the system to its users. Communication among units is limited or nonexistent, thereby ruling out the possibility of common or shared applications. This design approach can only be used where an existing organizational structure supports decentralized management. Further, it is not highly compatible with the management information system concept. An example of the decentralized design approach is shown in Figure 15–8d.

SUMMARY POINTS

■ A management information system (MIS) is a formal information network that uses computer capabilities to provide management with information necessary for decision making. The goal of an MIS is to get the correct information to the appropriate manager at the right time. The MIS should produce reports that are decision-oriented, have room for expansion and future growth, and contain results that the user needs.

■ The concept of an MIS involves three elements—management, information, and systems. The management element includes three levels of management, each with its own level of decision making: (1) Top-level management handles strategic decisions, (2) middle-level management handles tactical decisions, and (3) lower-level management handles operational decisions.

■ The information element of an MIS differs at each level of management. Because of these differences, the data must be organized and defined differently at each level to meet managers' information needs. Data is filtered at each level to provide summarized reports for use in higher-level decision making.

■ The system element operates as a cycle; inputs are processed to achieve outputs, and feedback affects future processing. Feedback is an output that is entered into the system as an input to control future events.

■ An MIS typically generates four kinds of reports: (1) scheduled listings, produced at regular intervals; (2) exception reports, generated when deviations from expected results occur; (3) predictive reports, used to project future outcomes; and (4) demand reports, which answer random requests for information.

■ Decision support systems emphasize effective decision making. Managers in strategic areas are provided with relevant information to help them make decisions. Support is provided for tasks which are not routine or structured. To be most useful, the decision support system should be compatible with the manager's decision-making processes.

■ The use of computers within decision support systems has primarily been to help speed the manager's analysis of decision alternatives.

■ A decision model acts as the heart of a decision support system. It is a mathematical representation of an actual system. The model should be developed by the manager who will use it so that it represents his or her perception of the actual system.

■ Simulation is the method used by managers to gain insight into the workings of a system; it employs a decision model to identify key variables, analyze the effects of changing key variables, and identify optimal solutions for decision alternatives. Three types of simulation include sensitivity analysis, "what if" analysis, and goal seeking.

■ A key factor in the acceptance of decision support systems within business is top managements' opinions of the value of DSS and decision modeling.

■ The future of DSS may lie in simultaneous decision support systems or corporate planning models, which are decision support systems designed to coordinate decision making within an entire organization.

■ The ways in which an MIS can be designed within the structure of an organization are virtually unlimited. Common approaches are centralized, hierarchical, distributed, and decentralized structures.

■ The centralized approach generally uses a single computer department to provide data processing for the entire organization.

■ In the hierarchical approach, each management level is given the computer power needed to support its task objectives.

■ In the distributed approach, computer support is placed in key activity centers, and information may be shared among the various functions.

■ In the decentralized approach, authority and responsibility for computer support are placed in relatively autonomous organizational units.

REVIEW QUESTIONS

1. Describe the type of information that should be provided by decision-oriented reports. What level(s) of management benefit most from this type of information?

2. What levels of management exist in a typical organization? What are the information requirements at each level? What are some difficulties for the MIS attempting to supply needed information to each level?

3. Briefly explain how tactical decision making differs from strategic decision making, and how operational decision making differs from strategic decision making.

4. Based on what you know about strategic decision making and what you have read about microcomputers, how do you think a microcomputer could be best used to serve the needs of a top-level manager?

5. Identify the types of reports an MIS generates. Describe the uses of each type of report and show, by examples, where each could be utilized.

6. In developing an MIS, who do you think is the most important individual or group? What role should this individual or group play in developing the MIS, and at what point should they be brought into the system development process?

7. What is a decision support system (DSS)? How does it differ from an MIS?

8. What is the purpose of a DSS? How should it interact with the manager who is using it?

9. What is a decision model? Is a model an exact replication of an actual system? Why, or why not?

10. Based on what you have read about software packages in general, what are some possible advantages and disadvantages associated with commercial planning packages versus planning packages developed in-house?

11. What are the three types of simulation discussed in the chapter? How do they differ from one another?

12. Contrast the distributed with the centralized MIS design alternative. Which of them is likely to be more responsive to user needs?

APPLICATION

Ford Motor Company

Since 1903, Ford Motor Company has grown from a tiny operation in a converted Detroit wagon factory to a multinational enterprise with more than 300,000 stockholders. Today, Ford serves tens of millions of customers throughout the United States and overseas. It is one of the world's largest industrial enterprises, with revenues totalling $44.5 billion and assets exceeding $24 billion; it is also the second largest auto company in the world.

Ford Motor Company entered the age of computers in 1955. Today there is data-processing equipment in every division plant, both in the United States and abroad. More than 400 computers are used for business applications; they vary in size and capacity and are supplied by a number of manufacturers, including IBM, Hewlett-Packard, Honeywell, Burroughs, Univac, and Amdahl. More than 1,500 computers are used in the industrial control area; most of them are minicomputers supplied by Control Data, Digital Equipment Corporation, and Hewlett-Packard. Corporate-wide, data processing at Ford involves more than 2,600 system analysts, programmers, and operations researchers and almost 2,400 personnel in computer operations; more than 2,500 systems; and more than 50,000 individual computer programs.

The Ford Communications and Data-Processing Center in Dearborn, Michigan, one of the largest such centers in private industry, houses large-scale computers to provide data-processing services to the company's Dearborn-area facilities. The center also is the headquarters for Ford's world-wide communication activities; a network of terminals connected to its communications processor transmits thousands of messages per day throughout the world.

Successful applications of computers in all phases of the company's activities range from product development to management control. With the aid of the computer, Ford analyzes market data to monitor customers' reactions to present products and to suggest possible product improvements to meet the changing needs of its customers. In the area of product design and devel-

opment, body-design engineers use a computer-directed scanner to translate the dimensions of clay models into digital coordinates. For capacity and product planning, a computer forecasting model projects total car and truck demand several years into the future. For production planning, a computer makes monthly forecasts of orders by body styles, options, and option combinations.

The development of computer systems has helped Ford management to improve operations related to the crucial area of customer service. By developing dealer-oriented applications close to the retail level, management can more efficiently control and monitor sales and inventory. For example, efficient parts service in an operation as extensive as Ford's is vital to customer service. Computer communication systems have improved parts service to dealers and independent service facilities. Dealers (more than 5,600 Ford and Lincoln-Mercury dealers and 1,500 independent distributors) cannot be expected to stock the 200,000 different parts needed to service all Ford vehicle products sold in the United States. Therefore, a system has been developed to allow dealers to order and receive parts as quickly as possible and at the same time allow corporate management to control inventory.

Figure 15–9 shows the flow of a parts order originated by any of the approximately 35 million customers

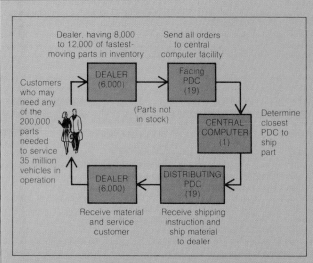

Dealer, having 8,000 to 12,000 of fastest-moving parts in inventory

Send all orders to central computer facility

Customers who may need any of the 200,000 parts needed to service 35 million vehicles in operation

DEALER (6,000)

Facing PDC (19)

(Parts not in stock)

CENTRAL COMPUTER (1)

Determine closest PDC to ship part

DEALER (6,000)

DISTRIBUTING PDC (19)

Receive material and service customer

Receive shipping instruction and ship material to dealer

Figure 15–9 ▪ Ford's Volume of Customers, Dealers, and Parts Distribution Centers

who own Ford-built vehicles in operation. Each dealer stocks from 8,000 to 12,000 parts and must depend on the Ford parts distribution system to replenish this inventory as well as to ship parts not normally stocked. Dealers are serviced by nineteen Parts Distribution Centers (PDCs) across the nation. The PDCs' inventories are based on a hierarchical stocking pattern, with the fastest-moving parts stocked at the greatest number of locations. Ten of the PDCs each stock from 14,000 to 15,000 of the fastest-moving parts. Eight other PDCs each stock from 30,000 to 40,000 different parts; stock is made up of the fastest-moving inventory as well as the inventory that moves at an intermediate speed. One PDC carries inventories of the slowest-moving parts. Each dealer places all parts orders in the same manner, even though the parts may be shipped from any one of the nineteen centers.

A system has been developed by the Ford Parts and Service Division to get parts from PDCs to dealers quickly. The system was designed in-house and has been in use for over fourteen years. Distributed processing capabilities allow an individual dealer to order any part from the closest PDC by use of a specialized input terminal; the PDC computer then transmits the order to the Central Order Processing System in Dearborn. Mail orders and phone orders requiring expediting or special assistance are processed by a Centralized Order Processing Center (See Figure 15–10). The Order Processing Center personnel utilize interactive computer terminals to follow up on orders in process, check stock availability, and enter order data in the Central Order Processing System. The Order

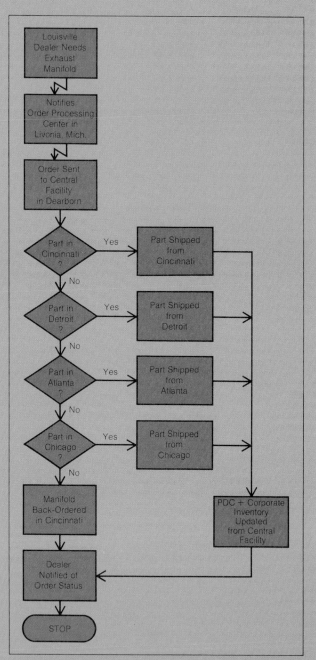

Figure 15–10 ▪ The Four-Step Logical Order Pattern for an Interim Order

Processing Center and the Order Processing System are centered around a data base located at the central facility. This data base is accessed to determine the location from which each ordered part should be sent.

An individual dealer has four ordering alternatives (see Table 15–2):

TABLE 15–2 ■ Ordering Alternatives

ORDER CONDITION	INCENTIVE	PART LOCATION SEARCH
Weekly stock order	5% discount	First normal stocking PDC
Interim order	No discount	Up to four closest stocking PDCs
Priority order	10% surcharge	Up to 19 PDCs
Inoperative vehicle order	10% surcharge	Up to 19PDCs; if nationally out of stock, refer to parts merchandiser

1. A weekly stock order. The stock supply normally ordered is replenished, and a 5 percent incentive discount is received.

2. An interim order. Parts are shipped every other day, and no discount is received.

3. A priority order. Parts are shipped within twenty-four hours, and a surcharge must be paid.

4. Inoperable vehicle order. Parts are shipped within 24 hours and a surcharge must be paid. Manual part sourcing is invoked if no stock is available.

Each type of order requires that a different search pattern be carried out against the data in the data base. For example, filling an interim order involves following a logical order pattern established in the data base for each dealer. When a dealer orders a part, the warehouse and transportation combination that can most economically supply the part is determined. If the part is not available at the closest location that normally stocks it, a computer search is made at the three next-closest stocking locations. If the part is not available at any of them, it is placed on a back-order at the closest location that normally stocks it.

If, for example, a Ford dealer in Louisville, Kentucky, needs an exhaust manifold for a 1980 Mustang, that dealer notifies the Order Processing Center (see Figure 15–10). From the Order Processing Center the order is transmitted to the Ford Parts and Service central computer facility in Dearborn; the central computer searches the data base and finds the PDC closest to the Louisville dealer that has the part. If the Cincinnati PDC normally stocks these exhaust manifolds, it is the first logical stocking location for the Louisville dealer. If the part is there, it is shipped. The master part file is updated to show the shipment of one exhaust manifold from the Cincinnati PDC. If the Cincinnati PDC is temporarily out of the part, the central system examines the master file for the exhaust manifold in the Detroit PDC, the next closest shipping location. Again, if the part is located, it is shipped, and the master file is updated. If it is still not located, the central computer examines the Atlanta PDC's inventory position for this part. If the part is located, the normal procedure occurs. If not, the procedure is repeated once again for Chicago. If the exhaust manifold is not found during the computer search of the fourth location, it is put on a back-order at the PDC in Cincinnati. The entire search process is done in a fraction of a second.

When the part has been located, the dealer's facing PDC in Cincinnati sends him a hard-copy listing to show that the part has been ordered and to identify the location from which it will be shipped. The central facility processes the order and updates the inventory for the PDC from which the part is being shipped as well as quantitatively controlling corporate inventory.

The system was designed for real-time operation to help dealers get out-of-stock parts quickly. It is also used for normal stock reordering; and by maintaining an inventory record of each part stored at each center, it provides up-to-date inventory information to management as well. An up-to-the-minute report can be generated to show exactly which parts, and how many of each, are in stock at any distribution center.

DISCUSSION POINTS

1. How could the parts-ordering system be used as a management tool for corporate decision making?

2. What benefits do individual Ford dealers derive from this system?

SECTION V
COMPUTERS IN SOCIETY

16

The Impact of Computers on People and Organizations

INTRODUCTION

Computers, although incapable of conventional thought and feeling, greatly affect our personal lives and the world in which we live. Because of computer technology, the way in which we live has changed drastically in recent history. The computer revolution has come with an impact that has been felt by individuals and organizations alike. While viewed on the whole as greatly beneficial, the computer revolution has had some negative effects on people and organizations.

This chapter will discuss a portion of the impact the computer has had on both our individual lives and on organizations and their struggle to survive in an ever-changing environment. The behavioral aspects of the impact of computers will be discussed, as will the nature of their impact on organizations in business, industry, and government. The chapter will also review some of the effects the computer has had on the office environment by exploring office automation. This chapter is by no means comprehensive. It is simply a review of a portion of the sweeping effect computers have had on our lives and our society.

ARTICLE

The Computer Backlash

Rod A. Scher

Andy Rooney, the radio commentator known for his wry insights into everyday life, recently told a nationwide audience that he has decided "not to become computer literate."

Using a now-familiar analogy, Rooney said that he has no idea how to build a car, and indeed has no desire to. It is enough that he can climb in his automobile, turn the key, and travel from one place to another. When the car is in need of repair, he can take it to an auto mechanic. Why, then, he wondered, does he need to know how a computer works?

From an entirely different sector we have the comments of Dr. Joseph Weizenbaum, noted professor of computer technology. In a recent interview, Weizenbaum said that technology "becomes dangerous when it becomes imperialistic; that is, when it takes over domains that aren't properly its own." He describes the drive toward computer literacy as an invention designed to sell an essentially unnecessary product, and compares his understanding of the term to the telephone: "People can use their phones perfectly without being 'telephone literate' in the sense of understanding what goes on at the exchange."

Rooney and Weizenbaum are just two proponents of the rising opposition to the campaign for computer literacy. What has brought on this backlash? Why do Rooney and Weizenbaum say the things they do?

Two basic misunderstandings, I think, feed their dark view of computers and computing: first, a misreading of the term "computer literacy," and second, a fear that it is something that will be force-fed to everyone, regardless of their interest or lack thereof.

What Computer Literacy Is

Though "computer literacy" has become a familiar buzzword, not to mention a powerful selling tool in the hands of computer and software manufacturers, it still means many different things to different people. To my mind, Rooney's and Weizenbaum's definition of the phrase is a distorted one. Though at first glance their car and phone analogies seem to hold up perfectly, a more careful examination reveals quite a different conclusion.

Few educators would suggest that all students become qualified auto mechanics. Classes exist for those who desire a sophisticated knowledge in that field, but those skills are not *required*. However, we do demand that students learn to *control* automative technology—to comply with the law, to increase the likelihood that this technology will be operated safely, and, most simply, to enable themselves to get quickly and easily from here to there.

Likewise, computer literacy is a familiarity with a device that enhances one's ability to live in and cope with the modern world. Like

driving and telephone skills, it should not be required of students, but as it becomes clearer and clearer that knowing the capabilities of the computer can be useful, it should become clear, also, that a need exists for opportunities to learn that skill.

What Computer Literacy Isn't

All of this does not mean, however, students should acquire the ability to program, but rather *the ability to manipulate computer technology*. While this skill may imply a minimal understanding of the manner in which the technology functions, it certainly does not require sophisticated programming knowledge.

As an accurate example of what computer literacy is (as well as what it isn't), consider the writing of this article. Rough drafts were produced on a computer using a piece of software called a word processor. Word processing allows almost effortless correcting, editing, and revision. In spite of the fact that I have some programming experience, I have nowhere near the expertise required to write the program I am using at this very moment. Further, I am not at all sure that I wish to engage in the intellectual exercise required to acquire that expertise. But I am literate enough to use the program someone has created for me.

There are many other examples. Recently Larry, a fellow teacher, came to me with a problem. He had with him a "test bank" of over 900 test and quiz questions he used in his science classes.

For a number of years, Larry had engaged in a practice commonly used by teachers in all disciplines. Prior to a test, he would thumb through the 100 or so pages of test questions, noting those he felt would be useful. He would then photocopy every page that contained one of the desired questions, cut and paste, and then once again photocopy to make a "master" test. Larry reasoned that there had to be an easier way, and he was right.

Intrigued by the problem, I began to see that there was a relatively simple solution. A few days later I had written a program called "testbank" that, in addition to storing questions and answers, allows the teacher to:

- add, delete, or change questions;
- use an index containing answers and difficulty levels;
- retrieve specific questions;
- have the computer generate any number of random questions;
- receive a printout of any or all data stored.

Larry has happily revised his procedures, and other teachers in the school will soon be following suit.

This case helps to illustrate the dichotomy between the ability to program and the ability to use a computer. Larry could not write the program needed to accomplish what he had in mind. However, Larry is computer literate in the sense that he is aware of possible uses of the technology. Having some background, he understands many of the potential uses and limitations of this technology. And, since most recent programs do at least a fair job of guiding the novice, Larry is more than capable of sitting at a keyboard and using a program someone else has written.

Larry may never become computer literate as the phrase is now being misused by many of us; that is, he may forever remain unable to write a program like "testbank." Like Larry, I may remain unable to write a truly sophisticated program such as the word processor I am now using. The real point of computer literacy is that neither of us is required to. It is enough that we can use the technology; we are not, and should not be,

required to possess an ability to program.

The drive toward computer literacy should not be seen as a headlong rush to create an entire nation of programmers. Instead, it is an attempt to ensure that we are capable of using those resources made available to us by emerging technology.

Andy Rooney, who used a word processor to write the column in which he celebrated his illiteracy, failed in his mission. He is already supremely computer literate as the phrase should be understood.

Computer literacy backlash is one of the more important behavioral aspects of how computers affect people and organizations. Computer literacy, computer anxiety, job displacement and retraining, and changes in the workspace are key behavioral issues that we must deal with nearly every day. It is important, therefore, that we, as a society, come to grips with what is truly meant by these terms.

BEHAVIORAL ASPECTS

Computer Anxiety

The rush, in recent history, to computerize has created a group of people who fear the effects computers have on their lives and society in general. Those who have this fear are said to be suffering from **computer anxiety** or **computerphobia.** In many cases these individuals are intimidated by computers. Business managers not familiar with computers, for example, fear that if they were to make a mistake and press the wrong button, valuable information would be destroyed. A fear of computers also results when people fear the loss of jobs due to computerization.

The overwhelming amount of jargon associated with the use of computers also leads to computer anxiety. Terms such as bits, bytes, 256K ROM, CPU, disk drives, emulators, and networks can be confusing and intimidating to the computer novice.

Another type of computer anxiety is thought to be gender related. Recent studies on women in computer fields, however, have shown that women can compete with men on equal ground in computer-related jobs. Genevieve Cerf, an instructor in electrical engineering at Columbia University, has found that women tend to make better programmers than do men. Studies have found that women are generally more organized, more verbal, and more likely to consider the end user when writing computer programs. Studies by biologists and psychologists also suggest that women are better than men at skills that depend on the left hemisphere of the brain—communication and logic skills. Logic skills, in particular, are essential to computer programming.

One of the more obvious benefits for women who obtain a computer science degree and enter the field is pay. According to a recent National Science Foundation study, women with computer science degrees earn nearly 100 percent of the salary that men holding a similar position earn. This fact may seem trivial; however, in some occupations women earn as little as 59 cents for every dollar earned by a man in a similar position. Equal pay draws much attention and may be one reason why women account for 26 percent of computer professionals. The National Science Foundation reported in 1980 that there were 90,200 female computer specialists—an increase of 44 percent from 1978. This suggests that women were just beginning to enter the computer area in force.

Age, too, is a factor that contributes to computerphobia. Those who grew up in an environment largely unaffected by computer technology tend to resist the role computers now play in society. Those who are more familiar with computers and have had much more contact with computers in their lives, on the other hand, tend to accept the role that computers play and are more willing to accept further advances in computer use as commonplace. This fear of the continuing advancement of computers into our lives—a fear of the unfamiliar—is often referred to as high tech anxiety. High tech anxiety is more predominant among older people, who have had limited contact with the computer in general.

Another type of computer anxiety is depersonalization. To many people, the use of a computer for such things as record keeping and billing often leads to a feeling of being treated as a number rather than as a person. This factor of impersonalization has led many people to develop negative attitudes concerning computers.

Computer Literacy

There is currently no standard definition of **computer literacy.** Most people, however, feel that being comfortable with using computers to solve problems of both an academic and a personal nature is important. This implies, therefore, that students need a knowledge of basic programming techniques and the functions of various hardware components. To prepare students for a highly technical society, computer literacy courses have been designed to meet these needs.

One goal of high school computer literacy courses is to give students an understanding of how computers work; for example, students examine microprocessor chips or circuit boards and take apart hand calculators, digital watches, and computer games. This way they learn to identify the parts of a computer; they can also follow the path that electricity takes and see firsthand the practical need for and use of the binary number system. Often, computer literacy courses also examine the effect of computers on society. Knowing the history of computers, examples of current uses, and projected future trends are all important to understanding how computers are changing our lives.

The importance of computer literacy was evidenced by the proposal introduced by the Federal Commission on Excellence in Education in May 1983 to implement new guidelines to stem the "rising tide of mediocrity" in our society. Among these guidelines was a suggestion that all students be required to take a half-year of computer science in high school. Among all the controversial opinions generated by the report, the wisdom of that suggestion was questioned by very few people. Why? The most likely answer is that parents and other adults have seen the computerization of their own workplaces and realize there is no turning back. Schools cannot be allowed the option of ignoring computers, because these machines alter jobs, entertainment, and home life so radically. It is becoming evident that those who learn about computers are advancing in their jobs, whereas those who avoid the use of computers are forfeiting promotions and even job security. Naturally, a problematic job future is not what parents want for their children. Although computer literacy is vital in the education of younger generations, it is also important that adults make an attempt to become computer literate. In order to prevent the forfeiture of promotions and job security, the members of the adult work force should also take steps to gain computer literacy.

Job Displacement and Retraining

Ever since the Industrial Revolution, automation has been of great concern to people. As technology has advanced, more and more processes have been automated, leading to greater efficiency and lower costs but also to machines replacing people in many jobs. With the advent of computers, fears that automation would lead to unemployment and depersonalization have taken on even greater significance. Whether these fears are justified is yet to be seen.

The evidence of the past three decades does not indicate that increased automation leads to increased unemployment. To be sure, workers have been displaced; but each new technology has created new employment opportunities that more than compensate for the jobs eliminated. For example, the invention of the automatic weaving machine eliminated many jobs in the garment industry; but this effect was offset by the creation of a whole new industry involved in the manufacture and marketing of the new equipment.

Nevertheless, many people argue that the impact of computers is going to be much more significant because computer technology provides for much more versatile and complex automation. Computers, instead of humans, can be used to control automatic machines and entire assembly lines. Grocery stores can be automated—that is, a person can call in an order; a computer can record it, find the required items, and even arrange for their delivery. Other computers can control entire processes in oil refineries, turning crude oil into tar, heating oil, diesel oil, gasoline, and so forth.

Several studies have been conducted to determine the effects of computer automation on jobs. The results have not been conclusive but have in general indicated that a certain amount of job displacement can be expected because

THE IMPACT OF COMPUTERS ON PEOPLE AND ORGANIZATION

the computer can take over many routine clerical jobs. However, the extent to which such displacement occurs also depends on other factors, including the following:

■ The goals that are sought from the use of the computer. Is the objective to be able to handle an increasing workload with the same personnel, or is it to reduce costs by eliminating jobs?

■ The growth rate of the organization. If the organization is expanding, it can more easily absorb workers whose jobs are being eliminated since many new jobs must be created to cope with the increasing business.

■ The planning that has gone into the acquisition and use of the computer. With careful preparation, an organization can anticipate the personnel changes a computer system will bring about. It can make plans either to reassign the affected people or to help them to find new jobs with other organizations. First-time use of a computer-based system will definitely create new jobs in the areas of computer operations, data entry, programming, and systems analysis and design. Usually, however, the skills and education required for these jobs differ from those required for the eliminated jobs. However, displaced employees can be trained to handle such jobs as operating computer equipment (loading and unloading tapes and the like) and keying in data; they can also be sent to schools for more formal training.

The current task of retraining displaced as well as unemployed workers has been taken on by groups such as businesses (which provide internal retraining), colleges, vocational schools, private training centers, and the federal government (through aid to states). Some of the more popular programs for retraining include robotics maintenance, computer programming, numerical control machinery programming and operation, word processing, computer maintenance, and electronics.

Changes in the Workplace

Since the advent of computers, changes in the workplace have been common. Farmers, secretaries, and business managers alike have experienced the effects computers can have in their workplace. The office is probably the area of greatest change and offers the greatest potential for automation. Office automation is discussed in the following section, while the impact the computer has had on the agricultural environment, workers themselves, and workstations will be discussed here.

The Agricultural Environment The farm with its fields of crops, stables of horses, and pastures of dairy cattle is feeling the presence of computers. Farmers are using computers to store animal health records and assist with feed selection and bookkeeping. Applications for microcomputers like those mentioned above have meant increased sales of microcomputers to farmers.

Studies of the agricultural market show dairy farming to be more record oriented than cattle or crop farming. For example, Mountain Dairy in Connecticut has turned to the personal computer to keep track of the 8,000 to 9,000 quarts of milk processed daily. In ways like this, farmers are able to reduce operating costs and improve management (see Figure 16−1).

Computers are also being used to control outbreaks of disease such as apple scab, a disease that can destroy an apple orchard within two years, and for horse breeding, farm accounting, and the monitoring of commodities and livestock prices.

Figure 16–1 ■ **Computers on the Farm**

This farmer examines a printout giving information on his dairy operation.

The Workers Workers' interaction with computers on a daily basis has meant new concerns. Perhaps the concerns that have received the most publicity have been those regarding worker health. The biggest complaint of office workers in automated offices is that of eyestrain, followed closely by complaints of backstrain. The issue of whether the small amount of radiation given off by the CRT screen is hazardous has not been resolved to the satisfaction of all concerned. CRTs have been shown to cause eyestrain, loss of visual acuity, changes in color perception, back and neck pain, stomachaches, and nausea when prolonged contact is experienced.

The Workstations To help alleviate some of the health concerns associated with the automated workplace, a new science has emerged. **Ergonomics,** the method of researching and designing computer hardware and software to enhance employee productivity and comfort, promises a better, more productive workplace. Its major areas of research include the different elements of the workstation and software.

To reduce such physical problems as eyestrain and backstrain, it is recommended that the time spent at a CRT be reduced to a maximum of two hours per day of continuous screen work, that periodic rest breaks be granted, and that pregnant women be permitted to transfer to a different working environment upon request. Recommendations have also been made regarding the design of the CRT and of the keyboard. Suggestions have been made regarding their slope, layout, adjustability, and use of numeric keypads and function keys (see Figure 16–2).

Other problems with the workstation include poor lighting and noise generated by printers. Sound-dampening covers and internal sound dampening are recommended but still do not reduce the noise sufficiently. The best solution to date is to put the printers in a separate room or at least away from the workers' area. Along with these suggestions, recommendations have been made regarding the tables and chairs used for data-processing work.

The application of ergonomics to workstations has resulted in a 10 to 15 percent improvement in performance in some offices.

Figure 16–2 ■ Ergonomic
Workstations

OFFICE AUTOMATION

As computer technology enters the workplace, the office environment is experiencing changes. Businesses are realizing that automating office procedures is efficient, cost effective, and in fact necessary in order to deal with the exploding information revolution. **Office automation**, the generalized and comprehensive term applied to this transition, refers to all processes that integrate computer and communication technology with the traditional manual processes. Virtually every office function can be automated—typing, filing, and communications, among others.

This section will discuss the characteristics of the elements that comprise office automation: word processing, communications, and local area networks.

Word Processing

Word processing is often considered the first building block in automating the workplace. It is the most widely adopted office automation technology; an estimated 75 percent of U.S. companies employ some type of word processing. **Word processing,** the manipulation of written text to achieve a desired output, bypasses the difficulties and shortcomings associated with traditional writing and typing. Word processors offer many functions to increase efficiency in the text manipulation process. Standard features include automatic centering, pagination (page numbering), alphabetizing, justification of type, and reformatting of paragraphs; word processors also usually have features enabling them to boldface, search and find, and move blocks of text.

Special function keys and codes are used to format the document being typed. The user may create, edit, rearrange, insert, and delete material—all electronically—until the text is exactly as desired. Then the text can be printed as well as stored on tape or disk for later use. Each copy of the text printed is an original; thus the output of a word-processing system is of a consistently high quality.

Word processing can be used for a variety of tasks. Some popular uses include editing lengthy documents (thus eliminating the need for having a document completely retyped every time it is edited), producing original form letters, and completing lengthy forms where tab stops can be automatically generated to increase the typist's speed. Some other functions that can be performed on certain word-processing systems are merging data with text, processing files, performing mathematical functions, generating the output of photocomposition devices, facilitating electronic filing, and distributing text after it has been created, which allows documents prepared in one location to be printed in others.

A typical word-processing system consists of a keyboard for data input, a CRT or LED display screen for viewing text material, a secondary storage unit (disk or tape), and a printer for generating output (see Figure 16–3). Word

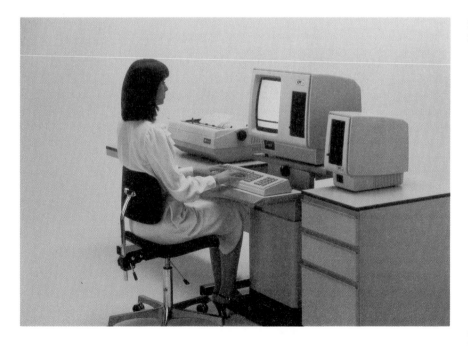

Figure 16–3 ■ A Typical Word-Processing System

processing is available in a variety of configurations, including electronic typewriters, dedicated word processors, dedicated data processors, and small business computers.

The major advantages of word processing over traditional text preparation are increased productivity and reduction in preparation time. Word processing, like data processing, relieves workers of time-consuming and routine tasks, thereby increasing standards of productivity and quality. It is estimated that, depending on the volume of typing done, a secretary's productivity can be increased 25 to 200 percent using word processing. Because a document does not have to be retyped every time a change is made, the preparation time is reduced dramatically.

One major disadvantage that has been noted is the increase in the number of times a document is revised. Because it is so easy to change a document, personnel make changes more often than when documents are prepared manually. To a point this can be useful; however, is there really that much difference in the quality of the document after it has been revised ten times? Another disadvantage in the past has been the cost of word-processing systems. However, the trend recently has been for the cost to decrease as the capabilities increase.

Only a tiny fraction of computer capabilities have been applied to current word-processing techniques. In the future, the word processor will have a spelling checker that will handle personal names, a built-in dictionary of definitions to provide the user with the meaning of an unfamiliar word, and a thesaurus that will provide the user with alternative words to be used. The word processor will automatically and correctly hyphenate words (it only guesses now), and it will check for correctness of standardized abbreviations, commas around dates, and written-out numbers compared to numerals. And in case the user's grammar is not up to par, the word processor will check and correct grammar and will even try to anticipate the next character to be typed. The user will be able to override the computer in case it does not select the correct character; however, this feature could save the user a considerable amount of time when lengthy words or phrases are duplicated throughout a document.

Color word processing should be available in the future. With this feature, each revision could be shown in a different color so that a distinction could be made as to the most recent revision. Also, different levels of management could have color codes so that informed decisions could be made as to what should be changed and what should not. Word processors will probably become much more portable; they will then be used on the airplane, in the car, or while on vacation. They will also have voice input capabilities eliminating the initial typing requirement. Word processing is in its infancy, with many future capabilities not even thought of yet.

Communications

An important benefit of office automation is the communication capabilities it makes possible. Such capabilities allow the electronic exchange of information between employees. Communications may be accomplished through forms such as electronic mail, teleconferencing, telecomputing, and telecommuting.

Electronic Mail **Electronic mail** is the transmission of messages at high speeds over telecommunication facilities (see Figure 16–4). It is used pri-

Figure 16–4 ▪ **Electronic Mail System**

marily for internal, routine communications; however, with the development of new technology, it is beginning to replace the traditional postal service. The concept behind these computer-based mail systems is the storage of messages in a special storage area until the recipient can access them. People using such systems can be in remote locations and need not be using their terminals simultaneously. Receivers are notified of waiting mail when they log on to their computer. They can then view the incoming mail items on a CRT screen or can have the items printed on their terminal. The mail can be revised, incorporated into other documents, passed along to new recipients, or filed like any other document in the system. Some electronic mail systems allow the sender to cancel the message if it has not yet been read by the recipient. The sender may also check to see if the messages he or she has sent have been read yet by the recipient by including a "receipt required" message with the document. Some systems also provide a delayed sending option, allowing the sender to create a message and have it sent at a set time in the future.

There are two basic forms of electronic mail: teletypewriter systems and facsimile systems. **Teletypewriter systems** transmit messages as strings of characters. **Facsimile systems,** sometimes called **telecopier systems,** produce a picture of a page by scanning it, as a television camera scans a scene or a copier scans a printed page. The image is then transmitted to a receiver, where it is printed.

Another type of electronic message system on which much work is currently being done is the **voice message system (VMS),** or **voice mail.** In VMS,

Telecommuting on Wheels

When one thinks of telecommuting, one generally thinks of a worker using a computer at home. However, thirty-one-year-old Steve Roberts of Columbus, Ohio, traveled on his eight-foot bicycle with a notebook-size computer. Traveling across the country, he worked on two books and numerous magazine articles. His objective was to learn how computers are changing people's lives.

Many people learned of Steve and his travels by using their home computers to access CompuServe, a national computer network; they began to communicate with him via the network. Steve rarely met any of his followers personally, but he did respond to their communications with him over CompuServe. During his trip, he became known by his network password, Wordy.

the sender presses a special "message" key on the telephone, dials the receiver's number, and speaks the message. The spoken message is converted by the VMS into digital form and stored in the computer's memory. A button lights on the receiver's phone. When he or she presses the "listen" key, the message is reconverted into voice form. Several characteristics distinguish VMS from standard answering machines. Recipients can fast-scan the messages, and voice mail also allows for longer messages than do answering machines.

Teleconferencing   In an effort to reduce travel time and expenses associated with out-of-town travel, businesses are turning to teleconferencing. **Teleconferencing,** the method of two or more remote locations communicating via electronic and image-producing facilities, offers businesses a viable alternative to long-distance, face-to-face communications.

Five forms of teleconferencing exist. The most basic form of conducting electronic meetings, **audio conferencing,** is simply a conference call linking three or more people. Ideal for impromptu conversations, audio conferencing requires no major equipment investments but is limited to voice only.

The next level, **augmented audio conferencing,** combines graphics with audio conferencing. In this situation, visual information accompanies the conversation in the form of facsimile, electronic blackboards or freeze-frame slide shows. Augmented audio conferencing is frequently used for technical discussions that require supplemental graphics to explain concepts.

Computer conferencing is well suited for ongoing meetings among a number of people. Information is exchanged at the participants' convenience using computer terminals; participants need not attend at the same time. New material can be added or previously submitted ideas can be critiqued. This differs from electronic mail in that discrete messages are not transmitted; instead comments are input in reference to specific issues. Computer conferencing has been found to reduce decision-making time considerably.

Video seminars represent the next level of sophistication. They employ one-way, full-motion video with two-way audio. The most common application of video seminars is for formal presentations that involve a question-and-answer session such as a press conference. Individuals from the audience communicate with the presentation headquarters via a separate two-way phone link. In turn, the entire audience can hear the question and view the official response. Special facilities with television equipment are needed for this type of conferencing.

Finally, there is **videoconferencing**—the technology currently receiving the most attention. Videoconferencing, employing a two-way, full-motion video plus a two-way audio system, provides the most effective simulation of face-to-face communication (see Figure 16–5). It is the only form that meets the need for full interaction; the participants are able to see and hear each other's responses. Videoconferencing is best suited for planning groups, project teams, and other groups that want a full sense of participation. It is not suitable for all situations, however. Videoconferencing resembles phone conversation rather than face-to-face communication. Thus, it does not seem to be effective when a participant is trying to persuade an audience or to sell something.

The cost effectiveness of videoconferences depends upon the geographic dispersion of the company, the number of intracompany meetings, and the management structure of the company. If the company does not have major offices throughout the country, videoconferencing would not be beneficial. Also, because different types of videoconferencing equipment are not compatible, it can only be used for conferences within the company, not with other companies. Some management structures such as committees or planning groups lend themselves to this structure.

Telecommuting   Probably the most exciting prospect for the automated office lies in the promise of employees commuting to the office by computer rather than in cars. **Telecommuting,** using a computer connected to the office from home via leased phone lines (see Figure 16 – 6), is already being tried by some companies on an experimental basis. The system has many advantages in areas where office rent is high and mass transit systems or parking facilities are inadequate, and in situations that do not require frequent face-to-face meetings among the office workers.

Telecomputing   Companies as well as individuals may subscribe to online information services—services that offer access to one or more data bases. This is often referred to as **telecomputing.** By accessing the online data bases, workers receive additional information and save considerable research time

Figure 16–5 ▪ **Videoconference**

Figure 16–6 ▪ **Telecommuting Terminal**

Working at Home

Many U.S. company employees are now working at home as telecommuters. Personal computers and communication devices such as modems are among the technological innovations that have made telecommuting a possibility. Blue Cross and Blue Shield of South Carolina have found that their sixteen telecommuters are 50 percent more productive than their office workers at keying insurance claims into the computer. Control Data Corporation reports a 35 percent gain in productivity with their telecommuters. Companies can hire disabled people or young mothers who would otherwise be unable to hold office positions.

Not all telecommuters work in the home. Best Western Hotels have hired residents of Arizona Center for Women, a minimum-security prison. It provided computer terminals and telephones to its employees.

Within the next ten years, about 18 percent of the work force will be telecommuting, predicts Marcia M. Kelly, president of Electronic Services.

(see Figure 16–7). There are many information services available that provide information on a wide variety of topics. Three of the more popular services are The Source, CompuServe, and Dow Jones News/Retrieval. Some of the services offered include: news stories; potentially news-making events; up-to-the-minute stock, bond, and commodity information; sporting events information; information on alcohol problems; and law libraries. This is by no means an all-inclusive list of the variety of topics offered by these services (other topics were mentioned in Chapter 6).

Usually, a membership fee is assessed from the user, and a password and account number are issued. The online service then usually charges the user for service time or connect time. Depending upon the network accessed and the time of day, service time costs $5 to $25 per hour. The only equipment needed is a computer, a modem, and a communications software package to instruct the user's computer how to talk to the computer at the other end. For such a small expense, employees can receive up-to-the-minute information with a minimal amount of effort and time.

Local Area Networks

Some experts believe that without integration of capabilities, office automation is a meaningless concept. This integration can be accomplished through local area networks. A **network** is a linking of CPUs and terminals by a communication system (see Figure 16–8). A **local area network (LAN)** is a special type of network that operates within a well-defined area with the stations being linked by cable. The workstations cannot be located more than two miles apart. The two factors limiting distance are the time required for the signal to travel from one workstation to the other and the decrease in the strength of the signal as it travels over the cables. A LAN allows users to share information, storage devices, and peripherals. It is best suited for environments where there is a great deal of information—either programs or data—that needs to be shared.

Figure 16–7 ■ Telecomputing

Figure 16—8 ▪ Local Area Network

LANs are classified on three different bases: physical layout, communication medium, and traffic management. There are three types of physical layouts that may be employed. A **star network** is comprised of a central station with multiple stations connected to it. The individual stations cannot communicate directly with each other; they must first go through the central station. The **bus network** has multiple stations connected to a main communication line. Any station can communicate directly with any other equipment on the bus. Finally, the **ring network** is comprised of multiple stations, each being connected to its adjacent station. In this fashion, communication must be relayed through adjacent stations to the desired station.

COMPUTERS IN BUSINESS AND INDUSTRY

As computers have entered American society, nowhere have they had more impact than in business and industry. Part of this is due to the fact that using computers speeds operations, reduces mistakes in calculations, and gives companies efficient, cost-effective analyses that would be nearly impossible with manual operations. Another major reason for the great impact of computers is the domino effect. If Business A speeds up its operations through the use of computers, then Business B must also computerize to compete. The same applies to the use of automation in industry. Once one factory incorporates automation, it sets a standard to be imitated and repeated.

These factors have caused a phenomenal increase in the number and types of computer applications in business and industry. Some experts even claim that these computer applications are helping to trigger a new type of industrial revolution.

Impact on Business

Because businesses are so varied in purpose and structure, it is nearly impossible to examine all business uses of computers. However, it is possible to look at how computers are used in most businesses, or at least in the average business. Of course, specific businesses will have special uses of computers. For example, a retail store might be interested in computerizing inventory, whereas a stock brokerage would be more interested in computerizing the files of its customers. In general, though, there are three areas in which computers are used in most businesses: (1) accounting and finance, (2) management, and (3) marketing and sales.

Accounting and Finance In the past, financial transactions were tediously calculated, either by hand or by calculator, and recorded using pencil and paper. This method has rapidly become obsolete as computers have moved into virtually every area of accounting and finance. To illustrate this point, let us examine how computers are being used in the areas of general accounting, financial analysis, and information management.

General accounting software is a very popular type of business software. In fact, it was the first business software to be offered for personal computers. Some of the most common uses of general accounting software are in preparing checks, reports, and forms (see Figure 16–9). Forms, because of their repetitive nature, are well suited to computer processing. General accounting packages that produce reports keep one informed of everything from inventory on-hand to monthly credit account balances. Checks seem to be the most popular type of form output by these programs—at least with those who receive them.

Today, the most common use of the computer in financial analysis is the electronic spreadsheet. Spreadsheets are used to design budgets, record sales, produce profit-and-loss statements, and aid in financial analysis. Refer to Chapter 12 for more information regarding spreadsheets.

Data management software for business computers gives them the capability of an electronic filing system. Data entered into selected categories can be retrieved by specifying, for example, those files on employees receiving a certain salary or employees hired on a certain date. Such a system makes file

Figure 16–9 ▪ Computers in Accounting

retrieval faster and more flexible, in addition to decreasing the amount of storage space required.

Small data management software packages designed for microcomputers enable a manager's appointments to be recorded and recalled as necessary. Some systems in this category also maintain expense account records. Chapter 12 also contains a discussion on data management software.

Management   The essence of business management is communication, and computer graphics are becoming an essential part of business communication. In the average business, computers are used to produce graphs that keep management informed and up-to-date on company statistics, sales records, and the like.

It is well known in business that executives make 80 percent of their decisions based on 20 percent of the data—that 20 percent representing the core data necessary to run their businesses. Finding that data can be difficult for managers if they are presented with pages upon pages of data. Graphically displayed data makes the task much easier. It is widely agreed that such displays can help managers to make better decisions. Also, comparisons, relationships and trends, and essential points can be clarified more easily with graphics (see Figure 16–10). Finally, computer graphics are the most cost-effective means of presenting the manager with that 20 percent core data.

Marketing and Sales   Businesses use computers in a variety of ways to facilitate sales, record sales, update inventories after sales, and make projections based on expected sales (see Figure 16–11). In addition to these standard functions, some computers are also being used in customer contact.

The Helena Rubenstein cosmetic firm served as a triggering force in the movement of computers onto the sales floor. The cosmetic computer assisted customers in their decisions about perfumes, makeup, and colorings. The firm's effort was very successful and inspired similar applications by other companies.

Impact on Industry

The financial and bookkeeping uses of computers apply to both business and industry. However, industry also uses computers in designing and manufac-

Figure 16–10 ▪ Computer Business Graphics

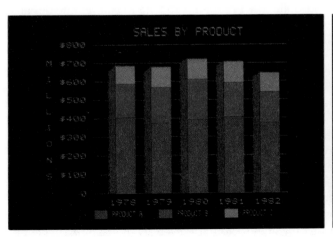

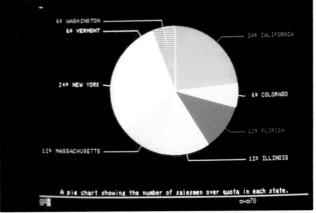

Figure 16–11 ■ Computers in Sales

turing products. It does this in two ways: (1) with the use of CAD/CAM and (2) with robotics.

CAD/CAM   One of the fastest growing areas of computer use in industry is **computer-aided design (CAD).** CAD allows the engineer to design, draft, and analyze a prospective product using computer graphics on a video terminal (see Figure 16–12). The designer, working with full-color graphics, can easily make changes, so he or she can test many versions of a product before the first prototype is ever built. The system is also able to analyze the designs for poor tolerance between parts and for stress points. This can save a great deal of money by eliminating defective designs before the money is spent to build a product.

Computer-aided design is often coupled with **computer-aided manufacturing (CAM),** and the combination is referred to as **CAD/CAM.** Using CAD/CAM, the engineer can analyze not only the product but also the manufacturing process.

Once the rough design of the product has been entered into the computer, the engineer can have the computer simulate any manufacturing step (see Figure 16–13). For example, if the product must be drilled, the engineer can create a computerized drill that can be guided, either by the engineer or the computer, to simulate the drilling process. This simulation can be very helpful in two ways. First, it should indicate any major problems that may be encountered on the assembly line—before it is even set up. Second, the com-

Figure 16–12 ■ Computer-Aided Design

Figure 16–13 ■ Computer-Aided Manufacturing

Figure 16–14 ▪ CAD/CAM at NIKE

(a)   (b)

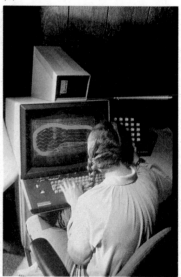

In an industry as competitive as the modern athletic shoe industry, the speed with which a new shoe model can be designed and manufactured is critical. Speed and accuracy in producing a new shoe model at NIKE is made possible in part by CAD/CAM (computer-aided design/computer-aided manufacturing). While CAD/CAM technology has been commonplace for years in the automotive and aerospace industries, its use by NIKE in the athletic shoe industry is revolutionary. It is a unique tool serving the product development area by decreasing the time necessary to bring a new design into production.

In the CAD stage of the development process, the designer inputs the specifications of the new shoe pattern into a computer graphics terminal (photo a). Each graphics terminal is connected to a sophisticated host computer. CAD technology permits a designer to create and modify computer-generated visual displays of new designs quickly and accurately. The image shown on the screen (photo b) is an air-sole mold. The final results of this process far exceed what could be expected from a conventional draftsman (photos c and d).

At the appropriate time, all pertinent information pertaining to the manufacture of the mold is passed from the CAD area to the CAM area. A computer in the CAM area instructs a numerical control milling machine how to machine the mold block (photo e). First, the milling machine mills out a sample of the design from a block of low-cost test material. This test milling is inspected to ensure the accuracy of the pattern. If everything is satisfactory, a finished part is milled out of metal (photo f). After the milling mold is completed, a four station, open-pour polyurethane machine is used for manufacturing sole units (photo g).

Computers are also used to test the new shoe. By measuring the energy cost of running on a treadmill, researchers can compare the effect of various shoe designs on running efficiency (photo h).

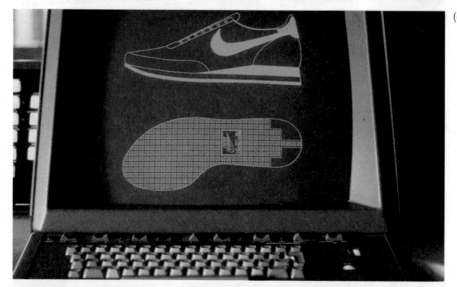

(c)

(d)

(e)

(f)

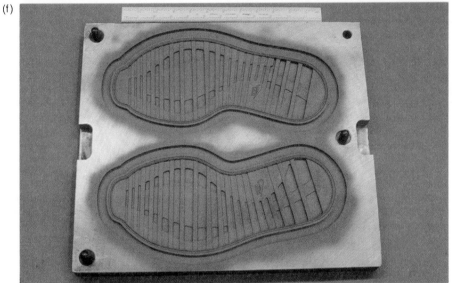

(g)

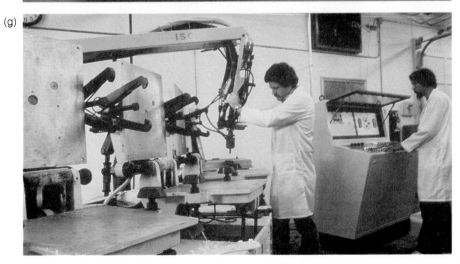

(h)

puter will record exactly how the tool moved and will store that information on magnetic tape. If that factory uses robotics and **numerically controlled machinery,** those tapes can be used to drive the actual machines in manufacturing the product. In this way, CAD/CAM can take the engineer from idea to final product. One of the more interesting applications of CAD/CAM is shown in Figure 16–14.

Robotics　Almost everyone is familiar with the terminology given workers: those who perform management-level jobs are referred to as white-collar workers; those performing unskilled tasks or factory jobs are called blue-collar workers. However, the influx of computers into the working world of the factories has created another category: the steel-collar worker. The steel-collar workers are nonhuman, and human workers are beginning to fear this new work force—the robots.

Science fiction writer Isaac Asimov coined the term robotics. **Robotics** is the science that deals with robots, their construction, capabilities, and applications.

Currently, American factories have over 6,000 robots hard at work (see Figure 16–15). This figure is expected to increase rapidly, reaching nearly 150,000 robots by 1990. General Motors, General Electric, and Westinghouse are the three leading users of industrial robots. These steel-collar workers perform standard jobs, such as spot welding and spray painting, as well as more complex jobs like fitting light bulbs into the dashboards of cars. The automobile industry is the leading user of robots in the United States.

The steel-collar worker is not always as efficient as one may think. Robots perform well on the factory floor, but they have been known to go berserk. Swinging its powerful steel arm, a robot can deliver blows to anything within its reach; the problem—a crossed wire. Also, robots lack common sense and intelligence. For example, consider the case of a robot that drills holes in the doors of cars as they pass on the assembly line. If the car is not in the right position, the robot will still drill holes.

Two generations of robots have appeared so far. The first generation possesses mechanical dexterity but no external sensory ability; that is, they cannot see, hear, touch, or smell. Second-generation robots, however, possess more human-like capabilities, including tactile sense or crude vision; they can "feel" how tightly they are gripping an object or "see" whether there are obstacles in their path.

Robots are appearing in places other than the factory, such as the area of sales. In Aurora, Colorado, an office supply store has robots for salespersons. They will, for example, tell customers about the specials within the store while pointing to the wares displayed.

The common sense required to make steel-collar workers more compatible with their white- and blue-collar counterparts is, however, still a long way in the future.

Impact on Government

The federal government is the single largest user of computers in the United States. As such, it gives rise to some of the worst fears (such as those generated by the movie *War Games*) and the highest hopes (for example, for far-reaching space exploration) computer observers can imagine.

Two major categories in which computers are used in government are simulation and modeling, and data bases.

Figure 16–15 ▪ Robotics

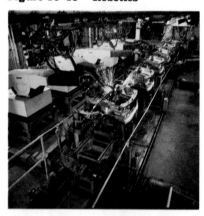

Simulation and Modeling Computers have long been a mainstay in the Department of Defense weapons development program, doing everything from simulating wars (see Figure 16–16) to designing and testing weapons to actually guiding missiles. As computers have nudged their way into the civilian school system, so have they advanced into military training programs.

The U.S. Navy is currently experimenting with a training device called NAVTAG (Navy Technical Action Game). The game is equipped with three terminals: one for "them," one for "us," and one for the referee. In addition to the several tactical scenes built into the game, players can invent their own. Essential information, such as target location and fuel on hand, is flashed onto the display terminals in written or graphic form. Players access the information and plan their battles accordingly. The referee can add factors into the game to make it more difficult. The game not only teaches tactics but also provides players with real information, such as real ship names and data on accuracy and range of weapons.

The forecasting of weather is one of the most interesting applications of computers in government. Several variables, such as air pressure, velocity, humidity, and temperature, are fed into huge computers for the processing of complex mathematical equations. The equations describe the interaction of these variables. Combining these data with mathematical models, forecasters can predict the weather.

The world's weather information is collected by the National Weather Service in Maryland from a variety of locations: hundreds of data-collection programs (DCPs), which are placed on buoys, ships, helium-filled balloons, and airplanes; about seventy weather stations; and four satellites (see Figure 16–17). Of the four satellites, two orbit the earth over the poles to send pictures revealing the movement and shape of clouds. The remaining two satellites are stationary and photograph the earth above the equator.

Although local forecasters use radar data directly, they also rely on the Weather Service information. The service's "brain" consists of fourteen computers housed at the meteorological center. These computers receive information from some of the DCPs whose data are beamed up to the two stationary satellites above the equator. The computers also receive information from other DCPs; the information travels from ground station to ground station. The fourteen computers use all of this incoming data to construct a mathematical description of the atmosphere. These weather reports—2,000 daily—are then sent to local weather offices.

Data Processing Machine Reads Russian

A scanning and processing system developed by Kurzweil Computer Products, Cambridge, Massachusetts, can convert printed (Cyrillic) Russian documents into computer-readable form. According to company personnel, designing the system wasn't as difficult as it seems to Americans. It only appears difficult because of the unusual structure of the Russian alphabet. The system's scanners can also recognize such things as italics, headings, and boldface.

The future holds the possibility of programming a computer to translate Russian to English. This could be especially helpful in government work and even in scientific research.

Figure 16–16 ▪ War Simulation

This participant uses the computer for war games simulation exercises. The display screens represent various situations that may be encountered in an actual war.

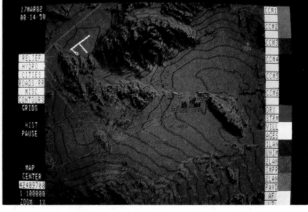

Figure 16–17 ▪ **Computerized Weather Forecasting**

Figure 16–18 ▪ **Library of Congress Computer Terminal**

Data Bases Data bases are most prevalent within the government. Much of the information in these data bases is acquired from the census returns filed each decade and the income tax returns filed annually. Three of the largest data bases are in the Library of Congress, the Federal Bureau of Investigation (FBI), and the Internal Revenue Service (IRS).

The work of the mammoth Library of Congress has been radically changed by the computer (see Figure 16–18). The library's storage, retrieval, and printing system now converts library cards into digital images on optical disks developed by Xerox. Under the old system, the library's file cabinets of catalog cards ran the length of a football field. The same information can now be stored on about thirty 14-inch optical disks. Each disk holds about 200,000 library cards.

Another keeper of enormous records is the FBI. The bureau's master index alone contains nearly five million index cards. To make its records more useful, the FBI has organized several computer-accessed data bases and is working toward having all of its 500 or so offices connected to the data bases by the end of the 1980s.

Every person living in the United States who earns more than a minimal

amount of money must report to the federal government for tax purposes. In addition, corporations and businesses file annual tax returns on their businesses. The IRS receives millions of tax returns each year. Computers are used by the IRS to monitor these returns and record the information (see Figure 16–19). Without the aid of computers, it would take many years to process just one year's worth of returns.

The IRS also performs audits on selected returns. Computers are used to randomly select tax returns for audits and perform some of the preliminary operations. This reduces the number of manual operations required to perform the audits, increasing the number of audits that can be performed each year.

The IRS recently lived up to its own publicity when one of its computers detected that a taxpayer had made a one-cent underpayment of his taxes because of an error in math. The computer automatically fired off a letter demanding payment of the penny, plus a fine of $159.78. ''Obviously, the computer has gone berserk,'' an IRS agent admitted.

Figure 16–19 ▪ **IRS Computers**

SUMMARY POINTS

▪ Computer anxiety is the fear people feel toward computers and the effects they have on individual's lives and society.

▪ In order to prepare students for the future, computer literacy courses are beginning to be taught throughout elementary and secondary education systems.

▪ Studies conducted by Genevieve Cerf at Columbia University have found that, overall, women may make better programmers than men.

▪ Computer-related fields are among the few that currently pay women and men equally for similar positions and work.

▪ Job displacement and retraining are issues that must be dealt with as computer technology continues to automate more and more jobs and processes.

▪ Ergonomics is the method of researching and designing computer hardware and software to enhance employee productivity and comfort. It has focused on recommendations for the workstation environment and for making software more user friendly.

▪ Office automation refers to all processes that integrate computer and communications technology with traditional manual office processes.

▪ The manipulation of written text to achieve a desired output is referred to as word processing; word processing is the most widely adopted office automation technology.

▪ Word processing is available on four major types of configurations: (1) electronic typewriters, (2) dedicated word processors, (3) dedicated data processors, and (4) small business computers.

▪ Communication capabilities derived from office automation allow the exchange of information electronically between employees.

▪ Electronic mail is the transmission of messages at high speeds over telecommunication facilities and can be in the form of a teletypewriter system, a facsimile system, or a voice message system.

▪ The method of two or more remote locations communicating via electronic and image producing facilities is called teleconferencing. Five forms of teleconferencing exist: (1) audio conferencing, (2) augmented audio conferencing, (3) computer conferencing, (4) video seminars, and (5) videoconferencing.

- Telecommuting refers to the use of a computer connected to the office from the home via leased phone lines. Telecommuting is growing in popularity.
- Accessing online information services, referred to as telecomputing, can provide a vast amount of information for a minimal amount of time and money.
- A local area network (LAN) is a linking of CPUs and terminals by a communication system within a well-defined area, usually less than two miles.
- Computerization in businesses has taken place primarily in three functional areas: (1) accounting and finance, (2) management, and (3) marketing and sales.
- General accounting software, electronic spreadsheets, and data management software have been heavily used in the area of finance.
- Computer graphics have become a very important factor in business communication.
- Computer-aided design (CAD) allows an engineer to design, draft, and analyze a potential product without leaving the computer terminal.
- The combination of computer-aided design and computer-aided manufacturing (CAD/CAM) allows the engineer to analyze both the design and manufacturing processes.
- Robots are being used in factories, primarily in the manufacture of automobiles, for such tasks as spot welding, spray painting, and fitting lightbulbs into dashboards.
- The federal government is the single largest user of computers in the nation. Computers are used by the military to simulate battle conditions, while the National Weather Service uses computers quite extensively in the prediction of weather. Three of the largest data bases within the government are maintained by the Library of Congress, FBI, and IRS.

REVIEW QUESTIONS

1. What is computer anxiety? List some reasons why you feel computer anxiety is important to those who design, implement, and maintain computer applications.
2. What is ergonomics? What are some recommendations that have been made as a result of ergonomics?
3. What are some of the advantages of office automation?
4. List the four types of word processors and describe the environment in which each might be best utilized.
5. Differentiate among the five forms of teleconferencing.
6. What is the difference between telecommuting and telecomputing?
7. What are the advantages of telecommuting?
8. Define a local area network and list some of its advantages.
9. Why have computer graphics become an important aspect of business management?
10. What impact has computer technology had on some of the services provided by the federal government?
11. In your opinion, what is the most identifiable effect computers have had on society?
12. Do you feel that we, as humans, will permit our society to be as automated as possible, or will there be some point in the future at which we will limit what computers can do? Briefly explain your answer.

APPLICATION

PRUPAC

Prudential Property and Casualty Insurance Company (PRUPAC) is a wholly owned subsidiary of The Prudential Insurance Company of America, the largest life insurance company in the United States. The company markets private passenger auto, homeowners, personal catastrophe liability, and dwelling fire insurance through Prudential agents. PRUPAC was created in 1971, after studies had indicated an interest on the part of the public in dealing with one agent for all their personal insurance needs: life, health, auto, and homeowners. At the same time, Prudential recognized a need to keep its agents competitive with those of several large property and casualty insurers (who had begun marketing life and health insurance through subsidiary companies) by adding auto and homeowners insurance to their portfolios.

PRUPAC began its operations in June of 1971, in a one-room office in Chicago, with 18 employees. By the end of that year, it had 112 employees and insured 14,200 cars and homes in Illinois alone. Within five years, the company had expanded countrywide, insuring nearly 1.5 million risks with a staff of more than 3,000. Today, with the same size staff, PRUPAC insures about 2 million cars and homes, making it one of the fifteen largest personal-line property and casualty insurers in the country.

Such rapid expansion would not have been possible without computers. Prudential bought its original computers in the early 1950s, when the first commercially available vacuum tube models appeared. As the computer evolved during the following decade, so did Prudential's applications. By the time PRUPAC was founded in 1971, it could build on the software and hardware expertise of its parent company and start its corporate life as a fully computerized operation. Unlike many of its competitors, PRUPAC never had to undergo the expense, both in terms of time and personnel dislocation, of converting a massive, manual record-keeping system to a computerized one. This heavy reliance on computers right from the start made it possible to handle more business with fewer people in less time, mak-

ing explosive growth financially and operationally feasible.

GENERAL DATA-PROCESSING ACTIVITIES

The basic product sold by insurance companies is an intangible: the promise to pay should a loss occur. The concrete embodiment of that promise is the insurance contract and all the records and paperwork that go with it. Computers have made it possible to handle the millions of transactions involved efficiently and economically.

Besides the computer systems which handle the records dealing with policyholders, their bills, and claims (which will be discussed in more detail a little later), other systems handle the finances of the company. These are the common general ledger, accounts payable, accounts receivable, tax, and payroll systems utilized by most companies, though specifically tailored for PRUPAC's needs.

While the basic product of insurance is simple—a promise to pay for a loss—the trick is in knowing how much to charge so that all losses can be paid off and the company can make a profit, without charging rates so high that customers go elsewhere. This is the realm of the actuaries, trained specialists in the mathematical discipline of probability theory. In addition to past experience with losses, the kinds of people who have had losses, and the circumstances under which those losses occurred, actuaries must take into consideration economic projections regarding inflation, return on investment, and so forth. Capturing and analyzing this mass of statistical data would be an awesome task without computer assistance. The computer has enabled insurance companies to analyze and adjust their rates on a more timely basis than previously possible.

Finally, all of these systems are a part of the management information system, which allows senior management to get a handle on what is happening with the company's business and financial picture before a crisis occurs. These include systems for projecting and planning for the future, analyzing current results against set objectives, and facilitating corrective action.

IMPACT OF COMPUTERS ON PEOPLE AND ORGANIZATION

While PRUPAC was born a child of the computer age, since its founding in 1971 there have been two major technological advances which have affected both the company's organization and its people. The first of these, which affected the structure of the organization and the way it operates, was the growth of telecommunications and of online storage capacity, allowing access to millions of records in a central location from anywhere in the company, and the ability to update those records quickly. The second was the advent of the microcomputer, which brought the power and the mystique of the computer out of the shrine of the programmers, the data-processing center, and placed it in the hands of the layperson.

TELECOMMUNICATIONS/ONLINE STORAGE

To get a feel for how telecommunications and on-line storage affect the day-to-day operation of the company, let's follow a policy through its "life cycle."

The process begins when the Prudential insurance agent completes an application for insurance. This app (as it is called in the trade) is then forwarded to one of five regional service offices throughout the country. Here the app is reviewed for acceptability by underwriters. If it passes muster, it is then keyed into an online terminal at the regional service office connected to Prudential's computer center in Pennsylvania. During a computer run that night, the information on the app becomes part of the policyholder record, the centralized computer file on which all future transactions with the policyholder will be based. At the same time, information on the new policy is passed to the billing system, which calculates what the coverage will cost. All of this information is transmitted from the Pennsylvania computer center to a computer at PRUPAC's corporate headquarters in Holmdel, New Jersey. There, the next morning, laser printers under control of PRUPAC's computer print out the Declarations page—a part of the policy that shows what coverages the person has and how much he or she paid for them—and the bill. These documents are then automatically assembled by electronic envelope stuffing machines, together with a printed copy of the policy and any special endorse-

ments required, and the whole package is sent to the agent for delivery to the policyholder.

From that point on, if the person calls any of the company's regional service offices with questions about the policy or the bill, the policyholder service representatives who take these calls can access the latest policyholder and bill records on terminals connected to the central computer in Pennsylvania and answer the questions while the client is still on the phone. They can also make changes to the policy online (for example, adding a new car).

When the return portion of the bill comes back with a check, the return portion is automatically read by a scanner, and the amount of the check is keyed in. This input goes to the billing and accounting systems, which automatically make up bank deposit slips and update the client's account with amount paid, still owed, and so on, and also update the company's accounts receivable and general ledger. If no check is received by the date due, the system automatically generates a notice of termination for nonpayment of premium.

When the policy comes up for renewal, the system generates a new Declarations page, based on the most recent version of the client's policyholder record, and a bill for the next policy period, and the cycle repeats itself.

In addition to the policyholder record and billing systems, claim files and claim activities are also maintained on online data bases. When a person calls to report a claim, the claim service representative can refer to all of the person's records on a terminal, verify coverage, make an appointment for an adjuster to inspect the damage, and check the history of previous claims. This ability to access company information instantly often makes it possible to handle the claim with only one phone call from the insured.

MICROS

The first application of microcomputer technology to a noncomputer environment in PRUPAC occurred with the introduction of IBM Displaywriter word processors in areas of the company with heavy document production needs. The machines were to be used primarily by secretaries and clerk/typists who, for the most part, had never used a terminal. Suddenly, they were confronted with a new keyboard, a screen where the paper used to be, and something called floppy disks. While manuals, teaching guides, and classes were held to instruct them in the use of the new equipment, there was still

an initial high level of anxiety about these new "wonders." Some of the users unconsciously began trying to raise their comfort level with the new equipment by relating the unfamiliar technology to familiar items in their daily lives. The CRT screen was referred to as the "TV," and the disk drive was dubbed "the toaster" (in fact, with its two slots for 8-inch disks, it does look like a toaster lying on its side).

As people began using the new equipment, three different stages in their development became clear. The first of these was marked by high anxiety: "It's too complicated. I'm afraid I'll do something wrong and break it." After some hands-on experience and further training, users advanced to the second stage—anger, confusion and frustration: "Why did the dumb machine do that?" (The usual explanation was that the machine was doing what it was told to do, not what it was meant to do—a common problem with all forms of computer programming.) "Why do we have to use these machines? I could have done this job faster on my typewriter!" The final stage, after still more experience using the machine for a month or more, was delighted acceptance:

"If you try to take away my machine, I'll break your arm! I don't want to share it; I want my own! Throw away all the typewriters!"

Shared learning replaced formal instruction at this point. As users learned more about the potential of the machine, sometimes by trial and error, assisted by the users' manuals or advice from technicians, they shared their new techniques with others in their area. It also became clear that users were developing an intuitive understanding of the program logic of the system. They were beginning to have a feel for how the machine would respond to instructions, or what commands would have to be used to accomplish a given result— even if the procedure was not explicitly explained in any of the manuals, and even though no one had shown them how to do it.

The reason for the acceptance of the equipment, once the barrier of unfamiliarity had been scaled, was that the users found it to be a powerful tool which removed much of the drudgery of typing and retyping the same document with minor changes, leaving them more time to be more creative in handling work. Their bosses, too, were delighted with the rapid turnaround time and the relief from the burden of guilt formerly felt when asking the secretary to type it "just one more time with these few changes."

Interestingly, there was a kind of transfer effect to a few of the management staff in areas where the machines were located. Some managers, with modest keyboard skills and a willingness to face technological challenge, learned (often from their secretaries) enough about how to use the machine that they could make simple editing changes in documents their secretaries had entered for them. Others entered memos or reports in very rough draft directly on the machine instead of on scratch paper or by dictation, leaving it to the secretary to "tidy it up." Still others, especially those whose jobs called for heavy writing—often involving typing initial drafts themselves which were then retyped in edited form by a typist—simply bypassed the middle person and did the whole job on the word processor, without the assistance of a typist. While this did not result in laying off any typists on staff, it did allow an increase in productivity without hiring any new typists. And those already on staff were able to expand their clerical (filing, correspondence, phone handling, and so on) activities, making them more junior administrative assistants than clerk/typists.

Of course, this effect was not universal. There are still managers who don't know (and don't want to know) anything about the machines, for whom touching a keyboard is still anathema, something beneath their job description. But the entire staff, whether direct users of the machines or not, evidenced a reaction similar to that which must have greeted the invention of the telephone. BEFORE: "What do we need it for? We've gotten along quite well with what we've got." AFTER: "How did we ever live without it?"

A second application of microcomputers is at the point of sale. Rating insurance policies is a complex process. For example, the variables involved in quoting an auto insurance premium in most states include, but are not limited to: the age, sex, and marital status of the drivers, the kind of car, how far the car is driven each year, what kind of use is made of the car, where the car is garaged, whether the driver has any points or convictions for motor vehicle violations, which of a dozen or more possible coverages the driver wants and in what amounts, and so forth. Take a family with two parents, two teenage drivers, and three cars, and the calculation involved in coming up with a rate is formidable. In fact, given all the variables, there are sev-

eral hundred thousand possible rate combinations. And to make matters even more complicated, these rates are subject to change on fairly short notice once or twice each year. For this reason (among others) many insurance agents have welcomed the personal computer into their offices to help them grapple with premium quotes. But Prudential agents faced a special problem. They don't work out of offices. Instead, they go out and transact business in the clients' homes at the clients' convenience. To expect them to lug a thirty-pound "portable" computer into a client's living room and ask "Where's the plug?" was out of the question.

In the search for easier ways to rate policies, PRU-PAC had begun with a looseleaf binder containing numerous tables of rates, rating rules, and worksheets to guide the agent through the calculations involved. When agents complained about the book being cumbersome and the process too complicated, a switch was made to a "slide-rule" kind of rater consisting of a sleeve into which cards containing the rate tables could be inserted. The agent slid the card to the proper description of the driver and his or her experience, and read the rates for the various coverages through windows in the sleeve. While this enabled the agent to dispense with the bulky rate manual, it still required adding together the rates for various drivers and cars in the family and a knowledge of the procedure for combining all the information into a single quote, a process which could take up to fifteen minutes—fifteen minutes while the clients sat and twiddled their thumbs. Not a dynamic sales approach! It was also difficult to use "what if" approaches. Recalculating the premium with different coverages or different amounts to try to come up with a package which met the client's needs was impeded by the difficulty of going through the whole process again.

The problem was solved by the advent of true computers in packages scarcely larger than the pocket calculators of a few years ago. These machines (SHARP 1500As) can fit easily into a briefcase or even into a jacket pocket yet provide more than 22K of storage. They are battery operated and have a non-volatile memory, so they "remember" the rating program as long as the batteries last, even when shut off. The computer is programmed in BASIC, with part of the program resident in RAM and part in a custom programmed PROM. And their cost, measured in hundreds of dollars rather than thousands as the result of decreasing prices for integrated circuit chips, makes it possible to equip Prudential's thousands of agent.

Instead of pulling out a manual or a bunch of cards, the agent simply turns on the Hand Held Computer (as the company calls it), indicates what policy he or she wants to rate, and answers a series of questions flashed on the computer's liquid crystal display. Most of the questions can be answered with a single keystroke (Y for "Yes"; N for "No") or by keying in an amount. Since the agent is asking the client for this information as he or she goes along, the client is kept involved in the process. When all the necessary data have been input, the computer takes over and calculates all the rates according to proper procedures, adds them up, and displays a final quote. The entire process, including keying in data, takes at most five minutes and keeps the agent involved with the client throughout the process. It is also simple to try "what if" possibilities by repeating the process as often as desired with changes in amounts—the computer "remembers" the previously entered figures or answers, so only new data has to be rekeyed.

When rates or the rating process changes, one computer in each agency office is connected to a modem which in turn is connected to a computer in the company's home office via regular telephone lines. The computer in the local office is then reprogrammed by remote control from the home office computer. That local computer, in turn, is connected to each of the other agents' computers in the office, copying the new rates and program into each.

The acceptance of the Hand Held Computer program by the agents has been overwhelmingly positive. They were quick to see the advantages in being relieved of lengthy computations, leaving them free to sell insurance—their real job. The size and "user friendliness" of the computer make it totally nonthreatening and easy to use. Agents like the fact that the computer, besides being useful, enhances their clients' perceptions of them as professionals working for a "state of the art" company. From the company's perspective, the Hand Held Computer means fewer rate misquotes, hence fewer dissatisfied customers, and more emphasis on analysis of client needs, hence more sales, instead of wasting time on brute calculations.

Since the Hand Held Computer program is relatively new, it is difficult to predict where it will eventually lead. It is probably true that as remote data links, either through phone or through radio, become more available and less expensive, an advanced form of the Hand Held Computer may one day make it possible for the information gathered by the agent to be fed directly into the company's central computer, bypassing the entire process of manually keying information from apps. But until the technology and the laws requiring companies to retain paper copies of signed applications change, the Hand Held Computer will remain state of the art.

DISCUSSION POINTS

1. Discuss how employees responded when microcomputers were first introduced at PRUPAC. Do you think that this is a fairly typical reaction when computers are introduced in similar situations?
2. Discuss the benefits the hand-held computers have had for PRUPAC's agents, its customers, and PRUPAC itself. How might a similar device be used in the future? (Point out ways not mentioned in the text.)

17

Computer Security, Crime, Ethics, and the Law

INTRODUCTION

There is no doubt that computers have had a very significant impact on our lives and our society. By the same token, extensive use of computers has created new problems that must be dealt with. Just as the computer's success is attributed to the imagination of people, many of the problematic situations that must be dealt with result from human nature. Computer crime and security, for example, are two issues that have created considerable concern among individuals who use computers for personal and business purposes. With computers being used as the main means of storage of personal information on credit, employment, taxes, and other aspects of a person's life, privacy is becoming a growing concern.

This chapter reviews some of the human issues associated with the use of computers. Computer crime and security as well as ethics and privacy are discussed. The chapter concludes with a discussion of issues relating to the law and how computers have affected it.

ARTICLE

For Better Security, Control Human Factor

Jerome Lobel

PHOENIX—It has been said that computer security is "technology driven," inferring that new computer-oriented tools may be the cause of new social, industrial and political problems. I do not agree, for although technology does contribute to the problems of computer abuse, I predict that the most important solutions that will evolve in the future will deal primarily with the control of human factors by human beings.

In other words, better decision making with regard to system design, implementation, operation, control, and legislation will have more impact on computer abuse than simply developing technical solutions to technology-induced problems. As increasing numbers of people are given "user friendly" access to a growing number of computers, problems of system abuse, crime, and privacy violations will also increase, and probably proportionately.

The significance of the total human factor problem is almost too large to comprehend. Consider, for instance, that there are over 100,000 computer sites in the United States and Europe that process, store and communicate valuable information.

The United States alone has well over three million computer terminals connected to tens of thousands of host computers, and it has been estimated that by 1990, automation will have grown to a point where more than 50 percent of the American labor force will have to know how to use computers.

We must take the following factors into consideration if computer abuse is to be controlled.

- Proper education and training of designers, operators and users in the proper ethical and physical application of computer technology. This can have a more positive impact on security and privacy than any other recommended solution.
- More extensive involvement of users in their systems' design, implementation and control responsibilities. Generally speaking, an information system will not be any more secure than its developers and owners want it to be.
- Recognition that only *people* can give or accept system security and privacy responsibilities. In addition, people (i.e., management, administrators, legislators) must decide what the penalties are going to be for security violations, and then enforce the rules.

Finally, the combination of prevention and detection through better computer design, and decisive penalty administration in the case of violation, should provide most organizations with the level of security they desire, even within the constraints of a constantly changing technology.

Currently, the human factor is the key element in relation to such topics as computer security, ethics, and crime. Issues such as hacking, employee loyalty, theft of services, physical threats to security, and software copying are all dependent on how humans interact with computers in an extremely dynamic environment.

COMPUTER CRIME
AND SECURITY

Computer crime is a greater problem than most people realize. Americans are losing billions of dollars to high-technology criminals whose crimes go undetected and unpunished; estimates of losses range from at least $2 billion to more than $40 billion a year. While no one really knows how much is being stolen, the total appears to be growing fast.

The earliest known instance of electronic embezzlement occurred in 1958, just a few years after IBM began marketing its first line of business computers. By the mid-1970s, scores of such crimes were being reported every year; yearly losses were estimated to be as high as $300 million.

Even worse problems appear to be ahead. Home computers and electronic funds transfer (EFT) systems pose a new threat to the billions of dollars in data banks accessible through telephone lines (see Figure 17–1). Already, criminals have made illegal switches of money over the phone, and more cases can be expected as EFT systems become widespread. Furthermore, the trend to distributed systems is relentless, and distributed systems present many opportunities for security and privacy violations.

Figure 17–1 ▪ Electronic Funds Transfer (EFT) From a Home Computer

Computer Crime Defined

What is meant by the term *computer crime*? There is no consensus on this question; however, the legal community has been focusing more attention on it through legislation and court opinions. Taking a broad but practical view, computer crime can be defined as a criminal act that poses a greater threat to a computer user than it would to a non–computer user, or a criminal act that is accomplished through the use of a computer.

Computer crime, as defined here, therefore, consists of two kinds of activity: (1) the use of a computer to perpetrate acts of deceit, theft, or concealment that are intended to provide financial, business-related, property, or service advantages; and (2) threats to the computer itself, such as theft of hardware or software, sabotage, and demands for ransom. Because computer crimes seldom involve acts of physical violence, they are generally classified as white-collar crimes. Computer criminals are often believed to be young and ambitious with impressive educational credentials. They tend to be technically competent and come from all employee levels, including technicians, programmers, managers, and high-ranking executives.

Types of Computer Crime

The variety of computer crimes is quite extensive and can be classified into four broad categories: (1) sabotage, (2) theft of services, (3) property crimes, and (4) financial crimes. This section examines each of these categories and gives examples drawn from actual crimes.

Sabotage Sabotage of computers results in destruction or damage of computer hardware. This type of computer crime often resembles traditional sabotage because the computer itself is not used to carry out the destruction. However, sabotage may require some sophistication if computer-assisted security systems must be thwarted or the system is manipulated to do harm to itself.

Computers are targets of sabotage and vandalism especially during times of political activism. Dissident political groups during the 1960s, for instance, conducted assaults on computer installations, often causing extensive damage. Other forms of physical violence have included shooting a computer with a revolver and flooding the computer room. One fired employee simply walked through the data storage area with an electromagnet, thereby erasing valuable company records. A computer's power source can also be the target of a saboteur.

Obviously, these acts of violence do not require any special expertise on the part of the criminal. Sabotage may, however, be conducted by dissatisfied former employees who may put to use some of their knowledge of company operations to gain access to and destroy both hardware and software.

Although computer sabotage is not the type of computer crime that people see as threatening in the same way as if the secrets of the computer were manipulated by a misguided genius, its potential threat should not be taken lightly. The degree of sophistication in a computer crime does not necessarily correlate with the cost of rectifying the damage.

Theft of Services Computer services may be abused in a variety of ways, depending upon the individual system. Some examples of theft of computer services have involved politicians using a city's computer to conduct campaign mailings or employees conducting unauthorized free-lance services on a company computer after working hours.

Time-sharing systems have been exposed to great amounts of abuse due to inadequate or nonexistent security precautions. It is much easier to gain unauthorized access to a time-sharing system than to a closed system. Though most require passwords to gain access, such a system is only as good as the common sense and caution of its users. A time-sharing system that does not require regular changing of access codes is inviting the theft of valuable computer time. The amazing lack of care exercised by supposedly sophisticated users in this regard made national headlines recently when it was discovered that a group of high school computer buffs in Milwaukee had accessed numerous information systems, including those of banks, hospitals, and even the defense research center in Los Alamos, New Mexico. The students reportedly gained access by using each system's password, some of which had not been changed for years and many of which were obtained from public sources.

Wiretapping is another technique used to gain unauthorized access to a time-sharing system. By "piggybacking" onto a legitimate user's line, one can have free use of the user's privileges whenever the line is not being used by the authorized party.

One of the prime examples of computer services theft took place at the University of Alberta. In 1976, a student at the university undertook an independent study under the supervision of a professor to investigate the security of the university's computer system, a time-sharing system with more than 5,000 users, some as far away as England. After discovering several gaps in the system's security, he was able to develop a program that reduced the possibility for unauthorized use as well as for other tampering. He brought this program to the attention of the computer center, which took no action on the student's recommendations because it was assumed that planned changes in the system would remove security shortcomings. However, the changes were not implemented for another nine months, and during this period, the program, which was capable of displaying passwords, was leaked to several students on campus. "Code Green," as the program was nicknamed, was eventually run several thousand times.

The university attempted to crack down on the unauthorized users and revoked several students' access privileges. Among these students were two who had been able to manipulate the program to get the computer to display the complete listing of all user passwords, including those at the highest privilege levels. In essence, this gave them unlimited access to the computer's files and programs. These students retaliated against the university administration by occasionally rendering the system inoperable and with less harmful acts, such as periodically inserting an obscenity into the payroll file. With an unlimited supply of IDs, they were able to escape detection, compiling a library of the computer's programs and even monitoring the implementation of the new security system. The desperate university computer personnel focused exclusively on this situation, keeping a detailed log of all terminal dialogues. This effort led them to a terminal in the geology department one evening, and the students were apprehended.

Theft of Property The most obvious computer crime that comes to mind in crimes of property is the theft of computer equipment itself. This has been more common with the increasing miniaturization of computer components and the advent of home computers. Such crimes, like acts of vandalism, are easily absorbed into traditional concepts of crime and present no unique legal problems. More intriguing is the issue of what actually constitutes property in the context of computer crimes. Different courts have come to very different conclusions on this issue.

Computer crimes of property theft frequently involve merchandise of a company whose orders are processed by computers. These crimes are usually committed by internal personnel who have a thorough knowledge of the operation. By record manipulation, dummy accounts can be created, causing orders of products to be shipped to an accomplice outside the organization. Similarly, one can cause checks to be paid out for receipt of nonexistent merchandise.

Theft of property need not be limited to actual merchandise but may also extend to software. Those with access to a system's program library can easily obtain copies for their own use or, more frequently, for resale to a competitor. Technical security measures in a computer installation are of little use when dishonest personnel take advantage of their positions of responsibility.

This kind of theft is by no means limited to those within the company structure, however. A computer service having specialized programs but poor security may open itself up to unauthorized access by a competitor. All that is necessary is that the outsider gain access to proper codes. This can be done in a number of ways, including clandestine observation of a legitimate user logging on from a remote terminal or use of a remote minicomputer to test for possible access codes.

Financial Crimes Although not the most common type, financial computer crimes are perhaps the most serious in terms of monetary loss. With the projected increasing dependence on electronic fund transfers, implications for the future are indeed ominous.

A common method of committing this kind of crime involves checks. These mass-produced, negotiable instruments can be manipulated in a number of ways. An employee familiar with a firm's operations can cause multiple checks to be made out to the same person. Checks can also be rerouted to a false address or to an accomplice. Such crimes do not seem so incredible when one realizes the scope of *unintentional* mistakes that have been made with computerized checks. For example, the Social Security Administration once accidentally sent out 100,000 checks to the wrong addresses while the system's files were being consolidated.

A form of a financial computer crime that has captured the attention of many authors, but has probably been used much less frequently than one would expect from media discussion, is known as the "round-off fraud." In this crime, the thief, perhaps a bank employee, collects the fractions of cents in customers' accounts that are created when the applicable interest rates are applied. These fractions are then stored in an account created by the thief. The theory is that fractions of cents collected from thousands of accounts on a regular basis will yield a substantial amount of money.

Another type of financial crime involves juggling confidential information, both personal and corporate, within a computer. Once appropriate access is gained to records, the ability to alter them can be highly marketable. At least one group operating in California engaged in the business of creating favorable credit histories to clients seeking loans.

Finally, one of the more ingenious financial crimes perpetrated through the use of a computer occurred in 1977 at Florida's Flagler Dog Track. The dog-racing odds were figured by computer, and often the races were conducted so quickly that the odds would not be figured completely until after the race was over. A conspiracy was developed whereby an operator of the computer received the race results from an accomplice observing the race. He then stopped the computer program in progress, deducted a number of losers and added a corresponding number to the pool of winners in computer storage. The program was restarted and shortly finished its run. False winning tickets were then printed, also by computer, and were cashed in the next day. Since winners were paid from a pool formed by the losers' money, there was no way to detect the loss. Rather, each winner's share was somewhat less than it should have been.

These cases exemplify the types of electronic crime being committed: manipulating input to the computer; changing computer programs; and stealing data, computer time, and computer programs. The possibilities for computer crime seem endless. It has recently been suggested that computers are used extensively by organized crime and that a computer-aided murder may already have taken place.

The unique threat of computer crime is that criminals often use computers to conceal not only their own identities but also the existence of the crimes. Law officers worry because solving computer crimes seems to depend on luck. Many such crimes are never discovered because company executives do not know enough about computers to detect them. Others are hushed up to avoid scaring customers and stockholders. It is estimated that only about 15 percent of computer thefts are reported to police. Many of these do not result in convictions and jail terms because the complexities of data processing mystify most police officials, prosecutors, judges, and jurors.

Crime Prevention and Detection Using Computers

The computer's ability to make statistical analyses has been called on in New York City to help authorities pinpoint buildings that are likely targets for arson. Several agencies contribute information to the computer about fires, and further data are available on fires that have occurred in the recent past. Out of this mass of data, the computer constructs profiles of the most probable targets of arsonists. The city can keep a watch on the likely buildings and tell their owners how to lessen the risk of fires. The program is also intended to decrease the owners' incentive to burn the buildings to collect the insurance proceeds. Part of the data mix fed into the computer is the names of landlords who are behind in their taxes or who have been cited for safety or occupancy violations.

Another computerized crime predictor, this one maintained by the FBI, has drawn a good deal of criticism—some of it from members of Congress. No complaints are heard about the system as it pertains to tracking known criminals. What worries people is that the Justice Department is using the system to monitor people who are considered a threat to officials but who have never been convicted of a crime. Under the plan, the Secret Service can place in the FBI's National Crime Information Center computer (see Figure 17–3) the names of persons considered to be threats to the President, Vice President, presidential candidates, visiting heads of state, or anyone else the Secret Service must protect. Among the most elaborate communication systems in the world, the National Crime Information Center is linked to 64,000 federal, state, and local justice agencies (see Figure 17–3).

Figure 17–2 ■ Computer technology has become an important tool for police work.

Figure 17–3 ■ FBI's National Crime Information Center (NCIC)

Theft Made Easier?

No longer do thieves have to enter one's house to steal money or valuable household items. They can now use telephone lines. Many home computer owners are using their computers, telephone lines, and a videotex service to do their banking, send mail, and order groceries. This is making possible a new type of crime—electronic theft.

The only equipment the thief needs is a computer, a telephone, and a modem. The thief can often determine user passwords and account numbers by random selection or by accessing an electronic bulletin board, where this information is often found.

Electronic theft is becoming a threat to security of information. Companies offering this type of service to home users must continue to improve the security of their phone-computer systems.

The head of the FBI said the Secret Service receives about 9,000 reports a year about people who might constitute a danger to public figures. Of these, 300 to 400 are considered dangerous. By putting these names in the bureau's massive computer, the Secret Service is able to learn immediately if any of its suspects are arrested and thus can keep track of their movements. In addition, any local law enforcement agency can quickly determine if a person they are considering arresting or have arrested is a Secret Service suspect. Those concerned about civil liberties express fears that through this system anyone's name might find its way into the computer, possibly causing damage to an innocent person.

Not only have computers aided in crime prevention, they have also made some headlines in crime detection. A far-ranging computer system helped put an end to the string of child killings in Atlanta. Using two IBM computers and several data bases, the Atlanta police department was able to pinpoint Wayne Williams as the prime suspect in the twenty-eight killings and ultimately convict him for the murder of two.

Because ten different law enforcement agencies were involved in the Atlanta cases, officials agreed early in the investigation that a system was needed for handling and cross-checking the great volume of investigative data and tips that poured in. The computer system was designed so that key words could be fed into it to generate a printout of all other data that contained those words. For example, if someone reported seeing a blue van in the area where a body was discovered, operators could ask the computer to bring up all other references to "blue" and "van." Through such repeated uses of the computer, Williams was finally apprehended. When Williams went to trial, the computer system was used to check defense testimony against prior statements, and the results were factored into the cross-examination.

After a machine gun raid on a Jewish restaurant in Paris, French President François Mitterand announced that his country was developing an antiterrorist data base whose systematical use could put an end to this type of activity. The French antiterrorist data base holds information from a number of legal agencies, among them those having to do with border security, military security, and terrorism. It is modeled after a similar data base in Austria.

Computer Security

Computer security involves the technical and administrative safeguards required to protect a computer-based system (hardware, personnel, and data) against the major hazards to which most computer systems are exposed and to control access to information.

Physical computer systems and data in storage are vulnerable to several hazards—fire, natural disaster, environmental problems, and sabotage.

Physical Threats to Security

■ *Fire.* Fire is one of the more apparent problems because most computer installations use combustible materials—punched cards, paper, and so on. Further, if a fire gets started, water cannot be used to extinguish it, because water can damage magnetic storage media and hardware. Carbon-dioxide fire-extinguisher systems are hazardous because they would endanger employees, if any were trapped in the computer room. Halon, a nonpoisonous chemical gas, can be used in fire extinguishers, but such extinguishers are costly.

- *Natural disasters.* Many computer centers have been damaged or destroyed by floods, cyclones, hurricanes, and earthquakes. Floods pose a serious threat to the computer hardware and wiring. However, water in the absence of heat will not destroy magnetic tapes unless the tapes are allowed to retain moisture over an extended period of time. Protection against natural disasters should be considered when the location for the computer center is chosen; for example, the center should not be located in an area prone to flooding.
- *Environmental problems.* Usually, computers are installed in buildings that were not originally planned to accommodate them. This practice can give rise to environmental problems. For example, water and steam pipes may run through a computer room; bursting pipes could result in extensive damage. Pipes on floors above the computer room are also potentially hazardous; so all ceiling holes should be sealed. Data on magnetic media can be destroyed by magnetic fields created by electric motors in the vicinity of the computer room. Other environmental problems include power failures, brownouts (temporary surges or drops in power), and external radiation.
- *Sabotage.* Sabotage represents the greatest physical risk to computer installations. Saboteurs can do great damage to computer centers with little risk of apprehension. For example, magnets can be used to scramble code on tapes, bombs can be planted, and communication lines can be cut. Providing adequate security against such acts of sabotage is extremely difficult and expensive.

Data Security Measures In addition to safeguarding their computer systems from these physical difficulties, companies must protect stored data against illegitimate use by controlling access to it. There is no simple solution to these security problems. Some ways to protect computer systems from physical dangers, such as fire and flood, are suggested in the list above. Organizations such as government agencies and businesses have instituted various other security measures—most to restrict access to computerized records, others to provide for reconstruction of destroyed data. Some examples are given below:

- Backup copies of data are stored outside the organization's location, and recovery procedures are established.
- Authorized users are given special passwords. Remote-terminal users have their own unique codes, and batch-processing users have specific job cards. Codes and passwords should be changed frequently.
- The scope of access to the computer system is proportionate to the user's security clearance and job responsibility. Access to specific portions of the data base can be gained only by those whose jobs necessitate it.
- Installations are guarded by internal security forces. For example, access to the data-processing department may be restricted to personnel with special badges and keys.
- Data is **encrypted,** or translated into a secret code, by complex coding devices that scramble information before it is transmitted or stored. When data is transmitted to or from remote terminals, it is encrypted at one end and **decrypted,** or translated back into plain text, at the other. Files can also be protected by the data's being encrypted before it is stored and decrypted after it has been retrieved. Data is principally encrypted on its way out of the computer and decrypted on its way back in.
- Computer installations use detectors that identify legitimate individual com-

On Locking the Barn Door after the (Trojan) Horse Has Been Stolen

Uses of computers in small businesses have been growing at a prodigious rate—and so have abuses. Small businesses are more vulnerable to computer crime than large corporations because they may be unable to absorb the losses resulting from "data diddling" in their computer programs.

One way to "diddle" the data is to insert a "Trojan horse" in the program. The Trojan horse, you remember from Greek legend, was left outside the gates of the city of Troy. The huge wooden horse was hollow. Being curious, the Trojans brought the horse inside the gates. At night, Greek soldiers poured out of the horse's insides, opened the gates to the Greek army, and destroyed Troy. So much for Troy. But Trojan horses can be "brought" into a computer program and cause the software to sabotage the data from within. Enough damage can be done to destroy a company.

How can small businesses protect themselves against data diddling? Computer controls such as encryption, backup procedures, and blocking techniques will help, but companies will have to remember to use the same precautions with a computer system as they once used with a manual system. Carelessness can cost a company its life.

puter users by fingerprints or voice patterns. For example, computer makers have developed attachments that grant access only to operators who put proper thumbprints on glass plates. Adoption of such expensive devices is slow, however, because they deter the main objectives of computers: economy and convenience.

Establishing Computer Security These security measures are not complete, however. They may not prevent internal sabotage, fraud, or embezzlement. For example, an employee with a special access code may steal classified information. Banks and insurance companies are especially susceptible. Often, these companies do not wish to report the incidents because of the bad publicity and the difficulty in solving such crimes.

How, then, can organizations establish computer security? First, computer users must recognize their role in security. If a high-level priority is assigned to security in the company, employees must be made aware of it and of the security measures that are being taken.

Second, many organizations recognize the need to have a well-trained security force—a department of security guards who specialize in maintaining data security, conducting system audits, and asking the right kinds of questions on a daily and continuing basis. Computerized records, like handwritten books, should be scrutinized regularly to see that everything is in order.

Third, a company should exercise a great deal of care in the selection and screening of the *people* who will have access to computers, terminals, and computer-stored data. Companies should choose programmers as carefully as they select attorneys or accountants.

Lastly, companies must discharge employees who stray beyond legal and ethical boundaries. Whenever these incidents occur, it is imperative that people be shown that they will not be tolerated and that, however hard the necessary course of action, those responsible for security and protection have the intellectual and ethical integrity to follow through.

ETHICS AND PRIVACY

Ethics

Another issue facing both organizations and individuals in relation to computer use is computer ethics. As is true in the cases of computer crime, security, and privacy, computer ethics are also largely dependent on human nature. The issue of computer ethics is just beginning to be recognized but will undoubtedly receive more attention in the near future.

Computer ethics is a term used to refer to the standard of moral conduct in computer use. Although some specific laws have been enacted in problem areas such as privacy invasion and crime, ethics are a way in which the "spirit" of some laws can be carried to other computer-related activities. Some of the topics currently being addressed under the ethics issue include hacking, the security and privacy of data, employee loyalty, and the copying of computer software. Security and privacy of data are discussed in other sections of the chapter, while discussions of hacking, employee loyalty and software copying will follow below.

Hacking   **Hacking** is a computer term used to describe the activity of computer enthusiasts who are challenged by the practice of breaking computer security measures designed to prevent unauthorized access to a particular computer system. Hackers do this for a number of reasons—to gain access to confidential data or illegal computer time, or just for the fun of it. Computer users should be aware that seemingly innocent activities such as hacking are actually criminal acts. Regardless of the reason, hacking is the same as intentionally committing a crime. Gaining unauthorized access to another computer can be as serious as breaking into someone's home.

The case in which a group of Milwaukee high school students gained access to the defense research center's computer in Los Alamos, New Mexico (see Theft of Services) is a prime example of hacking. The youths, after being caught, stated that they did not see any classified information, but that they did accidentally erase some files. The same group of students accessed another computer in a New York cancer center. The computer, which was used to monitor 250 cancer patients, failed for a short time due to the activity of these youths. The FBI is now investigating the activities of these students who reportedly broke into forty different computers. And what were the reasons given for their activity? They did not know it was a crime, and it gave them something to do in the evenings!

Employee Loyalty   The employee's duty of loyalty is another ethical issue that has surfaced in the area of data processing. Because the field of data processing is a dynamic environment with a shortage of qualified personnel, there are many job opportunities and, therefore, a considerable amount of job changing among data-processing personnel. Because an employee does have some obligations to his or her current employer, there have been a number of court cases that address the issue of employee loyalty to employers as a duty.

In one particular case, a data-processing consultant employed by Firm A was seeking a similar job with Firm B, which was in competition for consulting contracts with Firm A. Prior to being offered a position with Firm B, the consultant was asked to attend an interview with a potential client on behalf of Firm B. Unbeknownst to either the consultant or Firm B, Firm A was also seeking a contract from the client.

Upon becoming aware of the circumstances, Firm A then sued the consultant, who had left to join Firm B, alleging breach of his duty of loyalty. The day the consultant attended the interview, he had called in sick to Firm A. The trial court criticized the consultant for wanting to have it both ways, finding that the excuse not only permitted him to aid himself but also aid the competitor on the employer's time. However, an appellate court disagreed, based on the fact that neither Firm B nor the consultant knew Firm A was also competing for the contract and that an employee has the right to seek alternate employment if he or she is not bound by employment contract for a specific period of time. The court believed that an employee had the right to change jobs as long as he or she were not under contract for a definite term and that the right should be exercisable without the necessity of revealing the plans to the current employer.

Although the court opinions differed, it should be noted that the courts do recognize some degree of duty of loyalty to the employer on the part of the employee. For this reason, all employees in the area of data processing should be aware of their obligations and rights as employees and as potential

Is the Computer Raising New Ethical Questions?

Is the computer raising new ethical questions in industry, or is it just raising ones that have laid dormant for many years? Ethical considerations that have come up include: can an employee use a company computer for personal use? and how much data on employees or customers should be stored in personal computers?

A survey of 100 companies was recently conducted. Over half of the companies have policies regarding the use of company computers.

International Business Machines Corporation, General Electric Company, and Equitable Life Assurance Society have developed policies regarding personal use of company computers. IBM, for example, does not allow its employees to use the company computers for anything other than business. However, General Electric allows employees to use company personal computers for personal tasks on their own time. Equitable Life even allows employees to take company computers home.

The amount and type of data the company stores on its employees and customers can also be a problem; confidentiality is the major issue involved. Some companies have adapted standards in this area, also.

COMPUTER SECURITY, CRIME, ETHICS, AND THE LAW

employees. It should also be noted that actions taken in the process of changing positions should be conducted in an ethical fashion.

Software Copying   Another area of ethical concern is **software copying,** or **piracy.** Software piracy is the unauthorized copying of a computer program that has been written by someone else. Many software manufacturers write security measures into their programs so that they cannot be copied without authorization. However, some computer enthusiasts are challenged by trying to break this form of security as well. Whether done for personal use or to sell for profit, software piracy is a crime.

   Computer ethics cannot be emphasized enough. It is the responsibility of each computer user to evaluate his or her own actions and determine the standard of morals to be followed. Only through ethical behavior will the ultimate security and privacy of computers and computer data be assured.

Privacy

Privacy involves an individual's ability to determine what, how, and when information about him or her is communicated to others. With computers being used as the main means of storage of personal information relating to credit, employment, taxes, and other aspects of a person's life, the issue of privacy is becoming a matter of great importance. Since the early 1970s, regulations and laws regarding the protection of privacy have been enacted. These regulations and laws control the collection, use, distribution, and transmission of personal data.

Data Bases   Because of large data banks kept on individuals by the government (especially by the IRS), the workplace, banks, credit unions, and universities, many people feel that individual privacy is threatened.

Figure 17–4 ▪ FBI's Organized Crime Information System (OCIS) Data Base Shown Online

Because information is both easier to obtain and easier to store as a result of computers, there are more data being collected on individuals. An individual's data are stored in one main file and can be easily accessed by entering his or her social security number.

Also, the increased ease of obtaining information tempts organizations to collect more information than is really necessary. People then have less control over who has access to their personal information. They are unaware of whether or not their personal data files are complete and accurate. They may not even be aware that such information is being kept about them at all.

The major concerns about privacy can be summarized:

■ Too much personal information about individuals is being collected and stored in computerized files. The possibility of file integration exists because many of the systems use social security numbers as a common means of identification. This permits the various users to link files, easily correlating and matching scattered bits of data.

■ The accuracy, completeness, and currency of the information may be low.

■ Much of the personal information data may be irrelevant for the purposes for which they will be used.

■ Decisions are often made by organizations solely on the basis of these computerized records.

■ The security of stored data is a problem.

Despite the negative aspects of this use of computers as vast stores of personal information, it reduces costs of institutions and adds to efficiency. It is helpful, say, for a business to have adequate financial information about an individual before issuing credit. However, an appropriate balance must be struck between the need of organizations for information and the rights of individuals to maintain their privacy.

Figure 17–5 ■ Magnetic Tapes and Drives for the FBI's National Crime Information Center Data Base

Privacy Legislation   Efforts to protect our privacy have led government, particularly at the federal level, to pass several laws and regulations. The major legislation has been the Privacy Act of 1974, which covers information gathered by the federal government. This act, applying only to federal agencies, provides that:

■ There must be no secret data banks of personal information.
■ Individuals must be allowed to learn what information about themselves is being recorded and how it will be used.
■ A way must be provided for individuals to correct wrong information.
■ Information collected for one purpose should not be used for another without the consent of the individual involved.
■ Organizations creating, manipulating, using, or divulging personal information must ensure the data's reliability and take precautions to prevent its misuse.

Although the act did not extend to state and local governments, many states have followed suit with similar legislation. States are also becoming aware of the need to protect individuals from privacy invasion by private businesses. However, the laws vary from state to state, as does their potential effectiveness.

The lawmaking process is slow on this issue, perhaps partly due to the lack of litigation over privacy. Since the data may be disclosed without the knowledge or consent of the subjects, most people do not realize when their privacy has been breached. If they did know, many still would not go to court for fear of making public the very information they wanted protected.

COMPUTERS AND THE LAW

This portion of the chapter discusses two of the legal issues associated with owning a computer system. The purchase of computer hardware and software and the applicable warranties, and the copyright law and how it applies to computer software will be presented. A discussion of express and implied warranties in relation to the purchase of computer hardware and software will be followed by a review of copyright law and how it applies to the writing of computer programs.

Warranties

The **Uniform Commercial Code (UCC)** is a set of provisions proposed by legal experts to promote uniformity among the state courts in their legal treatment of commercial transactions. By using Article Two of the UCC, the courts have a common basis for rendering decisions concerning the sale of computer hardware and software by vendors.

Common law, on the other hand, is based on customs and past judicial decisions in similar cases. If Article Two of the UCC does not apply to a transaction, then the common law of contracts will apply. The UCC is a far better system since it is more modern and basically abolishes the concept of *caveat emptor* (a Latin legal maxim meaning "let the buyer beware"). Under Article Two, for example, the computer user is given implied warranty protection, whereas under common law, buyer protection is not presumed or implied and must therefore be negotiated and agreed upon in the final contract. Most computer vendors are reluctant to agree to such negotiations.

For the UCC to apply to computer acquisitions, two main conditions must be satisfied. First, the contract must be one for goods, not services. As a general rule, the UCC is not applicable to contracts for services. Second, the contract should be for the *sale* of goods. Article Two of the UCC does not normally apply to leases or licenses.

Express Warranties Under Article Two of the UCC, **express warranties** are created when the seller makes any promise or statement of fact concerning the goods being sold which the purchaser uses as a basis for purchasing the goods. By doing so, the seller warrants, or guarantees, that the goods are those that will meet the needs of the purchaser. An express warranty may be created by the supplier's use of a description, sample, or model in attempting to sell the goods, although the seller's contract terms will often attempt to limit or disclaim all such warranties. Express warranties are also found in the written contract, such as statements that defective equipment will be replaced or repaired for up to one year after delivery. A **breach of contract** occurs if the goods fail to conform to the express warranty, in which case the buyer is entitled to a reduction in price of the goods as compensatory damages. One drawback of express warranties is that the purchaser must keep the defective equipment. Therefore, unless expressly stated in the contract, the computer hardware or software would not have to be replaced, only reduced in price.

Implied Warranties Implied warranties were also created under Article Two of the Uniform Commercial Code. **Implied warranties** provide that a contract for the sale of goods automatically contains certain warranties that exist by law. An implied warranty need not be verbally made nor included in the written warranties of a contract to be effective. Two major types of implied warranties include implied warranty of merchantability and implied warranty of fitness for a particular purpose.

The **implied warranty of merchantability** only exists if the seller is considered a merchant. Computer and software vendors are classified as merchants because they are in the business of selling computer-related products on a repetitive basis. In the case of a purchased computer system, an implied warranty of merchantability guarantees the user that the system will function properly for a reasonable period of time. As in the case of express warranties, however, the purchaser must keep the defective equipment.

To create an **implied warranty of fitness** for a particular purpose, the purchaser must communicate to the supplier the specific purpose for which the product will be used. The purchaser must then rely upon the supplier's judgment, skill, and expertise to select suitable computer hardware and software. If the computer hardware or software later fails to meet those needs, the supplier has breached this implied warranty and is liable for damages. Again, however, the violation of this warranty permits the purchaser to recover only a certain amount of the sales price.

Copyright Law

Computer software, or computer programs, have been accepted for copyright registration since 1964. In order for a program to be protected under the copyright law, it must contain a notice of copyright that is visible to the user.

This notice of copyright must consist of three things: (1) the © symbol, the word *copyright,* or the abbreviation *copr.,* (2) the year of the work's first publication, and (3) the name of the copyright owner. If these three items are not given, however, the copyright is not necessarily forfeited—the duplicator of the program may not be liable for damages. Unpublished programs are also eligible for protection under the copyright law, and registration is not required since copyright protection exists from the moment of creation. Registration is only required to obtain the right to sue for copyright infringement.

Current copyright law only protects against unauthorized copying and not against unauthorized use. It is not against copyright law, however, to make a copy of a program that is in a magazine, for example, or for archival purposes. There is some question whether copyright law applies to a program in machine-readable form—such as object code—if a copyright was obtained on the source program. In some cases, though, the program output can also be copyrighted. This would prevent such things as screen displays from being used by programs that do not violate the copyright laws.

SUMMARY POINTS

- Taking a broad view, computer crime can be defined as any criminal act that poses a greater threat to a computer user than it would to a non–computer user, or a criminal act that is accomplished through the use of a computer.
- Computer crimes can be classified in four categories: sabotage, theft of services, theft of property crimes, and financial crimes.
- Uses of computers in the prevention and detection of crimes include pinpointing likely arson targets, monitoring people who are potential threats to public officials, and the handling and cross-checking of data and tips in murder investigations.
- Physical threats to computer security exist in the forms of fire, natural disasters, environmental problems (such as power failures, brownouts, and external radiation), and sabotage.
- Data security is an issue that must also be addressed by organizations that store sensitive data on computers. Illegitimate use of data must be controlled through access security measures.
- Computer ethics refers to the standard of moral conduct for computer use. Computer ethics are largely dependent on human nature.
- Hacking is the practice of breaking computer security measures to gain unauthorized access to a computer system. Hacking is a criminal act.
- Employee duty of loyalty is an ethical issue that can pose a serious problem to companies in competition for both business and employees.
- Unauthorized software copying, or piracy, is a crime, whether done for personal use or for profit.
- The major piece of legislation designed to protect individual privacy is the Privacy Act of 1974, which regulates information gathered by the federal government.
- The Uniform Commercial Code (UCC) is a set of provisions established by legal experts to act as a uniform guide to state courts for resolving contract disputes.
- For the UCC to be applicable, the contract must be one for goods rather than services, and the contract should be for the sale of goods, not for leases or licenses.

- Under Article Two of the UCC, express warranties and implied warranties can be created on behalf of the purchaser.
- Copyright law is one method of protecting computer programs from being illegally copied.
- Copyright registration is not required but is necessary if damages would ever be sought for a copyright infringement.

REVIEW QUESTIONS

1. What is computer crime? Do you feel computer crime is a serious problem in our society?
2. Describe some of the ways computers are being used in the detection and prevention of crimes.
3. Briefly explain some of the measures that can be taken by an organization to insure data security.
4. What is meant by the term *computer ethics?* Describe some instances, other than those discussed, in which computer ethics would be required.
5. Do you feel that computer ethics within an organization should be described through a formal company document that establishes what is ethical and what is not, or should computer ethics be a personal issue left to the discretion of each employee? Briefly explain your answer.
6. Why has the issue of privacy become so important? Do you feel that organizations that maintain information on individuals should be required to disclose this information to those people to verify its correctness—why, or why not?
7. Distinguish between express warranties and implied warranties. What are the two types of implied warranties?
8. Why is the copyright law important to a computer software vendor? Would a vendor be protected even if he or she neglected to register the software?

APPLICATION

General Accounting Office

The General Accounting Office (GAO), headed by the Comptroller General of the United States, was created by the Congress in 1921 as an independent, nonpartisan agency to assist in congressional oversight of the executive branch of the federal government. The GAO has approximately 5,000 employees, and its major responsibilities are carried out principally through auditing and evaluating federal programs, functions, and financial operations.

Based on its work, the GAO issues reports to the Congress and federal agency officials, testifies before congressional committees, provides written comments on proposed legislation, and lends support to the Congress in many other ways.

The GAO's basic mission is to investigate all matters regarding the receipt, disbursement, and application of public funds and to make recommendations leading to greater economy and efficiency in public expenditures. The GAO's job is thus as large and as diverse as the federal budget itself, reaching into virtually all aspects of our society and economy.

This application contains information included in a report prepared by the Information Management and Technology Division of the General Accounting Office on Computer Security in the federal government. The report, which was presented to the Subcommittee on Oversight of the Government Management Committee on Governmental Affairs of the United States Senate, addresses the issues of computer and telecommunications security and privacy.

The basic message of the report is that the vulnerabilities facing the government's computer systems and telecommunications networks are increasing as technology advances. The growing numbers of remote computer terminals that provide access to very large data bases make errors or deliberate attacks difficult to discover and fix. Legislation, policies, management roles, and audits provide a framework for counteracting these vulnerabilities, but further steps are needed. In particular, government agencies need to devote more

attention and resources to implementing total systems of control.

THE NATURE OF THE INFORMATION SECURITY PROBLEM

The federal government depends heavily on computers and telecommunications networks to handle information on functions ranging from defense and intelligence to banking and financial activities, health, and education. Much of this information is personal, proprietary, or otherwise sensitive and requires effective protection. Information security has three basic components: computer security, telecommunications security, and physical/administrative personnel security.

GAO reports since 1976 and examinations by others have repeatedly demonstrated that federal information systems are subject to three broad categories of threat: (a) natural hazards, (b) unintentional actions, and (c) intentional actions. Natural hazards include fire, floods, earthquakes, and so on, that can damage or totally destroy equipment, software, and data or seriously interrupt operations through extended power outages. Unintentional actions include equipment failures, malfunctions, and failures resulting from inadequate recovery mechanisms as well as personnel errors and inappropriate actions. The latter two pose the more serious threats. Intentional actions, which receive considerable attention, include attacks on equipment, improper access to and disclosure of information which should be held private, and unauthorized alteration of official records. A variety of technical methods can be used to penetrate computer systems for these purposes.

Providing a reasonable level of protection in today's technological environment is a formidable challenge because the range of vulnerabilities is increasing. The larger systems in use can store more sensitive information in electronic form. The expanded use of remote terminals provides more isolated points of access and makes it difficult to pinpoint errors or attacks. Similarly, the advent of microcomputers provides more individuals with the potential capability to access, create, and manipulate data bases by bypassing central controls. The trend toward linking computers and terminals through telecommunications networks provides potential penetrators with more opportunities, techniques, and devices to access systems, to insert communications, and to intercept and interpret communications.

In spite of the sophistication and complexities of the hardware, software, and communications networks, it must be kept in mind that information security is basically a management problem, not a technology problem, and requires a concerted management solution.

KEY FACTORS AFFECTING INFORMATION SECURITY

Legislation, policy, management by central and executive government agencies, and auditing are the key factors that support federal efforts to provide security.

Legislation

Legislation serves to define information security goals and objectives and to assign overall management responsibilities for security. A variety of laws have been enacted governing different security activities.

The Brooks Act of 1965, which amended the Federal Property and Administrative Services Act of 1949, assigned the Office of Management and Budget (OMB), the General Services Administration (GSA), and the De-

partment of Commerce collective responsibility for managing government agencies' acquisition and maintenance of ADP resources, but placed OMB in a leadership role. The Federal Communications Act of 1934, as later modified by the Omnibus Crime Control and Safe Streets Act of 1968, provided for the protection of electronic transmissions. The Privacy Act of 1974 prescribed controls over personal records dissemination and access. The Paperwork Reduction Act of 1980 broadened OMB's responsibilities in the context of information resources management. Finally, the Federal Managers' Financial Integrity Act of 1982 directed evaluations of administrative and financial internal control systems and agency accounting systems. In 1983 GAO published *Standards for Internal Controls in the Federal Government,* to be used by agencies to establish and maintain effective systems of internal control in compliance with the 1982 act.

Policy

Information security policy should provide government agencies with a clear and concise blueprint for implementing relevant legislation. It should faithfully reflect legislative intent, completely address all pertinent features of the legislation, and be compatible with other related policies.

OMB is the key policymaker in this area. A circular issued by OMB, entitled "Security of Federal Automated Information Systems," outlines basic policy and specifies agencies' responsibilities for the development and implementation of security. In particular, it assigns government-wide responsibilities to GSA, Department of Commerce, and the Office of Personnel Management (OPM). Another OMB circular, "Responsibilities for the Maintenance of Records about Individuals by Federal Agencies," requires agencies to establish reasonable safeguards against improper disclosure of such records. A circular entitled, "Internal Control Systems," revised after passage of the Financial Integrity Act, prescribes policies and guidance for establishing and maintaining internal controls over program and administrative activities. It mandates that all levels of agency management help assure the adequacy of these controls.

Management

Management responsibilities are divided among four "central agencies" (OMB, GSA, Department of Commerce, and OPM) and the remaining executive agencies.

The central agencies should issue policies, guidelines, and regulations that are consistent and coordinated with each other and contain "how-to" specifics where applicable to assist executive agencies in meeting legislative and Executive Office requirements. They also should oversee agencies' implementation of their guidance.

The central agencies have related yet separate responsibilities. OMB must review agencies' organizational structures and management procedures to ensure they meet policy requirements. GSA is required to issue policies and regulations for the physical security of computer rooms and to ensure that agency procurement requests for computers include appropriate security requirements. The Department of Commerce is responsible for developing uniform federal ADP standards, including security standards. It has delegated this responsibility to the National Bureau of Standards (NBS). OPM is responsible for establishing personnel security policies for federal personnel associated with the design, operation, or maintenance of computer systems or having access to data in these systems.

The executive agencies play the most vital role in protecting our information assets. They must develop and implement agency information security programs through a set of policies and procedures which conform to the requirements of applicable legislation and guidance. Their security programs should provide a reasonable, yet cost-effective, level of protection. Agency management should base their programs on assessments of risk and ensure that they incorporate administrative and physical, as well as technical, controls. Finally, agency management must monitor the implementation of their programs.

Agency managers employ a wide variety of techniques to achieve a total system of control. A technique known as risk analysis is used to ascertain the extent to which information systems are vulnerable to natural disaster, human error, and improper or illegal use. This provides a basis for a program to minimize the effects of such vulnerability. Other related techniques include background investigations for employees and contractors associated with computers; contingency plans for emergency response in the event of system failure; backup and recovery capabilities to keep systems operating in the wake of disaster; and the use of encryption devices to protect data transmissions.

Audits

Systematic internal audits provide management with periodic reports on the level of protection actually provided to automated systems in general, and to sensitive applications in particular. Management can use these reports to identify needed corrective measures. The OMB circular entitled "Security of Federal Automated Information Systems" requires agencies to conduct periodic audits of security safeguards. It specifies that these audits be performed by an organization independent of the user organization and computer facility managers.

The Comptroller General has issued specific standards for auditing programs supported by computer-based systems. These standards prescribe that auditors review both general systems and applications controls. They also suggest that reviews be conducted during the early stages of system design and development. The circular entitled "Internal Control Systems" requires that agency inspectors general assist in this process.

GAO AUDIT FINDINGS

Since April 1976 GAO has issued about forty reports related to information security within government agencies. These reports have identified deficiencies in the areas of legislation, policy, management, and audit, including such things as:

* Inadequate telecommunications security legislation.
* Need for revision of OMB circulars used for policy formulation.
* Inadequate effort on the parts of six executive agencies to implement information security program policies and guidance.
* Management that does not use risk analysis techniques to select, implement, and maintain a total system of controls.
* Required personnel background investigations were not always performed.
* A lack of appropriately skilled audit staffs throughout the agencies.

CURRENT ACTIVITIES TO IMPROVE SECURITY

To place the above findings in perspective, the GAO has attempted to identify current initiatives in the areas of legislation, policy, management, and audit that may become vehicles for enhancing security throughout government. These findings include such things as:

- The introduction of two bills in the House and Senate to establish criminal penalties for the fraudulent or illegal use of computers owned by, operated by, or under contract to the U. S. Government.
- Updates of existing information management circulars put out by the OMB to reflect better security measures.
- The various agencies' positive response to audits conducted by the GAO.
- The fact that the central agencies are now focusing more on information security.
- The fact that the Financial Integrity Act requires agencies to evaluate internal accounting and administrative controls and report the findings to Congress and the President.
- The possible sharing of information security techniques used by the Department of Defense.
- The President's Council on Integrity and Efficiency is emphasizing audit activities.

SUMMARY

As Warren G. Reed, Director of the Information Management and Technology Division of the General Accounting Office, has stated, "The potential for loss is increasing because we (the government agencies) are concentrating more information—a valuable resource—in automated systems." It is essential, therefore, that these agencies take the steps necessary to protect this information to the best of their ability.

DISCUSSION QUESTIONS

1. What types of threats does the GAO feel federal information systems are subject to? What types of problems do advances in microcomputer and telecommunication technology pose to federal information systems?
2. What are the key factors that support federal efforts to provide security? Describe how each of these factors can affect the security of federal information systems.

18

Computers in Our Lives: Today and Tomorrow

INTRODUCTION

As the previous chapter pointed out, computers have had, and will continue to have, a significant impact on organizations and the people who work in those organizations. However, computers have also significantly affected areas such as the arts and sciences and even our lives at home. Along with the computer revolution has come an irreversible impact on our lives and our entire society.

This chapter examines some of the effects computer technology has had on our personal lives, education, medicine and science, and arts and entertainment. The chapter will also examine some of the effects computers may have in the future. Because computer technology has moved at such a tremendous speed and is expected to continue to do so, a look at potential computer impact is somewhat difficult. A review of some of the research currently taking place, however, can provide us with some feeling for what our future, in relation to computer technology, holds.

ARTICLE

Tutoring by Telephone

Reach out . . . Reach out and *teach* someone. That's what the folks at Computer Curriculum Corp. aim to do in a educational experiment called Dial-A-Drill. The innovative system, linking a central computer with home telephones, temporarily turns the phone into a computer terminal to help tutor kids in math, spelling, and reading.

Dial-A-Drill automatically calls students at set times, quizzing them in an electronically synthesized voice, for 6 to 10 minutes in the selected subject. The youngsters answer questions by pressing the push buttons on their phone. A plastic overlay placed on the keypad makes certain numbers perform special functions—such as repeat, erase, sound softer or louder, and enter (which corresponds to a computer's Return key and is labeled Go).

For each session, the company's Data General minicomputer draws from a database of thousands of exercises, constantly adjusting the level of difficulty according to students' on-line performance. This approach allows children to progress at their own pace. When the youngster taps in a correct answer, the electronic voice offers words of encouragement, such as "Exactly right" or "Good work." If a wrong answer is entered, the student is asked to listen carefully and to try again. Sometimes a helpful hint is supplied, like "Try rounding the numbers first." Kids get two chances to answer problems; and at the end of each drill, the total number of correct responses is indicated.

The system is remarkably interactive. For instance, in this sixth-grade math problem, the voice responds specifically to an incorrect answer: "Stephanie bought two notepads for 15 cents each," states the computer. "She paid for them with a dollar bill. How much change did she get back?" If you press the number 30, you'll hear: "That was how much two notepads cost. How much change will Stephanie get from a dollar?"

Computer Curriculum Corp., based in Palo Alto, California, specializes in providing computer-assisted instruction to schools. The home phone service is intended to improve students' basic skills by furnishing supplemental work in mental arithmetic, reading, and spelling. Designed for any child—no matter how quickly or slowly he or she learns—each course has been planned for specific grade levels: arithmetic for the first through eighth grades; reading comprehension (through use of a student workbook) for grades one through four; and spelling, for the second through eighth grades.

Fees range from $18 for one course, with calls three times a week, to $52 for all three subjects and five weekly phone sessions. Sutdents' progress is continually tracked; and parents are sent a monthly report.

Rgiht now, Dial-A-Drill is available only in Palo Alto, but anyone can get a demonstration by calling (914) 856-3631. Plans call for expanding the service to other areas of the country this year, according to Nancy Smith, CCC's consumer products and services director. Apart from its convenience, computerized telephone tutoring is beneficial, she says, because the session is "a private, nonthreatening experience."

From Tutoring by Telephone by Bruce Foster, Rick Friedman, and Jane Wollman appearing in the March 1984 issue of Popular Computing magazine. Copyright 1984 Byte Publications, Inc. Used with the permission of Byte Publications, Inc.

Computer-assisted instruction has already had a significant impact on the field of education, and will undoubtedly have a greater impact in the future. As we've said, computers play an important role in our lives today, and that role will certainly grow tomorrow.

COMPUTERS AT HOME

Often, when you talk with people who have used or been affected by computers, you will observe one of two basic attitudes: They loved the computer, or they hated it. Most people enjoy computing and can think of ways in which the computer would be useful at home. This section of the chapter explores three home computer applications: home computer services, automated homes, and home robots.

Home Computer Services

Experiments in banking and shopping at home by computer have already been pronounced successful (see Figure 18–1). The know-how exists to make us all homebodies. If movement in this direction seems slower than predicted, it is mainly because the widespread application of computers is still too expensive. In addition, there is still some consumer resistance. After all, shopping at home does not allow one to actually touch the product which is purchased, and one may not be able to determine its quality or appropriateness. Also, banking at home by computer, may make one feel that the transaction is too impersonal or that his or her finances may be revealed to unauthorized eyes.

Once this initial resistance is overcome, though, the advantages of home-based shopping and banking become clear. When shopping by computer, the customer avoids the cost of driving to stores, the irritation of traffic, and

Figure 18–1 ▪ **Home Information System**

the other inconveniences of shopping in person. Also minimized are the dangers of impulse buying and the prospect of being mugged. Shoppers can call up catalogs from different stores on their video terminals and select the items for purchase. By inserting a keyed charge card into the terminal and pressing a button, the order is placed for home delivery or pickup.

With in-home, twenty-four-hour banking, customers can instantly and as often as desired get the same kind of details about their accounts that are now available only from the mailed monthly statements. The bank-linked computer will allow the user to pay bills automatically by instructing the bank's computers to transfer money out of the designated account and send it to designated creditors.

Another plus of computer ownership is being able to keep up with the changing world beyond your doorstep without leaving home. Research data that were once available only at the local public or university library can now be accessed in the home. Subscription to home information services can give the user video versions of major newspapers, stock market reports, restaurant listings, recipes, and movie reviews.

The information that people wish to access is compiled and stored in huge hard-copy data bases by **data-base producers.** Other companies, called online services, buy the rights to this information and make it available to home users through telecommunication networks and the user's personal computer. *Better Homes & Gardens* magazine, for example, sells the rights to electronically send the magazine to CompuServe, Inc., an online service company. To send *Better Homes & Gardens* to your home terminal, CompuServe uses either the Tymnet or its own telecommunications network.

The popularity of online services is evidenced by the growth in their numbers. In the fall of 1979, only 59 services were listed in the *Directory of Online Databases.* By the fall of 1982, the listings had jumped to 213. Three

of the current major data bases that provide in-home information are The Source, CompuServe, and Dow Jones News/Retrieval.

In most cases, these services can be accessed by the home user with a local phone call, since major telecommunications networks such as Telenet, Tymnet, and Uninet have spun their webs through all of the major American cities. One of the major functions of these networks is error checking. While phone line static may cause little problems with an ordinary phone call, it is a major problem with digital transmission. The files a user requests are checked for errors at regular points along the way from the online service to the user's home.

One of CompuServe's more exciting recent additions is an online encyclopedia. The entire twenty-one volume (28,000 articles, 9 million words) *Grolier's Academic American Encyclopedia* is now available to subscribers. A topic can be researched by requesting a list of articles with the topical key word in the heading.

Automated Homes

A microcomputer can be used to do one particular job, or several microcomputers together can be used to handle many of a home's physical functions. In Arizona a computer-controlled house has been built as a showcase of automated systems. Called Ahwatukee (a Crow Indian word meaning "house of dreams"), this house is described as the state of the art in technology, ecology, and sociology. Visitors come by the thousands each month to view the house in a half-hour tour.

Five microcomputers are linked to run the five systems in the house. Heating, cooling, and the opening and shutting of doors and windows is the primary function of the environmental control system. The security system protects against intruders with the use of television cameras, sensors, and a password-controlled front door. The sensors also watch for fire and will sound a warning if necessary. An electrical switching system uses sensors to note people moving through the house and adjusts lights as appropriate. Cost-efficient use of electricity is assured with the energy management system, and an information storage and retrieval system is provided for personal or home business needs.

Houses are now routinely designed to rely on computer assistance for their maintenance. Linked to sensors, computers can precisely control temperatures at locations throughout the house and make the best use of energy. They can raise shades, activate fans and switches, and turn on security lights (which go from an energy-saving dimness to an alarming brightness if a sensor detects an intruder). They can also dial the police should a break-in occur and activate the video camera that monitors the area of break-in (see Figure 18–2).

Home Robots

An application of computer technology for the home which has seen only limited use so far but could be used considerably more in the future is the home robot. The home robots developed so far perform small tasks such as welcoming guests, acting as sentinels, or retrieving objects (see Figure 18–3).

Androbot Inc., of Sunnyvale, California, has recently introduced B.O.B. (Brains-On-Board), who is described as "a mobile, multi-tasking, fully pro-

Satellites to Show the Way

By the year 2000, motorists may be using a satellite navigation system to show them where they are if they become lost on the highway. An Air Force system, the $3.2 billion Navstar Global Positioning System is scheduled for operation by 1982; although it is intended mainly for military navigation, its signals will also be used by motorists. Receivers in the car will pick up signals to plot routes and find locations on paper maps with satellite coordinates or on video screens.

Among the first vehicles to use the satellite navigation will be emergency vehicles. Rental cars, delivery trucks, and then passenger cars are expected to follow. The nation's automakers are interested. A General Motors spokesman predicts that simple-to-install models will be available to car owners for about $500. A similar portable system will be offered for hikers and boaters.

Figure 18–2 ■ **The Smarthome I**

This home control system may be used to control household appliances and lighting. Here a display screen shows the Tomorrow House home control system.

grammable robot for the home''. B.O.B. has many features, including the ability to wheel about the house, talk, and even retrieve cold beverages from a robot-accessible refirgerator (AndroFridge™) using a robot wagon (AndroWagon™).

Housed within B.O.B. are microprocessors and 3 million bytes of memory. B.O.B. has a vocabulary of over a hundred words and phrases in memory

Figure 18–3 ■ **RB5X Intelligent Robot Manufactured by RB Robot Corporation**

and can be programmed for both speech and motion using a high-level programming language called ACL (Androbot Control Language™). Androbot Inc. describes B.O.B. as, "a newly defined, fully expandable personal robot designed to entertain, to communicate, and to be a useful addition to the home environment."

Heath Company is also offering a home robot in the form of a kit called Hero I. Hero can be programmed by cassette or ordered about with a joystick linked to the robot via a cable. Although robots have a long way to go before they are common household figures, they will undoubtedly see considerably greater use in the homes of the future.

THE IMPACT ON EDUCATION

Computer-Assisted Instruction

Computer-assisted instruction (CAI) is a process in which a student interacts directly with a computer that serves as an instructor to guide the student through the learning material (see Figure 18–4). Each student receives instruction adapted to his or her learning pace, immediate feedback on progress, and motivation from sound and graphics provided by the CAI software.

Each student may progress through a CAI session at his or her own pace. The student's performance is monitored by the CAI program, which can present material to the student based on progress. A benefit of CAI is that the teacher-learner relationship is an unintimidating one. The computer is the ultimate in patience and good nature; it does not scold or lose its temper. Even very young children can learn to be at ease with teaching machines. In the long run, gaining this familiarity with computers at an early age may be the most durable lesson.

In its traditional form, however, CAI rarely teaches skills that are new, and it seldom presents the learning material in an unusual manner. This is not to

Figure 18–4 ▪ Computer-Assisted Instruction

PLATO® computer-based education is designed for the individual, offering personal, one-to-one learning with infinite patience and personalization.

say that CAI has no advantages, however. It has been found that the majority of students using CAI cover the required material in less time than it would have been covered in a traditional classroom setting. The question that has arisen, following several years of CAI use, is whether students who use this mode of learning are becoming computer literate. The answer from parents, educators, and students alike is a resounding "No!" Although CAI can be very effective in both teaching and helping the student to overcome computer anxiety, it does very little in the way of teaching computer programming and the working of computer hardware components.

Computer Camps for Young and Old

Computer camps were initially begun to provide children in the age range of eight to seventeen with the opportunity to use and learn about personal computers. The idea was so successful with the children that computer camps have now begun to offer a similar opportunity to adults on weekends.

Computer camps were started in 1978 as an alternative to the traditional summer camps where children spent one or two weeks swimming, boating, hiking, playing sports, and participating in arts and crafts. Although the traditional recreational activities are still available to computer campers, the children have the added opportunity to learn about computing (see Figure 18–5).

Prior to arriving at the camps, or upon arrival, the children are placed in one of three levels—beginner, intermediate, or advanced—based on their age and their computer skills. The camps' curricula generally include either small-group or individual instruction in programming languages such as Logo, Pilot, BASIC, Pascal, and Assembler—again based on the experience level of the camper.

Based on the acknowledged success of summer computer camps for children, computer camps have now begun offering off-season weekend computer camps for adults. The curricula of the camps are designed for both novice computer users and adults wishing to improve their computer literacy. Classes in word processing and electronic spreadsheet use, as well as traditional camping activities, are available to the adult campers.

Figure 18–5 ▪ Computer Camp
A day at computer camp means waking up, slipping into a t-shirt and shorts, eating a hearty breakfast, and then sitting down at your computer to work through your learning packet.

Innovations in Education

Topics such as CAI and computer camps were once innovations in the area of education. Innovations, however, are appearing all the time and will continue in a field that can greatly benefit from computer technology. As the degree of sophistication in educational software products increases, and as computer technology continues to advance, the uses of computers in education appear to be endless. A few of the recent innovations in education are described below.

In Hartford, Connecticut, a specialized learning tool called Urban Adventure was developed as a project of Encendiendo Una Llama (Lighting a Flame). This program combined the adventure game concept with the real urban environment to help children in grades three through six explore their city.

The children first explored landmarks of the city. Then, using a light pen and an Apple Graphics Tablet, they drew the landmarks and stored them in the computer's memory. They programmed an exploration game to go with the graphics, and a speech synthesizer was programmed to say certain words and phrases about the landmarks in both English and Spanish. Although the game they developed is a good learning activity for all children in this age group, the children who created it learned the most—about their city, how computers work, speaking in both languages, and working with others on a complex project.

At the University of Iowa, teachers are experimenting with a teaching device that combines computer and videodisc technology. The videodisc, unlike videotape, can be immediately accessed at a chosen point. Working through computerized controls, students have access on the discs to visual stills, sound tracks, or computer texts and graphics in a number of combinations. According to Joan Sustik, director of the school's Intelligent Videodisc Research and Development Project, "Motion sequences can be shown in slow motion or still frame to observe critical details. It is also possible to overlay computer text and graphics on top of projected videodisc images. This allows highlighting, cuing, and other visual techniques."

The system can operate automatically or at the direction of the student user. Teachers have so far used the system to teach dance students 190 ballet positions, plus the position names and how they are spelled. For architecture students, a program shows moving and still pictures while an interview with Frank Lloyd Wright is carried on the sound track.

As you can see from the issues and examples in this section, from preschool to graduate school to adult education, the computer presents both challenges and opportunities in education. How we meet them will determine the course of the future.

COMPUTERS IN MEDICINE AND SCIENCE

Medicine

Computers have many uses in medicine. Most of these applications are found in hospital settings. With the area of medicine growing at a fast rate—especially since the 1950s—computers have become essential for the health care profession.

Computer-Assisted Diagnosis   Computer-assisted diagnostic techniques evaluate numerical data and compare them with normal or standard values (see Figure 18–6). In this way a diagnosis can be reached. There are many applications of **computer-assisted diagnosis.** Two examples of computer-assisted diagnosis being used in clinics and hospitals are multiphasic health testing and computerized tomography scanning.

When a patient goes to a center that does **multiphasic health testing (MPHT),** he or she is asked to complete questions concerning family history; these data are put in computerized form. The results of the battery of tests that are then run, including perhaps eye, hearing, pain tolerance, chest X-ray, and blood tests, are also computerized. The computer can then compare a given test value against established normal limits or a mean. A printout of the test findings is then made, including any abnormal test results and necessary information from the patient's medical history. The tests are administered by nurses, and the printouts are reviewed by a trained physician. The final results, along with the physician's recommendations or remarks, are then sent on to the patient's family physician. A consultation with the family physician about the results can then be arranged by the patient.

A major advance in health care technology has been achieved through **computerized tomography (CT or CAT) scanning,** a method that combines X-ray techniques and a computer for quick and accurate physical diagnosis (see Figure 18–7). Although the equipment is still expensive to hospitals, and thus to patients, costs for scanning can be cut by linking several scanning units to a central computer. When this linking was done by three hospitals in Kansas, each one saved approximately $500,000 without impairing the qual-

Figure 18–6 ▪ Computer-Assisted Diagnosis

Many hospitals are using computers to assist doctors in diagnosis. Here, a radiologist views a computerized image to assist in the diagnosis.

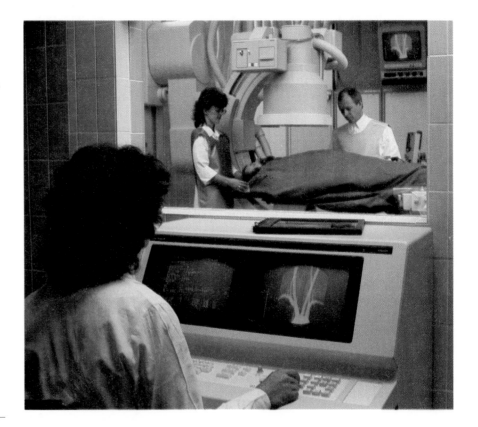

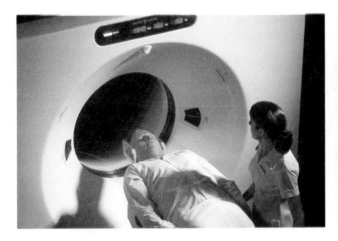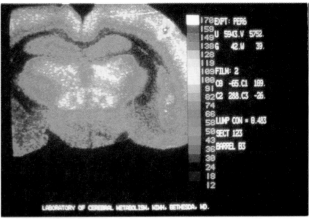

Figure 18—7 ▪ **CT Scan**

Computerized tomography is used for many diagnostic purposes. Shown here are the patient undergoing brain scan (left) and a resulting image (right). This image depicts area of brain activity using special tests. Colors shown indicate different levels of brain activity.

ity of the diagnoses. Because of this, the CT scan is becoming a common procedure in today's hospitals.

Computerized tomography can assist in surgery. For example, a child born in September 1982 was found to have a congenital deformity of the skull. After thirty-nine CT scans, a three-dimensional composite of the skull was assembled by computer. A lucite model of the child's skull was made, using the computer to plot the contours of each cross-section onto lucite sheets. These sheets were then placed on top of each other in order to construct a life-sized replica of the child's skull. Once the surgeon could examine the replica of the skull, he could determine the surgery necessary to correct the problem. Using the computer, the surgeon could see the probable results of the surgery before lifting a scalpel.

Computerized Life Support   Only a few years ago, twenty-four-hour nursing care was needed for a critically ill patient. But now computers are being used in intensive care and coronary care units to acquire and digest patient information. Mainly, computers monitor physiological variables such as heart rate, temperature, and blood pressure. The computer is also used in some cases to monitor the patient's urine output; whenever the output goes below a predetermined quantity, the computer can activate a pump to infuse a diuretic agent.

The computerized monitoring system frees the nurse from constant watch over the critically ill patient (see Figure 18—8). The computers provide an immediate alarm if any abnormality occurs, allowing the nurse to react promptly. Usually, information on as many as eight patients can be displayed at the nurse's station.

Science

Computers are capable of doing a wide variety of tasks in the area of science. Computers make mathematical calculations and projections in seconds compared to the months it once took humans. Using computers, the scientists' conclusions are made easier because the data can be retrieved, classified,

Figure 18–8 ▪ Monitoring System

The FLO-GUARD 8500 micro volumetric infusion pump is designed for use in critical care newborn and pediatric situations, as well as for microinfusion of critical drugs and chemotherapy in adults.

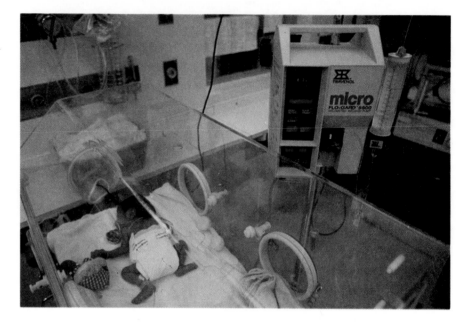

Figure 18–9 ▪ Computerized Modeling in the Laboratory

How medica's PCA knee, a new joint replacement, is manufactured with the aid of computer technology.

and displayed much more quickly. Computer applications in the area of science are perhaps some of the broadest. A few of them are considered below.

Three-Dimensional Electron Microscopy **Electron microscopy (EM),** in which individual electrons can be used to view biological material about, for example, the thickness of a baby's eyelash, has been in use for nearly a quarter of a century. However, only recently has a computer system been devised to accompany the EM techniques and to provide a three-dimensional image. This system, developed by scientists at Oak Ridge National Laboratory, Oak Ridge, Tennessee, will be used to determine the three-dimensional structure of biological specimens.

The negatives of the photographs taken with the electron microscope are viewed with a scanning television camera attached to a computer. The computer displays a representation of a three-dimensional structure on the television screen. Special glasses must be worn to view the image.

Recently, new, synthesized ribonucleic acid (RNA) in a gene of a water insect has been viewed using the new technique. The technique is referred to as **electron microscope tomography,** as it is based on a similar technique used in medicine—computerized tomographic (CT) scanning—discussed in the section on medicine.

Computers as Animal Replacements in Laboratory Tests A recent innovation in science has been the use of **computer modeling** in place of animal testing in laboratories (see Figure 18–9). Although these models are in a very early stage of development, it is hoped that in the future animal and human biological systems can be modeled, thereby using the computer models for laboratory testing of drugs and chemicals. The primary drawback to date has been the lack of complete understanding of both human and animal bodily functions. As advances are made in both computer technology and biological research, the value of modeling such bodily functions as heart beat, temperature, brain waves, and others will increase.

It is important to note, however, that the use of computer modeling in laboratory research will never fully replace the use of laboratory animals. It has, as many other computer applications have in the past, the potential to save millions of dollars. The cost of purchasing laboratory animals will be greatly reduced. The use of computer modeling will also prevent what some people have referred to as the needlessly redundant killing of laboratory animals for education and testing of chemicals such as cosmetics. The use of computer modeling in laboratory research, therefore, has a great future potential.

COMPUTERS IN THE ARTS AND RECREATION

The Arts

Computers have many uses in the arts, from controlling stage lighting to writing and editing through word processing. The word-processing capability is revolutionizing many of the arts. Choreographers employ word processing in dance notation (dance steps both graphically displayed and explained in a written type of shorthand), as do writers and editors in their craft.

Computer Art   The knowledge of programming to a computer artist can be as important as the knowledge of brushes, brush strokes, and paints is to the conventional artist. Computer art (see Figure 18–10) is becoming a well-known and popular art form.

One of the leading computer artists, Saul Bernstein, began his work in 1978 after receiving a microcomputer. Bernstein has won an Emmy Award and also has gained nationwide recognition as a result of his work in microcomputerized animation. In addition, Bernstein was commissioned by Hewlett-Packard to "paint" portraits of Prince Phillip and Queen Elizabeth using

Figure 18–10 ■ Computer Art

This example of computer art involves complex programming procedures required to produce the pattern of colored lines and curves.

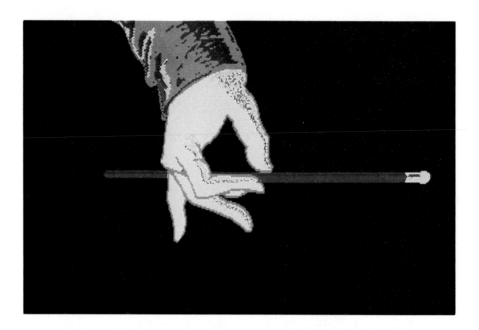

his computer. The Queen is reported to have had difficulty telling the computer images from photographs.

Computerized Music The popularity of the computer—especially the microcomputer—extends to the area of music (see Figure 18–11). French composer and former music director of the New York Philharmonic Orchestra, Pierre Boulez, used computer technology to produce an eighteen-minute work, *Repons*. The piece uses twenty-four musicians, six soloists, and a computer to alter and transform the musical sounds produced by the soloists. These altered sounds are carried over six loudspeakers, which are stationed around the performance hall.

The late John Lennon used computer editing during the recording of his last album, Double Fantasy. Lennon rejected take after take while making the

Figure 18–11 ▪ Microcomputer Music System

album. Finally, his producer, Jack Douglas, had the idea of using the computer as an editor. The best portions of the takes were pulled, and the computer merged them. The computer successfully completed the editing in ten minutes, and Lennon was very pleased with the results.

Besides being able to reproduce sounds of specific instruments, computers also produce other sound effects, such as stones scraping pavement or breaking glass. The sounds are then stored on a floppy disk and can be modified to imitate various moods.

Computerized music is also being heard by many people—sometimes unknowingly—in television commercials and music themes. Computer-designed music for TV commercials appears on such spots as Dr. Pepper, Club Med, and Kentucky Fried Chicken. In television show theme songs, the theme from the hospital series *St. Elsewhere* heads the list.

Recreation and Entertainment

We would probably think we were in the year 2001 if we could see all the ways computers are already being used in recreation and entertainment. The field of sports has in the past used the computer as it was originally intended—to calculate statistics. Recently, however, computer applications in recreation have begun to include sports research and athletic shoe construction. In the area of entertainment, Disney's EPCOT (Experimental Prototype Community of Tomorrow) Center, near Orlando, Florida, is a futuristic look at computerized society.

Computerized Sports Research   In the area of sports research, Dr. Gideon Ariel, co-founder and president of the Coto Research Center, has revolutionized the study of the human body in relation to sports. At the COTO Research Center, Dr. Ariel uses what he refers to as biomechanics to analyze human movement. Simply stated, **biomechanics** is the application of engineering methodologies to biological systems (see Figure 18–12).

The science of biomechanics involves the use of high-speed cameras, digitizer pens, computers, and computer software in the process of analyzing human movement. In the case of athletics, the high-speed cameras are used to film the athlete's motion. The film of the athlete in motion is then used along with the digitizer pen to enter the motions into the computer. Once the athlete's motion is stored in the computer, the computer software is used to analyze the motion and provide data concerning the distance the body moves, the speed at which it moves, and the forces acting on the body. Once this data is obtained, it can be used along with three-dimensional computer images to help the athlete to correct his or her motion so that it is the best possible for a given sport. A given individual's motion can be analyzed in such sports as swimming, diving, cycling, weight-lifting, and others.

One of the primary goals of the COTO Research Center, through its analysis of motion, is the prevention and treating of sport injuries. As an added feature, however, the Center's analysis can also be used in other areas, including: restoring as much mobility as possible to the disabled, the analysis of human motion at work, the analysis of industrial robots' movements, and the motion analysis of racing horses. The technique for analyzing motion developed by Dr. Ariel can, therefore, be used to improve our lives outside the area of sports as well.

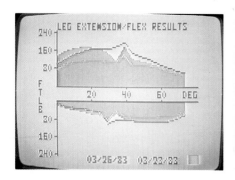

Figure 18–12 ▪ Biomechanics

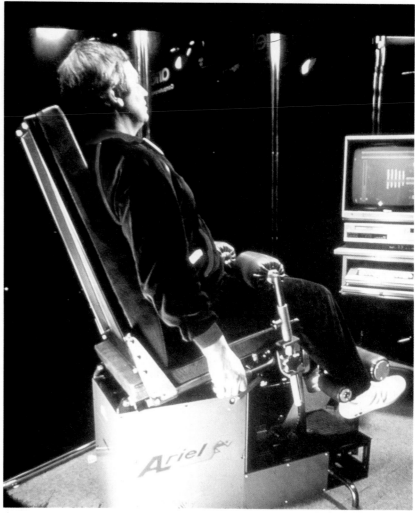

EPCOT—Computerization at Its Finest   Though visitors to EPCOT Center, at Walt Disney World, may not come expecting to learn about computers, learn they will (see Figure 18–13). EPCOT Center guests are completely surrounded by computerization in Future World. CommuniCore acts as the center of activity in Future World and puts guests in touch with the world through "an array of computer-fed, interactive video screens and high-technology electronic libraries." Here, visitors become accustomed to computers and gain confidence in their own ability to manage them.

Within Future World are a series of exhibits that ease bewilderment about emerging technologies. Computers become allies in games and the quest for information, through communicating and performing everyday tasks at EPCOT.

One such exhibit, Computer Central, gives visitors a look at the EPCOT central computer room and an explanation of how computers work, how they help to run EPCOT Center, and how they affect our lives. Explanations are given of how the wide variety of Sperry computer systems, from V77 mini-computers to large 1100 Series systems, control many functions at EPCOT and elsewhere within Disney World. The functions these computers control

include show presentations, guest services, security, environmental and business systems, and management information.

Within Computer Central there are also exhibits highlighting several specific computer applications such as manufacturing, computer-aided design (CAD), and airline operations. Terminals and CRT screens are also made available to give visitors hands-on experience (see Figure 18–14).

Another exhibit within CommuniCore is the WorldKey Information Service, which allows guests to seek information through a prototype audio, video, and text information system. Terminals with touch-sensitive screens provide instant information on EPCOT Center attractions, restaurants, shops, entertainment, and guest services.

Figure 18–14 ■ "Hands on" Participation Is Welcomed at EPCOT Center Computer Central

In addition, a WorldKey attendant can be contacted via a network of two-way television cameras and hands-free speaker-phones. The WorldKey attendant can answer questions and provide assistance.

By simply touching the attraction image, the filmed exteriors of all attractions are shown, or if the visitor prefers, a map tour selection may be chosen. Along with these capabilities, the WorldKey service can also be used as an index. A shop selling china, for example, may be found by first touching the letter C, which displays an alphabetical list of topics beginning with the letter C. Touch the word *china,* and the names of shops in EPCOT where china is sold will be displayed.

Designed by both Disney and Bell Systems, the WorldKey Information Service integrates the technologies of microelectronics, computer software, laser videodisc, television, touch-sensitive screens, and fiber-optic transmission systems.

Several other exhibits in a wide variety of areas can also be found in CommuniCore (see Figure 18–15). These areas include energy, telecommunications, travel, and news. Through each exhibit guests learn about the key role computers play in these areas and how they will affect the future.

FUTURE TECHNOLOGY

Brain-Wave Interface

An input method being researched and entering the development stage is the **brain-wave interface.** Although the hardware has been available, new software is bringing the idea closer to practical reality. To control a computer with this technology, a person gazes at a particular flashing light while wearing electrodes like those used for an electroencephalogram. The system board contains a grid of lights, each representing an action or data item. For instance, if a grid is set up with a light for each alphabetic character, the person

Figure 18–15 ▪ Energy Exhibit at EPCOT

Giant prehistoric creatures re-enact their role in the creation of fossil fuels.

could spell out a message to the computer by glancing at the lights in the proper order. The computer recognizes these messages because, although each light blinks in the same pattern, the lights are not in unison. This causes the viewer's brain waves to respond in a distinct pattern. The electrodes pick up the brain waves and send the messages to the computer. Once the message is decoded, the computer can respond accordingly. Currently, the brain-wave interface is very slow, particularly for a computer. As technology continues to advance, it is hoped that the interface will help the handicapped in a variety of ways. Hooked up to a voice synthesizer, the computer could pronounce the message being sent, enabling speechless people to communicate. The lights need not be on a grid; they could be located beside particular appliances, and the brain-wave interface would be used to turn the appliance on or off. One challenge at present is to eliminate interference coming from tense neck muscles, which also generate electrical impulses.

Artificial Intelligence

A major effort is being made in the field of software to build computers with **artificial intelligence (AI)**, the ability to think and reason as humans do. The field is certainly not new; so much research is being done that breakthroughs could occur at any moment.

Expert Systems **Expert systems** use what is known of the human thought process to build computer programs that mimic the decision-making process of human experts (see Figure 18–16). In such a system, software designers try to program the computer to follow the same path of thinking as top experts in that field. New expert systems are being designed right now; several are on the market. One of the more well-known experimental-stage expert systems is called **CADUCEUS,** which diagnoses medical problems.

Nonmonotonic Logic Theory All researchers want to go beyond expert systems, which do not exhibit the common sense of humans and which are very

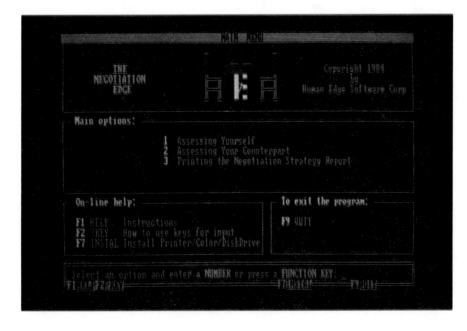

Figure 18–16 ▪ Expert System

The Negotiation Edge, by Human Edge Software, is an expert system that produces customized negotiation advice. Computer art designed on the Mindset Personal Computer.

Nuclear Power Plants Supervised by Computers

"Leak in progress. Based on current plant state, suggest emergency procedures three through five. Close valves to isolate systems." This is what might be flashed on the screen of a computer supervising a nuclear power plant.

Idaho National Engineering Laboratory (INEL) has designed programming for such an intelligent computer system. This system helps operators of nuclear power plants to find and solve sudden problems or malfunctions. Also, the new system gives warnings of breakdowns and, almost at the same time, gives suggestions on how the breakdowns can be repaired.

The computers will not take the place of a plant operator. The plant operator is free to either use personal judgment or take the suggestions of the computer.

narrow in application. The country's top researchers have taken different approaches to the way the wealth of human knowledge must be organized inside the computer. John McCarthy, director of Stanford's Artificial Intelligence Laboratory, is optimistic about the use of **nonmonotonic logic** in building computer knowledge.

Monotonic logic allows conclusions to be drawn from assumptions, and if more assumptions are added, the new conclusions will not make the previous conclusions wrong. For example, "If X is a bird and birds can fly, then X can fly" is monotonic logic. But what if X is a dead bird or a penguin? As you can see, monotonic logic doesn't always hold true. McCarthy's nonmonotonic logic adapts to this by saying, "X can fly *unless something prevents it.*" By defining human knowledge and thinking this way, McCarthy hopes to get the computer to allow for such unusual situations.

Script Theory A second approach is being taken by other researchers, primarily Marvin Minsky at Massachusetts Institute of Technology and Roger Schank at Yale University. It is based on the **script theory,** which says that in any particular situation humans have an idea of how the thinking or dialogue would go. For instance, we each have a dentist's office script, a classroom script, or a restaurant script. Memories of past events are usually filed in our minds under keys associated with the structure of these scripts.

What these researchers want is to give the computer a way to make inferences based on the situation at hand. They realize, though, that the inferences need some boundaries. Thus, to endow computers with common sense, a vast store of information must be conveniently categorized and triggered. Teaching computers to learn—perhaps the ultimate goal—is a very long way in the future.

SUMMARY POINTS

■ Home computer services including banking, shopping, and access to home information services are all available to the personal computer owner.

■ Information for home information services is compiled by data-base producers who then sell the large data bases to online service companies, such as CompuServe, Inc.

■ Microcomputers are now in limited use to control functions within the home. Microcomputers are being used to control the environmental, security, and maintenance functions within individual homes.

■ Personal robots represents an area of computer technology that has just recently begun to market products. Initial introductions to the market include B.O.B. (Brains-On-Board), manufactured and sold by Androbot, Inc., and Hero I, a personal robot kit sold by Heath Company.

■ Computer-assisted instruction (CAI) allows students to learn subject matter at their own learning pace in a one-on-one interaction, with the computer acting as instructor.

■ Computer camps are being used to instruct both children and adults in the use of computers.

■ Education is a field that can benefit greatly with advances in computer technology. As education benefits, so will society in general.

■ Computer innovations in the area of medicine include computer-assisted diagnosis and computerized life support systems.

■ The use of computers to model both human and animal body functions is a recent innovation in science that could eventually mean computer replacement of some of the animals used in laboratory tests.

■ Displays and exhibits of how computers can be used in our everyday lives can be found at EPCOT Center in Walt Disney World. EPCOT exhibits and displays use emerging computer technologies such as microelectronics, laser videodiscs, touch-sensitive screens, and fiber-optic transmission systems.

■ Areas in which current research may lead to future technology include brain-wave interface and artificial intelligence.

REVIEW QUESTIONS

1. What types of services are currently available to the personal computer owner through networks? Are there any services that you feel could be valuable to the home computer user in the future that currently are not available?

2. Do you think that home robots have any practical applications within the home, or are they simply for our entertainment? List any practical applications you may think of.

3. Explain why computer literacy has become such an important issue in education. At what point do you feel children should be exposed to computers? Is there a danger in exposing them to computers at too young an age?

4. How is computer-assisted instruction used in comparison with traditional methods of teaching? What are a few of the advantages and disadvantages of CAI?

5. Do you think it is important for an adult who is computer illiterate to attend either a computer camp or computer class to increase his or her computer literacy? Why or why not?

6. By using computer technology in medicine, do you think that we have impersonalized the field of medicine? Explain your answer.

7. What are some advantages associated with using computer models in place of laboratory animals? List some other applications for which you think computer modeling could be a great asset.

8. Do you think that the use of computers in the various areas of art is limiting the creativity of humans in these areas. Why or why not?

9. Briefly explain the manner in which computers are used to analyze the movements of athletes. What is this science called?

10. Briefly explain how you think an attraction like EPCOT Center benefits our lives and our society. That is, is it purely a tourist attraction, or does it serve some additional purpose?

11. Do you think that human existence as we know it will be threatened by introducing artificial intelligence into computer technology? Explain your answer.

APPLICATION

NASA

James L. Raney

HISTORY AND BACKGROUND OF NASA

The present-day NASA (National Aeronautics and Space Administration) had its foundation in an amendment the Congress of 1915 attached to a naval appropriations bill. It thereby established an Advisory Committee for Aeronautics "to supervise and direct the scientific study of the problems of flight, with a view to their practical solution." At its first meeting, this committee changed its name to the National Advisory Committee for Aeronautics. This new "NACA" began making surveys of the state of aeronautical research and development facilities around the country. Its first real contribution came during the First World War when it aided significantly in the formulation of national policy on such critical problems as the cross-licensing of patents and aircraft production. In 1920, the first NACA research facility, Langley Memorial Aeronautical Laboratory, named after the "aerodrome" pioneer, was opened at Langley Field, Virginia.

In the 38 years that followed, the NACA grew in size, ability, and function, adding several facilities and developing a staff of highly qualified and motivated scientists and engineers. It was involved in many innovative improvements leading to significant reductions in aerodynamic drag on aircraft shapes and consequent increases in speed and performance. These efforts received much national attention beginning in 1940 when more new research facilities were created to aid in the war effort. During the war the NACA was primarily involved only with aerodynamic improvements to production models and not with developing new technologies needed to improve aircraft design, construction, and propulsion. However, after the war these facilities and the function of NACA evolved into a major research base for jet- and rocket-powered exploration of the atmosphere and near-space environment.

As the intensity and significance of space exploration developed, the NACA slowly broadened its research scope to involve "man in space." In 1958, official recognition of this metamorphosis was gained in the establishment of the NASA. This new NASA absorbed the NACA and assumed responsibility for guiding the United States into the Space Age. New operational facilities were established to manage the design, development, and operation of manned space projects, the major ones being the Mercury, Gemini, Apollo, and Space Shuttle Programs. The Mercury Program put the first man in Earth orbit for the United States. The Gemini Program demonstrated the ability to rendezvous two vehicles in Earth orbit. The Apollo Program put the first man on the Moon and returned many lunar samples to the Earth. The Space Shuttle Program is the current program of NASA and provides the first and only reusable Earth-to-orbit-and-return transportation system. Each of these programs was a major accomplishment in itself, but the final result is a major national industry and experience base capable of conceiving and completing complex engineering and operations projects.

DATA PROCESSING AS A BASIS FOR NASA'S ACCOMPLISHMENTS

None of the major accomplishments of NASA could have been possible without the modern digital computer. From the early days in the development of the computing industry, when the Army sponsored the first major research on stored program digital computers for computing ballistics tables for weaponry purposes, until the present, computing devices have been of importance to aeronautics and space efforts. Prior to the advent of manned spacecraft, the important applications of digital computers were for research, engineering computations, and reduction and analysis of instrumentation data obtained from test facilities and actual test flights. The NACA did little to lead to new computing technologies, but was an eager user of new computing equipment and procedures as they became commercially available.

In the case of computer systems for test aircraft, rockets, and space vehicles, the NASA has participated in the development of new computing technologies. The evolution of rocketry and man-rated space-craft has centered around the evolution of attitude command and control systems. Early command and control systems were simple analog devices with little or no externally generated command response capability. Most were preprogramed and provided specific time- or event-driven commands as well as an automated attitude control capability. As the need arose to provide man-rated spacecraft, these command and control systems evolved into specialized, extremely complex systems based on digital computers operating real-time, sampled data simulations of feedback control loops. They were developed based on special-purpose digital computers interfaced with sensors and effectors, sophisticated mathematical control laws, and real-time programing technologies. They matured when the special-purpose equipment and programming were replaced with commercially available systems that provided the same real-time performance.

As special processing and interface technologies were advanced to provide digital command and control, the state of the art in general-purpose computing was also advancing significantly. As the sophistication of spacecraft as well as the capabilities of space-qualified digital computers grew, the embedded nature of on-board digital systems grew. In modern space vehicles, digital computers also support complex system management functions, instrumentation data collection, formatting, and routing, uplink telemetry data receipt, storage, and processing, and other on-board engineering and mission support functions.

The embedded nature of computing systems in ground-based space mission operations has grown in a manner parallel to the on-board systems. The more complex spacecraft and mission profiles of modern space ventures require real time processing to provide training, flight avionics maintenance, and fail-safe mission operations. More on-board systems and capabilities dictate more accurate real-time simulations, more ground-based tracking and analysis of those systems, and more automation in these capabilities. Large computer complexes dedicated to these real-time simulations for training, mission design verification, and flight equipment maintenance are necessities of space missions. Complex statistical models of projected orbital paths, cross-range potentials for launch or entry trajectories, and on-orbit maneuvers are important computation capabilities commonplace in the modern space operations scenario.

It is of significance to note that the cost of providing computer systems for space operations, both on-board and ground-based, is far exceeded by the cost of providing facilities needed to support the engineering, development, and delivery of those operational systems. Therefore, the significance of support computer planning and development methodologies is a major component of the NASA systems expertise of today. Many of these tools depend on computer-based system modeling techniques, on the expertise and experience of NASA personnel, and on the ability of the computing industry to provide advances in the state of the art in computing systems as needed. The classic example of this is the emerging capability to facilitate local area networks of computers. This approach is required to support the management methodologies needed to develop future generations of space vehicles and missions.

It is also of significance to note that the trend in planning for future space programs is towards increasing the quality and quantity of embedded computing systems in space. Evolving hardware, operating system, and networking technologies support this advance. The increasing need to have space vehicles that function automatically or that have many autonomous component systems must be met. The utilization of knowledge-based systems, robotics, telepresence, and other artificial intelligence technologies to resolve real operational problems is being realized. Their adaptation to the space environment follows naturally, where human limits could be expanded enormously through such aids.

CURRENT COMPUTER APPLICATIONS AT NASA

In current space missions, computers and general data processing are utilized in all phases of a project, from conceptual studies to operational status, and in all portions of the systems that support the mission. Some examples of the utilization of digital computers in a typical modern space mission environment follow.

Engineering Support—All aspects of a space mission can now be simulated. Using the experience base available in NASA and computer processes developed from data obtained in previous space missions, new components, space vehicles, or even complete missions can be conceived to meet new requirements. They can be sized, shaped, and tested without bending one piece of metal; these analyses can be conducted in a very short time (sometimes, in only a matter

of minutes) and poor designs eliminated or improved. Trade studies can be constructed and conducted in such a way that summary results can be automatically provided. Through mechanized drafting and manufacturing aids, also based on digital processes, actual spacecraft hardware can be manufactured and assembled by NASA contractors. Through complete mission simulations, initialization parameter sets can be developed for testing, hardware integration, mission planning, or an actual space mission.

Spacecraft systems—Essentially all spacecraft systems involve digital computing in some form. Guidance, navigation, and control of spacecraft are probably the most widely recognized applications of data processing in spacecraft operation. Here, complex systems of sensors, effectors, and command inputs are all interfaced with complex, real-time digital programs in on-board processors to provide these functions. All these components, as well as most other functional systems in a spacecraft, are interfaced with the on-board digital systems for intrumentation, communications, and systems management roles. In addition, the on-board computers provide a computing resource and display system capable of supporting most crew activities. In the current era, the on-board computer system of the Space Shuttle also provides payloads (experiments carried up in the Shuttle) with a sophisticated level of computer support.

Ground-based Systems—Large volumes of instrumentation and communications data are received by the ground-based mission support systems. Here this data is received, error-checked, reduced or processed in the appropriate manner, and used immediately or stored for future use. As appropriate, real-time support is provided for the control and operation of space missions. Other support is provided on an as-needed basis from data that has been archived, either earlier in the mission or during some previous, related mission. The ground based system must also be able to prepare and transmit uplink commands to active space vehicles. All of this data handling involves world-wide communications complexes, large data processing and storage centers, and complex data display systems, all of which are based on digital computers.

Research and training facilities—Simulation modeling, like that provided for engineering applications, is also available for research and training efforts. These facilities play a very important role in maintaining the operational status of any space program. They commonly provide real-time simulations of the space vehicle and the Universe in which it will fly for research, development, maintenance, or training applications. However, of equal importance to these efforts is the instrumentation and communications support, along with its companion data reduction and analysis processing and systems control capability. Large wind tunnel, space environment, life science, and training facilities can be controlled and operated accurately, efficiently, safely, and profitably with real-time digital control systems. The information received from such facilities forms a very valuable resource for the evolution of space projects by the NASA.

Business support—All of the classic areas of conducting business on a day-to-day basis are supported by digital processing in the NASA. The regime reaches from payroll processing to automatic control of building utilities to electronic communication of budgets to electronic searches of library contents. All aspects have some form of digital computer support. Some systems are fully automated with online terminal interfaces while many only provide batch processing support. However, more systems are being brought online each year and most will receive online support in the near future.

Office Automation—The recent availability of inexpensive, sophisticated word processing systems, electronic mail, and appointment management capabilities has established office automation as a cost effective process for NASA. For memoranda and interoffice notes, distributed word processing systems equipped with a local area network communications capability allow the secretarial staff to provide a high level of inter- and intra-office correspondence, both formal and informal. For documents, centralized word processing systems with remotely located terminal interfaces (with high quality print capabilities) provide an effective system of producing and managing the configuration of large, space mission information data bases. Personal computers with word processor emulation packages and local area network communications support many managers, engineers, and scientists by providing the capability of flowing information between individuals in a fast and efficient manner. These distributed systems also allow the engineers and managers to do much conceptual modeling right at their desks. This provides them with an efficient method of doing work; it also offloads the central support computer systems.

Mission Reconfiguration—With the advent of the Space Shuttle, the first reusable spacecraft, a significant new function is evolving within the NASA. To provide the Shuttle as a cost effective, reusable space transportation system is a major objective of NASA. A large data base of information about past and planned Space Shuttle flights must form the basis for the planning and execution of subsequent missions. The processing of information from that data base into the actual forms required to "reconfigure" the Space Shuttle systems and all of their supporting facilities, such as Mission Control Center, research and training facilities, and payload integration processes, must be done in an efficient, effective, and rapid manner. A large complex of digital computers, processes, procedures, and data distribution mechanisms is being developed to support this function.

SUMMARY AND CONJECTURE ABOUT THE FUTURE

The modern-day NASA and its supporting industries would not exist without digital computers. Some say the evolution of the computer would not have progressed to its present state without the impetus of the space effort. It is certainly true that as the requirements for more complex space computers have evolved, the computing industry has responded with the necessary improvements. In fact, it is difficult to identify which technology advancement drives which; the interdependencies are obvious and the future of both is apparently unlimited.

DISCUSSION QUESTIONS

1. Discuss the significance of the digital computer to the NASA space program.
2. Identify and discuss some of the applications in which NASA uses computers in the current space missions.

Appendix A
Careers

PEOPLE AND THEIR ROLES

Men and women with technical or managerial skills in data processing are employed in almost every industry. The need for data-processing personnel exists not only in business firms but also in hospitals, schools, government agencies, banks, and libraries. However, the major emphasis of this section will be on computer-related career opportunities in a business environment.

A typical computer installation in a business organization is expected to perform at least three basic functions: system analysis and design, programming, and computer operation. Personnel with the education and experience required to work in these areas are needed; in addition, data-base technology has created the need for specialists in data-base analysis and administration. Further, an information system manager is needed to coordinate activities, set goals for the data-processing department, and establish procedures to control and evaluate both personnel and projects in progress.

Information System Managers

Historically, data-processing managers have been programmers or systems analysts who worked their way up to management positions with little formal management training. But the increasing emphasis on information systems and information management has brought a change; professional managers with demonstrable leadership qualities and communication skills are being hired to manage information system departments.

The **management information system (MIS) manager** is responsible for planning and tying together all the information resources of the firm. The manager must organize the physical and human resources of the department to achieve company goals and must devise effective control mechanisms to monitor progress. This means that the MIS manager must possess the following knowledge and skills:

- A thorough understanding of the organization, its goals, and its business activities.
- Leadership qualities to motivate and control highly skilled people.
- Knowledge of data-processing methods and familiarity with available hardware and software.

A man or woman seeking a career in information system management should have a college degree. For managing business data-processing centers, a degree in business administration with a concentration in the area of management information systems is desirable. Some employers prefer to hire someone with an MBA degree. Furthermore, to handle high-level management responsibilities such as those outlined above, a candidate for a position as MIS director should have at least two years of extensive management experience, as well as advanced knowledge of the industry and competence in all technical, professional, and business skills.

System Development Personnel

Programmers Generally, three types of programming are done in an organization: application programming, maintenance programming, and system programming. Persons working in any of these areas should possess the following basic skills:

- Good command of the programming language or languages in which programs are written.
- A knowledge of general programming methodology and of the relationships between programs and hardware.
- Analytical reasoning ability and attention to detail.
- Creativity and discipline to develop new problem-solving methods.
- Patience and persistence.
- Good communication skills.

APPLICATION PROGRAMMER Application programs perform data-processing or computational tasks to solve specific problems facing an organization. This type of programming constitutes the bulk of all programming tasks. It involves taking a broad system design prepared by an analyst and converting it into instructions for the computer. The responsibilities of application programmers also include testing, debugging, documenting, and implementing programs.

An **application programmer** in business data processing must apply the capabilities of the computer to problems such as customer billing and inventory control. In addition to the basic skills outlined earlier, a business-oriented application programmer should know the objectives of the organization and have a basic understanding of accounting and management science.

Besides business-oriented application programmers, there are scientific application programmers who work on scientific or engineering problems, which usually require complex mathematical solutions. Thus, a scientific application programmer needs a basic knowledge of science or engineering.

MAINTENANCE PROGRAMMER Program maintenance is a very important but often neglected activity. Many large programs are never completely debugged, and there is a continuing need for changes to and improvement of major programs. It is the responsibility of **maintenance programmers** to change and improve existing programs. In some organizations, maintenance programming is done by application programmers. To be effective, a maintenance programmer needs considerable programming experience and a high level of analytical ability.

SYSTEM PROGRAMMER A different type of specialist, the **system programmer,** is responsible for creating and maintaining system software. System programmers are not concerned with writing programs to solve day-to-day organizational problems. Instead, they are expected to develop utility programs; maintain operating systems, data-base packages, compilers, and assemblers; and be involved in decisions concerning additions and deletions of hardware and software. Because of their knowledge of operating systems, system programmers typically offer technical help to application programmers. To be able to perform these duties effectively, a system programmer should have: (1) a background in the theory of computer language structure and syntax and (2) extensive and detailed knowledge of the hardware being used and the software that controls it.

In hiring any of these types of programmers, employers may also look for specialized skills. For example, the increasing impact of minicomputers and microcomputers is creating a demand for programmers with experience in real-time or interactive systems using mini and micro hardware. Also, the advanced technology of today's communication networks provides excellent opportunities for programmers skilled in designing, coding, testing, debugging, documenting, and implementing data communication software.

Educational requirements for programmers vary, because employers' needs vary. For a business-oriented application programming job, a college degree, though desirable, is usually not required. However, most employers prefer applicants who have had college courses in data processing, accounting, and business administration. Sometimes, workers experienced in computer operation or specific functional areas of business are promoted to programming jobs and, with additional data-processing courses, become fully qualified programmers.

Scientific application programming usually requires a degree in computer or information science, mathematics, engineering, or a physical science. Some jobs require graduate degrees. Few scientific organizations are interested in applicants with no college training.

Persons seeking to enter the system programming field should have at least one year of assembly language programming experience or a college degree in computer science. In addition to a degree, work experience, although not essential for a job as a programmer, is extremely beneficial.

Computer programming is taught in technical and vocational schools, community and junior colleges, and universities. Many high schools offer computer programming courses.

Application and system programmers will continue to be in exceptionally high demand. Application programmers with some exposure to data-base management and direct-access techniques, remote processing, conversational programming, structured design, and distributed processing will be in greatest demand. As the use of minicomputers and microcomputers increases, knowledge of BASIC, RPG, and Pascal will be valuable. System programmers knowledgeable in data communications, network planning and analysis, data-base concepts, and terminal-oriented systems will be in great demand. With these trends in mind, data processing, computer science, and business administration students may choose to direct their education toward some degree of specialization.

LEAD PROGRAMMER Within an organization, a programmer's chances for advancement are usually good. A programmer who has demonstrated his or her technical competence and ability to handle responsibility may be promoted to **lead programmer,** or **project leader,** and given supervisory responsibilities. Some application programmers become system programmers, and vice versa.

Systems Analysts   The **systems analyst** is the key person in the analysis, design, and implementation of a formal information system. The analyst has the following responsibilities:

■ Helping the user determine information needs.
■ Gathering facts about existing systems and analyzing them to determine the effectiveness of current processing methods and procedures.
■ Designing new systems, recommending changes to existing systems, and being involved in implementing these changes.

The analyst's role is critical to the success of any management information system. He or she acts as an interface between users of the MIS and technical personnel such as programmers, machine operators, and data-base specialists. This role becomes more important as the cost of designing, implementing, and maintaining information systems rises.

To be effective, the systems analyst should possess the following characteristics:

■ A general knowledge of the firm, its goals and objectives, and the products and services it provides.
■ Familiarity with the organizational structure of the company and management's rationale for selecting that structure.
■ Comprehensive knowledge of data-processing methods and current hardware and familiarity with available programming languages.
■ The ability to plan and organize work and to cooperate and interact effectively with both technical and nontechnical personnel.
■ A high level of creativity.
■ The ability to communicate clearly and persuasively with technical personnel as well as with persons who have little or no computer background.

The minimum requirements for a job as a systems analyst generally include work experience in system design and programming and some specialized industry experience. Systems analysts seeking jobs in a business environment should be college graduates with backgrounds in business management, accounting, economics, computer science, information systems, or data processing. An MBA or some graduate study is often desired. For work in a scientifically oriented organization, a college background in the physical sciences, mathematics, or engineering is preferred. Many universities offer majors in management information systems; their curricula are designed to train people to be systems analysts.

Some organizations, particularly small ones, do not employ systems analysts. Instead, **programmer/analysts** are responsible for system analysis and programming. In other companies, systems analysts begin as programmers and are promoted to analyst positions after gaining experience. However, the qualities that make for a good analyst are significantly different from those that characterize a good programmer. Hence, there is no clear career path *from* programming *to* analysis, though such movement is possible.

System analysis is a growing field. According to data from the United States Department of Labor, computer systems analysts can look forward throughout the 1980s to employment prospects brighter than those for workers in almost any other occupation. There is a continuing growth of management consulting firms and computer services organizations, as well as a high demand for system professionals by computer manufacturers. The growth rate in jobs is estimated to be 37 percent by 1990. Also, the increasing use of minicomputers and microcomputers will cause an increase in the small user's needs for analysts to design systems for small computers.

Data-Base Specialists

Data-Base Analyst Data-base specialists are responsible for designing and controlling the use of the organization's data resources. A **data-base analyst**—the key person in the analysis, design, and implementation of data structures—must plan and coordinate data use within the system. The analyst has the following responsibilities:

- Helping the user or systems analyst to analyze the interrelationships of data.
- Defining physical data structures and logical views of data.
- Designing new data-base systems, recommending changes to existing ones, and being involved in the implementation of these changes.
- Eliminating data redundancy.

In some organizations, the function of data analysis and coordination is incorporated in the systems analysis function.

A data-base analyst needs technical knowledge of programming and system methodologies. A background in system software is valuable for persons planning physical data-base structures. The job requires a college education with concentration in the areas of computer science, business data processing, and data-base management system design. Many colleges offer courses in data-base management to train people to be data analysts.

Data-Base Administrator The career path within the data-base specialty often leads to the position of corporate **data-base administrator (DBA).** Data-base administrator is a management-level position responsible for control of all the data resources of the organization. The primary responsibilities of this position include:

- Developing a dictionary of standard data definitions so that all records are consistent.
- Designing data bases.
- Maintaining the accuracy, completeness, and timeliness of data bases.
- Designing procedures to ensure data security and data-base backup and recovery.
- Facilitating communications between analysts and users.
- Advising analysts, programmers, and system users as to the best ways to use data bases.

To handle these responsibilities, a data-base administrator must have a high level of technical expertise as well as an ability to communicate effectively with diverse groups of people. This person must exhibit supervisory and leadership skills developed through experience.

Demand is strong for data-base specialists. With the increasing trend toward data-base management, the need for persons with the technical knowledge to design data-base-oriented application systems is increasing.

Data-Processing Operations Personnel

Data-processing operations personnel are responsible for entering data and instructions into the computer, operating the computer and attached devices, retrieving output, and ensuring the smooth operation of the computing center and associated libraries. An efficient operations staff is crucial to the effective use of an organization's computer resources.

Librarian   The **librarian** is responsible for classifying, cataloging, and maintaining files and programs stored on cards, tapes, disks, diskettes, and all other storage media and kept in a computer library for subsequent processing or historical purposes. The librarian's tasks include transferring backup files to alternate storage sites, purging old files, and supervising the periodic cleaning of magnetic tapes and disks.

The librarian's job is important because he or she controls access to stored master files and programs. Computer operators and programmers do not have access to the tapes or disks without the approval of the librarian. This prevents unauthorized changes or processing runs.

The educational background required for this particular job is not extensive; a high-school diploma is adequate. In addition, the individual must have some knowledge of basic data-processing concepts and should possess clerical record-keeping skills.

Computer Operator   A **computer operator's** duties include setting up equipment for particular jobs; mounting and removing tapes, disks, and diskettes as needed; and monitoring the operation of the computer. This person should be able to identify operational problems and take appropriate corrective actions. Most computers run under sophisticated operating systems that direct the operator through messages generated during processing. However, the operator is responsible for reviewing errors that occur during operation, determining their causes, and maintaining operating records.

People seeking jobs as computer operators should enjoy working with machines and be able to read and understand technical literature. A computer operator has to act quickly and properly; a good operator can prevent the loss of a great deal of valuable computer time, as well as the loss or destruction of files and input data. An operator must also possess communication skills so that he or she can explain to users why programs worked or did not work.

Most operators receive training as apprentice operators. Few have college degrees. However, formal operator training is available through technical schools and junior colleges. To be effective, training must include several weeks of on-the-job experience with equipment similar to that the operator will be using.

Data-Entry Operator   A **data-entry operator's** job involves transcribing data into a form suitable for computer processing. A **keypunch operator** uses a keypunch machine to transfer data from source documents to punched cards. Operators of other key-entry devices transfer data to magnetic tape or magnetic disk for subsequent processing. Due to a significant increase in the use of remote data-entry by a remote terminal operator, very little data-entry by keying to cards, tape, or disks is currently being done.

Remote Terminal Operator   A **remote terminal operator** is also involved with the preparation of input data. The operator is located at a remote site, probably some distance from the computer itself. The data is entered into the computer directly from the location at which it is generated.

Data-entry jobs usually require manual dexterity, typing or keying skills, and alertness. No extensive formal education is required; a high-school diploma is sufficient. However, all personnel in this category should be trained carefully to minimize the incidence of errors. Usually several weeks of on-the-job training is provided for new operators to familiarize them with the documents they will be reading and the data-entry devices they will be using.

Occupations in computer operations are being affected by changes in data-processing technology. The demand for keypunch operators will continue to decline as new methods of data preparation are developed and as the use of computer terminals and direct data-entry techniques continues to flourish. However, as the use of computers continues to expand, especially in small businesses, demand for computer operating personnel should remain strong.

MANAGING INFORMATION SYSTEMS

Organization of Data Processing

Traditionally, data-processing activities have been performed within the functional departments of organizations. However, because of increased record-keeping requirements, the ever-present need for current information, and the necessity to adapt to a complex, changing environment, many organizations have consolidated their data-processing operations. The computer has been used increasingly as a tool to manage the paper explosion that threatens to engulf many organizations.

The rapid growth of computer-based data processing has affected the location of the EDP department in an organization's structure. In most organizations, data processing originated in the accounting area, since most record keeping was done there. However, management has recognized that information is a scarce and valuable resource of the entire organization and has increasingly emphasized the data-processing activity and elevated it in the organizational structure.

Figure A–1 shows two versions of an organizational chart for a typical manufacturing firm, each with a different general location for the EDP department. Figure A–1a shows the traditional location: the EDP manager reports to the vice-president of finance and accounting. This location is satisfactory only if the other functional areas do not demand extensive use of computer capabilities. Unless the processing requirements of the accounting and finance department are extensive, the computer is not used to its full potential under such an arrangement. Further, this location has the following drawbacks:

■ It is biased toward accounting and financial applications in the setting of job priorities. Since the data-processing manager reports to the controller, he or she will obviously give high priority to financial applications.
■ It discourages involvement of data-processing personnel with the other functional divisions and inhibits overall integration of the data-processing function.

Figure A–1b shows an alternative location that overcomes these limitations. Elevating the data-processing activity to the same status as the traditional line functions (production, marketing, finance) reflects its corporate-

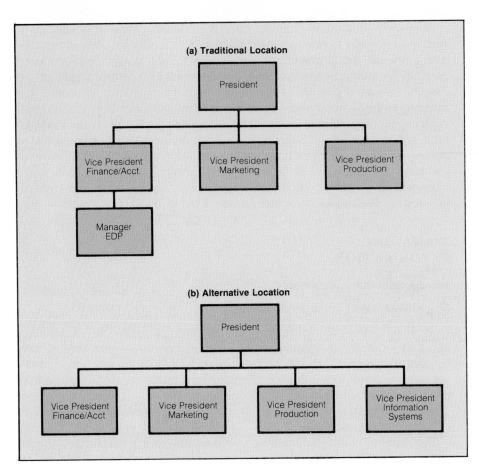

Figure A–1 ▪ Possible Locations for EDP Department in Organizational Structure

(a) Traditional Location

President

Vice President Finance/Acct.

Vice President Marketing

Vice President Production

Manager EDP

(b) Alternative Location

President

Vice President Finance/Acct.

Vice President Marketing

Vice President Production

Vice President Information Systems

wide scope. When it occupies this position, the EDP department's name is often changed to management information system (MIS) department, to stress the importance of its function. The independent status of the MIS department helps to ensure that each functional area gets impartial service and that their particular information requirements are integrated to meet organizational goals.

The internal organizational structure of the MIS department can take various forms. Perhaps the most common breakdown is by data-processing function—system analysis and design, programming, and computer operations—as illustrated in Figure A–2.

An alternative structure emphasizes project assignments. Analysts and programmers work on specific projects in teams that include personnel from user departments. As projects are completed, teams are restructured and team members are assigned to new projects. Such an approach is illustrated in Figure A–3.

Managing System Development

System analysis, design, and implementation were discussed in detail in Chapter 13. It is the responsibility of the MIS (data-processing) manager to monitor the total system development cycle to ensure that projects are completed within reasonable time schedules. Various formal network techniques

```
                    Vice
                  President
                 Information
                   Systems

     Manager              Manager             Manager
     System             Programming          Computer
   Analysis &                                Operations
     Design

  System    System    Applications  Maintenance   Data-Entry   Equipment
  Support   Analysts  Programmers   Programmers   & Control    Operators
  Specialists
```

like PERT (Program Evaluation and Review Technique) and CPM (Critical Path Method) are available for project planning and control. To use such techniques, the manager must break the project into distinct activities, determine the sequence in which the activities are to be performed, and establish a time estimate for each activity. Then, a scheduling chart can be designed. The responsible manager monitors the progress of the project by comparing estimated completion times with actual times. If delays occur, the reasons behind them must be identified and corrective actions taken.

Managing Computer Operations

Most modern computer systems cost millions of dollars; thus, there is increasing concern that the systems' CPUs and peripheral devices be used efficiently. Management can collect data and analyze it to determine the degree

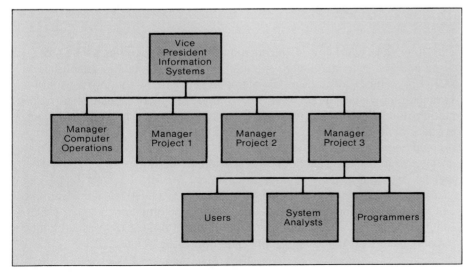

Figure A–3 ▪ Project Organization
of MIS Department

of utilization of the hardware and encourage higher efficiency and increased throughput by proper job scheduling and balancing of hardware capabilities.

In addition to improving hardware utilization, the data-processing manager must strive for a high degree of maintainability and reliability; preventive maintenance schemes must be developed for both hardware and software. Better systems can be achieved through use of the following practices:

- Establishing standard procedures to control actions that initiate and implement change.
- Using a modular approach for both hardware and software so that systems can be expanded; a complete switch to new equipment and new programs is a costly undertaking and should be avoided if possible.
- Strictly adhering to documentation standards. Software maintenance is impossible without extensive documentation to clarify how specific programs work.
- Implementing standard control and audit procedures to ascertain that the administrative policies and procedures established by management are followed.
- Planning for all contingencies so that data-processing interruptions are not catastrophic.

Managing an MIS is a difficult but important task. Managers must keep in mind that an MIS is an integrated set of people and machines. No matter how sophisticated the MIS, success in using it can be achieved only through its acceptance by users at all levels of the organization.

PROFESSIONAL ASSOCIATIONS

Professional societies have been formed to increase communication among professional people in computer fields, to continue the professional education of members, and to distribute current knowledge through publications of professional journals.

AFIPS

The **American Federation of Information Processing Societies (AFIPS),** organized in 1961, is a national federation of professional societies established to represent member societies on an international basis and to advance and disseminate knowledge of these societies. There are two categories of AFIPS participation: (1) member societies that have a principal interest in computers and information processing and (2) affiliated societies that, although not primarily concerned with computers and information processing, have a major interest in this area. Some of the prominent constituent societies of AFIPS are the Association for Computing Machinery (ACM), the Data Processing Management Association (DPMA), the Institute of Electrical and Electronic Engineers (IEEE), and the American Society for Information Science (ASIS). Affiliated societies of AFIPS include the American Institute of Certified Public Accountants (AICPA) and the American Statistical Association (ASA).

ACM

The **Association for Computing Machinery (ACM)** is the largest scientific, educational, and technical society of the computing community. Founded in 1947, this association is dedicated to the development of information processing as a discipline and to the responsible use of computers in increasingly complex and diverse applications. The objectives of the association are:

- To advance the science and art of information processing, including the study, design, development, construction, and application of modern machinery, computing techniques, and programming software.
- To promote the free exchange of ideas in the field of information processing in a professional manner between specialists and the public.
- To develop and maintain the integrity and competence of individuals engaged in the field of information processing.

The ACM has established special interest groups (known as SIGs) to address the wide range of interests in the computing field. For example, SIGSMALL was established for ACM members interested in small computers; SIGPLAN, for those interested in programming languages; and SIGCSE, for those interested in computer science education.

DPMA

Founded in Chicago as the National Machine Accountants Association, the **Data Processing Management Association (DPMA)** was chartered in December 1951. At that time the first electronic computer had yet to come into commercial use. The name "machine accountants" was chosen to identify persons associated with the operation and supervision of punched-card equipment. The society took its present name in 1962.

DPMA is one of the largest world-wide organizations serving information-processing and management communities. It includes all levels of management personnel. Through its educational and publishing activities, DPMA seeks to encourage high standards in the field of data processing and to promote a professional attitude among its members.

One of DPMA's specific purposes is to promote and develop educational and scientific inquiry in the field of data processing and data-processing management. As such, it sponsors college student organizations interested in data processing and encourages members to serve as counselors for the Scout computer merit badge. The organization also presents the "Computer Sciences Man of the Year" award for outstanding contributions to the profession.

ASM

The **Association for Systems Management (ASM),** founded in 1947, is headquartered in Cleveland, Ohio. The ASM is an international organization engaged in keeping its members abreast of the rapid growth and change occurring in the field of systems management and information processing. It provides for the professional growth and development of its members and of the systems profession through:

- Extended programs in local and regional areas in the fields of education and research.

- Annual conferences and committee functions in research, education, and public relations.
- Promotion of high standards of work performance by members of the ASM and members of the systems profession.
- Publication of the *Journal of Systems Management,* technical reports, and other works on subjects of current interest to systems practitioners.

The ASM has five technical departments: Data Communications, Data Processing, Management Information Systems, Organization Planning, and Written Communications. An ASM member can belong to one or more of these departments.

ICCP

The **Institute for Certification of Computer Professionals (ICCP)** is a non-profit organization established in 1973 to test and certify knowledge and skills of computing personnel. A primary objective of the ICCP is to pool the resources of constituent societies so that the full attention of the information-processing industry can be focused on the vital tasks of development and recognition of qualified personnel.

The establishment of the ICCP was an outgrowth of studies made by committees of the DPMA and the ASM, which developed the concept of a "computer foundation" to foster testing and certification programs. In 1974, the ICCP acquired the testing and certification programs of DPMA, including the Certificate in Data Processing (CDP) examination, which DPMA had begun in 1962. All candidates for the CDP examination must have at least five years of work experience in a computer-based information system environment. The examination consists of five sections: data-processing equipment, computer programming and software, principles of management, quantitative methods, and system analysis and design. Any qualified person may take the examination; he or she must successfully complete all five sections to receive the certificate. Another certification, the Certificate in Computer Programming (CCP), recognizes experience and professional competence at the senior programmer level. Candidates for this certification must also pass a basic five-part examination.

The ICCP is involved in improving existing programs and establishing new examinations for various specialties. A framework for a broad spectrum of tests and the relationship of these tests to job functions and curricula is under development.

SMIS

The **Society for Management Information Systems (SMIS)** was founded in 1968 to serve persons concerned with all aspects of management information systems in the electronic data-processing industry, including business system designers, managers, and educators. The organization aims to be an exchange or marketplace for technical information about management information systems and to enhance communications between MIS directors and executives responsible for the management of the business enterprise. SMIS also offers educational and research programs, sponsors competitions, bestows awards, and maintains placement programs.

BASIC
Supplement

CONTENTS

PREFACE

BASIC has traditionally been accepted as the most effective programming language for instructional purposes. In recent years, business and computer manufacturers have recognized the vast potential for the BASIC language beyond education. Therefore, the availability and usage of BASIC has increased dramatically. Today most small business computer systems and home computer systems rely exclusively on BASIC programming support.

One major problem associated with such tremendous growth has been the lack of controls on the implementation of the language. Although there is a national standard (ANSI) version of BASIC, it is normally not followed by computer designers. Thus there are differences in the BASIC language found on various computers. The material in this book not only presents BASIC found on a typical large time-shared computer system (Digital Equipment Corp.), but also includes coverage of microcomputer implementations (PET, Apple, Apple Macintosh, IBM, TRS-80). Whenever a BASIC instruction deviates from the national standard, it is highlighted.

Color coding has been used extensively throughout the material to assist the reader. The following legend should prove valuable:

BLUE	Computer Output
BROWN SHADING	Statements Referenced in Text
RED	User Response
GREY SHADING	Nonstandard BASIC

Every program has been both class tested and run on the various computer systems. Our primary goal has been to develop a student-oriented BASIC text that is both logical and consistent in its presentation. I would appreciate receiving any suggestions that might improve the material.

BACKGROUND

BASIC was developed in the mid-1960s at Dartmouth College by Professors John G. Kemeny and Thomas E. Kurtz and has become one of the most popular programming languages. **BASIC,** short for **Beginner's All-purpose Symbolic Instruction Code,** is easy to learn, can be used for a wide variety of useful tasks, and is well suited for classroom teaching.

BASIC, like any language, includes rules for spelling, syntax, grammar, and punctuation. Just as the rules in English help us understand one another, so the rules in BASIC help the computer understand what we want it to do. In BASIC, the rules link abstract algebraic expressions with easy-to-understand English words like LET, GOTO, FOR/NEXT, INPUT, PRINT, and END.

BASIC was originally developed for use in a large, interactive computer environment: one or more BASIC users could communicate with the computer *during* processing and feel as though they had the computer all to themselves. As the demand for minicomputers and microcomputers increased, manufacturers of such computers felt pressure to develop simple but effective languages for them. Rather than create entirely new languages, most opted to offer BASIC because of its interactive capability—where the user can communicate directly with the computer in a conversational fashion. Many altered the original BASIC, however, to suit their equipment. The result is that, although the BASIC language has a universally accepted set of standard rules called **ANSI BASIC**, each manufacturer adds its enhancements, or extensions, to this standard to make use of special features of its machines.

This supplement discusses BASIC commands common to most computer systems but notes the language variations among vendors. The programming examples have been executed on seven different computers: A DECSYSTEM 20 to represent the major time-sharing systems; and the Apple II, Apple Macintosh, IBM Personal Computer, IBM Personal Computer Junior, TRS-80 Model IV, and PET/Commodore 64 to represent popular microcomputer systems. For the scope of this book, the IBM Personal Computer and the IBM Personal Computer Junior are considered the same and thus are included together under the title IBM. Most other microcomputers are capable of using a dialect called BASIC-80 from Microsoft Consumer Products and an operating system called CP/M produced by Digital Research. Since the IBM's BASIC and operating systems were also designed by Microsoft, they are similar to BASIC-80 and CP/M. Therefore, references for those systems will parallel the IBM instructions. The programming examples are run on the DECSYSTEM 20 computer, but important changes required to execute them on the other computers are noted. Although there are a variety of models and languages for the Apple and TRS-80 computers, this supplement discusses only the Apple II computer with the Applesoft language and the Apple Macintosh with Microsoft BASIC and the TRS-80 Model III computer with Model III language (essentially the same as level II BASIC for Model I).

INTRODUCTION TO COMPUTER PROGRAMMING

Computer programs (also called software) are step-by-step instructions to solve a problem. Since the computer must be able to read and interpret each instruction, each must be precisely written. To know what instructions are required to solve a problem, the programmer follows five steps (commonly called the **programming process**):

1. Define the problem.
2. Design a solution.
3. Write the program.
4. Compile, debug, and test the program.
5. Document the program (see Chapter 9).

In order to show how these steps are used in the programming process, let us take a sample data-processing problem: calculating the area of a rectangle.

The first step is to define the problem. To do so, we analyze it by using the basic flow of all data processing—**input, processing, output**—but with a twist. It is often easier to determine what processing is needed by working backwards. First, determine what output is required, and then see what input is available for the program. The gap between the available input and required output will be the processing needed in the program.

Determining the output required for the problem is quite simple—we need to know the area of a rectangle. The input available is the length and width of the rectangle. We now need to develop a series of steps, called an algorithm, that will enable us to produce the desired output from the available input. We need an arithmetic equation that translates length and width into area. Length multiplied by width equals area; hence, the algorithm to calculate area is area = length × width. We have now defined the problem.

The second step, designing a solution, requires developing a logical sequence of instructions, or statements, to solve the problem. Documentation for this step consists of written descriptions and explanations of the instructions and statements used to solve the problem. Good documentation makes the program easier for others to understand and can simplify modification or updating of the program. A tool that is commonly used at this point is the flowchart. **Flowcharts** (detail flowcharts) are a form of documentation and are composed of symbols that stand for program statements. For example, the symbol for a processing step is this:

The following is the symbol for a step that involves either input from the terminal or output to the terminal or printer:

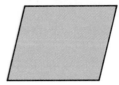

This symbol shows where the program starts or stops:

To create a flowchart for our example, we only need these three symbols. Some additional symbols that we will use later in this book include the following:

1. The symbol that shows where a comparison (decision) is to be made and where alternative processing is to occur based upon the results of the comparison is this:

2. To indicate an entry from or an exit to another part of the program flowchart, use this symbol:

3. The following symbol represents a preparation step, such as defining the dimensions of an array (discussed in Section IX):

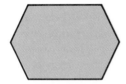

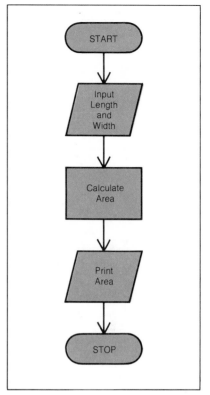

Figure I–1 ▪ Flowchart Example

Figure I–1 shows a flowchart depicting the steps of the programming example. Notice how the symbols are shown in logical order, top down, connected by flowlines (arrows). The first symbol shows the start of the program. It may correspond to one or more remarks at the beginning of the program statements. The second symbol shows an input step—we enter length and width. The third shows the processing done by the program—multiplying length by width to obtain area. After that, we want to see the result, so we output the area to the terminal. Finally, another start/stop symbol signifies the end of the program. The flowchart makes it easy to see the input, processing, and output steps of the program.

If the solution has been designed carefully, the third step—writing the program—should be relatively easy. All that is required is to translate the flowchart into BASIC statements. Figure I–2 shows this program written in BASIC. As you can see, many BASIC words, such as INPUT and PRINT, are easy to interpret. The symbol * means "multiply." The REM statement is used to document the program. Compare the coded BASIC statements in Figure I–2 to the flowchart in Figure I–1, noting the correspondence between the two.

In the program in Figure I–2, each statement starts with a **line number.** Line numbers tell the computer the order in which to execute statements.

Line 110 is a comment describing the program. The computer ignores all

Figure I–2 ▪ Area Program

```
00100 REM ************************************************************
00110 REM ***   THIS PROGRAM CALCULATES THE AREA OF A RECTANGLE   ***
00120 REM ************************************************************
00130 INPUT "ENTER THE LENGTH OF THE RECTANGLE IN CENTIMETERS";L
00140 INPUT "ENTER THE WIDTH OF THE RECTANGLE IN CENTIMETERS";W
00150 LET A = L * W
00160 PRINT "THE AREA OF THE RECTANGLE IS";A;"SQUARE CENTIMETERS"
00999 END
```

Boxes and ANSI Standards

Throughout the BASIC portion of this book, boxes are used to separate the main body of text from short discussions dealing with peculiarities, warnings, problems, and items of special interest. This, the first box, deals with the ANSI standards.

The purpose of a programming standard is to make it possible for a program to have *transportability*. In other words, if you write a program whose syntax lies completely within the BASIC standard, then this program will run correctly on *any* brand of computer that claims its BASIC meets the standards.

The American National Standards Institute, Inc., (ANSI) 1430 Broadway, New York, NY 10018, has published the ANSI Standard for Minimal BASIC. You can obtain a copy by writing the above address for document X3.60. As the title of the document suggests, the standard fails to include many features implemented by computer manufacturers. Material presented in this supplement that extends beyond the ANSI standard is shaded and identified as nonstandard.

such comment statements; they are for documentation purposes. Lines 130 and 140 tell the computer to print out a statement (shown in quotes)—the prompt (your cue) to enter the length and the width—and then to accept the input after it is typed in. Line 150 is an example of an assignment statement, which assigns values on the right side of the equal sign to special variables on the left (this is discussed in Section III). Line 160 instructs the computer to print out first a heading (shown in quotes) and then the computed area. Finally, line 999 tells the computer to stop processing. Again, you can see how the program follows the flow of input, processing, and output.

The fourth step involves sitting down at the terminal and typing the program, line for line, into the computer. Many interactive BASIC interpreters and compilers check for syntax errors as each statement is typed in. The statements necessary to use the BASIC interpreter or compiler are given in Table I–1 (found near the end of this section). **Syntax** refers to the way instructions have to be written (rules must be followed, just as grammatical rules must be followed in English). A syntax check can save considerable debugging time. Figure I–3 shows an interactive session with syntax checking.

After all syntax errors have been eliminated, the program can be tested with sample data (the fourth step). During this stage, the logic of the program is checked for correctness; for instance, were the correct statements used to determine the area? Figure I–4 shows the execution of the area program.

During each of these five steps, it is important that adequate documentation be written and maintained. During the last step, any revisions to the documentation that may be required should be made.

This example is relatively simple, but it shows each of the steps required to complete a program. Although other problems may be more complex, the steps involved are the same; successful programming can only come about through diligent application of the five steps in the programming process.

INTERACTING WITH THE COMPUTER

An important step in BASIC programming is learning to control the computer. Although this book cannot present the full operational details for each computer, it can discuss the principles of how to turn the computer on, use the BASIC programming language, retrieve a program from secondary storage, display the program, alter the program, and save the program for future reference.

Figure I–3 ▪ Syntax Checking

```
00010 REM *** EQUAL SIGN IS IN THE WRONG PLACE ***
00020 LET L * M = N
20 LET L *
? Found "*" when expecting "="


00010 REM *** INPUT IS SPELLED I-N-P-U-T ***
00020 INPUR "MY NAME IS";N$
20 INPUR "MY NAME IS";N$

? Statement not recognized
```

Figure I—4 ▪ Execution of Area
Program

```
RUNNH
ENTER THE LENGTH OF THE RECTANGLE IN CENTIMETERS ? 4
ENTER THE WIDTH OF THE RECTANGLE IN CENTIMETERS ? 3
THE AREA OF THE RECTANGLE IS 12 SQUARED CENTIMETERS
```

Manipulating Programs

BASIC programming requires the use of different types of commands. Some of the commands, like GOTO, LET, and READ, are program language statements. They are assembled into programs to solve specific business, scientific, engineering, and mathematical problems. The remainder of the BASIC supplement describes their characteristics and how they are used.

There are also **system commands,** used by the programmer to communicate with the operating system of the computer to perform functions like saving programs for future reference and making changes to programs. Some commands, like LIST, RUN, and DELETE, are almost universally used but are not covered by ANSI standards. A description of such commands as they relate to the five computer systems used in programming examples in this supplement follows.

APPLE

Hardware The APPLE II (Figure I—5) initially contains INTEGER BASIC. Since INTEGER BASIC lacks many important features of the ANSI standard, this discussion only refers to this computer once APPLESOFT floating point BASIC has been loaded.

Starting the Computer The power switch is located in the left rear portion of the computer. Since an external monitor or CRT is required, you must remember to turn on power to this device also. If a disk drive is attached, it

**Figure I—5 ▪ Apple II
Microcomputer**

will whir and try to *boot* the disk operating system (DOS), so be sure that a diskette is placed in the disk drive before the computer is turned on. (When the disk drive "boots the DOS," it loads from a diskette the instructions that tell the computer how to manage the disk. This must be done before the computer can perform any disk-related tasks.)

The computer "comes up" with **floating-point BASIC,** as indicated by the use of the] character as a prompt.

Saving and Loading Programs   Programs are commonly accessed from either cassette tape or disk on this system.

■ *Cassette:* To recall a program from a cassette tape into main memory, you must first position the tape to the beginning of the program. This means that you must keep a record of where programs are located on the tape. Next, push the PLAY button and pull out the earphone plug on the recorder until you can hear the tape sounds. When you hear a constant, high-pitched tone, stop the recorder and plug the earphone jack back in. Then type LOAD, push the PLAY button, and hit RETURN. The program has been loaded when you hear a beep and the cursor appears on the screen. (The **cursor** is usually a flashing character such as an underline or a block that shows where the next typed character will appear on the screen.)

To store a program, position the tape to a blank area, type SAVE, push the PLAY and RECORD buttons simultaneously, and then press RETURN. Again you will hear a beep, and the cursor will return when the program has been written to the tape.

■ *Disk:* The Apple has a convenient file-by-name catalog system for the DOS. To save an APPLESOFT (this is Apple's name for its floating-point BASIC) program—for example, one named PROGRAM 1—on disk, type

SAVE PROGRAM1

and press RETURN. To load the same program from disk, type:

LOAD PROGRAM1

and press RETURN. You can then run the program. Alternatively, you can type RUN PROGRAM1 without loading it; this causes the DOS to both load and run the program.

APPLE MACINTOSH

Hardware   The Apple Macintosh (Figure I–6) comes with a built-in 3 ½-inch disk drive and makes use of a pointing device called a mouse. The Macintosh runs Microsoft BASIC.

Starting the Computer   The power switch is located on the left side of the rear panel about halfway up the computer. When you turn the switch on, the Macintosh will beep to let you know it's started and then a picture (icon) representing a Macintosh disk appears on the screen. The blinking question mark shows that the Macintosh is ready for you to insert a disk. Insert a Macintosh disk (the Microsoft BASIC disk to start BASIC) into the disk drive, metal end first, label side up. The disk should be pushed in until it clicks into place. A message will then appear welcoming you to the Macintosh. You could also have inserted the disk first and then turned the power on.

To start MS-BASIC double-click the MS-Basic icon.

Figure I–6 ▪ **Apple Macintosh Microcomputer**

Saving and Loading Programs   The commands to save and load a program on disk are found in the File Menu located at the top of the screen on the Menu Bar.

The OPEN command brings in a program from the disk so that it can be run, listed, or edited. When OPEN is chosen from the File Menu, a display box appears on the screen requesting the name of the program to be loaded. After entering the name of the file, move the pointer to the box where OK appears and then click the button on the mouse once. The program will then be loaded into memory.

The SAVE command saves a program on the disk after you have typed it or made changes to it. When SAVE is chosen from the File Menu, a dialog box appears on the screen requesting the name of the program to be saved. It assumes you want the current name, but the name can be changed.

DEC

Hardware   The DECSYSTEM 2050 (see Figure I-7) is a large minicomputer that can have up to several million bytes of addressable primary storage for

Figure I–7 ▪ **DECSYSTEM 2050 and VT-100 Terminal**

programs—as opposed to a few tens of thousands of bytes in the microcomputers discussed here. The exact form of BASIC employed here is called BASIC PLUS 2 by the manufacturer.

The detailed hardware description very much depends on what CRT terminal is used with this computer. The one used here is the standard VT-100 terminal.

Signing On   The power switch (toggle variety) is located in the lower left on the back of the terminal. If the terminal is linked directly to the computer, press the CONTROL and C keys at the same time. If the terminal is linked to the computer by telephone, dial the correct number. When you hear a constant high-pitched tone, place the phone receiver in the modem; most modems have a light that comes on when the connection is made properly. Then press CONTROL-C.

Now a header will appear, followed by the symbol @.

```
TOPS-20 MONITOR 5.1(5622)
@
```

This is the prompt for the TOPS-20 MONITOR—the housekeeping program that controls the computer. You must now type LOGIN and account identifier followed by a password. The password should be privileged information—known only to those who need access to the programs in this particular account. For example, the programs for this manual were kept in an account called IACCT.MIS; access to the account was controlled by the password BASIC. The screen looked like this after log-in:

```
@LOGIN IACCT.MIS
```

The password did not appear on the screen, because the *monitor* knows that any characters following the blank after an account identifier are not to be made public.

After the RETURN key is pressed, the computer responds with a header giving the date and time. Then the monitor prompt (@) is displayed. To use the BASIC language, just type BASIC. When the computer is prepared to accept BASIC commands, it responds READY. To write a program, type NEW, and the computer asks for a name for the program.

```
READY
NEW
New program name--PAYROLL

READY
```

If you hit RETURN without supplying a name, the computer will call the program NONAME. You can now proceed to type in your program.

Saving and Loading Programs   We assume this computer uses disks for secondary storage. To save a program named PAYROLL, simply type SAVE PAYROLL.

```
READY
SAVE PAYROLL

READY
```

To load it at a later time, type OLD after the computer responds READY. The computer will ask for the old program's name. Type PAYROLL.

```
READY
OLD
Old file name--PAYROLL

READY
```

After the computer again responds READY, you may run or list the program or perform editing operations on it.

Signing Off When you are finished, type GOODBYE. After the computer acknowledges your message, turn the terminal off.

IBM

Hardware The IBM personal computer (Figure I–8) contains an enhanced version of Microsoft BASIC. We will discuss the hardware configuration using disk only. Consult your documentation for cassette commands.

Starting the Computer Place the DOS diskette into Drive A, the left-hand drive. Then turn the computer on. The power switch is located on the right side (toward the rear) of the system unit. Don't forget to turn on the TV monitor, too. When the computer is turned on, it will try to load the DOS. (If no diskette has been placed into the disk drive, the computer will "come up" in Cassette BASIC.)

The IBM has three BASIC dialects—Cassette BASIC, Disk BASIC, and Advanced BASIC. For the purposes of this book, they are the same.

Once DOS has been booted (loaded), the computer asks for the date as follows:

```
Current date is Tue  1-01-1980
Enter new date:
```

After you have typed the date and pressed the carriage return, the computer asks for the time as follows:

```
Current time is  0:00:16.86
Enter new time:
```

Figure I–8 ▪ **IBM Personal Computer**

After you have typed the time and pressed the carriage return, it responds with:

```
The IBM Personal Computer DOS
Version 1.10 (C)Copyright IBM Corp 1981, 1982

A>
```

The A> is the DOS prompt. Simply type BASIC and press the carriage return to load the disk BASIC translator. The BASIC prompt is "OK." Now you are ready to start programming.

Saving and Loading Programs   The IBM has a convenient file-by-name catalog system for the DOS. To save a program on disk (for example, one named SALES), type:

```
SAVE "SALES"
```

The name of the program should be less than or equal to eight characters. Do not embed any spaces. To load the same program from disk, type:

```
LOAD "SALES"
```

You can then LIST and RUN the program. The IBM provides you with a set of predefined function keys on the left-hand side of the keyboard. These keys can be used as an alternative to typing out some system commands. The function key number and its function are given at the bottom of the screen.

PET/CBM

Hardware   The PET (Figure I–9) and CBM computers are made by the same manufacturer, Commodore Business Machines. For each number series, the two computers are nearly identical. For example, the PET 2001 and the CBM 2001 differ only as follows:

Figure I–9 ▪ **PET Microcomputer**

- The PET keyboard has graphics characters labeled; the CBM keyboard does not.
- The SHIFT key on a PET switches between capital letters and graphics characters, whereas the SHIFT key on a CBM switches between lower case and capital letters.

(See your manual to find out how to make the PET mimic the CBM and vice-versa with a simple POKE command.)

PET/CBM computers come in three basic styles. The oldest PETs have a small keyboard and a self-contained tape cassette. A later PET has a standard typewriter-style keyboard, but the tape cassette no longer fits inside the computer. Both of these styles have nine-inch diagonal CRT screens allowing twenty-five lines of forty characters each to be displayed. Recently, a larger screen allowing eighty-character rows has been introduced. All of these computers come with 8K, 16K, 24K, and 32K memories.

Starting the Computer   The power switch is in back near the left-hand corner underneath the body of the computer. When the power switch is turned on, you see something like this:

```
***COMMODORE BASIC 4.0***
31743 BYTES FREE
READY
```

The first line tells which version of the BASIC language is available.[1] The second line tells how much memory your computer has (32K in this example). The third line indicates that you can immediately begin typing in BASIC line numbers and statements.

Saving and Loading Programs   Programs are commonly accessed from either cassette tape or disk on this system.

- *Cassette:* The PET has a convenient file-by-name cataloging system. To save a program, position the tape to a blank area, and type SAVE and the program name in quotes. For example:

```
SAVE "REPORT"
```

You must also remember to press the RECORD and PLAY buttons on the cassette. If you have more than one cassette tape drive, you may have to specify the device number—otherwise, it will default to 1. For example, if you want to save REPORT on cassette tape drive 2, type

```
SAVE "REPORT",2
```

To load a stored program, you need only type LOAD and the program name (enclosed in quotes); for example:

```
LOAD "REPORT"
```

Then, when the cassette PLAY button is pressed, the computer will search for the named program. The names of other programs found during the search will be displayed on the screen. Therefore, the tape does not have to be

---

[1]All programming examples in this book were run on version 4.0; but no changes should be necessary to run them on versions 2.0 and 3.0, since the main differences are in disk commands that are beyond the scope of this book.

positioned precisely for loading. The computer will tell you when it has found the desired program and when it is loading the program into primary memory. An example—loading a program named IDIDIT, the fourth one on a tape—is shown below.

```
LOAD "IDIDIT"

PRESS PLAY ON TAPE #1
OK

SEARCHING FOR IDIDIT
FOUND COMMISSION
FOUND LAST
FOUND WEIGHT
FOUND IDIDIT
LOADING
READY.
```

■ *Disk:* The PET floppy disk system has two drives housed in one cabinet and a file-by-name catalog. To save a program named REPORT on drive 0, you type:

```
DSAVE "REPORT"
```

To specify drive 1, type:

```
DSAVE "REPORT",D1
```

If you alter a program that was read in from a disk and you want to replace the existing version on the disk, use @ as follows:

```
DSAVE "@REPORT",D1
```

To load a program from disk, you need only type:

```
DLOAD "REPORT"
```

or

```
DLOAD "REPORT",D1
```

The first example loads from drive 0, since that is the default unit.

TRS-80

Hardware These programs have all been tested on the TRS-80 Model III with the Model III BASIC language (see Figure I-10). An older computer, the Model I with Level II BASIC, is very similar to the Model III. The comments about BASIC programs here generally apply to either computer but do not deal with the Level I BASIC language.

Starting the Computer All peripherals should first be turned on. The computer is then turned on by a rocker switch located beneath the keyboard on the right hand side. All disk drives should be empty when the computer is turned on or off. If diskettes remain in the disk drives, the information on the diskettes could be destroyed. Next the TRSDOS diskette should be inserted in Drive 0. The RESET button must be pressed to enable the computer to load TRSDOS. The TRSDOS version number and date of creation will be displayed followed by the amount of RAM and the number of drives in the system. TRSDOS then prompts the user to enter the date in the form MM/DD/YY. The date in correct form must be entered and the ENTER key pressed before

Figure I–10 ▪ **Radio Shack's TRS-80 Microcomputer**

TRSDOS will continue. Next the time in 24 -hour for HH:MM:SS must be entered and the enter key pressed. To set the time at 00:00:00 the ENTER key may simply be pressed. The monitor will then display:

TRSDOS READY

The computer is then in the TRSDOS READY mode and TRSDOS commands may be entered.

To load the BASIC interpreter type:

BASIC

Press the ENTER key.
The computer will display:

HOW MANY FILES?

then:

MEMORY SIZE?

Press ENTER in response to each of these questions.
Next the computer will display a heading followed by:

READY

>

You may now begin to use Disk BASIC.
To use cassette BASIC hold down the reset and break keys after turning on the computer.

Saving and Loading Programs Programs are commonly accessed from either cassette tape or disk on this system.

▪ *Cassette:* The TRS-80 has a convenient file-by-name cataloging system. To save a program:

1. Position the tape to a blank area.
2. Type SAVE "program-name"; for example, SAVE "TRIAL".
3. Press the RECORD and PLAY buttons on the cassette.

To load a stored program, you need only type:

```
CLOAD
```

When the cassette PLAY button is pressed, the computer will search for the program. The names of the programs found during the search will be displayed on the screen. After the computer has found the desired program, it will load it into main memory.

■ *Disk:* To save a program (for example, TRIAL) just type:

```
SAVE "TRIAL"
```

and hit the ENTER button. To load the same program from disk, type

```
LOAD "TRIAL"
```

BASIC SYSTEM AND EDITING COMMANDS

The system and editing commands are **immediate-mode commands;** that is, they are executed as soon as the carriage control key (RETURN, ENTER) is pressed. They differ from BASIC language commands, which are not executed until the program is run. The most commonly used system commands are discussed below.

System Commands

NEW

This command tells the computer to erase any program currently in active memory. After typing this command, you can start entering a new program.

LIST

After typing in a long program, you may want to admire the finished product. Type LIST to see the program commands displayed at the terminal. If you have a very short program, LIST can display the whole program on the screen. However, if the program has more lines than the screen does, only the last part of the program will remain on the screen. Some screens permit only twenty-four lines to be displayed. You can display portions of programs by specifying the lines to be listed—LIST 250 – 400, for example. Most computers also allow you to suppress scrolling, that is, to freeze the listing temporarily (see "Controlling the Scroll" later in this section).

SAVE

After you have typed many program lines, you will want to avoid losing them when the computer is turned off, or if there is a power failure. To do this, you have to move a program from primary memory to a secondary storage medium such as a cassette tape or disk. This move is accomplished by the SAVE command. There are generally several options to this command; for example, you may supply a name that distinguishes this particular program from all others.

LOAD

This command moves the designated program from secondary storage to primary memory. Before moving the program. LOAD closes all open files and deletes all variables and program lines currently residing in memory.

Controlling the Scroll If your program's output consists of forty lines of information but your screen only has a twenty-four-line capacity, how will you see all your output? The forty lines will be displayed so quickly that you will not be able to read them until the listing is finished. By then, however, the first sixteen lines will be gone—scrolled off the top of the screen.

Most computers have a means of controlling the scroll of the screen. The programmer can simply push one or two keys to freeze the display and then press the same keys to resume listing when desired. This method also can be used to freeze the output listing of a program during execution. Table I–1 summarizes the method of scroll freezing, as well as the type of editor (discussed below) used on each of the five computers.

Table I–1 ▪ Common System Commands

	DEC	APPLE	APPLE MACINTOSH	PET/COMMODORE 64
POWERSWITCH LOCATION	Left rear of terminal	Left rear of terminal	Left rear terminal	Right side panel (rear)
SIGNON PROCEDURES			No response Icon of disk with blinking question mark	
User	Control-C	No response		No response
Computer response	TOPS-20 MONITOR	APPLE II	No response Insert appropriate disk	***COMMODORE 64 BASIC V2***
Users	LOG ACCT. # PASSWORD	No response		No response
STARTING BASIC				
User	BASIC	Comes up in BASIC	Insert MS-BASIC disk	Comes up in BASIC
Computer response	READY	Flashing cursor	Display directory of MS-BASIC disk	READY
User	NEW		Double click MS-BASIC icon	(Flashing block)
Computer response	NEW FILENAME—		Command box appears	
User	Enter name of program; begin typing program	Begin typing program	Begin typing program	Begin typing program
SYSTEM COMMANDS		LIST	(The following can be typed or selected from a menu)	LIST
List	LIST	RUN		RUN
Execute a program	RUN	Type line #, then RETURN	LIST	Type line #, then RETURN
Delete a line	DELETE line #		RUN	
Store program on disk	SAVE	SAVE name	Type line #, then RETURN	SAVE "name",8
Store program on tape	Does not apply	SAVE	SAVE filename	SAVE "name"
Retrieve program from disk	OLD FILENAME—	LOAD name	Does not apply	LOAD "name",
Retrieve program from tape	Does not apply	or RUN name8	LOAD	LOAD "name"
List of file names	CATALOG	LOAD CATALOG	OPEN filename Does not apply Files automatically appear	For Disk: LOAD "$", 8 LIST For Cassette: LOAD "$" LIST
SIGN-OFF PROCEDURES				
User	GOODBYE or BYE	No response	Select QUIT from File Menu	No response
Computer response	KILLED JOB	No response	Displays directory window	No response
User	Power off	Power off	Select CLOSE and then select EJECT from File Menu to quit MS-BASIC; Turn power off	Power off

Table continued on next page

Table I–1 ▪ Continued

	TRS-80	IBM/Cassette BASIC	IBM/disk BASIC
POWERSWITCH LOCATION	Right front under keyboard	Right rear of computer	Right rear of computer
SIGN-ON PROCEDURES			
User	No response	No response	No response
Computer response	CASS?	IBM Personal Computer BASIC	Enter today's date (m-d-y); time
	MEMORY SIZE?	Version C1.00 Copyright IBM	The IBM Personal Computer
	RADIO SHACK MODEL III	Corp. 1981	DOS Version 1.10 (C) Copyright
	BASIC	61404 Bytes Free	IBM Corp. 1981, 1982
	(C) 80 TANDY	OK	A >
User	Respond to CASS? and	No response	Respond to date query
	MEMORY SIZE?		
	Queries		
STARTING BASIC			
User	Comes up in BASIC	Comes up in BASIC	Type BASIC or BASICA (For Advanced BASIC) after computer types A >
Computer response	READY	OK	OK
User	Begin typing program	Begin typing program	Begin typing program
SYSTEM COMMANDS			
List	LIST	LIST	LIST
Execute a program	RUN	RUN	RUN
Delete a line	DELETE line #	DELETE line #	DELETE line #
Store program on disk	SAVE "name"	Does not apply	SAVE "name"
Store program on tape	SAVE "name"	SAVE "name"	Does not apply
Retrieve program from disk	LOAD "name"	Does not apply	LOAD "name
Retrieve program from tape	CLOAD "name"	LOAD "name"	Does not apply
List of file names	Return to system level and type DIR	FILES	FILES
SIGN-OFF PROCEDURES			
User	No response	No response	No response
Computer response	No response	No response	No response
User	Power off	Power off	Power off

CATALOG

A **catalog** is a program that supplies a complete alphabetical list of a user's file. This command is used to list the file names of your programs and data files. To use this command, type CATALOG or just CAT and press RETURN. The command to list the file names may vary for the different computers (see Table I–1).

Editing Commands

Everyone makes typing mistakes. You should quickly learn how to correct yours. You may find a mistake before you press the RETURN key, or you may find it later. These two conditions call for different methods of correction.

BEFORE RETURN HAS BEEN PRESSED

Suppose you type LOST when you wish to LIST a program. If you notice the error before pressing RETURN, you can move the computer's cursor back to the O in LOST by pressing the DELETE key (on the DEC), the ← key (on the Apple, IBM, and TRS-80), or the INST DEL key (on the PET/Commodore 64), or the BACKSPACE key on the Macintosh. Then you can retype LIST correctly.

AFTER RETURN HAS BEEN PRESSED

If you notice an error after RETURN has been pressed, the simplest correction, in principle, is to retype the whole line. This may get tiresome for long lines, however—especially if you need to change only one character. Each computer has a means of correcting mistakes within a given line. There is not enough space here for a full explanation of these methods, but there are two general kinds—the screen editor and the line editor.

To use the screen editor, list the portion of the program containing the error. Then move the cursor to the position of the error—typically by pressing four keys with arrows that move the cursor up, down, left, or right. The incorrect characters then can be typed over or deleted, or new characters can be inserted between existing characters.

The line editor works on individual lines. The user specifies the line containing the error and uses commands such as REPLACE, INSERT, and DELETE instead of moving the cursor to the error.

Type of Editor and Scroll Control

COMPUTER	SCREEN EDITOR?	LINE EDITOR?	SCROLL STOP/START
DECSYSTEM 20	X	X	NO SCROLL[1]
Apple	X		CTRL-S[2]
IBM/Microsoft	X		CTRL-NUMLOCK[3]
TRS-80		X	SHIFT-@[4]
PET/Commodore 64	X		None[5]
Apple Macintosh		X	Scroll bars[6]

NOTES:
[1] NO SCROLL is a separate single key.
[2] CTRL-S means hold down the CONTROL key and the S key at the same time.
[3] CTRL-NUMLOCK means hold down the control key and the NUMLOCK key at the same time.
[4] SHIFT-@ means hold down the SHIFT key and the @ key at the same time.
[5] There is no scroll stop/start key: however, pressing the shift key slows down the scroll to one line at a time.
[6] "Clicking" on the scroll bar or scroll arrow will scroll the display. "Dragging" the scroll box will also scroll the display.

SUMMARY POINTS

■ BASIC (Beginner's All-purpose Symbolic Instruction Code) was developed in the mid-1960s by Professors John G. Kemeny and Thomas E. Kurtz.

■ BASIC has rules of grammar (syntax) to which programmers must adhere.

■ The following are the five steps in the programming process: (1) define the problem; (2) design a solution; (3) write the program; (4) compile, debug, and test the program; and (5) document the program.

■ System commands are used by the programmer to communicate with the operating system of the computer. Some commonly used ones are NEW, LIST, and SAVE.

■ Editing commands help the programmer correct mistakes.

■ Table I–1 summarizes start-up procedures and common system commands.

REVIEW QUESTIONS

1. What is BASIC?
2. List the five steps of the programming process.
3. What is documentation, and why is it important?
4. What are the system and editing commands used for? List three system commands.

OVERVIEW

One of the best ways to learn any programming language is to examine sample programs. This and the remaining sections in the BASIC supplement will intersperse discussions of the language's general characteristics with program examples.

This section discusses some BASIC fundamentals: line numbers, BASIC statements, constants, character strings, and variables. All are demonstrated so that you can use them properly when you write programs.

FUNDAMENTALS OF THE BASIC LANGUAGE

A BASIC program is a sequence of instructions that tells the computer how to solve a problem. Figure II–1 is an example. This program calculates the sales tax of an item that costs $5.50.

Notice that each instruction contains a line number and a BASIC statement. BASIC statements are composed of special programming commands, numeric or character string constants, numeric or string variables, and formulas (also called expressions). Line 160 from the sample program is a typical BASIC statement. It tells the computer to multiply two values together and place the result in a location called T. T is the location in memory where the sales tax is stored.

Note that pseudocode rather than flowcharting has been used to describe the processing steps to be performed in the program. For more information about pseudocode, see Chapter 9.

On the DECSYSTEM 20 there are two commands, RUN and RUNNH, that can be used to execute (run) a program. If RUN is used, as in Figure II–1, the computer will print a header giving the name of your program, the date, and the time as well as the output of the program. The RUNNH (Run No Header) command will eliminate the header and print only the output of the program. Throughout the remainder of this book we will use the RUNNH format. (See box titled "Important Keys and Commands.")

LINE NUMBERS

The **line number** must be an integer between 1 and 99999. The upper limit for line numbers may vary according to the system being used. Program statements are executed by the computer in the sequence in which they are numbered. (Later we will explain how this sequence can be altered.) Line numbers also can be used as labels to refer to specific statements in the program.

Line numbers do not have to be specified in increments of 1. Using increments of 10, for example, makes it easier to insert new statements between existing lines at a later time without renumbering all the old statements in the program. For example, if we wanted to insert a new statement in the sample program between statements 150 and 160, we could number the new statement 155 without disturbing the order or numbering of the existing statements (see Figure II–2). The BASIC interpreter or compiler arranges all the program statements in ascending order according to line number, even though the lines actually may have been entered in some other order.

Another advantage of BASIC line numbers is that they permit changes to be made to the program as it is being entered. For example, if two lines are

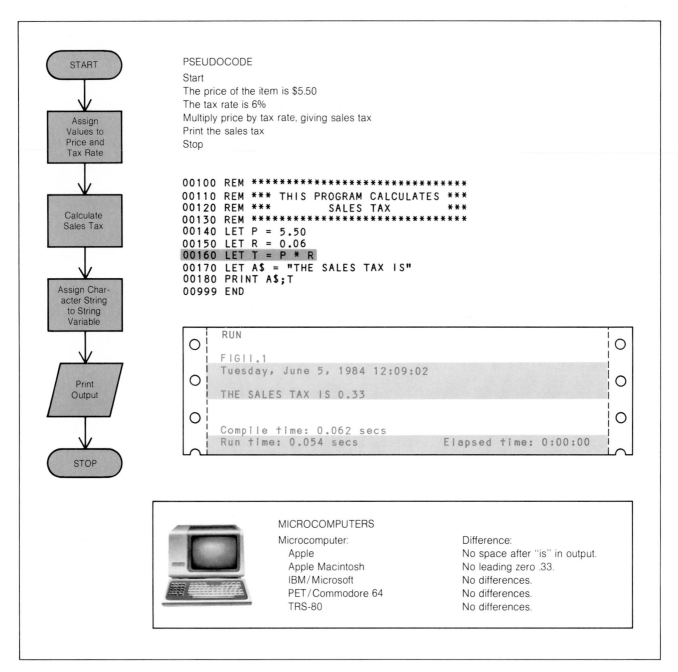

Figure II–1 ▪ Sales Tax Program

typed in with the same line number, the computer will accept the last one entered as the correct one. Thus, if we make a mistake in a statement, we can simply type in the same line number and the correct statement. Suppose that in the sales tax example, we gave P the wrong price; it should have been $6.50, not $5.50. All we have to do to correct this is type the number of the line to be changed and then retype the statement with the correct price:

```
00140 LET P = 6.50
```

The line just entered will be put into computer memory in place of the original line 140.

Important Keys and Commands

COMPUTER	EXECUTION COMMAND	CARRIAGE CONTROL KEY	COMMENTS
DECSYSTEM 20	RUN or RUNNH	RETURN	RUNNH means "RUN No Header." When RUN alone is pressed, the computer points out the date and a system-identifying label.
Apple	RUN	RETURN	
Apple Macintosh	RUN	RETURN	
IBM/Microsoft	RUN	↵	Although there is no lettering on the key, we will refer to it as *carriage return*.
TRS-80	RUN	ENTER	The ENTER key is located on the right side of the keyboard. This is the location of the RETURN key on the other computers. The two keys serve the same purpose.
PET/Commodore 64	RUN	RETURN	

Figure II–2 ▪ Sales Tax Program with Inserted Line

```
00100 REM ********************************
00110 REM *** THIS PROGRAM CALCULATES ***
00120 REM ***          SALES TAX       ***
00130 REM ********************************
00140 LET P = 5.50
00150 LET R = 0.06
00155 REM ***    TAX = PRICE * RATE    ***
00160 LET T = P * R
00170 LET A$ = "THE SALES TAX IS"
00180 PRINT A$;T
00999 END


RUNNH
THE SALES TAX IS 0.33
```

MICROCOMPUTERS

Microcomputer:	Difference:
Apple	No space after "is" in output.
Apple Macintosh	No leading zero .33.
IBM/Microsoft	No differences.
PET/Commodore 64	No differences.
TRS-80	No differences.

BASIC STATEMENT COMPONENTS

In the remaining portion of this section, we will take a closer look at numeric and character string constants and numeric and string variables.

Constants

Constants are values that do not change during a program's execution. There are two kinds: numeric and character string.

NUMERIC CONSTANTS

BASIC permits numbers to be represented in two ways: as real numbers or in exponential notation.

Real Numbers   Real numbers can be either integers or decimal fractions. The following are some examples of real numbers.

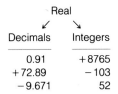

Decimals	Integers
0.91	+8765
+72.89	−103
−9.671	52

There are some rules to remember when using numbers in BASIC:

1. No commas can be embedded within numbers:

42305 (valid)   1,295 (invalid)

BASIC interprets the invalid example not as the number one thousand two hundred ninety-five, but as the number one and the number two hundred ninety-five.

2. If the number is negative, it must be preceded by a minus sign:

−1.23 (valid)   1.23− (invalid)

3. If no sign is included, the number is assumed to be positive:

7146 is the same as +7146

Exponential Notation   Exponential notation (scientific notation) usually is used for very large or very small numbers. Some examples follow:

9.26347E+07   2.984E−04

The E represents base 10, and the signed number following the E is the power to which 10 is raised. The number preceding the E is called the mantissa and in most systems lies between 1.000 and 9.999. A plus sign (+) by the power indicates that the decimal point is to be shifted to the right that number of places, whereas a minus sign (−) indicates that the decimal point should be shifted left the power number of places (see Figure II–3).

The following are examples of exponential notation:

Decimal	Power Equivalent	Exponential Notation
6783	6.783×10^3	6.783E+03
0.0002217	2.217×10^{-4}	2.217E−04
−4132784	-4.132784×10^6	−4.132784E+06

Figure II–3 ■ **Exponential Notation**

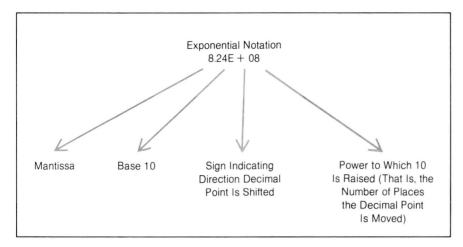

Exponential Notation
8.24E + 08

Mantissa Base 10 Sign Indicating Direction Decimal Point Is Shifted Power to Which 10 Is Raised (That Is, the Number of Places the Decimal Point Is Moved)

CHARACTER STRING CONSTANTS

The other type of constant is the character string. Character strings are composed of alphanumeric data—a sequence of letters, numbers, and special characters enclosed in quotation marks. The maximum number of characters allowed in a character string varies from system to system. On some systems it is not necessary to enclose character strings within quotation marks in data statements unless commas and semicolons are to be included within the character string. It is generally considered good practice to use the quotes, however. The following are examples of character strings:

```
"STEVE"
"11/12/84"
"BOWLING GREEN, OHIO"
```

The program in Figure II–1 contains a character string in line 170:

```
00170 LET A$ = "THE SALES TAX IS"
```

Variables

Any data values to be used by a program must be stored in the computer either before or during execution of the program. The computer has a great number of memory locations, which are assigned names by the programmer. These names are called variable names, because the value stored in a memory location can change as the program is executed. A variable is the name of the location or the address in memory where the value is stored and can only represent one value at a time. Memory works something like post office boxes. The variable is the P.O. box number, the memory cell is the actual box itself, and the value that is stored in memory is like the mail; however, in a computer memory "box" there can only be one piece of "mail" at a time. Each time a new piece of "mail" is put in the memory "box," the old one is taken out.

There are two types of variables: numeric and string. In our examples, P, R, and T are numeric variables, and A$ is a string variable.

NUMERIC VARIABLES

A numeric variable name represents a number that is either supplied to the computer by the programmer or internally calculated by the computer during execution of the program. A numeric variable name can be either one letter alone or one letter followed by one numeric digit. (Almost all BASICs permit the use of two letters, and many computer systems permit more descriptive variable names—see box.) The following examples show valid and invalid numeric variable names:

Valid	Invalid and Why	
X	33	(must begin with a letter)
B4	*C	(must begin with a letter)
A9	6	(cannot be a single digit)

Note lines 140,150, and 160 in the program in Figure II–2:

```
00140 LET P = 5.50
00150 LET R = 0.06
00160 LET T = P * R
```

P contains the price of the item—$5.50. R holds the tax rate, and the location of T has the result of price multiplied by rate.

STRING VARIABLES

A string variable name can represent the value of a character string—for example, a name, an address, or a Social Security number. String variable names are distinguished from numeric variable names by the use of the dollar sign ($) following a single alphabetic character. The following are examples of valid and invalid string variable names:

Valid	Invalid and Why
H$	6$ (first character must be alphabetic)
T$	X (last character must be $)

Many computer systems permit the use of more descriptive string variable names. However, all systems require that the first character be alphabetic and the last character be $. See the box for description of names permitted by other systems.

Numeric Variable Names

MICROCOMPUTER	NUMBER OF UNIQUE CHARACTERS RECOGNIZED	ADDITIONAL CHARACTERS PERMITTED
DECSYSTEM 20	35	No
Apple	2	Yes
Apple Macintosh	40	Yes
IBM/Microsoft	40	No
TRS-80	2	Yes
PET/Commodore 64	2	Yes

String Variable Names

MICROCOMPUTER	NUMBER OF UNIQUE CHARACTERS RECOGNIZED	ADDITIONAL CHARACTERS PERMITTED
DECSYSTEM 20	34 (plus $)	No
Apple	2 (plus $)	Yes[1]
Apple Macintosh	40 (plus $)	Yes
IBM/Microsoft	40 (plus $)	No
TRS-80	2 (plus $)	Yes[1]
PET/Commodore 64	2 (plus $)	Yes[1]

[1]When additional characters are used, the last character must be a dollar sign ($).

Typical examples of the proper use of string variables can be seen in lines 170 and 180 of the sample program:

```
00170 LET A$ = "THE SALES TAX IS"
00180 PRINT A$;T
```

The character string "THE SALES TAX IS" is assigned to the string variable name A$. In line 180, the values of A$ and T are printed out. This is the output:

```
RUNNH
THE SALES TAX IS 0.33
```

Reserved Words

Reserved words are words that have a special meaning to the translator program (the interpreter or compiler) of the computer. These words cannot be used as variable names. The "Common DECSYSTEM 20 Reserved Words" box shows some of the most commonly used reserved words for the DECSYSTEM 20. Refer to your system's manual for additional reserved words or any differences in your system.

Common DECSYSTEM 20 Reserved Words

ABS	CALL	CHR	COS
DATA	DEF	DEL	DELETE
DIM	ELSE	END	EXP
FOR	GET	GO	GOSUB
GOTO	IF	INPUT	INT
LEFT$	LET	LOG	MAT
MID$	NEXT	NOT	ON
OPEN	OR	PRINT	PUT
READ	REM	RESTORE	RETURN
RIGHT	RND	SGN	SIN
SQR	SQRT	STEP	STOP
STR$	SYS	TAB	TAN
THEN	TO	UNTIL	VAL
WHILE			

SUMMARY POINTS

■ A BASIC program is a series of instructions. Each one is composed of a line number and a BASIC statement.

■ The line numbers serve (1) as labels by which statements can be referenced and (2) as instructions to specify the order of execution of the program.

■ Using line numbers in increments of 5 or 10 permits easy insertion of new statements.

■ BASIC statements contain special reserved words (programming commands), numeric or character string constants, numeric or string variables, and formulas.

■ Constants are values that do not change. A valid numeric constant is any real number expressed as an integer, decimal fraction, or in exponential notation. Character strings are alphanumeric data enclosed in quotation marks.

■ Variable names are programmer-supplied names that specify locations in memory where data values may be stored. Numeric variable names represent numbers. String variables contain alphanumeric values, and their names are distinguished from numeric variable names by the symbol $.

■ Reserved words are words which have a special meaning to the translator program of the computer, so they may not be used as variable names.

REVIEW QUESTIONS

1. What are the two components of a BASIC instruction?
2. What types of things are BASIC statements composed of?
3. What are two main uses of line numbers? Why is it advantageous to use them in increments of five or ten?
4. What is a variable? Name two types and explain how they differ.

OVERVIEW

This section describes four elementary BASIC statements—REM, LET, PRINT, and END. The LET statement is used to input, or assign, data to variables and to perform arithmetic calculations. The PRINT statement allows the programmer to see the results of processing. Processing is stopped with the END statement. The REM statement is presented here to underscore the importance of program documentation.

THE REM STATEMENT

The remark (REM) statement provides information for the programmer or anyone else reading the program; it provides no information to the computer. The REM statement is used to document the program; the programmer generally uses it to explain program segments, to define variables used within the program, or to note any special instructions. Because they are non-executable statements, REM statements can be placed anywhere throughout the program.

The general format of the REM statement is this:

line# REM comment

Some REM statements that could be used to document or explain a program are presented next. For example:

```
00010 REM *** THIS PROGRAM CALCULATES COMPANY PAYROLL ***
```

This example illustrates the use of a REM statement to explain the purpose of a program. A REM statement such as this could be used anywhere in a program to explain the purpose of individual program segments. Notice the asterisks that surround the descriptive statement. Many programmers will use the asterisks (although any character could be used) to set off the REM statement from the other statements in a program. This technique allows the REM statements to be easily identified when the programmer is looking through long program listings.

The following example illustrates the use of a REM statement to define a variable used within the program:

```
00030 REM *** O = OVERTIME PAY ***
```

It is a good practice to define the variables used in a program, especially if other people will be using it.

It is possible to have a REM statement with no comment following it, or one followed by asterisks (*):

```
00070 REM
00080 REM ****************************************
```

In these cases, the REM statement could be used to set off comments from executable statements and thus improve the readability of the program.

THE LET STATEMENT

The purpose of the LET, or assignment, statement is to assign values to variables. It can be used to enter data into a program as well as to process it.

The general format of the LET statement is this:

line# LET variable = expression

The expression may be a constant, arithmetic formula or a variable. The following are examples:

Statement	Expression	Type
00010 LET Z = 35	35	Numeric constant
00020 LET B$ = "STEVE"	"STEVE"	Character string constant
00030 LET R = G	G	Numeric variable
00040 LET N$ = C$	C$	String variable
00050 LET Y = T * 4	T * 4	Arithmetic formula

The LET statement can be used to assign values to numeric or string variables directly or to assign the result of a calculation to a numeric variable. In either case, the value or calculated result of an expression on the right side of the equal sign is assigned to the variable on the left side. It is important to note that the statement is not evaluated in the same way as an algebraic expression.

When BASIC assigns a value to a variable on the left side of the equation, it really is putting that value in a storage location in memory labeled by that variable name. Since a storage location can only be represented by a variable name, only a variable can be on the left.

The following examples of LET statements are presented along with a short description of how they are executed.

LET Statement	Computer Execution
00010 LET N = 25	The numeric value 25 is assigned to the location called N.
00050 LET R = S + T	The values in S and T are added together and assigned to R.
00100 LET N$ = "THE WHITE HOUSE"	The character string enclosed in quotes is placed into the string variable N$ (the quotes are not).
00130 LET T = T + 1	1 is added to the current value of T, and the result is assigned to T. This result replaces whatever was in T previously. Notice that this procedure effectively counts how many times line 130 is executed.
00170 LET O = (2.25 + K − J) / (L * 20)	The arithmetic expression to the right of the equal sign is evaluated and assigned to 0.

The reserved word LET identifies a statement in BASIC as an assignment statement. However, some compilers and interpreters do not require it. These versions accept the statement without the reserved word LET as follows:

00050 R = 4.55

This shorthand method can save both time and memory space.

Arithmetic Expressions

In BASIC, arithmetic expressions are composed of constants, numeric variables, and arithmetic operators. The arithmetic operators that can be used are the following:

BASIC Arithmetic Operation Symbol	Operation	Arithmetic Example	BASIC Arithmetic Expression
+	Addition	A + B	A + B
−	Subtraction	A − B	A − B
*	Multiplication	A × B	A * B
/	Division	A ÷ B	A / B
∧ or ** or ↑ or [	Exponentiation	A^B	A ∧ B or A ** B or A ↑ B or A [B

Some examples of valid expressions in LET statements follow:

```
00010 LET A = T - U
00020 LET B = Q1 + Q2 + Q3 + Q4
00030 LET X = N ^ 5 / 2 * T
00040 LET Y = 2.5 * W
```

Hierarchy of Operations

When more than one operation is to be performed within an arithmetic expression, the computer follows a hierarchy, or priority, of operations. When parentheses are present in an expression, the operation within the parentheses is performed first. If parentheses are nested, the operation in the innermost set of parentheses is performed first. Thus, in the expression

```
(X + (Z - 2) * Y) / 15
```

the first operation to be performed is to subtract 2 from the value in Z. The result of that operation is then multiplied by Y and added to X because of the rules of priority discussed below. Once the expression within the outer parenthesis has been evaluated, that result is divided by 15.

Parentheses aside, operations are performed according to the following rules of priority:

Priority	Operation	Symbol
First	Exponentiation	∧ or ** or ↑ or [
Second	Multiplication or division	* or /
Third	Addition or subtraction	+ or −

Operations with high priority are performed before operations with lower priority (subject to our discussion on parentheses). If more than one operation is to be performed at the same level, for example,

```
5 ^ 4 ^ 2
```

the computer evaluates them from left to right. In this example, the 5 would be raised to the fourth power and then the result, 625, raised to the second power. The answer is 390,625.

The following are examples of these hierarchical rules:

Expression	Computer Evaluation
Expression 1	
2 * 5 + 1	
First: 2 * 5 = 10	Multiplication has a higher priority than addition, so it is done first.
Second: 10 + 1 = 11	Then the addition is done. The result is 11.
Expression 2	
2 * (5 + 1)	
First: (5 + 1) = 6	In this case, the addition must be done first, because it is enclosed in parentheses.
Second: 2 * 6 = 12	The result is multiplied by 2. Compare this result with the result in Expression 1.
Expression 3	
2 ∧ 3 / 4 − 2	
First: 2 ∧ 3 = 8	The priority order tells the computer to start with exponentiation.
Second: 8 / 4 = 2	Next is division.
Third: 2 − 2 = 0	Last, the subtraction is done. The result is 0.
Expression 4	
4 * 5 + 1 / 2 * 21	
First: 4 * 5 = 20	There are three operations at the same level: *, /, and *. They are performed from left to right. Last, the addition is done; the result is 30.5.
Second: 1 / 2 = 0.5	
Third: 0.5 * 21 = 10.5	
Fourth: 20 + 10.5 = 30.5	

Assigning Character Strings

The LET statement also can be used to assign a character string value to a string name. A character string is composed of alphanumeric data enclosed in quotes. For example,

```
00010 LET N$ = "MY NAME IS"
00020 LET K$ = N$
```

The following examples show valid and invalid LET statements:

Valid	Invalid and Why	
00010 LET X = Y / Z	00010 LET Y / Z = X	(Only a variable can appear on the left side of the equal sign.)
00020 LET N$ = "STEVE"	00020 LET N = "STEVE"	(A character string must be assigned to a string variable.)
00030 LET T = N1 + N2	00030 LET T = N1 + N$	(A string variable cannot be part of an arithmetic expression.)

Figure III–1, which calculates average monthly salary, illustrates several uses of the LET statement. The logic in this program is straightforward: First enter the total amount of salary for the year; second, calculate the monthly average; and third, print the results.

Line 140 is a LET statement used to enter the total amount of salary for the year, $15,000.00, into the numeric variable T. The expression in line 150 calculates the monthly average—that is, the total amount of salary for the year divided by 12, the number of months in a year. Line 160 assigns a character string to the string variable name T$. The character string and the results of the calculation are printed by line 170.

Figure III–1 ▪ Average Monthly Salary Program

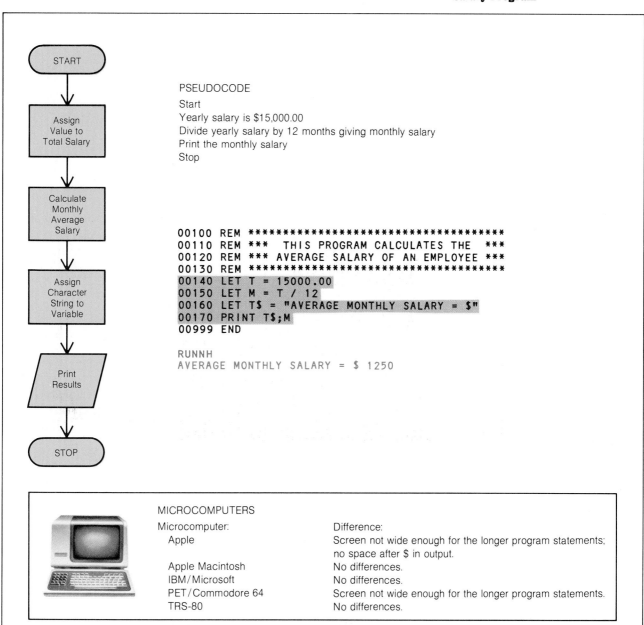

PSEUDOCODE
Start
Yearly salary is $15,000.00
Divide yearly salary by 12 months giving monthly salary
Print the monthly salary
Stop

```
00100 REM *****************************************
00110 REM ***   THIS PROGRAM CALCULATES THE  ***
00120 REM *** AVERAGE SALARY OF AN EMPLOYEE ***
00130 REM *****************************************
00140 LET T = 15000.00
00150 LET M = T / 12
00160 LET T$ = "AVERAGE MONTHLY SALARY = $"
00170 PRINT T$;M
00999 END

RUNNH
AVERAGE MONTHLY SALARY = $ 1250
```

MICROCOMPUTERS

Microcomputer:	Difference:
Apple	Screen not wide enough for the longer program statements; no space after $ in output.
Apple Macintosh	No differences.
IBM/Microsoft	No differences.
PET/Commodore 64	Screen not wide enough for the longer program statements.
TRS-80	No differences.

THE PRINT STATEMENT

The PRINT statement is used to print or display the results of computer processing. It also permits the formatting, or arranging, of output. The general form of the PRINT statement is as follows:

line# PRINT $\begin{cases} \text{Variables} \\ \text{Literals} \\ \text{Arithmetic expressions} \\ \text{Combination of above} \end{cases}$

PRINT statements can take several forms, depending on the output required. Let us look at some examples.

Printing the Values of Variables

We can tell the computer to print values assigned to memory locations by simply using the keyword PRINT with the variable names after it, separated by commas:

```
00200 PRINT X,Y,Z
```

The comma is used to separate one variable from another; it also is used for carriage control (more on this in Section IV).

Printing has no effect on the contents of memory. The PRINT statement is a simple reading of the value of a variable that allows the user to see what the contents are. Normally, each time the computer encounters a PRINT statement, it begins printing output on a new line. Exceptions to this are discussed in Section IV.

Printing Literals

A literal is an expression consisting of alphabetic, numeric, or special characters or a combination of all three. The following are examples of literals:

ABC	32.57	Q1B97
DEF	100	N$*#!

CHARACTER STRINGS

A character string literal is a group of letters, numbers, or special characters that you want printed on the output page. To have that done, enclose the group in quotation marks (''). Whatever is inside the quotation marks is printed exactly as it is; for example,

```
00040 PRINT "EXAMPLE - %)*&^%$#@!"
```

would appear on the output page as

```
EXAMPLE - %)*$^%$#@!
```

To print column headings, put each heading in quotes and separate each group by a comma. The comma instructs the printer to skip to the next print zone (more on this in Section IV). An example follows:

```
00070 PRINT "DATE","NAME","CLASS"
```

When line 70 is executed, the character strings are printed out exactly as typed, except that the quotation marks do not appear:

```
DATE            NAME            CLASS
```

NUMERIC LITERALS

Numeric literals do not have to be enclosed in quotation marks to be printed. For example, the statement

```
00100 PRINT 99
```

will print the following result:

```
99
```

Printing the Values of Expressions

The computer can print not only the values of literals and the values of variables but also the values of arithmetic expressions.

```
00010 LET A = 66
00020 LET B = 23
00030 PRINT A * 57 / B
```

First, the computer evaluates the expression according to the rules of priority. The result is printed as follows:

```
163.5652
```

If the value of the expression is extremely large or extremely small, the computer may print it in exponential notation.

Figure III–2 deals with the expressions in both decimal and exponential forms. When the PRINT statement in line 40 is executed, the three expressions are evaluated and their values printed. Notice that the first and last numbers are too large to be printed conventionally and are printed instead in exponential notation.

Printing Blank Lines

A PRINT statement with nothing typed after it will provide a blank line of output. For example,

```
00150 PRINT
```

To skip more than one line, simply include more than one of these PRINT statements:

```
00180 PRINT
00190 PRINT
```

THE END STATEMENT

The END statement indicates the end of the program and so must be assigned the highest line number in the program. The general format of the END statement is this:

line# END

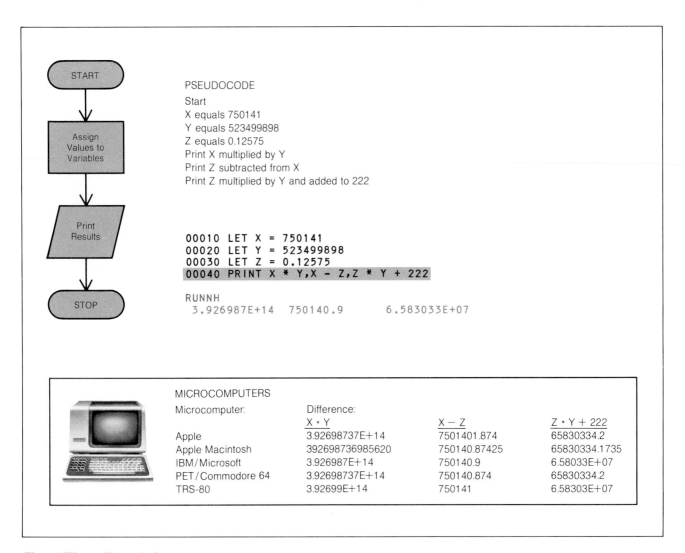

Figure III–2 ■ Numeric Output

The use of an all-nines number for the END statement is a common programming practice, although it is not required. This convention serves as a reminder to the programmer to include the END statement and helps insure that it is positioned properly. See line 999 in the salary program (Figure III–1) for an example of an END statement.

A PROGRAMMING PROBLEM

Problem Definition

A university sorority was offered the following profits on candy by a local candy shop.

- 35 percent profit on pecan turtles.
- 42 percent profit on peanut clusters.
- 45 percent profit on chocolate bars.

Figure III–3 ▪ Candy Profit Program

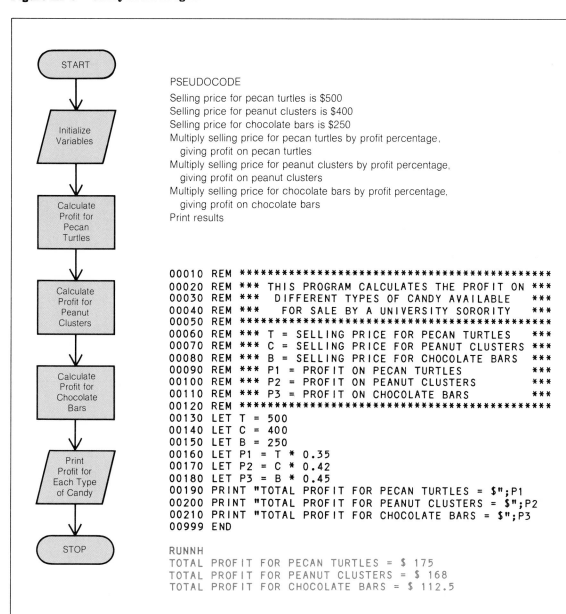

PSEUDOCODE

Selling price for pecan turtles is $500
Selling price for peanut clusters is $400
Selling price for chocolate bars is $250
Multiply selling price for pecan turtles by profit percentage,
    giving profit on pecan turtles
Multiply selling price for peanut clusters by profit percentage,
    giving profit on peanut clusters
Multiply selling price for chocolate bars by profit percentage,
    giving profit on chocolate bars
Print results

```
00010 REM **********************************************
00020 REM *** THIS PROGRAM CALCULATES THE PROFIT ON ***
00030 REM ***   DIFFERENT TYPES OF CANDY AVAILABLE  ***
00040 REM ***    FOR SALE BY A UNIVERSITY SORORITY  ***
00050 REM **********************************************
00060 REM *** T = SELLING PRICE FOR PECAN TURTLES   ***
00070 REM *** C = SELLING PRICE FOR PEANUT CLUSTERS ***
00080 REM *** B = SELLING PRICE FOR CHOCOLATE BARS  ***
00090 REM *** P1 = PROFIT ON PECAN TURTLES          ***
00100 REM *** P2 = PROFIT ON PEANUT CLUSTERS        ***
00110 REM *** P3 = PROFIT ON CHOCOLATE BARS         ***
00120 REM **********************************************
00130 LET T = 500
00140 LET C = 400
00150 LET B = 250
00160 LET P1 = T * 0.35
00170 LET P2 = C * 0.42
00180 LET P3 = B * 0.45
00190 PRINT "TOTAL PROFIT FOR PECAN TURTLES = $";P1
00200 PRINT "TOTAL PROFIT FOR PEANUT CLUSTERS = $";P2
00210 PRINT "TOTAL PROFIT FOR CHOCOLATE BARS = $";P3
00999 END

RUNNH
TOTAL PROFIT FOR PECAN TURTLES = $ 175
TOTAL PROFIT FOR PEANUT CLUSTERS = $ 168
TOTAL PROFIT FOR CHOCOLATE BARS = $ 112.5
```

MICROCOMPUTERS

Microcomputer:	Difference:
Apple	No space after $ in output.
	Screen not wide enough for long program statements.
Apple Macintosh	No differences.
IBM/Microsoft	No differences.
PET/Commodore 64	Screen not wide enough for long program statements.
TRS-80	No differences.

The selling price for each case of candy is as follows:

Item	Price
Pecan Turtles	$500
Peanut Clusters	$400
Chocolate Bars	$250

Before deciding which type of candy to sell, the sorority asks you to write a program to determine which type of candy is the most profitable (see Figure III–3).

Solution Design

The first step in the program is to enter the selling price per case for each candy type. Next, determine the profit for each type of candy by multiplying the selling price by the appropriate percentage of profit. Finally, print out the results.

The Program

Figure III–3 shows a listing and output of the program as well as a flowchart. The REM statements in lines 10 through 120 document the purpose of the program and the meanings of the variables. The REM statement in line 120 is used to set off the remarks from the executable statements. Lines 130 through 150 use LET statements to enter the selling price of each type of candy. Lines 160 through 180 calculate the profit for each type of candy. The results are printed out in lines 190 through 210.

SUMMARY POINTS

■ REM statements are used to document a program; they are not executed by the computer.
■ The purpose of the LET statement is to assign values to variables; LET is an optional keyword in some BASIC implementations.
■ The LET statement is not evaluated as an algebraic equation. The computer first evaluates the expression on the right side of the equal sign and then assigns that result to the variable on the left side of the equal sign.
■ Arithmetic expressions are evaluated according to the following hierarchy of operations: (1) operations in parentheses, (2) exponentiation, (3) multiplication or division, and (4) addition or subtraction. Multiple operations at the same level are evaluated left to right.
■ The PRINT statement is used to print or display the results of processing.
■ The END statement indicates the physical end of a program and stops execution.

REVIEW QUESTIONS

1. Why is it important to document your programs by using the REM statement?
2. What is the purpose of the LET statement?
3. Give the hierarchy, or priority, of operations followed by BASIC.
4. What is the purpose of the PRINT statement?

DEBUGGING EXERCISES

Debug the following program segments.

```
1. 10 *** THIS PROGRAM PRINTS A CITY ***
   15 REM *** AND ITS POPULATION ***
   20 LET C$ = 500
   25 LET P = "HICTON"
   30 PRINT C$,P


2. 40 LET 5 * X = B
   45 LET C$ = 54.7
   50 PRINT X B C$
```

PROGRAMMING PROBLEMS

1. Mr. Morley needs you to write a program for him which will calculate his gross pay if he receives his raise to $15.50 per hour. He plans to work 40 hours a week for 51 weeks. He wishes the output to appear as follows:

GROSS PAY	RATE PER HOUR
XXXXXX	15.50

Be sure to document your program.

2. You have been asked to write a program which will calculate the average score of bowling contestants and print the contestant's name, three game scores, and average score. Your output should contain column headings; be sure to document your program using the REM statement. Use the following data:

Name	Game 1	Game 2	Game 3
Bill Davis	103	136	145
Tonya Rae	150	172	167

OVERVIEW

This section will introduce new ways of entering data into a program. Although the LET statement can be used to enter small amounts of data, the INPUT statement and the READ/DATA statements are the most commonly used methods.

When programming, it is often necessary to have organized and formatted output. This yields a better appearance and readability. We will show you how to produce output with headings, columns, and appropriate spacing.

Figure IV–1 is a sample of the type of output you will be able to produce with the tools in this chapter. It also makes use of the INPUT statement.

THE INPUT STATEMENT

The INPUT statement is used for inquiry and response when a user application calls for a question-and-answer environment. The last section explained how the LET statement can be used to enter data values into a program. The INPUT statement differs from the LET statement in that it allows the user to enter data at the terminal while the program is running. The general format of the INPUT statement is as follows:

line# INPUT variable list

For example,

```
00100  INPUT H,R
00110  INPUT N$,S$,A$
```

These also could be combined into one line as follows:

```
00100  INPUT H,R,N$,S$,A$
```

or they could be on separate lines:

```
00100  INPUT H
00110  INPUT R
00120  INPUT N$
00130  INPUT S$
00140  INPUT A$
```

Figure IV–1 ▪ Formatted Output

```
RUNNH
ENTER QUANTITY AND PRICE OF SHIRTS
 ? 11,5.98
ENTER QUANTITY AND PRICE OF DRESSES
 ? 5,9.99
ENTER QUANTITY AND PRICE OF PANTS
 ? 9,7.99


                    INVENTORY LIST


            QUANTITY      PRICE         TOTAL

SHIRTS         11        $ 5.98        $ 65.78
DRESSES        5         $ 9.99        $ 49.95
PANTS          9         $ 7.99        $ 71.91
                                       $ 187.64
```

The variables listed in the INPUT statements may be string or numeric. Just be sure to enter the correct value to be assigned to each variable. In other words, the type of data must be the same as that designated by the variable.

INPUT statements are placed where data values are needed in a program. This is determined by the logic of the program. After the program has been keyed in, the user types the execution command RUNNH on the DECSYS-TEM 20; the computer then starts to execute the program. Whenever the computer reaches an INPUT statement, it stops, prints a question mark at the terminal, and waits for the user to enter data. After typing in the data, the user presses the RETURN key. The computer then assigns the data value to the variable indicated in the INPUT statement and resumes processing. More than one variable can be listed in the INPUT statement; the user must know how many values to enter. When there are not enough data entered, an error message is printed, telling the user there are insufficient data. For example, when line 100 is executed with only one value entered, the result would look like this:

```
00100 INPUT H,R
RUNNH
 ? 3.35

? 59   Insufficient data at line 00100 of MAIN PROGRAM
 ?
```

If the user knew what entries to make and how many, the output would look like this:

```
RUNNH
 ? 3.35,45
```

The variable H would have the value 3.35, and R would be assigned the value 45. As you can see, the INPUT statement offers a great deal of flexibility. Each time the program is executed, new values can be entered without changing any program statements.

Prompts

The INPUT statement is usually preceded by a PRINT statement. This PRINT statement is referred to as a prompt. Since the INPUT statement signals the need for data with only a question mark, it is good programming to precede each INPUT statement with a PRINT statement that explains to the user what data is to be entered. This practice is particularly important in a BASIC program that contains numerous INPUT statements; otherwise, when users see only a question mark requesting data, they may not know what data values are to be entered and in what order.

Figure IV–2 is a program with a prompt that calculates a percentage score on a test. Lines 130 and 140 cause the program to be executed in a question-and-answer mode (also called inquiry-and-response, or conversational mode). When the program is run, line 130 causes the computer to print a message at the terminal that says, "ENTER TOTAL POINTS AND POINTS RECEIVED." A question mark then appears to signal the user that the data values are to be entered. At this point, the user types in the requested data values, separating them with commas, and then presses the RETURN key to continue execution of the program:

```
RUNNH                                        ←Program Prompt
ENTER TOTAL POINTS AND POINTS RECEIVED
? 75,67                                      ←Computer Prompt (?), User Data Entry
TEST PERCENTAGE = 89.33332 %                 ←Computer Continues Execution after User Pushes RETURN
```

```
00100 REM ************************************************
00110 REM ***        TEST PERCENTAGE PROGRAM         ***
00120 REM ************************************************
00130 PRINT "ENTER TOTAL POINTS AND POINTS RECEIVED"
00140 INPUT T,R
00150 LET P = R / T * 100
00160 PRINT "TEST PERCENTAGE =";P;"%"
00999 END
```

```
RUNNH
ENTER TOTAL POINTS AND POINTS RECEIVED
? 75,67
TEST PERCENTAGE = 89.33333 %
```

MICROCOMPUTERS

Microcomputer:	Difference:
Apple	No space before percent symbol.
Apple Macintosh	No differences.
IBM/Microsoft	No differences.
PET/Commodore 64	No differences.
TRS-80	No differences.

Figure IV-2 ▪ Test Percentage Program Using A Prompt And An Input Statement

Most computers permit the prompt to be an integral part of the INPUT statement. For example, the following line could be substituted for lines 130 and 140 in the test percentage program:

```
00130 INPUT "ENTER TOTAL POINTS AND POINTS RECEIVED";T,R
```

When the program is run with this new line, the question mark appears immediately after the prompt, and no separate PRINT statement for the prompt is needed:

```
RUNNH
ENTER TOTAL POINTS AND POINTS RECEIVED? 90,75
TEST PERCENTAGE = 83.33333 %
```

THE READ AND DATA STATEMENTS

The READ and DATA statements provide another way to enter data into a BASIC program. These two statements always work together. Values contained in the DATA statements are assigned to variables listed in the READ statements.

The general format of the READ and DATA statements is this:

line# READ variable list
line# DATA data list

Here some examples of READ and DATA statements:

```
00100 READ S$,N$,C
00110 READ Q,P
   .
   .
   .
00420 DATA "297-49-2210","J. DOE"
00430 DATA 25,3,2547
```

This method of entering data into a program works a little differently than the INPUT statement. The READ statement tells the computer to search through the BASIC program until it finds the first DATA statement. The computer then assigns the data values consecutively to the variables in the READ statement. Each READ statement causes as many values to be taken from the data list as there are variables in the READ variable list. Figure IV—3 illustrates this process of assigning values from the data list to variables.

Statement 40 says to the computer: "Take the value from the top of the data list and put it in the storage location named N$. (Anything that was previously in storage location N$ is destroyed when the new information is put in N$.) Next take the following value from the data list and assign it to variable P (which also destroys anything that was previously in location P). Then take the next value from the data list and place it in the storage location H (the previous contents of H are also destroyed)." After statement 40 has been executed, the character string JERRY MORRIS is in storage location N$, the number 107 is in storage location P, and the number 40 is in storage location H. This leaves the character string KENNY SANDERS at the top of the data list.

When statement 70 is executed, the character string at the top of the data list (KENNY SANDERS) is assigned to the variable N$. The character string JERRY MORRIS, which was assigned to N$ by statement 40, is replaced by the new value (KENNY SANDERS). In the same manner, the number 96 is assigned to the variable P and the number 30 is assigned to H in statement 80. When these values are assigned, the values previously stored in the variables are destroyed.

This process illustrates the basic concept of nondestructive read, destructive write. This means that, once the data items have been assigned to storage locations, they remain there and are not destroyed when read; however, when a new value is assigned to a storage location, the previous value in that location is destroyed. Thus, all four variables represent more than one value during execution, but never more than one at a time.

If a READ statement is attempted after the data list has been exhausted, a message is produced to indicate that the end of the data list has been reached. The message points out the line number of the READ statement in

Figure IV–3 ▪ READ/DATA Example

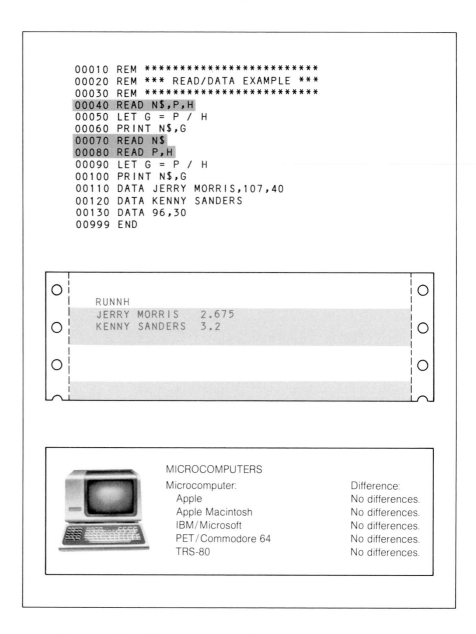

```
00010 REM ***************************
00020 REM *** READ/DATA EXAMPLE ***
00030 REM ***************************
00040 READ N$,P,H
00050 LET G = P / H
00060 PRINT N$,G
00070 READ N$
00080 READ P,H
00090 LET G = P / H
00100 PRINT N$,G
00110 DATA JERRY MORRIS,107,40
00120 DATA KENNY SANDERS
00130 DATA 96,30
00999 END
```

```
RUNNH
JERRY MORRIS    2.675
KENNY SANDERS   3.2
```

MICROCOMPUTERS

Microcomputer:	Difference:
Apple	No differences.
Apple Macintosh	No differences.
IBM / Microsoft	No differences.
PET / Commodore 64	No differences.
TRS-80	No differences.

error; for example, if line 80 were such a READ statement, the computer would print the following:

```
? 57 End of DATA found at line 00080 of MAIN PROGRAM
```

READ statements, like INPUT, are located wherever the logic of the program indicates the need for data. Data statements, however, are nonexecutable and may be located anywhere in the program. Although DATA statements may be anywhere in a program, it is common practice to group them together either at the beginning or the end of a program. This makes debugging easier. The BASIC interpreter or compiler simply takes all the data items in all the DATA statements and forms one combined data list, ordering the DATA statements from lowest line number to highest and then using the data from left to right. For example, the following three program segments look different, but the data lists they produce are alike:

DATA Statements	DATA List

```
00100 DATA 63                      63
00110 DATA "EDWIN"                 EDWIN
00120 DATA 21                      21
00130 DATA "ALICIA"                ALICIA
```

or

```
00100 DATA 63,"EDWIN"
00110 DATA 21,"ALICIA"
```

or

```
00100 DATA 63,"EDWIN",21,"ALICIA"
```

Note that when two or more data values occupy a line, they are separated by commas. Character strings may or may not be enclosed in quotation marks in DATA statements. However, if the character strings are to contain leading or trailing blanks, commas, and semicolons, they must be enclosed in quotation marks.

We would assign the previous data items in the following manner:

```
00070 READ R
00080 READ S$
00090 READ C
00100 READ B$
```

or

```
00070 READ R,S$
00080 READ C,B$
```

or

```
00070 READ R,S$,C,B$
```

It does not matter in this example how many READ or DATA statements are used. However, the order of the variables and values is important. Make sure that the arrangement of values in the DATA statements corresponds to the data required in the READ statements—that is, that character strings are assigned to string variables and numeric constants to numeric variables.

Let us return to the test percentage program and change it to use READ/DATA statements (see Figure IV–4). Lines 130 and 140 perform the same function as the INPUT statement did previously. With INPUT, the data values are assigned by the user as the program is running. With READ/DATA statements, on the other hand, the total points and points received already are contained in program line 130, the DATA statement. If we wanted to run this program again using different data, we would have to change the DATA statement.

COMPARISON OF THE THREE METHODS OF DATA ENTRY

LET, INPUT, and READ/DATA all can be used to enter data into BASIC programs. You may wonder, then, which command is best to use. That depends on the particular application. Here are some general guidelines:

1. When the data to be used by a program are constant, use the LET statement. The LET statement is often used to assign a beginning value to a variable, such as zero. This is called **initialization.** For example: LET T = 0

```
00100 REM ****************************************
00110 REM ***     TEST PERCENTAGE PROGRAM       ***
00120 REM ****************************************
00130 DATA 75,67
00140 READ T,R
00150 LET P = R / T * 100
00160 PRINT "TEST PERCENTAGE =";P;"%"
00999 END
```

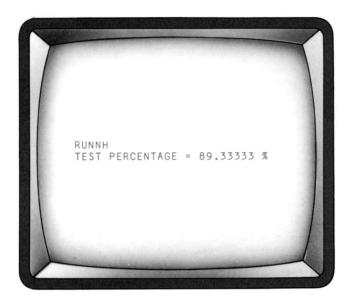

```
RUNNH
TEST PERCENTAGE = 89.33333 %
```

MICROCOMPUTERS

Microcomputer:	Difference:
Apple	No space before percent symbol.
Apple Macintosh	No differences.
IBM/Microsoft	No differences.
PET/Commodore 64	No differences.
TRS-80	No differences.

Figure IV–4 ▪ Test Percentage Program Using READ/DATA Statements

2. The INPUT statement is used when a question-and-answer mode is desired. It is also a good method to use when data values are likely to change frequently. A good application for the use of the INPUT statement might be entering data about hospital patients—a situation in which people are checking in and out every day, and data about a particular patient changes frequently.

3. When many data values must be entered, READ/DATA statements are a good option. These statements often are used to read data into arrays (to be discussed in Section IX).

PRINTING PUNCTUATION

Section III explained that the PRINT statement lets us get the results of processing printed. When more than one item is to be printed on a line, commas and semicolons can be used to control the spacing of the output.

Print Zones and Commas

The number of characters that can be printed on a line varies with the system used. On some terminals, such as the DEC VT-100 used with the DECSYSTEM 20 computer, each output line consists of eighty print positions. The line is divided into five print zones, each fourteen characters wide. The beginning columns of the five print zones are shown here:

ZONE 1	ZONE 2	ZONE 3	ZONE 4	ZONE 5
COL	COL	COL	COL	COL
1	15	29	43	57

When the computer encounters the PRINT statement in this program segment:

```
00010 READ A$,B$,C$
00020 PRINT A$,B$,C$
00030 DATA "COMPUTERS","ARE","FUN"
```

the value in A$, which is COMPUTERS, will be printed starting in the first print zone. The comma between A$ and B$ tells the computer to space over to the next zone and print the value contained in B$. After ARE is printed, the comma directs the computer to space over to the third print zone and print the value in C$. The output is as follows:

Zone 1	Zone 2	Zone 3
RUNNH		
COMPUTERS	ARE	FUN

If there are more items listed in a PRINT statement than there are print zones, the computer starts printing in the first zone of the next line. If the value to be printed exceeds the width of the print zone, the computer will completely print out the value, even though part of it goes into the next print zone. The comma then directs printing to start in the following print zone. Take a look at the following example and note where the value of A (30) is printed:

```
00010 LET A = 30
00020 PRINT "MY BIRTHDAY IS ON JULY",A
```

```
RUNNH
MY BIRTHDAY IS ON JULY        30
```

Zone 1   **Zone 2**   **Zone 3**

Also note that since 30 is a positive number, most computers will leave a blank before the number for the sign. Of course, if the value in A were negative, the minus sign would be printed starting in the first column of Zone 3.

Table IV–1 presents the formatting differences among our five computers. The first column identifies the computer. Columns 2 and 3 give the number of columns and rows on the CRT screen. Columns 4 and 5 give the number

TABLE IV–1 ■ **Computer Display Characteristics**

COMPUTER	SCREEN WIDTH (CHARACTERS)	SCREEN HEIGHT (LINES)	NUMBER OF PRINT ZONES	ZONE WIDTH	SPACE FOR SIGN?	SPACE FOLLOWING?	NUMBER OF DIGITS PRINTED, SINGLE PRECISION
DECSYSTEM 20	80/312*	24/16*	5/9*	14	Yes	Yes	7
Apple	40	24	2.5	16	No	No	9
Apple Macintosh	†	**	†	†	Yes	Yes	6
IBM/Microsoft	80	24	5	14	Yes	Yes	7
TRS-80	64/32*	15	4/2*	16	Yes	Yes	6
PET/Commodore 64	40	25	4	10	Yes	Yes	9

See example
below

Example: With the Apple computer, the statement

`10 PRINT 39;-2;9;2;-39`

would print

`39-292-39`

With the Apple Macintosh, DECSYSTEM 20, IBM/Microsoft, TRS-80, and PET/Commodore 64 computers, the same statement would print

`39 -2  9  2 -39`

*Slash indicates both options are available to user.

**Up to 18 depending on which window is being used.

†This is determined by the WIDTH statement. Check the Microsoft BASIC Manual for the Apple Macintosh for details.

of print zones (when commas are used as spacing control in PRINT statements) and print zone widths. Columns 6 and 7 indicate whether a space is always left in front of a number for a positive or negative sign and whether a space follows a number for ease in reading. The use of semicolons is discussed next in this section. Finally, column 8 gives the maximum number of digits output to the screen. If the number to be printed contains more characters than that listed, all remaining characters will be truncated—the number will not be rounded. (The DECSYSTEM 20, IBM, TRS-80, and Apple Macintosh have provisions for double precision; however, caution must be used, because the BASIC internal functions might not be any more accurate with double precision than with single precision—see your manual.)

SKIPPING PRINT ZONES

A print zone can be skipped by the use of a technique that involves enclosing a space (the character blank) in quotation marks. This causes the entire zone to appear empty:

`00100 PRINT "STREET"," ","PRECINCT"`

Most computers (all five of ours) also allow the user to skip a zone by typing two consecutive commas:

`00100 PRINT "STREET",,"PRECINCT"`

Both of these techniques cause the literal "STREET" to be printed in zone 1, the second zone to be blank, and the literal "PRECINCT" to be printed in the third zone:

Zone 1	Zone 3

```
RUNNH
STREET                    PRECINCT
```

ENDING WITH A COMMA

As mentioned earlier, output generated by a PRINT statement normally begins in the first zone of a new line. However, if the previously executed PRINT statement ends with a comma, the output of a PRINT statement starts in the next available zone. Thus, the statements

```
00010 DATA "MY","BIRTHDAY","IS","JULY 30, 1960"
00020 READ A$,B$,C$,D$
00030 PRINT A$,B$,
00040 PRINT C$,D$
00999 END
```

produce the following output:

```
RUNNH
MY            BIRTHDAY        IS              JULY 30, 1960
```

Using Semicolons

Using a semicolon instead of a comma causes output to be packed more closely on a line. This alternative gives the programmer greater flexibility in formatting output. In the following examples, notice the difference in spacing when semicolons are used instead of commas:

Using Commas

```
00100 PRINT 409,352,-1
RUNNH
 409          352            -1
```

Using Semicolons

```
00100 PRINT 409;352;-1
RUNNH
 409  352 -1
```

The semicolon between the items tells the computer to skip to the next **column** to print the next item—not to the next print zone, as with the comma. Generally, when the number is positive, a space is left in front of the number for the sign.

SEMICOLONS AND CHARACTER STRINGS

The following example shows what happens when semicolons are used with character strings:

```
00070 PRINT "BOBBY";"LEE"
RUNNH
BOBBYLEE
```

Since letters do not have signs, they are run together. The best way to avoid this problem is to enclose a space within the quotes:

```
00070 PRINT "BOBBY ";"LEE"
RUNNH
BOBBY LEE
```

ENDING WITH A SEMICOLON

If the semicolon is the last character of the PRINT statement, carriage control is not advanced when the printing of the statement is completed; therefore, the output generated by the next PRINT statement continues on the same line; for example,

```
00070 PRINT 22435;
00080 PRINT " BOBBY";" LEE"
RUNNH
 22435  BOBBY LEE
```

Line 70 causes 22435 to be printed out. The semicolon after this number keeps the printer on the same line; then, when line 80 is encountered, BOBBY LEE is printed on the same line.

THE TAB FUNCTION

The comma causes the results of processing to be printed according to pre-defined print zones. The semicolon causes them to start printing in the next position on the output line. Both are easy to use, and many reports can be formatted in this fashion. However, there are times when a report should be structured differently.

The TAB function allows output to be printed in any column in an output line, providing the programmer greater flexibility to format printed output.

The general format of the TAB function is this:

TAB(expression)

The expression in parentheses may be a numeric constant, numeric variable, or arithmetic expression; it tells the computer the column in which printing is to occur. The TAB function (as used in a PRINT statement) must immediately precede the variable or literal to be printed out. For example, the statement

```
00100 PRINT TAB(12);N;TAB(20);N$
```

causes the printer to be spaced to column 12 (indicated in parentheses) and to print the value stored in N. The printer then spaces over to column 20, as indicated in the next parentheses, and prints the value in N$. On many computers, such as the DECSYSTEM 20, IBM/Microsoft, and TRS-80, the value in N in this example would begin in column 13 and N$, in column 21. In other words, the computer tabs to column 12 and the semicolon instructs it to begin printing in the next column (column 13, or check the systems manual for your specific system). The program in Figure IV–5 illustrates the use of the TAB function.

Note that we have used the semicolon as the punctuation mark with the TAB function. The semicolon separates the expression from the values to be printed. If commas were used instead, the printer would default and use the predefined print zones, ignoring the columns specified in parentheses. For example, if line 60 of the program in Figure IV–5 had been

```
00060 PRINT TAB(5),"NAME",TAB(20),"HIRE DATE"
```

the output would have been:

Figure IV–5 ▪ **Employee Program**

```
00010 REM *****************************************
00020 REM ***         EMPLOYEE REPORT        ***
00030 REM *****************************************
00040 PRINT TAB(10);"EMPLOYEE REPORT"
00050 PRINT
00060 PRINT TAB(5);"NAME";TAB(20);"HIRE DATE"
00070 PRINT
00080 READ N$,D$
00090 PRINT TAB(5);N$;TAB(20);D$
00100 READ N$,D$
00110 PRINT TAB(5);N$;TAB(20);D$
00120 READ N$,D$
00130 PRINT TAB(5);N$;TAB(20);D$
00140 DATA N. WALKER,3/12/82,S. MANDELL,5/3/79
00150 DATA T. BROOKS,9/30/83
00999 END
```

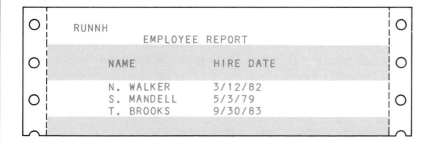

```
RUNNH
            EMPLOYEE REPORT

     NAME            HIRE DATE

     N. WALKER       3/12/82
     S. MANDELL      5/3/79
     T. BROOKS       9/30/83
```

MICROCOMPUTERS

Microcomputer:	Difference:
Apple	No differences.
Apple Macintosh	No differences.
IBM/Microsoft	No differences.
PET/Commodore 64	No differences.
TRS-80	No differences.

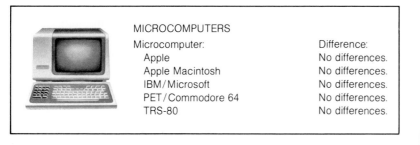

```
RUNNH
        EMPLOYEE REPORT

            NAME                                HIRE DATE

     N. WALKER       3/12/82
     S. MANDELL      5/3/79
     T. BROOKS       9/30/83
```

The computer spaced over the five columns indicated by the first TAB function, but when it saw the comma following the parentheses, it skipped over to the next predefined print zone to print HIRE DATE. The same thing happens again with NAME. Use semicolons rather than commas in PRINT statements containing the TAB function.

As another caution, remember that when the TAB function is used, the printer cannot be backspaced. Once a column has been passed, the printer cannot go back to it. This means that if more than one TAB function is used in a PRINT statement, the column numbers in parentheses must increase from left to right. For example,

Valid:

```
00100 PRINT TAB(8);"H";TAB(18);"I";TAB(28);"I"
RUNNH
        H         I              I
```

Invalid:

```
00100 PRINT TAB(28);"I";TAB(18);"I";TAB(8);"H"
RUNNH
                                    I I H
```

```
00100 PRINT TAB(18);"I";TAB(8);"H";TAB(28);"I"
RUNNH
                    I H              I
```

The first invalid example tells the computer to print an exclamation point at column 28. The computer does this, but because the printer cannot backspace to column 18 and column 8, it prints letters I and H as it normally would using semicolons.

THE PRINT USING STATEMENT

Another convenient feature for controlling output is the PRINT USING statement; with it, the programmer can avoid print zone restrictions and can "dress up" the output. PRINT USING is an extension of the ANSI standards—not part of the standards. Its syntax is quite varied among different brands of computers. This section briefly describes its use on the DECSYSTEM 20 computer; the principles should be similar for other computers with this feature. Many microcomputers do not have a PRINT USING capability: The Apple and PET/Commodore 64 do not; the Apple Macintosh, IBM/Microsoft, and TRS-80 do. The general format of the PRINT USING statement is as follows:

line# PRINT USING image statement line#, expression-list

The PRINT USING statement tells which statement in the program has the print line image and what values are to be used in that print line. The expression list consists of a sequence of variables or expressions separated by commas; it is similar to the expression list in any PRINT statement. The line number of the image statement is the number of the BASIC statement that tells the computer how to print the items in the expression list.

The image statement is denoted by a colon (:) following the line number:

line#: format control characters

It is a nonexecutable statement, like DATA, and it can be placed anywhere in the program. The PRINT USING command, however, is placed where the logic demands. A single image statement can be referred to by several PRINT USING statements. Special format control characters are used in the image statement to describe the output image and to control spacing.

The major DECSYSTEM 20 formal control characters are listed in the following table (a **mask** specifies the maximum number of characters to be printed in one field):

FORMAT CONTROL CHARACTER	CONTROL IMAGE FOR	EXAMPLE
#	Numeric data; used in a mask; one symbol for each number to be printed; pads zeros to the left of decimal point	###
$	Dollar sign; printed exactly as is	$###
$$	Causes dollar sign to be printed immediately before first digit	$$##.##
**	Leading asterisks; printed in place of blanks or spaces	**###.#
	Decimal point; printed exactly as is	$##.##
E	Alphanumeric data; preceded by apostrophe ('); permits overflow to be printed to the right; left justifies; pads with blanks	'E
L	Alphanumeric data; preceded by apostrophe ('); used as a mask; left justifies; pads with blanks	'LLLLLL
R	Alphanumeric data; preceded by apostrophe ('); used as a mask; right justifies; pads with blanks	'RRRRRR
C	Alphanumeric data; preceded by apostrophe ('); used as a mask; centers in the field; pads with blanks	'CCCCCCC

Format Control Characters for Apple Macintosh, IBM, and TRS-80

APPLE MACINTOSH	IBM	TRS-80	EXPLANATION
#	#	#	Same as DECSYSTEM 20.
.	.		Same as DECSYSTEM 20.
		$	Same as DECSYSTEM 20.
$$	$$	$$	Two dollar signs cause the dollar sign to be floating, meaning that it will be in the first position before the number.
**$	**$	**$	Vacant positions will be filled with asterisks, and the dollar sign will be in the first position to the left of the number.
+	+	+	When a + sign is placed at the beginning or end of a number, it causes a + sign to be printed if the number is positive and a − sign to be printed if the number is negative.
−	−	−	When a − sign is placed at the end of a number, negative numbers will have a negative sign, and for positive numbers it will appear as a space after the number.
∧∧∧∧	∧∧∧∧	↑ ↑ ↑ ↑ or [[[[	This causes the number to be printed in exponential format.
\spaces\	\spaces\	%space%	This specifies a string field to be two plus the number of spaces below the characters.
!	!	!	This causes the computer to print only the first string character.
&	&		This specifies a variable-length field. The string is output exactly as it is entered.
___	___		Underscore causes the next character in the format string to be printed out. The character itself may be underscored by preceding it with two underscores (_____).
%	%		If the number to be printed is larger than the specified field, a percent sign will appear before the number. If rounding caused the number to exceed the field, the percent sign will be printed in front of the rounded number.

The program in Figure IV–6 illustrates some of these control characters on the DECSYSTEM 20.

The Apple Macintosh, IBM/Microsoft and TRS–80 PRINT USING statements are somewhat different. The general format for both of these systems looks like this:

line# PRINT USING "format"; expression-list

Figure IV–6 ▪ PRINT USING Statement on DECSYSTEM 20

```
00010 REM **************************************************************
00020 REM ***          PROGRAM UTILIZING PRINT USING STATEMENTS      ***
00030 REM **************************************************************
00040 PRINT
00050 PRINT
00060 PRINT USING 170,"AGENT","TICKETS SOLD","PRICE PER TICKET","TOTAL PRICE"
00070 PRINT
00080 PRINT
00090 READ N$,N,P
00100 IF N$ = "END" THEN GOTO 999
00110 LET T = N * P
00120 PRINT USING 180,N$,N,P,T
00130 GOTO 90
00140 DATA AARON,4,110.25,BURBANK,2,75.99
00150 DATA SELLERS,10,89,TRAVERS,1,150.89
00160 DATA VALE,5,125,ZINK,2,239,END,0,0
00170: 'LLLLL              'CCCCCCCCCCCC       'CCCCCCCCCCCCCCCCC     'RRRRRRRRRR
00180: 'LLLLLLLLLLLLLLL          ##             $###.##              $###.##
00999 END
```

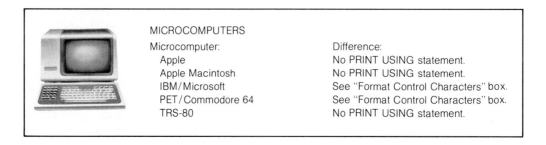

```
RUNNH

AGENT                TICKETS SOLD      PRICE PER TICKET      TOTAL PRICE

AARON                     4              $110.25             $441.00
BURBANK                   2              $ 75.99             $151.98
SELLERS                  10              $ 89.00             $890.00
TRAVERS                   1              $150.89             $150.89
VALE                      5              $125.00             $625.00
ZINK                      2              $239.00             $478.00
```

MICROCOMPUTERS

Microcomputer:	Difference:
Apple	No PRINT USING statement.
Apple Macintosh	No PRINT USING statement.
IBM/Microsoft	See "Format Control Characters" box.
PET/Commodore 64	See "Format Control Characters" box.
TRS-80	No PRINT USING statement.

For a list of the control characters for the Apple Macintosh, IBM and TRS-80, see box.

Figure IV–7 shows examples of the PRINT USING statement on the Apple Macintosh and the IBM Personal Computer.

A PROGRAMMING PROBLEM

Problem Definition

The Clothing Store sells shirts, dresses, and pants. It needs a program to list its quantity, selling price, and total inventory price. The output should be formatted as follows:

```
                    INVENTORY LIST
        QUANTITY          PRICE          TOTAL

SHIRTS
DRESSES
PANTS
```

Solution Design

To produce the desired report, we need to ask the user to enter the quantity and price for each item. To find the inventory price, all we need to do is multiply the quantity and the price. To find the total inventory price, we just add the totals of each item.

Figure IV–7 ▪ **PRINT USING Statement on Apple Macintosh and IBM Personal Computer**

```
PRINT USING "##.##    ";25.58,143.22,9.5,6.775        25.58   %143.22   9.50      6.78

PRINT USING "$###.##    ";927.25,34.44                $927.25   $ 34.44

PRINT USING "$$###.##    ";927.25,34.44                $927.25       $34.44

PRINT USING "**##.##    ";66.65,2.33                  **66.65   ***2.33

PRINT USING "**$##.##    ";66.65,2.33                 **$66.65   ***$2.33

PRINT USING "+###.##    ";-284.25,835.1,-99.99        -284.25   +835.10      -99.99

PRINT USING "###.##-    ";-284.25,835.1,-99.99        284.25-   835.10      99.99-

PRINT USING "#####,.##    ";589001,3657.75            58,900.00    3,657.75

PRINT USING "##.####^^^^    ";29.352,34.9761           2.9352E+01    3.4976E+01

PRINT USING "_$##.##_$    ";19.95,21.36                $19.95$  $21.36$


10 LET R$ = "CANDY"
20 LET S$ = "MAN"
30 PRINT USING "!";R$;S$
40 PRINT USING "\    \";R$;S$


10 LET R$ = "CANDY"
20 LET S$ = "MAN"
30 PRINT USING "!";R$
40 PRINT USING "&";S$
```

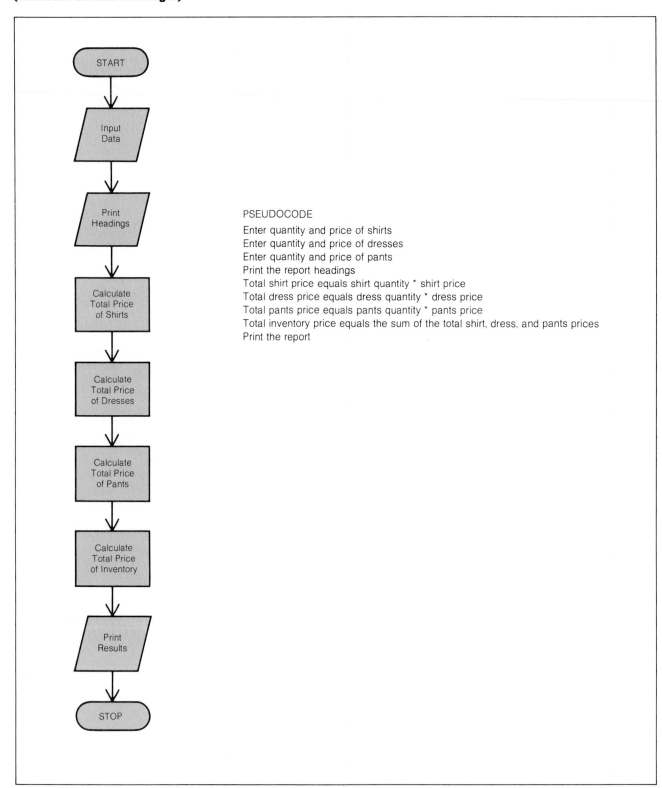

The Program

The program in Figure IV–8 documents the major variables used in lines 40 through 70. Lines 90 through 140 request the user to enter data. Lines 90, 110, and 130 are prompts telling the user what values to enter. After the data have been entered, program execution continues. The headings are printed

Figure IV–8 ▪ Continued

```
00010 REM *******************************************************
00020 REM ***              FIGURE PRICE OF INVENTORY          ***
00030 REM *******************************************************
00040 REM *** S1,D1,P1 - QUANTITY OF THE ITEMS                ***
00050 REM *** PS,PD,PP - PRICE OF THE ITEMS                   ***
00060 REM *** TS,TD,TP - TOTALS OF EACH ITEM                  ***
00070 REM *** T - TOTAL INVENTORY PRICE                       ***
00080 REM *******************************************************
00090 PRINT "ENTER QUANTITY AND PRICE OF SHIRTS"
00100 INPUT S1,PS
00110 PRINT "ENTER QUANTITY AND PRICE OF DRESSES"
00120 INPUT D1,PD
00130 PRINT "ENTER QUANTITY AND PRICE OF PANTS"
00140 INPUT P1,PP
00150 PRINT
00160 PRINT
00170 PRINT TAB(25);"INVENTORY LIST"
00180 PRINT
00190 PRINT " ","QUANTITY","PRICE","TOTAL"
00200 PRINT
00210 LET TS = S1 * PS
00220 LET TD = D1 * PD
00230 LET TP = P1 * PP
00240 LET T = TS + TD + TP
00250 PRINT "SHIRTS",S1,"$";PS,"$";TS
00260 PRINT "DRESSES",D1,"$";PD,"$";TD
00270 PRINT "PANTS",P1,"$";PP,"$";TP
00280 PRINT " "," "," ","$";T
00999 END
```

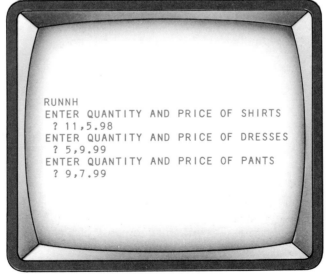

```
RUNNH
ENTER QUANTITY AND PRICE OF SHIRTS
? 11,5.98
ENTER QUANTITY AND PRICE OF DRESSES
? 5,9.99
ENTER QUANTITY AND PRICE OF PANTS
? 9,7.99
```

```
INVENTORY LIST

              QUANTITY        PRICE          TOTAL

SHIRTS          11          $ 5.98         $ 65.78
DRESSES          5          $ 9.99         $ 49.95
PANTS            9          $ 7.99         $ 71.91
                                           $ 187.64
```

MICROCOMPUTERS

Microcomputer:	Difference:
Apple	Screen not wide enough; output must be reformatted.
Apple Macintosh	No differences.
IBM / Microsoft	No differences.
PET / Commodore 64	Screen not wide enough; output must be reformatted.
TRS-80	No differences.

Figure IV–8 ▪ Continued

in lines 150 through 200. Notice how line 170 uses the TAB statement to center the heading. The total price of shirts is figured in line 210, the total price of dresses in line 220, the total price of pants in 230, and the total price of all inventory, T, in line 240. Lines 250 through 280 print the results in the desired format.

SUMMARY POINTS

▪ The INPUT statement is used to enter data into a program in a question-and-answer mode.

▪ Another way of entering data into a program is to use READ and DATA statements. The READ statement causes values contained in the DATA statements to be assigned to variables.

▪ READ and INPUT statements are located where the logic of the program indicates. DATA statements are nonexecutable and may be located anywhere in the program.

▪ When more than one item is to be printed on a line of output, the spacing can be indicated by the use of commas and semicolons.

▪ Each line of output is divided into a predetermined number of print zones. The comma is used to cause results to be printed in the print zones.

▪ Using a semicolon instead of a comma to separate printed items causes output to be packed more closely on a line.

▪ Using the TAB function in a PRINT statement permits results to be printed anywhere on an output line.

▪ The PRINT USING feature provides a flexible method of producing output. The format control characteristics in the image statement define how the output will look.

REVIEW QUESTIONS

1. Why would you want to use the INPUT statement to enter data rather than the LET, and what is the purpose of the prompt?
2. When are the READ and DATA statements preferred to enter data?
3. LET statements are most often used for what?
4. In addition to commas and semicolons, the TAB function can also be used to format output. How does the TAB function work? Can the TAB function be used to backspace the printer?

DEBUGGING EXERCISES

```
1. 10 REM ***   READ IN DATA   ***
   20 READ P,A,T$
   30 PRINT P,A,T$
   40 READ P,T$,A
   60 DATA 5,10,Z00,8,16
   99 END

2. 10 INPUT "ENTER YOUR NAME",N$
   20 INPUT "ENTER YOUR AGE";A$
   30 PRINT TAB(10),"NAME",TAB(25),"AGE"
   40 PRINT TAB(10);N$;TAB(5);A$
```

PROGRAMMING PROBLEMS

1. The Dairy Delight ice cream store needs a program which will calculate the amount of ice cream to order for milkshakes. Write a program which requests the user to enter the number of milkshakes he or she wishes to make. Each milkshake requires 6 ounces of ice cream. Your output should look like this:

FOR XXX MILKSHAKES YOU WILL NEED XXX OUNCES OF ICE CREAM

2. Dr. Barker wishes to find the average height in inches of his male patients. You are to write a program which will do this using the READ/DATA statements to enter the data below.

NAME	HEIGHT (in inches)
JIM GERFER	67
FRED PFEIFER	74
HENRY HOLLOW	72

Your output should include each patient's name and height. Format your output as follows:

NAME	HEIGHT
XXXX	XXX
XXXX	XXX
XXXX	XXX

AVERAGE HEIGHT IS XX INCHES

(The column of names should start in column 10, and height should start in column 25.)

OVERVIEW

The programs described to this point contained instructions that were always executed one right after the other—from the lowest line number to the highest. This section will discuss ways of transferring control to program statements out of sequence by using the GOTO, IF/THEN, and ON/GOTO statements. One of the most valuable programming techniques, looping, will also be discussed.

In the previous sections, we have been able to run a program with only one set of data without having to repeat a program segment multiple times or rerun the program. For example, if we had a program that computed a goal tender's goals against average, chances are that we probably would want to calculate the average of more than just one goal tender. Without the control statements discussed in this chapter, we would have to rerun the program for each set of data or rewrite the program segment that calculates the average as many times as we had goal tenders. Using one of these control statements, however, allows us to process multiple sets of data more efficiently. We might want, for example, the output of the goals against average program to appear as follows:

NAME	AVERAGE
PETE PETERS	3.6
JERRY MCPHEE	4.625
TOM ANDREWS	2.2

In this section we will see how these control statements allow us to obtain this output.

THE GOTO STATEMENT: UNCONDITIONAL TRANSFER

All BASIC programs consist of a series of statements that normally are executed in sequential order. Sometimes, however, it is desirable to alter the flow of execution. This is called **branching,** and the programmer can use the GOTO statement to do it. The general format of the GOTO statement is as follows:

line# GOTO transfer line#

The programming command GOTO can be written as one word or as two words, GO TO.

The GOTO statement is called an **unconditional transfer statement** because the flow of execution is altered to the transfer line number every time the statement is encountered.

A typical GOTO statement follows:

```
00210 GOTO 100
```

This statement tells the computer that the next statement to be executed is line 100. If line 100 is an executable statement, that statement and those following are executed. If it is a nonexecutable statement, execution proceeds at the first executable statement encountered after line 100.

Let us see how the GOTO statement might be used in an application by first looking at Figure V–1, which calculates the goals against average for

Figure V–1 ▪ Goals Against Average Program

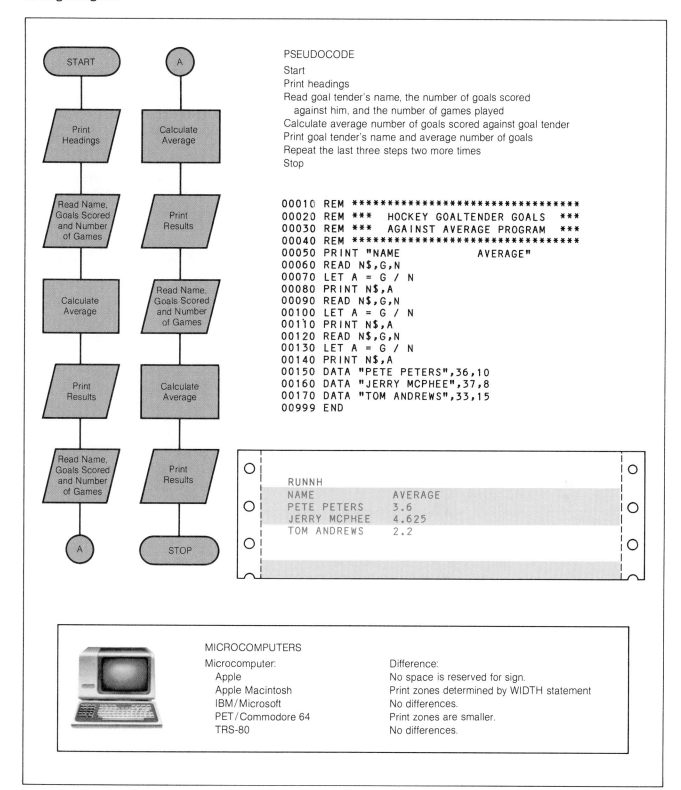

PSEUDOCODE

Start
Print headings
Read goal tender's name, the number of goals scored
   against him, and the number of games played
Calculate average number of goals scored against goal tender
Print goal tender's name and average number of goals
Repeat the last three steps two more times
Stop

```
00010 REM *******************************
00020 REM ***   HOCKEY GOALTENDER GOALS   ***
00030 REM ***   AGAINST AVERAGE PROGRAM   ***
00040 REM *******************************
00050 PRINT "NAME                AVERAGE"
00060 READ N$,G,N
00070 LET A = G / N
00080 PRINT N$,A
00090 READ N$,G,N
00100 LET A = G / N
00110 PRINT N$,A
00120 READ N$,G,N
00130 LET A = G / N
00140 PRINT N$,A
00150 DATA "PETE PETERS",36,10
00160 DATA "JERRY MCPHEE",37,8
00170 DATA "TOM ANDREWS",33,15
00999 END
```

```
RUNNH
NAME            AVERAGE
PETE PETERS     3.6
JERRY MCPHEE    4.625
TOM ANDREWS     2.2
```

MICROCOMPUTERS

Microcomputer:	Difference:
Apple	No space is reserved for sign.
Apple Macintosh	Print zones determined by WIDTH statement
IBM/Microsoft	No differences.
PET/Commodore 64	Print zones are smaller.
TRS-80	No differences.

three goal tenders and prints the results without using a GOTO statement. What we really have here is a single process (dividing the goals against the goal tender by the number of games) repeated three times. The programmer typed in the following three lines as many times as was necessary:

```
READ N$,G,N
LET A = G / N
PRINT N$,A
```

Although this is not a very difficult task with a small, uncomplicated problem, imagine how time consuming and inefficient it would be for a hundred sets of data!

The same result can be achieved much more simply by using a GOTO statement. In Figure V–2, the GOTO statement in line 90 directs the computer back to statement 60. A **loop** is formed. In this example, the error message "End of DATA found at line 00060 of MAIN PROGRAM" was printed because an attempt was made to read data after the data list had been exhausted. The execution of the program was terminated.

Note how the loop is indicated in the flowchart. A flow line is drawn from the process step immediately preceding the GOTO statement to the process step indicated by the transfer line number.

Later, this section will show how to control the number of times a loop is repeated (eliminating any error messages and the need to manually interrupt the program).

THE IF/THEN STATEMENT: CONDITIONAL TRANSFER

The GOTO statement always transfers control. Often, however, it is necessary to transfer control only when a specified condition exists. The IF/THEN statement is used to test for such a condition. If the condition does not exist, the next statement in the program is executed. The general format of the IF/THEN statement is this:

line# IF condition THEN transfer line#

A condition has the following general format:

relational
expression   symbol   expression

For example, in the statement "110 If $X < Y + 1$ THEN 230", $X < Y + 1$ is the condition.

Conditions tested can involve either numeric or character string data. Relational symbols that can be used include the following:

Symbol	Meaning	Examples
$<$	Less than	$A < B$
$< =$ or $\leq$	Less than or equal to	$X < = Y$
$>$	Greater than	$J > 1$
$> =$ or $\geq$	Greater than or equal to	$A > = B$
$=$	Equal to	$X = T$
		$N\$ = $ "NONE"
$<>$ or $><$	Not equal to	$R <> Q$
		"APPLE" $<>$ R\$

Figure V–2 ▪ Goals Against Average Program with GOTO Statement

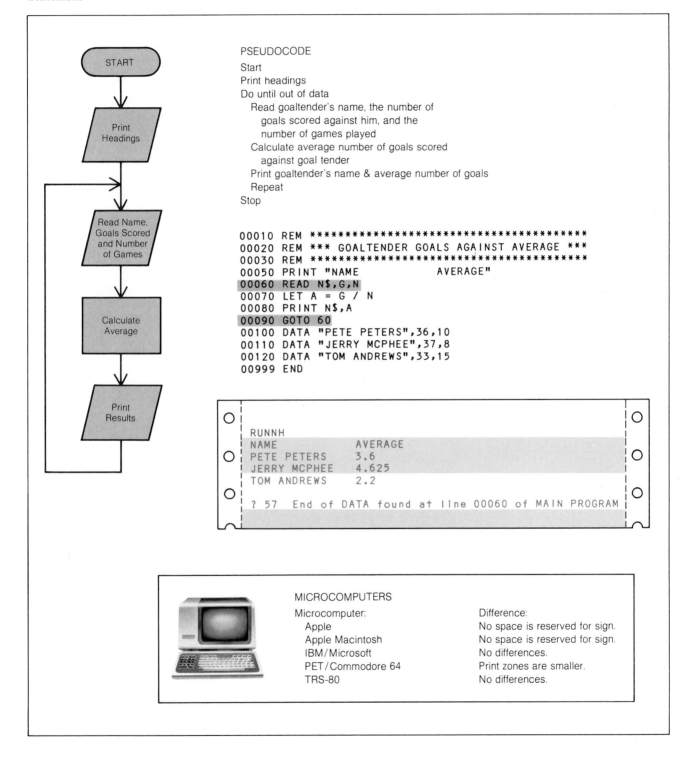

PSEUDOCODE

Start
Print headings
Do until out of data
    Read goaltender's name, the number of
      goals scored against him, and the
      number of games played
    Calculate average number of goals scored
      against goal tender
    Print goaltender's name & average number of goals
    Repeat
Stop

```
00010 REM ***************************************
00020 REM *** GOALTENDER GOALS AGAINST AVERAGE ***
00030 REM ***************************************
00050 PRINT "NAME              AVERAGE"
00060 READ N$,G,N
00070 LET A = G / N
00080 PRINT N$,A
00090 GOTO 60
00100 DATA "PETE PETERS",36,10
00110 DATA "JERRY MCPHEE",37,8
00120 DATA "TOM ANDREWS",33,15
00999 END
```

```
RUNNH
NAME              AVERAGE
PETE PETERS       3.6
JERRY MCPHEE      4.625
TOM ANDREWS       2.2

? 57   End of DATA found at line 00060 of MAIN PROGRAM
```

MICROCOMPUTERS

Microcomputer:	Difference:
Apple	No space is reserved for sign.
Apple Macintosh	No space is reserved for sign.
IBM/Microsoft	No differences.
PET/Commodore 64	Print zones are smaller.
TRS-80	No differences.

Some examples of valid IF/THEN statements follow:

Statement	Computer Execution

```00050 IF Q >= 9 THEN 100```
```00060 LET T = T + Q```
```00070 PRINT Q```
	If the value contained in Q is greater than or equal to 9, the computer branches to line 100. If not, the computer executes the next sequential instruction, line 60.

```00080 IF A < B + 54 THEN 50``` ```00090 LET A = B + 54```	If A is less than B + 54, the computer transfers to statement 50. Otherwise, it executes the next statement, line 90.

```00030 IF R$ = "TRUE" THEN 100```
```00040 LET F = F + 1```
```00050 PRINT "FINISHED"```
	If the value contained in R$ is TRUE, control is passed to line 100. If R$ contains anything else, control goes to line 40.

The program in Figure V–3 uses numeric comparisons to search student records to find all eligible students so they can be placed on a mailing list. The program reads the name, grade point average, and major grade point average for each student. A numeric comparison is made to determine if the student is eligible to apply for an internship.

```
00080 IF GPA < 3.0 THEN 140
```

The test is stated in such a way that only if the student's grade point average is greater than or equal to 3.0 will the program continue to evaluate his or her record. Otherwise, control is transferred to line 140.

The other qualification for the mailing list is that the student's major grade point average is greater than or equal to 3.2. This is also a comparison of numbers.

```
00120 IF MGPA < 3.2 THEN 140
```

If the student's major grade point average is less than 3.2, control is transferred to line 140.

BASIC EXTENSIONS
IF/THEN/ELSE

The BASIC implementation on the Apple Macintosh and on the IBM/Microsoft allows the use of the IF/THEN/ELSE statement. This statement can be useful because it uses one IF/THEN/ELSE statement instead of many IF/THEN statements. The general format of the IF/THEN/ELSE statement is this:

line # IF condition THEN clause ELSE clause

The clause can be a BASIC statement or statements or a line number to branch to.

If the condition being tested is true, the clause following the THEN statement is executed. If the condition is false, the THEN statement is bypassed and the clause following the ELSE statement is executed.

Examples of the IF/THEN/ELSE statement are shown below:

```
10 IF A <> B THEN PRINT A ELSE PRINT B
20 IF C$ = "END" THEN 200 ELSE 150
30 IF K = 8 THEN K = -1 ELSE K = 1
40 IF T = Q / N THEN P = Q * N ELSE P = T
```

Any person who satisfies both conditions is mailed an internship application. The program output indicates that only two students, Jeff Lewis and Amy Smith, should be mailed an application.

THE ON/GOTO STATEMENT: CONDITIONAL TRANSFER

The ON/GOTO, or computed GOTO, statement transfers control to other statements in the program based on the evaluation of a mathematical expres-

Figure V-3 ▪ Internship Program

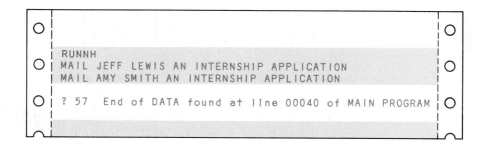

```
00010 REM ********************************************
00020 REM ***           INTERNSHIP PROGRAM         ***
00030 REM ********************************************
00040 READ N$,GPA,MGPA
00050 REM ********************************************
00060 REM ***    REJECT IF GRADE POINT < 3.0     ***
00070 REM ********************************************
00080 IF GPA < 3.0 THEN 140
00090 REM ********************************************
00100 REM *** REJECT IF MAJOR GRADE POINT < 3.2 ***
00110 REM ********************************************
00120 IF MGPA < 3.2 THEN 140
00130 PRINT "MAIL ";N$;" AN INTERNSHIP APPLICATION"
00140 GOTO 40
00150 DATA DON WILSON,2.5,2.8
00160 DATA JEFF LEWIS,3.4,3.5
00170 DATA AMY SMITH,3.2,3.2
00180 DATA DONNA TRAVERS,2.9,3.0
00999 END
```

```
RUNNH
MAIL JEFF LEWIS AN INTERNSHIP APPLICATION
MAIL AMY SMITH AN INTERNSHIP APPLICATION

? 57  End of DATA found at line 00040 of MAIN PROGRAM
```

MICROCOMPUTERS

Microcomputer:	Difference:
Apple	?OUT OF DATA ERROR IN 40.
Apple Macintosh	OUT OF DATA in line 40.
IBM/Microsoft	OUT OF DATA in 40.
PET/Commodore 64	?OUT OF DATA ERROR 40.
TRS-80	?OD ERROR in 40.

sion. The computed GOTO often operates as would multiple IF/THEN statements; any one of several transfers can occur, depending on the result computed for the expression. Since transfers depend on the expression, the computed GOTO is another **conditional transfer** statement. Its general format is this:

line# ON expression GOTO line#1,line#2,line#3, . . .,line#n

The arithmetic expression always is evaluated to an integer, and the line numbers following GOTO must identify statements in the program.

The general execution of the ON/GOTO statement proceeds as follows:

1. If the value of the expression is 1, control is transferred to the first line number indicated.
2. If the value of the expression is 2, control is transferred to the second line number indicated.

.   .   .
.   .   .
.   .   .

n. If the value of the expression is n, control is transferred to the nth line number indicated.

Several examples are presented here to illustrate the operation of this statement:

Statement	Computer Execution
00010 ON T GOTO 40,70,100	IF T = 1, control goes to line 40. IF T = 2, control goes to line 70. IF T = 3, control goes to line 100.
00020 ON Q / 2 GOTO 70,100	IF Q/2 = 1, control goes to line 70. IF Q/2 = 2, control goes to line 100.

If the computed expression in an ON/GOTO statement does not evaluate to an integer, the value is either rounded or truncated (digits to the right of the decimal are ignored), depending on the BASIC implementation. For example,

Statement	Value of Variable	Action
00030 ON N / 4 GOTO 20,150	N = 10	10 ÷ 4 = 2.5. The expression is evaluated as 2.5. The remainder is truncated, and the result becomes the integer 2. Control passes to statement 150.

If the expression evaluates to an integer less than 1, larger than the number of statements indicated, or greater than the maximum number of line numbers allowed, either the program will terminate with an error message or the ON/GOTO statement will be bypassed. For example,

Statement	Value of Variable	Action
00080 ON C GOTO 110,150,200 00090 LET C = Q + R	C = 5	The value of C exceeds the number of line numbers in the GOTO list. Control passes to statement 90.

ON/GOTO Errors

COMPUTER	ACTION IF NUMBER EVALUATED IS GREATER THAN NUMBER OF LINE NUMBERS	ACTION IF NUMBER EVALUATED IS LESS THAN 1 OR GREATER THAN MAXIMUM ALLOWED
DECSYSTEM 20	Execution stops/Error message displayed	"ON STMT OUT OF RANGE" error
Apple	ON/GOTO bypassed	"ILLEGAL QUANTITY" error
Apple Macintosh	Execution continues with the next executable statement	"ILLEGAL FUNCTION CALL" error*
IBM/Microsoft	ON/GOTO bypassed	"ILLEGAL FUNCTION CALL" or "OVERFLOW" error
TRS-80	ON/GOTO bypassed	"?FC" error
PET/Commodore 64	ON/GOTO bypassed	"ILLEGAL QUANTITY" error

*If the value of the expression 0 (zero), execution will continue with the next executable statement.

The box "ON/GOTO Errors" illustrates how various BASIC implementations respond to these conditions.

MENUS

A menu is a listing that displays the functions that can be performed by a program. The desired function is chosen by entering a code (typically a simple numeric or alphabetic character) from the terminal keyboard. A computer menu is like a menu in a restaurant. The user (diner) reads a group of possible selections on the screen (menu) and then enters a selection (describes the desired meal to the waiter or waitress).

The state capital menu program (Figure V– 4) illustrates a common use of the ON/GOTO statement in making a menu selection. The user tells the computer which state capital she wishes to find by entering either 1, 2, 3, 4, or 5. Line 130 transfers the program execution to the appropriate operation.

In the example, the user indicates that she wishes to know the state capital of New Jersey by typing in the number 3, which is assigned to the variable N. Line 130, an ON/GOTO statement, causes program execution to branch to the third line number 180. The operation is then performed, and the result is printed.

LOOPING PROCEDURES

There are several things to consider in setting up a loop. The programmer must decide not only what instructions are to be repeated, but also how many times the loop is to be executed. There are three techniques for loop control. This section covers trailer values and counters. Section VI will discuss the other method, FOR and NEXT statements.

Trailer Value

A loop controlled by a trailer value contains an IF/THEN statement that checks for the end of the data. The last data item is a **dummy value** that is not part of the data to be processed. Either numeric or alphanumeric data can be used as a trailer value. However, the programmer must always select a trailer value that will not be confused with real data. For example, a customer account number is never 0, which implies that zero may be safely used as a dummy value.

Figure V–4 ■ ON/GOTO Example Using a Menu

```
00010 REM ********************************
00020 REM *** STATE CAPITAL MENU PROGRAM  ***
00030 REM ********************************
00040 PRINT
00050 PRINT
00060 PRINT "STATE CAPITAL MENU SELECTION, ENTER:"
00070 PRINT "        1 FOR OHIO"
00080 PRINT "        2 FOR NEW YORK"
00090 PRINT "        3 FOR NEW JERSEY"
00100 PRINT "        4 FOR PENNSYLVANIA"
00110 PRINT "        5 FOR KANSAS"
00120 INPUT N
00130 ON N GOTO 140,160,180,200,220
00140 LET C$ = "COLUMBUS"
00150 GOTO 230
00160 LET C$ = "ALBANY"
00170 GOTO 230
00180 LET C$ = "TRENTON"
00190 GOTO 230
00200 LET C$ = "HARRISBURG"
00210 GOTO 230
00220 LET C$ = "TOPEKA"
00230 PRINT
00240 PRINT
00250 PRINT "THE STATE CAPITAL IS ";C$
00999 END
```

```
RUNNH


STATE CAPITAL MENU SELECTION, ENTER:
        1 FOR OHIO
        2 FOR NEW YORK
        3 FOR NEW JERSEY
        4 FOR PENNSYLVANIA
        5 FOR KANSAS
    ? 3


THE STATE CAPITAL IS TRENTON
```

MICROCOMPUTERS

Microcomputer:	Difference:
Apple	No differences.
Apple Macintosh	No differences.
IBM / Microsoft	No differences.
PET / Commodore 64	No differences.
TRS-80	No differences.

Here is how it works. An IF/THEN statement is placed within the set of instructions to be repeated, usually at the beginning of the loop. One of the variables to which data is entered is tested. If it contains the dummy value, control is transferred out of the loop. If the variable contains valid data (does not equal the trailer value), looping continues.

Figure V–5 contains a loop pattern controlled by a trailer value. The program calculates the sales price of several different flowers. Statement 140 tests the value I$ for the dummy value:

```
00140 IF I$ = "END" THEN 240
```

If the condition is true, the flow of processing drops out of the loop to line 240. If the condition is false, processing continues to the next line in sequence, line 150. Note that since we used the INPUT statement to enter the data, it is necessary to tell the user how to end the looping process. This is done in line 90. The user has to enter two dummy values, END and 0, because the INPUT statement expects two values to be entered.

Counter

A second method of controlling a loop requires the programmer to create a counter—a numeric variable that is incremented each time the loop is executed. Normally, the increment is 1. A counter is effective only if the programmer notifies the computer how many times a loop should be repeated. The following steps are involved in setting up a counter for loop control:

1. Initialize the counter to give it a beginning value.
2. Increment the counter each time the loop is executed.

Figure V–5 ▪ Flower Sales (Continued Next Page)

```
00010 REM ********************************
00020 REM ***    FLOWER SALES PROGRAM    ***
00030 REM ********************************
00040 LET D = 0.85
00050 REM ********************************
00060 REM ***      BEGINNING OF LOOP     ***
00070 REM ********************************
00080 PRINT "ENTER ITEM AND REGULAR PRICE"
00090 PRINT "ENTER END,0 WHEN FINISHED"
00100 INPUT I$,R
00110 REM ********************************
00120 REM ***    TEST FOR TRAILER VALUE  ***
00130 REM ********************************
00140 IF I$ = "END" THEN 240
00150 LET S = R * D
00160 PRINT
00170 PRINT "ITEM","SALES PRICE","REGULAR PRICE"
00180 PRINT I$,S,R
00190 PRINT
00200 GOTO 80
00210 REM ********************************
00220 REM ***          END OF LOOP       ***
00230 REM ********************************
00240 PRINT
00250 PRINT "JOB IS COMPLETED"
00999 END
```

Figure V–5 ■ Continued

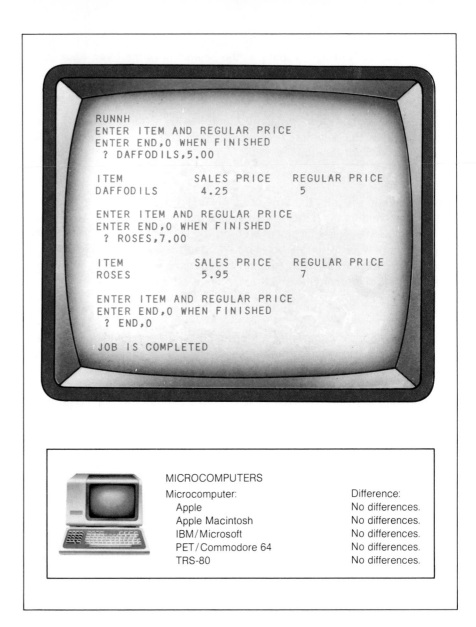

```
RUNNH
ENTER ITEM AND REGULAR PRICE
ENTER END,0 WHEN FINISHED
 ? DAFFODILS,5.00

ITEM            SALES PRICE   REGULAR PRICE
DAFFODILS         4.25          5

ENTER ITEM AND REGULAR PRICE
ENTER END,0 WHEN FINISHED
 ? ROSES,7.00

ITEM            SALES PRICE   REGULAR PRICE
ROSES             5.95          7

ENTER ITEM AND REGULAR PRICE
ENTER END,0 WHEN FINISHED
 ? END,0

JOB IS COMPLETED
```

MICROCOMPUTERS

Microcomputer:	Difference:
Apple	No differences.
Apple Macintosh	No differences.
IBM/Microsoft	No differences.
PET/Commodore 64	No differences.
TRS-80	No differences.

3. Test the counter to determine if the loop has been executed the desired number of times.

The flower sales program used in Figure V–5 can be modified to use a counter, as shown in Figure V–6. Since there are three flowers, the loop must be executed three times. The counter in this example is C. It is initialized to 0 in line 80. The IF/THEN statement in line 140 tests the number of times the loop has been executed, as represented by the counter C. Line 190 causes C to be incremented each time the loop is executed. The loop instructions will be executed until C equals 4.

**Figure V–6 ▪ Flower Sales
Program with Counter**

```
00010 REM ****************************
00020 REM ***   FLOWER SALES PROGRAM   ***
00030 REM ****************************
00040 LET D = 0.85
00050 REM ****************************
00060 REM ***    INITIALIZE COUNTER    ***
00070 REM ****************************
00080 LET C = 0
00090 PRINT " ","REGULAR","SALES"
00100 PRINT "ITEM"," PRICE","PRICE"
00110 REM ****************************
00120 REM ***    TEST COUNTER VALUE   ***
00130 REM ****************************
00140 IF C = 4 THEN 999
00150 READ I$,R
00160 LET S = R * D
00170 PRINT
00180 PRINT I$,R,S
00190 LET C = C + 1
00200 REM ****************************
00210 REM *** UNCONDITIONAL TRANSFER ***
00220 REM ****************************
00230 GOTO 130
00240 DATA DAFFODILS,5.00,ROSES,7.00
00250 DATA CARNATIONS,4.00,DAISIES,3.00
00999 END
```

```
RUNNH
                REGULAR        SALES
ITEM            PRICE          PRICE

DAFFODILS       5              4.25

ROSES           7              5.95

CARNATIONS      4              3.4

DAISIES         3              2.55
```

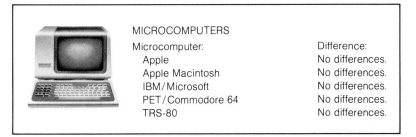

MICROCOMPUTERS

Microcomputer:	Difference:
Apple	No differences.
Apple Macintosh	No differences.
IBM/Microsoft	No differences.
PET/Commodore 64	No differences.
TRS-80	No differences.

A PROGRAMMING PROBLEM

Problem Definition

The Office of the Registrar at Ed U. K. Shun College needs a program that will assign class rank to students based on their earned credit hours. In addition, office personnel want to know how many students in each class rank are registered for a class and how many total students are in the class.

The class rank scale is as follows:

Credit Hours	Class Rank
90 or more	Senior
60 to 89	Junior
30 to 59	Sophomore
Less than 30	Freshman

The students and their credit hours earned follow:

Student	Credit Hours
Shirley Simon	66
Ed Taylor	15
Steve Dun	92
Kelly Cole	100
Gerry Hill	45
Shelly Cable	28
Beth Anderson	33
Karen Redford	89
Henry Kullen	78
Mary Mars	55

Solution Design

The first step in the program is to read each student's name and number of credit hours. Next, 1 must be added to the total number of students. The appropriate class rank should then be assigned and the total number of students in that class should be incremented. Finally, print the results.

The Program

The counter variables are initialized to 0 by the READ and DATA statements in lines 40 and 50 of Figure V–7. The name and credit hours for each student are read in line 110. Line 160 tests for the trailer value END. As long as the student's name does not equal END, the loop is re-executed. The total number of students is accumulated in line 170. The first test to determine the class rank is made in line 180. If the credit hours are less than 90, the student is not a senior. Control is transferred to line 220, where the credit hours are tested again to see if they total fewer than 60 (required for junior class status). In this fashion, credit hours less than the lowest number required for a particular class rank are passed down to the next lowest level until the correct class ranking is found. Line 300 requires no test; any credit hours fewer than 30 give the student freshman status. When the trailer value END is detected, control drops to line 380, where printing of the totals occurs.

Figure V–7 ▪ **Class Rank** **(Continued on Next Two Pages)**

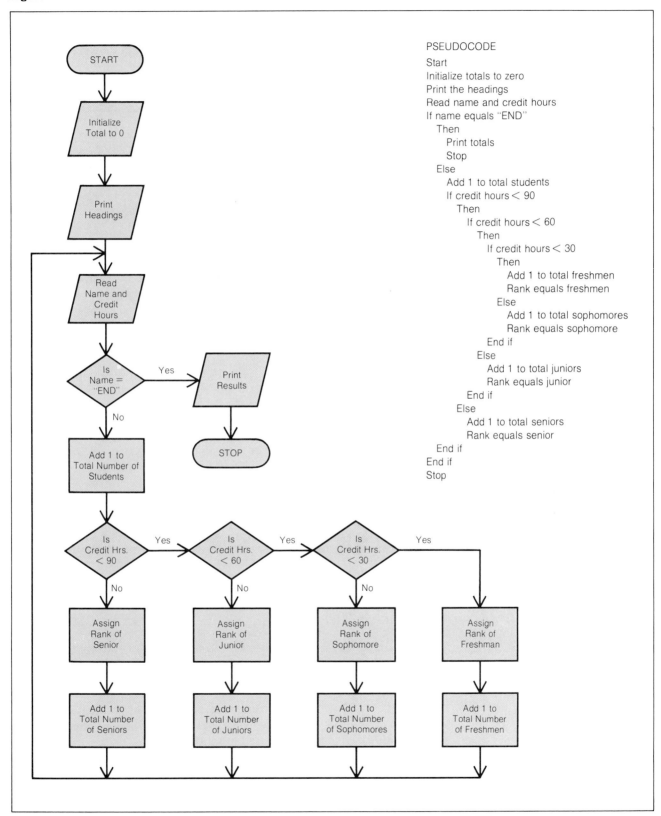

PSEUDOCODE

Start
Initialize totals to zero
Print the headings
Read name and credit hours
If name equals "END"
    Then
        Print totals
        Stop
    Else
        Add 1 to total students
        If credit hours < 90
            Then
                If credit hours < 60
                    Then
                        If credit hours < 30
                            Then
                                Add 1 to total freshmen
                                Rank equals freshmen
                            Else
                                Add 1 to total sophomores
                                Rank equals sophomore
                        End if
                    Else
                        Add 1 to total juniors
                        Rank equals junior
                End if
            Else
                Add 1 to total seniors
                Rank equals senior
    End if
End if
Stop

Figure V–7 ▪ **Continued**

```
00010 REM **************************************
00020 REM ***          ASSIGN CLASS RANK        ***
00030 REM **************************************
00040 DATA 0,0,0,0,0
00050 READ F,S,J,SE,T
00060 PRINT "NAME"," ","CREDIT HOURS","CLASS RANK"
00070 PRINT
00080 REM **************************************
00090 REM ***        THE LOOP BEGINS HERE       ***
00100 REM **************************************
00110 READ S$,C
00120 REM **************************************
00130 REM ***        TEST FOR TRAILER VALUE     ***
00140 REM ***          CONDITIONAL TRANSFER     ***
00150 REM **************************************
00160 IF S$ = "END" THEN 380
00170 LET T = T + 1
00180 IF C < 90 THEN 220
00190 LET R$ = "SENIOR"

00200 LET SE = SE + 1
00210 GOTO 320
00220 IF C < 60 THEN 260
00230 LET R$ = "JUNIOR"
00240 LET J = J + 1
00250 GOTO 320
00260 IF C < 30 THEN 300
00270 LET R$ = "SOPHOMORE"
00280 LET S = S + 1
00290 GOTO 320
00300 LET R$ = "FRESHMAN"
00310 LET F = F + 1
00320 PRINT S$," ",C,R$
00370 GOTO 110
00380 PRINT
00390 PRINT "TOTAL # OF FRESHMAN = ";F
00400 PRINT "TOTAL # OF SOPHOMORES = ";S
00410 PRINT "TOTAL # OF JUNIORS = ";J
00420 PRINT "TOTAL # OF SENIORS = ";SE

00430 PRINT
00440 PRINT "TOTAL # OF STUDENTS = ";T
00450 DATA "SHIRLEY SIMON",66,"ED TAYLOR",15
00460 DATA "STEVE DUN",92,"KELLY COLE",100
00470 DATA "GERRY HILL",45,"SHELLY CABLE",28
00480 DATA "BETH ANDERSON",33,"KAREN REDFORD",89
00490 DATA "HENRY KULLEN",78,"MARY MARS",55
00500 DATA "END",0
00999 END
```

SUMMARY POINTS

▪ The GOTO statement is an unconditional transfer of control that allows the computer to bypass or alter the sequence in which instructions are executed.
▪ The GOTO statement often is used to set up loops.
▪ The IF/THEN statement permits control to be transferred only when a specified condition is met. If the condition following IF is true, the clause following the word THEN is given control; if it is false, control passes to the next line.

Figure V–7 ▪ Continued

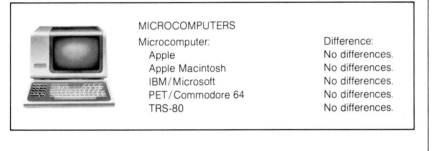

```
RUNNH
NAME                          CREDIT HOURS    CLASS RANK

SHIRLEY SIMON                      66         JUNIOR
ED TAYLOR                          15         FRESHMAN
STEVE DUN                          92         SENIOR
KELLY COLE                        100         SENIOR
GERRY HILL                         45         SOPHOMORE
SHELLY CABLE                       28         FRESHMAN
BETH ANDERSON                      33         SOPHOMORE
KAREN REDFORD                      89         JUNIOR
HENRY KULLEN                       78         JUNIOR
MARY MARS                          55         SOPHOMORE

TOTAL # OF FRESHMAN =    2
TOTAL # OF SOPHOMORES =  3
TOTAL # OF JUNIORS =     3
TOTAL # OF SENIORS =     2

TOTAL # OF STUDENTS =   10
```

MICROCOMPUTERS

Microcomputer:	Difference:
Apple	No differences.
Apple Macintosh	No differences.
IBM/Microsoft	No differences.
PET/Commodore 64	No differences.
TRS-80	No differences.

▪ The ON/GOTO statement instructs the computer to evaluate an expression and, based on its value, to branch to one of several points in a program.

▪ A menu is a listing that displays the functions a program can perform. The user selects the desired function by entering a code from the keyboard.

▪ The number of times a loop is executed can be controlled by the use of a trailer value or a counter.

▪ The trailer value is a dummy value entered at the end of all the data.

▪ A counter can be set up if the programmer knows ahead of time how many times a loop is to be executed.

REVIEW QUESTIONS

1. How do unconditional and conditional transfers differ? Give an example of each.

2. Why is the IF/THEN statement a conditional transfer? If the condition after the IF in an IF/THEN statement is false, where is control transferred to?

3. Where will control be transferred to when the following ON/GOTO statement is executed? X has the value of 270.

$$20 \ \ ON \ X/90 \ GOTO \ 90,270,310$$

4. What is a menu?

5. Give two methods discussed in this section of controlling the number of times a loop is executed.

DEBUGGING EXERCISES

```
1.  50 LET C = 4
    55 ON C GOTO 60,70,80
    60 PRINT "C = ";1
    65 GOTO 99
    70 PRINT "C = ";2
    75 GOTO 100
    80 PRINT "C = ";3
    99 END
```

```
2.  05 REM *** PRINT THE EVEN NUMBERS FROM 10 DOWN THROUGH Z ***
    10 LET Z = -6
    15 LET X = 10
    20 IF X THEN 99
    25 PRINT X * 10
    30 LET X = x - 2
    35 GOTO 10
    99 END
```

PROGRAMMING PROBLEMS

1. Write a program using the GOTO statement to implement a loop, and a counter to control the number of times the loop is executed. The output from this program should appear as follows:

10	20	30
40	50	60
70	80	90
100	110	120

2. Using a menu and the ON/GOTO statement, write a program which allows the user to enter his or her body weight (in pounds) and gives him or her the choice of calculating: (1) the average number of calories which should be eaten per day to maintain that body weight (weight * 16) or (2) the recommended number of grams of protein which should be consumed per day (weight * 0.453).

OVERVIEW

Section V discussed two methods of controlling loops—counters and trailer values. The IF/THEN and GOTO statements were used to implement these methods. This section presents another method for loop control—FOR and NEXT statements. In addition, it discusses nested loops (loops within loops).

Let us review what happens when a counter is used to control a loop, since the logic of FOR/NEXT loops is very similar. First, the counter variable is set to some initial value. Statements inside the loop are executed once and the counter incremented. The counter variable then is tested to see if the loop has been executed the required number of times. When the variable exceeds the designated terminal, or ending, value the looping process ends, and the computer proceeds to the rest of the program. For example, assume we want to write a program that will multiply each of the numbers from 1 to 6 by 2. The program in Figure VI–1 does this using a loop controlled by the counter method. We will see later how the FOR/NEXT loop allows us to accomplish the same steps in a more efficient manner.

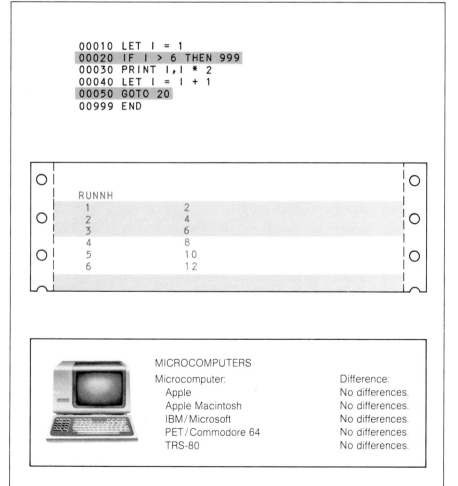

Figure VI–1 ▪ **Looping with a Counter**

```
00010 LET I = 1
00020 IF I > 6 THEN 999
00030 PRINT I,I * 2
00040 LET I = I + 1
00050 GOTO 20
00999 END
```

```
RUNNH
   1           2
   2           4
   3           6
   4           8
   5          10
   6          12
```

```
MICROCOMPUTERS
Microcomputer:              Difference:
   Apple                    No differences.
   Apple Macintosh          No differences.
   IBM/Microsoft            No differences.
   PET/Commodore 64         No differences.
   TRS-80                   No differences.
```

THE FOR AND NEXT STATEMENTS

The FOR and NEXT statements allow concise loop definition. The general format of the FOR and NEXT loop is as follows:

line# FOR loop variable = initial value TO terminal
value STEP step value

.

.

.

line # NEXT loop variable

The FOR statement tells the computer how many times to execute the loop. The loop variable (also called the index) is set to an initial value. This value is tested against the terminal value to determine whether or not the loop should be repeated. The initial and terminal values may be constants, variables, expressions, or decimals, all of which must be numeric.

To set the initial value and test the counter took two lines (lines 10 and 20) in Figure VI–1. The FOR statement combines these two steps into one statement:

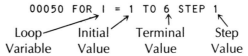

00050 FOR I = 1 TO 6 STEP 1

Loop   Initial   Terminal   Step
Variable   Value   Value   Value

Lines 40 and 50 in Figure VI–1 increment the loop variable (the counter) and send control back to line 20. The functions of these two statements are combined in the NEXT statement. In Figure VI–1, after control is transferred back to line 20, the value of the loop variable is again tested against the terminal value. Once the terminal value is exceeded, control passes to line 999. When FOR and NEXT are used, control goes to the statement immediately following the NEXT statement.

Thus, the loop used in Figure VI–1 can be set up to use FOR and NEXT statements, as shown in Figure VI–2. The FOR statement in line 10 tells the computer to initialize the loop variable, I, to one. Between the FOR and NEXT statements is line 20, the instruction that is to be repeated; it prints out I and the result of I * 2. Line 30, the NEXT statement, increments the loop variable by the step indicated in the FOR statement. The step value may be a constant, real number, variable, or expression, and it must have a numeric value.

Flowcharting FOR and NEXT loops

Figure VI–3a illustrates the standard method of flowcharting the FOR/NEXT loop. We have developed our own shorthand symbol for FOR and NEXT loops, which is shown in Figure VI–3b. This is very convenient for representing a loop, since it shows the initial, terminal, and step values for the loop variable in one symbol.

Processing Steps of FOR and NEXT Loops

Let us review the steps followed by the computer when it encounters a FOR statement:

Figure VI–2 ■ FOR/NEXT Loop

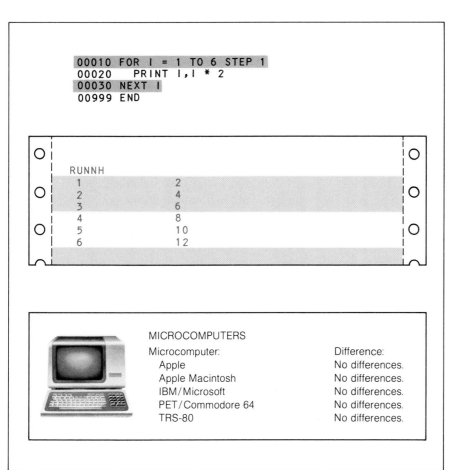

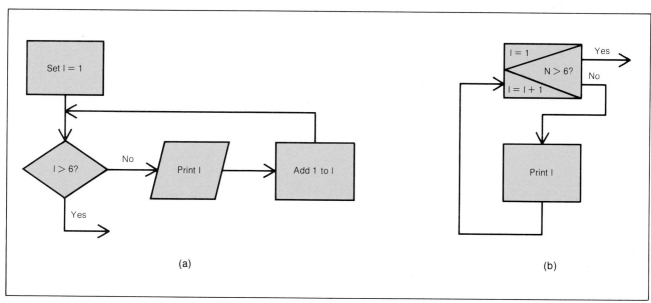

Figure VI–3 ■ Flowcharting
FOR/NEXT Loops

1. It sets the loop variable to the initial value indicated.

2. The first time the FOR/NEXT loop is executed, the FOR statement tests to see if the value of the loop variable exceeds the indicated terminal value. If the value of the loop variable does not exceed the terminal value, the statements in the loop are executed. Otherwise, control is transferred to the statement following the NEXT statement.

When the NEXT statement at the end of a loop is encountered, the computer does the following:

1. It adds the step value (given in the FOR statement) to the value of the loop variable. If no step value is indicated in the FOR statement, the value is assumed to be +1. Thus, the following two statements are equivalent:

```
00050 FOR I = 1 TO 6 STEP 1
```

or

```
00050 FOR I = 1 TO 6
```

2. It tests to see if the value of the loop variable exceeds the indicated terminal value.

3. If the value of the loop variable does not exceed the terminal value, the statements in the loop are executed.

4. If the value of the loop variable exceeds the terminal value, control is transferred to the statement immediately following.

Rules for Using FOR and NEXT Statements

Some rules to be aware of when you use FOR and NEXT statements follow:

1. The initial value must be less than or equal to the terminal value when using a positive step. Otherwise, the loop will never be executed; for example,

```
Valid: FOR J = 1 TO 30 STEP 3
Invalid: FOR J = 20 TO 10 STEP 2
```

2. There are times when it is desirable to use a negative step value, for example, to count backward from 15 by 1s (see Figure VI–4). The loop is terminated when the value of the loop variable N "exceeds" the specified terminal value, 5. In this case, though, the value of N "exceeds" in a downward sense—the loop is terminated when N is smaller than the terminal value. The initial value of the loop variable should be greater than the terminal value when using a negative step; for example,

```
Valid: FOR K = 30 TO 20 STEP -5
Invalid: FOR N = 20 TO 30 STEP -5
```

3. The step size in a FOR statement should never be 0. This value would cause the computer to loop endlessly. Such an error condition is known as an infinite loop:

```
Invalid: FOR R = 1 TO 10 STEP 0
```

4. Transfer can be made from one statement to another within a loop. For example, the program in Figure VI–5 reads in five tourist attractions and their state of residence. It will print out only those tourist attractions that are not in

Figure VI–4 ▪ **Using a Negative Step Value**

```
00010 FOR N = 15 TO 5 STEP -5
00020   PRINT N
00030 NEXT N
00999 END
```

```
RUNNH
 15
 10
  5
```

MICROCOMPUTERS

Microcomputer:	Difference:
Apple	No differences.
Apple Macintosh	No differences.
IBM/Microsoft	No differences.
PET/Commodore 64	No differences.
TRS-80	No differences.

Figure VI–5 ▪ **Transferring Control Within a FOR/NEXT Loop**

```
00010 FOR K = 1 TO 5
00020   READ P$,S$
00030   IF S$ = "OHIO" THEN 50
00040   PRINT P$
00050 NEXT K
00060 DATA EMPIRE STATE BUILDING,NEW YORK
00070 DATA CEDAR POINT AMUSEMENT PARK,OHIO
00080 DATA ALAMO,TEXAS
00090 DATA WASHINGTON MEMORIAL,WASHINGTON DC
00100 DATA SEA WORLD,OHIO
00999 END
```

```
RUNNH
EMPIRE STATE BUILDING
ALAMO
WASHINGTON MEMORIAL
```

MICROCOMPUTERS

Microcomputer:	Difference:
Apple	No differences.
Apple Macintosh	No differences.
IBM/Microsoft	No differences.
PET/Commodore 64	No differences.
TRS-80	No differences.

Ohio. Note, however, that a transfer from a statement within the loop to the FOR statement of the loop is illegal. Such a transfer would cause the loop variable to be reset (rather than simply continuing the loop process):

Invalid Transfer

```
00010 FOR J = 1 TO 15
00020    IF J = 10 THEN 10
00030    PRINT J + 1
00040 NEXT J
```

If you want to continue the looping process but want to bypass some inner instruction, branch (transfer control) to the next statement, as was done in Figure VI–5 (line 30).

Transferring outside the loop before it is normally terminated should also be avoided. If such a transfer is made, the loop variable will not have the value which you would expect.

5. The value of the loop variable should not be modified by program statements within the loop. For example, line 30 here is invalid:

```
00010 FOR I = 1 TO 10
00020    LET T = T + 1
00030    LET I = T
00040 NEXT I
```

6. The initial, terminal, and step expressions can be composed of any valid numeric variable, constant, or mathematical formula. The following examples are valid where A = 7, B = 3, C = 1:

```
00010 FOR L = A TO (B + 10) STEP 2
00020    PRINT L * A
00030 NEXT L
```

```
00010 FOR N = 1 TO A STEP B
00020    LET T = T + 1
00030 NEXT N
```

```
00010 FOR J = (A * B) TO (A + B) STEP -C
00020    PRINT J,J * 3
00030 NEXT J
```

7. Each FOR statement must be accompanied by an associated NEXT statement. In addition, the loop variable in the FOR statement must be specified in the NEXT statement.

Figure VI–6 demonstrates the application of a FOR/NEXT loop. The purpose of this program is to find out the number of dropouts of a marathon race at each checkpoint of the race. There are six checkpoints. The FOR/NEXT loop is set to be executed six times—once for each checkpoint. Each time through the loop, the user enters the number of racers who have checked in at the checkpoint; then the computer prints the number of dropouts to the checkpoint, and at the end prints the total number of racers who have completed the rate and the total number of racers who dropped out.

NESTED FOR AND NEXT STATEMENTS

Loops can be nested; that is, all of one loop can be inside another loop or many other loops. An example of a nested loop follows:

Figure VI–6 ▪ **FOR/NEXT Loop**

```
00010 REM ***************************************************************
00020 REM *** PROGRAM TO COMPUTE THE NUMBER OF MARATHON DROP-OUTS ***
00030 REM ***************************************************************
00040 LET T = 100
00050 FOR J = 1 TO 6
00060    PRINT "ENTER NUMBER OF RACERS AT CHECKPOINT # ";J
00070    INPUT N
00080    PRINT "NUMBER OF DROP-OUTS AT CHECKPOINT # ";J;" = ";T - N
00090    PRINT
00100    LET T = N
00110 NEXT J
00120 PRINT
00130 PRINT "TOTAL NUMBER OF RACERS WHO COMPLETED THE RACE = ";T
00140 PRINT "TOTAL NUMBER OF RACERS WHO DROPPED OUT OF THE RACE = ";100 - T
00999 END
```

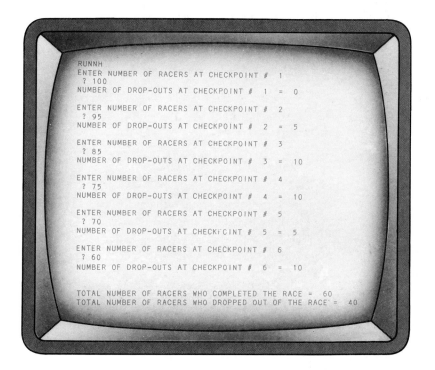

```
RUNNH
ENTER NUMBER OF RACERS AT CHECKPOINT #  1
? 100
NUMBER OF DROP-OUTS AT CHECKPOINT #  1  =  0

ENTER NUMBER OF RACERS AT CHECKPOINT #  2
? 95
NUMBER OF DROP-OUTS AT CHECKPOINT #  2  =  5

ENTER NUMBER OF RACERS AT CHECKPOINT #  3
? 85
NUMBER OF DROP-OUTS AT CHECKPOINT #  3  =  10

ENTER NUMBER OF RACERS AT CHECKPOINT #  4
? 75
NUMBER OF DROP-OUTS AT CHECKPOINT #  4  =  10

ENTER NUMBER OF RACERS AT CHECKPOINT #  5
? 70
NUMBER OF DROP-OUTS AT CHECKPOINT #  5  =  5

ENTER NUMBER OF RACERS AT CHECKPOINT #  6
? 60
NUMBER OF DROP-OUTS AT CHECKPOINT #  6  =  10


TOTAL NUMBER OF RACERS WHO COMPLETED THE RACE =  60
TOTAL NUMBER OF RACERS WHO DROPPED OUT OF THE RACE =  40
```

MICROCOMPUTERS

Microcomputer:	Difference:
Apple	Output must be reformatted.
Apple Macintosh	No differences.
IBM/Microsoft	No differences.
PET/Commodore 64	Output must be reformatted.
TRS-80	No differences.

```
┌─FOR K = 1 TO 5
│  ┌─FOR L = 1 TO 4
│  │   •
│  │   •                        Valid
│  │   •
│  └─NEXT L
└─NEXT K
```

The inner loop often is indented to improve readability. In this case, each time the outer loop (K loop) is executed once, the inner loop (L loop) is executed four times. When the L loop is terminated, control passes to the statement immediately below it, NEXT K. When control is transferred to FOR K (and the value of K does not exceed the terminal value, 5), the FOR L statement is soon encountered again. L is reinitialized, and the L loop is again repeated four times.

In nested FOR and NEXT statements, be careful not to mix the FOR from one loop with the NEXT from another. In other words, be sure one loop is completely inside another. The following example will not execute:

```
┌──┌─FOR K = 1 TO 5
│  ├─FOR L = 1 TO 4
│  │   •
│  │   •                        Invalid
│  │   •
│  └──NEXT K
└─NEXT L
```

You must also be careful not to give nested loops the same index variable:

```
┌─FOR N = 1 TO 3
│  ┌─FOR N = 1 TO 6
│  │   •
│  │   •                  Invalid
│  │   •
│  └─NEXT N
└─NEXT N
```

If you do this, each time the inner loop is executed, it changes the value of the outer loop variable. This violates Rule 5.

The following segment illustrates the mechanics of the nested loop. The outer loop will be executed four times, since I varies from 1 to 4. The inner loop will be executed three times each time the outer loop is executed once, so the inner loop will be executed a total of twelve times (3 × 4):

```
                    ┌─FOR I = 1 TO 4
                    │ ┌─FOR J = 1 TO 3│
Outer Loop ─────────┤ │    PRINT I,J   │───── Inner Loop
                    │ │  NEXT J        │
                    └─NEXT I
```

		I	J	
a.	First time through outer loop; I = 1	1	1	First time through inner loop; J = 1
		1	2	Second time through inner loop; J = 2
		1	3	Third time through inner loop; J = 3
b.	Second time through outer loop; I = 2	2	1	First time through inner loop; J = 1
		2	2	Second time through inner loop; J = 2
		2	3	Third time through inner loop; J = 3
c.	Third time through outer loop; I = 3	3	1	First time through inner loop; J = 1
		3	2	Second time through inner loop; J = 2
		3	3	Third time through inner loop; J = 3

d. Fourth time through   4   1   First time through inner loop; J = 1
    outer loop; I = 4   4   2   Second time through inner loop; J = 2
                          4   3   Third time through inner loop; J = 3

Figure VI–7 is an application of nested loops that generates three division tables. The inner loop controls the printing of the columns in each row, and the outer loop controls how many rows will be printed.

First I is initialized to 1. Then execution of the inner loop begins. Line 30 tells the computer (when J = 1) to print "1/1 = 1." The comma at the end of that line tells the computer not to start the output of the next PRINT statement on a new line, but rather to continue in the next print zone. Line 40 increments J to 4. The value of I has not changed. The terminal value of J is not exceeded, so "$\frac{1}{4}$ = 0.25" is printed in the second print zone. The inner loop executes one more time and prints out "$\frac{1}{7}$ = 0.1428571." After the inner loop has executed the third time, one complete row has been printed:

$$\frac{1}{1} = 1 \qquad\qquad \frac{1}{4} = 0.25 \qquad\qquad \frac{1}{7} = 0.1428571$$

To have printing start on the next line instead of in the next print zone, it is necessary to have the rest of the line printed with blanks. That is accom-

Figure VI–7 ▪ Nested Loops

```
00010 FOR I = 1 TO 10
00020    FOR J = 1 TO 8 STEP 3
00030       PRINT I;"/";J;"=";I / J,
00040    NEXT J
00050    PRINT
00060 NEXT I
00999 END
```

```
RUNNH
 1 / 1 = 1        1 / 4 = 0.25     1 / 7 = 0.1428571
 2 / 1 = 2        2 / 4 = 0.5      2 / 7 = 0.2857143
 3 / 1 = 3        3 / 4 = 0.75     3 / 7 = 0.4285714
 4 / 1 = 4        4 / 4 = 1        4 / 7 = 0.5714286
 5 / 1 = 5        5 / 4 = 1.25     5 / 7 = 0.7142857
 6 / 1 = 6        6 / 4 = 1.5      6 / 7 = 0.8571429
 7 / 1 = 7        7 / 4 = 1.75     7 / 7 = 1
 8 / 1 = 8        8 / 4 = 2        8 / 7 = 1.142857
 9 / 1 = 9        9 / 4 = 2.25     9 / 7 = 1.285714
10 / 1 = 10      10 / 4 = 2.5     10 / 7 = 1.428571
```

MICROCOMPUTERS

Microcomputer:	Difference:
Apple	Output must be reformatted.
Apple Macintosh	No differences.
IBM/Microsoft	No differences.
PET/Commodore 64	Output must be reformatted.
TRS-80	No differences.

plished by line 50. Finally, I is incremented when line 60 is encountered. The whole process continues until I exceeds the terminal value, 10.

A PROGRAMMING PROBLEM

Problem Definition

The Association of Business Management needs a program to display a bar chart of attendance at its annual convention. The attendance is given as follows:

MONDAY	250
TUESDAY	300
WEDNESDAY	330
THURSDAY	270
FRIDAY	140

The required output lists a three-letter abbreviation for each day in a column headed by "WEEK" and a horizontal bar chart labelled "ATTENDANCE" and marked off by units of 100.

Solution Design

The first thing which must be done is to print the headings. Then, nested loops must be set up. Each time through the outer loop the day of the week and the attendance for that day must be read, and the day printed. Then the inner loop will print the appropriate number of asterisks. Finally the key must be printed.

The Program

Figure VI–8 is a good illustration of nested FOR and NEXT loops. Statements 40 and 50 contain the names of the weekdays and their associated attendance figures. Lines 60 to 140 contain PRINT statements that adjust spacing and column headings. The outer loop (lines 150 to 220) runs five times (once for each day). Nested inside, statements 180 to 200 form a loop whose ter-

Figure VI–8 ▪ Convention Attendance Chart Program (Continued on Next Page)

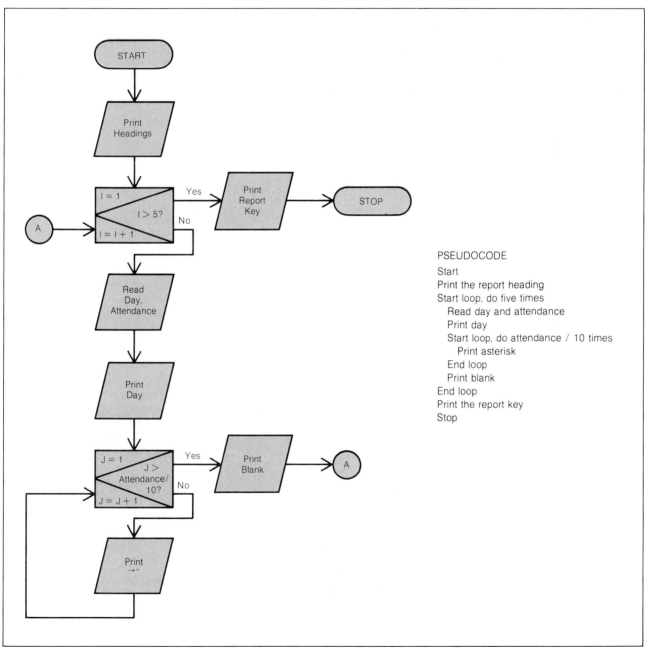

PSEUDOCODE
Start
Print the report heading
Start loop, do five times
   Read day and attendance
   Print day
   Start loop, do attendance / 10 times
     Print asterisk
   End loop
   Print blank
End loop
Print the report key
Stop

```
00010 REM *****************************************************************
00020 REM *** BAR CHART OF ANNUAL CONVENTION ATTENDANCE PROGRAM ***
00030 REM *****************************************************************
00040 DATA MON,250,TUE,300,WED,330
00050 DATA THU,270,FRI,140
00060 PRINT
00070 PRINT
00080 PRINT
00090 PRINT TAB(8);"ANNUAL CONVENTION ATTENDANCE"
00100 PRINT
00110 PRINT "DAY";TAB(8);"ATTENDANCE"
00120 PRINT
00130 PRINT TAB(7);"10";TAB(16);"100";TAB(26);"200";TAB(36);"300"
00140 PRINT
00150 FOR I = 1 TO 5
00160    READ D$,A
00170    PRINT D$;TAB(8);
00180    FOR J = 1 TO A / 10
00190      PRINT "*";
00200    NEXT J
00210    PRINT " "
00220 NEXT I
00230 PRINT
00240 PRINT "KEY"
00250 PRINT
00260 PRINT "* = 10 MEMBERS"
00999 END
```

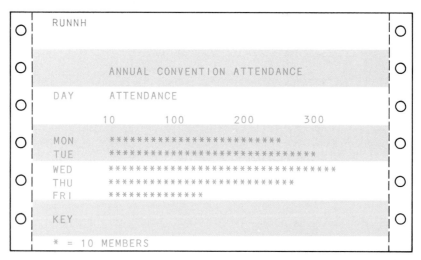

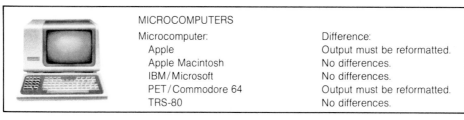

Figure VI–8 ▪ Continued

minal value is the value of the variable A divided by 10. The value of A is the attendance during a particular day. A is divided by ten in order to print one asterisk for ten attending members. Statement 190 prints an asterisk for every ten members who attended the convention. The semicolon at the end of line 190 prevents a carriage return as long as the inner loop is executing.

After the inner loop is finished, however, it is necessary to prepare for the next day's line by the printing of a blank space in line 210, which completes the carriage return.

Many variations can be made to the basic bar chart display. The asterisk can be replaced by any other character.

SUMMARY POINTS

■ BASIC provides for concise loop definition with the FOR and NEXT statements. The FOR statement tells the computer how many times to execute the loop. The NEXT statement increments the loop variable and sends control back to the FOR statement.

■ Some rules to remember when using FOR and NEXT loops follow:

1. The initial value must be less than or equal to the terminal value when using a positive step value.
2. The step value can be negative. If it is, the initial value must be greater than or equal to the terminal value.
3. The step value should never be 0; this would cause the computer to loop endlessly.
4. Transfer can be made from one statement to another within a loop. However, transfer from a statement within a loop to the FOR statement is illegal.
5. The value of the loop variable should not be modified by program statements within the loop.
6. The initial, terminal, and step expressions can be composed of any valid numeric variable, constant, or mathematical formula.
7. Each FOR statement must be accompanied by an associated NEXT statement.
8. FOR and NEXT loops can be nested.
9. The NEXT statement of the inner loop must come before the NEXT statement of the outer loop.

REVIEW QUESTIONS

1. Give the two steps followed by the computer when it encounters a FOR statement.
2. What are the four steps followed by the computer when it encounters a NEXT statement?
3. Transfer can be made from one statement to another within a loop. True or false?
4. Name two things to be careful not to do when nesting FOR/NEXT loops.

DEBUGGING EXERCISES

```
1.  10 FOR I = 1 TO 20 STEP -2
    15    READ N
    20    IF N > 15 THEN 10
    25    PRINT N
    30 NEXT I
```

```
2. 10 FOR J = 1 TO 5
   15    FOR K = 3 TO 9
   20       LET J = J + 2
   25    NEXT J
   30 NEXT K
```

PROGRAMMING PROBLEMS

1. Write a program which will read in a list of ten names and print each one after it is read. Use a FOR/NEXT loop. Here is the list of names.

JOHN	CANDY
KAREN	ROBERT
EDWARD	MIKE
DAVID	JOSE
TONYA	LISA

2. The Home Economics Department needs a program which will display in a horizontal bar graph the number of students enrolled in each nutrition class, sections 210 through 219. Use the following data.

SECTION NUMBER	NUMBER of STUDENTS
210	33
211	23
212	36
213	29
214	25
215	10
216	18
217	28
218	24
219	33

Your output should have the following format:

```
                        CLASS ENROLLMENT
SECTION
NUMBER                  STUDENTS
              1       10      20      30
210           ********************************
211              .
212
213              .
214
215              .
216
217              .
218
219           **************************************
```

OVERVIEW

BASIC has numerous built-in functions that perform specific mathematical operations, such as finding the square root of a number or generating random numbers. These functions are useful to the programmer, who is spared the necessity of writing the sequence of statements otherwise needed to perform these operations. At other times, however, it may be useful for the programmer to define a function to meet the particular needs of an application. This section discusses these two tools: library functions (also called **built-in,** or **predefined functions**) and user-defined functions.

LIBRARY FUNCTIONS

Table VII–1 lists the ANSI standard library functions found on most systems. The functions have been built into the BASIC language because many applications require these types of mathematical operations. The functions are included in the BASIC language library, where they can be referred to easily—hence, the name **library functions.**

The general format for referencing a library function is as follows:

function name(argument)

In the function references in Table VII–1, the variable X is used as the **argument.** In BASIC, the argument of a function can be a constant, a variable, a mathematical expression, or another function. These functions are used in place of constants, variables, or expressions in BASIC statements such as PRINT, LET, and IF/THEN.

Trigonometric Functions

The first four library functions in Table VII–1—SIN(X), COS(X), TAN(X), and ATN(X)—are trigonometric functions, which are very useful in mathematics, engineering, and scientific applications. They use radian measures of angles, since computers find them easier to understand than degrees. People, however, prefer to use degrees. The following examples show how to convert from one unit to the other:

Table VII–1 ▪ **Common ANSI Standard Library Functions**

FUNCTION	PURPOSE
SIN(X)	Trigonometric sine function, X in radians
COS(X)	Trigonometric cosine function, X in radians
TAN(X)	Trigonometric tangent function, X in radians
ATN(X)	Trigonometric arc tangent function, X in radians
LOG(X)	Natural logarithm function
EXP(X)	e raised to the X power
SQR(X)	Square root of X
INT(X)	Greatest integer less than X
SGN(X)	Sign of X
ABS(X)	Absolute value of X
RND	Random number between 0 and 1

$$1 \text{ radian} = 57.29578 \text{ degrees}$$

$$N \text{ radians} = N * 57.29578 \text{ degrees}$$

To convert 2.5 radians to degrees, multiply 2.5 by 57.29578. The product is about 143 degrees.

$$1 \text{ degree} = 0.01745 \text{ radians}$$

$$N \text{ degrees} = N * 0.01745 \text{ radians}$$

To convert 180 degrees to radians, multiply 180 by 0.01745. The result is 3.14 radians (exactly equal to π).

Exponentiation Functions

The LOG(X), EXP(X), and SQR(X) functions deal with raising a number to a particular power.

EXP(X)

The exponential, or EXP(X), function makes the calculation EXP(X) = e^x. The constant e is equal to 2.718. We will not dwell on e, but it is useful in advanced topics in science, mathematics, and business statistics.

LOG(X)

The **natural logarithm,** or LOG(X), function is the reverse of the EXP(X) function. For example, if X = e^y, then LOG(X) = Y. In other words, Y (the LOG of X) is the power e is raised to in order to find X. If we know X but need Y, we can use the following BASIC statement to find it:

```
10 Y = LOG(X)
```

SQR(X)

The square root, or SQR(X), function determines the square root of an argument. In most BASIC implementations, the argument must be a positive number. For example,

X	SQR(X)
4	2
16	4
11.56	3.4

Mathematical Functions

INT(X)

The integer, or INT(X), function is used to compute the greatest integer less than or equal to the value specified as the argument. The integer function does not round a number to the nearest integer. If the argument is a positive value with digits to the right of the decimal point, the digits are truncated (cut off). For example,

X	INT(X)
8	8
5.34	5
16.9	16

Be careful when the argument is a negative number. Remember the number line:

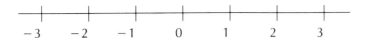

The farther left you go, the less value the number has. For example,

X	INT(X)
−2	−2
−2.5	−3
−6.3	−7

Using INT(X) to Round. Although the INT(X) function does not round by itself, it can be used in an expression that rounds to the nearest integer, tenth, hundredth, or to any degree of accuracy wanted. The program in Figure VII–1 rounds a number to its nearest dollar amount and its nearest penny amount. Since the INT(X) function returns the greatest integer less than or equal to the argument, it is necessary to add 0.5 to the argument to round to the nearest integer (see line 30). Line 40 rounds the same number to the

Figure VII–1 ▪ Rounding Program

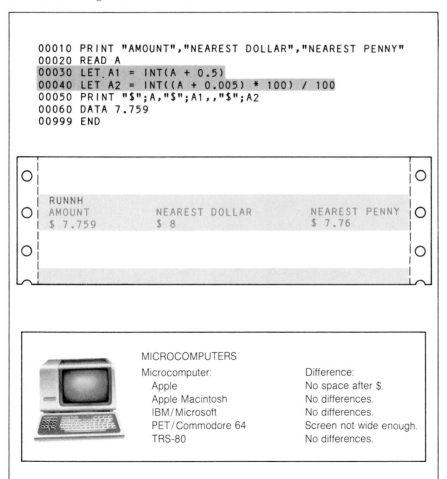

```
00010 PRINT "AMOUNT","NEAREST DOLLAR","NEAREST PENNY"
00020 READ A
00030 LET A1 = INT(A + 0.5)
00040 LET A2 = INT((A + 0.005) * 100) / 100
00050 PRINT "$";A,"$";A1,,"$";A2
00060 DATA 7.759
00999 END
```

```
RUNNH
AMOUNT          NEAREST DOLLAR        NEAREST PENNY
$ 7.759         $ 8                   $ 7.76
```

MICROCOMPUTERS

Microcomputer:	Difference:
Apple	No space after $.
Apple Macintosh	No differences.
IBM/Microsoft	No differences.
PET/Commodore 64	Screen not wide enough.
TRS-80	No differences.

nearest hundredth. We add 0.005 to N and then multiply that result by 100. The INT(X) function is then applied, and the result is divided by 100.

SGN(X)

The sign, or SGN(X), function yields one of three possible values. If $X > 0$, SGN(X) = +1; if $X = 0$, SGN(X) = 0; and if $X < 0$, SGN(X) = −1. For example,

X	SGN(X)
8.34	+1
0	0
−3.5	−1
0.5	+1

This function might be used to quickly identify when a sales representative has gone over his or her allotted amount of travel expenses (15 percent of sales), as shown in Figure VII–2. After the salesperson's name, sales, and

Figure VII–2 ▪ Travel Expense Program

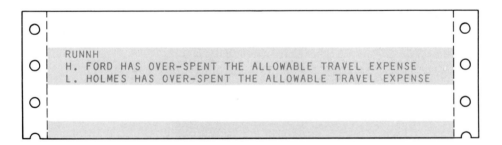

```
00010 LET T = 3
00020 FOR I = 1 TO T
00030    READ S$,S,E
00040    LET A = S * .15
00050    LET D = A - E
00060    IF SGN(D) > −1 THEN 80
00070    PRINT S$;" HAS OVER-SPENT THE ALLOWABLE TRAVEL EXPENSE"
00080 NEXT I
00090 DATA S. MANDELL,500,35
00100 DATA H. FORD,650,100
00110 DATA L. HOLMES,725,175
00999 END
```

```
RUNNH
H. FORD HAS OVER-SPENT THE ALLOWABLE TRAVEL EXPENSE
L. HOLMES HAS OVER-SPENT THE ALLOWABLE TRAVEL EXPENSE
```

MICROCOMPUTERS

Microcomputer:	Difference:
Apple	No differences.
Apple Macintosh	No differences.
IBM/Microsoft	No differences.
PET/Commodore 64	No differences.
TRS-80	No differences.

travel expenses are read, the computer calculates the allotted expenditure and then checks to see whether the balance between the allotted expenditure and the actual expenses is negative (line 60). If the balance is negative, the computer prints the overdrawn message; otherwise, the next salesperson's name is read.

ABS(X)

The absolute value, or ABS(X), function returns the absolute value of the argument. The absolute value is always positive, even if the argument is a negative value. For example,

X	ABS(X)
−2	2
0	0
3.54	3.54
−2.68	2.68

We can use this function to identify all values that differ from a given value. For example, a bank may want to know which individuals have large deposits or have loans. Figure VII–3 shows how the absolute value function

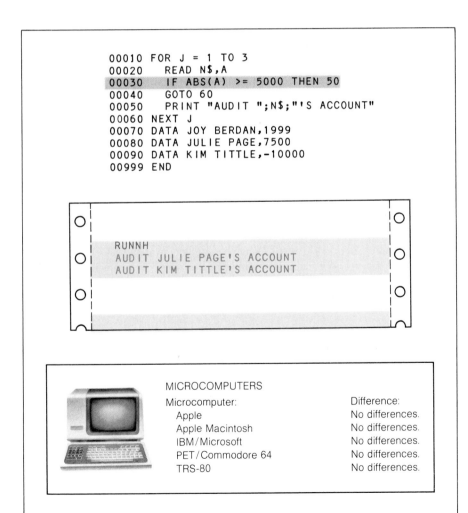

Figure VII–3 ■ Audit Search Program

```
00010 FOR J = 1 TO 3
00020    READ N$,A
00030    IF ABS(A) >= 5000 THEN 50
00040    GOTO 60
00050    PRINT "AUDIT ";N$;"'S ACCOUNT"
00060 NEXT J
00070 DATA JOY BERDAN,1999
00080 DATA JULIE PAGE,7500
00090 DATA KIM TITTLE,-10000
00999 END
```

```
RUNNH
AUDIT JULIE PAGE'S ACCOUNT
AUDIT KIM TITTLE'S ACCOUNT
```

MICROCOMPUTERS

Microcomputer:	Difference:
Apple	No differences.
Apple Macintosh	No differences.
IBM/Microsoft	No differences.
PET/Commodore 64	No differences.
TRS-80	No differences.

might be used to help identify these individuals. Line 30 tests for users who either deposited at least $5,000 or are being loaned at least $5,000.

RND

The randomize, or RND, function is used to generate a random number between 0 and 1. The term random means that any value between 0 and 1 is equally likely to occur. This function is especially important in applications involving statistics, computer simulations, and games. Some systems require that the RND function be used with an argument; other systems do not (see the "Random Numbers" box).

We can use the RND function to generate numbers greater than 1 by using it with other mathematical operations (see Figure VII– 4). Suppose we need a random number between 1 and 10 instead of between 0 and 1. Line 30 in Figure VII– 4 computes a random number between N1 (the lower limit in a selected range) and N2 (the upper limit in the range).

Lines 10 and 20 set N1 to 1 and N2 to 10. In line 30, the computer subtracts N2 from N1. The result is multiplied by a random number generated by the RND function. Finally, that product is added to N2.

USER-DEFINED FUNCTIONS

The definition (DEF) statement can be used by the programmer to define a function not already included in the BASIC language. Once the function has been defined, the programmer can refer to it as a function when necessary.

BASIC Extensions
CINT Function

The Apple Macintosh and the IBM/Microsoft allow the use of the CINT function which is useful when rounding. The format of the CINT function is shown below:

$$\text{line \# } Y = CINT(X)$$

The CINT function converts X to an integer by rounding the fraction portion of the number. X must be within the range of -32768 to 32767 or else an overflow error will occur.

An example of the CINT function is shown below.

```
10 PRINT "NUMBER","INTEGER"
20 FOR I = 1 TO 3
30    READ N
40    LET C = CINT(N)
50    PRINT N,C
60 NEXT I
70 DATA 5.2980734,778.98,64.5
99 END

RUN
NUMBER          INTEGER
 5.298073        5
 778.98          779
 64.5            65
```

Figure VII–4 ▪ Random Number Program

```
00010 LET N1 = 1
00020 LET N2 = 10
00030 LET R = RND * (N1 - N2) + N2
00040 PRINT R,N1,N2
00999 END


RUNNH
 8.246632        1                10
```

The DEF statement can be placed anywhere in the program before the first reference to the function. Its general format is as follows:

line# DEF function name(argument) = expression

The function name consists of the letters FN followed by any one of the twenty-six alphabetic characters. There can be only one argument. However, an argument is not required within the DEF statement. The expression can contain any mathematical operations desired, although a function definition cannot exceed one line.

When the computer encounters line 10 in the following program, it stores in memory the definition for the function FNR. Line 20 initializes T to 7. When the computer encounters line 30, it uses the definition for FNR and substitutes the value of T, which in this case is 7, for N in the expression (N * 2) + 5. The printed result is 19:

```
00010 DEF FNR(N) = (N * 2) + 5
00020 LET T = 7
00030 PRINT FNR(T)

RUNNH
 19
```

Line 10 in Figure VII–5 defines a function to round a number multiplied by 0.25 to the nearest hundredth and then to add 150 to the result. After the

Figure VII–5 ▪ Calculating Packaging Expense

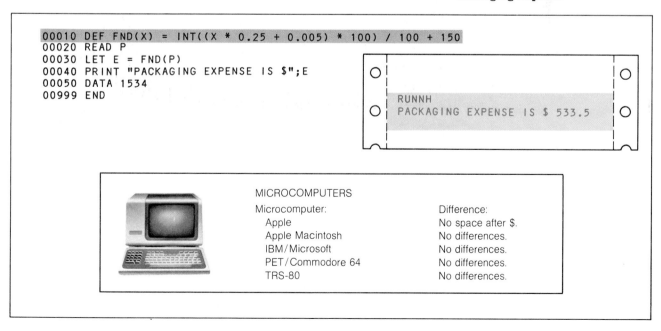

```
00010 DEF FND(X) = INT((X * 0.25 + 0.005) * 100) / 100 + 150
00020 READ P
00030 LET E = FND(P)
00040 PRINT "PACKAGING EXPENSE IS $";E
00050 DATA 1534
00999 END
```

```
RUNNH
PACKAGING EXPENSE IS $ 533.5
```

MICROCOMPUTERS

Microcomputer:	Difference:
Apple	No space after $.
Apple Macintosh	No differences.
IBM/Microsoft	No differences.
PET/Commodore 64	No differences.
TRS-80	No differences.

Random Numbers

At first it might not seem hard to make up numbers whose values are arrived at only by chance. However, this task is difficult for machines with precise structure and logic (such as computers). The various computer manufacturers use different methods for obtaining random numbers. You can obtain random numbers between 0 and 1 using each of our computers as follows.

DECSYSTEM 20

Two statements are needed with the DECSYSTEM 20 computer. The RND function needs no argument. The function used alone will give the same numbers each time a program is run; therefore, they are not truly random. Once you know that a program works the way you want it to, you should precede the statement containing RND by a RANDOMIZE statement. Now each time the program runs, RND will give a different unpredictable number. An example follows:

```
00050 RANDOMIZE

00090 LET Y = RND
```

APPLE

Only one statement is needed with the Apple microcomputer. The RND function needs an argument. A positive argument will return a random real number greater than or equal to 0 and less than 1. For example,

```
10 LET Y = RND(17)
```

If the argument is 0,

```
10 LET Y = RND(0)
```

the most recently generated random number will be returned. A negative argument generates a particular random number that is the same every time RND is used with that argument. If an RND statement with a positive argument follows an RND statement with a negative argument, it will generate a particular, repeatable sequence of random numbers.

value for the number of boxes packaged has been read, the computer is instructed to calculate the packaging expense and round it to the nearest hundredth. This is accomplished by substituting the result of P for X in the expression defined in line 10. The result is then printed out.

A PROGRAMMING PROBLEM

Problem Definition

Honesty Realty, Inc. rents apartments to college students. The apartments need new carpeting, and you have been asked to write a program to determine how many square yards of carpeting are needed. The apartment manager has given you the length and the width of each room in a standard apartment in feet.

Random Numbers

IBM/MICROSOFT

Two statements are needed to give a truly random result with the IBM/Microsoft microcomputer (works similar to the RND function on the DECSYSTEM 20). The argument for RND is optional. An example follows:

```
10 RANDOMIZE
20 PRINT RND
```

When the program is run, the computer prompts you with: Random number seed (−32768 to 32767)? You must enter a number within this range. Then the processing will continue.

PET/COMMODORE 64

Two statements are needed to give a truly random result with the PET/Commodore 64 microcomputer. The function RND needs an argument. RND(0) and RND(−N) should precede the use of RND(N). In other words, RND(0) and RND(−N) work much as RANDOMIZE does on the DECSYSTEM 20.
An examples follows:

```
10 LET X = RND(-RND(0))
```

```
70 LET X = RND(2)
```

Now X should be a valid random number. Line 40 "seeds" the random number generator.

TRS-80

Two statements are needed with the TRS-80 microcomputer. An argument is needed for RND (you should use 0 to get a number between 0 and 1). An example follows:

```
40 RANDOM
```

```
90 LET Y = RND(0)
```

Solution Design

Since we know the length and the width of each room, we can use the following formula to calculate the area in square feet:

$$\text{Area} = \text{Length} * \text{Width}$$

The next step is to convert the area in square feet into the area in square yards. This is done by dividing the area in square feet by 9 (the number of square feet in a square yard). We can define a function to do this as follows:

$$\text{FNA(Area)} = \text{Area} / 9$$

The last step is to add the area of each room to give the total area of the apartment.

The Program

Line 100 of the program in Figure VII–6 defines a function, FNA, to convert square feet into square yards. The next several lines print the headings. Line

Figure VII–6 ▪ **Area of Room Program, Flowchart, and Pseudocode (Continued on Facing Page)**

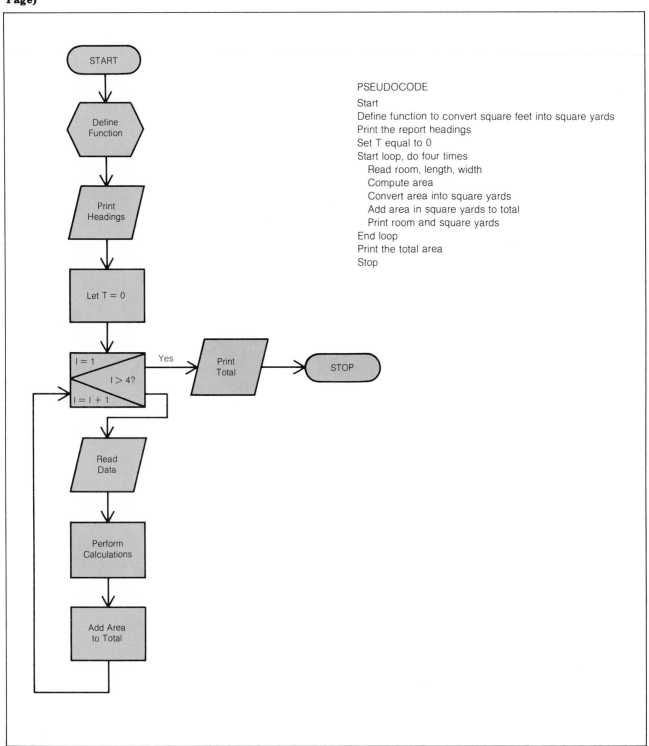

PSEUDOCODE

Start
Define function to convert square feet into square yards
Print the report headings
Set T equal to 0
Start loop, do four times
   Read room, length, width
   Compute area
   Convert area into square yards
   Add area in square yards to total
   Print room and square yards
End loop
Print the total area
Stop

Figure VII–6 ▪ **Continued**

```
00010 REM **************************************************
00020. REM *** THIS PROGRAM CALCULATES THE SQUARE YARDS ***
00030 REM ***           TO CARPET AN APARTMENT          ***
00040 REM **************************************************
00050 DATA LIVING ROOM,20,15,BEDROOM,17.5,12.5
00060 DATA DINING ROOM,15,10,BATHROOM,10,7
00070 REM **************************************************
00080 REM *** FUNCTION CONVERTS SQ FEET INTO SQ YARDS ***
00090 REM **************************************************
00100 DEF FNA(X) = X / 9
00110 PRINT
00120 PRINT
00130 PRINT "ROOM","SQUARE YARDS"
00140 PRINT
00150 LET T = 0
00160 REM **************************************************
00170 REM ***           THE LOOP BEGINS HERE            ***
00180 REM **************************************************
00190 FOR I = 1 TO 4
00200    READ R$,L,W
00210    LET A = L * W
00220    LET S = INT(FNA(A)) + 1
00230    LET T = T + S
00240    PRINT R$,S
00250    PRINT
00260 REM **************************************************
00270 REM ***           THE LOOP ENDS HERE              ***
00280 REM **************************************************
00290 NEXT I
00300 PRINT "TOTAL AREA  =",T;" SQUARE YARDS"
00999 END
```

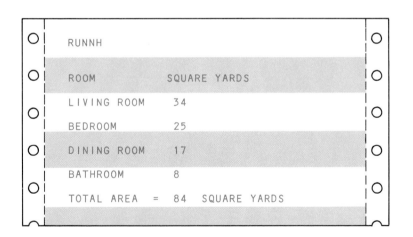

```
RUNNH

ROOM              SQUARE YARDS

LIVING ROOM       34

BEDROOM           25

DINING ROOM       17

BATHROOM          8

TOTAL AREA  =  84  SQUARE YARDS
```

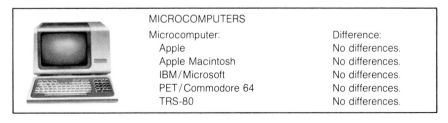

MICROCOMPUTERS

Microcomputer:	Difference:
Apple	No differences.
Apple Macintosh	No differences.
IBM/Microsoft	No differences.
PET/Commodore 64	No differences.
TRS-80	No differences.

190 initiates the FOR/NEXT loop that reads the data, calculates the area in square feet, converts the area into square yards, and then prints the results. In line 220, the programmer refers to FNA to convert the area in square feet into square yards. Also, line 220 adds 1 to the area in order to ensure that there will be enough carpeting for each room. Line 290 marks the end of the FOR/NEXT loop. Line 300 prints the total.

SUMMARY POINTS

- The BASIC language includes several library functions that can make complicated mathematical operations easier to program.
- The trigonometric functions are SIN(X), COS(X), TAN(X), and ATN(X).
- The exponentiation functions are EXP(X), LOG(X), and SQR(X).
- Other mathematical functions are INT(X), SGN(X), ABS(X), and RND.
- It is also possible for the programmer to define functions by using the DEF statement.

REVIEW QUESTIONS

1. What are library functions?
2. What are the four trigonometric functions? When are angles used as an argument to one of the four functions? What unit of measure is used?
3. What are the three exponentiation functions and what does each function do?
4. List the four mathematical functions. What does each function do?
5. Give the general format of a user-defined function. What does the function name consist of and where are user-defined functions located in a program?

DEBUGGING EXERCISES

```
1. 10 REM ***           GENERATE A RANDOM NUMBER           ***
   15 REM ***              BETWEEN 5 AND 15                ***
   20 LET R = RND


2. 10 LET R = FNAB(Y)
   15 REM ***           FUNCTION TO ROUND NUMBER           ***
   20 REM ***               NEAREST TENTH                  ***
   25 FNAB(X) = INT ((X + 0.005) * 100) / 100
```

PROGRAMMING PROBLEMS

1. Write a program which calculates the square roots and natural logarithms of the numbers from 1 to 10. Round each number to three decimal places. The output should have the following format.

NUMBER	SQUARE ROOT	NATURAL LOGARITHM
1	XX.XXX	XX.XXX
2	.	.
3	.	.
	.	.
10	XX.XXX	XX.XXX

2. Write a program to print a table giving the sine, cosine, and tangent of the following angles: 15, 30, 45, 60, 75, and 90 degrees. (Note: 1 degree = 0.01745 radians.) The table should be in the following format:

ANGLE	SINE	COSINE	TANGENT
15	XX.XX	XX.XX	XX.XX
30	.	.	.
.	.	.	.
.	.	.	.
90	XX.XX	XX.XX	XX.XX

SECTION VIII

Subroutines and String Functions

OVERVIEW

Sometimes it is necessary to have the computer execute an identical sequence of instructions at several different points in a program. The programmer need not write the set of instructions over and over again; instead, it can be placed in a subroutine. A subroutine is a sequence of statements, typically located at the end of the main program body; it performs a particular function and may be used in several different parts of the main program. By doing this, the instructions need only be written once.

For example, oil prices are expected to increase by 10 percent. A local gas station would like a report that lists the type of gasoline, its price now, and its expected selling price after the 10 percent increase. When writing the solution to this problem, we find that the same procedure is needed to round today's prices (since gasoline prices are usually carried to four decimal places) and tomorrow's expected prices. Instead of writing this rounding procedure two different times, we have written a subroutine that will be executed twice for each type of gasoline. The program will transfer control to the subroutine and back to the main program through the use of two statements: GOSUB and RETURN. These statements, along with the STOP statement and the string functions, will be discussed in this section.

THE GOSUB STATEMENT

The GOSUB statement is used to transfer the flow of control from the main logic of a program to a subroutine. The general format of the GOSUB statement is as follows:

line# GOSUB line#

The line number following GOSUB identifies the first statement of the subroutine.

The GOSUB statement is something like an unconditional GOTO statement. The difference is that the GOSUB command also makes the computer remember where to return after the subroutine has been executed. Here is a typical example of a GOSUB statement:

```
00170 GOSUB 750
```

Figure VIII–1 uses GOSUB statements in lines 210 and 270. Notice the line number of the subroutine. Subroutines often are assigned distinctive line numbers so that they are easier to locate. Although subroutines may be placed anywhere in a program, they are usually at the end, with a line number quite a bit higher than the line numbers in the main program. This leaves sufficient room for statements to be added to the main program.

THE RETURN STATEMENT

After processing within a subroutine has been completed, control must be transferred back to the main logic flow of the program. That is accomplished by the RETURN statement. The general format of the RETURN statement is as follows:

line# RETURN

Figure VIII–1 ▪ **Calculating Gas Prices (Continued on Next Page)**

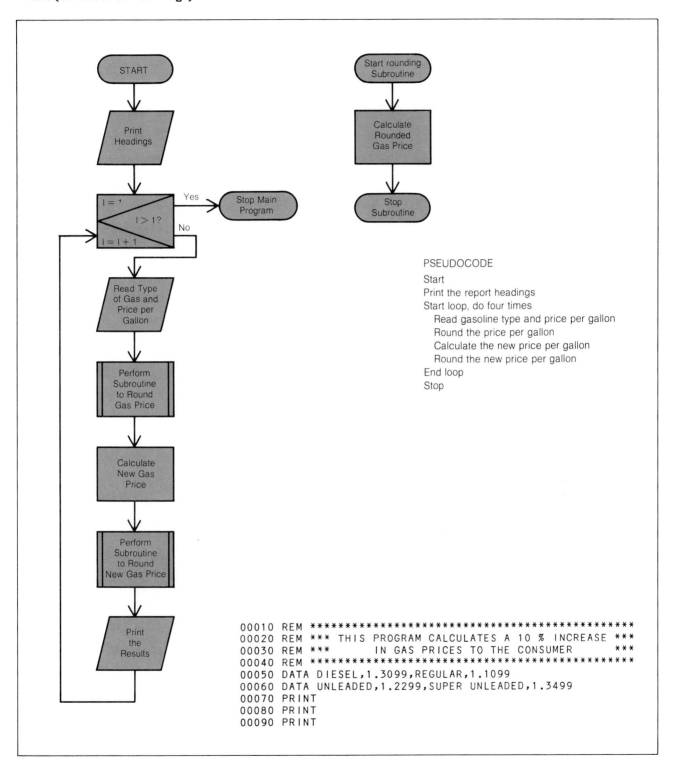

PSEUDOCODE

Start
Print the report headings
Start loop, do four times
   Read gasoline type and price per gallon
   Round the price per gallon
   Calculate the new price per gallon
   Round the new price per gallon
End loop
Stop

```
00010 REM ****************************************************
00020 REM *** THIS PROGRAM CALCULATES A 10 % INCREASE ***
00030 REM ***      IN GAS PRICES TO THE CONSUMER      ***
00040 REM ****************************************************
00050 DATA DIESEL,1.3099,REGULAR,1.1099
00060 DATA UNLEADED,1.2299,SUPER UNLEADED,1.3499
00070 PRINT
00080 PRINT
00090 PRINT
```

Figure VIII–1 ▪ **Continued**

```
00100 PRINT "TYPE OF GASOLINE";TAB(20);"PRICE PER GALLON";TAB(40);"NEW PRICE"
00110 PRINT
00120 REM ********************************************
00130 REM ***           LOOP BEGINS HERE          ***
00140 REM ********************************************
00150 FOR I = 1 TO 4
00160    READ G$,P
00170    REM ********************************************
00180    REM ***           ROUND PRICE            ***
00190    REM ********************************************
00200    LET X = P
00210    GOSUB 1000
00220    LET N1 = N
00230    REM ********************************************
00240    REM ***      DETERMINE NEW GAS PRICE       ***
00250    REM ********************************************
00260    LET X = P * 1.1
00270    GOSUB 1000
00280    PRINT G$;TAB(25);N1;TAB(41);N
00290    REM ********************************************
00300    REM ***           LOOP ENDS HERE         ***
00310    REM ********************************************
00320 NEXT I
00330 STOP
01000 REM ********************************************
01100 REM ***   SUBROUTINE TO ROUND THE GAS PRICES   ***
01300 REM ********************************************
01400 LET N = INT((X + 0.005) * 100) / 100
01500 RETURN
09999 END
```

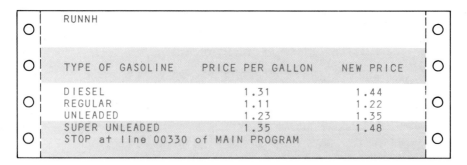

```
RUNNH


TYPE OF GASOLINE      PRICE PER GALLON      NEW PRICE

DIESEL                    1.31               1.44
REGULAR                   1.11               1.22
UNLEADED                  1.23               1.35
SUPER UNLEADED            1.35               1.48
STOP at line 00330 of MAIN PROGRAM
```

MICROCOMPUTERS

Microcomputer:	Difference:
Apple	Break in 330; output must be reformatted.
Apple Macintosh	Break in 330.
IBM/Microsoft	Break in 330.
PET/Commodore 64	Break in 330; output must be reformatted.
TRS-80	Break in 330.

No line number need follow RETURN, because the BASIC interpreter remembers to return to the statement immediately following the most recently executed GOSUB statement. For example,

```
00100 GOSUB 1000
00110 PRINT T
      :
      :
01000 REM *** SUBROUTINE ***
      :
      :
01100 RETURN
```

The RETURN statement in line 1100 sends control back to the instruction following the GOSUB statement that called the subroutine, so the RETURN statement in line 1100 sends the computer back to line 110. The RETURN statement in line 1500 of Figure VIII–1 will return control to line 220 if the subroutine was called in line 210. If the subroutine was called in line 270, control will be returned to line 280.

THE STOP STATEMENT

The STOP statement halts execution of a program; it is placed wherever a logical end to a program should occur. The general format of the STOP statement follows:

line# STOP

The STOP statement differs from the END statement in that STOP can appear as often as necessary in a program, whereas the END statement can appear only once and must have the highest line number in the program.

Using STOP with Subroutines

One of the major uses of the STOP statement is with subroutines. For convenience, subroutines generally are placed near the end of a program, but the subroutine may be referred to several times in the program. A STOP statement usually is placed just before the beginning of the first subroutine to prevent unnecessary execution of the subroutine when the computer comes to the logical end of the program. Figure VIII–1 illustrates how the STOP statement is used before subroutines (line 330).

Using STOP with Exception Handling

Many programs contain **exception-handling instructions.** These sequences of statements help the computer prevent the input of invalid data, which is referred to as a **garbage in–garbage out error.** The STOP statement can be used to stop execution of a program after such a sequence has been executed.

Figure VIII–2 calculates the square root of a number. Since the computer can find the square root of positive numbers only, the program includes an exception-handling instruction in line 120. If the user of the program enters a number less than or equal to 0, the computer will branch to line 250, print an error message, and stop processing. Notice that this program also contains a stop statement in line 210; this is the logical end of the main program. In lines 180 through 200, the user is directed to input YES to continue finding the square roots of numbers. If the user does not wish to continue finding the

Figure VIII–2 ▪ **Exception Handling (Continued on Facing Page)**

```
00010 REM **********************************
00020 REM ***    ABNORMAL STOP PROGRAM    ***
00030 REM **********************************
00040 PRINT
00050 PRINT "THIS PROGRAM RETURNS THE SQUARE ROOT OF A NUMBER"
00060 PRINT
00070 PRINT "ENTER A NUMBER WHOSE SQUARE ROOT YOU WANT"
00080 INPUT N
00090 REM **********************************
00100 REM *** TEST FOR ZERO OR NEGATIVE ***
00110 REM **********************************
00120 IF N <= 0 THEN 250
00130 LET S = SQR(N)
00140 PRINT
00150 PRINT
00160 PRINT "THE SQUARE ROOT OF ";N;" IS ";S
00170 PRINT
00180 PRINT "DO YOU WANT TO TRY AGAIN? (YES OR NO)"
00190 INPUT C$
00200 IF C$ = "YES" THEN 60
00210 STOP
00220 REM **********************************
00230 REM ***     PRINT ERROR MESSAGE    ***
00240 REM **********************************
00250 PRINT "YOU HAVE ATTEMPTED TO TAKE THE"
00260 PRINT "SQUARE ROOT OF ZERO OR A NEGATIVE NUMBER"
00270 STOP
00999 END
```

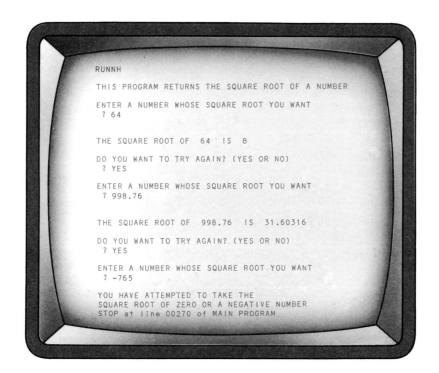

```
RUNNH

THIS PROGRAM RETURNS THE SQUARE ROOT OF A NUMBER

ENTER A NUMBER WHOSE SQUARE ROOT YOU WANT
? 64


THE SQUARE ROOT OF  64  IS  8

DO YOU WANT TO TRY AGAIN? (YES OR NO)
? YES

ENTER A NUMBER WHOSE SQUARE ROOT YOU WANT
? 998.76


THE SQUARE ROOT OF  998.76  IS  31.60316

DO YOU WANT TO TRY AGAIN? (YES OR NO)
? YES

ENTER A NUMBER WHOSE SQUARE ROOT YOU WANT
? -765

YOU HAVE ATTEMPTED TO TAKE THE
SQUARE ROOT OF ZERO OR A NEGATIVE NUMBER
STOP at line 00270 of MAIN PROGRAM
```

MICROCOMPUTERS

Microcomputer:	Difference:
Apple	Break in 270; output must be reformatted.
Apple Macintosh	Break in 270.
IBM/Microsoft	Break in 270.
PET/Commodore 64	Break in 270; output must be reformatted.
TRS-80	Break in 270.

Figure VIII–2 ▪ Continued

square roots of numbers, he or she types NO, and program execution ends. The STOP statement prevents subsequent lines from being executed (and thus prevents the error message from being printed unnecessarily).

STRING FUNCTIONS

Up to this point, we have manipulated numbers but have done little with strings except print them out or compare them in IF and THEN tests. Many business applications require more sophisticated manipulations of strings.

A string is simply a series of alphanumeric characters such as %#$Z, HONEYWELL, or TED. Usually, BASIC requires that quotation marks be placed around strings.

BASIC string functions allow programmers to modify, **concatenate** (join together), compare, and analyze the composition of strings. These functions are useful for sorting lists of names, finding out subject matter in text, printing mailing lists, and so forth. For example, we can help the computer understand that Franklin Oswald III is the same as Oswald III, Franklin. The most common string functions are listed in Table VIII–1.

Table VIII–1 ▪ String Functions

BASIC STRING FUNCTION	OPERATION	EXAMPLE
string 1$ + string 2$	Concatenates; joins two string together	KUNG + FU is KUNGFU
LEN(string)	Finds the length of a string	If H$ is HELLO HOWARD, then LEN(H$) is 12
LEFT$(string,expression)	Returns the number of leftmost characters of a string specified by the expression	LEFT$("ABCDE",2) is AB
RIGHT$(string,expression)	Returns the rightmost characters of a string, starting with the character specified by the expression	RIGHT$("ABCDE",2) is BCDE
MID$(string,expression 1, expression 2)	Starting with the character at expression 1, returns the number of characters specified by expression 2	MID$("ABCDE",3,2) is CD
ASCII(string)	Returns the ASCII code for the first character in the string	If A$ contains DOG, then ASCII(A$) is 68
CHR$(expression)	Returns the string representation of the ASCII code of the expression	If CHR$(F$) > Z, then 20
VAL(expression)	Returns the numeric equivalent of the string expression	X = VAL (H$)
STR$(expression)	Converts a number to its string equivalent	STR$(123) is 123

The Concatenation Function

It is possible to join strings together using the concatenation function. In business this is often desirable when working with names or addresses. The program in Figure VIII–3 demonstrates what happens.

The LEN Function

The LEN function returns the number of characters in the string. An example of how the LEN function might be used is given in Figure VIII–4. In this example, if the value in C$ is less than ten characters long, we do not wish

Figure VIII–3 ▪ Concatenation

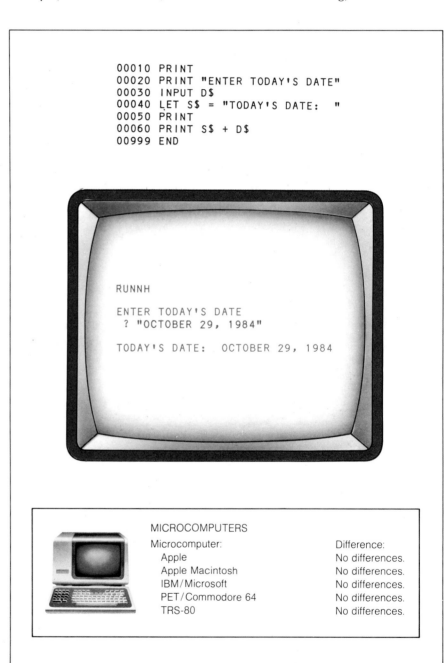

```
00010 PRINT
00020 PRINT "ENTER TODAY'S DATE"
00030 INPUT D$
00040 LET S$ = "TODAY'S DATE:   "
00050 PRINT
00060 PRINT S$ + D$
00999 END
```

```
RUNNH

ENTER TODAY'S DATE
 ? "OCTOBER 29, 1984"

TODAY'S DATE:   OCTOBER 29, 1984
```

MICROCOMPUTERS

Microcomputer:	Difference:
Apple	No differences.
Apple Macintosh	No differences.
IBM/Microsoft	No differences.
PET/Commodore 64	No differences.
TRS-80	No differences.

to know the length of the string. Otherwise, we wish to know the length of the string.

The LEFT$ and RIGHT$ Functions

The LEFT$ function returns the number of characters specified in the argument, starting from the beginning of the string. The RIGHT$ function returns a substring, which starts with the character specified by the expression. The LEFT$ and RIGHT$ functions are illustrated in Figure VIII–5. In this example, the computer stores a character string in G$. Line 20 tells the computer to print the first seven characters of G$. Line 30 tells the computer to start printing with the twentieth character. The microcomputer handles the RIGHT$ function differently than the DECSYSTEM20. On the microcomputers, the instruction

```
30 PRINT RIGHT$(G$,20)
```

instructs the computer to print the last twenty characters of the string. The output would look like this:

```
THE SUN
SUN IS SHINING TODAY
THE SUN IS SHINING TODAY
```

Figure VIII–4 ▪ The LEN Function

```
00010 PRINT "ENTER ANY STRING LARGER THAN 10 CHARACTERS"
00020 INPUT C$
00030 IF LEN(C$) < 10 THEN 80
00040 PRINT
00050 PRINT
00060 PRINT "THE LENGTH OF ";C$;" IS ";LEN(C$);" CHARACTERS"
00070 STOP
00080 PRINT "THE LENGTH OF ";C$;" IS LESS THAN 10 CHARACTERS"
00999 END



RUNNH
ENTER ANY STRING LARGER THAN 10 CHARACTERS
 ? IT'S A BEAUTIFUL DAY IN THE NEIGHBORHOOD


THE LENGTH OF IT'S A BEAUTIFUL DAY IN THE NEIGHBORHOOD IS  40  CHARACTERS
STOP at line 00070 of MAIN PROGRAM
```

MICROCOMPUTERS

Microcomputer:	Difference:
Apple	Output must be reformatted.
Apple Macintosh	Output must be reformatted.
IBM/Microsoft	No differences.
PET/Commodore 64	Output must be reformatted.
TRS-80	Output must be reformatted.

```
00010 LET G$ = "THE SUN IS SHINING TODAY"
00020 PRINT LEFT$(G$,7)
00030 PRINT RIGHT$(G$,20)
00040 PRINT G$
00999 END
```

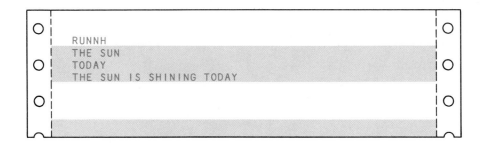

```
RUNNH
THE SUN
TODAY
THE SUN IS SHINING TODAY
```

MICROCOMPUTERS

Microcomputer:	Difference:
Apple	RIGHT$ function finds last characters of a given string. RIGHT$ (G1,20) outputs "SUN IN SHINING TODAY".
Apple Macintosh	Same as above.
IBM / Microsoft	Same as above.
PET / Commodore 64	Same as above.
TRS-80	Same as above.

Figure VIII–5 ▪ The LEFT$ and RIGHT$ Functions

The LEFT$ function is often useful when comparing character strings. Suppose a program asks the user to answer a yes or no question but does not specify whether the question should be answered by typing the entire word YES or NO or just the first letter, Y or N. We can use the LEFT$ function to compare just the first character of the user's response, allowing the user to type either YES/NO or Y/N. The program in Figure VIII– 6 illustrates this.

The MID$ Function

The MID$ function is more complicated. Here is the general format:

line#   MID$(string, expression#1, expression#2)

String Constant or Variable   Starting Point in String   Numbers of Characters to Be Returned

Figure VIII–6 ▪ Comparing Character Strings

```
00010  INPUT "ARE YOU A REGISTERED STUDENT ";C$
00020  LET C$ = LEFT$(C$,1)
00030  IF C$ = "Y" THEN 60
00040  PRINT "YOU MAY NOT USE THE RECREATION FACILITIES"
00050  GOTO 99
00060  PRINT "YOU MAY USE THE RECREATION FACILITIES"
00099  END
```

```
RUNNH
ARE YOU A REGISTERED STUDENT  ? YES
YOU MAY USE THE RECREATION FACILITIES
```

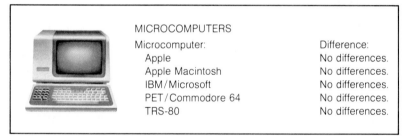

MICROCOMPUTERS

Microcomputer:	Difference:
Apple	No differences.
Apple Macintosh	No differences.
IBM/Microsoft	No differences.
PET/Commodore 64	No differences.
TRS-80	No differences.

Sometimes expression 2 is omitted; in that case, the characters—from the starting point to the end of the string—are returned. This function is useful when you want to look at a string in the middle of another string. For instance, assume you have a calendar, and you want to print out the events on May 15. Here are the dates with important events.

```
5/2/84
5/10/84
5/15/84
5/15/84
5/17/84
```

The program in Figure VIII–7 will compare the day to "15" and print the events that occurred on the fifteenth.

The ASCII and CHR$ Functions

The ASCII function returns the decimal ASCII value of the first character specified in the string argument. The argument must be a variable name. Figure VIII–8 lists characters and their corresponding ASCII value. An example is shown in Figure VIII–9.

The CHR$ function works just the opposite of the ASCII function. This function returns the character that corresponds to the decimal ASCII value. The program in Figure VIII–10 illustrates the use of the CHR$ function.

The ASCII and CHR$ functions are helpful in allowing programs to respond to both lowercase and uppercase input. By using these functions, we can write a program that will allow the user to answer a yes or no question with either y or Y and n or N. Looking at Figure VIII–8, you can see that lowercase letters range from 97 to 122, and uppercase letters range from 65 to 90. An IF/THEN statement can be used to compare the ASCII value to 96. If the value

Figure VIII–7 ▪ The MID$ Function

```
00010 FOR I = 1 TO 5
00020    READ D$,E$
00030    IF MID$(D$,3,2) = "15" THEN PRINT E$
00040 NEXT I
00050 DATA 5/2/84,SALES MEETING
00060 DATA 5/10/84,MEETING WITH PRESIDENT
00070 DATA 5/15/84,SALES MEETING
00080 DATA 5/15/84,ACQUISITION
00090 DATA 5/17/84,BUSINESS SEMINAR
00999 END
```

```
RUNNH
SALES MEETING
ACQUISITION
```

MICROCOMPUTERS

Microcomputer:	Difference:
Apple	No differences.
Apple Macintosh	No differences.
IBM/Microsoft	No differences.
PET/Commodore 64	No differences.
TRS-80	No differences.

Figure VIII–8 ▪ **ASCII Codes**

```
       32        l  33        "  34        #  35
  $  36        %  37        &  38        '  39
  (  40        )  41        *  42        +  43
  ,  44        -  45        .  46        /  47
  0  48        1  49        2  50        3  51
  4  52        5  53        6  54        7  55
  8  56        9  57        :  58        ;  59
  <  60        =  61        >  62        ?  63
  @  64        A  65        B  66        C  67
  D  68        E  69        F  70        G  71
  H  72        I  73        J  74        K  75
  L  76        M  77        N  78        O  79
  P  80        Q  81        R  82        S  83
  T  84        U  85        V  86        W  87
  X  88        Y  89        Z  90        [  91
  \  92        ]  93        ^  94           95
  `  96        a  97        b  98        c  99
  d  100       e  101       f  102       g  103
  h  104       I  105       j  106       k  107
  I  108       m  109       n  110       o  111
  p  112       q  113       r  114       s  115
  t  116       u  117       v  118       w  119
  x  120       y  121       z  122       {  123
  I  124
```

Figure VIII–9 ▪ **The ASCII Function**

```
00010 LET A$ = "]"
00020 LET B$ = "%"
00030 LET C$ = "@"
00040 LET D$ = "Q"
00050 PRINT ASCII(A$),ASCII(B$)
00060 PRINT ASCII(C$),ASCII(D$)
00999 END
```

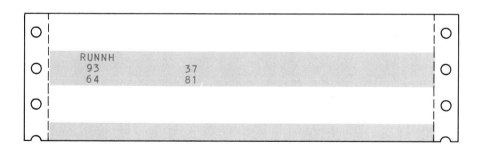

```
RUNNH
93            37
64            81
```

MICROCOMPUTERS

Microcomputer:	Difference:
Apple	Line 50:PRINT ASC(A1),ASC(B$);
	Line 60:PRINT ASC(C$),ASC(D$).
Apple Macintosh	Same as above.
IBM/Microsoft	Same as above.
PET/Commodore 64	Same as above.
TRS-80	Same as above.

**Figure VIII–10 ▪ The CHR$
Function**

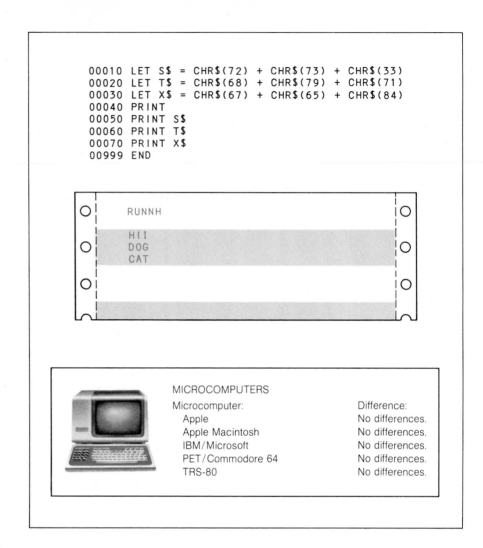

```
00010 LET S$ = CHR$(72) + CHR$(73) + CHR$(33)
00020 LET T$ = CHR$(68) + CHR$(79) + CHR$(71)
00030 LET X$ = CHR$(67) + CHR$(65) + CHR$(84)
00040 PRINT
00050 PRINT S$
00060 PRINT T$
00070 PRINT X$
00999 END
```

```
RUNNH

HII
DOG
CAT
```

MICROCOMPUTERS

Microcomputer:	Difference:
Apple	No differences.
Apple Macintosh	No differences.
IBM/Microsoft	No differences.
PET/Commodore 64	No differences.
TRS-80	No differences.

is greater than 96, a lowercase letter has been typed; if the value is less than 96, the letter is uppercase. Once you know what type of letter you have, it can be converted to either uppercase or lowercase for comparison. An uppercase letter can be changed to lowercase by adding 32 to the ASCII value, and a lowercase letter can be changed to uppercase by subtracting 32.

The program segment in Figure VIII–11 illustrates this use of the ASCII and CHR$ functions. This program segment checks the user's reply to see if it is lowercase. If it is lowercase, 32 is subtracted from the ASCII value to give the ASCII value for the uppercase of the same letter. After subtracting, CHR$ assigns the character corresponding to the ASCII value to C$. C$ then can be compared with uppercase characters.

The VAL Function

The VAL function turns a numeric string (for example, 21893074) into a number that can be used in arithmetic calculations. Figure VIII–12 illustrates this.

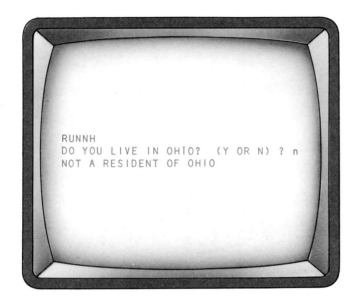

```
00010 INPUT "DO YOU LIVE IN OHIO?  (Y OR N)";C$
00020 LET X = ASCII(C$)
00030 IF X > 96 THEN C$ = CHR$(X - 32)
00040 IF C$ = "N" THEN PRINT "NOT A RESIDENT OF OHIO"
00999 END
```

```
RUNNH
DO YOU LIVE IN OHIO?  (Y OR N) ? n
NOT A RESIDENT OF OHIO
```

MICROCOMPUTERS

Microcomputer:	Difference:
Apple	00020 LET X = ASC(C$).
Apple Macintosh	Same as above.
IBM/Microsoft	Same as above.
PET/Commodore 64	Same as above.
TRS-80	Same as above.

Figure VIII–11 ▪ **Converting Lowercase Letters to Uppercase Letters**

By using the VAL function, it is possible to change the number in character string format to a real number so that the number can be used in mathematical computations. If the character string contains any nonnumeric characters, the VAL function will replace these with zeros.

The STR$ Function

The STR$ function is just the opposite of the VAL function; it converts a real number to a string. Figure VIII–13 illustrates the STR$ function. Remember that once a number has been converted to a character string, it no longer can be used in mathematical computations.

```
00010 PRINT "ENTER A NUMBER"
00020 INPUT N$
00030 LET N = VAL(N$)
00040 PRINT
00050 PRINT "THE NUMERIC STRING ";N$;" HAS BEEN CONVERTED TO A REAL NUMBER ";N
00999 END



RUNNH
ENTER A NUMBER
 ? 21893074

THE NUMERIC STRING 21893074 HAS BEEN CONVERTED TO A REAL NUMBER  2.189307E+07
```

MICROCOMPUTERS

Microcomputer:	Difference:
Apple	Real number = 21893074; Output must be reformatted.
Apple Macintosh	Real number = 21893074; Output must be reformatted.
IBM/Microsoft	Real number = 2.189308E+07.
PET/Commodore 64	Real number = 21893074; Output must be reformatted.
TRS-80	Real number = 2.18931E+07; Output must be reformatted.

Figure VIII–12 ▪ The VAL Function

A PROGRAMMING PROBLEM

The Problem

The goal in this problem is to write a program that accepts a bride's name and groom's name (see Figure VIII-14). The program's output will consist of the bride's name, the groom's name, and the bride's married name. For example:

INPUT	OUTPUT
Elizabeth Taylor	Elizabeth Taylor
Richard Burton	Richard Burton
	Elizabeth Burton

Solution Design

The process used to get the bride's married name can be outlined as follows:

1. Set up a loop to search the groom's name for a blank.
2. The string to the right of the blank is the last name.
3. Set up a loop to search the bride's name for a blank.
4. The string to the left of the blank is the first name.
5. Print the first name and the last name.

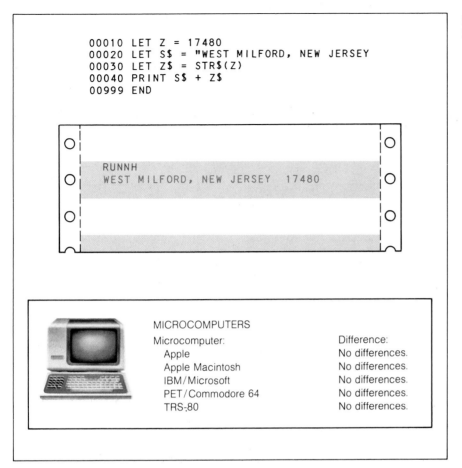

Figure VIII–13 ■ The STR$
Function

```
00010 LET Z = 17480
00020 LET S$ = "WEST MILFORD, NEW JERSEY
00030 LET Z$ = STR$(Z)
00040 PRINT S$ + Z$
00999 END
```

RUNNH
WEST MILFORD, NEW JERSEY   17480

MICROCOMPUTERS

Microcomputer:	Difference:
Apple	No differences.
Apple Macintosh	No differences.
IBM/Microsoft	No differences.
PET/Commodore 64	No differences.
TRS-80	No differences.

The Program

Lines 40 and 60 prompt the user to enter the bride's name and the groom's name. Lines 110 to 200 form a FOR/NEXT loop that searches for a blank between the groom's first and last names. The loop is set up to look at each character. The terminal value for the loop is the length of the groom's name. Line 120 looks at each character of the string and places it in R$. In this example, the first four values of I produce the following:

I	R$
1	C
2	A
3	L
4	V

Line 160 tests whether RS$ is a blank by using the CHR$ function (the ASCII code for a blank is 32). If a blank is found, line 160 sends the computer to line 240 to search for the first name. Lines 240 to 330 form a FOR/NEXT loop which searches for the first name in the same manner as the last name

BASIC SUPPLEMENT

B–119

Figure VIII–14 ▪ Married Names Program (Continued on Next Two Pages)

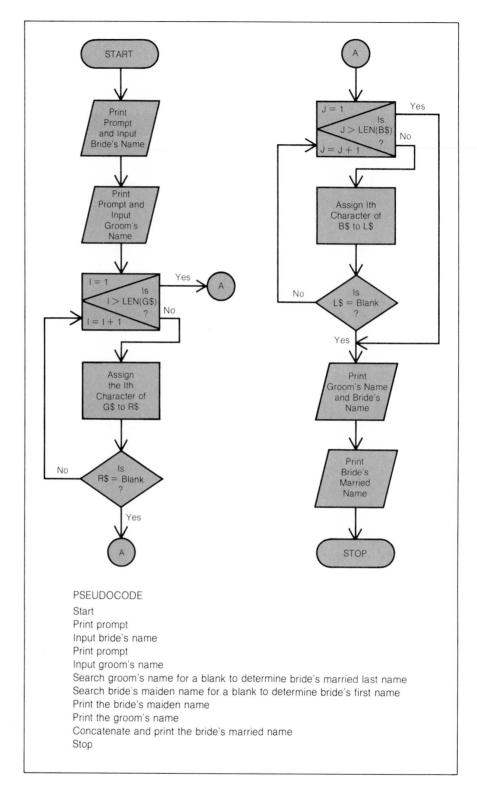

PSEUDOCODE

Start
Print prompt
Input bride's name
Print prompt
Input groom's name
Search groom's name for a blank to determine bride's married last name
Search bride's maiden name for a blank to determine bride's first name
Print the bride's maiden name
Print the groom's name
Concatenate and print the bride's married name
Stop

```
00010 REM **********************************************************
00020 REM *** PROGRAM TO PRINT OUT A BRIDE'S MARRIED NAME ***
00030 REM **********************************************************
00040 PRINT "ENTER BRIDE'S NAME"
00050 INPUT B$
00060 PRINT "ENTER GROOM'S NAME"
00070 INPUT G$
00080 REM **********************************************************
00090 REM *** SEARCH UP TO THE LENGTH OF THE GROOM'S NAME ***
00100 REM **********************************************************
00110 FOR I = 1 TO LEN(G$)
00120    LET R$ = MID$(G$,I,1)
00130    REM ****************************************************
00140    REM ***              TEST FOR BLANK              ***
00150    REM ****************************************************
00160    IF R$ = CHR$(32) THEN 240
00170    REM ****************************************************
00180    REM ***         IF NOT BLANK, THEN CONTINUE      ***
00190    REM ****************************************************
00200 NEXT I
00210 REM **********************************************************
00220 REM *** SEARCH UP TO THE LENGTH OF THE BRIDE'S NAME ***
00230 REM **********************************************************
00240 FOR J = 1 TO LEN(B$)
00250    L$ = MID$(B$,J,1)
00260    REM ****************************************************
00270    REM ***              TEST FOR BLANK              ***
00280    REM ****************************************************
00290    IF L$ = CHR$(32) THEN 370
00300    REM ****************************************************
00310    REM ***         IF NOT BLANK, THEN CONTINUE      ***
00320    REM ****************************************************
00330 NEXT J
00340 REM **********************************************************
00350 REM ***         PRINT OUT BRIDE'S MARRIED NAME         ***
00360 REM **********************************************************
00370 PRINT
00380 PRINT
00390 PRINT "BRIDE'S NAME IS ";B$
00400 PRINT "GROOM'S NAME IS ";G$
00410 PRINT
00420 PRINT "BRIDE'S MARRIED NAME IS ";LEFT$(B$,J - 1);RIGHT$(G$,I)
00999 END
```

Figure VIII–14 ▪ Continued

was found. When line 290 finds the blank between the bride's first and last name, control is sent to line 370. Lines 390 to 400 print the bride's name and the groom's name. Line 420 prints the bride's married name. Since the counter J in the second FOR/NEXT loop marks where the blank is, we use J-1 to count the number of characters in the first name of the bride's married name. The counter I in the first FOR/NEXT loop marks where the blank is, we use I to begin the RIGHT$ function for the last name of the bride's married name.

SUMMARY POINTS

▪ Two statements define a subroutine: GOSUB and RETURN.
▪ The GOSUB statement is used to transfer the flow of control from the main logic of a program to a subroutine.

```
RUNNH
ENTER BRIDE'S NAME
 ? BONNIE BELL
ENTER GROOM'S NAME
 ? CALVIN KLEIN


BRIDE'S NAME IS BONNIE BELL
GROOM'S NAME IS CALVIN KLEIN

BRIDE'S MARRIED NAME IS BONNIE KLEIN
```

MICROCOMPUTERS

Microcomputer:	Difference:
Apple	Line 420 would use RIGHT$(G$,LEN(G$) − I).
Apple Macintosh	Line 420 would use RIGHT$(G$,L(G$) − I + 1).
IBM/Microsoft	Same as Apple.
PET/Commodore 64	Same as Apple.
TRS-80	Same as Apple.

Figure VIII–14 ▪ Continued

▪ The RETURN statement transfers control from a subroutine back to the line in the main program immediately following the last GOSUB statement that was executed.

▪ The STOP statement halts execution of a program.

▪ BASIC string functions permit modification, concatenation, comparison, and analysis of the composition of strings.

REVIEW QUESTIONS

1. What is a subroutine and why is it useful?

2. What do the GOSUB and RETURN statements do? Where is the RETURN located in a program?

3. How is the STOP statement used with subroutines? What is the difference between the STOP statement and the END statement?

4. What is a string?

5. BASIC string functions allow programmers to
   a. modify strings.
   b. concatenate strings.
   c. compare strings.
   d. analyze the composition of strings.
   e. all of the above.

DEBUGGING EXERCISES

```
1.  10 READ N$,B$
    15 LET A = STR$(A$)
    20 LET A = A + 3
    25 LET A$ = VAL(A)
    30 LET C$ = B$ + A$
    35 DATA 10,30

2.  10 REM *** PRINT THE FIRST 4 CHARACTERS ***
    15 REM *** AND THE LAST 3 CHARACTERS OF A STRING ***
    20 LET A$ = "GOOD FRIDAY"
    25 PRINT LEFT(A$,4)
    30 PRINT RIGHT(A$,3)
```

PROGRAMMING PROBLEMS

1. Write a program which will use one subroutine to calculate the average number of points that the following basketball players score per game, and another subroutine to reverse the player's name so that it is in the format LASTNAME, FIRSTNAME.

PLAYER	GAME 1	GAME 2	GAME 3
Ed Miller	22	20	18
John Long	12	19	17
Joe Barros	7	3	5
Mike Hawn	15	12	12
Gary Storts	10	13	7

Your OUTPUT should include the players' names and averages with column headings.

2. Write a program to print a chart of the capital letters from A to L and their corresponding ASCII value in the following format:

CHAR	VALUE	CHAR	VALUE
A	65	B	66
.	.	.	.
.	.	.	.
.	.	.	.
K	75	L	76

OVERVIEW

So far, our programs have used simple variables such as N, C$, and T1 to represent single values. Now let us say we want to write a program that reads the weekly grocery bills for six people, calculates the average, and prints the difference between each person's weekly grocery bill and the average in the following format:

```
RUNNH
                                    DIFFERENCE
NAME            GROCERY BILL     FROM AVERAGE

F. BROCKMAN        $ 50             $ 16

T. TURNER          $ 30             $-4

G. MCMILLIAN       $ 25             $-9

J. OLSEN           $ 32             $-2

K. FISK            $ 39             $ 5

S. SPOCK           $ 28             $-6


AVERAGE WEEKLY GROCERY BILL = $ 34
```

Up to this point, we have been calculating averages by reading one value at a time into a single variable when using the READ/DATA statements and accumulating the values as they are read. In this procedure, however, each time a new value is read, the previous value stored in the variable is destroyed; thus, in the previous example, we would not be able to compare each person's grocery bill with the calculated average grocery bill. To make the comparison, each person's grocery bill would need to be stored in a separate memory location. One way of accomplishing this is by using a distinct variable name for each value. This approach will work (provided you know the number of values you will be working with beforehand) but can become cumbersome when dealing with a large number of values.

There is an easier way: BASIC permits us to deal with groups of related values as arrays. Figure IX–1 shows the coding necessary to produce the previously listed output. Array names are distinguished from simple variable names through the use of subscripts. The DIM statement tells the computer how much storage is necessary to hold an array. Arrays may be one-dimensional (sometimes called lists), two-dimensional (often called tables, or **matrices**), or of higher dimensions. A method for sorting arrays is also discussed in this section.

SUBSCRIPTS

An array is a group of storage locations in memory in which data elements can be stored. The entire array is given one name; the programmer indicates individual elements in the array by referring to their positions. The general concept is simple. Let us say there are three teachers who teach accounting classes. We would like to store the names of the teachers in an array T$. It might look like this:

```
00010 REM *********************************
00020 REM ***    GROCERY BILL PROGRAM    ***
00030 REM *********************************
00040 DIM N$(6)
00050 DIM B(6)
00060 LET T = 0
00070 FOR I = 1 TO 6
00080    READ N$(I)
00090    READ B(I)
00100    LET T = T + B(I)
00110 NEXT I
00120 LET A = T / 6
00130 PRINT " "," "," DIFFERENCE"
00140 PRINT "NAME","GROCERY BILL","FROM AVERAGE"
00150 FOR I = 1 TO 6
00160    PRINT
00170    PRINT N$(I);TAB(17);"$";B(I);TAB(31);"$";B(I) - A
00180 NEXT I
00190 PRINT
00200 PRINT
00210 PRINT "AVERAGE WEEKLY GROCERY BILL = $";A
00220 DATA F. BROCKMAN,50,T. TURNER,30
00230 DATA G. MCMILLIAN,25,J. OLSEN,32
00240 DATA K. FISK,39,S. SPOCK,28
00999 END
```

MICROCOMPUTERS

Microcomputer:	Difference:
Apple	Output must be reformatted.
Apple Macintosh	No differences.
IBM/Microsoft	No differences.
PET/Commodore 64	Output must be reformatted.
TRS-80	No differences.

Figure IX–1 ▪ Array Example

Array T$

T$(1)	ROBERT NEER
T$(2)	ANGELA LORING
T$(3)	SUSAN COOKE

We can gain access to an individual name within the array by telling the computer which position in the list it occupies. This is done through the use of subscripts. For example, Robert Neer is in the first position in the array—that is, T$(1). Angela Loring is in the second location, T$(2). Susan Cooke is in T$(3). The subscripts are enclosed in parentheses.

In BASIC, the same rules that apply to naming simple variables apply to naming arrays. Remember that only numbers can be stored in numeric variable array names, and only character strings can be stored in string variable arrays. It is good programming practice not to use the same name for both a simple variable and an array in a program.

The subscript (index) enclosed in parentheses can be any legal expression; for example, $T(Q)$, $I(15)$, and $C(X * Y)$ are valid references to array elements.

When an array element is indicated by an expression, the computer carries out the following steps:

1. It evaluates the expression inside the parentheses.
2. It translates the result to the nearest integer.
3. It accesses the indicated element in the array.

For example, if the computer encounters T(Q), it looks at the current value of Q. This value indicates the position of the desired element in array T.

Array T

10
15
16
17
32

Assume that I = 2, N = 3, and Q = 5. Then

T(I) refers to T(2)—the second element in array T, or 15.

T(N) refers to T(3)—the third element in array T, or 16.

T(I + N) refers to T(5)—the fifth element in array T, or 32.

T(Q) refers to T(5)—the fifth element in array T or 32.

References to specific elements of arrays are called **subscripted variables.** In contrast, simple variables are **unsubscripted variables.** An unsubscripted variable—say, P3—is used to refer to a single storage location named P3; the subscripted variable P(3), in contrast, represents the third item in an array called P.

THE DIM STATEMENT

When a programmer uses an array, the BASIC compiler does not automatically know how many elements the array will contain. Unless told otherwise, it makes provisions for a limited number. Usually the compiler is designed to assume that an array will have no more than ten elements (eleven elements in some systems: 0 through 10). Consequently, it reserves space for ten elements in the array. The programmer cannot write a statement that refers to an array element for which space has not been reserved.

The programmer can specify the number of elements for which space must be reserved by means of a DIM (dimension) statement. A DIM statement is not required for arrays of ten or fewer elements (or whatever number of elements the system assumes); however, many programmers will specify DIM statements for small arrays to help document the array usage.

The general format of the DIM statement follows:

line# DIM variable 1(limit 1), variable 2(limit2), . . .

The variables are the names of arrays. Each limit is an integer constant that represents the maximum number of storage locations required for a particular array.

Assume that space is needed to store fifty elements in an array named A. The following statement reserves storage for fifty elements:

```
00050 DIM A(50)
```

There is no problem if fewer than fifty values are actually read into array A, but it cannot contain more. Array subscripts can vary in the program from 0 to the limit declared in the DIM statement, but no subscript can exceed that limit. More than one array can be declared in a DIM statement; for example,

```
00040 DIM N(10),Q(55),B(125)
```

declares N, Q, and B as arrays. Array N may contain up to 10 elements; Q, up to 55 elements; and B, up to 125 elements. (If an index of 0 is used, up to 11, 56, and 126 elements can be stored, respectively.)

DIM statements must appear in a program before the first references to arrays they describe. A good programming practice is to place them at the beginning of the program. The following standard preparation symbol is often used to flowchart the DIM statement:

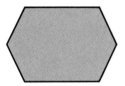

ONE-DIMENSIONAL ARRAYS

This section has been discussing lists of related values stored under a single variable name—one-dimensional arrays. Let us look at some applications involving the use of one-dimensional arrays.

Reading Data into an Array

Using FOR and NEXT statements can be an efficient method of reading data into an array. The following program segment reads and stores a list of seven prices in an array named P:

```
00010 FOR J = 1 TO 7
00020   READ P(J)
00030 NEXT J
00040 DATA 3.75,2.25,5.99,19.99
00050 DATA 1.99,0.87,4.74
```

The first time through this program loop, the loop variable J equals 1. When statement 20 is executed, the computer reads a price from the data lists and stores it in P(1)—the first storage location in array P. The second time through the loop, J equals 2. The next price is read into P(2)—the second location in the array. The loop processing continues until all seven prices have been read and stored.

Printing Data in an Array

Now assume we are to print the seven prices in array P in a single column. The following statements do just that:

```
00060 FOR I = 1 TO 7
00070    PRINT P(I)
00080 NEXT I

RUNNH
 3.75
 2.25
 5.99
 19.99
 1.99
 0.87
 4.74
```

As the loop variable I varies from 1 to 7, the index changes, and the computer prints elements 1 through 7 of array P.

Computations with Arrays

The program in Figure IX–2 generates a library book report that outlines the number of days overdue, the amount per day, and the amount due. In addition, the program prints out the total amount due from all of the overdue books.

This problem solution can be broken into the following steps:

1. Read the data into arrays.
2. Calculate the amount for each book by multiplying the amount/day and the number of days overdue.
3. Calculate the total amount due by adding the amount due from each book.

Three arrays are used in Figure IX–2. Two one-dimensional arrays are read as input: a list of the number of days each book is overdue, stored in array D, and a list of the amount due per day, stored in array A. In the main part of the program, a third array, T, is generated. It is a list of the total amount due from each book.

The program begins with a segment that establishes the number of days array, D. In lines 100 through 120, the variable L is set equal to 1, and a number is read from the data list and assigned to D(1). As the looping continues, D(2) is given a value, then D(3), and so on. When the looping is finished, array D contains the number of days each book is overdue. That is, D(1) is 5, D(2) is 3, and so on.

The next segment of the program fills array A with values in the same manner. The values read into A are the amounts due per day for each book. Thus, after execution of the loop (lines 130 through 150) has been completed, A(1) is 0.25, A(2) is 0.25, A(3) is 0.50, and so on.

Once the array elements have been stored, it is possible to manipulate them to obtain the desired information. For example, the main part of the program calculates the amount due for each book and stores the results in the array T. These computations are accomplished by multiplication of the elements in the array of the number of days overdue, D, by the corresponding elements in the amount per day array, A. All these arrays are then printed.

We also are to determine the total amount due from all of the books. We know that the array T contains the total amount due for each book. Therefore, we need to add all the elements in array T. This is accomplished in lines 200 through 230.

Figure IX–2 ■ Overdue Book Program (Continued on Next Page)

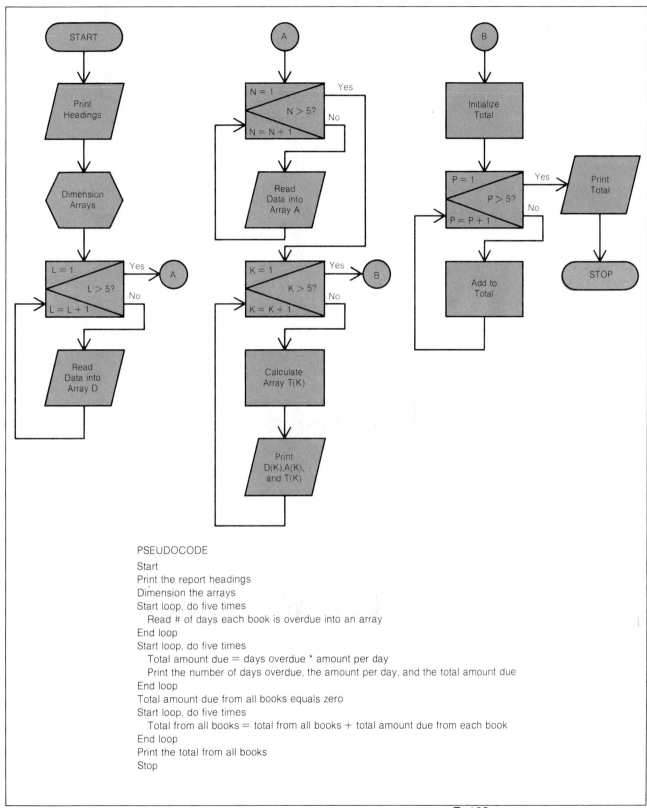

PSEUDOCODE

Start
Print the report headings
Dimension the arrays
Start loop, do five times
  Read # of days each book is overdue into an array
End loop
Start loop, do five times
  Total amount due = days overdue * amount per day
  Print the number of days overdue, the amount per day, and the total amount due
End loop
Total amount due from all books equals zero
Start loop, do five times
  Total from all books = total from all books + total amount due from each book
End loop
Print the total from all books
Stop

Figure IX–2 ▪ **Continued**

```
00010 REM ****************************************
00020 REM *** OVERDUE LIBRARY BOOKS PROGRAM ***
00030 REM ****************************************
00040 PRINT
00050 PRINT
00060 PRINT
00070 PRINT "DAYS OVERDUE","AMOUNT/DAY","AMOUNT DUE"
00080 PRINT
00090 DIM D(5),A(5),T(5)
00100 FOR L = 1 TO 5
00110    READ D(L)
00120 NEXT L
00130 FOR N = 1 TO 5
00140    READ A(N)
00150 NEXT N
00160 FOR K = 1 TO 5
00170    LET T(K) = D(K) * A(K)
00180    PRINT D(K),A(K),T(K)
00190 NEXT K
00200 LET TD = 0
00210 FOR P = 1 TO 5
00220    LET TD = TD + T(P)
00230 NEXT P
00240 PRINT
00250 PRINT "THE TOTAL AMOUNT DUE IS $";TD
00260 DATA 5,3,14,10,2
00270 DATA 0.25,0.25,0.50,0.25,0.75
00999 END
```

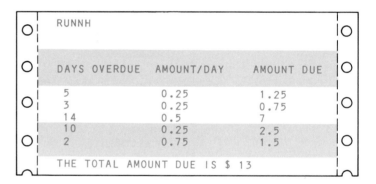

```
RUNNH

DAYS OVERDUE    AMOUNT/DAY      AMOUNT DUE

5               0.25            1.25
3               0.25            0.75
14              0.5             7
10              0.25            2.5
2               0.75            1.5

THE TOTAL AMOUNT DUE IS $ 13
```

MICROCOMPUTERS

Microcomputer:	Difference:
Apple	No differences.
Apple Macintosh	No differences.
IBM/Microsoft	No differences.
PET/Commodore 64	No differences.
TRS-80	No differences.

If we wanted the total amount due from the first three books, we could simply alter the number of times the FOR/NEXT loop is executed:

```
00200 LET TD = 0
00210 FOR P = 1 TO 3
00220    LET TD = TD + T(P)
00230 NEXT P
```

TWO-DIMENSIONAL ARRAYS

An array does not have to be a single list of data; it can be a table or matrix. For example, assume that Connor Video, Inc. operates three video games in four different arcades. Mr. Connor has received the following table of data concerning the number of games played in each of the four arcades:

Arcade	Millipede	Star Wars	Tron
Video Madness	100	250	200
Sappy Sam's	500	600	700
Krazy Kevin's	200	225	230
City Arcade	120	520	500

The rows in the table refer to the arcades, and the columns refer to the video games. Thus, the number of games of Millipede played at Krazy Kevin's can be found in the third row, first column.

This arrangement of data—a table consisting of rows and columns—is called a **two-dimensional array.** In this case, the two-dimensional array of data comprises four rows and three columns—a total of twelve elements (4 × 3).

Two-dimensional arrays are named in the same way as other variables. A name used for a two-dimensional array cannot be used for a one-dimensional array in the same program (and vice versa). An individual element in a table is indicated by a pair of subscripts in parentheses. The first subscript indicates the row; the second, the column. The row and column subscripts are separated by a comma.

If we name the array G for Connor Video Inc., the number of video games played at the individual arcades can be indicated by G(r,c), where r stands for the row in which a value is found, and c stands for the column in which it is found:

Array G		
G(1,1) 100	G(1,2) 250	G(1,3) 200
G(2,1) 500	G(2,2) 600	G(2,3) 700
G(3,1) 200	G(3,2) 225	G(3,3) 230
G(4,1) 120	G(4,2) 520	G(4,3) 500

Thus, G(2,3) represents the number of games of Tron played at Sappy Sam's, found in row 2, column 3. G(1,1) indicates the number of games of Millipede played at Video Madness.

Notice that it is necessary to store the arcades' names in a separate array, because we cannot mix character string values with numeric values in the same array:

Array A$

Array A$	
A$(1)	Video Madness
A$(2)	Sappy Sam's
A$(3)	Krazy Kevin's
A$(4)	City Arcade

As with one-dimensional arrays, individual subscripts in two-dimensional arrays may be indicated with any legal expression:

$$G(2,3)$$
$$G(L,1)$$
$$G(L,K)$$
$$G(1, L - K)$$

As with one-dimensional arrays, the space needed to store a two-dimensional array must be stated if the array size exceeds a certain limit. Unless told otherwise, most BASIC compilers reserve enough space for an array with up to ten rows and up to ten columns. Therefore, for an array to exceed either the row limit or the column limit, the programmer must specify its size in a DIM statement. For example,

```
00070 DIM T(50,20)
```

reserves space for array T, which has fifty rows and twenty columns.

Reading and Printing Data in Two-Dimensional Arrays

Reading data into and printing data from two-dimensional arrays can be accomplished with nested FOR/NEXT statements. Thus, in Figure IX–3, we read Connor Video, Inc. data into a two-dimensional array called G. The reading of the table follows a row-by-row sequence from left to right across each column. The loops in lines 50 through 90 perform this reading process:

```
00050 FOR I = 1 TO 4
00060    FOR J = 1 TO 3
00070       READ G(I,J)
00080    NEXT J
00090 NEXT I
00100 DATA 100,250,200,500,600,700
00110 DATA 200,225,230,120,520,500
```

When the program is executed, each data value is represented by the variable G followed by a unique pair of subscripts telling its location by row, I, and column, J. As the data values are read, they fill the table row by row (that is, after row 1 has been filled, row 2 is filled, then 3, and then row 4). The outer FOR/NEXT loop controls the rows (using the variable I); the inner loop controls the columns (using the variable J). Thus, every time the outer loop is executed once, the inner loop is executed three times. While I is equal to 1, J is equal to 1, 2, and 3. The first three numbers from the data list are read into G(1,1), G(1,2), and G(1,3). Then I is incremented to 2. The inner loop again is executed three times, and the next three numbers from the data list are read into the second row, G(2,1), G(2,2), and G(2,3). I is finally incremented to 4 and the fourth row of the table is filled.

To print the entire table, a PRINT statement in a nested loop can be used.

```
00010 REM *******************************
00020 REM ***   VIDEO GAME PROGRAM   ***
00030 REM *******************************
00040 DIM G(4,3)
00050 FOR I = 1 TO 4
00060   FOR J = 1 TO 3
00070     READ G(I,J)
00080   NEXT J
00090 NEXT I
00100 PRINT
00110 PRINT "ARCADE","MILLIPEDE","STAR WARS","TRON"
00120 PRINT
00130 FOR I = 1 TO 4
00140   READ A$
00150   PRINT A$,
00160   FOR J = 1 TO 3
00170     PRINT G(I,J),
00180   NEXT J
00190   PRINT
00200 NEXT I
00210 DATA 100,250,200,500,600,700
00220 DATA 200,225,230,120,520,500
00230 DATA VIDEO MADNESS,SAPPY SAM'S,KRAZY KEVIN'S,CITY ARCADE
00999 END
```

```
RUNNH

ARCADE          MILLIPEDE     STAR WARS     TRON

VIDEO MADNESS   100           250           200
SAPPY SAM'S     500           600           700
KRAZY KEVIN'S   200           225           230
CITY ARCADE     120           520           500
```

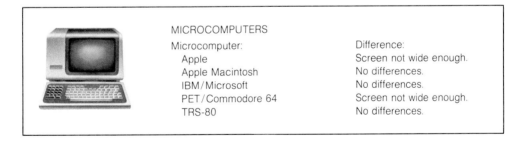

MICROCOMPUTERS

Microcomputer:	Difference:
Apple	Screen not wide enough.
Apple Macintosh	No differences.
IBM/Microsoft	No differences.
PET/Commodore 64	Screen not wide enough.
TRS-80	No differences.

Figure IX–3 ▪ Video Game Program

This is illustrated in lines 160 through 230. Let us examine the PRINT statements in this segment:

```
00160 FOR I = 1 TO 4
00170   READ A$
00180   PRINT A$,
00190   FOR J = 1 TO 3
00200     PRINT G(I,J),
00210   NEXT J
00220   PRINT
00230 NEXT I
```

The comma in line 200 signals the computer to print the three values in predefined print zones on the same line. After the inner loop has been executed, the blank PRINT in line 220 sets the carriage return so that the next row is printed on the next line.

Adding Rows of Items

After data has been read and stored as an array, it is possible to manipulate the array elements. For example, Mr. Connor may want to find out how many video games were played at City Arcade or how many games of Star Wars were played.

Figure IX–4 ▪ Complete Video Game Program 2 (Continued on Next Three Pages)

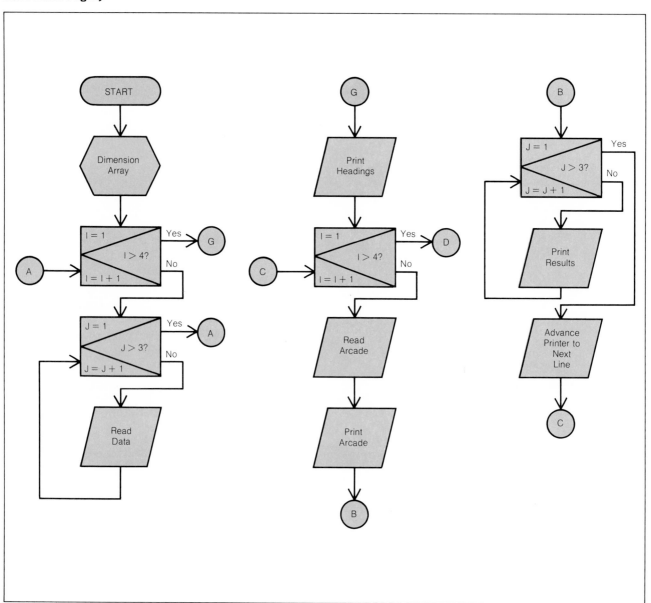

Since the data for each arcade are contained in a row of the array, we need to total the elements in one row of the array (the fourth row) to find out how many video games were played at City Arcade. This can be done with the following statements:

```
00240 LET T = 0
00250 FOR L = 1 TO 3
00260    LET T = T + G(4,L)
00270 NEXT L
```

Notice that G(4,L) restricts the computations to the elements in row 4, while the column, L, varies from 1 to 3.

Figure IX–4 ▪ Continued

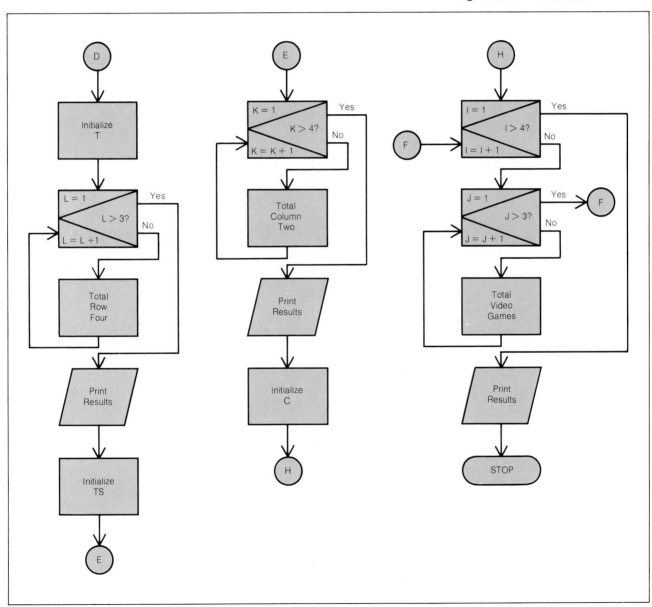

Figure IX—4 ▪ Continued

PSEUDOCODE

Start
Dimension the arrays
Start loop, do four times
  Start loop, do three times
    Read number of games into a two-dimensional array
  End loop
End loop
Print the report headings
Start loop, do four times
  Read the arcade name into an array
  Print the arcade name from the array
  Start loop, do three times
    Print the number of games from the two-dimensional array
  End loop
  Print a blank
End loop
Total of City Arcade equals zero
Start loop, do three times
  Total of City Arcade = total of City Arcade + # of each video game played at City Arcade
End loop
Print the total of City Arcade
Total of Star Wars equals zero
Start loop, do four times
  Total of Star Wars = total of Star Wars + # games of Star Wars played at each arcade
End loop
Print the total of Star Wars
Total equals zero
Start loop, do four times
  Start loop, do three times
    Total = total + # of each video game played at each arcade
  End loop
End loop
Print total
Stop

```
00010 REM ******************************
00020 REM ***   VIDEO GAME PROGRAM   ***
00030 REM ******************************
00040 DIM G(4,3)
00050 FOR I = 1 TO 4
00060   FOR J = 1 TO 3
00070     READ G(I,J)
00080   NEXT J
00090 NEXT I
00100 PRINT
00110 PRINT "ARCADE","MILLIPEDE","STAR WARS","TRON"
00120 PRINT
00130 FOR I = 1 TO 4
00140   READ A$
00150   PRINT A$,
00160   FOR J = 1 TO 3
00170     PRINT G(I,J),
00180   NEXT J
00190   PRINT
```

Figure IX–4 ▪ Continued

```
00200 NEXT I
00210 DATA 100,250,200,500,600,700
00220 DATA 200,225,230,120,520,500
00230 DATA VIDEO MADNESS,SAPPY SAM'S,KRAZY KEVIN'S,CITY ARCADE
00240 LET T = 0
00250 FOR L = 1 TO 3
00260    LET T = T + G(4,L)
00270 NEXT L
00280 PRINT
00290 PRINT T;" VIDEO GAMES WERE PLAYED AT CITY ARCADE"
00300 LET TS = 0
00310 FOR K = 1 TO 4
00320    LET TS = TS + G(K,2)
00330 NEXT K
00340 PRINT TS;" GAMES OF STAR WARS WERE PLAYED"
00350 LET C = 0
00360 FOR I = 1 TO 4
00370    FOR J = 1 TO 3
00380       LET C = C + G(I,J)
00390    NEXT J
00400 NEXT I
00410 PRINT C;" VIDEO GAMES WERE PLAYED ALTOGETHER"
00999 END
```

```
RUNNH

ARCADE          MILLIPEDE       STAR WARS       TRON

VIDEO MADNESS   100             250             200
SAPPY SAM'S     500             600             700
KRAZY KEVIN'S   200             225             230
CITY ARCADE     120             520             500

 1140   VIDEO GAMES WERE PLAYED AT CITY ARCADE
 1595   GAMES OF STAR WARS WERE PLAYED
 4145   VIDEO GAMES WERE PLAYED ALTOGETHER
```

MICROCOMPUTERS

Microcomputer:	Difference:
Apple	Screen not wide enough.
Apple Macintosh	No differences.
IBM/Microsoft	No differences.
PET/Commodore 64	Screen not wide enough.
TRS-80	No differences.

Adding Columns of Items

To find the number of games of Star Wars that were played, we want to total the elements in the second column of the array:

```
00300 LET TS = 0
00310 FOR K = 1 TO 4
00320   LET TS = TS + G(K,2)
00330 NEXT K
```

In these statements, G(K,2) restricts the computations to the elements in the second column, while the row, K, varies from 1 to 4.

Totaling a Two-Dimensional Array

Now suppose we need to know how many video games were played altogether. This means we must add all the elements in the array:

```
00350 LET C = 0
00360 FOR I = 1 TO 4
00370   FOR J = 1 TO 3
00380     LET C = C + G(I,J)
00390   NEXT J
00400 NEXT I
```

C is the variable that will be used to accumulate the total. It is initialized outside the loop. To add all the elements in array G, we are going to use a nested loop. The outer loop will control the rows and the inner loop, the columns. Line 380 does the actual accumulation. The first time through the loop, both I and J equal 1; thus, G(1,1) is added to 0. J is then incremented, and G(1,2) is added to C to make 350. Then G(1,3), or 200, is added. At this point, I is incremented to 2 so that we can begin adding the second-row values and so on until all the elements in G have been totaled. Figure IX–4 shows the complete program for Connor Video, Inc. and the resulting output.

ADVANTAGES OF ARRAYS

Although it may not be obvious at this point, arrays are useful in many applications. By using arrays, we can avoid having to make up names for numerous items. Also, once data are stored in an array, the data items (elements) can be referred to over and over again without being reread. Arrays also are used extensively in file processing (discussed in Section X).

Arrays can also be manipulated in a number of ways other than the basic computational examples previously given. For instance, some of the more common manipulation techniques include array merges, array searches, and array sorts. We will discuss one method of sorting the elements of an array in this section; however, there are many other methods of sorting.

SORTING

Many applications require that data items be sorted, or ordered, in some way. For example, names must be alphabetized, Social Security numbers arranged from lowest to highest, basketball players ranked from high scorer to low scorer, and the like.

Suppose that an array, X, contains five numbers that we would like ordered from lowest to highest:

It is a simple matter for us to mentally reorder this list as follows:

Array X (Unsorted)	Array X (Sorted)
10	2
30	10
15	15
100	30
2	100

What if there were seven hundred numbers instead of five? Then it would not be so easy for us to order the number list. However, the computer is perfectly suited for such tasks. One method of sorting with the computer is illustrated in Figure IX–5.

Figure IX–5 ▪ Sorting Program (Continued on Next Two Pages)

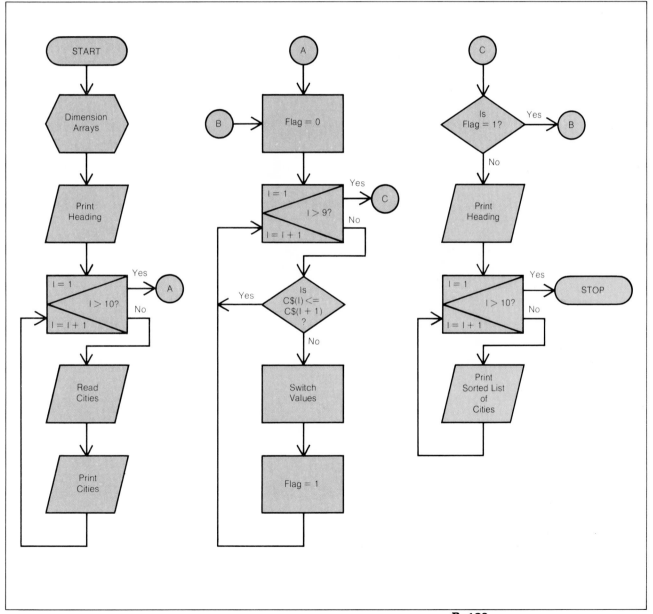

```
PSEUDOCODE                            00010 REM ****************************************************
Start                                 00020 REM ***      THIS PROGRAM SORTS THE CITIES IN      ***
Dimension the arrays                  00030 REM ***         THE USA INTO ALPHABETIC ORDER       ***
Print the heading for the first listing 00040 REM ****************************************************
Start loop, do ten times              00050 DIM C$(10)
   Read the cities into an array      00060 PRINT "UNSORTED LIST OF CITIES IN THE USA"
   Print the cities from an array     00070 PRINT
End loop                              00080 REM ****************************************************
Print blank lines                    00090 REM ***         READ THE NAMES INTO AN ARRAY        ***
Flag equals zero                     00100 REM ****************************************************
Start loop, do nine times            00110 FOR I = 1 TO 10
   If city$(I) > city$(I + 1)        00120    READ C$(I)
      Then                           00130    PRINT C$(I)
         Switch city$(I) with city$(I + 1)  00140 NEXT I
         Flag equals 1              00150 PRINT
   End if                           00160 PRINT
End loop                            00170 REM ****************************************************
If flag equals 1                    00180 REM ***                THE BUBBLE SORT               ***
   Then                             00190 REM ****************************************************
      Flag equals zero              00200 LET F = 0
      Repeat preceding loop         00210 FOR I = 1 TO 9
   Else                             00220    IF C$(I) <= C$(I + 1) THEN 270
      Print heading for the second listing  00230    LET H$ = C$(I)
      Start loop, do ten times      00240    LET C$(I) = C$(I + 1)
         Print the cities from the array  00250    LET C$(I + 1) = H$
      End loop                      00260    LET F = 1
End If                              00270 NEXT I
Stop                               00280 IF F = 1 THEN 200
                                   00290 PRINT "SORTED LIST OF CITIES IN THE USA"
                                   00300 PRINT
                                   00310 FOR I = 1 TO 10
                                   00320    PRINT C$(I)
                                   00330 NEXT I
                                   00340 DATA LOS ANGELES,CHICAGO,DETROIT,NEW YORK CITY,DALLAS
                                   00350 DATA CLEVELAND,BOSTON,WASHINGTON,MIAMI,DENVER
                                   00999 END
```

Figure IX–5 ▪ Continued

The Bubble Sort

The **bubble sort** works by comparing two adjacent values in an array and then interchanging them according to the desired order—either ascending or descending order.

The program in Figure IX–5 sorts ten U.S. cities into alphabetical order. To the computer, the letter A is less than the letter B, B is less than C, and so on. Lines 110 through 140 simply read the city names into an array called C$ and print them. Lines 200 through 280 perform the bubble sort. Let us examine them carefully to see what happens.

Line 200 refers to the variable F, short for flag. It is initialized to 0. Its value is checked later by the computer to determine if the entire array has been sorted.

Notice the terminal value of the FOR/NEXT loop that sorts the array. The terminal value is one less than the number of items to be sorted. This is because two items at a time are compared. I varies from 1 to 9, which means that the computer eventually will compare item 9 with item 9 + 1. If the terminal value were 10 (the number of cities), the computer would try to compare item 10 with item 11, which does not exist in our array.

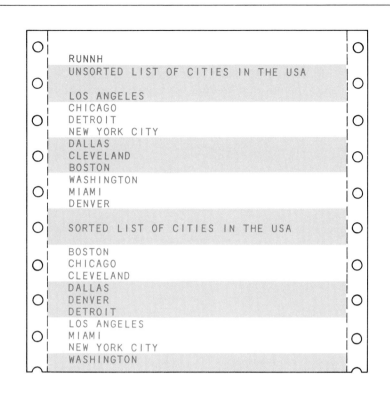

MICROCOMPUTERS

Microcomputer:	Difference:
Apple	No differences.
Apple Macintosh	No differences.
IBM/Microsoft	No differences.
PET/Commodore 64	No differences.
TRS-80	No differences.

Figure IX–5 ▪ Continued

The IF/THEN statement in line 220 tells the computer whether to interchange two compared values. For example, when I = 1, the computer compares LOS ANGELES with CHICAGO. Since C comes before L in the alphabet, there is need to switch these two items:

LOS ANGELES	I = 1	CHICAGO	
	Switch		
CHICAGO	I = 2	LOS ANGELES	DETROIT
	Switch		
DETROIT	I = 3	LOS ANGELES	
	No switch		
NEW YORK CITY	I = 4		
.			
.			
.			
DENVER			

Then I is incremented to 2, and LOS ANGELES is compared with DETROIT. These two names must be interchanged. This is performed by lines 230 through 250. Note that we have created a holding area, H$, so that the switch can be made. We move LOS ANGELES to the holding area, H$, and then move DETROIT to LOS ANGELES'S previous position. Now LOS AN-GELES is placed in the position previously occupied by DETROIT. Whenever the computer interchanges two values, F is set to 1 in line 260. This loop continues until every item in the array has been examined. After once through this entire loop, the array C$ looks like this:

CHICAGO
DETROIT
LOS ANGELES
DALLAS
CLEVELAND
BOSTON
NEW YORK CITY
MIAMI
DENVER
WASHINGTON

Although several switches have been made, the list is not sorted completely. That is why we need line 280. As long as F equals 1, the computer knows that switches have been made, and the sorting process must continue. When the computer loops through the entire array without setting F equal to 1—that is, when no switches are made—the computer finds F equal to 0 and knows that the list is ordered.

Numbers, of course, can be sorted by this same method. Two-dimensional arrays can be sorted with nested loops.

A PROGRAMMING PROBLEM

The Problem

The *New York Times* needs to determine quickly the standings for the Patrick Division of the NHL. Six teams are included in the Division. Their names, wins, and losses follow:

New York Islanders	10	5
New York Rangers	8	7
Washington Capitals	8	7
Philadelphia Flyers	7	8
Pittsburg Penguins	2	13
New Jersey Devils	0	15

Solution Design

Since we know each team's win and loss record, the wins and losses can be introduced to the program along with the teams' names in READ and DATA statements. Last night's game should be entered by an INPUT statement. Next, the total scores must be calculated and then sorted from the highest to lowest wins (there are no ties). A crucial point is that as the win records are

BASIC Extensions
SWAP

The Apple Macintosh and the IBM/Microsoft have additional capabilities which allow the use of the SWAP statement. The SWAP statement exchanges the values of two variables and is useful when sorting. The general format of the SWAP statement is shown below:

line # SWAP variable 1, variable 2

Following is a sorting program using the SWAP statement.

```
10 FOR I = 1 TO 8
20    READ D$(I)
30 NEXT I
40 LET F = 0
50 FOR I = 1 TO 7
60    IF D$(I) <= D$(I + 1) THEN 90
70    SWAP D$(I),D$(I + 1)
80    LET F = 1
90 NEXT I
100 IF F = 1 THEN 40
110 PRINT "BUSINESS COLLEGE"
120 PRINT
130 FOR I = 1 TO 8
140    PRINT D$(I)
150 NEXT I
160 DATA ECONOMICS,ACCOUNTING,STATISTICS
170 DATA FINANCE,OPERATIONS RESEARCH
180 DATA MIS,BUSINESS EDUCATION,MANAGEMENT
999 END


RUN
BUSINESS COLLEGE

ACCOUNTING
BUSINESS EDUCATION
ECONOMICS
FINANCE
MANAGEMENT
MIS
OPERATIONS RESEARCH
STATISTICS
```

rearranged in the sorting section, the corresponding team's name and its loss record must be carried with each win record (although the team name and the loss record are not sorted). Finally, the results must be printed.

The Program

Figure IX–6 shows this problem's solution. Line 40 sets aside room for the variables (although this DIM statement is not strictly necessary, since the arrays have fewer than ten elements per index). Lines 130 through 150 read the data into a one-dimensional array. Lines 190 through 220 enter the win or loss for each team from last night's game. Lines 260 through 290 accumulate the wins or the losses for each team. The win records of the teams are sorted from highest to lowest in lines 330 through 470. The variables H1 and H2 in lines 370 and 380 are the holding places for the team's win record and loss

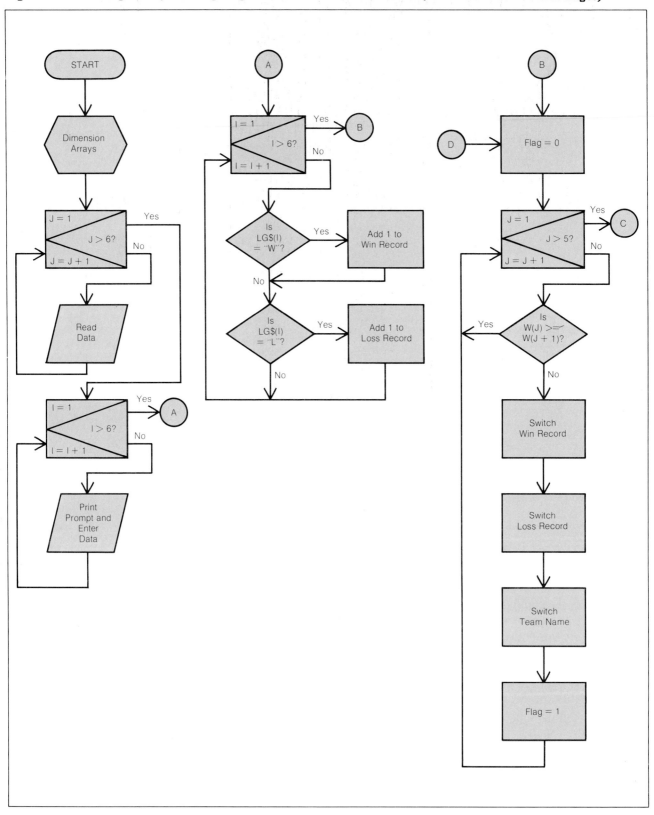

Figure IX–6 ▪ Continued

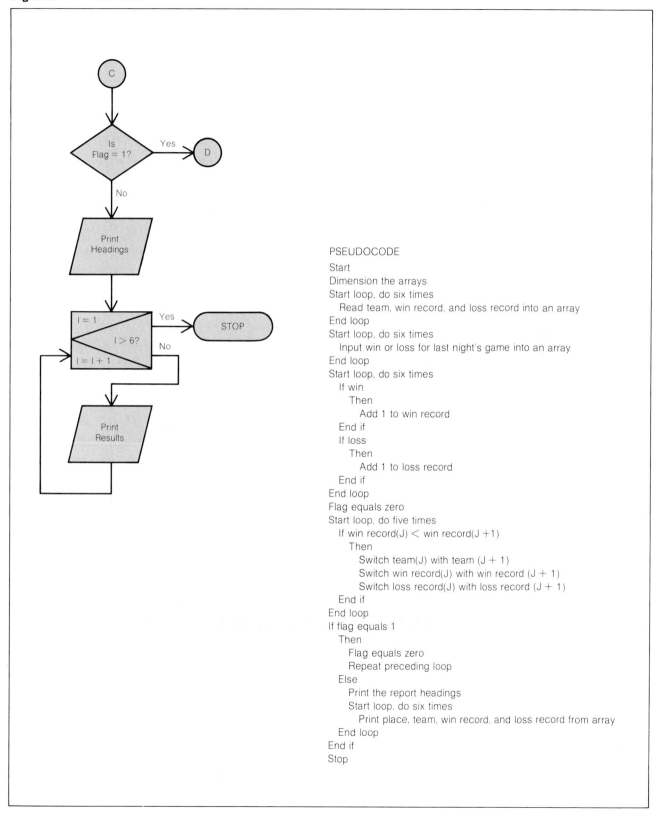

PSEUDOCODE

Start
Dimension the arrays
Start loop, do six times
   Read team, win record, and loss record into an array
End loop
Start loop, do six times
   Input win or loss for last night's game into an array
End loop
Start loop, do six times
   If win
     Then
       Add 1 to win record
   End if
   If loss
     Then
       Add 1 to loss record
   End if
End loop
Flag equals zero
Start loop, do five times
   If win record(J) < win record(J +1)
     Then
       Switch team(J) with team (J + 1)
       Switch win record(J) with win record (J + 1)
       Switch loss record(J) with loss record (J + 1)
   End if
End loop
If flag equals 1
   Then
     Flag equals zero
     Repeat preceding loop
   Else
     Print the report headings
     Start loop, do six times
       Print place, team, win record, and loss record from array
   End loop
End if
Stop

Figure IX–6 ■ **Continued**

```
00010 REM ***************************************
00020 REM ***    HOCKEY STANDING STATISTICS    ***
00030 REM ***************************************
00040 DIM T$(6),W(6),L(6)
00050 PRINT
00060 PRINT
00070 DATA NEW YORK ISLANDERS,10,5,NEW YORK RANGERS,8,7
00080 DATA NEW JERSEY DEVILS,0,15,WASHINGTON CAPITALS,8,7
00090 DATA PHILADELPHIA FLYERS,7,8,PITTSBURGH PENGUINS,2,13
00100 REM ***************************************
00110 REM ***   READ DATA FOR FIRST 15 GAMES   ***
00120 REM ***************************************
00130 FOR J = 1 TO 6
00140    READ T$(J),W(J),L(J)
00150 NEXT J
00160 REM ***************************************
00170 REM *** INPUT SCORES FOR THE LAST GAME  ***
00180 REM ***************************************
00190 FOR I = 1 TO 6
00200    PRINT "ENTER WIN OR LOSS (W OR L) FOR THE ";T$(I)
00210    INPUT LG$(I)
00220 NEXT I
00230 REM ***************************************
00240 REM *** CALCULATE TOTAL WINS AND LOSSES ***
00250 REM ***************************************
00260 FOR I = 1 TO 6
00270    IF LG$(I) = "W" THEN LET W(I) = W(I) + 1
00280    IF LG$(I) = "L" THEN LET L(I) = L(I) + 1
00290 NEXT I
00300 REM ***************************************
00310 REM *** SORT TEAMS INTO PROPER STANDING ***
00320 REM ***************************************
00330 LET F = 0
00340 FOR J = 1 TO 5
00350    IF W(J) >= W(J + 1) THEN 460
00360    LET H$ = T$(J)
00370    LET H1 = W(J)
00380    LET H2 = L(J)
00390    LET T$(J) = T$(J + 1)
00400    LET W(J) = W(J + 1)
00410    LET L(J) = L(J + 1)
00420    LET T$(J + 1) = H$
00430    LET W(J + 1) = H1
00440    LET L(J + 1) = H2
00450    LET F = 1
00460 NEXT J
00470 IF F = 1 THEN 330
00480 REM ***************************************
00490 REM ***    PRINT OUT THE TEAM STANDINGS   ***
00500 REM ***************************************
00510 PRINT
00520 PRINT
00530 PRINT "PLACE","TEAM",,"WINS","LOSSES"
00540 FOR I = 1 TO 6
00550    PRINT I,T$(I),W(I),L(I)
00560 NEXT I
00999 END
```

Figure IX–6 ■ **Continued**

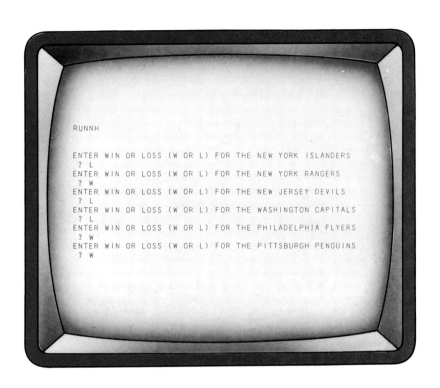

```
RUNNH

ENTER WIN OR LOSS (W OR L) FOR THE NEW YORK ISLANDERS
? L
ENTER WIN OR LOSS (W OR L) FOR THE NEW YORK RANGERS
? W
ENTER WIN OR LOSS (W OR L) FOR THE NEW JERSEY DEVILS
? L
ENTER WIN OR LOSS (W OR L) FOR THE WASHINGTON CAPITALS
? L
ENTER WIN OR LOSS (W OR L) FOR THE PHILADELPHIA FLYERS
? W
ENTER WIN OR LOSS (W OR L) FOR THE PITTSBURGH PENGUINS
? W
```

PLACE	TEAM	WINS	LOSSES
1	NEW YORK ISLANDERS	10	6
2	NEW YORK RANGERS	9	7
3	WASHINGTON CAPITALS	8	8
4	PHILADELPHIA FLYERS	8	8
5	PITTSBURGH PENGUINS	2	13
6	NEW JERSEY DEVILS	0	16

MICROCOMPUTERS

Microcomputer:	Difference:
Apple	Screen not wide enough.
Apple Macintosh	Screen not wide enough.
IBM/Microsoft	No differences.
PET/Commodore 64	Screen not wide enough.
TRS-80	Screen not wide enough.

record, respectively. The variable H$ in line 360 performs the same duty for the teams' names. Every time the computer switches a win record, W(J), it also must switch the corresponding team name and loss record. The computer performs the switches in lines 360 through 440. Lines 510 through 560 print the results.

SUMMARY POINTS

■ Arrays are lists or tables of related values stored under a single variable name.
■ Access to individual elements in an array can be gained through the use of subscripts.
■ The DIM statement sets up storage space for arrays.
■ Array manipulation is carried out through the use of FOR/NEXT loops.
■ Two-dimensional arrays also are called tables or matrices.
■ Two subscript numbers identify individual items in a matrix. The first number indicates the row; the second indicates the column.
■ The bubble sort is one method of ordering values contained in an array.

REVIEW QUESTIONS

1. What is an array? Name two types of arrays and give two advantages of arrays.
2. We can reference individual elements in an array referring to their position in the array. This is done through the use of _____ _____. When the array element is referenced by an expression, what are the three steps carried out by the computer?
3. What is the purpose of the DIM statement and where is it located in a program?
4. Manipulation of arrays is often achieved through the use of _____. _____.

DEBUGGING EXERCISES

1.
```
10 DIM T$(25)
15 FOR I = 1 TO 30
20    READ T$(I)
25    PRINT T$(I)
30 NEXT I
```

2.
```
100 REM ***    TOTAL THE ELEMENTS IN    ***
105 REM ***    ROW THREE OF ARRAY G     ***
110 DIM G(5,6)
115 LET T = 0
120 FOR I = 1 TO 5
125    LET T = T + G(I,6)
130 NEXT I
```

PROGRAMMING PROBLEMS

1. Write a program to read fifteen data items (integers) into each of two arrays, X and Y. Calculate the products of the corresponding elements in X and Y and store the results in a third array, Z. Print a three-column table, with headings, displaying the contents of X, Y, and Z. Then compute the sum of the elements in each array and print the results. Make up your own data.

2. Write a program to accept the answers to a ten-question true/false exam given in an economics class and the corresponding student identification number. The student identifications should be placed in an array N$, and the student's answers should be entered into a two-dimensional array G. Use the following data:

STUDENT ID NO.	ANSWERS (1 = True; 0 = False)
0009	0010010010
0108	0101000011
0187	0111010011
0309	1101010101
0256	0111010010

The correct answers are: 0111010011. These answers should be entered into array A. Calculate each student's score, forming a third array, S. Find the best score, then determine each student's grade as follows: Give the best score an A; best - 1 a B; best - 2 a C; best - 3 a D; and otherwise give an F. Print a two-column table with headings, displaying the students' identification numbers and their corresponding grades.

SECTION X

File Processing

OVERVIEW

Business applications often involve large amounts of data. It is not uncommon for programs dealing with inventory, payroll, or customer balances to process hundreds, thousands, or millions of data items. Since the main memory of the computer is limited, users need some means of storing programs and data so that they do not have to retype them into the computer every time it is necessary to run the programs. Some microcomputers are so small that they cannot store internally all the data needed. In addition, it is useful to establish a single data file that several programs can use in different ways at different times. For example, personnel data can be used in applications such as handling payroll, processing medical claims, and printing mailing lists. For all these reasons, data often is stored on secondary storage media (secondary storage devices)—usually magnetic disks and tapes. Groups of data stored on disks or tapes are known as files.

Unfortunately, there is no standardized method for performing operations on files stored on secondary storage devices. Many BASIC implementations include unique file manipulation commands. Fortunately, the principles on which the commands are based are similar. We look first at the fundamentals of file processing and later differentiate among implementations on the computers we have been discussing.

WHAT IS A FILE?

A file is a way of organizing data. Think of a typical office, which probably has a number of file drawers. Usually each file drawer contains related information about one general topic. For example, one drawer might contain all the information about the firm's clients and be called the client file. Within this drawer might be a separate information sheet for each client giving the name, address, and so on. Each of these information sheets are referred to as a record. The individual data items, such as the client's name recorded on the information sheet, are called **fields.** A group of one or more related fields is known as a **record,** and a group of one or more related records is known as a **file** (see Figure X–1).

Figure X–1 ■ File Organization

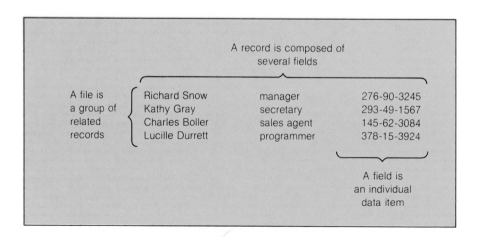

The computer has allowed us to store and manipulate files much more efficiently than its predecessor, the file cabinet. The computer uses two main types of file access methods: sequential and random access. Our discussion will concentrate mainly on accessing sequential files (opening, writing to, reading from, and closing). Random files will also be introduced. However, we will not give specific examples of random file accessing on each computer. Please refer to your system manual for more information concerning random files.

SEQUENTIAL DATA FILES

Magnetic tape is one type of sequential media (see Figure X–2). In a **sequential file,** the data items are recorded one after another and must also be read one after another in the same order in which the recording took place. For example, to recall the fifth item stored in a sequential file, you must start at the beginning of the file and read the first four items successfully to get to the fifth one.

Data also can be stored sequentially on disk (see Figure X–3). A disk is divided into concentric circles called **tracks.** The data items are recorded one after another on the tracks of the disk. Figure X–3 shows how a disk containing our client file might be organized. The number 13 is the ASCII code for the carriage return, which is used to separate fields.

In a sequential file, each field takes only the amount of space required by its length. To record data in a sequential file, the following three steps are needed:

1. *Opening a sequential data file for writing to the file.* When opening a file, the programmer must tell the computer the name of the file to which data is to be output. Using this name, the computer sets up a location on a disk or tape in which the data are to be placed.

2. *Writing data to a sequential data file.* After opening a data file, data may be written onto the disk. A special statement is used to write data onto a disk, with the processing being similar to printing output on the screen or printer, except the data are being written onto the disk instead.

3. *Closing a sequential data file.* The last step in creating a sequential data file is to close it. After all the data have been written on the disk, the file must be closed to prevent loss of its contents. Closing also indicates to the computer that the use of the file is finished for the present time.

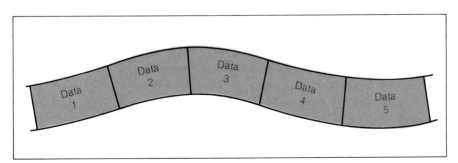

Figure X–2 ▪ **Magnetic Tape**

Figure X–3 ▪ **Disk**

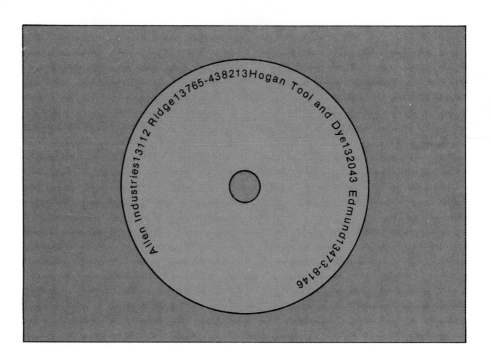

Reading from a sequential file also requires three steps:

1. *Opening a sequential data file for reading from the file.* The opening of a sequential file for reading may be either identical to the opening format for writing to a file or slightly modified. For example, to open a data file to write to a disk may require that a word or character be included to indicate this, such as WRITE or W. To read from the data file, these might need to be changed to READ or R.

2. *Reading data from a sequential data file.* After the file has been opened, the data can be read from the disk and placed in variables—numeric data in numeric variables and string data in string variables. Remember that in a sequential file, data are always read in the same order in which they were written.

3. *Closing a sequential data file.* Closing the file after reading the disk is identical to closing it after writing to the disk.

No matter what type of computer you are using, these general steps apply in using sequential data files. An example follows of sequential data file use on the DECSYSTEM 20 (also referred to as **terminal format files**). Following this, we will show the same example for each of our computers, the Apple, IBM/Microsoft, TRS-80, and PET/Commodore 64. Refer to the appropriate section for your computer. The discussion on implementing files will be limited to files on disk. Consult your manual for any differences in commands for tape.

DECSYSTEM 20

CREATING OR ACCESSING A SEQUENTIAL DATA (TERMINAL FORMAT) FILE

The general format of the command that creates or accesses a data file for the DECSYSTEM 20 is as follows:

line# OPEN "filename" AS FILE #number

If a file already exists with the filename specified, the computer will give us access to it. Otherwise, a new file will be created. The number can be used to refer to the file. The following is an example:

```
00010 OPEN "TELEPHONE" AS FILE #2
```

WRITING DATA TO A FILE

After the file has been created, we can write data to it:

line# PRINT #number, expression

The number is the one used in the OPEN statement. The expression is the data to be written onto the disk. For example,

```
00020 PRINT #2,"352-8952"
```

Pressing RETURN at the end of the line tells the computer that this is the end of the data item.

CLOSING A FILE

The general format of the CLOSE command is as follows:

line# CLOSE #number

The program in Figure X–4 creates a file called TELEPHONE as file #2 and writes some data to it.

Line 10 creates a file called TELEPHONE. The file number at the end of the line is used later to refer to the file. Line 20 sets up a FOR/NEXT loop to read some data items (in line 30) and write them to the file. Line 40 prints the values in T$ to file 2, TELEPHONE. Line 60 closes the file.

READING DATA FROM A FILE

To use the data stored on a file, we read it. The INPUT command can be used, and its format is as follows:

line# INPUT #file number, variable list

The following is an example:

```
00020 INPUT #2,T$
```

Figure X–4 ▪ Creating and Writing Data to a File

```
00010 OPEN "TELEPHONE" AS FILE #2
00020 FOR I = 1 TO 6
00030    READ T$
00040    PRINT #2,T$
00050 NEXT I
00060 CLOSE #2
00070 DATA "BONNIE COOK:  287-6562","TIM SMITH:  315-3537"
00080 DATA "JOHN ROGERS:  425-2920","BOB HILL:  287-7171"
00090 DATA "STEVE SIMON:  425-3172","SARAH JOHNS:  425-0061"
00999 END
```

The program in Figure X–5 reads data stored in the file called TELEPHONE.
Line 10 gives access to TELEPHONE as file 2. Line 20 sets up for a FOR/NEXT loop that reads the items from the file one by one into the array T$ and prints them out for us to see. Line 40 prints the data on the screen. Line 60 closes the file.

Apple

CREATING OR ACCESSING A SEQUENTIAL DATA FILE

The Apple system calls data files **text files.** To tell the system to use the disk, we need to cue the computer by pressing the control (CTRL) key and the D key simultaneously. Since this has to be done several times in a file manipulation program, we may want to initialize a variable, D$, to CTRL-D by doing the following:

```
10 LET D$ = CHR$(4)
```

Check section VIII to refresh your memory about what CHR$ does.

The general format of the command for creating or opening a text file is the following:

line# PRINT D$; "OPEN filename"

D$ is the CTRL-D command. The file name must begin with a letter and be less than thirty characters long. An example follows:

```
10 LET D$ = CHR$(4)
20 PRINT D$;"OPEN TELEPHONE"
```

A file called TELEPHONE now is listed in our catalog. A **catalog** is a program that supplies a complete alphabetical list of a user's files. It is designated as a text (data) file by the letter T in the catalog listing. The OPEN command is used in this manner whenever we want to gain access to data in a file.

WRITING DATA TO A FILE

After the file has been created, we can alert the computer that we want to put some data into the file by using this command:

line# PRINT D$; "WRITE filename"

Figure X–5 ▪ Reading Data from a File

```
00010 OPEN "TELEPHONE" AS FILE #2
00020 FOR I = 1 TO 6
00030   INPUT #2,T$(I)
00040   PRINT T$(I)
00050 NEXT I
00060 CLOSE #2
00999 END
```

This line is followed by the command that actually does the writing to the disk:

line# PRINT expression

This PRINT command writes the expression to the disk. Since a sequential file is simply a long list of data, the computer needs to know where one data item ends and the next one begins. Pressing the RETURN button at the end of the PRINT line tells the computer this.

CLOSING A FILE

The general format of the CLOSE command is as follows:

line# PRINT D$; "CLOSE filename"

The program in Figure X–6 opens a file named TELEPHONE, writes some data out to it, and finally closes it.

Line 10 initializes D$ to the disk command; this tells the computer we are dealing with disk files. Line 20 creates the file. Line 30 tells the computer that we are going to write some data to the disk.

In this example, the data items are different lengths: BONNIE COOK: 287–6562 is twenty-two characters long; TIM SMITH: 315–3537 is twenty characters long, and so forth. The items are separated from one another by the fact that they are on different lines. Therefore, the file is a list of items, each of which ends with the ASCII character 13, the carriage return:

TELEPHONE: BONNIE COOK: 287–656213TIM SMITH: 315–353713

READING DATA FROM A FILE

Once a file has been established, it can be read whenever the user wants to use the data. The following command alerts the computer that reading from a file on disk is to occur:

line# PRINT D$; "READ filename"

Figure X–6 ▪ Creating and Writing Data to a File

```
10 LET D$ = CHR$(4)
20 PRINT D$;"OPEN TELEPHONE"
30 PRINT D$;"WRITE TELEPHONE"
40 PRINT "BONNIE COOK:  287-6562"
50 PRINT "TIM SMITH:  315-3537"
60 PRINT "JOHN ROGERS:  425-2920"
70 PRINT "BOB HILL:  287-7171"
80 PRINT "STEVE SIMON:  425-3172"
90 PRINT "SARAH JOHNS:  425-0061"
100 PRINT D$;"CLOSE TELEPHONE"
999 END
```

To read the data items, we use an INPUT statement, as shown in Figure X–7. After the file is opened, line 130 signals the computer that we are going to read data from a disk file. The FOR/NEXT loop then reads the data into the array T$. The file is closed by line 170.

IBM/Microsoft

CREATING OR ACCESSING A SEQUENTIAL DATA FILE

The general format for creating or accessing a sequential data file for the IBM/Microsoft microcomputer follows:

line# OPEN "filename" FOR OUTPUT AS #number
line# OPEN "filename" FOR INPUT AS #number

The filename in quotes must be less than or equal to eight characters. OUTPUT specifies sequential output mode; it allows data to be written to the specified file on disk. INPUT specifies sequential input mode; it allows data to be read from the specified file on disk. The number after the pound (#) sign will be used later as a shorthand reference to the file in the program. An example statement creating a file called TELEPHONE follows:

```
10 OPEN "TELEPHONE" FOR OUTPUT AS #1
```

WRITING DATA TO A FILE

Once a file has been created, we can write some data to it by using a variation of the PRINT statement. Notice, however, that the following PRINT statement looks different from that used to display the results of processing:

line# PRINT #number,expression

The #number distinguishes this statement from a regular PRINT command. The number should be the same one that was specified in the OPEN statement. The expression can be any valid variable, string, numeric constant, and so on. Since a sequential file is simply a long list of items, the computer knows where one data item ends and the next one begins by the pressing of the carriage return at the end of the PRINT line.

Figure X–7 ▪ Reading Data from a File

```
110 LET D$ = CHR$(4)
120 PRINT D$;"OPEN TELEPHONE"
130 PRINT D$;"READ TELEPHONE"
140 FOR I = 1 TO 6
150    INPUT T$(I)
160 NEXT I
170 PRINT D$;"CLOSE TELEPHONE"
999 END
```

CLOSING A FILE

The general format of the CLOSE command follows:

line# CLOSE #number

Again, the number should be the same one that was used to open the file.

The program in Figure X–8 opens a file named TELEPHONE, writes some data to it, and closes the file.

Line 10 creates the file as #1. That same number is used throughout the program in the file statements as a shorthand reference to TELEPHONE. Lines 20 through 70 simply write data items to the file. Line 80 closes the file.

READING DATA FROM A FILE

Once a file has been created, it can be read to access the data using the following:

line# INPUT #number, expression

The #number distinguishes this as a file statement. The following is an example:

```
40 INPUT #1,T$
```

The program in Figure X–9 reads data stored in a file called TELEPHONE.

Line 10 accesses TELEPHONE as file #2. Line 20 sets up a FOR/NEXT loop that reads the items from the file one by one into the array T$. The items are displayed by line 40. Line 60 closes the file.

Apple Macintosh and TRS–80

CREATING OR ACCESSING A SEQUENTIAL DATA FILE

On the TRS–80, the computer will ask,

```
HOW MANY FILES?
```

Figure X–8 ▪ **Creating and Writing Data to a File**

```
10 OPEN "TELEPHONE" FOR OUTPUT AS #1
20 PRINT #1,"BONNIE COOK:  287-6562"
30 PRINT #1,"TIM SMITH:  315-3537"
40 PRINT #1,"JOHN ROGERS:  425-2920"
50 PRINT #1,"BOB HILL:  287-7171"
60 PRINT #1,"STEVE SIMON:  425-3172"
70 PRINT #1,"SARAH JOHNS:  425-0061"
80 CLOSE #1
99 END
```

Figure X-9 ■ Reading Data from a File

```
10 OPEN "TELEPHONE" FOR INPUT AS #2
20 FOR I = 1 TO 6
30    INPUT #2,T$(I)
40    PRINT T$(I)
50 NEXT I
60 CLOSE #2
99 END
```

Since we are going to deal with fewer than three files, we can simply press the ENTER button in response.

The following command permits access to files on both the Apple Macintosh and TRS-80.

line# OPEN "mode", buffer number, "filename"

The "mode" will be either I for sequential input (reading data from an existing file) or O for sequential output (writing data on the disk). After the "mode" is specified, we designate the number of the buffer where data will temporarily be held. The filename can be from one to eight characters long; the first character must be alphabetic (do not embed any blanks). An example follows:

```
10 OPEN "O",1,"TELEPHONE"
```

This line creates a file called TELEPHONE. After the file is opened, we can use buffer 1 to write data to the file ("mode" = O). We will see how this works later.

WRITING DATA TO A FILE

After a file has been created (opened), data can be written to it. The general format of the PRINT command is:

line# PRINT #buffer number, expression

For example,

```
20 PRINT #1,"BONNIE COOK:  287-6562"
```

prints the character string BONNIE COOK: 287-6562 as the first item in the file called TELEPHONE. The #1 is the buffer number used in the OPEN statement for TELEPHONE above.

Now we can write a simple program that creates a file and writes some data to it, as shown in Figure X-10.

Line 10 opens the file called TELEPHONE. We use buffer #1 to write data to the file. Pressing ENTER at the end of each line separates one item from another on the disk file. Line 80 closes the file.

Figure X–10 ▪ **Creating and Writing Data to a File**

```
10 OPEN "O",1,"TELEPHONE"
20 PRINT #1,"BONNIE COOK:  287-6562"
30 PRINT #1,"TIM SMITH:  315-3537"
40 PRINT #1,"JOHN ROGERS:  425-2920"
50 PRINT #1,"BOB HILL:  287-7171"
60 PRINT #1,"STEVE SIMON:  425-3172"
70 PRINT #1,"SARAH JOHNS:  425-0061"
80 CLOSE #1
99 END
```

CLOSING A FILE

The following command closes a file:

line# CLOSE #buffer number

Make sure that the buffer number is the one specified in the OPEN statement for the file. (See lines 10 and 80 in Figure X–10.)

READING DATA FROM A FILE

To read data from a file, we first must gain access to it by using the OPEN statement. However, the mode is now I, for sequential input. The following statement should be used to gain access on an already existing file:

line# OPEN"I",buffer number,"filename"

The command that reads data from the file follows:

line# INPUT #buffer number,variable

The program segment in Figure X–11 reads data that have been stored in TELEPHONE.

Line 10 gives access to an already existing file called TELEPHONE. A FOR/NEXT loop then is established to read the data into the array T$. Data is read from the file by line 30. Note that the buffer number is the same as was

Figure X–11 ▪ **Reading Data from a File**

```
10 OPEN "I",1,"TELEPHONE"
20 FOR I = 1 TO 6
30    INPUT #1,T$(I)
40 NEXT I
50 FOR I = 1 TO 6
60    PRINT T$(I)
70 NEXT I
80 CLOSE #1
99 END
```

designated in the OPEN statement. Lines 50 through 70 simply print out the file. Line 80 closes the file.

PET/Commodore 64

CREATING OR ACCESSING A SEQUENTIAL DATA FILE

The general format of the command for creating or accessing a data file for the PET/Commodore 64 microcomputer follows:

line# OPEN file#,device#,channel#,"0:name,type,direction"

The file number is used to refer to the file. The device number is 8, which tells the computer to open the file on disk. The channel number is a data channel, numbers 2 through 14. For convenience, it is suggested that you use the same number for both the channel and file numbers to keep them straight. The name is the file name. For our purposes here, the type is SEQ (sequential), which can be abbreviated by using just the first letter, S. The direction must be READ or WRITE, or at least the first letter of each. An example follows:

```
10 OPEN 3,8,3,"0:TELEPHONE,S,W"
```

If the file TELEPHONE already exists and we need only read what is on it, the W should be changed to R. The following example gives us access to an existing file TELEPHONE:

```
10 OPEN 3,8,3,"0:TELEPHONE,S,R"
```

WRITING DATA TO A FILE

After a filename has been created, we can write data to the file by using a PRINT command. The general format is:

line# PRINT #file number, expression

The file number is the one specified in the OPEN statement. The expression is the data to be written onto the disk. For example,

```
30 PRINT #3,"BONNIE COOK:  287-6562"
```

writes BONNIE COOK: 287–6562 to file 3. Pressing RETURN at the end of the line signals the computer that this is the end of the data item.

CLOSING A FILE

The general format of the CLOSE statement follows:

line# CLOSE #file number

Let us put these commands together in Figure X–12 to create a file called TELEPHONE, write some data to it, and close it.

Figure X–12 ▪ Creating and Writing Data to a File

```
10 OPEN 2,8,2,"O:TELEPHONE,S,W"
20 PRINT #2,"BONNIE COOK:  287-6562"
30 PRINT #2,"TIM SMITH:  315-3537"
40 PRINT #2,"JOHN ROGERS:  425-2920"
50 PRINT #2,"BOB HILL:  287-7171"
60 PRINT #2,"STEVE SIMON:  425-3172"
70 PRINT #2,"SARAH JOHNS:  425-0061"
80 CLOSE #2
99 END
```

READING DATA FROM A FILE

Once a file has been established, it can be read so that manipulations can be performed on the data. First, the file should be reopened:

line# OPEN file#, device#,channel#, "O:name, type, direction"

Then we use the following command to read the data items:

line# INPUT #file number, expression

The file number, of course, must be the same as the file number in the OPEN statement. The expression is the variable that specifies where the data will be stored in internal memory.

The program in Figure X–13 reads data from the file called TELEPHONE. Line 10 opens file 2. Since the file already has been established, R is specified as the direction (that is, to read from the file). A FOR/NEXT loop is initiated in line 20. Line 30 reads data from file 2 into the array T\$. Line 40 is a PRINT statement. No file number is specified; it simply prints the data items on the screen of the PET/Commodore 64. Finally, the file is closed in line 60.

RANDOM DATA FILES

Random data files are files that allow you to write to or read from a file in random order. Figure X–14 illustrates how a random file is organized on disk.

```
10 OPEN 2,8,2,"O:TELEPHONE,S,R"
20 FOR I = 1 TO 6
30    INPUT #2,T$(I)
40    PRINT T$(I)
50 NEXT I
60 CLOSE #2
99 END
```

Figure X–13 ▪ Reading Data from a File

Figure X–14 ▪ **Random Data Files**

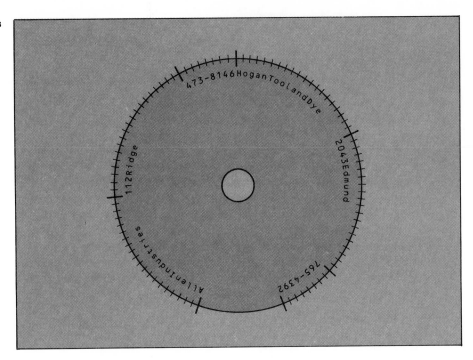

For the purposes of this book, all records must be the same length in a random file. (Check your manual for other options.) This enables the computer to find them without reading all the preceding records. Since the fields that make up each record may not be the same length, blank characters are placed after them. Because of this, random files tend to take up more disk space than sequential files, but this disadvantage is outweighed by the associated advantages, such as speed of access.

Our discussion of random files will deal with relative files. A record file with relative organization contains records that are stored in numbered locations. The number associated with a position represents its location relative to the beginning of the file. For example, record 1 would occupy the first record position; record 2, the second record position; and so forth. Thus, with a relative file we can access a record either sequentially or randomly by record number.

Like sequential files, random files have to be opened before use and closed after use. When reading or writing with a random file, the number of the record to be read or written to must be specified. Record numbers start with 1 and continue to as high as necessary to store all the records. The methods used to perform these steps vary from computer to computer.

RANDOM VERSUS SEQUENTIAL FILES

The following is a short summary of the differences between random and sequential files:

▪ Records in sequential files are written to the disk one after the other, starting with record 1.

- Records in random files may be written in any order desired.
- Records in sequential files are read from the disk one after the other, starting with record 1.
- Records in random files may be read in any order desired.
- Records in sequential files can be of varying lengths.
- Records in random files must all be the same length.

Another method of randomly accessing data in a file is through the use of indexed files. Indexed files initiate random access by means of a key, or a field within a record that uniquely identifies the contents of a particular record. For a more detailed discussion of indexed files, see your systems manual.

A PROGRAMMING PROBLEM

The Problem

Safeway National Bank keeps a file of all its customers and their account balances. They have asked you to write a program that will update their master file by using a transaction file they have processed for you.

Solution Design

The twenty customers and their account balances are described on a file called MASTER.FILE. There are ten customers and the amounts of their transactions on a file called TRANS.FILE. A negative amount on the TRANS.FILE indicates a withdrawal, while a positive amount shows a deposit. The data in these files can be read into arrays. Then the MASTER.FILE can be updated and written to a file called NEW.MASTER.

The Program

Figure X–15 gives the program listing. Line 40 sets dimensions for the arrays that will hold the data from the files. Lines 50 and 60 open the master file and the transaction file, respectively. Line 70 opens the new master file that will be an updated version of the master file. Lines 150 through 190 put data from the MASTER.FILE into arrays A$ and A. Lines 270 through 310 put the data from the TRANS.FILE into arrays N$ and T.

Now we must update the MASTER.FILE. We close files 1 and 2 with lines 320 and 330. Lines 370 through 460 determine each customer's new account balance. Lines 370 through 390 set each new account balance (B) equal to each old account balance (A). If the name from the MASTER.FILE (A$) does not equal the name from the TRANS.FILE (N$), then line processing continues at line 450 until the two names are equal. When the two names are equal, then line 430 replaces the number in B with the result of the transaction amount (T) added to the old balance (A). Lines 540 through 580 form a FOR and NEXT loop that stores each customer's name and new account balance on disk and also prints out the file listing. Line 590 closes file 3.

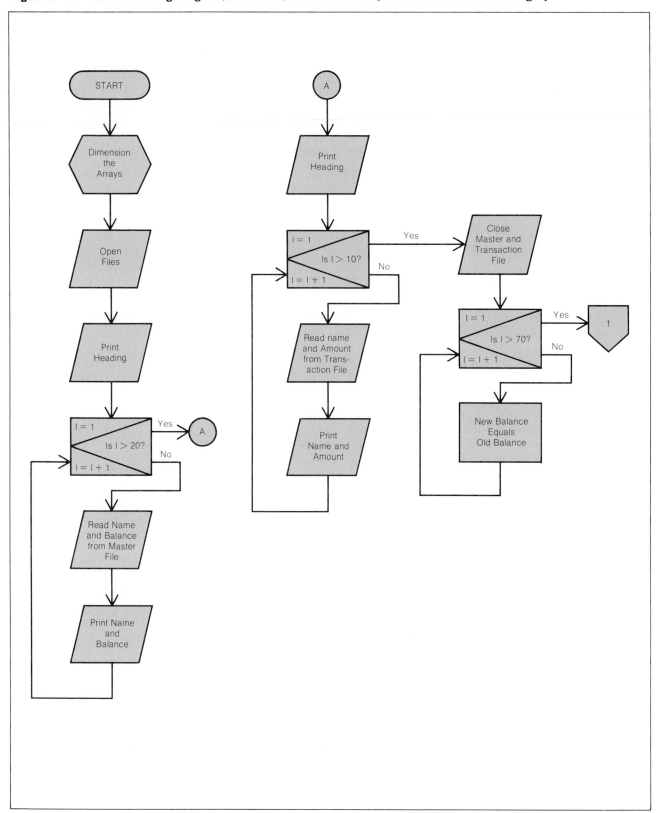

Figure X–15 ▪ **Continued**

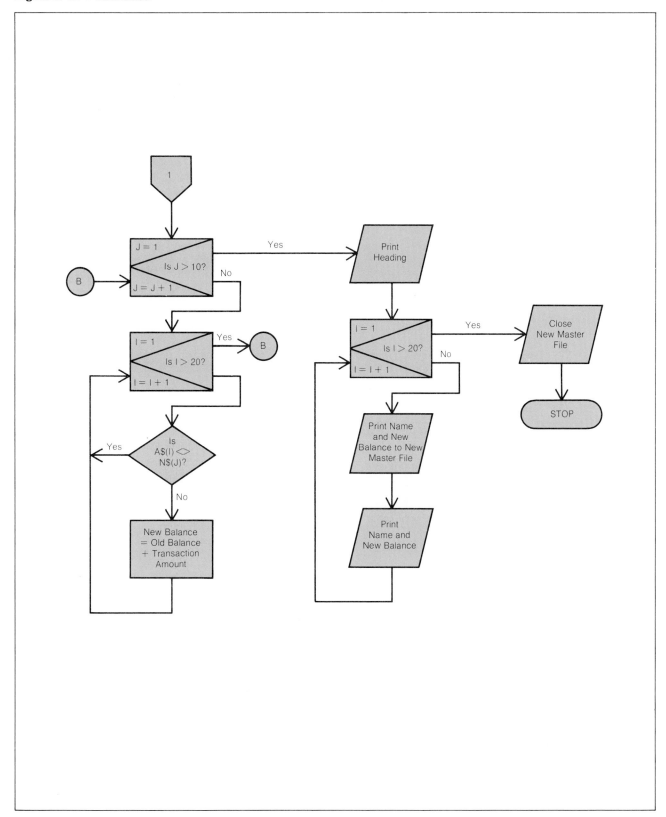

Figure X–15 ▪ **Continued**

PSEUDOCODE
Start
Dimension the arrays
Open master file, transaction file, and new master file
Print the master file report headings
Start loop, do twenty times
  Read name
  Read account balance
  Print name and account balance
Endloop
Print the transaction file report headings
Start loop, do ten times
  Read name
  Read transaction amount
  Print name and transaction amount
Endloop
Close master file and transaction file
Start loop, do twenty times
  New balance of each account equals its old balance
Endloop
Start loop, do ten times
  Start loop, do twenty times
    If master file name equals transaction file name
      Then
        New balance of the account equals old account balance + transaction amount
    Endloop
  Endloop
Print the new master file report headings
Start loop, do twenty times
  Write each name to the new master file
  Write each new account balance to new master file
  Print name and new account balance
Endloop
Close new master file
Stop

```
00010 REM *************************************************
00020 REM ***          FILE PROCESSING PROGRAM        ***
00030 REM *************************************************
00040 DIM A$(20),A(20),N$(10),T(10),B(20)
00050 OPEN "MASTER.FILE" AS FILE #1
00060 OPEN "TRANS.FILE" AS FILE #2
00070 OPEN "NEW.MASTER" AS FILE #3
00080 REM *************************************************
00090 REM ***        READ MASTER.FILE INTO PROGRAM    ***
00100 REM *************************************************
00110 PRINT
00120 PRINT "MASTER FILE"
00130 PRINT "ACCOUNT","BALANCE"
00140 PRINT
```

Figure X–15 ▪ Continued

```
00150 FOR I = 1 TO 20
00160    INPUT #1,A$(I)
00170    INPUT #1,A(I)
00180    PRINT A$(I),A(I)
00190 NEXT I
00200 PRINT
00210 REM ************************************************
00220 REM ***       READ TRANS.FILE INTO PROGRAM       ***
00230 REM ************************************************
00240 PRINT "TRANSACTION FILE"
00250 PRINT "ACCOUNT","AMOUNT"
00260 PRINT
00270 FOR I = 1 TO 10
00280    INPUT #2,N$(I)
00290    INPUT #2,T(I)
00300    PRINT N$(I),T(I)
00310 NEXT I
00320 CLOSE #1
00330 CLOSE #2
00340 REM ************************************************
00350 REM ***       DETERMINE NEW ACCOUNT BALANCE      ***
00360 REM ************************************************
00370 FOR I = 1 TO 20
00380    LET B(I) = A(I)
00390 NEXT I
00400 FOR J = 1 TO 10
00410    FOR I = 1 TO 20
00420       IF A$(I) <> N$(J) THEN 450
00430       B(I) = A(I) + T(J)
00440       GOTO 460
00450    NEXT I
00460 NEXT J
00470 REM ************************************************
00480 REM *** WRITE NEW BALANCE TO FILE AND PRINT OUT ***
00490 REM ************************************************
00500 PRINT
00510 PRINT "NEW MASTER FILE"
00520 PRINT "ACCOUNT","BALANCE"
00530 PRINT
00540 FOR I = 1 TO 20
00550    PRINT #3,A$(I)
00560    PRINT #3,B(I)
00570    PRINT A$(I),B(I)
00580 NEXT I
00590 CLOSE #3
00999 END
```

Figure X–15 ▪ **Continued**

```
RUNNH

MASTER FILE
ACCOUNT        BALANCE

CLEMMENS       7841.91
CONRAD         287.03
GIRNUS         5786.45
GOUGH          888.23
GREENE         87.55
HARRIS         45.9
HILL           443.67
KRAMMER        20.34
LEWIS          72.11
MILLER         839.89
MUGG           345.39
NEWHART        8.32
POOR           109.7
SMITH          103.28
SOMMERS        49.23
SPITERY        34.92
TWILLY         874.97
WEINSTEIN      9032.97
WILLE          656.28
YALE           834.88

TRANSACTION FILE
ACCOUNT        AMOUNT

CLEMMENS       -800
GIRNUS         -150
GOUGH          45.14
GREENE         89.23
HARRIS         99.45
HILL           443.1
KRAMMER        -10
MUGG           -175
WEINSTEIN      107.93
YALE           -200

NEW MASTER FILE
ACCOUNT        BALANCE

CLEMMENS       7041.91
CONRAD         287.03
GIRNUS         5636.45
GOUGH          933.37
GREENE         176.78
HARRIS         145.35
HILL           886.77
KRAMMER        10.34
LEWIS          72.11
MILLER         839.89
MUGG           170.39
NEWHART        8.32
POOR           109.7
SMITH          103.28
SOMMERS        49.23
SPITERY        34.92
TWILLY         874.97
WEINSTEIN      9140.9
WILLE          656.28
YALE           634.88
```

SUMMARY POINTS

■ Data is organized in the following manner. A single data item is called a field. Related fields are organized into a record. A file is composed of a group of related records.

■ There are two main types of files: sequential and random access.

■ There is no standardized method for performing operations on files stored on secondary storage devices.

REVIEW QUESTIONS

1. What are files and some of their advantages? What are fields and records?
2. Give the three steps needed to record data in a sequential file. How do these differ from the steps needed to read data from a sequential file?
3. What two things does closing a sequential file do?
4. What is the main difference between random and sequential access?

DEBUGGING EXERCISES (Designed for DECSYSTEM 20)

```
1. 100 OPEN CUSTOMER AS FILE #4
   105 FOR I = 1 TO 100
   110    READ X
   115    PRINT #2,X
   120 NEXT I
   125 CLOSE #4
```

```
2. 50 REM *** READ DATA FROM FILE ***
   55 OPEN PAYROLL FILE #3
   60 FOR I = 1 TO 5
   65    READ #3 A$(I)
   70    PRINT A$(I)
   75 NEXT I
   80 CLOSE #2
```


PROGRAMMING PROBLEMS

1. Write a program which will create a sequential file containing the following names of bodybuilders:

HANEY	BANNOUT
BERTIL	MAKKAWY
PLATZ	WILKOSZ
FULLER	BECKLES
ZANE	METZ

2. The IFBB wants to send information about the next Mr. Olympia contest to potential contestants. They need an alphabetically sorted list of bodybuilders. Write a program to read the list of names from the file you created in Programming Problem 1, sort the names alphabetically, and print them out.

BASIC Glossary

Alphanumeric data   A character set that contains any combination of letters, numbers, and special characters (such as punctuation marks).

ANSI BASIC   A programming language that has a universally accepted set of standard rules. BASIC is short for Beginners All-purpose Symbolic Instruction Code.

Argument   The quantity to be evaluated by a function. It can be a constant, a variable, a mathematical expression, or another function and is enclosed in parentheses.

Array   A one- or two-dimensional group of storage locations in memory given a single variable name. Individual elements of an array are referenced by using subscripts.

BASIC   (Beginners' All-purpose Symbolic Instruction Code) A high-level programming language commonly used for interactive problem solving by beginning programmers.

Boot   A term used to describe the process in which the disk drive loads the instructions that tell the computer how to manage the disk.

Branching   A method of transferring control from one part of the program to another by skipping past some statements in the program.

Bubble sort   A method of sorting that works by comparing two adjacent values in an array and then interchanging them according to the desired order.

Built-in function   See Library function.

Catalog   The contents of a disk.

Character string constant   A group of letters, numbers, or special characters enclosed in quotation marks; the value does not change during program execution.

Character string literal   A group of letters, numbers, or special characters assigned when a program is written that are to be printed exactly as is on the output page.

Column   Vertical segregations on the print line.

Concatenate   To append; attach; to join together two or more character strings. The addition (+) operand is used.

Conditional transfer   A transfer of control to other statements in the program based on the evaluation of a mathematical expression.

Constant   Numeric or character string value that does not change during program execution.

Conversational mode   A mode in which the user can communicate with the computer while a program is being executed.

Cursor   Usually a flashing character such as an underline or a block that shows where the next typed character will appear on the screen.

Decision block   A diamond-shaped symbol used in flowcharting to represent an IF/THEN test.

Dummy value   See Trailer value.

Exception-handling   A sequence of statements that helps the program to handle problems that would otherwise lead to a premature stop.

Expression   A valid literal, variable, or mathematical formula.

Field   A meaningful item of data, such as a student's name.

File   A grouping of related records, such as student records.

Floating-point BASIC   A version of the BASIC language that allows use of decimal fractions.

Flowchart   A symbolic chart showing the processing steps needed to solve a problem.

Garbage-in-garbage out   A phrase meaning that output can be no more accurate than the input fed into the computer.

Hierarchy of operations   The priority path a computer follows when performing more than one mathematical operation in a single formula.

Immediate mode command   A command used without a line number; executed as soon as the return key is pressed.

Index   The loop variable of a FOR/NEXT loop. This value is tested to see if the loop has been executed the desired number of times.

Infinite loop   A loop that repeats endlessly.

Initialization   Assign a beginning value to a variable; used with accumulators and counters.

Input   The step in the data-processing flow where data are entered and coded for computer use.

Inquiry-and-response mode   A mode in which the program requests information from the user and the user responds; see also Conversational mode.

Library function   Functions that have been built into the BASIC language because many applications require these types of mathematical operations; included in the BASIC language library.

Line number   The number that preceeds each statement. Line numbers tell the computer the order in which the statements are to be executed.

List   See One-dimensional array.

Literal   A numeric or string constant used in a PRINT statement.

Loop   A series of instructions in a program that is executed repeatedly as long as specific conditions are met.

Mantissa   The number preceding the "E" which in most systems lies between 1.000 and 9.999.

Mask   Symbols that specify the number of characters to be printed in a field.

Matrix   Another name for a one- or two-dimensional array.

Natural logarithm   A function that is the reverse of the EXP(x) function.

Numeric constant   A real number that does not change when a program is executed.

Numeric literal   A real number assigned when a program is written (not calculated) that is to be printed exactly as is on the page. Numeric literals are used in the PRINT statement.

Numeric variable   A real number that is either supplied to the computer by the programmer or internally calculated by the computer. All variables can change during the execution of the program.

One-dimensional array   An array with just one column of values.

Output   Information that comes from the computer as a result of processing.

Predefined function   See Library function.

Processing   The manipulation of data provided as input in order to generate information; includes classifying, sorting, calculating, summarizing, and storing.

Programming process   A 5-step process used for problem solving: (1) Define the problem, (2) Design a solution, (3) Write the program, (4) Submit the program, and (5) Test and debug.

Prompt   A message printed out to explain to the user what data should be entered. Usually used in conjunction with the INPUT statement.

Real number Numbers composed of either integers or decimal fractions.

Record A collection of data items, or fields, that are related; such as data about a single student.

Relational symbol A symbol that can be used for condition testing. These symbols include :$<$, $>$, $=$, $>=$, $<=$, $><$, and $<>$.

Reserved word Words that are reserved for special purposes, such as programming commands; they cannot be used in variable names.

Sequential file A file where data items are recorded one after another and must be read one after another in the same order in which they were recorded.

Statement The fundamental building-block of a computer program. Each BASIC statement must include a line number and a BASIC command.

String variable A value composed of letters, numbers or special characters that is enclosed in quotation marks. This value may change when the program is executed.

Subroutine A sequence of statements not within the main line of the program; used primarily to avoid having to re-write program segments. All subroutines must end with a RETURN statement.

Subscripted variable Elements of an array. The subscript is the integer enclosed in parentheses that allows reference to a specific element; for example X(3).

Syntax Refers to the way rules must be followed while coding instructions, just as grammatical rules must be followed in English.

System command A command used by the programmer to communicate with the operating system of the computer.

Table See Two-dimensional array.

Terminal format file See Sequential file.

Text files What the Apple system calls data files.

Tracks Concentric circles on the surface of a disk.

Trailer value A value added to the end of a data list to indicate that a loop should stop executing.

Two-dimensional array The arrangement of data in a table consisting of rows and two or more columns.

Unconditional transfer Another name for a GOTO statement. A statement that changes the flow of execution every time it is executed (unconditionally).

Unsubscripted variable Simple variables that use no subscripts, such as N1.

Variable A numerical or string value that can change during the execution of the program.

Variable name The name the programmer assigns to data stored in the computer's memory whose value can change as the program is executed.

BASIC
Index

GLOSSARY

A

Access mechanism The physical device that positions the read/write head of a direct-access storage device over a particular track.

Accounting machine Forerunner of the computer; could mechanically read data from punched cards, perform calculations, rearrange data, and print results in varied formats.

Accumulator A register that accumulates results of computations.

Accuracy The constancy of computer-generated results.

Action entry One of four sections of a decision logic table; specifies what actions should be taken.

Action stub One of four sections of a decision logic table; describes possible actions applicable to the problem to be solved.

Activity Refers to the proportion of records accessed during an update run of the data file.

Ada A high-level programming language developed for use by the Department of Defense. Named for Augusta Ada Byron, Countess of Lovelace and daughter of Lord Byron the poet.

Address A unique identifier assigned to each memory location within primary storage.

Alphanumeric A character set that contains letters, digits, and special characters such as punctuation marks.

American National Standards Institute (ANSI) The institute that adopted a standard set of flowchart symbols which are commonly accepted and used by programmers.

American Standard Code for Information Interchange (ASCII) A seven-bit standard code used for information interchange among data-processing systems, communication systems, and associated equipment.

Amount field The field where a clerk manually inserts the amount of the check; used in the processing of bank checks.

Analog computer A computer that measures continuous electrical or physical magnitudes rather than operating on digits; contrast with digital computer.

Analog transmission Transmission of data over communication channels in a continuous wave form.

Analytical engine A machine created by Charles Babbage, capable of addition, subtraction, multiplication, division, and storage of intermediate results in a memory unit; too advanced for its time, the analytical engine was forgotten for nearly one hundred years.

APL (a Programming Language) A terminal-oriented symbolic programming language especially suitable for interactive problem solving.

Application-oriented language A language that focuses on the computational and logical procedures required to solve a problem.

Application program A sequence of instructions written to solve a specific problem facing organizational management.

Application programmer The person who writes application software.

Architecture Another name for the internal design of a computer.

Arithmetic/logic unit (ALU) The section of the CPU that handles arithmetic computations and logical operations.

Array An ordered set of data items; also called a table or matrix.

Array variable A symbol that can be used to represent groups of similar data items.

Artificial intelligence A field of research currently developing techniques whereby computers can be used to solve problems that appear to require imagination, intuition, or intelligence.

ASCII-8 An eight-bit version of ASCII.

Assembler program The translator program for an assembly language program; produces a machine language program (object program).

Assembly language A symbolic programming language that uses convenient abbreviations rather than groupings of 0s and 1s; intermediate-level language in terms of user orientation.

Atanasoff-Berry Computer (ABC) Determined to be the first electronic computer; developed by John Vincent Atanasoff and Clifford Berry.

Attributes A field containing information; a descriptive property associated with a name to describe a characteristic of items that the name may represent.

Audio conferencing A conference call that links three or more people.

Audio input system See Voice recognition device.

Augmented audio conferencing A form of teleconferencing that combines graphics and audio conferencing.

Automatic data processing (ADP) The collection, manipulation, and dissemination of data by electromechanical machines to attain specified objectives.

Automatic teller machine (ATM) Remote terminals that allow bank customers to communicate with the bank's central computer; user can perform such functions as check account balances, transfer funds, make deposits, withdrawals, and loan payments.

Auxiliary storage Also known as external storage or secondary storage; supplements primary storage but operates at slower speeds.

B

Back-end processor A small CPU serving as an interface between a large CPU and a large data base stored on a direct-access storage device.

Background partition In a multiprogramming system, a partition holding a lower-priority program that is executed only when high-priority programs are not using the system.

Background program In a multiprogramming system, a program that can be executed whenever the facilities of the system are not needed by a high-priority program.

Backup Alternate procedures, equipment, or systems used in case of destruction or failure of the original.

Bandwidth The range, or width, of the frequencies available for transmission on a given channel.

Bar-code reader A device used to read a bar code by means of reflected light, such as a scanner that reads the Universal Product Code on supermarket products.

Base 2 See Binary number system.

Base 8 See Octal number system.

Base 16 See Hexadecimal number system.

BASIC (Beginners' All-Purpose Symbolic Instruction Code) A programming language commonly used for interactive problem solving by users who may not be professional programmers.

Batch sequential processing The grouping of user jobs for processing one after another in a continuous stream—a batch processing environment.

Binary number system The numeric system used in computer operations that uses the digits 0 and 1 and has a base of 2.

Binary representation Uses a two-state, or binary, system to represent data; as in setting and re-setting the electrical state of semiconductor memory to either 0 or 1.

Binary system See Binary number system.

Biochip A primary memory chip that uses the grouping of molecules to create an electronic circuit; none have actually been made.

Biomechanics The application of engineering methodologies to biological systems.

Bit (short for BInary digiT) The smallest unit of information that can be represented in binary notation.

Bit cells The name for storage locations in semiconductors.

Block In block-structured programming languages, a section of program coding treated as a unit.

Block diagram See Flowchart.

Blocked records Records grouped on magnetic tape or magnetic disk to reduce the number of interrecord gaps and more fully utilize the storage medium.

Brain-wave interface A technology that allows a user to control computer resources by using his or her brain wave patterns.

Branch A statement used to bypass or alter the normal flow of execution.

Breach of contract The instance when goods fail to meet the terms of either an express warranty or implied warranty.

Broad-band channels Communication channels that can transmit data at rates of up to 120,000 bits per second; for example, laser beams and microwaves.

Bubble memory A memory device in which data is represented by magnetized spots (magnetic domains) that rest on a thin film of semiconductor material.

Buffer Storage used to compensate for a difference in the rate of flow of data, or time of occurrence of events, when transmitting data from one device to another.

Built-in functions A common or often-used procedure that is permanently stored in the computer; examples include square root, absolute value, and logarithms.

Bus network A local area network in which multiple stations connected to a communication line can communicate directly with any other station on the line.

Byte A fixed number of adjacent bits operated on as a unit.

C

Cache memory Also known as a high-speed buffer; a working buffer or temporary area used to help speed the execution of a program.

CAD/CAM See Computer-aided design and Computer-aided manufacturing.

CADUCEUS An artificial intelligence, expert system that diagnoses medical problems.

Calculate The arithmetic and/or logical manipulation of data.

Capacitor The device that holds the electrical charge within a bit cell of semiconductor memory.

Card punch See Keypunch.

Cathode-ray tube (CRT) A visual-display device that receives electrical impulses and translates them into a picture on a television-like screen.

Cell The unique location within an electronic spreadsheet where a row and a column intersect.

Central processing unit (CPU) Also known as the mainframe, or heart of the computer; composed of three sections—the primary storage unit, arithmetic/logic unit (ALU), and control unit.

Chain printer An output device that has the character set engraved in type and assembled in a chain that revolves horizontally past all print positions; prints when a print hammer (one for each column of the paper) presses the paper against an inked ribbon that presses against the characters on the print chain.

Channel A limited-capacity computer that takes over the tasks of input and output in order to free the CPU to handle internal processing operations.

Character-at-a-time printer Prints just one character of information at a time.

Charge-coupled device (CCD) A storage device that is made of silicon; is nearly one-hundred times faster than magnetic bubbles.

Check bit See Parity bit.

Chief programmer team (CPT) A method of organization used in the management of system projects where a chief programmer supervises the programming and testing of system modules; programmer productivity and system reliability are increased.

Classify To categorize data according to certain characteristics so that it is meaningful to the user.

Clustered-key-to-tape device Several keyboards are tied to one or two magnetic-tape units.

COBOL (COmmon Business-Oriented Language) A high-level programming language generally used for accounting and business data processing.

CODASYL (COnference on DAta SYstems Languages) A committee formed by the Department of Defense to examine the feasibility of establishing a common business programming language.

Code To convert data from various sources and assemble them at one location.

Collect To gather data from various sources and assemble them at one location.

Command area The area at the bottom of some electronic spreadsheets that displays the available commands to the user.

Common law Law that is based on customs and past judicial decisions in similar cases.

Communicate A step in the output phase of data flow; to transfer information in intelligible form to a user.

Communication channel A medium for carrying data from one location to another.

Comparison A statement that allows two items to be compared.

Compiler program The translator program for a high-level language such as FORTRAN or COBOL; translates source-program statements into machine-executable code.

Computer A general-purpose machine with applications limited only by the creativity of the humans who use it; its power is derived from its speed, accuracy, and memory.

Computer anxiety A fear individuals have of the effects computers have on their lives and society in general.

Computer conferencing A form of teleconferencing that uses computer terminals for the transmission of messages; participants need not be using the terminal in order to receive the message—it will be waiting the next time he or she uses the terminal.

Computer crime A criminal act that poses a greater threat to a computer user than it would a non-computer user, or a criminal act that is accomplished through the use of a computer.

Computer ethics A term used to refer to the standard of moral conduct in computer use; a way in which the "spirit" of some laws are applied to computer-related activities

Computer literacy A broad, general knowledge of how to use comptuers to solve problems, of the functioning of the software and hardware, and an understanding of the societal implications of computers.

Computer modeling The use of computers to model animal biological systems, for example, in place of the animals themselves; using computers to act as a real system for testing purposes.

Computer operator An individual that is responsible for setting up computer equipment for particular jobs like mounting and removing tapes, disks, and diskettes, and monitoring the operation of the computer.

Computer output microfilm (COM) Miniature photographic images of output. Computer output is placed on magnetic tape which serves as the input to a microfilm processor.

Computer security Instituting the technical and administrative safeguards necessary to protect a computer-based system against the hazards to which computer systems are exposed and to control access to information.

Computer store A retail store that sells computers and is structured to appeal to the small-business person or personal user.

Computer-aided design (CAD) The process of designing, drafting, and analyzing a prospective product using computer graphics on a video terminal.

Computer-aided manufacturing (CAM) The process of using the computer to create a magnetic tape that will guide the machine tool in creating the particular part.

Computer-assisted diagnosis A technique that allows the computer to compare numerical data gathered from a patient to normal or standard data; helps the physician to make a diagnosis.

Computer-assisted instruction (CAI) Direct interaction between a computer and a student in which the computer serves as an instructor.

Computerized tomography (CT or CAT) scanning A form of

computer-assisted diagnosis in which X-ray techniques are combined with computer technology to provide for quick and accurate physical diagnosis.

Computerphobia See Computer anxiety.

Concentrator A device that systematically allocates communication channels among several terminals.

Concurrently Over the same period of time; in multiprogramming, processing rotates between different programs, giving the illusion of simultaneous (or concurrent) processing.

Condition entries One of four sections of a decision logic table; answers all questions in the condition stub.

Condition stub One of four sections of a decision logic table; describes all factors (options) to be considered in determining a course of action.

Continuous form A data-entry form, such as cash register tape, utilized by OCR devices.

Control program A routine, usually part of an operating system, that aids in controlling the operations and management of a computer system.

Control unit The section of the CPU that directs the sequence of operations by electrical signals and governs the actions of the various units which make up the computer.

Convert To translate information into a form people can read.

Corporate planning models See Simultaneous decision support systems.

Counters A method of controlling a loop in which a specific value is entered into the program and that value is tested each time the loop is executed; when the proper value is reached, the loop can be terminated.

Crash conversion Also known as direct conversion; a method of system implementation in which the old system is abandoned and the new one implemented at once.

Cursor Usually a flashing character such as an underline or a block that shows where the next typed character will appear on the computer display screen.

Cut form Data-entry form such as a phone or utility bill; used by OCR devices.

Cylinder All tracks on a magnetic disk that are accessible by the read/write heads with one movement, or positioning, of the access mechnaism.

D

Daisy-wheel printer An output device resembling an office typewriter; it employs a flat disk with petal-like projections with characters on the surfaces; printing occurs one character at a time.

Data Facts; the raw material of information.

Data base The cornerstone of a management information system; basic data are commonly defined and consistently organized to fit the information needs of a wide variety of users in an organization.

Data-base administrator (DBA) A manager responsible for the control of all the data resources of the organization.

Data-base analyst The person responsible for analysis, design, and implementation of data structures.

Data-base management system (DBMS) A set of programs that serves as an interface between the data base and three principal users—the programmer, the operating system, and the user; provides a method of arranging data to limit duplication, an ability to make changes easily, and a capability to handle direct inquiries.

Data-base producers Companies that compile and store huge, hard-copy data bases for use by online service companies.

Data buffering Reading data into a separate storage unit normally contained in the control unit of the input/output system.

Data communication The electronic transmission of data from one site to another, usually over communication channels such as telephone/telegraph lines or microwaves.

Data-entry operator A person who transcribes data into a form suitable for computer processing.

Data processing A systematic set of procedures for collecting, manipulating, and disseminating data to achieve specified objectives.

Data set A grouping of related records; also called a file.

Datacom handlers See Multiplexer and Concentrator.

Debugging The process of locating, isolating, and resolving errors within a program.

Decimal number system A number system based on the powers of ten.

Decision logic table (DLT) A standardized table that organizes relevant facts in a clear and concise manner to aid in the decision-making process.

Decision support system (DSS) Information obtained from this system is used as a supportive tool for managerial decision making.

Decrypted Data that are translated back into regular text after being encrypted for security reasons.

Dedicated machines A computer that has been specifically adapted to perform specific tasks.

Dedicated word-processing system A computer system designed solely for the purpose of word processing.

Default A course of action chosen by the compiler when several alternatives exist but none have been stated explicitly by the programmer.

Definition mode When APL is used in this mode, a series of instructions is entered into the memory, and the entire program is executed on command from the programmer.

Deletion A word-processing feature that allows deletion of characters, words, sentences, or blocks of text.

Demodulation The process of retrieving data from a modulated carrier wave.

Density The number of characters that can be stored on one inch of tape; storage capacity of the tape depends in part on its density.

Desk-checking A method used in both system and application program debugging in which the sequence of operations is mentally traced to verify the correctness of the processing logic.

Desk-debugging See Desk-checking.

Detail diagram Used in HIPO to describe the specific function performed and data items used in a module.

Detail flowchart Depicts the processing steps required within a particular program.

Difference engine A machine developed by Charles Babbage in 1822; used to compute mathematical tables with results up to five significant digits in length.

Digit rows The lower ten rows, numbers 0 through 9, that are found on an 80-column punched card.

Digital computer The type of computer commonly used in business applications; operates on distinct data (for example, digits) by performing arithmetic and logic processes on specific data units.

Digital transmission The transmission of data as distinct "on"/"off" pulses.

Digitizer An input device that allows for the input of two-dimensional images into computer memory; the images are traced in the X/Y plane and the coordinates are transformed into object form by the digitizer software.

Direct conversion See Crash conversion.

Direct access Also random-access processing; a method of processing in which data are submitted to the computer as they occur; individual records can be located and updated without reading all proceeding files.

Direct-access storage A method of storing data whereby they can be retrieved in any order, at random.

Directory Consists of two columns, the first containing the key of the record and the second containing the address of the record with that key.

Disk address The method used to uniquely identify a data record on a magnetic disk; consists of the disk surface number, the track number, and the record number.

Disk drive The mechanical device used to rotate a disk pack during data transmission; common speeds range between 40 and 1,000 revolutions per second.

Disk pack A stack of magnetic disks.

Distributed data processing (DDP) Data processing that is done at a site other than that of the central computer.

Document-oriented word processor A word processor that treats a text file as a document, rather than as a series of pages; a greater portion of the file is held in primary storage thereby reducing the amount of secondary-storage accesses that must be done.

Dot-matrix printer A type of impact printer that creates characters through the use of dot-matrix patterns.

Drum printer An output device consisting of a metal cylinder that contains rows of characters engraved across its surface; one line of print is produced with each rotation of the drum.

Dummy modules A temporary program module that is inserted at a lower level to facilitate testing of the higher-level modules; used in top-down design to enable higher-level program modules to be coded prior to completion of lower-level modules.

Dump A hard-copy printout of the contents of computer memory; valuable in debugging programs.

Dump program A printout that lists the contents of registers and primary-storage locations.

E

Edit checks Program statements designed to test data that are entered as input to a program for such things as reasonableness; a very critical part of online applications where information is updated immediately.

EDSAC (Electronic Display Storage Automatic Computer) The first stored-program computer.

EDVAC (Electronic Discrete Variable Automatic Computer) A stored-program computer developed at the University of Pennsylvania.

Eight-column punched card See Hollerith card.

Electron microscope tomography The use of a computer and individual electrons to view microscopic biological material as a three-dimensional image.

Electron microscopy (EM) The use of individual electrons to view microscopic material as a two-dimensional image.

Electronic bulletin board A communication network used to send messages to members of a group which share a common interest; uses existing communication networks.

Electronic data processing (EDP) Data processing performed largely by electronic equipment, such as computers, rather than by manual or mechanical methods.

Electronic drawing pen See Light pen.

Electronic funds transfer (EFT) A cashless method of paying for services or goods; the amounts of the two parties involved in the transaction are adjusted by electronic communication between computers.

Electronic mail The transmission of messages at high speeds over telecommunication facilities.

Electronic spreadsheet An electronic ledger sheet used to store and manipulate any type of numerical data.

Electrostatic printer A nonimpact printer in which electromagnetic impulses and heat are used to affix characters to paper.

Electrothermal printer A nonimpact printer that uses special heat-sensitive paper; characters are formed when heated rods in a matrix touch the paper..

Encrypted A term describing data that is translated into a secret code for security reasons.

ENIAC (Electronic Numerical Integrator a And Calculator) Developed by J. Presper Eckert and John W. Mauchly at the University of Pennsylvania; early electronic computer; sponsored by the War Department.

Erasable programmable read-only memory (EPROM) This memory unit can be erased and reprogrammed, but only by being submitted to a special process.

Ergonomics The method of researching and designing computer hardware and software to enhance employee productivity and comfort.

Even parity A method of coding in which an even number of 1 bits represent each character; used to enhance the detection of errors.

Execution mode When APL is used in this mode, the terminal can be used much like a desk calculator.

Expert system A form of artificial intelligence in which the software is designed to program the computer to follow the same decision-making process as top experts in a specific field.

Express warranty Created when the seller makes any promise or statement of fact concerning the goods being sold which the purchaser uses as a basis for purchasing the goods.

Extended Binary Coded Decimal Interchange Code (EBCDIC) An 8-bit code for character representation.

External storage See Auxiliary storage.

F

Facsimile system Produces a picture of a page by scanning it.

Feedback A check within a system to see whether or not predetermined goals are being met.

Field A meaningful item of data, such as a social security number.

File A grouping of related records; sometimes referred to as a data set.

File handler A data manager application package which is capable of operating on only one file at a time.

First-generation computer Used vacuum tubes; developed in the 1950s; much faster than earlier mechanical devices, but very slow in comparison to today's computers.

Fixed disk A magnetic disk system used on microcomputers that is a sealed unit and cannot be accessed by the user; relatively low-priced, reliable, secure, small in size, and has large storage capacity.

Flexible diskette A low-cost random-access form of data storage made of plastic; a flexible magnetic disk currently made in 3½-, 5¼-, and 8-inch diameter sizes.

Floppy diskette See Flexible diskette.

Flowchart Of two kinds: the program flowchart, which is a graphic representation of the types and sequences of operations in a program; and the system flowchart, which shows the flow of data through an entire system.

Flowlines The lines that connect flowchart symbols.

Foreground partition Also called foreground area; in a multiprogramming system, a partition containing high-priority application programs.

Foreground program In a multiprogramming system, a program that has high priority.

Formal design review Also called structured walk-through; an evaluation of the documentation of a system by a group of managers, analysts, and programmers to determine completeness, accuracy, and quality of deisgn.

FORTRAN (FORmula TRANslator) A programming language used primarily in performing mathematical or scientific operations.

Four-bit Binary Coded Decimal (BCD) A four-binary-digit computer code that uses the unique combinations of zone bits and numeric bits to represent specific characters.

Fourth-generation computers Use large-scale integration and offer significant price and performance improvements over earlier computers.

Front-end processor A small CPU serving as an interface between a large CPU and peripheral devices.

Full-duplex A type of communication channel capable of the most versatile mode of data transmission; can transmit data in both directions simultaneously.

G

Game paddle An input device that is normally used with microcomputers for game applications; it is used to position a figure that is required to move across or up and down the display screen.

Garbage-in-garbage-out (GIGO) A phrase used to exemplify the fact that the meaningfulness of data-processing results relies on the accuracy or relevancy of the data fed into the processor.

General-purpose machines Computers that can be used for a variety of purposes.

Goal seeking A form of simulation that allows the user to specify a desired result from which the values of the variables necessary to achieve the desired result are calculated by the DSS.

Grade The range, or width, of the frequencies available for data transmission on a given channel.

Graphic display device A visual-display device that projects output in the form of graphs and line drawings and accepts input from a keyboard or light pen.

Graphics software packages Application software packages designed to allow the user to display images on the display screen or a printer.

Grid chart A chart used in system analysis and design to summarize the relationships between the components of a system.

H

Hacking A term used to describe the activity of computer enthusiasts who are challenged by the practice of breaking computer security measures designed to prevent unauthorized access to a particular computer system.

Half-duplex A type of communication channel through which communication can occur in both directions, but in only one direction at a time.

Hard copy Printed output.

Hard magnetic disks Magnetic disks that can be used on microcomputer systems; they are found in two configurations—fixed disk and removable disk.

Hardware The physical components that make up a computer system.

Hard-wired Memory instructions that cannot be changed or deleted by other stored-program instructions.

Hashing See Randomize.

Hexadecimal number system A base 16 number system commonly used when printing the contents of primary storage to aid programmers in detecting errors.

Hierarchical configuration A multi-level CPU configuration that is controlled by a single computer at the top of the multiple CPU hierarchy; the lowest level of the hierarchy is the user level.

Hierarchical structure A method of organizing data within a data base that consists of one owner record and any number of member records.

High-level languages English-like coding schemes that are procedure-, problem-, and user-oriented.

HIPO (Hierarchy plus Input-Process-Output) A documentation technique used to describe the inputs, processing, and outputs of program modules.

Hollerith card An 80-column punched card; a commonly used, sequential-storage medium in which data are represented by the presence or absence of strategically placed holes.

Hollerith code A method of data representation in which the placement of holes in 80-column punched cards represents numbers, letters, and special characters.

Horizontal software integration In a business sense, application software packages that are general in nature and can be used for a variety of applications; in a design sense, the combination of various types of application software packages.

I

I/O control unit A device that performs code conversion and is located between one or more I/O devices and the CPU; is used only to facilitate I/O operations.

Impact printer A printer that forms characters by physically striking print element, ribbon, and paper together.

Implied warranty A warranty that provides for the automatic inclusion of certain warranties in a contract for the sale of goods.

Implied warranty of fitness A situation where the purchaser relies on a seller's expertise to recommend a good that will meet his or her needs; if the good later fails to meet the purchaser's needs the seller has breached the warranty.

Implied warranty of merchantability Guarantees the purchaser that the good purchased will function properly for a reasonable period of time.

In-house An organization's use of its own personnel or resources to develop programs or other problem-solving systems.

Index An ordered reference list of the contents of a file, or the keys for identification or location of the contents.

Indexed-sequential design A file organization design that allows for both sequential access and direct access of data records.

Informal design review An evaluation of system-designed documentation by selected management, analysts, and programmers prior to the actual coding of program modules to determine necessary additions, deletions, and modifications to the system design.

Information Data that have been organized and processed so that they are meaningful.

Ink-jet printer A nonimpact printer that uses a stream of charged ink to form dot-matrix characters.

Input Data that are submitted to the computer for processing.

Input/output management A subsystem of the operating system that controls and coordinates the CPU while receiving input from channels, executing instructions of programs in storage, and regulating output.

Input/output statements Used to bring data into primary storage for use by the program and to transfer data from primary storage to output media such as printer listings.

Input/output-bound A situation in which the CPU is slowed down because of I/O operations which are extremely slow in comparison to CPU internal processing speeds.

Insertion A word processing feature that allows characters, words, sentences, or blocks of text to be inserted into a document.

Instruction set The fundamental logical and arithmetic procedures that the computer can perform, such as addition, subtraction, and comparison.

Integrated circuit (IC) A small chip less than 1/8-inch square containing hundreds of electronic components, permitting much faster processing at a greatly reduced price.

Intelligent terminal A terminal with an internal processor that can be programmed to perform specified functions, such as data editing, data conversion, and control of other terminals.

Interblock gap (IBG) A space on magnetic tape that facilitates processing; records are grouped together and separated by interblock gaps.

Internal storage See Primary storage.

Interpreter A high-level language translator that evaluates and translates a program one statement at a time; used extensively on microcomputer systems because it takes less primary storage than a compiler.

Interpreter program See Interpreter.

Interrecord gap A space that separates records stored on magnetic tape; allows the tape drive to regain speed during processing.

Interrupt A condition or event that temporarily suspends normal processing operations.

Inverted structure A file structure that permits fast, spontaneous searching for previously unspecified information; independent lists are maintained in record keys which are accessible to the values of specified fields.

J

Job-control language (JCL) A language that serves as the communication link between the programmer and the operating system.

Job-control program A control program that translates the job-control statements written by a programmer into machine-language instructions that can be executed by the computer.

Josephson Junction A primary storage unit that, when completed, will be housed in liquid helium to reduce the resistance to the flow of electricity that currently exists in semiconductor memory.

Joystick   An input device that is normally used with micro-computers for game applications; it is used to position some object, such as a cursor, on the display screen.

K

K   A symbol used to denote $1024(2^{10})$ storage units when referring to a computer's primary storage capacity.

Key   A unique identifier for a record; used to sort records for processing or to locate a particular record within a file.

Keypunch   A keyboard device that punches holes in a card to represent data.

Keypunch operator   A data-entry operator that uses a keypunch to transcribe data in a form suitable for computer processing.

Key-to-disk   Hardware designed to transfer data entered via a keyboard to magnetic disk or diskette.

Key-to-diskette   A floppy disk is used instead of the conventional (hard) disk.

Key-to-tape   Hardware designed to transfer data entered via a keyboard to magnetic tape.

L

Label   A name written beside an instruction that acts as a key or identifier for it.

Language-translator program   Software that translates the English-like programs written by programmers into machine-executable code.

Large-scale integrated (LSI) circuits   Circuits containing thousands of transistors densely packed on a single silicon chip.

Laser printer   A type of nonimpact printer that combines laser beams and electrophotographic technology to form images on paper.

Laser storage system   A secondary storage device using laser technology to encode data onto a metallic surface; usually used for mass storage.

Lead programmer   An individual who oversees a small group of programmers working on one project, or a number of projects; provides technical assistance to junior level programmers.

Librarian   Data-processing personnel responsible for the control and maintenance of files, programs, and catalogs; also responsible for subsequent processing or historical record-keeping.

Librarian program   Software that manages the storage and use of library programs by maintaining a directory of programs in the system library and appropriate procedures for additions and deletions.

Library programs   User-written or manufacturer-supplied programs and subroutines that are frequently used in other programs; they are written and stored on secondary storage and called into primary storage when needed.

Light pen   A pen-shaped object with a photoelectric cell at its end; used to draw lines on a visual-display screen.

Line editor   A word processor that allows the user to operate on only one line of text at a time; contrast to a screen editor.

Line-at-a-time printer   Prints an entire line of information at a time.

Linear structure   A specific ordered sequence of data records within a data base.

Linkage editor   A subprogram of the operating system that links the object program from the system residence device to primary storage.

List   See Simple structure.

Local area network (LAN)   A specialized network that operates within a well-defined area, such as a building or complex of buildings, with the stations being linked by cable.

Local area networking   An alternate form of distributed processing; involves interconnecting computers in a single building or a complex of buildings.

Local system   Peripherals connected directly to the CPU.

Logic diagram   See Flowchart.

Logical design   The way in which data elements are arranged within a data base; independent of physical design.

Logo   An education-oriented, procedure-oriented, interactive programming language designed to allow anyone to begin to program and communicate with computers.

Loop   A series of instructions that are executed repeatedly as long as specified conditions remain constant.

M

Machine language   The only set of instructions that a computer can execute directly; a code that designates the proper electrical states in the computer as combinations of 0s and 1s.

Machine-oriented language   A language which describes program functions and execution; very similar to actual machine language.

Macro flowchart   See Modular program flowchart.

Magnetic core   An iron-alloy, doughnut-shaped ring about the size of a pinhead of which memory can be composed; an individual core can store one binary digit (its state is determined by the direction of an electrical current).

Magnetic disk   A storage medium consisting of a metal platter coated on both sides with a magnetic recording material upon which data are stored in the form of magnetized spots; suitable for direct processing.

Magnetic domain   A magnetized spot representing data in bubble memory.

Magnetic drum   A cylinder with a magnetic outer surface on which data are stored.

Magnetic tape   A storage medium consisting of a narrow strip upon which spots of iron-oxide are magnetized to represent data; a sequential storage medium.

Magnetic-ink character recognition (MICR) device   A device that reads characters composed of magnetized particles; often used to sort checks for subsequent processing.

Main control module   The highest level in the module hierarchy; controls other modules below it.

Main memory   See Primary storage.

Main storage   See Primary storage.

Mainframe   See Central processing unit.

Maintenance programmer   A programmer that makes changes to and modifies existing programs.

Management information system (MIS)   A formal network that extends computer use beyond routine reporting and into the area of management decision-making; its goal is to get the correct information to the appropriate manager at the right time.

Management information system manager   The individual who oversees the entire system development cycle to insure that projects are completed within reasonable time schedules.

Mark I   The first automatic calculator.

Mark-sensing   See Optical mark recognition.

Mass storage   High-density magnetic tapes or disks used to store infrequently used data while retaining accessibility.

Master file   A file that contains relatively permanent data; updated by records in a transaction file.

Maxicomputers   See Supercomputers.

Memory   The part of the computer that provides the ability to recall information.

Memory management   In a multiprogramming environment, the process of keeping the programs in primary storage separate.

Memory protection   See Memory management.

Menu-drive   An application program is said to be menu-driven when it provides the user with ''menus'' displaying available choices or selections to help guide the user through the process of using the software package.

Message-switching   A communications processor with the principal task of receiving messages and routing them to appropriate destinations.

Micro flowchart   See Detail flowchart.

Microcomputer   A computer small in size but not in power; now available in 8-, 16-, and 32-bit microprocessor configurations.

Microprocessor   The CPU of a microcomputer.

Microprogram   A sequence of instructions wired into read-only memory; used to tailor a system to meet the user's processing requirements.

Minicomputer   A computer with the components of a full-sized system but having a smaller primary storage capacity.

Mnemonics   A symbolic name (memory aid); used in symbolic languages (for example, assembly language) and high-level programming languages.

Model   A representation of a real world system; used to construct a decision support system to help managers with their decision making tasks.

Modeling package   An application software program incorporating a representation of a real world situation; used on mainframe computers and minicomputer.

Modem   Also called a data set; a device that modulates and demodulates signals transmitted over communication facilities.

Modular approach   Simplifying a project by breaking it into segments or subunits.

Modular program flowchart   A diagram that represents the general flow and major processing steps (modules) of a program.

Modulation   A technology used in modems to make data-processing signals compatible with communication facilities.

Module   A part of a whole; a program segment; a subsystem.

Monitor   A housekeeping program that controls the computer. A display device used on microcomputer systems.

Mouse   A small device used primarily on microcomputers for the positioning of the cursor; its primary advantage is that it eliminates a great deal of typing for some applications.

Multiphasic health testing (MPHT)   A form of computer-assisted diagnosis that compiles information on patients and their test results, which are compared to norms or means in order to aid the physician in making a diagnosis.

Multiplexer   A device that permits more than one I/O device to transmit data over the same communication channel.

Multiplexor channel   A limited-capacity computer that can handle more than one I/O device at a time; normally controls slow-speed devices such as card readers, printers, or terminals.

Multiprocessing   A multiple CPU configuration in which jobs are processed simultaneously.

Multiprogramming   A technique whereby several programs are placed in primary storage at the same time, giving the illusion that they are being executed simultaneously; this results in increased CPU active time.

N

Narrow bandwidth channels   Communication channels that can only transmit data at a rate of forty-five to ninety bits per second; for example, telegraph channels.

Natural languages   Designed primarily for novice computer users; use English-like sentences usually for the purpose of accessing data in a data base.

Network   The linking together of several CPUs.

Next-sequential-instruction feature   The ability of a computer to execute program steps in the order in which they are stored in memory unless branching takes place.

Nondestructive read/destructive write   The feature of computer memory that permits data to be read and retained in their original state, allowing them to be referenced repeatedly during processing.

Nonimpact printers   The use of heat, laser technology, or photographic techniques to print output.

Nonmonotonic logic   The theory that logic should develop in steps, consistent with all preceding steps, and that additional assumptions will not make the previous conclusions false.

Numeric bits   The four rightmost bit positions of 6-bit BCD used to encode numeric data.

Numerically controlled machinery   Manufacturing machinery that is driven by a magnetic punched tape created by a tape punch that is driven by computer sofware.

O

Object program   A sequence of machine executable instructions derived from source-program statements by a language translator program.

Octal number system   Each position represents a power of eight.

Odd parity   A method of coding in which an odd number of 1 bits is used to represent each character; facilitates error checking.

Office automation   The integration of computer and communication technology with traditional manual processes found in business offices.

"On us" field   The section of a check that contains the customer's checking account number.

Online   In direct communication with the computer.

Online storage symbol   A symbol that indicates the file is kept on an online external storage medium such as disk or tape.

Operand   The part of an instruction that tells where to find the data or equipment to be operated on.

Operating system   A collection of programs designed to permit a computer system to manage itself and to avoid idle CPU time while increasing utilization of computer resources.

Operation code   Also known as op code; the part of an instruction that tells what operation is to be performed.

Optical character   A special type of character that can be read by an optical-character reader.

Optical disk   Also known as a laser disk; stores data as the presence or absence of a pit burned into the surface of the disk by a laser beam.

Optical-character recognition (OCR)   A capability of devices with electronic scanners that read numbers, letters, and other characters, and convert the optical images into appropriate electrical signals.

Optical-mark page reader   A device that senses marks on an OMR document as the document passes under a light source.

Optical-mark recognition (OMR)   Also mark sensing; a capability of devices with electronic scanners that read marks on a page and convert the optical images into appropriate electrical signals.

Output   Information that comes from the computer as a result of processing.

Overlapped processing   A method of processing where the computer works on several programs instead of one.

Overview diagram   Used in HIPO to describe, in greater detail, a module shown in the visual table of contents.

P

Page frame   In a virtual storage environment, one of the fixed-size physical areas into which primary storage is divided.

Page-oriented word processor   A word processor that treats a document as a series of pages; contrast to document-oriented word processor.

Page   In a virtual storage environment, the portion of a program that is kept in secondary storage and loaded into real storage only when needed during processing.

Paging   A method of implementing virtual storage; data and programs are broken into fixed-size blocks, or pages, and loaded into real storage when needed during processing.

Parallel conversion   A system implementation approach in which the new system is operated side-by-side with the old one until all differences are reconciled.

Parallelism   The process of simultaneous data movement through a number of communication channels on a computer system.

Parity bit   A means of detecting erroneous transmission of data; internal self-checking to determine if the number of 1 bits in a bit pattern is either odd or even.

Partition   In multiprogramming, the primary storage area reserved for one program; may be fixed or variable in size; see also Region.

Pascal   An example of a language developed for education purposes, to teach programming concepts to students; named after French mathematician Blaise Pascal.

Peripheral device   A device that attaches to the CPU, such as secondary storage devices and input/output devices.

Phased conversion   A method of system implementation in which the old system is gradually replaced by the new one; the new system is segmented and gradually applied.

Physical design   Refers to how the data within a data base are kept on storage devices and how they are accessed.

Pilot conversion   The implementation of a new system into the organization on a piecemeal basis; also known as modular conversion.

Piracy   The unauthorized copying of a computer program written by someone else.

Pixel   The individual dots on a display screen that are used to create characters and images.

PL/I   Programming Language One; a general-purpose language used for both scientific and business applications.

Plotter   An output device that convertes data emitted from the CPU into graphic form; produces hard-copy output.

Point-of-sale (POS) system   A computerized system that records information required for such things as inventory control and accounting at the point where a good is sold; see also Source data automation.

Poll   Or polling; the process used by a concentrator to determine if an input/output device wants to send a message to the CPU.

Primary memory   Also known as internal storage or main storage; the section of the CPU that holds instructions, data, and intermediate and final results during processing.

Primary storage   Also known as internal storage, memory, main storage the section of the CPU that holds instructions, data, and intermediate and final results during processing.

Print formatting   The process in which the word processor communicates with the printer to tell it how the text should be printed.

Print-wheel printer An output device consisting of 120 print wheels, each containing 48 characters. The print wheels rotate until an entire line is in the appropriate position, then a hammer presses the paper against the print wheel.

Printer-keyboard An output device similar to an office typewriter; prints one character at a time and is controlled by a program stored in the CPU of the computer.

Printer A device used to produce permanent (hard-copy) computer output; impact printers are designed to work mechanically; nonimpact printers use heat, laser, or chemical technology.

Privacy An individual's right regarding the collection, processing, storage, dissemination, and use of data about his or her personal attributes and activities.

Problem-oriented language A language that describes the problem and solution without detailing the computational procedures; RPG is an example of this type of language.

Procedure-oriented language Examples consist of COBOL, FORTRAN and PL/1.

Process To transform raw data into useful information.

Process-bound A condition that occurs when a program monopolizes the processing facilities of the computer, making it impossible for other programs to be executed.

Processing program A routine, usually part of the operating system, that is used to simplify program preparation and execution.

Program A series of step-by-step instructions that provides a problem solution and tells the computer exactly what to do; of two types—application and system.

Programmable communications processor A device that relieves the CPU of the task of monitoring data transmissions.

Programmable read-only memory (PROM) Read-only memory that can be programmed by the manufacturer or by the user for special functions to meet the unique needs of the user.

Programmer The person who writes step-by-step instructions for the computer to execute.

Programmer/analyst This person is responsible for system analysis and programming and is usually found in small organizations.

Project leader See Lead programmer.

Prompt A message printed out to explain to the user what data are to be entered for the program's use.

Proper program A program using the structured approach and top-down design, and having only one entrance and one exit.

Pseudocode An informal design language used to represent the logic patterns of structured programming.

Pulse form A pulse of current used to store data in computers.

Punched card An outdated form of sequential storage in which the data is represented by the presence or absence of strategically placed holes.

Q

Query language See Natural languages.

Queue A list or collection of programs waiting for execution by the CPU; normally ordered on a first-in, first-out basis.

R

RAM (random-access memory) chips The most popular of the microchips; a continuous supply of power is needed.

Randomize To compute record numbers from actual keys through any of a number of mathematical techniques.

ROM (read-only memory) The part of computer hardware containing items that cannot be deleted or changed by stored-program instructions because they are wired into the computer.

Read/write head An electromagnet used as a component of a tape or disk drive; in reading, it detects magnetized areas and translates them into electrical pulses; in writing, it magnetizes appropriate areas, thereby erasing data stored previously.

Real storage See Primary storage; contrast with virtual storage.

Record A collection of data items, or fields, that relates to a single unit.

Region In multiprogramming with a variable number of tasks, a term often used to mean the internal space allocated; a variable-size partition.

Register An internal computer component used for temporary storage of an instruction or data; capable of accepting, holding, and transferring that instruction or data very rapidly.

Remote input Input that must be sent to a central computer for processing.

Remote system A system where terminals are connected to the central computer by a communication channel.

Remote terminal operator A person who uses a remote terminal to enter data into a computer system.

Remote terminal A terminal that is placed at a location distant from the central computer.

Removable disk A hard magnetic disk unit that can be used on a microcomputer for secondary storage; allows for one disk to be removed and another inserted.

Resident routines The most frequently used components of the supervisor which are initially loaded into primary storage.

Retrieve The accessing of previously stored information by the computer so that it can be referenced by the user.

Ring configuration A type of distributed system in which a number of computers are connected by a single transmission line in a ring arrangement.

Ring network A classification of local area network in which multiple stations are each connected to its adjacent station; communication must be relayed through adjacent stations to the desired station.

Robotics The science that deals with robots, their construction, capabilities, and applications.

RPG (report program generator) An example of a problem-oriented language originally designed to produce business reports.

Run book Also known as operator's manual; program documentation designed to aid the computer operator in running a program.

S

Screen editor A word processor that allows for the editing of text that appears on the entire display screen; contrast with a line editor.

Screen formatting Features within a word processor that control the way in which text appears on the display screen.

Script theory An approach to artificial intelligence that says that memories of a situation within our minds dictate how we, as humans, would think or act in a particular situation; this is an attempt to apply this logic to giving computers intelligence.

Scrolling The process of positioning a portion of a text file onto the display screen; used to view portions of a document while using a word processor.

Search A word processing feature that allows the user to specify a word or set of characters to be searched for throughout the document.

Second-generation computers Used magnetic cores for primary storage and magnetic tapes for secondary storage; first use of high-level programming language; 1959–1964.

Secondary storage Also known as external or auxiliary storage; supplements primary storage but operates at slower speeds.

Segment A variable-size block or portion of a program used in a virtual storage system.

Segmentation A method of implementing virtual storage; involves dividing a program into variable-size blocks, called segments, depending on the program logic.

Selection Program logic that includes a test; depending on the results of the test, one of two paths is taken.

Selector channel A channel that can accept input from only one device at a time; usually used with high-speed I/O devices such as a magnetic-tape or magnetic-disk unit.

Semiconductor memory Circuitry on silicon chips that are smaller than magnetic cores and allow for faster processing; more expensive than core memory and requires a constant power source.

Sensitivity analysis A form of simulation that allows the user to identify the key variables within a decision support system model.

Sequential file Data (records) stored in specific order, one right after the other.

Sequential processing See Batch processing.

Sequential-access storage Auxiliary storage from which records must be read, one after another, in a fixed sequence, until the needed data are located; for example, magnetic tape.

Serial processing A method of processing where programs

are executed one at a time, usually found in simple operating systems such as the earliest computer systems.

Silicon chip Solid-logic circuitry used in primary storage units of third- and fourth-generation computers.

Simple sequence Program logic where one statement after another is executed in order, as stored.

Simple structure A sequential arrangement of data records within a data base.

Simple variable A variable within the FORTRAN programming language that stands for a single data item.

Simplex A type of communication channel that provides for unidirectional, or one-way, transmission of data.

Simulation The process used by decision-support-system users to gain insight into the workings of an actual system.

Simultaneous decision support system A decision support system that attempts to incorporate into one system the decision making of various functional areas of an organization so that consistent, overall decisions can be made by management.

Single variables See Simple variables.

Six-bit binary coded decimal A data representation scheme that is used to represent the decimal digits 0 through 9, the letters A through Z, and 28 special characters.

Soft-copy Data displayed on a CRT screen; not a permanent record; contrast with hard-copy.

Software Programs used to direct the computer for problem solving and overseeing operations.

Software copying See Piracy.

Software package A set of standardized computer programs, procedures, and related documentation designed to solve problems of a specific application; often acquired from an external supplier.

Sort To arrange data elements into a predetermined sequence to facilitate processing.

Sort/merge programs A part of the operating-system utility programs; used to sort records to facilitate updating and subsequent combining of files to form a single, updated file.

Source program A sequence of instructions written in either assembly language or high-level language that is translated into an object program.

Source-data automation The use of special equipment to collect data at their source.

Special-purpose machines See Dedicated machines.

Spreadsheet Also known as a ledger sheet; used by accountants for performing financial calculations and recording transactions.

Stand-alone key-to-tape device A self-contained unit that takes the place of a key-punch device.

Stand-alone mode A strategy that allows the user to keep applications in a local mode, allowing no access to remote computer facilities, thus avoiding potential problems of on-line use.

Star configuration A multiple CPU configuration in which all transactions must go through a central computer prior to being routed to the appropriate network computer.

Star network A classification of a local area network in which multiple stations are connected to a central station;

communication between stations must take place through the central station.

Status area A portion of an electronic spreadsheet that appears at the top of the display and shows the location of the cursor within the spreadsheet and what was entered into a particular cell of the spreadsheet.

Store To retain processed data for future reference.

Stored program Instructions stored in the computer's memory in electronic form; can be executed repeatedly during processing.

Stored-program computer A computer that stores instructions for operations to be performed in the electronic form, in primary storage.

Stored-program concept The idea that program instructions can be stored in primary storage in electronic form so that no human intervention is required; allows computer to process the instructions at its own speed.

Structure chart A graphic representation of top-down programming, displaying modules of the problem solution and relationships between modules; of two types—system and process.

Structured programming A top-down modular approach to programming that emphasizes dividing a program into logical sections in order to reduce testing time, increase programmer productivity, and bring clarity to programming.

Structured walk-through See Formal design review.

Subroutine A sequence of statements not within the main line of the program; saves the programmer time by not having to write the same instructions over again in different parts of the program.

Subscript The integer enclosed within parentheses that allows reference to a specific element.

Summarize To reduce large amounts of data to a more concise and usable form.

Supercomputers Large, sophisticated computers that are capable of performing millions of calculations per second and processing enormous amounts of data.

Supervisor program Also known as a monitor or executive; the major component of the operating system; coordinates the activities of all other parts of the operating system.

Swapping In a virtual-storage environment, the process of transferring a program section from virtual storage to real storage, and vice versa.

Symbolic language Also known as assembly language; uses mnemonic symbols to represent instructions; must be translated to machine language before it can be executed by the computer.

Syntax Refers to the way rules must be followed while coding instructions, just as grammatical rules must be followed in English.

System A group of related elements that work together toward a common goal.

System analysis A detailed, step-by-step investigation of an organization and its systems for the purpose of determining what must be done in relation to the systems and the best way to do it.

System analysis report A report given to top management

after the system analysis phase has been completed to report the findings of the system study; includes a statement of objectives, constraints, and possible alternatives.

System analyst The person who is the communication link or interface between users and technical persons (such as computer programmers and operators); responsible for system analysis, design, and implementation of computer-based information systems.

System design report A report given to top management after the system analysis phase that explains how various designs will satisfy the information requirements; includes flowcharts, narratives, resources required to implement alternatives, and recommentations.

System flowchart The group of symbols that represent the general information flow; focuses on inputs and outputs rather than on internal computer operations.

System library A collection of files in which various parts of an operating system are stored.

System program A sequence of instructions written to coordinate the operation of all computer circuitry and to help the computer run quickly and efficiently.

System programmer A programmer responsible for writing and maintaining system software.

System residence device An auxiliary storage device (disk, tape, or drum) on which operating-system programs are stored and from which they are loaded into primary storage.

T

Tabular chart See Grid chart.

Tape cartridge See Tape cassette.

Tape cassette A sequential-access storage medium (similar to cassettes used in audio recording) used in small computer systems for high-density digital recording.

Tape drive A device that moves tape past a read/write head.

Teleconferencing The method of two or more remote locations communicating via electronic and image-producing facilities.

Telecommunication The combined use of communication facilities, such as telephone systems and data-processing equipment.

Telecommuting Computer hookups between offices and homes, thereby allowing employees to work at home.

Telecomputing A term referring to the use of online information services that offer access to one or more data bases; for example, CompuServe, The Source, and Dow Jones News/Retrieval.

Telecopier system See Facsimile system.

Teletypewriter system Transmits messages as strings of characters.

Template A predefined set of formulas for use on an electronic spreadsheet.

Terminals Input/output devices that are hooked into a communication network.

Text-editing The process of using a word processor to enter and store a text file in the computer's secondary storage and then retrieve it for editing and storing as the old file, or as a new file.

Third-generation computers Characterized by the use of integrated circuits, reduced size, lower costs, and increased speed and reliability; 1965–1970.

Thrashing Programs in which little actual processing occurs in comparison to the amount of swapping.

Time-sharing An arrangement in which two or more users can access the same central computer system and receive what seem to be simultaneous results.

Time-sharing system A central computer that can be used by various users at the same time for diverse tasks.

Time slicing A technique used in a time-sharing system that allocates a small portion of processing time to each user.

Top-down design A method of defining a solution in terms of major functions to be performed, and further breaking down the major functions into subfunctions; the further the breakdown, the greater the detail.

Touch-sensitive screen A display screen that serves as an input device; the display is divided into a grid and sensors are placed in the screen to allow the terminal to sense being touched; a method of input that does not require the use of a keyboard.

Touch-tone device A terminal used with ordinary telephone lines to transmit data.

Trace Hard-copy list of the steps followed during program execution in the order they occurred.

Trace program A program that is used for a trace.

Track A horizontal row stretching the length of a magnetic tape on which data can be recorded; one of a series of concentric circles on the surface of a magnetic disk; one of a series of circular bands on a magnetic drum.

Trailer value A method of controlling a loop in which a unique item signals the computer to stop performing the loop.

Train printer See Chain printer.

Transaction file A file that contains new records or modifications to existing records; used to update a master file.

Transfers of control A type of instruction that allows the sequence of instruction execution to be altered by transferring control.

Transient routine A supervisor routine that remains in primary storage with the remainder of the operating system.

Transistor A type of circuitry characteristic of second-generation computers; smaller, faster, and more reliable than vacuum tubes but inferior to third-generation, large-scale integration.

Transit field The section of a check, preprinted with magnetic ink, that includes the bank number.

Tree structure See Hierarchical structure.

Turtle A triangular object used in the Logo programming language to allow users to program graphics interactively.

U

Undo A word-processing feature that allows the user to recover text that has been accidentally deleted.

Uniform Commercial Code (UCC) A set of provisions proposed by legal experts to promote uniformity among state courts in the legal treatment of commercial transactions between sellers and purchasers.

Unit record One set of information; the amount of data on one punched card.

UNIVAC I (UNIVersal Automatic Computer) One of the first commercial electronic computers; became available in 1951.

Universal Product Code (UPC) A code consisting of ten pairs of vertical bars that represent the manufacturer's identity and the identity code of the item; commonly used on most grocery items.

Updating Transferring new information from a transaction file to a master file by computer-matching the two files.

User friendly An easy-to-use, understandable software design that makes it easy for non-computer personnel to use an application software package.

Utility program A program within an operating system that performs a specialized function.

V

Variables Meaningful names assigned by the programmer to storage locations.

Verify To check the accuracy and completeness of data.

Vertical software integration In a business sense, a software package designed for a specific purpose such as legal word processing; in a design sense, the enhancement of a single package.

Very-large-scale integration (VLSI) Use of large-scale integration to offer significant price and performance improvements over earlier computers.

Videoconferencing A technology that employs a two-way, full-motion video plus a two-way audio system for the purpose of conducting conferences between two remote locations through communication facilities.

Video seminar A form of teleconferencing that employs a one-way, full-motion video with two-way audio.

Virtual memory See Virtual storage.

Virtual storage An extension of multiprogramming in which portions of programs not being used are kept in secondary storage until needed, giving the impression that primary storage is unlimited; contrast with real storage.

Visual display terminal A terminal capable of receiving output on a cathode-ray tube (CRT) and, with special provisions, is capable of transmitting data through a keyboard.

Visual table of contents Similar to a structure chart; each block is given an identification number that is used as a reference in other HIPO diagrams.

Voice mail See Voice message system.

Voice message system (VMS) The sender activates a special "message" key on the telephone, dials the receiver's number, and records the message. A button lights on the receiver's phone, and when it is convenient, the receiver can activate the phone and listen to the message.

Voice synthesizer   The output portion of a voice communication system; used to provide verbal output from the computer system to the user.

Voice-grade channel   A communication channel that has a wider frequency range and can transmit data at a rate of forty-five to ninety bits per second, for example, a telegraph channel.

Voice-recognition device   See Voice recognition device.

Voice-recognition module (VRM)   A module, or dictionary, that contains the words and phrases that can be recognized by a voice-recognition device.

Voice-recognition system   The input portion of a communication system; used to provide verbal input from the user to the computer system.

Volatility   Refers to the frequency of changes that are made to a file over a certain time period.

W

Wand reader   A device used in reading source data represented in optical bar-code form.

What-if analysis   A form of simulation that allows the user to interactively process various decision alternatives to determine which one may be the best.

Window environment   An operating system enhancement that allows more than one application software package to run concurrently.

Window   See Window environment.

Wire-matrix printer   See Dot-matrix printer.

Word processing   The manipulation of text data to achieve a desired output.

Word processor   An application software package that performs text-editing functions.

Word wrap   Also known as word wraparound; the word processor automatically positions text so that full words are positioned within declared margins.

Word-processing system   The computer system on which word processing can be performed; of two types—a dedicated word processor and a word processor used on a general-purpose computer system.

Word   A memory location within primary storage; varies in size (number of bits) from computer to computer.

X

Xerographic printer   A type of nonimpact printer that uses printing methods similar to those used in common xerographic copying machines.

Z

Zone bit   Used in different combinations with numeric bits to represent numbers, letters, and special characters.

Zone rows   The upper three rows, numbered 12, 11, and 0, that are found on an 80-column punched card.

Index